SHEILA LUKINS

U★S★A

COOK ★ BOOK

Illustrations by Carolyn Vibbert
Wine & beer selections made with Steve Olson

WORKMAN PUBLISHING
NEW ★ YORK

Lukins, Sheila.

Sheila Lukins USA cookbook/by Sheila Lukins: illustrations by Carolyn Vibbert:

wine and beer selections by Steve Olson.

p. cm.

Includes index.

ISBN 0-7611-0775-4 (hc); ISBN 1-56305-807-3 (pb)

1. Cookery, American. I. Title.

TX715.L938 1997

641.5973—dc21   97-9411

CIP

Thanks to the following for sharing their recipes with me: page 33: Marion Cunningham's Raised Waffles. From *The Breakfast Book* by Marion Cunningham. Copyright © 1987 by Marion Cunningham. Reprinted by permission of Alfred A. Knopf, Inc.; page 69: Queen's Cake and page 549: Colonial Gingerbread. Recipes from the *Raleigh Tavern Bake Shop*. Published by The Colonial Williamsburg Foundation, Williamsburg, VA; page 293: Portobellos in Tomato Sauce and page 321: Polenta with Mascarpone. From *Cafe Pasqual's Cookbook: Spirited Recipes from Santa Fe* by Katharine Kagel. Copyright © 1993 by Katharine Kagel. Reprinted by permission of Chronicle Books; page 359: Country Meat Loaf with Mushroom Gravy. From *The Mushroom Book* by Michael McLaughlin. Copyright © 1994 by Michael McLaughlin. Reprinted by permission of Chronicle Books.

Cover design by Paul Hanson

Book design by Lisa Hollander and Lori S. Malkin

Typesetting by Book Publishing Enterprises

Workman books are available at special discounts when purchased in bulk for premium and sales promotions as well as for fund-raising or educational use. Special editions or book excerpts can also be created to specification. For details, contact the Special Sales Director at the address below.

Workman Publishing Company, Inc.

708 Broadway

New York, NY 10003-9555

Manufactured in the U.S.A.

First printing April 1997

10 9 8 7 6 5 4 3 2 1

I dedicate this book to Molly and Annabel,

my extraordinary daughters,

with great hope that during

their beautiful and joyful lives,

they have the chance to experience

the U.S.A. the way their mother did.

I love you both more than words can say.

And to

Laurie Griffith,

my unfailing friend, kitchen soulmate,

and traveling companion, without whom

this book might still be just one

of those great ideas.

ACKNOWLEDGMENTS

★ ★ ★

I can't imagine that most large publishing projects begin the way mine did. I think they require several meetings and elaborate presentations. Nevertheless, while on my book tour for *All Around the World Cookbook,* I called the best editor in the world, Suzanne Rafer, and told her my idea for the *U.S.A. Cookbook,* and she told me to hurry back. This is our fourth book together, and once again, great love and thanks go out to her . . . and Suzanne, I have this great idea . . .

I called Suzanne first because I don't know Peter Workman's direct number, but it is the truth to say that Peter and the entire Workman team have been supportive, loving, enthusiastic, and sensitive to my work, and it's been an honor working with them since 1981.

I can't imagine a day going by without talking to Arthur Klebanoff, my agent and wonderful friend. His wisdom and guidance have helped lead me forward, and there's always time for his "special" sense of humor.

Walter Anderson, editor of *Parade* magazine, will always be a great inspiration to me. He has given me the opportunity to speak to so many Americans, and for this privilege I am constantly grateful. He's also dynamite to work for. Speaking of *Parade,* a week wouldn't be complete without a work session with Fran Carpentier, my editor at the magazine. She's the greatest.

A million thanks to the best in their fields, who shared their expertise with me for this book: Jon Rowley, Dale DeGroff, Steve Olson, Judith Choate, and Lynnia Milliun.

Love and kisses to my devoted sister, Elaine Yanell, and my adorable mother, Berta Olderman, who have been there for me every minute. Thanks to Sandi Butchkiss, Francesca Peretti, and Sally Waxman, who have given their help when called upon.

Bravo to Paul Hanson, who keeps those cover designs coming. This one I loved at first sight. And to Lisa Hollander, thank you for a bright and spirited book design. Thanks, too, to Lori S. Malkin for bringing the design to life and to Carolyn Vibbert for her lively illustrations. My sincerest appreciation for their editorial help goes to Kathie Ness, Margery Tippie, Emily Nolan, Carrie Schoen, Lori Eisenkraft-Palazzola, Cathy Dorsey, and editorial consultant Laura Stanley, as well as to my other friends at Workman, including Nancy Murray (production), Steve Pesola (pre-press), Andrea Glickson (marketing), Ellen Morganstern and Kim Yorio (publicity), Janet Harris (sales), David Schiller (copy writer), and Carolan Workman (foreign rights).

Last but not least, I could have never attempted another book without Lula Mae Green, who knows how to fry up some really good chicken! Bless you.

CONTENTS

★ ★ ★

PART ONE: THE BREAKFAST NOOK

Breakfast Fruits & Cereals

★ 3 ★

Quick, nourishing, and intensely flavorful, a Raspberry Melon Smoothie or a big bowl of Morning Glory Granola can be just the right way to start a busy weekday. Other soul-satisfying starts include Cranberry Walnut Maple Oatmeal, Sunburst Salad, and an eye-opening Fresh Blueberry Compote.

Eggs & Hash

★ 11 ★

Upscale or down, eggs are glorious in any guise—from a simple Fried Egg Sandwich to Go, to an elegant Cheddar Chive Omelet or Wild Mushroom Scramble. Or instead, rustle up a few leftovers and enjoy Chicken Apple Hash or a Hot and Smooth Breakfast Burrito stuffed with ripe avocado and spicy Cajun sausage. Pure heaven any time of the day.

Pancakes, Waffles & Sides

★ 25 ★

Could anything be more festive than Gingerbread Buttermilk Pancakes, Apple Cinnamon Waffles, or Annabel's French Toast on a Sunday morning? Here they are, along with lots of hearty, savory sides, including Ham Steak with Sheila's Redeye Gravy, Breakfast Chicken Livers and Onions, Creamy Grits, and a light-as-air Cheese Grits Soufflé.

PART TWO: COFFEE BREAK

Muffins & Sweet Breads

★ 51 ★

Rise and Shine Coffee Cake, Flaherty's Maple Pecan Scones, Cakey Buttermilk Doughnuts, Pumpkin Pecan Tea Bread, Oatmeal Raisin Muffins. They're a particularly gratifying way to enjoy a midmorning break—especially alongside a steaming mug of Santa Fe Heavenly Hot Chocolate or a cup of good, strong coffee.

Loaf. New Deli Rye Bread. Dense, savory Boston Brown Bread. Jalapeño Cheese Bread. Rolled Buttermilk Biscuits hot from the oven. Here is an easy-to-make selection of favorites to enclose a sandwich, sop up gravy, or to just butter and enjoy.

Soups
★ 217 ★

Robust or delicately flavored, soups are ideal one-pot feasts for every season and mood. There's Roasted and Fresh Vegetable Gazpacho to cool the fire of summer; Chippewa Wild Rice Soup to banish the chill of winter; Creamy Fiddlehead Fern Soup to celebrate spring; Velvet Squash Soup to give thanks in early autumn; and deep-flavored Beef and Vegetable Barley Soup to satisfy the soul. Plus lots more, including Guacamole Soup and Sunset Red Lentil Soup.

Dinner Side Salads
★ 257 ★

From woodsy, delicately dressed spring greens to a lush salad of tender spinach leaves topped with caramelized sweet pears and fresh chèvre, these salads are deliciously inviting. There's a light, tangy Cherry Carrot Salad, Fabulous Fennel Bread Salad, New World Succotash Salad, and Walla Walla Onion Salad—just right for serving with grilled sourdough bread. Just as winning are salads bursting with summer-ripened tomatoes, peppers, sugar snaps, and asparagus.

The Farmers' Market
★ 277 ★

Turn the market's freshest offerings into Maple Butter Carrots, Fennel and Acorn Squash Whip, and Smothered Red, Red Cabbage (flavored with tart cherries and hot Cajun sausage). Along with such colorful dishes as Maque Choux, Golden Eggplant Curry, and Creamy Leek Ribbons, here are familiar favorites, too: Silky Corn Pudding, Mashed Yukon Golds, and Blue Plate Creamed Spinach.

Noodles, Grains & Beans
★ 313 ★

As side dishes or entrées they are, perhaps, America's most popular comfort foods. Enjoy hearty helpings of American Macaroni and Cheese, Monday Red Beans and Rice, Penne with Summertime Red and Yellow Peppers, Down-and-Dirty Rice. Polenta with Mascarpone. Austin Baked Beans. Hughes's Spaghetti with Venison, and Morels and Butterflies.

Beef
★ 339 ★

Roasted or barbecued, grilled or fried, ground for burgers or diced for pie, beef is infinitely versatile. Not to mention sublime. Think of short ribs blanketed in a lush onion gravy. Ponder Aromatic Meat Loaf. Or dream of a Sumptuous Southwestern Brisket, sauced with olives, capers, and raisins. But don't overlook the equally transcendent Meat-and-Potatoes Pot Pie, Neat Sloppy Joes, or elegant Roasted Tenderloin of Beef.

Pork & Ham
★ 369 ★

Succulent and marvelously agreeable to seasonings and sauces, pork is wedded here with an inspiring, sometimes surprising array of fruits and spices: There are Gentleman Jack Country Pork Ribs and Iowa Fruit-Stuffed Pork Chops. Plus Cider-Splashed Roasted Pork Loin, North Carolina–Style Pulled Pork Barbecue, and Glazed Country Ham.

Lamb
★ 385 ★

From fancy, festive Herb-Crusted Rack of Lamb to dressed-down and delicious Los Angeles Lamb Burgers, lamb's lush texture and distinctive taste is perfectly suited to contrasting ingredients. Try Chinatown Lamb Chops, earthy Lamb Stew with Beans and Escarole, Too, and the crowd-pleasing New York–Style Cincinnati Chili, spiked with a handful of Mediterranean spices.

Poultry & Game
★ 401 ★

Roasted to a turn, fried to a crisp, tucked into jambalaya or a savory pot pie, curried, creamed, stuffed, or barbecued, here is a chicken for every pot! As well as Sweet-and-Sour Squabs, Roasted Pheasant with Kentucky Bourbon Sauce, and Midseason's Eve Duck. For even more of a good thing, try Berry-Stewed Rabbit or creamy Thyme-Scented Rabbit with Onions.

Fish
★ 435 ★

Deep South Catfish, Macadamia-Crusted Halibut with Coconut Curry, Seared Tuna Steaks, Pompano with Papaya Cream and Papaya Salsa, and Broiled Swordfish with Lemon-Caper Sauce are just a few of the highlights. Other fish favorites include an easy-to-prepare, utterly delectable Grilled Trout, crispy, sweet-tasting Pan-Fried Sole on a Bun, and The Great U.S.A. Salmon Cake—light, delicate, and fragrant with thyme.

Shellfish
★ 467 ★

Distilling the very essence of the sea, nothing tastes better than a big bowl of Freddie Gautreau's Beer Steamers, a mess of Pacific Northwest Light Mussels, Grilled Scampi on a

Stick, or Broiled Stuffed Lobster. Other tasty offerings include Frogmore Stew for a Crowd, Grilled Soft-Shell Crabs with Roasted Tomato Sauce, and Seared Scallops in Chipotle Cream.

PART SIX: FOR DESSERT

Fruit Desserts, Puddings & Pies

★ 491 ★

Double Berry Cobbler, Blushing Peach Crunch, Harvest Baked Pears, and a Big Beautiful Berry Salad. Sumptuous Double Dip of Chocolate Pudding. Soothing Carolina Rice Pudding. And lots  and lots of fabulous pies, including: King Orchards' Sour Cherry Pie, Wende's Blue-Ribbon Apple Pie with Candied Ginger, Harvest Sweet Potato Pie, and tart-sweet Lemon Chess Pie.

Cakes & Cookies

★ 525 ★

The best cheesecake. The Queen of Coconut Cakes. Granny Ruth's perfect brownies. Lady Baltimore Cake. "School's Out" Strawberry Shortcake, oozing with summer sweetness. Liberty Bar's Chocolate Cake, the densest, richest one imaginable. And all those other wonderful treats that are just a little fancier than the ones we used to find in our lunchboxes: Steffi's Best Chocolate Chip Cookies, Cookie Jar Peanut Butter Cookies, and Oatmeal Cherry Cookies.

The Big Scoop

★ 551 ★

A winning array of traditional and innovative ice cream parlor treats, including Bittersweet Chocolate Ice Cream, New Orleans Praline Ice Cream, Blood Orange Sorbet, Summertime Peach Ice Cream, and Homey Vanilla Ice Cream. Not to be missed, too, are the luscious sauces and syrups—everything from Silky Hot Chocolate Sauce to Old-Fashioned Butterscotch Sauce and Deep Blueberry Syrup. Plus easy-to-make recipes for cherry cola and three different lemonades.

Introduction
ALL AROUND THE U.S.A

★ ★ ★

The American food front is not at all quiet. It's been active and dynamic as long as I've been cooking and writing, some twenty-five years. And today the buzz is louder and more interesting than ever: Americans have become avid readers of sophisticated cooking columns, food magazines, and cookbooks, and discriminating consumers of the fresher, more diverse and flavorful goods now stocked in so many grocery stores. We seek out the local bounty that spills from our farmers' markets (which are common now—another exciting change). And we routinely buy the very best ingredients we can get: stone-ground meals and flours, extra virgin olive oils, free-range chickens, and aromatic fresh herbs.

For my last book, the *All Around the World Cookbook,* I traveled through Europe, Asia, North Africa, Latin America, and the Caribbean, exploring the cookery of dozens of foreign cultures. I was both fostering and riding a great wave of interest in "exotic" cuisines, which were fast becoming familiar. Americans were looking outward for nourishment and inspiration—a healthy curiosity that I was happy to support. And what a thrill it was to travel the globe tasting new dishes and collecting ideas, and then tasting all I had collected back home in my own kitchen. But once I'd finished that book, I found myself looking *inward* with renewed enthusiasm at homegrown American foods. I was in the Pacific Northwest, beginning my book tour, when I felt a spark ignite. Perhaps it was the colorful spectrum of Pacific oysters, laid out in the Pike Place Market in Seattle that did it. Or was it the season's first Copper River salmon, perfectly grilled

by old friends and complemented by a fruity, flowery Oregon Pinot Noir? Or my first taste of caramelized Kasu cod at Seattle's Dahlia Lounge? I can't say. But I knew it was time to start the *U.S.A. Cookbook.*

Eager as I was to be back home again, my impulse to hit the road in search of ideas proved stronger. I wanted to go everywhere and sample each region's diners, luncheonettes, inns, and fine restaurants. I wanted to observe the harvest of fruits, grains, vegetables, and fish, and I wanted to celebrate these harvests at local festivals and county fairs. Along the way, I hoped to find great home cooking—cozy, classic food—and meet gifted but unsung home cooks. Over the next three years, my research expeditions took me from Maine to the Florida Panhandle, from Chesapeake Bay crabcakes to crab Louis on San Francisco's Fisherman's Wharf. I ate buffalo in South Dakota, wild boar in Texas hill country. I toured the pineapple groves of Hawaii and fished the icy Gulf of Alaska, ever in search of the newest, oldest, boldest, most authentic, *best* American fare.

Getting Started

★ ★ ★

I began my work with a visit to the annual Lima Bean Festival in West Cape May, New Jersey, a tiny town in the center of a major lima-growing region. It was a splendid cookoff of dozens of lima dishes, prepared by church groups, civic organizations, even elementary school classes (first-graders served up one of my favorite soups, which you'll find in the soup chapter). There was so much creativity and civic pride in evidence, and such deep and pure pleasure in local, traditional recipes. The day's high spirit was infectious; it helped set the tone for my new book.

I moved next to Plymouth, Massachusetts, cradle of so much of our history and culture. The town is bordered by cranberry bogs, a startling crimson sea of them—and all of them descendants of the indigenous "crane berry" that Native Americans introduced to white settlers. I plunged through this red landscape to Hancock Shaker Village, once a settlement and now a museum of Shaker architecture, crafts, and culture in the Berkshire Mountains. The austere Shakers were imaginative cooks. Poring over old menus for community dinners, I found dishes as innovative as anything created by today's high-profile chefs. A pot roast simmered in whole cranberry sauce caught my eye in particular—such a marriage of sweet and savory seemed so contemporary (you'll find my version in the beef chapter). Pressing north, in Middlebury, Vermont, I found myself beginning a meal with condiments served from a spinning relish wheel. This was a treat I'd loved as a child:

pickled beets, cottage cheese, apple butter, and other savories. I'd taste more of New England before I was through, in Nantucket, Maine, and Connecticut.

And I'd only just begun! Contemplating the enormity of what lay ahead, it was impossible to guess what foods would become my favorites. Vast stretches of the United States—the South, the Midwest, and the mountain states—were still virgin territory for me.

Down South, Then Heading West

★ ★ ★

In New Orleans and Louisiana bayou country, I learned the distinctions and similarities between the spicy, soulful Cajun and Creole cuisines. I quickly developed a powerful appetite for both; you'll find their flavors throughout this book. Georgia was gracious, especially at table, where Southern-style fried chicken, fried green tomatoes, and homey potato salad were regular guests. On the quiet island of St. Helena, off the South Carolina coast, I sampled a local specialty called Frogmore stew—a liberally spiced boil of shrimp, smoked sausage, and corn. Dining was outdoors, off a newspaper-lined picnic table. In Wakefield, Virginia, in a bower of towering loblolly pines, I watched the "planking" (wood smoking on cured oak boards) of some 2,000 pounds of freshly caught spring shad—the centerpiece of another great festival. The nearby Virginia Diner was serving a breakfast special of creamy grits under sausage gravy, with dropped ham biscuits on the side—whew! I couldn't leave the state without paying homage to Smithfield ham; in the smokehouse I was privileged to stand under 240,000 pounds of it, inhaling its distinctive fragrance. The first Smithfield hams were smoked in 1779, before the close of the Revolution.

The Heartland is vast, and splendid with plenty. I began in Wisconsin, which produces more than 2 billion pounds of cheese a year. In the state's northwest corner, the most productive dairyland in the nation, tranquil Holsteins dot endless miles of lush green landscape. Sour cherries grow in profusion on Lake Michigan; when they're in season *everyone* feasts on pie. Great Lakes whitefish is a year-round favorite, especially at the popular Door County fish boils. In the wilds of northern Minnesota, I visited the wetlands with Chippewa (Ojibwa) hand-harvesters of wild rice. Down in St. Paul, I walked in awe through the St. Paul Farmers' Market, which was that day a late-autumn spectacular of local apples, squashes, pumpkins, greens, ciders, doughnuts, and hardy cold-weather flowers. In Kansas City I headed straight for Stroud's, the roadhouse of legend, where the fried chicken has been admired far and wide since opening day, in 1933. My next stop was the revered Arthur Bryant's, where I warmed up with pork ribs dripping with the restaurant's famed sauce (a fiercely guarded secret), then shamelessly moved on to a juicy brisket sandwich. Barbecue aficionados from coast to coast venerate this place; on this trip, I joined their ranks.

In Texas, too, and throughout the South, people are passionate about smoky, slow-roasted barbecue; they watch over cooking meat as one would a baby, tenderly and for hours at a time. No one in those parts would laugh were I to call barbecue an art form! At Sonny Bryan's, in Dallas, I saw devotees eat theirs in rapt silence, like appreciative museum goers before the world's greatest paintings.

Chile Country and the Coast

★ ★ ★

In the Southwest, I turned my attention to chiles. Their fruity heat permeates much of that region's cooking, and many of the recipes in this book. When I arrived in New Mexico on my travels for this project, I was no stranger to the state or its fare; like many American cooks, I'd been a fan for years. So popular is this region's cuisine now that mesquite-smoked chipotles, fiery little serranos, even incendiary habaneros are widely available all over the nation (you may not need look further than your local grocery!). But the food's still hottest in Santa Fe, where I feasted for four days. I can still taste the lamb quesadillas at Mark Miller's Coyote Cafe and the grilled portobello mushrooms over creamy mascarpone polenta I had at Katharine Kagel's Cafe Pasqual. The venerable Pink Adobe was a must for drinks—and for eating among some of the Southwest's finest artworks. Even breakfast was regional and distinctive—everything from piñon hotcakes at the Tecolote Cafe to a morning burrito at Inn of the Anasazi, where I stayed.

More legendary restaurants awaited in California, birthplace of so much of America's modern culinary genius. In the Bay Area, Alice Waters's Chez Panisse is very much a Mecca, as important for its active promotion of sustainable, organic agriculture as it is for its world-renowned kitchen artistry. But all San Francisco is dotted with culinary giants. I'd never leave town without stopping in at Judy Rodgers's Zuni Cafe or Jeremiah Towers's Stars. Sampling the food of such talented chefs is always a thrill for me, since so much that is new in American cooking starts with them. Once out of town, there was no time to break my pace, not with Thomas Keller's French

Laundry and Michael Chiarello's Tra Vigne to dine at in Napa, and Wolfgang Puck's Spago and Chinoise on Main and Mark Peel and Nancy Silverton's Campanile in Los Angeles. And I couldn't miss the Gilroy Garlic Festival, mother of all American food fairs. Some 150,000 people turn up each year to don garlic leis and gorge themselves on everything garlic—even ice cream, which I still can't believe I ate.

I could go on—I made some fifty trips, so there's a lot to tell. There were other great restaurants and other fun festivals—honoring catfish, artichokes, cheese, strawberries, crab, peaches, apples, corn, onions–all over the nation. If it grows here or we make it, we're sure to celebrate it each year. The surge of interest in good eating has heightened our pride in old culinary practices. Vermonters still gather in maple sugaring season to eat fresh snow drizzled with new syrup (with dill pickles on the side, to cut the sweetness). Each April, during Fiesta, thousands of San Antonians still flock to the city's historic district to cook and eat at an enormous street party they've been having since 1938. These days, the banquet is as multicultural as the city itself has become. The Amish and Mennonite people of Pennsylvania Dutch country have been farming, marketing, and cooking more or less the same way they did when they settled there, more than 250 years ago. The Wyam Indians of the Pacific Northwest still herald the arrival in spring of the Chinook salmon by what was once their dipnetting site on the Columbia River. Although the original ceremonial grounds were submerged when the river was dammed in 1957, ancient practice is much the same. Tribal thanksgiving rites—prayer,

music, dancing, feasting—go back a millennium or more.

I encountered much blending of traditions, too, often with spectacular results. In Hawaii, brilliant young chefs with classical French training have employed the flavors and methods of all the state's peoples—Polynesian, Japanese, Chinese, Thai, and Philippine—in creating an astonishing new, 100-percent-American cuisine. The tropics provide a vivid palette of flavors, everything from passion fruit and kaffir lime to coconut mint and pineapple sage.

The Hawaiians are not alone in their insistence on fine indigenous ingredients. Chefs all over the nation now work with seasonal local produce, meat, poultry, and fish whenever they can. American farmhouse cheeses are impressive, widely respected at home and abroad. California now produces some of the world's great wines; Oregon, Washington, and New York are heading in that direction too. With wine now being made in every state but Alaska, the possibilities are exciting. American beers aren't playing catch-up anymore either, not with hundreds of microbreweries and a thousand brewpubs turning out so many interesting new beers each year. Look out for ales, lagers, wheat beers, pilsners from throughout the U.S. to accompany your dinner.

Home at My Range

★ ★ ★

Between trips, and since finishing travel, I've been back where I belong, cooking up a storm. My memories, my photos, and the foods I carried home inspired me to write a book that reflects the culinary richness of my country. Baking fruit and custard pies, flipping Blue Wally pancakes at home, I've relived dozens of wonderful experiences. Mornings, at work over fruit smoothies and waffles, I would imagine myself in a warm, cozy diner somewhere in Pennsylvania. Nighttime work on the Big Time Banana Split took me back to the soda fountain

at Congdon's Pharmacy on Nantucket. In between, I'd travel in my mind back to the Blue Willow Inn of Social Circle, Georgia, and its groaning board resplendent with good Southern cooking—fried shrimp and catfish, barbecued ribs, mashed yams, black-eyed peas, turnip greens, spiced peaches, and more, so much more. Testing an "Indian taco" on Native American fry bread, I'd reminisce about the Cheyenne Crossing Cafe in Lead, South Dakota. Creating a signature sour-cherry salsa, I'd remember harvest season on Lake Charlevoix in northwestern Michigan, the orchards on Lake Michigan aflame with ripe fruit.

As you read about my experiences and try some of my recipes, I hope that you'll feel as if you've traveled the nation, too—breakfasted, lunched, and dined with me, stood with me in fields of ripening vegetables and grains, and eaten with me at community fish fries and seaside clambakes. This book is a celebration that I'd like you to join—a celebration of American pride, ingenuity, and individuality. It's a paean to our fearless style of cooking, free to be anything it wants in a brave new culinary world.

—Sheila Lukins

PART ONE

THE
BREAKFAST
NOOK

Breakfast Fruits & Cereals

On weekdays, it's hard not to short-change breakfast. Most of us are too bleary and rushed to fuss, so we grab a doughnut on the way to the train. If we eat something hot, it's usually instant—oatmeal or creamed wheat from a single-serving packet, maybe with a banana if there's one lying around. It's hard to get fancy and usually impossible to linger first thing in the morning, especially before coffee!

But if you're going to eat, even just a little, it should be nourishing, satisfying, *good*. And it can be. The simple, light breakfasts that follow—fruit salads, smoothies, and cereals—can be whipped up in minutes. My granola is easily made in advance—in large quantities, of course, for use over many days. Got an extra ten minutes? Spoon some lemony Blueberry Compote over yogurt or hot cereal. With such treats to look forward to, you may greet your jam-packed days cheerful, eager, and a little earlier than before.

RASPBERRY MELON SMOOTHIE

★ ★ ★

In the early morning, I often find it difficult to take the time to cook for myself, so I rely on the refreshing, quick pick-me-up of a fresh fruit smoothie. You can substitute other fruit, of course, according to what's in season. If you don't mind a wake-up call in a shocking color, try blueberries in place of the raspberries.

3 cups diced ripe cantaloupe
½ cup fresh raspberries, gently rinsed
1 cup plain nonfat yogurt
1 tablespoon sugar
2 sprigs fresh mint, for garnish

Place the cantaloupe, raspberries, yogurt, and sugar in a blender and purée until smooth. Serve over ice cubes, if desired, garnished with mint sprigs.
Serves 2

ROSY STRAWBERRY BANANA SMOOTHIE

★ ★ ★

My local Long Island strawberries combine with ripe bananas to make this fantasy smoothie

one of the most ambrosially healthful ways to begin a summer day. All it takes is a quick spin in the blender and then you're ready to go out the door! For the most brilliant color and deepest flavor, just be sure that your berries are fragrantly ripe.

2 cups ripe strawberries, rinsed and hulled
1 ripe banana
1 cup plain nonfat yogurt
2 tablespoons honey, or to taste
2 whole ripe strawberries, for garnish

Combine the hulled strawberries, banana, yogurt, and honey in a blender and purée until smooth. Pour into two glasses, and perch a whole strawberry on the rim of each glass.
Serves 2

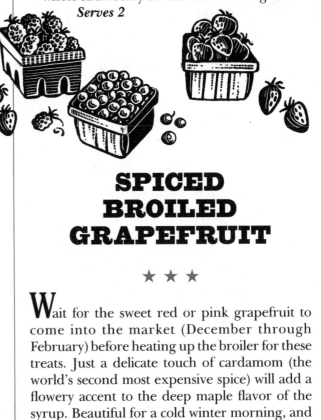

SPICED BROILED GRAPEFRUIT

★ ★ ★

Wait for the sweet red or pink grapefruit to come into the market (December through February) before heating up the broiler for these treats. Just a delicate touch of cardamom (the world's second most expensive spice) will add a flowery accent to the deep maple flavor of the syrup. Beautiful for a cold winter morning, and easily doubled or tripled.

A TASTY SURPRISE

—❧—

*I*n 1929, an unsuspecting worker picked six grapefruit from a tree in an orchard in the lower Rio Grande Valley, only later to discover that their flesh was colored red. The worker could not remember exactly which tree produced this ruby fruit, so the owner had to wait an entire year for the next harvest before he finally located the source. Remarkably, it was only one limb on one tree that produced this special variety. Several grafts were taken from the limb and from it whole orchards were spawned.

The meat of the red grapefruit variety is a beautiful, lush color, lively enough to begin any morning. Another perk is they are so naturally sweet there is no need for additional sugar. If you have never tried a Ruby Red grapefruit, do seek them out. They can be mail-ordered from Frank Lewis's Alamo Fruit, 100 North Tower Road, Alamo, Texas 78516; (800) 477-4773.

1 grapefruit, preferably Ruby Red, halved
1 tablespoon light brown sugar
½ teaspoon ground cardamom
1 tablespoon pure maple syrup
1 teaspoon unsalted butter

1. Preheat the broiler.
2. Section the grapefruit with a small sharp knife, removing the seeds as you go, and place the halves on a baking sheet or in a small baking pan.
3. Combine the brown sugar and the cardamom and set aside.
4. Drizzle the maple syrup over the grapefruit halves. Sprinkle them with the brown sugar mixture, and dot with the butter.
5. Place the grapefruit halves under the broiler, 3 inches from the heat source, and cook until bubbly and slightly browned, 4 to 5 minutes. Serve immediately.

Serves 2

SUNBURST SALAD

★ ★ ★

This salad is a welcome eye-opening wake-up call with its burst of tart-sweet flavor! You can vary the citrus, adding blood oranges or tangelos to the grapefruit sections.

1 pink or red grapefruit
1 white grapefruit
2 navel oranges
1 lime
2 tablespoons honey
2 tablespoons chopped fresh mint leaves
4 small sprigs fresh mint, for garnish

1. Using a sharp knife, carefully remove the peel and all of the white pith from the grapefruits, oranges, and lime. (It's easiest to begin by cutting a slice off the top and bottom of the fruit.) Cut the fruit into segments, removing any seeds and reserving the juices. Combine the fruit in a bowl.

2. In a small bowl, dissolve the honey in the reserved juices. Gently toss with the fruit.

3. To serve, gently toss the chopped mint into the salad. Divide it among four bowls, and garnish each one with a mint sprig.

Serves 4

DEW DROP FRUIT SALAD

★ ★ ★

O n hot, humid mornings, this breakfast salad will ease you into the day. Cool, colorful, and summery, it is the perfect accompaniment to fresh blueberry muffins. Be sure that the melon is juicy and ripe, and use a medium-size melon baller to scoop out perfect rounds.

2 cups ripe honeydew balls
2 cups ripe cantaloupe balls
1 cup fresh blueberries, gently rinsed
1 cup fresh raspberries, gently rinsed
2 tablespoons fresh orange juice
2 tablespoons fresh lemon juice
2 tablespoons chopped fresh
   mint leaves

1. Place all the melon balls in a medium-size bowl. Pat the blueberries and raspberries dry, add to the bowl, and toss gently.

2. Just before serving, sprinkle with the orange and lemon juices and lightly toss with the mint. Serve immediately.

Serves 4

RED, WHITE, AND BLUE BREAKFAST PARFAIT

★ ★ ★

W hether you're celebrating Memorial Day or the Fourth of July, this is *the* patriotic way to start the morning. June and July are ripe berry months from Seattle to Maine, timed just right for this celebratory parfait. Raise the flag, gather up your long-handled dessert spoons, declare your allegiance, and celebrate the Red, White, and Blue.

1 pint ripe strawberries, rinsed and hulled
1 tablespoon sugar
1 tablespoon fresh orange juice
1 quart plain nonfat yogurt
2 tablespoons honey
2 teaspoons finely grated orange zest
2 cups fresh raspberries
2 cups fresh blueberries
1 tablespoon chopped fresh mint leaves
4 small sprigs fresh mint, for garnish

1. Pat the strawberries dry and cut into ¼-inch pieces. Place them in a bowl and toss with the sugar and orange juice. Set aside to macerate at room temperature for 1 hour.

2. Place the yogurt in a fine-mesh strainer and let it drain for 30 minutes. Then place the yogurt in a bowl and stir in the honey and orange zest. Set aside.

3. Combine the raspberries and blueberries in a bowl, and toss with the chopped mint.

4. To assemble the parfaits, place ¼ cup of the raspberry-blueberry mixture in each of four 8-ounce glasses. Top with ¼ cup of the yogurt mixture, followed by 1 tablespoon of the strawberry mixture. Repeat the three layers. Finish each parfait with 2 tablespoons of the yogurt and 1 tablespoon of the strawberries. Garnish with a mint sprig, and serve immediately.

Serves 4

CRANBERRY WALNUT MAPLE OATMEAL

★ ★ ★

Winter offers the best weather for cozying up to a bowl of oatmeal filled with New England's best trimmings. When I was developing this recipe, I used maple syrup from the spring tapping outside Burlington, Vermont, cranberries from a batch harvested in Plymouth, Massachusetts, and Yankee ingenuity!

2½ cups unsweetened apple juice
½ cup water
½ teaspoon ground cinnamon
Pinch of salt
1½ cups rolled oats
½ cup dried cranberries
¼ cup pure maple syrup
½ cup chopped walnuts
Heavy (or whipping) cream, for serving
Brown sugar, for serving

1. Bring the apple juice, water, cinnamon, and salt to a boil in a heavy saucepan. Stir in the rolled oats, cranberries, and maple syrup. Return the mixture to a boil and reduce the heat to medium. Cook, stirring occasionally, for 10 minutes or until the desired consistency is reached.

2. Stir in the walnuts, and serve immediately with heavy cream and brown sugar.

Serves 4

CINNAMON-RAISIN OATMEAL

★ ★ ★

My friend Francesca Bill is a true oatmeal aficionado, and she carefully explained to me why she makes it the way she does. According to Francesca, old-fashioned rolled oats are essential. Always use a 2:1 ratio of liquid to oats. The key to creamier oatmeal, she says, is slow cooking; if the oats cook too quickly, they won't absorb the liquid. The low heat also means they needn't be stirred constantly.

As she avoids sugar whenever possible, Francesca adds raisins for sweetness. Instead of sugar or sweet syrup on top, she adds mashed bananas just as the steamy bowl is ready. Once in a while, I choose a pat of butter or a sprinkling of chopped nuts to add a pleasant contrasting texture, but try these delicious oats Francesca's way before adopting any further frills.

HAUTE OATS

—❦—

I understand better as an adult than I did as a kid how wintry mornings and creamy bowls of oatmeal are made for each other. When I was young, to me oatmeal was mush or gruel, something Oliver Twist might have wanted more of, but that's because he hadn't tasted the good stuff—pancakes and waffles. Now I know better, and keep a couple of different kinds of oats in my cupboard—slow cooking and rolled—for breakfasts and bakings. I doubt poor young Oliver's breakfast bowlfuls were as good as the ones I offer here. When shopping for oats, it's important to know what you're buying:

OAT GROATS: Natural, complete, whole-grain oats, which look like long-grain brown rice and are packed with fiber, vitamins B and E, and protein. They have a sweet, nutty flavor, and can be eaten as a hot cereal or substituted for rice in many recipes. Since they take about 45 minutes to cook, they probably aren't the best choice for breakfast during the week.

SCOTCH, IRISH, OR STEEL-CUT OATS: These are made from oats that have been cut into two or three pieces, and still retain most of their B vitamins. At 30 minutes cooking time, they, too, probably take too long for most mornings, but are so flavorful and chewy, if you're an oatmeal fan, you owe it to yourself to enjoy an occasional weekend bowl.

OLD-FASHIONED ROLLED OATS: Made from groats that have been steamed, then flattened, these are the oats many of us think of as oatmeal. Cooked plain, they take a reasonable 5 or so minutes to cook and make a delicious start to a cold day. When I call for rolled oats, I'd prefer you use these, but you can also use the oats that are listed next.

QUICK-COOKING ROLLED OATS: These are made from rolled oats that have been cut into smaller pieces and processed so that they cook in pratically no time flat. They make for a nice bowl of cereal in about 1 minute's time.

INSTANT OATS: Made from groat pieces that have been refined and partially cooked, these oats result in a cereal that's practically nutrient-free. Often they are packaged already flavored and sweetened, and although they make for a quick start in the morning, they shouldn't be used in baking.

1½ cups rolled oats
3 cups cold milk
½ teaspoon ground cinnamon
½ cup golden raisins or dried cherries
2 ripe bananas, mashed

1. Combine the oats, milk, and cinnamon in a heavy saucepan and cook over very low heat, stirring to combine, for about 5 minutes.

2. Add the raisins and cook until the oatmeal thickens to your taste, 3 to 5 minutes longer. Serve immediately, topped with the mashed bananas.

Serves 4

MORNING GLORY GRANOLA

★ ★ ★

Homemade granola is easy to prepare and far better than any packaged mixture. Once the dry ingredients are combined, you simply need to warm some honey with a touch of brown sugar and toss everything together. A dash of salt pops the flavors but is purely optional. Once it's finished, let the mixture dry thoroughly before packing it into airtight containers. Granola is delicious with milk and sliced bananas or sprinkled over yogurt with Fresh Blueberry Compote. A handful makes a nutritious snack any time of the day.

2 cups rolled oats
½ cup coarse wheat bran
½ cup shredded sweetened coconut
½ cup coarsely chopped almonds
½ cup sunflower seeds
½ cup safflower oil
¼ cup honey
¼ cup (packed) light brown sugar
1 teaspoon pure vanilla extract
½ teaspoon ground cinnamon
¼ teaspoon ground nutmeg
  ¼ teaspoon salt (optional)
   ½ cup coarsely chopped dried apricots
   ½ cup dried cherries
½ cup golden raisins
Finely grated zest of 1 orange
Plain nonfat yogurt, for serving (optional)
Fresh Blueberry Compote (recipe
    follows), for serving (optional)

1. Preheat the oven to 325°F. Lightly oil a rimmed baking sheet or shallow baking dish.

2. Combine the oats, bran, coconut, almonds, and sunflower seeds in a large bowl. Set aside.

3. Combine the oil, honey, brown sugar, vanilla, cinnamon, nutmeg, and salt, if using, in a small saucepan, and cook over medium-low heat, stirring, until the sugar has dissolved. Add to the reserved dry ingredients and toss well.

4. Spread the mixture evenly on the baking sheet, and bake, shaking the pan once or twice, until the mixture is golden brown, 30 minutes.

5. Return the granola to the bowl and add the remaining ingredients. Stir well and set aside to cool and dry completely, tossing once or twice. Pack into airtight containers.

6. For each breakfast serving, place 1 cup yogurt in a bowl and top with the granola and some of the compote.

Makes about 6 cups granola

Fresh Blueberry Compote

★

Early summer is when the time is ripe for blueberry picking. Devotees of this indigenous American food bake blueberry pies, blueberry muffins, put up blueberry preserves in every guise, and eat blueberries out of bowls with pitchers of cream at hand. The sweet blue gems that are plentiful in local markets are mostly from cultivated high bushes, but the smaller, more intensely flavored low-bush wild blueberries can also be found; both types are available frozen.

For me, berry picking is a lost cause because inevitably it is one for my basket and two for me—I never come home with enough to cook up anything substantial. So the farmers' market is where I head when I want to make this compote. To avoid mushy or jam-like berries, I remove them from the syrup just as soon as they've absorbed enough yet still maintain their shape. At this consistency they're ideal to spoon over my granola, waffles, pancakes, or ice cream sundaes. The lemon zest keeps the compote from being cloyingly sweet.

2 pounds fresh blueberries, lightly rinsed
½ cup sugar
1 tablespoon finely grated lemon zest
2 tablespoons fresh lemon juice

1. Place the berries in a heavy nonreactive saucepan. Add the sugar and lemon zest. Shake the pan so that the ingredients are well distributed. Then add the lemon juice and toss gently with a rubber spatula.

2. Place the pan over medium heat and cook, shaking the pan occasionally, until the sauce just starts to bubble, 15 minutes. Remove from the heat, stir, and cool to room temperature.

3. Using a slotted spoon, remove the blueberries from the liquid (reserve the liquid for use later, if desired, as an ice cream topping or in a milkshake). Refrigerate until ready to use.

Makes about 3 cups

Eggs & Hash

Across the United States, eggs are regarded as breakfast food—a sunny-yellow, protein-rich starter that tastes friendly and goes down easy. Our vast repertoire of egg dishes is largely geared toward early eating. In some diners (very few now, alas), a colorful, old-fashioned morning lingo is still used for popular fast favorites: "dead-eyes" (two poached), "Adam and Eve on a raft" (two poached, on toast), "cackle-berries and grunt" (eggs and ham), and "stars and stripes" (eggs and bacon). Fancier fare such as the classic Denver omelet and eggs Benedict is reserved for weekend brunch or the rare leisurely breakfast, while scrambled eggs can be simple, or easily dressed up; try them with wild mushrooms, Sonoma chèvre, or Vermont Cheddar.

In this chapter, I've recommended wines and beers to complement some of the egg and hash dishes. Surprised? Hash has gone upscale. It's no longer a hasty way to use up leftovers, but a star main or side dish that, like scrambled eggs, is great any time of day. So update any outdated egg and hash thoughts—read on, get out that skillet, and try something new!

SHEILA'S BASIC SCRAMBLED EGGS

★ ★ ★

It seems to me that everyone has a particular system of scrambling up eggs. Some add milk and others water to lighten the finished scramble. Some like to see bits of browned, well-cooked eggs while another group opts for soft and runny. I like the creamy texture that results when you add a spoonful of sour cream and then cook over very low heat to produce soft, pale yellow clouds. Here is my basic recipe, which I enjoy accompanied by a crusty piece of sourdough toast topped with homemade sour cherry preserves. This is not to say that you couldn't add some small pieces of smoked fish or meat or fresh herbs for a nice variation on the breakfast plate.

2 large eggs
1 heaping teaspoon sour cream
Salt and freshly ground black pepper, to taste
1 teaspoon unsalted butter

1. In a small bowl, whisk the eggs well with the sour cream and salt and pepper.
2. Melt the butter over medium-low heat in a nonstick skillet until it foams. Add the eggs and cook, stirring with a fork, bringing the set eggs in from the side, until they are just cooked through, about 1½ minutes for perfect soft eggs or 2 minutes if you like them firmer. Serve immediately.

Serves 1

CALIFORNIA GARDEN GOAT CHEESE SCRAMBLE

★ ★ ★

To me, nothing says "California" with more gusto than fresh vegetables and goat cheese. Incorporate these two West Coast symbols into some eggs, and you have a lovely brunch centerpiece for a late spring morning. To keep the texture light and fresh, sprinkle the cheese on top instead of stirring it in. If you desire a firmer scramble, cook for another 30 seconds or so, but no more than that or the eggs will be chewy.

Wine: Sonoma County (CA) Sauvignon Blanc

½ small zucchini, trimmed
½ small yellow squash, trimmed
½ cup small broccoli florets
8 large eggs
2 tablespoons sour cream
1 teaspoon finely chopped fresh dill
Salt and freshly ground black pepper,
    to taste
1 tablespoon unsalted butter
¼ cup diced (¼ inch) red bell pepper
2 ounces soft goat cheese, crumbled,
    for garnish

1. Cut the zucchini and yellow squash into ¼-inch dice, avoiding the seeds. You should have ¼ cup of each.
2. Blanch the broccoli florets in boiling water for 30 seconds. Drain well and set aside.
3. Whisk the eggs, sour cream, dill, and salt and pepper together in a large bowl.
4. Melt the butter in a nonstick skillet over

medium heat until it foams. Add the broccoli, squash, zucchini, and bell pepper and cook, stirring, until just tender, 5 minutes.

5. Reduce the heat to medium-low, add the eggs, and cook, stirring with a fork, bringing the set eggs in from the sides, until they are just cooked through, 4 to 5 minutes.

6. Serve immediately, topped with crumbled goat cheese.

Serves 4

POPEYE SCRAMBLED EGGS

★ ★ ★

Lightly steamed fresh spinach is the key to this great-tasting all-occasion dish. The garnishes of sour cream and crumbled bacon add a flavorful kick to the finished eggs. Even Popeye would approve of this variation on his number-one food.

2 strips of bacon
About ¾ pound tender fresh spinach
4 large eggs
3 tablespoons sour cream
⅛ teaspoon ground nutmeg
Salt and freshly ground black pepper, to taste
2 teaspoons unsalted butter

1. Cook the bacon in a nonstick skillet over medium-high heat until just crisp, about 5 minutes. Drain the bacon on a paper towel, then crumble it and set it aside.

2. Rinse the spinach well, shaking most of the water off. Remove the tough stems and cut the leaves crosswise into ½-inch strips. Place in a large saucepan over high heat, cover, and steam the spinach in the water that clings to the leaves for about 3 minutes, shaking the pan occasionally. Drain, then wrap the spinach in a kitchen towel and squeeze out as much liquid as possible.

3. Whisk the eggs, 1 tablespoon of the sour cream, the nutmeg, and the salt and pepper together in a large bowl. Add the spinach and mix well with a fork.

4. Melt the butter in a nonstick skillet over medium-low heat until it foams. Add the eggs and cook, stirring with a fork, bringing the set eggs in from the side, for 1½ minutes for perfect soft eggs or 2 minutes if you like them firmer.

5. Serve immediately, dolloped with the remaining 2 tablespoons sour cream and sprinkled with the reserved crumbled bacon.

Serves 2

WILD MUSHROOM SCRAMBLE

★ ★ ★

I used to find that no matter how long or at what heat I sautéed mushrooms, they always managed to let off liquid after I thought they were done. This was particularly frustrating when I added them to eggs, as the liquid ruined the texture and turned the dish a most unwelcome brownish color. I knew I needed a solution and I found one. I begin by cleaning the mushrooms with a damp paper towel and trimming the stems. (Never wash them—it will give them a spongy texture.) Once they're clean, I cook them separately and then combine them with the eggs at the last minute. The resulting presentation is of two wonderfully complementary tastes and textures.

Wine: Napa Valley (CA) Pinot Noir

2 ounces fresh shiitake mushrooms
2 ounces fresh cremini or other mushrooms,
*   such as chanterelles or cèpes*
2 teaspoons unsalted butter
1 teaspoon vegetable oil
Pinch of ground nutmeg
4 large eggs
1 tablespoon sour cream
Salt and freshly ground black
*   pepper, to taste*
1 teaspoon snipped fresh
*   chives or chopped*
*   fresh chervil*

1. Clean the mushrooms well with a damp paper towel. Trim off the stems and cut the caps into julienne strips.

2. Heat 1 teaspoon of the butter and the oil in a nonstick skillet over medium-high heat until it foams. Add the mushrooms, sprinkle with the nutmeg, and cook quickly, shaking the skillet, until just tender, about 4 minutes. Transfer the mushrooms to a bowl and set aside. Wipe out the skillet with a paper towel.

3. Whisk the eggs, sour cream, and salt and pepper together in a medium-size bowl. Melt the remaining 1 teaspoon butter in the skillet over medium-low heat until it foams. Add the eggs and cook, stirring with a fork, bringing the set eggs in from the sides, about 1½ minutes for

soft eggs, 30 seconds longer for firmer eggs.

4. Spoon the eggs into two small bowls or plates, and top evenly with the mushrooms. Sprinkle with the chives and serve immediately.
Serves 2

UPTOWN HAM AND EGGS

★ ★ ★

The usual breakfast order of ham and eggs features two fried eggs and a couple of thin slices of ham, along with overly buttered white toast and a plastic container of grape jelly. I love the mix, but I sure like it better my way! If you come by a piece of great baked ham and brown it up just right, you'll be heading toward a model morning repast.

1 tablespoon unsalted butter
4 ounces coarsely sliced baked ham
4 large eggs
2 tablespoons sour cream
Salt and freshly ground black pepper, to taste
2 teaspoons snipped fresh chives

1. Melt the butter in a nonstick skillet over medium heat until it foams. Add the ham and cook, stirring, until it just begins to brown, 5 minutes. Reduce the heat to medium-low.

2. Meanwhile, beat the eggs, sour cream, and salt and pepper together in a medium-size bowl until well mixed.

3. Add the eggs to the ham and cook, stirring with a fork, bringing the set eggs in from the sides, for 1½ minutes for perfect soft eggs, 30 seconds more for firmer eggs. Sprinkle with the chives and serve immediately.
Serves 2

SATURDAY MORNING SALAMI AND EGGS

★ ★ ★

When I was a kid, my mother frequently made this combination for me, though without the embellishment of tomatoes and chives. I still feel that the combination makes one of the best simple breakfasts. Orange marmalade on rustic wheat toast will nicely complete the picture.

1 tablespoon unsalted butter
4 ounces thinly sliced kosher salami
4 large eggs
¼ cup milk
Salt and freshly ground black pepper, to taste
1 plum tomato, thinly sliced
1 tablespoon snipped fresh chives

   1. Melt the butter in a nonstick skillet over medium-high heat until it foams. Add the salami and cook, turning, until it browns slightly, 5 minutes. Reduce the heat to medium-low.
   2. Meanwhile, beat the eggs, milk, and salt and pepper together in a medium-size bowl until well mixed.
   3. Add the eggs to the salami and cook, stirring with a fork, bringing the set eggs in from the sides, for 1½ minutes for soft eggs, 30 sec-

onds longer for firmer eggs. Spoon the eggs onto two plates, cover with the tomato slices, and sprinkle with the chives. Serve immediately.
   Serves 2

FRIED EGG SANDWICH TO GO

★ ★ ★

Since Laurie Griffith moved from Kansas and started working with me, she's brightened many a work break with this fried egg sandwich, her childhood favorite. Since Laurie and I both adore this unusual pairing of savory and sweet, we're a match made in heaven, especially in the early hours.

1 teaspoon unsalted butter
1 slice (2 ounces) ham
1 soft deli roll
1 tablespoon strawberry preserves
1 large egg
Salt and freshly ground black pepper, to taste
1 slice (2 ounces) Swiss cheese

   1. Melt the butter in a nonstick skillet over medium heat until it foams. Add the ham and cook, turning, until slightly browned, 3 to 4 minutes.
   2. Meanwhile, lightly toast the roll.
   3. Spread the preserves over the bottom half of the roll, and cover with the ham.
   4. Break the egg into the skillet and fry over medium heat until set and slightly browned, 1 to 2 minutes. Using a spatula, gently turn the egg over. Sprinkle with salt and pepper, and top with

the cheese. Cover the skillet and cook until the cheese has melted, about 1 minute more. Place the egg on top of the ham, and cover with the top of the roll. Serve immediately.

Serves 1

MOLLY'S EGG-IN-THE-HOLE

★ ★ ★

We first saw this egg dish being made by Olympia Dukakis in the movie *Moonstruck,* and now my daughter, Molly, has adopted it for her own. Even without a patent, I can't imagine anyone doing a better job. The olive oil sinks into the bread, giving it a fragrant, fruity flavor. If neatly breaking an egg gives you trouble, crack it into a cup and then pour it into the hole.

1 slice crusty sourdough peasant bread,
    about ½ inch thick
1 tablespoon extra virgin olive oil
1 large egg
Salt and freshly ground black pepper, to taste

1. Cut a 1½- to 2-inch circle out of the bread, using a cookie or biscuit cutter.
2. Heat the oil in a nonstick skillet over medium heat. Add the bread slice, with the cut-out circle next to it, and cook until brown on one side, 2 minutes. Turn the pieces over, and break the egg into the hole. Sprinkle with salt and pepper, cover the pan, and cook for about 4 minutes, or until the egg white is set and the yolk is cooked as desired. (As the egg cooks, the bread will brown on the other side.) Serve immediately, with the toasted circle alongside.

Serves 1

HAM AND EGG SALAD FOR BRUNCH

★ ★ ★

This favorite breakfast combination makes a quick transition to the brunch menu when blended with a mustard-mayonnaise dressing. A touch of chopped scallions and crisp red bell peppers brightens the texture. Pile this high on a thick slice of pumpernickel and top it with a slice of ripe tomato.

THE BEST HARD-COOKED EGGS

—❦—

Gently rinse the eggs in warm water, to prevent them from cracking, and drain them. Place the eggs in a saucepan, cover with cold water, and bring to a boil over medium-high heat. Then reduce the heat to a gentle simmer and cook for exactly 13 minutes. Drain the eggs and rinse them under cold water. Peel, and use as directed.

6 hard-cooked eggs
Salt and freshly ground black pepper, to taste
2 ounces thinly sliced baked ham
1 small scallion (1 inch green left on), finely chopped
1 tablespoon finely diced red bell pepper
1 tablespoon coarsely chopped fresh flat-leaf parsley
¼ cup mayonnaise
2 teaspoons Dijon mustard

1. Quarter the eggs, then coarsely chop them. Place in a bowl, and season with salt and pepper. Shred the ham and add it to the eggs along with the scallion, bell pepper, and parsley. Mix together with a fork.

2. In a separate bowl, combine the mayonnaise and the mustard. Fold it into the salad and serve immediately, or cover and refrigerate for up to 2 days.

Makes about 2 cups; serves 4

BACON AND EGG SALAD

★ ★ ★

Try this breakfast egg salad heaped on a thick slice of white toast. Instead of the plain ketchup often served with bacon and eggs, I've added a zesty dash of it to a mayonnaise dressing, making this "salad" diner-authentic.

6 hard-cooked eggs
3 ounces (3 slices) thick-cut bacon,
   cut into ¼-inch dice
Salt and freshly ground black pepper, to taste
½ cup mayonnaise
1 teaspoon ketchup

1. Quarter the eggs, then coarsely chop

them. Place the chopped eggs in a bowl.

2. Cook the bacon in a nonstick skillet over medium heat until just crisp and browned, 4 to 5 minutes. Using a slotted spoon, transfer the bacon to paper towels to drain.

3. Add the bacon to the eggs, season with salt and pepper, and toss well.

4. Mix the mayonnaise and ketchup together in a small bowl, and stir into the eggs with a fork. Serve immediately.

Makes about 2 cups; serves 4

SOUTHWESTERN SUNRISE

★ ★ ★

Here's a dish to snap even the sleepiest of taste buds awake. The eggs are baked in individual ramekins and are surrounded by an array of Southwestern flavors. A brunch star, this also works beautifully as an appetizer, particularly before a meal of Hog Neck or Vegetable Chili. Pungent bursts of fresh cilantro or chives add a finishing touch of liveliness to the assertive flavors.

Wine: New Mexico sparkling wine

2 teaspoons unsalted butter
2 red pepper halves, roasted (see How to Roast
   a Bell Pepper, page 132)
½ small ripe avocado, pitted, peeled,
   and cut into ½-inch dice
2 large eggs
Salt and freshly ground black pepper, to taste
2 tablespoons grated Monterey Jack cheese
2 teaspoons sour cream
1 tablespoon chopped fresh cilantro or
   freshly snipped chives

1. Preheat the oven to 325°F.

2. Divide the butter between two 8-ounce ramekins. Place the ramekins on a baking sheet and put them into the oven to melt the butter, about 2 minutes.

3. Place a red pepper half in the bottom of each ramekin, and top with the diced avocado. Carefully break an egg into each ramekin, and sprinkle with salt and pepper. Top each with 1 tablespoon of the grated cheese. Return the ramekins to the oven and bake until the eggs have reached the desired doneness, about 15 minutes. Dollop each with a teaspoon of sour cream and sprinkle with cilantro or chives. Serve immediately.

Serves 2

HOT AND SMOOTH BREAKFAST BURRITO

★ ★ ★

To make a great burrito, you need the bite of a Tex-Mex salsa, the smooth creaminess of a ripe avocado, and extra-fresh, warm-from-the-oven flour tortillas. This scrumptious burrito could be eaten out of hand, but I think it really shines when eaten with a knife and fork at the brunch table.

Wine: Santa Barbara County (CA) Pinot Blanc

2 flour tortillas (7½-inch diameter)
1 spicy cured sausage, such as andouille or chorizo, cut into ¼-inch slices
4 large eggs
2 tablespoons milk
1 teaspoon chopped fresh cilantro leaves
Salt and freshly ground black pepper, to taste
1 teaspoon unsalted butter
½ ripe avocado, pitted, peeled, and cut into ¼-inch dice
½ cup grated Monterey Jack cheese
2 tablespoons sour cream or plain nonfat yogurt
Roasted Rosy Salsa (page 196), for serving
Creamy Salsa Verde (page 195), for serving

1. Preheat the oven to 350°F.

2. Wrap the tortillas in aluminum foil, and warm them in the oven while you prepare the filling.

3. Cook the sausage in a nonstick skillet over medium heat until browned, 3 to 4 minutes. Set them aside on paper towels to drain. Wipe out the skillet.

4. Whisk the eggs in a medium-size bowl with the milk, cilantro, and salt and pepper. Melt the butter in a nonstick skillet over medium heat until it foams. Add the egg mixture and cook, stirring with a fork, bringing the set eggs in from the sides, until they just start to become firm. Add the reserved sausage and the avocado, and cook until the eggs are done to your liking (about 1½ minutes total).

5. Remove the tortillas from the oven. Spoon the egg mixture evenly down the center of each tortilla. Sprinkle with the grated cheese, and top with sour cream. Fold the two sides over to cover the eggs, turn the burritos over, and place them seam side down on a plate. Top each serving with a generous spoonful of both salsas and serve immediately.

Serves 2

THE CLASSIC DENVER OMELET

★ ★ ★

Originating with the hardworking folks in Colorado and Utah, this American classic began life as an overstuffed white bread sandwich. The omelet filling was laden with chopped onions, green peppers, and ham. A Denver, or Western, omelet was another one of my favorite childhood Saturday morning breakfasts, and my mother, a fellow lover, always made one big enough for both of us. Today's short-order cooks seem to feel that more is better. Personally, I think this eggy treat is best when the ingredients are as close to the original as possible. A salsa topping can be the innovation that brings new taste and refreshing flavor. But if you're like me and can't resist the traditional splash of ketchup, go ahead!

Wine: Texas Chenin Blanc
Beer: Colorado amber ale

1 thick slice of bacon, cut into ½-inch pieces
2 tablespoons diced (¼ inch) red bell pepper
2 tablespoons diced (¼ inch) green bell pepper
2 tablespoons diced (¼ inch) red onion
1 slice baked ham, torn into shreds
2 large eggs
¼ cup milk
Salt and freshly ground black pepper,
   to taste
1 teaspoon snipped fresh chives
2 teaspoons unsalted butter
1 tablespoon sour cream, for garnish (optional)
Mellow Breakfast Salsa (recipe follows; optional)

1. Place the bacon in a nonstick skillet and cook over medium-low heat until just crisp, 5 minutes. Using a slotted spoon, transfer the bacon to a paper towel to drain. Remove and discard all but 1 tablespoon of the bacon fat.

2. Add both of the peppers and the onion to the skillet and cook over low heat, stirring, until just wilted, 5 minutes. Transfer the vegetables to a bowl, and add the bacon and ham.

3. In a separate bowl, beat the eggs with the milk. Season with salt and pepper, and whisk in the chives. Stir in the vegetable mixture.

4. Melt the butter in a nonstick skillet over medium heat until it foams. Add the egg mixture and cook without stirring until the omelet begins to set around the edges, about 10 seconds. Then, using a fork, push the set eggs into the center, letting the uncooked eggs run out to the edges. Continue cooking, making sure the filling is distributed evenly, until the eggs are almost set, 45 seconds. Cover the pan with a lid and cook for 30 to 45 seconds more, or until the eggs are cooked to the desired doneness.

5. Slide the omelet halfway onto a plate, then flip it over itself. Serve dolloped with sour cream and Mellow Breakfast Salsa, if using.
Serves 1 or 2

Mellow Breakfast Salsa

★

This mild, velvety salsa of avocado, ripe tomatoes, and red onion is the perfect accompaniment to Denver (and other) omelets. If you crave a spicier salsa, a teaspoon or two of finely minced jalapeño pepper will add some zest.

*½ ripe avocado, pitted, peeled, and cut into
    ¼-inch dice*
1 tablespoon fresh lime juice
*1 ripe tomato, halved, seeded, and cut into
    ¼-inch dice*
3 to 4 tablespoons diced (¼ inch) red onion
1 tablespoon snipped fresh chives
Salt and freshly ground black pepper, to taste

Place the avocado cubes in a bowl and toss with the lime juice. Gently fold in the remaining ingredients. Serve alongside the omelet for spooning atop.

Makes about 1½ cups

CHEDDAR CHIVE OMELET

★ ★ ★

When enveloped in a mild-tasting omelet, the marvelous tang of well-aged Vermont Cheddar will really stand out. The rule of thumb is the older a cheese, the sharper the flavor, so look for vintage cheese to create this truly elegant meal. A confetti of fresh herbs accents the meltingly fragrant interior.

Wine: California sparkling Moscato
Beer: Vermont copper ale

2 large eggs
*2 teaspoons snipped fresh chives or chopped fresh
    tarragon or chervil*
Salt and freshly ground black pepper, to taste
2 teaspoons unsalted butter
¼ cup grated Cheddar cheese

1. Whisk the eggs, chives, and salt and pepper together in a small bowl.

2. Melt the butter in a nonstick skillet over medium heat until it foams. Shake the pan to coat the entire surface with the butter. Add the eggs and cook, stirring, until the omelet begins to set around the edges, about 10 seconds. As it begins to set, use a fork to pull the cooked eggs into the center while tilting the pan so that the uncooked eggs run to the outside.

3. When the eggs are nearly set, 1 to 1½ minutes, sprinkle the cheese across one side of the omelet. Slide the omelet halfway onto a plate, then flip it over onto itself. Serve immediately.

Serves 1

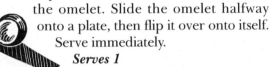

WEEKEND EGGS BENEDICT

★ ★ ★

You might consider this classic a bit of culinary retro, but to me it will always be special. The key is a great hollandaise sauce; there is nothing like it to turn ordinary into luxurious. Steamed, well-drained spinach or even asparagus spears may be substituted for the Canadian bacon.

Sunny Hollandaise Sauce (recipe follows)
4 large eggs
4 slices Canadian bacon
2 English muffins
1 tablespoon unsalted butter
Fresh flat-leaf parsley sprigs, for garnish

★★★★★★★★★★★★★★★★★★★★★★★★★

HOW TO POACH AN EGG

—❧—

Bring 4 cups of water and 1 tablespoon of white or cider vinegar to a gentle simmer over medium-low heat in a medium-size nonreactive saucepan. Break an egg into a cup, and then slip it into the simmering water. (It is best to cook just one egg at a time, as they tend to stick to each other.) Cook to the desired consistency, 3 to 4 minutes. Using a slotted spoon, remove the egg from the water and immediately dip it into a bowl of cold water to stop the cooking. To keep them from cooling off, place the cooked eggs in a bowl of warm water until you are ready to use them, but no longer than 5 or 10 minutes. Before serving, transfer the eggs to paper towels to drain, and trim away any unsightly strands of egg white.

★★★★★★★★★★★★★★★★★★★★★★★★★

1. Prepare the hollandaise sauce and keep it warm while you prepare the rest of the dish.

2. Poach the eggs following the directions in the box above.

3. Heat a medium-size nonstick skillet over medium-high heat. Add the Canadian bacon and cook until slightly browned, about 2 minutes. Turn and brown the second side, 1½ minutes more. Remove the bacon and drain on paper towels.

4. Split and toast the English muffins. Lightly butter each half.

5. Place 2 English muffin halves on each plate. Top each half with a slice of Canadian bacon. Place a well-drained poached egg on top of the bacon. Spoon the hollandaise sauce over the eggs. Garnish each with a small sprig of parsley and serve immediately.
Serves 2

Sunny Hollandaise Sauce

—★—

3 large egg yolks
1 tablespoon fresh lemon juice
8 tablespoons (1 stick) unsalted butter, melted
Salt and freshly ground white pepper, to taste
Dash of Tabasco sauce

1. Fill the bottom pot of a double boiler slightly less than half full with water and heat it till it steams. Then lower the heat so that the water remains at that temperature. It should not simmer.

2. Off the heat, place the egg yolks and lemon juice in the top pot of the double boiler and whisk well to combine, about 1 minute. Then place the top pot over the hot water (the bottom of the top pan should not touch the water) and whisk until the yolks are smooth, and the consistency of heavy cream. Add the butter in a slow, steady stream, whisking constantly until it has been completely incorporated. Remove the sauce from over the hot water.

3. Season to taste with the salt, white pepper, and Tabasco. Serve warm (see Note).
Makes about ¾ cup

NOTE: If the sauce should separate or curdle, add 1 ice cube and whisk briskly until it has melted. This will bring the sauce back together.

GARDEN HASH

★ ★ ★

Colorful, nutritious, and delicious, this skillet-ful of vegetables will lure even the most ardent meat eater. Unlike the other hashes, when cooked, it doesn't form a pancake but rather has a confetti-like consistency. When topped with poached eggs, it is every bit as gratifying as its corned beef cousin. Garden Hash also doubles nicely as dinner fare.

Wine: North Carolina Scuppernong
Beer: American lager

1 large white turnip (about 8 ounces)
1 large boiling potato (about 8 ounces)
¼ cup vegetable broth, preferably homemade
    (page 255)
1 cup diced (¼ inch) onion
1 cup diced (¼ inch) red bell pepper
1 cup diced (¼ inch) green bell pepper
1 cup corn kernels, thawed if frozen
1 teaspoon dried thyme
Salt and freshly ground black pepper, to taste
4 tablespoons chopped fresh flat-leaf parsley
2 tablespoons olive oil, plus more if needed
6 poached eggs (page 21; optional)

1. Peel and cut the turnip and the potato into ¼-inch dice. Place in a large saucepan and add water to cover. Bring to a boil and cook until just tender, about 8 minutes. Drain, and transfer to a large bowl.
2. Pour the broth into a large nonstick skillet, and add the onion and both bell peppers. Cook over medium heat, stirring, until softened, 4 to 5 minutes. Add the corn and cook for 1 minute. Add this to the turnip and potato mixture, and toss with the thyme, salt, pepper, and 3 tablespoons of the parsley.

3. Add 2 tablespoons olive oil to the skillet. Add the hash mixture, spread it out evenly, and weight it down with something heavy, like a plate or a smaller skillet. Cook over medium heat until the bottom is slightly golden, 5 to 7 minutes. Turn the hash over, in sections, with a spatula, adding more oil if necessary, and cook for 5 minutes, until that side is slightly golden.
4. Transfer the hash to a platter, and sprinkle with the remaining 1 tablespoon parsley. Serve as is or, if desired, top with the poached eggs.

Serves 6

PASTRAMI VEGETABLE HASH

★ ★ ★

Corned beef, roast beef, and red bell peppers have traditionally been considered standard fare for a hash foundation, but the ratios have changed over the last two decades and vegetables now play a more prominent role. I do love hash made with New York deli corned beef, but here I prepare it with lean pastrami for an even richer flavor. Of course, corned beef or leftover roast beef make fine substitutes.

Wine: Russian River Valley (CA) Pinot Noir

*2 russet potatoes (8 ounces each), peeled and
    cut into ¼-inch dice*
*½ pound lean pastrami, roast beef, or corned beef,
    cut into ¼-inch dice*
*¼ pound thick-sliced bacon, cut into ¼-inch
    dice*
1 onion, coarsely chopped
*1 red bell pepper, stemmed, seeded, and cut into
    ¼-inch dice*
*1 green bell pepper, stemmed, seeded, and cut into
    ¼-inch dice*
¼ teaspoon ground nutmeg
Salt and freshly ground black pepper, to taste
Finely grated zest of 1 orange
3 tablespoons chopped fresh flat-leaf parsley
6 poached eggs (page 21), for serving

1. Cook the potatoes in boiling salted water until just tender, about 8 minutes. Drain well and place in a large bowl. Add the pastrami.

2. Cook the bacon in a nonstick skillet over medium heat to render the fat, 5 minutes. Add the onion and both bell peppers. Cook, stirring, until just wilted, 5 minutes. Remove with a slotted spoon and add to the potatoes and pastrami. Discard all but 2 tablespoons of the fat.

3. Add the nutmeg, salt, pepper, orange zest, and 2 tablespoons of the parsley to the hash mixture and toss well with a rubber spatula.

4. Spread the hash mixture evenly in the skillet, and weight it down with something heavy, like a plate or a smaller skillet. Cook over medium-high heat until golden brown on the bottom, 5 minutes. Turn the hash over with a spatula, and cook until golden brown, 5 to 7 minutes. Spoon the hash onto plates and serve as is, or, if desired, top with the poached eggs and sprinkle with the remaining 1 tablespoon parsley.

Serves 6

DISHING HASH

— ❧ —

*I*f you think of hash as a humble, economical assemblage of leftovers, consider this: Fifty years ago, it was the most expensive item on the à la carte menu at New York's Ritz Carlton. Although the French-style "Ritz Chicken Hash" was a far cry from lunch counter and "hash house" fare, its cachet boosted the image of hash everywhere.

Hash has been with us since colonial times. Martha Washington is said to have made it of meat, onion, and herbs, from a recipe her daughter Nelly wrote down. Corned beef hash, or "cornbeef Willie," was a well-known diner standard by 1900. This, especially with the traditional fried egg plopped on top, is delicious, if somewhat heavy and cholesterol-laden. But creative, health-minded cooks have lightened and brightened hash, using more vegetables, less meat, and high notes—fresh herbs, sweet peppers, raw scallions—that were missing before. Will one of these new, all-American versions ever achieve the status once enjoyed by that hash at the Ritz? I certainly would like to think so.

CHICKEN APPLE HASH

★ ★ ★

Before hash reached culinary heights on exalted menus around the country, nothing more than refrigerator leftovers was needed to come up with the ingredients for this brunch favorite. Nowadays it's a trip to the market for some special fixings. Diced apple adds a surprising crispness to this hash, while lots of fresh thyme gives it a pungent flavor. Top the hash with a poached egg and garnish it with a spicy Garden Chili Sauce, and a breakfast favorite moves up to entrée status.

Wine: New England Vidal Blanc
Beer: San Francisco Anchor Steam Beer

1 russet potato, peeled and cut into ¼-inch dice
3 tablespoons extra virgin olive oil
1 onion, cut into ¼-inch dice
½ cup diced (¼ inch) red bell pepper
½ cup diced (¼ inch) green bell pepper
1 whole skinless, boneless chicken breast, cooked,
*   cut into ¼-inch pieces*
1½ teaspoons fresh thyme leaves, or ½ teaspoon dried
Salt and freshly ground black pepper, to taste
1 cup unpeeled diced (¼ inch) Golden Delicious
*   apple*
¼ cup chopped fresh flat-leaf parsley
4 poached eggs (page 21), for serving (optional)
Garden Chili Sauce (page 197), for serving (optional)

1. Place the potatoes in a small saucepan and cover with salted water. Bring to a boil and cook until just tender, about 8 minutes. Drain, and set aside.

2. Heat 2 tablespoons of the oil in a medium-size nonstick skillet over medium heat. Add the onion and cook, stirring, until just wilted, about 5 minutes. Add both of the peppers and cook, shaking the pan, 5 minutes more.

3. Raise the heat to medium-high and add the remaining 1 tablespoon olive oil, the chicken, and the potatoes. Sprinkle with the thyme, salt, and pepper. Cook, stirring, for 5 minutes. Weight the hash down with something heavy, like a plate or a smaller skillet, and cook until browned, 5 minutes. Turn the hash over, in sections, with a spatula and cook, weighted down, until it is browned, 5 minutes.

4. Add the apple and parsley, turn with the spatula, and continue cooking for another 5 minutes, turning again once or twice. The apple should soften and take on some color. Transfer the hash to a platter and serve as is, or, if desired, top with the poached eggs and chili sauce.

Serves 4

Pancakes, Waffles & Sides

It's Sunday, you've slept late, and you have no plans to speak of. You'll lounge in your bathrobe for hours, reading that fat newspaper, all of it. This is one of your week's high points, an occasion that calls for a treat to eat. How about pancakes, waffles, or French toast? They can be superb plain, with nothing more than maple syrup. Or jazz them up with fruit, ginger, bacon, or even a jelly filling. And if you'd like something hearty on top or on the side, you'll find plenty of suggestions: creamed mushrooms, sausage gravy, home fries, and more. All of these "sides" are great with eggs, too.

Making these dishes is easy, but achieving perfection requires technique. For pancakes, heed the advice from griddle guru Doug Grina, of Al's Breakfast in Dinkeytown, Minneapolis. You'll get lots of other help here from me and a few of my friends. So, eat up, and take your time, because tomorrow is, well, *not* Sunday.

BLUE WALLY PANCAKES

★ ★ ★

Al's Breakfast, centered in Dinkeytown, the university area of Minneapolis, serves up celestial pancakes. Whether your appetite craves a "short stack," a pile of "regulars," or a "long haul," these blueberry walnut pancakes, luxuriating in a veil of melted butter and pure Minnesota maple syrup, will get your day off to just the right start. Al's is reputed to be the one-time haunt of Bob Dylan when he played at The Ten O'Clock Scholar, a nearby folk house, before going to New York. While some may think that's a claim to fame, I don't think it can hold a candle to the talent of Doug Grina, co-owner, who is often seen flipping the cakes right up by the front window. I managed to come away with a few of Doug's secrets, some great flapjack advice, and more than a long haul of his signature cakes.

AL'S WAY WITH PANCAKES

Al's Breakfast is a tiny, wildly popular diner in the Dinkeytown section of Minneapolis, near the University of Minnesota, where breakfast only is served every day from 6:00 A.M. to 1:00 P.M. Al Bergstrom started flipping pancakes in 1950 and remained sole proprietor until 1973. Today the griddle has been turned over to co-owners Doug Grina and Jim Brandes, who continue Al's tradition with some of the best-tasting pancakes, waffles, and eggs in the U.S.A. The serpentine lines around the block are testimony to Al's! Here are their tips:

• Mixing the dry ingredients into the wet (and not vice versa) makes for a smoother batter.

• When mixing fruits and nuts into pancake batter, first stir them into the dry ingredients so that they are well coated; this will make sure they're evenly distributed throughout the batter. If not everyone wants nuts, sprinkle them on top of the individual pancakes just after you've ladled the batter into the skillet.

• To make very light pancakes, let the batter rest for 30 minutes at room temperature; this gives the baking powder a chance to aerate the batter as it begins the leavening process.

• Never use a blender to beat pancake batter. Overmixing will prevent the baking powder from aerating the batter, resulting in flat pancakes.

• The first pancake in the skillet may be unattractive, but after you get the rhythm and you're more adept, you'll soon achieve pancake perfection.

• At Al's, a "short stack" is two pancakes, a "regular" is three, and a "long haul" is four. Checking diner history, this seems to be a general pancake-counting rule of thumb.

1½ cups all-purpose flour
1½ cups whole-wheat flour
2½ teaspoons baking powder
1 teaspoon salt
1 cup fresh blueberries
1 cup chopped walnuts
3 large eggs
3 cups milk
6 tablespoons (¾ stick) plus 1 or more
    teaspoons unsalted butter
1 tablespoon honey
Pure maple syrup,
    for serving

1. Combine both of the flours, the baking powder, and salt in a large bowl. Mix in the blueberries and walnuts and set aside.

2. In another large bowl, lightly beat the eggs. Then add the milk and stir to combine. Melt the 6 tablespoons butter with the honey in a small saucepan over low heat, and stir this into the eggs.

3. Add the flour mixture to the liquid, and whisk together until the batter is just smooth. Let rest at room temperature for 30 minutes for the batter to aerate.

4. Melt the remaining 1 teaspoon butter in a medium-size nonstick skillet over medium heat until it foams. Tilt the skillet, making sure the butter coats the entire surface. Ladle ¼ cup of batter into the skillet, and cook for about 30 seconds, until small bubbles form on the top of the pancake. Turn it over and cook for about 30 seconds longer or until golden brown. Repeat with the remaining batter, adding more butter as necessary to the pan to prevent sticking. Serve the pancakes as you make them, with syrup, or keep warm, loosely covered with aluminum foil, in a low (200°F) oven.

Makes 24 pancakes; serves 6 to 8

BUTTERMILK CORN PANCAKES

★ ★ ★

In addition to a visit to the Walker Art Center, these flawless pancakes are a compelling reason for making a stop in Minneapolis. They're light as a feather and corny as Kansas in you-know-when. I had to pester Doug Grina, the cook and co-owner of Al's Breakfast, for the secret to his art. He said, "No secret, just combine baking powder with buttermilk to produce a leavening agent far greater than when you use sweet milk." Secret or not, what a taste!

3 cups all-purpose flour
2½ teaspoons baking powder
1½ teaspoons sugar
1 teaspoon salt
1½ cups cooked corn kernels
2 large eggs
1 quart buttermilk
3 tablespoons plus 1 or more teaspoons
    unsalted butter, melted
Pure maple syrup, for serving

1. Combine the flour, baking powder, sugar, and salt in a large bowl. Stir in the corn, and set aside.

2. Lightly beat the eggs in a large bowl, and combine with the buttermilk and the 3 tablespoons melted butter.

3. Add the flour mixture to the liquid, and

whisk until the batter is just smooth. Let rest at room temperature for 30 minutes for the batter to aerate.

4. Lightly brush a nonstick skillet with the remaining 1 teaspoon melted butter, and place it over medium heat. Ladle ¼ cup of batter into the skillet, and cook for about 40 seconds, until small bubbles form on the top of the pancake. Turn it over and cook for 40 seconds longer or until golden brown. Repeat with the remaining batter, adding more butter as necessary to the pan to prevent sticking. Serve the pancakes as you make them, with syrup, or keep warm, loosely covered with aluminum foil, in a low (200°F) oven.

Makes 24 pancakes; serves 6 to 8

GINGERBREAD BUTTERMILK PANCAKES

★ ★ ★

Spicy as warm, fresh-from-the-oven gingerbread, these pancakes send out all the homey flavors of autumn. The combination of butter-milk and baking powder gives them a nice rise, so they're marvelously light.

2 cups all-purpose flour
1 teaspoon baking powder
½ teaspoon salt
1 teaspoon ground ginger
½ teaspoon ground nutmeg
½ teaspoon ground cinnamon
¼ teaspoon ground cloves
2 large eggs
2 cups buttermilk
1 cup milk
¼ cup unsulfured molasses
2 tablespoons dark brown sugar
2½ tablespoons unsalted butter, melted
1 teaspoon unsalted butter
Pure maple syrup, for serving
Shaker Applesauce (page 200), for serving

1. Combine the flour, baking powder, salt, and all of the spices in a bowl and set aside.

2. Lightly beat the eggs in a large bowl, and combine with the buttermilk, milk, molasses, brown sugar, and melted butter.

3. Add the flour mixture to the liquid, and whisk until the batter is just smooth. Let the batter rest at room temperature for 30 minutes to aerate.

4. Melt the 1 teaspoon butter in a nonstick skillet over medium heat, making sure it coats the entire surface of the pan. Ladle ¼ cup of batter into the skillet and cook for about 40 seconds per side or until golden brown. Repeat with the remaining batter, adding more butter as necessary to the pan to prevent sticking. Serve the pancakes as you make them, with the syrup and applesauce, or keep warm, loosely covered with aluminum foil, in a low (200°F) oven.

Makes 20 pancakes; serves 6 to 8

★★

A PANCAKE BY ANY OTHER NAME

—❦—

As East, West, North, and South grow ever more alike, so do our names for the foods we all eat. Take pancakes. Once tagged everything from "flapjacks" to "griddle cakes" to "sweatpads," they're now almost universally called "pancakes"—a term which didn't come into wide use until the late nineteenth century. But anyone who relishes this classic American breakfast food (and who doesn't?) knows that there's a staggering array of recipes out there, with more being created all the time. Bored with the standard, white-flour variety? A typical pancake house lists offerings made with buckwheat, buttermilk, and sourdough, plus additions of banana, berries, apple, pumpkin, chocolate, nuts, or whatever else suits your fancy. And that's not even getting into toppings and size variations, such as "silver dollars" (small pancakes beloved by small children).

More refined pancake varieties include the soufflé-like puff or oven pancake, raised pancakes (blini), made with yeast and whipped egg white, and the thin French crêpe, which has been with us for generations; Virginians of yore made them with a white-wine batter and called them "quire of paper pancakes."

The hardy johnnycake, made of cornmeal, salt, and milk or water, is one of our first national dishes, introduced by Native Americans who called them *joniken* (or so some scholars say—others dispute this). Rhode Islanders, who in years past were great millers of corn, are passionate about authenticity. A fifty-year-old state law requires that only whitecap flint corn, an old Indian variety, be used in any mix labeled "Rhode Island johnnycakes."

★★

APPLE PUFF PANCAKE

★ ★ ★

Light and fluffy, this apple-laden German-style pancake is baked rather than fried. Choose a decorative ovenproof serving dish for the baking so you can present breakfast, piping hot and gloriously risen, right from the oven. Dust the hot pancake with confectioners' sugar, then cut it into wedges. Pass crisp bacon strips or sausage patties and a pot of black cherry jam alongside.

4 tablespoons (½ stick) unsalted butter, melted

3 apples (Golden Delicious or McIntosh), peeled, cored, and cut into 1-inch chunks

1 tablespoon light or dark brown sugar

1 teaspoon ground cinnamon

4 large eggs

½ cup milk

1 teaspoon pure vanilla extract

Pinch of salt

½ cup all-purpose flour

1 tablespoon confectioners' sugar

1. Preheat the oven to 450°F. Butter or oil a 12-inch ovenproof pie plate or cast-iron skillet.

2. Place 2 tablespoons of the melted butter in a nonstick skillet over medium heat. Add the apples, sprinkle with the brown sugar and cinnamon, and cook, stirring, until tender, 10 minutes.

3. Whisk the eggs, milk, remaining 2 tablespoons melted butter, vanilla, and salt together in a medium-size bowl. Add the flour and mix well.

4. Spread the apples over the bottom of the prepared pie plate, and pour the egg mixture over them.

5. Bake until puffed and golden brown, 20 minutes. Dust with confectioners' sugar and serve immediately, cut into wedges.

Serves 4

SHEILA'S BASIC WAFFLES

★ ★ ★

Although whole eggs are generally mixed into waffle batters, for my basic method I separate the whites from the yolks, beat them until stiff and fold them into the finished batter. This results in a much lighter texture, a crispier crust, and lots of calls for seconds.

2 cups all-purpose flour
2 tablespoons light brown sugar
1 tablespoons baking powder
½ teaspoon salt
3 large eggs, separated
1½ cups milk
⅓ cup unsalted butter, melted
1 teaspoon pure vanilla extract
Unsalted butter, for serving
Pure maple syrup, for serving
Fresh berries, for serving

1. Preheat a nonstick waffle iron.

2. Combine the flour, brown sugar, baking powder, and salt in a bowl, and set aside.

3. In another bowl, whisk together the egg yolks, milk, melted butter, and vanilla. Stir the flour mixture into the liquid, and mix just to combine.

4. Beat the egg whites until stiff, and then fold them into the batter with a rubber spatula.

5. Pour ½ cup of batter into the center of the preheated waffle iron. Quickly spread it out toward the edges with a rubber spatula. Close the top and cook for 2 minutes. Remove the waffle, and repeat with the remaining batter. Serve immediately with butter, syrup, and fresh berries.

Makes 8 waffles; serves 4

NOTE: Not long ago, I ordered a terrific bacon waffle for breakfast. I thought there had to be some great magic going on in the restaurant kitchen, but once I tried it out at home, I found a little magic myself. All I did was fry up some bacon nice and brown but not quite crisp, and drain it on a paper towel. Then, just before closing the waffle iron, I laid a couple of strips over the batter. Voilà! Great bacon waffles. Serve them with butter, syrup, and berries alongside, just as you would the basic waffles.

WHOLE-WHEAT SOUR CREAM WAFFLES

★ ★ ★

Tasting both sunny and earthy, whole-wheat waffles enhanced with pecans are ideal fare for breakfast on a cold winter day, particularly when they are draped in melted butter and real maple syrup. To ensure equal distribution of pecans in each waffle, I sprinkle them on top of the batter just before closing the waffle iron. The hint of cinnamon in the batter adds a slightly spicy tinge that I like.

1½ cups whole-wheat flour
½ cup all-purpose flour
2 tablespoons light brown sugar
1 tablespoon baking powder
½ teaspoon salt
¼ teaspoon ground cinnamon
3 large eggs, separated
1 cup sour cream
1 cup milk
⅓ cup unsalted butter, melted
½ cup chopped pecans (optional)
Unsalted butter, for serving
Pure maple syrup, for serving

1. Preheat a nonstick waffle iron.
2. Combine both of the flours, the brown sugar, baking powder, salt, and cinnamon in a bowl. Set aside.
3. In another bowl, whisk together the egg yolks, sour cream, milk, and melted butter. Sift the flour mixture into the liquid, and mix just to combine.
4. Beat the egg whites until stiff, and then fold them into the batter with a rubber spatula.
5. Pour ½ cup of the batter into the center of the preheated waffle iron. Quickly spread it out toward the edges with a rubber spatula. If desired, sprinkle 1 tablespoon of the chopped pecans over the batter. Close the top and cook for 2 minutes. Remove the waffle and repeat with the remaining batter and pecans. Serve immediately, with butter and syrup.
   Makes 8 waffles; serves 4

APPLE CINNAMON WAFFLES

★ ★ ★

Granny Smith apples, cinnamon, and vanilla add great wintry flavor to waffles. As in the basic recipe, beating the egg whites before folding them into the batter will give the waffles a light texture. Serve these hot and fresh on a lazy Sunday morning with some homemade sausage patties, sautéed apples, sweet butter, and maple syrup for a perfect beginning to a restful day.

2 cups all-purpose flour
2 tablespoons light brown sugar
1 tablespoon baking powder
½ teaspoon ground cinnamon
½ teaspoon salt
3 large eggs, separated
1 cup milk
1 cup plain nonfat yogurt
⅓ cup unsalted butter, melted
1 teaspoon pure vanilla extract
1 tablespoon fresh lemon juice
2 Granny Smith apples, cored and peeled
Unsalted butter, for serving
Pure maple syrup, for serving
Butter-Sautéed Apples (recipe follows), for serving
Zesty Sausage Patties (page 40), for serving

1. Preheat a nonstick waffle iron.

2. Combine the flour, brown sugar, baking powder, cinnamon, and salt in a bowl. Set aside.

3. In another bowl, whisk together the egg yolks, milk, yogurt, melted butter, and vanilla. Sift the flour mixture into the liquid, and mix just to combine.

4. Place the lemon juice in a bowl. Grate the apples into the bowl, and toss well with the lemon juice. Add to the batter and combine well.

5. Beat the egg whites until stiff, and then fold them into the batter with a rubber spatula.

6. Pour ½ cup of the batter onto the center of the preheated waffle iron. Quickly spread it out toward the edges with a rubber spatula, close the top, and cook for 2 minutes. Remove the waffle, and repeat with the remaining batter.

Serve immediately with butter, syrup, sautéed apples, and sausage patties.

Makes 10 waffles; serves 5

Butter-Sautéed Apples

—★—

3 tablespoons unsalted butter
4 apples (Golden Delicious, McIntosh, or
  Granny Smith), peeled, cored, and
  cut into 1-inch chunks
2 tablespoons light brown sugar
1 teaspoon ground cinnamon

WAFFLING AROUND

—❦—

Waffles first came to America from the Netherlands, via our Dutch colonial forebears. They kept their waffle irons—long-handled instruments that worked directly over open flames—at the hearthside. These irons were rarely found outside the Dutch settlements, but we know that Thomas Jefferson had one—and that he brought his home from France.

The introduction of the first electric waffle iron was in the 1890s, but it wasn't until the 1940s that they became more mainstream in American households.

Today's electric irons do their work in four minutes or less and their nonstick coatings allow them to be wiped clean with a dry towel. Waffle batters are simple, too. They usually have slightly more butter than pancake batters, for crispness. Some recipes also call for whipped egg whites, for lightness. "Belgian waffles," the thicker variety commonly sold at county fairs, require yeast and an iron with deeper grids than normal. (These, by the way, were the sensation of the mid 1960s, when, topped with strawberries and whipped cream, they were served to hungry hordes at the New York City World's Fair.)

Batter can be prepared ahead of time, but waffles can't. Serve them fresh out of the iron, and top them with syrup, honey, or fresh fruit right before eating. (If it's morning, that is. After breakfast, I prefer them with scoops of ice cream and plenty of hot fudge!)

Melt the butter in a large nonstick skillet over medium-high heat. Add the apples and sprinkle with the brown sugar and cinnamon. Cook for 10 to 15 minutes, stirring, until tender.

Serves 4 to 6

BANANA BUTTERMILK WAFFLES

★ ★ ★

Coarsely mashed bananas and a pinch of nutmeg make these intensely flavored waffles more moist than most, while the yogurt cuts the sweetness. As a complementary taste, I top them with a dollop of cool sour cream or more yogurt and fresh raspberries to make a delightful late morning breakfast or a light supper.

2 cups all-purpose flour
2 tablespoons light brown sugar
1 tablespoon baking powder
½ teaspoon salt
½ teaspoon ground cinnamon
¼ teaspoon ground nutmeg
3 large eggs, separated
1 cup plain nonfat yogurt
1 cup milk
⅓ cup unsalted butter, melted
1 teaspoon pure vanilla extract
2 very ripe bananas
1 tablespoon fresh lemon juice
Unsalted butter, for serving
Pure maple syrup, for serving

1. Preheat a nonstick waffle iron.

2. Combine the flour, brown sugar, baking powder, salt, cinnamon, and nutmeg in a bowl. Set aside.

3. In another bowl, whisk together the egg yolks, yogurt, milk, melted butter, and vanilla. Sift the flour mixture into the liquid, and mix just to combine.

4. Coarsely mash the bananas with the lemon juice in a bowl, and stir them into the batter.

5. Beat the egg whites until stiff, and then fold them into the batter with a rubber spatula.

6. Pour ½ cup of the batter onto the center of the preheated waffle iron, and quickly spread it out toward the edges with a rubber spatula. Close the top and cook for 2 minutes. Remove the waffle, and repeat with the remaining batter. Serve immediately, with butter and maple syrup.

Makes 10 waffles; serves 5

MARION CUNNINGHAM'S RAISED WAFFLES

★ ★ ★

Once I got into creating and sharing waffle recipes, my waffle-specialist friend told me I had to try Marion Cunningham's ethereal Raised Waffles. Marion, our modern-day Fannie Farmer, is responsible for some of the best breakfast creations I know and these raised waffles are no exception. Make them for breakfast, brunch, or even a devilish late supper served with a dollop of sour cream and caviar. I promise the beginning of a love affair. Just note the timing; the batter is prepared a day ahead.

½ cup warm water
1 package active dry yeast
2 cups milk, warmed
½ cup (1 stick) unsalted butter, melted
1 teaspoon salt
1 teaspoon sugar
2 cups all-purpose flour
Vegetable oil cooking spray
2 large eggs
¼ teaspoon baking soda

1. Place the warm water in a large mixing bowl and sprinkle the yeast over it. Let stand to dissolve for 5 minutes.

2. Add the warm milk, melted butter, salt, sugar, and flour, and beat until smooth and blended. (A whisk or hand mixer may be used to get rid of the lumps.) Cover the bowl with plastic wrap and let it stand overnight at room temperature.

3. Preheat a nonstick waffle iron, first spraying it with vegetable oil cooking spray.

4. Just before cooking the waffles, beat the eggs and baking soda into the batter, stirring until well mixed (the batter will be very thin). Pour ½ to ¾ cup of the batter into a very hot waffle iron. Quickly spread it out toward the edges with a rubber spatula, and close the top. Bake the waffle until it is golden and crisp, 2 to 3 minutes. Repeat with the remaining batter.

Makes 8 waffles

NOTE: The batter will keep well for several days in the refrigerator.

ANNABEL'S FRENCH TOAST

★ ★ ★

For years, my daughter has been making her marvelous French toast for breakfast on the weekends. I never interfere and have always stayed out of the way until I'm called. She finally gave me the recipe for this book and I found that the ratio of eggs to half-and-half is what gives her toast just the right degree of richness. Soaking the challah in the batter is the final touch of perfection. Serve with melted butter, maple syrup, and jam and you'll understand one of the reasons why I know my daughter is a treasure!

4 large eggs
½ cup half-and-half or milk
¼ teaspoon pure vanilla extract
2 tablespoons sugar
¼ teaspoon ground cinnamon
¼ teaspoon salt
3 teaspoons unsalted butter, plus more
    if needed
8 slices challah or other bread, cut
    1 inch thick
Melted unsalted butter, for serving
Pure maple syrup, for serving
Jam, for serving

1. Whisk the eggs, half-and-half, vanilla, sugar, cinnamon, and salt together in a shallow bowl.

2. Melt 1 teaspoon of the butter in a medium-size nonstick skillet over medium-high heat. Soak 2 slices of the bread in the batter for about 1 minute, pressing down on the bread so it absorbs as much batter as possible. Then place the slices in the skillet and cook until golden, about 3 minutes on each side.

3. Serve immediately or keep warm, loosely

covered with foil, in a 250°F oven while you cook the remaining slices, adding more butter to the skillet as necessary.

4. Pass the butter, syrup, and jam.

Serves 4

FRENCH TOAST AND JELLY

I always think of French toast as a purely American dish, but it actually originated across the sea. Making excellent use of stale day-old bread, the ever thrifty French call the dish *pain perdu,* or "lost bread," and that's also what it's called in the Cajun and Creole cooking of Louisiana. Generously soaked in a light batter, the bread requires nothing more than a quick turn in a skillet to make our much-loved morning treat. After trying many breads, I have found that challah or an eggy brioche produces the finest French toast. In this recipe, the surprise of a pocket filled with jam makes a unique treat.

4 large eggs
1 cup milk
½ teaspoon pure vanilla extract
½ teaspoon sugar
¼ teaspoon ground cinnamon
⅛ teaspoon ground nutmeg
8 slices challah, brioche, or other egg bread,
    cut 1 inch thick
½ cup strawberry, raspberry, or apricot
    preserves
4 teaspoons unsalted butter
Pure maple or raspberry syrup,
    for serving

1. Beat the eggs, milk, vanilla, sugar, cinnamon, and nutmeg together in a shallow bowl. Set aside.

2. Carefully slice a 2-inch opening in one crust side of each of the bread slices to create a pocket. Do not cut through the other three crust sides. Gently spread the inside of each pocket with 1 tablespoon of the preserves.

3. Melt 1 teaspoon of the butter in a nonstick skillet over medium heat until it foams. Dip 2 bread slices in the egg mixture, coating them completely, and place them in the skillet. Cook until nicely browned on the first side, about 3 minutes. Turn and cook for about 2 minutes longer. Repeat with the remaining bread slices, adding more butter to the pan as necessary. Serve immediately, with syrup, or keep warm, loosely covered with foil, while you cook the remaining slices.

Serves 4

BRUNCH HAM-AND-CHEESE FRENCH TOAST

★ ★ ★

French toast is always a winner for breakfast or brunch, but wait until you taste this one! A rich batter combined with a mild Vermont Cheddar and Black Forest ham brings this version to the

★★

AMERICAN MAPLE SUGARING

—🍒—

*M*aple sugaring is a picturesque business. It's done in the same lovely places that maple trees are tapped, in wooden "sugarhouses" at the edges of snowy groves in cold, woodsy places all over North America. Vermont is the biggest producer, responsible for more than a third of the national output. So I started my maple studies there, at the Butternut Mountain Farm, minutes north of the ski-resort town of Stowe. It was a typical day for early March—gray, with temperatures in the high 30s that kept the orchard pleasantly melty. The cold, heavy damp pressed the clouds of steam close to the weathered barn where freshly gathered sap was boiling down, or "evaporating," to its sweet brown essence. It takes roughly thirty to fifty gallons to make a single gallon of syrup, depending on the time of year and the weather.

Native Americans slashed trees to gather sap and dropped red-hot stones into it to make syrup. Colonials introduced tapping through holes bored into maple trunks, and boiled over open fires. Today's methods are similarly low-tech. Sap is often still gathered by hand and emptied into storage tanks that travel on tractors or horse-drawn sleighs. Sometimes it's funneled directly into a tank via plastic tubing (miles of it, at some farms). From there, it's strained and emptied into an elevated tank in the sugarhouse. This tank is attached to an "evaporator," an open pan heated over a wood fire that's divided into a maze of shallow channels. The evaporating liquid flows through slowly, emerging at the end as finished syrup.

All this is simple in principle, but complicated in practice. As with wine, soil and location are key. The species of maple matters, too, as not all saps are created equal. Weather is a big concern: since sap runs best when the woods freeze by night and thaw by day, a season that's too cold or too warm can be disappointing. Sugar farmers have to race with spring each year, since warmer days can also turn sap milky and bitter. In February the sap is more concentrated, therefore less is needed per gallon of syrup. By April, the sap is more fluid, requiring up to fifty gallons to make a gallon of syrup. Once collected, sap must be cooked immediately, since it spoils quite easily. And for a light, high-quality result, it should be cooked down fast, ideally in just an hour.

I had never quite understood what "grade A," "grade B," or "fancy" meant on a tin of syrup, but I'd always picked up the "fancy" kind because I assumed it was the best. David Marvin, the owner of Butternut Mountain Farm, set me straight about that. The grade, he explained, refers to when in the sugaring season the sap for a given batch was drawn. "Fancy" or "Grade AA," made earliest, is lightest in color and flavor, best for cake icings and other delicate sweets.

★★

"**Grade A Medium**," the most common kind, is somewhat more intense, good on pancakes, waffles, and French toast. "**Grade A Dark**" and "**Grade B**" are progressively bolder and darker, great for baked beans, meat glazes, candied yams, and any dessert recipes that call for robust flavoring.

People who make maple syrup usually love to cook with it. When I visited Flaherty's Maple Sugar Farm and Maple Trails Resort, cross country in Bemidji, Minnesota, the Flahertys laid out a superb breakfast of their own maple-pecan scones (yes, they gave me the recipe and I've included it in the **Coffee Break** chapter), maple butter (a form of reduced syrup), and coffee brewed from sap. Dan Flaherty uses all the modern methods to collect his sap (flexible plastic tubing links the trees to a 600-gallon stainless-steel collection tank), but he still also uses a few old-fashioned collection buckets for his family's personal needs. Although the Flahertys sell their maple syrup commercially, their biggest market are the guests who stay at the resort. Dan, his wife, Donna, and their daughter Molly sent me home with a few bottles of amber elixir for my own kitchen, which I've stored (per their instructions) in the refrigerator to prevent fermentation and crystallization.

top of the chart. The drizzle of pure maple syrup may sound too rich, but try it—it adds just the right touch.

2 large eggs
⅓ cup half-and-half
2 teaspoons pure vanilla extract
1 tablespoon sugar
⅛ teaspoon ground cinnamon
⅛ teaspoon salt
4 slices best-quality white bread
4 teaspoons unsalted butter, at room
*   temperature*
1 tablespoon honey mustard
2 slices (1 ounce each) Vermont white
*   Cheddar*
4 thin slices (1 ounce each) baked or cured
*   ham, such as Black Forest, or Canadian*
*   bacon or Italian pancetta*
Pure maple syrup or confectioners' sugar,
*   for serving*

1. Whisk the eggs, half-and-half, vanilla, sugar, cinnamon, and salt together in a shallow bowl. Set aside.

2. Spread 2 of the slices of bread with a teaspoon each of the butter. Spread the remaining slices of bread with the mustard. Lay 1 slice of cheese and 2 slices of ham over the mustard, and top with the buttered bread, buttered side down.

3. Melt 1 teaspoon of the butter in a non-stick skillet over medium heat. Dip one of the sandwiches in the egg batter, making sure both sides are well soaked. Place it in the skillet and cook until it is golden brown and the cheese has melted, 2 to 3 minutes on each side. Add the remaining 1 teaspoon butter to the skillet, and repeat with the second sandwich.

4. Cut the sandwiches in half diagonally, and serve immediately with maple syrup or confectioners' sugar.

Serves 2

LAURIE'S LUSCIOUS CINNAMON TOAST

★ ★ ★

Other than once at the Okura Hotel in Tokyo, I have never tasted better cinnamon toast than my friend and associate Laurie makes. She prefers white bread, but my choice would be challah or a brioche loaf sliced about ½ inch thick. Whichever you use, the butter and cinnamon sugar will form a thin, crackling crust on the toast. Served directly from the oven, no enhancement is necessary. Besides being perfect breakfast food, this toast is an ideal after-school snack.

2 tablespoons sugar
1 teaspoon ground cinnamon
4 slices best-quality white bread
8 teaspoons unsalted butter, at room temperature

1. Preheat the broiler.
2. Combine the sugar and cinnamon in a small bowl.
3. Place the bread slices on a baking sheet and toast under the broiler, on one side only, until golden brown, about 45 seconds. (Watch closely to avoid burning.)
4. Turn the bread over. Spread 2 teaspoons of butter evenly on the untoasted side of each slice of bread. Sprinkle 1½ teaspoons of the cinnamon sugar evenly over each buttered side.

Place the baking sheet under the broiler, and broil the toast until the top is golden and bubbly, about 1½ minutes. Serve immediately.
Serves 2

HAM STEAK WITH SHEILA'S REDEYE GRAVY

★ ★ ★

Redeye gravy originated in the Old South. To mellow the flavor of richly seasoned sautéed Smithfield ham, a sauce was made by adding some water and strong coffee to the skillet. The little red specks of almost-burned fat that were scraped up from the bottom of the pan were said to resemble red eyes as they floated to the top of the gravy—therefore the strangely enticing name.

One day, while drinking coffee and ruminating on this culinary tale, I was inspired to create my version of this age-old favorite. Since I had already drunk the coffee, I scraped up my red eyes with a combination of tawny and ruby ports and a bit of chicken broth. A little red currant jelly was the extra touch for a true red color. In all, a splendid dish for brunch or dinner with Creamy Grits and a mess of greens.

1 baked Virginia ham steak (2½ to 2¾ pounds), cut 1½ inches thick
2 onions, halved lengthwise and slivered
½ cup golden raisins
½ cup defatted chicken broth, preferably homemade (page 253)
½ cup tawny port
2 tablespoons ruby port
1 tablespoon red currant jelly

1. Trim the fat off the ham steak, and cut it into small pieces. Render the fat in a large non-stick skillet over medium-low heat for about 10 minutes. Using a slotted spoon, remove the pieces of fat from the pan and discard them.

2. Add the ham to the skillet, and cook over medium heat until browned on each side, 10 minutes. Transfer the ham to a warm platter, and pour off all but 2 tablespoons of the fat from the skillet.

3. Add the onions and raisins to the skillet. Cook over medium heat until soft, about 10 minutes, stirring occasionally.

4. Add the broth, both ports, and the red currant jelly. Bring to a boil and continue to boil for 5 minutes, scraping up any brown bits on the bottom of the pan. Reduce the heat to medium, and simmer for another 5 minutes.

5. Before serving, thinly slice the ham steak crosswise. Arrange several slices on each plate, and top with the gravy.

Serves 6

CAROLYN'S CREAMED DRIED BEEF ON BISCUITS

★ ★ ★

When Carolyn Maxwell and I were room-mates in New York during the 1960s, there were only three things that we could afford to eat: canned tuna fish, spaghetti, and for Sunday breakfast, Carolyn's Pennsylvania Dutch specialty, creamed dried beef served over toast. Although I had never before tasted this stick-to-your-ribs wake-up call, I grew to like it almost as

much as I liked Carolyn—so much that it still has a place on my breakfast menu. These days I serve it over Rolled Buttermilk Biscuits with soft scrambled eggs on the side.

This dish tastes best if the beef is rinsed before cooking, to remove some of the salt that it absorbs during its long curing. Pat it dry and then let it air-dry thoroughly before shredding.

½ pound thinly sliced dried beef
2 tablespoons unsalted butter
3 tablespoons finely minced shallots
2 tablespoons all-purpose flour
1 cup defatted chicken broth, preferably homemade (page 253)
2 tablespoons medium-dry sherry
¾ cup heavy (or whipping) cream
Pinch of ground nutmeg
Pinch of cayenne pepper
4 Rolled Buttermilk Biscuits (page 215) or toasted English muffins, for serving

1. Separate the slices of dried beef, put them in a strainer, and rinse them under running water to remove some of the salt. Drain well, and pat dry with a paper towel. Spread the slices out on a dry towel, and allow them to dry completely. Coarsely shred the dried beef.

2. Meanwhile, melt the butter in a medium-size nonstick skillet over medium-low heat. Cook the shallots, stirring, until wilted, 4 to 5 minutes. Do not brown them.

3. Add the flour and cook, stirring, for 2 minutes, making a light brown roux.

4. Add the broth, sherry, cream, nutmeg, and cayenne pepper. Stir over low heat until slightly thickened, about 6 minutes. (Do not add any salt.) Add the beef and heat through. Serve over warm split biscuits.

Serves 4

ZESTY SAUSAGE PATTIES

★ ★ ★

Homemade sausage patties are easy to prepare and a delicious surprise, especially when they're flavored with orange zest. These little patties are just spicy enough to be served at breakfast or brunch instead of bacon or link sausages. If you prefer a spicier rendition, use hot instead of sweet Italian sausage. Serve these with waffles, pancakes, eggs, or Butter-Sautéed Apples.

1 pound ground pork shoulder
½ pound sweet Italian sausage, removed
*   from casing*
2 tablespoons chopped fresh flat-leaf parsley
1 tablespoon chopped fresh thyme, or
*   1 teaspoon dried*
2 teaspoons finely grated orange zest
½ teaspoon salt, or to taste
½ teaspoon coarsely ground black pepper

1. Combine all the ingredients in a large bowl, mixing them together well with your hands. Wash your hands thoroughly after working with the meat. Cover and chill the mixture for 30 minutes.
2. Form the meat into 14 to 16 flat patties, about 2 inches across and ½ inch thick. If the meat is too sticky to work with, wet your hands.
3. Fry the patties in a dry nonstick skillet over medium heat for about 4 minutes per side, until the meat is nicely browned and cooked through.
Makes 14 to 16 patties; serves 8

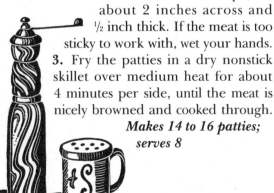

SOUTHERN SAUSAGE GRAVY

★ ★ ★

I caught the spirit of sausage gravy served over a split biscuit at the Restaurant Miche Mache, which was until recently in Stamford, Connecticut. My friends and I were there to enjoy a gospel brunch, featuring the singing of Jean Cheek and her trio, Faces, and the mouthwatering soul food of chef-owner Michel Nischan. Plates were piled high with onion-smothered pork chops, fried catfish, crispy fried chicken, and all the go-withs—fried okra, black-eyed peas, molasses corn, spicy collards, grits, and mashed potatoes—whew! When I got home, my particular ardor for the sausage gravy fueled an attempt to invent my own home-cooked version. To jazz it up a bit, I used a spicier sausage than the traditional mildly flavored bulk sausage, then added a good dose of fresh thyme for a Cajun accent as well. This makes a hearty power breakfast or brunch dish when served with scrambled eggs, fried ham, and some Fresh Pineapple Relish.

½ pound mild or sweet sausage, removed
*   from casings*
½ pound spicy Italian sausage, removed
*   from casings*
3 tablespoons all-purpose flour
¾ cup milk
¾ cup defatted chicken broth, preferably
*   homemade (page 253)*
1½ teaspoons chopped fresh thyme leaves, or
*   ¼ teaspoon dried*
Salt and freshly ground black pepper,
*   to taste*
6 Rolled Buttermilk Biscuits (page 215),
*   for serving*

1. Cook both of the sausage meats in a large nonstick skillet over medium-high heat, breaking the meat up with the spoon, until browned and cooked through. Using a slotted spoon, transfer the meat to a bowl.

2. Remove all but 3 tablespoons of the fat from the skillet. Sprinkle the flour into the skillet, stir well, and cook over medium-high heat for 1 minute, stirring constantly. Remove from the heat.

3. Slowly add the milk and the broth, whisking constantly until the mixture is smooth. Return the skillet to the heat and cook until the gravy is slightly thickened, 2 to 3 minutes. Add the thyme, and season with salt and pepper.

4. Add the crumbled sausage meat and combine well. Cook over medium heat until warmed through. Serve immediately over split biscuits.

Serves 6

BREAKFAST CHICKEN LIVERS AND ONIONS

★ ★ ★

Although the cholesterol-counting game keeps many of us from frequently eating liver, when it is time to cheat, I recommend this tasty chicken liver dish. I cook the onions until they are just lightly browned before adding the livers. Be sure to snip off any extra fat and to pat the livers very dry to ensure perfect crispness. To really satisfy my urge, I always serve them piled right beside two perfectly fried or scrambled eggs.

1 onion
1 tablespoon olive oil
1 tablespoon unsalted butter
¾ pound chicken livers, cleaned
⅛ to ¼ teaspoon dried thyme
Salt and freshly ground black pepper,
  to taste

1. Halve the onion and cut it into thin slivers.

2. Heat the oil and butter in a large nonstick skillet. Add the onion and cook over medium heat, stirring, until soft and lightly browned, 10 minutes.

3. Add the chicken livers and sprinkle with the thyme, salt, and a generous grinding of pepper. Cook, shaking the pan, until the livers are browned on the outside but still pink inside, 5 to 7 minutes. Serve immediately.

Serves 4

LIGHTLY CREAMED MUSHROOMS

★ ★ ★

Soft mushrooms napped in velvety cream sauce are a brunch classic, particularly when served over toasted biscuits or English muffins with a side of fried ham or thick bacon. In most preparations, a heavy flour roux is used to thicken the cream sauce, but I don't feel it's necessary. I just let the cream reduce as the mushrooms cook, creating a luscious light sauce.

2 tablespoons unsalted butter
2 tablespoons finely chopped shallots
10 ounces white mushrooms, cleaned and sliced
Pinch of cayenne pepper
Pinch of ground mace
¼ cup defatted chicken broth, preferably homemade
    (page 253)
2 tablespoons tawny port
½ cup heavy (or whipping) cream
Salt, to taste
1 tablespoon snipped fresh chives
2 Rolled Buttermilk Biscuits (page 215), or
    1 lightly toasted English muffin, for serving

1. Melt the butter in a large nonstick skillet over low heat. Add the shallots and cook, stirring, until wilted, 5 minutes.

2. Add the mushrooms, raise the heat to medium-high, and cook, stirring, until softened, 5 minutes. Sprinkle with the cayenne pepper and mace.

3. Add the broth and port, reduce the heat to medium, and cook for 5 minutes. Then add the cream and simmer gently to blend the flavors, 5 minutes. Season with salt and stir in the chives. Serve immediately, spooned over split biscuits or toasted English muffin halves.
    Serves 2

DENVER PETE'S HOME FRIES

★ ★ ★

On the way to the airport at five o'clock one morning, I stopped at Pete's Kitchen, a funky circa-1942 Denver landmark where every breakfast is diner textbook-perfect. At Pete's, the potatoes are baked in their jackets before being fried up with green bell peppers and onions. The mixture is heavenly—as near perfection as a breakfast potato can get. Two fried eggs and a splash of ketchup, and I heard the angels sing.

Whenever you're baking potatoes, put a few extra in the oven to keep on hand, refrigerated, to make Pete's special home fries the morning after. A sprinkling of chopped parsley just before serving will add a burst of freshness as well as great color.

4 russet potatoes (about 8 ounces each)
¼ cup olive oil, or more if necessary
1 large green bell pepper, stemmed, seeded,
    and cut into 1-inch pieces
1 large onion, cut into 1-inch
    pieces
Coarse salt and freshly
    ground black pepper,
    to taste
1½ tablespoons chopped
    fresh flat-leaf
    parsley, for garnish

1. Preheat the oven to 375°F.

2. Wash the potatoes, pat them dry, and prick them with the tines of a fork. Bake for 1 hour. Let the potatoes cool slightly, and then cut them into 1-inch chunks.

3. Heat the oil in a large nonstick skillet over medium heat. Add the bell pepper and onion and cook, stirring, until wilted and lightly browned, 10 minutes.

4. Add the potatoes to the skillet and toss with the vegetables. Season generously with coarse salt and pepper. Cook until crispy and lightly browned, turning occasionally with a spatula, 10 to 12 minutes. Sprinkle with the parsley and serve hot.
    Serves 4 to 6

★★★

HASH BROWNS OR HOME FRIES

—❦—

There was a time when I would never order hash browns over home fries, but since I've started making my own at home, it's a pretty close call these days. To take the confusion out of these two delectable breakfast potato favorites, I thought I'd get down to specifics.

Hash browns: The domain of the short-order cook, coarsely chopped or grated raw potatoes are fried in flat cakes in hot bacon fat or butter until they are crusty brown on both sides.

Home fries: The domain of the home cook, home

fries can be made a couple of ways. Traditionally, potatoes are first boiled, then sliced and fried in bacon fat or butter in a skillet until they are brown on both sides. My preference, however, is to bake some russets a day before use, cut them (skin and all) into large chunks, and sauté them with onions in olive oil until the potato skins are crisp and the onions are slightly golden. I season generously with coarse salt and freshly ground black pepper. When I'm really into making them special, I chop up a green pepper à la Denver Pete's (see recipe, facing page). Either way—yum!

★★★

HASH-BROWN PANCAKE

★ ★ ★

I've never sat down in a diner at breakfast time where the cook wasn't frying up hash browns on the griddle. And this presents a problem. First, I really like home fries better than hash browns, and second, the hash browns are nearly always served up pale brown on the outside and under-cooked on the inside. So I put on my short-order hat and fried up a batch for this book. They were spectacular! To get the best results, you will need a medium-size nonstick skillet to fry the grated potatoes into a well-browned pancake. It's large, but it will hold together. Cut it into four wedges and serve them warm, with ketchup.

2 russet potatoes, peeled
Salt and freshly ground black pepper,
    to taste
1 tablespoon peanut or vegetable oil
1 tablespoon unsalted butter

1. Using the medium holes on a grater, grate the potatoes into a bowl. Season with salt and pepper.
2. Heat the oil and butter in a medium-size nonstick skillet over medium heat until hot. Add the potatoes and pat them down to form a pancake.
3. Cover the skillet and cook until the bottom of the "pancake" is browned, 10 to 12 minutes. Turn it over carefully, cover, and cook 10 minutes longer or until nicely browned. Cut into four sections and serve immediately.
Serves 4

GRITS—SOUL OF THE SOUTH

—❧—

More than just a traditional Southern food, grits are a Southern institution—in fact, it's been said that to fathom grits is to glimpse a facet of the Southern soul.

As any Southerner will tell you, there's just *something* about eating grits. No one eats them plain—plain is bland. And while they do well just with a little butter and salt, they're tastier still with a spoonful of sugar, a light lashing of maple sugar, or a sprinkling of sharp cheese. Look around your breakfast plate for additional seasonings—a touch of leaky egg yolk, a "smothering" of gravy, a forkful of bacon, sausage, or country ham. And don't limit them to breakfast—Southerners enjoy visiting with grits any time of day, in stews and casseroles, soufflés and stuffings, meatballs and fritters; they're mixed into breads, pizza crusts, and biscuits. Make them with egg, and they firm up when cooled, like polenta.

"Grits" (from the Old English *grytte*) originally described the bran and chaff that was left over from grinding grains, but by the sixteenth century grits had come to mean the coarsely ground grain itself. While any grain that can be hulled and ground is nominally a candidate for grits, what *we* call grits comes from the hulled, dried kernels of mature corn, called *ustatahamen* by the Native Americans who first made it, and hominy by the new Americans who inherited it—first in the Northeast and then, lastingly, down in the South.

How Are Your Grits Ground?

While grits may be an institution in the South, they are also available above the Mason-Dixon line, though not always, perhaps, in the greatest variety. Quaker Oats, Carnation, and Martha White Foods distribute grits nationwide, and stone-ground—the finest—are available in some specialty food stores and readily by mail-order (see the listing of sources below). To avoid spoilage and infestation by kitchen pests, keep uncooked grits tightly sealed in your refrigerator. They'll stay fresh there for up to three months, and up to one year in the freezer.

Stone-ground: These grits are made by grinding the whole dried corn kernel, including germ and endosperm, in an old-fashioned grist mill. Stone-ground grits have more nutritional value, oil, and flavor than the commercial (steel-ground) varieties, but they will go rancid if not refrigerated or frozen. They take 20 to 30 minutes to cook completely and are the grits preferred for these recipes.

★★★★★★★★★★★★★★★★★★★★★★★★★★★★★★★★

Regular: The coarsest of the three commercially produced grits products, regular require a longer cooking time (20 to 30 minutes) than quick or instant, but the resulting flavor is superior.

Quick-cooking: The grits most commonly found on grocery shelves. To make them, regular grits are lightly steamed and then compressed to fracture the particles. These grits cook in 3 to 5 minutes.

Instant: Southerners don't like to talk about instant grits because they don't consider them grits at all. They're made by cooking regular grits, then taking the water out so they can be easily reconstituted with boiling water; they are not recommended for these recipes.

Good whole-heart grits can be hard to find in stores outside the South. If you're having trouble, consider mail-ordering from Adams Milling Company in Dolthan, Alabama (205-983-4233), Callaway Gardens in Pine Mountain, Georgia (404-663-5100), or Falls Mill in Belvidere, Tennessee (615-469-7161).

★★★★★★★★★★★★★★★★★★★★★★★★★★★★★★★★

CREAMY GRITS

★ ★ ★

Homey, cozy, and thoroughly delicious, grits are a much-beloved staple of Southern cooking. This low-country classic recipe is as appreciated at dinner as it is for breakfast. I've eaten creamy grits in the morning with a sprinkling of brown sugar, and in the evening with a shrimp and sausage gravy. I do believe I understand why Southerners long for them when they're away from home.

6 cups water
1½ cups grits (not quick-cooking or instant),
*   preferably stone-ground*
1 teaspoon salt
1½ tablespoons unsalted butter
3 tablespoons heavy (or whipping) cream

1. Bring the water to a rapid boil in a large heavy pot.

2. Stir in the grits and salt all at once, and mix well. Reduce the heat to low, cover, and cook, stirring occasionally, until smooth and thick, 20 minutes.

3. Stir in the butter and the cream, mix well, and serve immediately.
Serves 4

CHEESE GRITS SOUFFLE

★ ★ ★

This popular recipe has become a standard from Kansas City to Memphis. And no wonder, as the casserole is delicious, easy to prepare, and a welcome change from potatoes or rice. It also sits just as well at the dinner table as it does at brunch. Before adding the eggs to the grits mixture, temper them by whisking a cup of hot grits into them. Then all the ingredients can be mixed together without the risk of making scrambled eggs.

6 cups water
Salt
1½ cups grits (not quick-cooking or instant),
*   preferably stone-ground*
2 eggs
1½ cups (6 ounces) grated Cheddar cheese
2 tablespoons unsalted butter
½ teaspoon Tabasco sauce, or to taste
Freshly ground black pepper, to taste
Paprika, to taste

1. Preheat the oven to 350°F. Lightly butter a 2-quart soufflé or baking dish.
2. Bring the water and 1 teaspoon salt to a boil in a large heavy pot. Gradually stir in the grits. Reduce the heat to low, cover, and cook, stirring occasionally, until thick, 20 minutes. Remove from the heat.
3. Lightly beat the eggs in a small bowl. Add 1 cup of the cooked grits to the eggs, and beat well to combine. Stir the egg mixture into the remaining cooked grits along with the cheese, butter, and Tabasco. Season with salt and pepper. Stir until the mixture is well combined and the cheese and butter have melted.
4. Pour the mixture into the prepared soufflé dish and sprinkle with the paprika. Bake until set and golden brown on top, 45 minutes. Serve immediately.

Serves 4 to 6

SOUTHERN FRIED GRITS

★ ★ ★

These stellar grits have replaced the mounds of polenta I have prepared in recent years. When shopping, seek out superb traditional stone-ground grits; avoid the instant variety if possible. But be ready to stir and then to wait: once the grits have set, they need to be chilled for about 3 hours before frying. (If you feel a rush of creativity, cut the chilled grits into decorative shapes, using biscuit or cookie cutters, before frying.)

1 quart milk
4 large cloves garlic, peeled and bruised
1 cup grits (not quick-cooking or instant),
*   preferably stone-ground*
1 cup shredded Monterey Jack cheese
¼ cup finely minced red bell pepper
¼ cup finely minced green bell pepper
½ cup chopped fresh basil leaves
Salt and freshly ground black pepper, to taste
½ cup all-purpose flour
1 tablespoon olive oil, or more as needed
1 tablespoon unsalted butter, or more as
*   needed*

1. Lightly butter a 9-inch square baking dish.

2. Combine the milk and the garlic in a heavy saucepan over medium-high heat and bring just to a boil. Remove the garlic. Stirring constantly, slowly add the grits. Simmer gently, stirring constantly, until the mixture is thick and

the milk has been completely absorbed, about 20 minutes.

3. Remove from the heat and stir in the cheese, both bell peppers, the basil, salt, and pepper. Spread the mixture in the prepared pan with a rubber spatula. Cool to room temperature, cover, and refrigerate until firm, 2 to 3 hours.

4. Cut the grits into nine 3-inch squares and dust lightly with the flour.

5. Heat the oil and butter in a large nonstick skillet over medium-high heat. Fry the grits, in batches, until golden brown, about 1 minute per side. Add more oil and butter to the skillet as necessary.

Serves 8

PART TWO

COFFEE
BREAK

Muffins & Sweet Breads

It's 11 A.M., time for a coffee break. You've settled in, set the day's pace, got some work done, made it through another morning. So reward yourself. Steal a moment at your desk, or find a cozy spot in front of the television before yet another household chore presents itself. A little indulgence will fortify you for the day ahead. Rise and Shine Coffee Cake, Jelly Muffins, or Flaherty's Maple Pecan Scones can soothe a cranky mood, especially if accompanied by a cup of Santa Fe Heavenly Hot Chocolate. For something less filling, choose from a basket of Cakey Buttermilk Doughnuts, delicate Cranberry Orange Bread, and surprisingly light Steffi's Bran Muffins. If it's summer, bake the season's natural sweetness into Zesty Blueberry Muffins or Carole Solie's Fresh Berry Bundt Cake. Between sips and nibbles, read up on the well-roasted bean. Follow the easy steps detailed in this chapter, and you'll soon have a home brew as fine as your favorite coffee bar's.

ZESTY BLUEBERRY MUFFINS

★ ★ ★

When blueberries are in season, these muffins make a glorious start to the day. But, even when berries are out of season, they're still pretty sensational. For fresh berries, substitute the kind that are individually quick-frozen and let them thaw slightly before folding them into the batter. (Never use frozen berries packed in syrup.) These muffins are just as delicious when made with wild black raspberries. Adding cornmeal to the batter gives a slight coarseness to the texture, which I particularly like.

½ cup (1 stick) unsalted butter, at room temperature
1 cup plus 2 tablespoons sugar
2 large eggs
2 teaspoons baking powder
1 teaspoon pure vanilla extract
½ teaspoon finely grated lemon zest
1¾ cups all-purpose flour
¼ cup finely ground yellow cornmeal
¼ teaspoon salt
⅛ teaspoon ground cinnamon
½ cup milk
2½ cups fresh blueberries

1. Preheat the oven to 375°F. Grease 12 regular muffin cups or line them with paper liners.

2. Using an electric mixer, cream the butter and 1 cup of the sugar together in a large bowl. Add the eggs, one at a time, beating well after each addition. Add the baking powder and mix well. Add the vanilla extract and lemon zest, and mix well.

3. In another bowl, combine the flour, cornmeal, salt, and cinnamon. Add half of the dry ingredients to the batter, and mix lightly. Then add the milk and stir well. Add the remaining dry ingredients and stir just to combine. Do not overmix.

4. Fold in the blueberries. Spoon the batter into the muffin cups, and sprinkle them evenly with the remaining 2 tablespoons sugar. Bake in the center of the oven until the muffins are golden brown and a toothpick inserted in the center comes out just clean, 25 to 35 minutes.

5. Cool the muffins in the pan on a wire rack for 15 minutes. Then unmold them onto a rack to cool completely.
Makes 12 muffins

CRANBERRY BLUEBERRY- BUCKLE MUFFINS

★ ★ ★

These fruity muffins are a wonderful change from the heavier bran and whole-wheat muffins that are the usual breakfast offering during the colder months. Their light, cakey texture nicely absorbs the addition of cranberries and blueberries. Since I usually make them in the winter, I use frozen blueberries, which are perfectly acceptable if they are individually quick-frozen—never use berries packed in syrup. Make sure that the berries are nearly thawed before you stir them in. The cranberries add a pleasant tartness that is offset by the spicy sweetness of the streusel topping.

STREUSEL TOPPING
1/4 cup sugar
2 tablespoons all-purpose flour
1/2 teaspoon ground cinnamon
2 tablespoons unsalted butter, cut into
    little pieces

BATTER
2 cups all-purpose flour
1/2 cup sugar
2 teaspoons baking powder
1 teaspoon salt
1 large egg
1 cup buttermilk
1/2 cup (1 stick) unsalted butter, melted
1/2 cup fresh cranberries
1/2 cup fresh or frozen blueberries
    (see headnote)

1. Preheat the oven to 400°F. Grease 12 regular muffin cups or line them with paper liners.
2. Prepare the streusel topping: Place all the streusel ingredients in a food processor and process until the mixture has a sandy texture. Set aside.
3. Prepare the batter: Combine the flour, sugar, baking powder, and salt in a large bowl. Mix well.
4. In another bowl, beat the egg. Add the buttermilk and melted butter, and mix well.
5. Stir the egg mixture into the dry ingredients, and mix until just combined. Then fold in the cranberries and blueberries.
6. Fill the muffin cups three-quarters full with the batter. Sprinkle each muffin with 2 teaspoons of the streusel topping. Bake in the center of the oven until a wooden pick inserted in the center comes out just clean, about 30 minutes.

7. Cool the muffins in the pan on a wire rack for 15 minutes. Then unmold them onto a rack to cool completely.
Makes 12 muffins

CRANBERRY WALNUT MUFFINS

★ ★ ★

Light and delicate, yet pungent with the tart bite of autumn's cranberries, these seasonal muffins really hit their mark with breakfast coffee or afternoon tea. They can also be a pleasant surprise in a basket of mixed breads served with a New England boiled dinner.

2 cups all-purpose flour
1 1/4 cups sugar
2 teaspoons baking powder
1/2 teaspoon salt
2 large eggs
1/2 cup buttermilk
1/4 cup (1/2 stick) unsalted butter, melted
1 tablespoon fresh lemon juice
1 cup fresh cranberries
1/2 cup coarsely chopped walnuts
1 teaspoon finely grated lemon zest

1. Preheat the oven to 400°F. Grease 12 regular muffin cups or line them with paper liners.
2. Combine the flour, sugar, baking powder, and salt in a bowl. Mix well and set aside.
3. In another bowl, beat the eggs lightly. Stir in the buttermilk, melted butter, and lemon juice.
4. Add the egg mixture to the dry ingredients, and mix until just combined. Fold in the cranberries, walnuts, and lemon zest.

5. Fill the muffin cups evenly with the batter. Bake in the center of the oven until a wooden pick inserted in the center comes out just clean, 20 minutes.

6. Cool the muffins in the pan on a rack for 15 minutes. Then unmold them onto a rack to cool completely.

Makes 12 muffins

JELLY MUFFINS

★ ★ ★

I love jelly doughnuts! However, since they take more time to make than I usually have to spend, I thought a jelly-filled muffin, warm from the oven, might be just the substitute. This all-in-one luxury breakfast treat has become a real favorite in my house. I use raspberry preserves, but you may use any you prefer. The muffins are a snap to make and sure to please.

1¾ cups all-purpose flour
½ cup sugar
2 teaspoons baking powder
½ teaspoon baking soda
½ teaspoon salt
1 large egg
¾ cup buttermilk
6 tablespoons (¾ stick) unsalted butter,
  melted
1 teaspoon finely grated orange zest
8 generous teaspoons raspberry preserves

1. Preheat the oven to 400°F. Grease 8 regular muffin cups or line them with paper liners.

2. Combine the flour, sugar, baking powder, baking soda, and salt in a bowl. Mix well and set aside.

3. In another bowl, lightly beat the egg. Add the buttermilk, melted butter, and orange zest and stir well.

4. Add the dry ingredients to the egg mixture, and stir with a wooden spoon until just combined.

5. Fill each muffin cup half full with batter. Using your index finger or the back of a teaspoon, make a slight indentation in the center of the batter and fill it with a teaspoon of the raspberry preserves. Spoon the remaining batter over the preserves, spreading it gently to cover them.

6. Bake the muffins in the center of the oven until a wooden pick inserted in the center comes out just clean, about 20 minutes.

7. Cool the muffins in the pan on a wire rack for 15 minutes. Unmold them onto a rack to cool completely.

Makes 8 muffins

STEFFI'S BRAN MUFFINS

★ ★ ★

Steffi Berne, friend and baker par excellence, has created a recipe for ambrosial bran muffins—the only bran muffins I've ever really liked! Steffi usually makes them in mini muffin tins and takes them along on early morning forays to the flea market. She offers this crucial tip: Do not overmix the batter; just gently fold in the dry ingredients, or the muffins will be tough and lopsided. I found the dried blueberries to be a welcoming surprise, but currants, raisins, or dried cherries would be satisfying substitutes. When you're making minis, make a double batch because they freeze beautifully!

1½ cups wheat bran cereal
1¼ cups milk
1 cup all-purpose flour
¼ cup whole-wheat flour
⅓ cup sugar
1 tablespoon baking powder
¼ teaspoon freshly grated nutmeg
Pinch of salt
¼ cup (generous) dried blueberries or currants
1 large egg
¼ cup vegetable oil

1. Preheat the oven to 400°F. Grease 12 regular or 24 mini muffin cups or line them with paper liners.

2. In a large bowl, combine the bran cereal and milk. Set aside.

3. In a medium-size bowl, combine both of the flours, the sugar, baking powder, nutmeg, salt, and dried blueberries. Stir with a fork until the ingredients are evenly distributed.

4. Add the egg and oil to the softened cereal, and beat with a wooden spoon or electric mixer until thoroughly combined. Fold in the dry ingredients just until the flour is barely visible. Do not overmix.

5. Fill the muffin cups evenly with the batter. Bake in the center of the oven for 20 minutes, or until the muffins are firm to the touch and a wooden toothpick inserted in the center comes out just clean.

6. Allow the muffins to cool in the pan for 5 minutes before unmolding them. Serve warm.
Makes 12 regular or 24 mini muffins

NOTE: These muffins freeze very successfully for up to 1 month. After baking, let them cool to room temperature, and then place them in a self-sealing plastic bag to freeze. To serve, place the frozen muffins on a baking sheet and heat them in a preheated 350°F oven for 10 minutes.

OATMEAL RAISIN MUFFINS

★ ★ ★

Slightly rustic, these breakfast muffins get their substance from old-fashioned oats, an American favorite. They're especially good served with sweet butter and bitter orange marmalade. A sip from a steaming cup of freshly brewed coffee or rich hot chocolate is all that's needed to complete the taste.

1 cup plus 1 tablespoon rolled oats
1 cup buttermilk
¾ cup whole-wheat flour
¾ cup all-purpose flour
2 teaspoons baking powder
½ teaspoon ground cinnamon
½ teaspoon salt
2 large eggs
½ cup (packed) light brown sugar
¼ cup honey
6 tablespoons (¾ stick) unsalted butter, melted
1 teaspoon pure vanilla extract
½ cup golden raisins

1. Preheat the oven to 400°F. Grease 12 regular muffin cups or line them with paper liners.

2. Place 1 cup of the rolled oats and the buttermilk in a small bowl, and combine well. Set aside.

3. Combine both of the flours, the baking powder, cinnamon, and salt in another bowl. Mix well and set aside.

4. In a third bowl, beat the eggs and the brown sugar together with an electric mixer. Add the honey and mix well. Add the melted butter and the vanilla, and mix well.

5. Add the flour mixture to the egg mixture, and stir with a wooden spoon until just combined. Then add the oats and the raisins, and stir until just mixed.

6. Fill the muffin cups three-quarters full with batter. Sprinkle the tops with the remaining tablespoon of oats. Bake in the center of the oven until a toothpick inserted in the center comes out just clean, 20 minutes.

7. Cool the muffins in the pan on a wire rack for 15 minutes. Then unmold them onto a rack to cool completely.

Makes 12 muffins

BERTA'S CARROT MUFFINS

★ ★ ★

I have never completed a book without some rendition of my mother's classic carrot cake. These muffins are my most recent and most delicious adaptation. They are great with a "schmear" (New York deli slang for a spread of cream cheese), or if you want to dress them up, top them with your favorite cream cheese icing.

1 cup all-purpose flour
1 cup whole-wheat flour
2 teaspoons baking powder
1 teaspoon baking soda
½ teaspoon salt
1 teaspoon ground cinnamon
1 large egg
½ cup (packed) dark brown sugar
¾ cup sour cream
½ cup (1 stick) unsalted butter, melted
¾ cup puréed cooked carrots
⅓ cup drained canned or crushed pineapple
1 teaspoon pure vanilla extract
½ cup coarsely chopped walnuts
½ cup shredded coconut

1. Preheat the oven to 400°F. Grease 12 regular muffin cups or line them with paper liners.

2. Combine both of the flours, baking powder, baking soda, salt, and cinnamon in a bowl. Stir well and set aside.

3. In another bowl, beat together the egg and the brown sugar until well combined. Stir in the sour cream, melted butter, puréed carrots, crushed pineapple, and vanilla extract.

4. Add the dry ingredients to the liquid, and stir with a wooden spoon until just combined. Fold in the walnuts and coconut.

5. Fill the muffin cups a generous three-quarters full with batter. Bake in the center of the oven until a wooden pick inserted in the center comes out just clean, 20 minutes.

6. Cool the muffins in the pan on a wire rack for 15 minutes. Then unmold them onto a rack to cool completely.

Makes 12 muffins

LET'S HAVE THE PERFECT CUP OF COFFEE

—❦—

One of the most significant food developments of the 1990s has been the coffee explosion—the groundswell of interest in better, more interesting beans and exotic preparations. Spearheaded by the people of foggy San Francisco and the rainy Pacific Northwest, who presumably need more caffeine than the rest of us, the movement has rapidly spread south and east. In Manhattan, where I live, I'm rarely more than three or four blocks away from a soigné "coffee bar" purveying everything from nerve-tingling espresso to milky, comforting caffe latte.

No cup is more important than the morning's first. I like to make this one myself. It's nothing fancy, but it tastes fabulous. I start with the best beans, purchased from a coffee bar or specialty shop that keeps them in airtight containers, to maintain freshness. Mail-ordered beans, which come vacuum-packed, can be even fresher. I store them carefully at home, too, sealed up in a cool, dark place (the refrigerator is best). Those I don't plan on using for a few weeks go straight into the freezer. I grind right before brewing, and use fresh, cold tap water (try filtered or bottled water if your tap water has an "off" taste). I prefer the drip method. Plunger-pots, or "French presses," are also good, best for those who want a rich, thick consistency. Just remember to use the appropriate grind: coarse for a plunger-pot, medium for a flat-bottomed filter and fine for cone-shaped filters. And measure correctly—2 tablespoons ground coffee per 6 ounces water yields the best flavor.

Many kinds of beans are available, so there's something for everyone. You can brew a varietal or a blend. You can even create your own blend, combining two or more types that have different qualities that you enjoy. Varietals range from the light-bodied, delicate Hawaiian Kona to the bold, spicy species of the Indonesian archipelago. The coffees of other regions fall in between these extremes: East African types are more brisk and lively; Central and South American varieties tend to be medium-bodied and only mildly acidic. How beans are roasted has a big effect on taste. "American roast" (or "regular roast") is neither light nor heavy, while "French roast" produces a darker, stronger result. "European roast" contains two parts French roast and one part American roast; "Viennese roast" has just the opposite. "Italian roast" is used for espresso.

Any beans can be decaffeinated. Chemical decaffeination, which involves direct contact with a solvent containing methylene chloride, produces a better-tasting coffee—almost as good as the "real thing." The water process, which employs hot water and steam to extract caffeine, removes more oil and more flavor. Chemically decaffeinated coffee is harmless, as far as anyone knows; yet some wary consumers still prefer the second type.

One last thing: Coffee that's been sitting for more than 20 minutes on a low burner or hot plate tastes terrible. To keep it fresh, keep it warm in a preheated, stainless-steel thermos. Then enjoy!

APPLESAUCE PECAN MUFFINS

★ ★ ★

If you are ambitious and make pots of applesauce come autumn, be sure to save some to add to these muffins. Rich sour cream anchors the flavor, and my favorite apple pie spices give these beauties a winter holiday feel. Do not overwork the muffin batter or you will have a tough muffin; stir until the dry ingredients are just incorporated into the wet ingredients. If you don't have fresh applesauce on hand, a good-quality store-bought brand will do just fine.

1½ cups all-purpose flour
2 teaspoons baking powder
1 teaspoon baking soda
½ teaspoon salt
1 teaspoon ground cinnamon
½ teaspoon ground allspice
⅛ teaspoon ground cloves
⅛ teaspoon ground nutmeg
1 large egg
½ cup sugar
½ cup (1 stick) unsalted butter, melted
⅓ cup sour cream
1 teaspoon pure vanilla extract
½ cup applesauce, preferably homemade
  (page 200)
¾ cup coarsely chopped pecans
10 pecan halves

1. Preheat the oven to 400°F. Grease 10 regular muffin cups or line them with paper liners.
2. Combine the flour, baking powder, baking soda, salt, cinnamon, allspice, cloves, and nutmeg in a bowl. Stir well and set aside.
3. In another bowl, beat the egg and the sugar together until well combined. Stir in the melted butter, sour cream, vanilla, and applesauce.
4. Add the dry ingredients to the liquid, and stir with a wooden spoon until just combined. Stir in the chopped pecans.
5. Fill the muffin cups three-quarters full with batter. Top each muffin with a pecan half. Bake in the center of the oven until a wooden pick inserted in the center comes out just clean, 20 minutes.
6. Cool the muffins in the pan on a wire rack for 15 minutes. Then unmold them onto a rack to cool completely.
Makes 10 muffins

PUMPKIN PECAN TEA BREAD

★ ★ ★

Pumpkin tea bread has always been one of my favorites. While baking, it fills the kitchen with such sweet smells that I make it all year round, not just for holidays. The cream cheese in the batter makes the bread slightly richer than you might expect. Sharp Vermont Cheddar cheese and ripe persimmons are perfect autumnal go-withs, while sliced ripe peaches and a dollop of whipped cream are ideal summer toppings.

2 cups all-purpose flour
2 teaspoons baking powder
1 teaspoon baking soda
1 teaspoon ground cinnamon
1 teaspoon ground allspice
½ teaspoon ground ginger
½ teaspoon ground nutmeg
½ teaspoon salt
½ cup (1 stick) unsalted butter, at room
    temperature
½ cup cream cheese, at room temperature
1 cup granulated sugar
½ cup (packed) light or dark brown sugar
2 large eggs
1 cup canned pumpkin pie filling
½ cup sour cream
1 teaspoon pure vanilla extract
1 cup chopped pecans

1. Preheat the oven to 350°F. Lightly grease two 9 x 5 x 2¾-inch loaf pans. Line the bottom of each pan with a piece of waxed paper, and grease the paper. Lightly dust the pans with flour and shake out the excess.

2. Sift the flour, baking powder, baking soda, cinnamon, allspice, ginger, nutmeg, and salt together into a bowl and set aside.

3. In another bowl, cream the butter, cream cheese, and both sugars with an electric mixer until smooth. Add the eggs, one at a time, mixing well after each addition. Add the pumpkin pie filling, sour cream, and vanilla, and mix well.

4. Stir in the dry ingredients until just combined. Fold in the pecans.

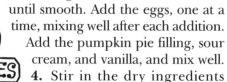

5. Spread the batter in the prepared pans, and bake in the center of the oven until a toothpick inserted into the center comes out clean, about 1 hour.

6. Cool the loaves in the pans on a wire rack for 15 minutes. Then run a knife around the edges of the pans to loosen the loaves, and turn them out onto the rack. Peel off the paper, and allow the loaves to cool completely.

Makes 2 loaves

CRANBERRY ORANGE BREAD

★ ★ ★

This is a tradition for the winter holidays, when fresh cranberries are plentiful. The sweet-tart flavor of the cranberries and the zest of fresh orange juice create a bread that is a wonderful treat—especially when it's thickly sliced, toasted, and spread with cream cheese. It's also a natural to top with thinly sliced baked Virginia ham and serve with some softly scrambled eggs alongside. Of course, the bread is a gift-giving classic for Thanksgiving and Christmas, too.

2 cups all-purpose flour
1 cup sugar
1 teaspoon baking powder
1 teaspoon baking soda
½ teaspoon salt
1 large egg
½ cup fresh orange juice
¼ cup buttermilk
¼ cup (½ stick) unsalted butter, melted
1½ cups fresh cranberries, coarsely chopped
½ cup coarsely chopped pecans
1 tablespoon finely grated orange zest

1. Preheat the oven to 350°F. Lightly grease a 9 x 5 x 2¾-inch loaf pan.

2. Combine the flour, sugar, baking powder, baking soda, and salt in a large bowl. Mix well.

3. Beat the egg in another bowl. Add the orange juice, buttermilk, and melted butter and mix well.

4. Add the egg mixture to the dry ingredients, and mix until just combined. Fold in the cranberries, pecans, and orange zest.

5. Spread the batter in the prepared pan. Bake in the center of the oven until a wooden pick inserted in the center of the loaf comes out just clean, about 1 hour.

6. Cool the bread in the pan on a wire rack for 15 minutes. Then run a knife around the edges of the pan to loosen the bread, and turn it out onto the rack to cool completely.

Makes 1 loaf

ZUCCHINI LEMON LOAF

★ ★ ★

Moist and piquant, with just the right lemon bouquet, this well-flavored loaf gets another intriguing dimension from the addition of tangy sour cream. It's lovely at teatime or for a coffee break, or topped with lemon ice cream for dessert. A simple lemon glaze adds elegance and extra flavor as it infuses the cake while it is still warm. When your zucchini patch hits its August overflow, make a few extra loaves and freeze them for the proverbial rainy day!

BATTER
1½ cups all-purpose flour
1½ teaspoons baking powder
½ teaspoon baking soda
½ teaspoon salt
1 teaspoon ground cinnamon
½ teaspoon ground nutmeg
¼ teaspoon ground cloves
2 large eggs
½ cup vegetable oil
1 cup granulated sugar
¼ cup sour cream
1 teaspoon pure vanilla extract
Finely grated zest of 1 lemon
1 cup grated unpeeled zucchini
½ cup chopped walnuts

GLAZE
½ cup confectioners' sugar
2 tablespoons fresh lemon juice

1. Preheat the oven to 350°F. Grease and lightly flour a 9 x 5 x 2¾-inch loaf pan.

2. Prepare the batter: Sift the flour, baking powder, baking soda, salt, cinnamon, nutmeg, and cloves together into a bowl and set aside.

3. Using an electric mixer in large bowl, beat the eggs just to mix. Add the oil and granulated sugar, and beat until combined. Add the sour cream, vanilla extract, and lemon zest and mix well. Add the dry ingredients and mix until just combined. Fold in the zucchini and the nuts.

4. Scrape the batter into the prepared pan, and bake in the center of the oven until a wooden pick inserted in the center comes out just clean, 55 to 60 minutes. Cool the loaf in the pan on a rack for 10 minutes. Then run a knife around the edges of the pan to loosen the bread, and turn it out onto the rack to cool completely.

5. Meanwhile, prepare the glaze (see Note): Place the confectioners' sugar and the lemon juice in a small saucepan and bring to a boil, stirring occasionally. Boil for 2 minutes, stirring, and remove from the heat. While the cake is still warm, use a skewer or a long pick to poke holes about 1 inch apart all over the surface of the cake. Brush the glaze all over and then let it cool completely.

Makes 1 loaf

NOTE: If you are freezing the loaf, freeze it unglazed. Once the loaf is fully defrosted, warm it slightly before continuing with step 5.

LEMON POPPY-SEED LOAF

★ ★ ★

The meltingly rich texture of an old-fashioned pound cake with a pleasant pucker of lemon, makes this little loaf scrumptious to serve with tea or at coffee break. It is also delicious paired with Laurie's Winter Lemon Ice Cream. I've cut down on the usual hefty amount of poppy seeds, preferring to add just a subtle hint.

1½ cups all-purpose flour
2 teaspoons baking powder
½ teaspoon salt
½ cup (1 stick) unsalted butter, at room
*   temperature*
1 cup sugar
2 large eggs
½ cup sour cream
¼ cup poppy seeds
2 tablespoons fresh lemon juice
1 tablespoon finely grated lemon zest

1. Preheat the oven to 350°F. Grease and lightly flour a 9 x 5 x 2¾-inch loaf pan.

2. Sift the flour, baking powder, and salt together into a bowl and set aside.

3. In a large bowl, cream the butter and the sugar together with an electric mixer. Add the eggs, one at a time, mixing well after each addition. Add the sour cream, poppy seeds, lemon juice, and zest and combine well.

4. Mix in the dry ingredients until just combined. Scrape the batter into the prepared pan, and bake in the center of the oven until a pick inserted in the center comes out just clean, 55 to 60 minutes.

5. Cool the loaf in the pan on a rack for 10 minutes. Then run a knife around the edges of the pan to loosen the bread, and turn it out onto the rack to cool completely.

Makes 1 loaf

BANANA GINGERBREAD

★ ★ ★

The bananas and sour cream both add a desired moistness to this well-spiced loaf. It is ideal at brunch, coffee or teatime, or for dessert, with the delicate honey mellowing the pungent

HERE'S TO TEA

—🍎—

*I*f Congress were looking for an official national beverage, I would nominate tea. Although very little is grown here, our national identity was born when rebel colonists angrily heaved tea leaves into Boston Harbor in 1773. Any drink that overcomes that abuse to be enjoyed by so many deserves recognition.

Today, we consume some 7.1 gallons per capita each year. Bracing, uncomplicated "orange pekoe" blends are the biggest sellers in supermarkets, along with cold bottled teas and iced tea mixes. Many of us also relish finer, costlier teas. We may not know exactly what goes into "Earl Grey," "Oolong," and "English Breakfast," but we do buy and enjoy them.

Learning more can be rewarding. Tea is as vast a subject as wine, and there are so many varieties grown around the world that it would take a lifetime to sample them all. To get started, check out a specialty shop that sells loose tea (all black teas are made from dried and fermented leaves; green-tea leaves are unfermented). There you'll find some or all of the following:

Assam: A full-bodied black tea from the Assam district of India.

Darjeeling: A dark, winey tea (the favorite of many aficionados) from the Indian foothills of the Himalayas.

Ceylon: Various dark teas from Ceylon, or Sri Lanka (also the source of much orange pekoe, a term that refers not to fruit but to a grade of tea).

Earl Grey: A charming black tea (sometimes a blend) flavored with a touch of oil of bergamot, giving it a distinct character.

English Breakfast: A brisk blend of Indian and Ceylon teas, perfect for a morning cup.

Lapsang Souchong: A smoky-flavored black tea from China.

Russian Caravan: Made from bold black Chinese teas.

Gunpowder (from China) and **Bancha** (from Japan)**:** Both grassy green teas.

Jasmine: A delicate combination of jasmine flowers and green tea.

Oolong: A mixture of green and black Chinese teas.

Only one tea is grown in the United States, on Wadmalaw Island, off the coast of South Carolina. Though a newcomer to the industry (it was founded in 1987), the Charleston Tea Plantation has already attracted a fair amount of attention with its smooth American Classic Tea. It's served in some of the best Charleston restaurants, and even in the White House (where to drink any other might be construed as unpatriotic!). To order some for your own house, call the plantation at (800) 443-5987.

gingerbread spices. It would be heavenly served warm with Homey Vanilla Ice Cream or New Orleans Praline Ice Cream and either Lanai Sweet Pineapple-Ginger Sauce or Old-Fashioned Butterscotch Sauce.

2 cups all-purpose flour
1 teaspoon baking powder
½ teaspoon salt
1½ teaspoons ground ginger
1 teaspoon ground cinnamon
½ teaspoon ground allspice
¼ teaspoon ground cloves
¼ teaspoon ground nutmeg
½ cup (1 stick) unsalted butter, at room temperature
½ cup (packed) dark or light brown sugar
½ cup unsulfured molasses
¼ cup honey
2 large eggs
½ cup sour cream
1 cup mashed ripe bananas (about 2 large)

1. Preheat the oven to 350°F. Grease and lightly flour a 9 x 5 x 2¾-inch loaf pan.

2. Sift the flour, baking powder, salt, ginger, cinnamon, allspice, cloves, and nutmeg together into a bowl and set aside.

3. In a large bowl, cream the butter, brown sugar, molasses, and honey with an electric mixer until smooth. Add the eggs, one at a time, mixing well after each addition. Add the sour

cream and the mashed bananas, and mix until combined.

4. Add the dry ingredients and mix until just combined. Scrape the batter into the prepared pan. Bake in the center of the oven until a pick inserted in the center comes out just clean, 55 to 60 minutes.

5. Cool the bread in the pan on a rack for 10 minutes. Then run a knife around the edges of the pan to loosen the bread, and turn it out onto the rack to cool completely. Or serve still warm, but not hot.

Makes 1 loaf

FLAHERTY'S MAPLE PECAN SCONES

★ ★ ★

After a tour of Dan Flaherty's maple sugar farm in Bemidje, Minnesota (see Index for American Maple Sugaring), his, wife, Donna, friend Robyn, and daughter Molly prepared an unusual coffee break for me. Instead of water, the liquid sap collected from the trees was used to brew a rich sweet coffee in a drip pot. A soft spread, made from butter whipped with an equal amount of the newly boiled batch, was served with maple syrup–flavored scones. I usually drink my coffee black with no sugar, so the Flaherty's home brew was quite a surprise, but not an unpleasant one. I have never experienced this kind of intense flavor in my coffee; the coffee they used must have been strong enough to counter all the sweetness. And it was delicious enough for me to ask for a refill to accompany these fragrant scones.

3½ cups all-purpose flour
1 cup finely chopped pecans
4 teaspoons baking powder
1 teaspoon salt
⅔ cup solid vegetable shortening
1 cup plus 1 tablespoon milk
½ cup pure maple syrup

1. Preheat the oven to 425°F. Grease a baking sheet.

2. Combine the flour, pecans, baking powder, and salt in a large bowl. Mix well. Using a pastry blender, cut in the shortening until the mixture resembles coarse crumbs.

3. Add the milk and 6 tablespoons of the maple syrup to the dry ingredients. Mix lightly with a fork until the mixture clings together and forms a soft dough.

4. Turn the dough out onto a lightly floured surface, and knead it gently 5 or 6 times. Divide the dough in half. Roll out one half of the dough to form a 7-inch round. Cut it into 4 wedges, and place them 1 inch apart on the prepared baking sheet. Repeat with the remaining dough.

5. Prick the tops of the scones all over with the tines of a fork. Brush the tops with the remaining 2 tablespoons maple syrup.

6. Bake the scones until golden brown, 15 to 18 minutes.

7. Cool the scones on a wire rack for 10 minutes, then serve warm.

Makes 8 scones

KEYS CARAMEL ROLLS

★ ★ ★

Barbara Hunn has generously shared her recipe for these delicious rolls, which are famous in the Twin Cities. They became one of her trademarks soon after she began making them, in 1974, one year after opening her first Keys Restaurant. She now has eight Keys Restaurants in the Minneapolis–St. Paul area, all serving generous portions of good home cooking family-style, and thanks to each of her four children joining in, the business continues to expand. Barbara says the success of Keys lies in the quality of the food, served at a good price with efficient service and a friendly smile. She must be right, because from 6:30 A.M. on there are lines of eager diners waiting to enjoy these rolls before they disappear for the day.

½ cup granulated sugar
1 teaspoon ground cinnamon
½ cup (1 stick) unsalted butter
1½ cups (packed) dark brown sugar
½ cup heavy (or whipping) cream
2 loaves (1 pound each) frozen white bread dough
    (see Note), thawed

1. Stir the granulated sugar and cinnamon together in a small bowl.

2. In a small saucepan, combine the butter, brown sugar, and cream over low heat, stirring until smooth. Pour the mixture into a 12 x 9 x 2-inch glass baking dish. Set aside.

3. On a lightly floured surface, flatten out one of the bread doughs to form a rectangle about 14 inches by 4½ inches (it will be very elastic). Sprinkle it evenly with half the sugar-cinnamon mixture, and roll it up from the short end. Cut the roll into 3 pieces, each 1½ inches wide.

Repeat with the remaining bread dough and sugar-cinnamon mixture.

4. Place the cut rolls in the baking dish, arranging them in two lengthwise rows of three rolls each, on top of the caramel mixture (there will be space around the edges, but as the rolls rise and bake, they will fill out the baking dish). Cover lightly and set aside in a warm place to rise until doubled in size, 45 minutes to 1 hour.

5. Meanwhile, preheat the oven to 350°F.

6. Bake the rolls in the center of the oven until golden brown, 25 to 30 minutes.

7. Let the rolls rest in the baking dish for about 15 minutes. Then carefully invert the baking dish over a platter or tray (there will be a good amount of caramel sauce, so be careful), and serve warm.

Makes 6 large rolls

NOTE: Frozen bread dough is available in supermarket frozen-food cases.

CAKEY BUTTERMILK DOUGHNUTS

★ ★ ★

It's no secret that we are a country of doughnut eaters. I prefer the cakey kind with my coffee— and they're less time-consuming to make than the yeast type.

2 large eggs
1 cup granulated sugar
1 cup buttermilk
3 tablespoons unsalted butter, melted
3½ cups all-purpose flour
1 tablespoon baking powder
1 teaspoon salt
¼ teaspoon ground allspice
¼ teaspoon ground mace
Vegetable oil, for frying
Confectioners' sugar, for dusting (optional)

1. Whisk the eggs in a large bowl until light and lemon-colored. Gradually add the granulated sugar, whisking constantly until the mixture is thick and ribbony.

2. Stir in the buttermilk and the melted butter.

3. In another bowl, sift the flour, baking powder, salt, allspice, and mace together. Add this to the egg mixture, and stir to combine. Do not overwork the dough. Let the dough rest in the refrigerator for 20 minutes.

4. Pour oil to a depth of 2 to 3 inches in a large heavy pot, and place it over medium-high heat. Heat it to a temperature of 370°F.

5. While the oil is heating, roll the dough out on a lightly floured surface to about ¼-inch thickness. Using a floured 2½-inch doughnut or biscuit cutter, cut it into rounds. (If you don't have a doughnut cutter, cut out the center holes with an apple corer.) Save the holes!

6. When the oil has reached 370°F, fry the doughnuts in it in small batches until golden brown, turning once, 1½ minutes per side (see Note). Use a slotted spoon to remove them from the oil, and set them on paper towels to drain. Then fry the doughnut holes (they'll take about 30 seconds per side). Watch the temperature of the oil; let it reheat between batches if necessary.

7. Sprinkle the doughnuts with confectioners' sugar, if desired, and serve warm.
Makes 28 doughnuts and holes

NOTE: It's best to stand back and wear a long-sleeved shirt or chef's jacket to prevent burns from splashing oil.

ORANGE SOUR CREAM DOUGHNUTS

★ ★ ★

A bite of these cakey doughnuts reveal a hint of orange and the tang of sour cream. When served hot on a chilly winter morning, they are a sweet way to start the day. Wrap them loosely in a linen napkin so they'll stay warm.

2 large eggs
1 cup granulated sugar
¾ cup sour cream
¼ cup milk
3 tablespoons unsalted butter, melted
1 tablespoon orange marmalade, melted
2 teaspoons finely grated orange zest
3½ cups all-purpose flour
1 tablespoon baking powder
1 teaspoon salt
½ teaspoon ground nutmeg
Vegetable oil, for frying
Confectioners' sugar, for dusting
*   (optional)*

1. Whisk the eggs in a large bowl until light and lemon-colored. Gradually add the granulated sugar, whisking constantly until the mixture is thick and ribbony.

2. Stir in the sour cream, milk, melted butter, melted orange marmalade, and orange zest.

3. In another bowl, sift the flour, baking powder, salt, and nutmeg together. Add this to the egg mixture, and stir to combine. Do not overwork the dough. Let the dough rest in the refrigerator for 20 minutes.

4. Pour oil to a depth of 2 to 3 inches in a large heavy pot, and place it over medium-high heat. Heat it to a temperature of 370°F.

5. While the oil is heating, roll the dough out on a lightly floured surface to about ¼-inch thickness. Using a floured 2½-inch doughnut or biscuit cutter, cut it into rounds. (If you don't have a doughnut cutter, cut out the center holes with an apple corer.) Save the holes!

6. When the oil has reached 370°F, fry the doughnuts in small batches until golden brown, turning once, 1½ minutes per side (see Note, top of this page). Use a slotted spoon to remove them from the oil, and set them on paper towels to drain. Then fry the doughnut holes (they'll take about 30 seconds per side). Watch the temperature of the oil; let it reheat between batches if necessary.

7. Sprinkle the doughnuts with confectioners' sugar, if desired, and serve warm.
Makes 28 doughnuts and holes

RISE AND SHINE COFFEE CAKE

★ ★ ★

Flecked with raisins and dates, this dense, buttery cake is luxurious. While it may take extra effort to make a yeast cake in these fast-moving times, the payoff is that first warm bite. The glaze helps keep the cake fresh for as long as it lasts, but if your house is like mine, don't count on it being around for more than a day or two.

SPONGE
1 package active dry yeast
1/4 cup warm water
1/2 cup milk, warmed
1 cup all-purpose flour

DOUGH
1 cup golden raisins
3/4 cup (1 1/2 sticks) unsalted butter, at room temperature
3 large eggs, lightly beaten
6 tablespoons granulated sugar
1 teaspoon salt
1/2 teaspoon ground nutmeg
1/2 cup milk, warmed
2 tablespoons honey
1 teaspoon pure vanilla extract
Finely grated zest of 2 oranges
4 1/2 cups all-purpose flour
1 cup pitted dates, coarsely chopped

GLAZE
1/4 cup (1/2 stick) unsalted butter
3/4 cup confectioners' sugar
2 tablespoons water
1 tablespoon cognac

1. Prepare the sponge: Stir the yeast into the warm water in a medium-size bowl. Allow it to sit until foamy, 5 minutes. Then add the warm milk and the flour and stir until combined. Cover and set aside for 30 minutes.

2. Prepare the dough: While the sponge is proofing, soak the raisins in enough cold water to cover for 30 minutes, then drain.

3. Place the sponge in a large mixing bowl, and add the butter, eggs, granulated sugar, salt, nutmeg, warm milk, honey, vanilla, and orange zest. Mix well. Using a heavy-duty mixer with a paddle, add the flour 1 cup at a time, mixing until the dough is smooth. (If you don't have a heavy-duty stand mixer, add the flour to the bowl 1 cup at a time, stirring, until incorporated; then turn the dough out onto a lightly floured surface and knead it until it is smooth, about 10 minutes.) Add the raisins and dates, and mix until incorporated. The dough will be silky, smooth, and slightly sticky. Place the dough in a large buttered bowl, cover it loosely, and set it aside in a warm place to rise for 1 hour.

4. Turn the dough out onto a lightly floured surface and punch it down. Form the dough into a round.

5. Line the bottom of a 9 1/2-inch springform pan with a circle of waxed or parchment paper. Butter the paper and the sides of the pan. Press the dough evenly into the pan, cover, and let rise until it has doubled in volume, about 1 hour.

6. Twenty minutes before the dough has finished rising, preheat the oven to 350°F.

7. Bake the coffee cake in the center of the oven until a wooden pick inserted in the center comes out clean, 1 1/4 hours. If it is browning too quickly, cover it with aluminum foil.

8. Cool the cake in the pan on a rack for 10 to 15 minutes.

9. Meanwhile, prepare the glaze: Combine the butter, confectioners' sugar, and water in a small saucepan. Heat to melt the butter and blend the ingredients, and then bring to a boil. Reduce the heat to low and cook for 5 minutes. Remove from the heat and stir in the cognac. Stir until the glaze is translucent.

10. Remove the sides of the springform pan. Place a baking sheet underneath the cooling rack. Pour the warm glaze over the warm cake, allowing it to run down the sides. Let the cake cool completely.

Serves 12

CAROLE SOLIE'S FRESH BERRY BUNDT CAKE

★ ★ ★

While visiting Appleton, Wisconsin, for their annual cheese festival, I spent the night at the Solie House Bed and Breakfast. The following morning, I awoke to the aromas of what would be a most elegant breakfast. In the dining room, this delicious bundt cake sat on an antique cake stand, overflowing with strawberries and ready for slicing. As if this weren't enough of a treat,

a full breakfast of oatmeal pancakes served with local maple syrup, scrambled eggs, and bacon was set before me. What a delightful way to start a new Wisconsin day!

¾ cup (1½ sticks) unsalted butter, at room temperature
2 cups granulated sugar
3 large eggs
3 cups plus 1 tablespoons all-purpose flour
1 tablespoon baking powder
½ teaspoon salt
¾ cup milk
1½ cups sliced fresh strawberries or whole blueberries
Confectioners' sugar, for dusting
1 cup whole fresh strawberries or blueberries

1. Preheat the oven to 350°F. Grease and lightly flour a 12-cup bundt pan.

2. In a large bowl, cream the butter and granulated sugar together with an electric mixer. Add the eggs, one at a time, mixing well after each addition. The mixture will be firm.

3. In another large bowl, sift together the 3 cups of flour, the baking powder, and salt. Gradually add this to the butter mixture, alternating with the milk. Toss the sliced strawberries with the remaining 1 tablespoon flour, and fold them into the batter.

4. Scrape the batter into the prepared bundt pan. Bake in the center of the oven until a wooden pick inserted in the center of the cake comes out just clean, 1¼ hours.

JAVA JIVE

Want to try something different? Learn some coffee-bar speak and order up!

Espresso: A concentrated, thick brew made in an espresso machine from water forced through finely ground, dark-roasted beans at high pressure. This is the strongest of coffees, usually drunk in 1.5-ounce "shots."

Espresso doppio: For those who can handle it, double the pleasure.

Espresso macchiato: A shot of espresso topped with a spot of foamed milk.

Espresso con panna: Same as the above, with whipped cream instead of milk.

Caffe americano: A shot of espresso diluted with hot water.

Cappuccino: Steamed milk and a shot of espresso, capped with foamed milk. Purists drink theirs ungarnished, while others like a dusting of cinnamon or cocoa powder.

Caffe latte: Also a shot of espresso with steamed milk, but with more milk than cappuccino.

Caffe mocha: A grown-up version of hot chocolate—one shot of espresso with steamed milk and chocolate syrup, often topped with whipped cream.

Café au lait: Equal portions brewed coffee and scalded or steamed milk.

"Skinny": Made with skim milk—i.e. "skinny latte."

Espresso granita: The name given to cold, iced coffee "slushies" that can be thick as milkshakes and almost as sweet. These cooling, fortifying treats are an American innovation that call to mind the coffee ice of Italy.

5. Cool the cake in the pan on a rack for 15 minutes. Then unmold it onto the rack to cool completely.

6. To serve, carefully transfer the cake to a serving platter and dust it all over with confectioners' sugar. Fill the center with the whole berries.

Serves 16

QUEEN'S CAKE

★ ★ ★

I spent a good part of my visit to Colonial Williamsburg at the Raleigh Tavern Bake Shop, enjoying the baked goods made from authentic

★★★★★★★★★★★★★★★★★★★★★★★★★★★

BREWING TEA

—❧—

Brewing most teas is simple. Start with a teapot and loose tea. Boil fresh, cold water, then swirl a little in the pot, to warm it. Measure out the leaves— 1 heaping teaspoon per cup, plus one for the pot. Pour the water over the leaves, stir, cover, and let steep for 5 to 7 minutes. Warm your cups with a little boiling water, too. If you like your tea with milk, pour it into the cup before you add your tea, not vice versa. Pour tea through a fine-mesh strainer.

★★★★★★★★★★★★★★★★★★★★★★★★★★★

eighteenth-century colonial recipes. Completely unlike what you might find in twentieth-century bakeries, the dozen or so items were all tastefully simple and thoroughly satisfying. Enjoy a slice of Queen's Cake with a morning cup of coffee or an afternoon cup of tea.

1 cup (2 sticks) unsalted butter, at room
    temperature
1 cup sugar
5 large eggs, at room temperature
1 teaspoon lemon extract
1 teaspoon orange extract
2 cups plus 1 tablespoon all-purpose flour
½ teaspoon baking powder
½ teaspoon ground cinnamon
2 cups currants

1. Preheat the oven to 325°F. Lightly butter a 9 x 5 x 2¾-inch loaf pan. Line the bottom of the pan with a piece of waxed or parchment paper and butter the paper. Then lightly flour the pan and shake out any excess.

2. In a large bowl, cream the butter and sugar with an electric mixer. Add the eggs one at a time, mixing well after each addition. Add the lemon and orange extracts, and mix well.

3. In another large bowl, sift the 2 cups of flour, the baking powder, and cinnamon together. Gradually add the flour mixture to the batter, stirring well after each addition.

4. Toss the currants with the remaining 1 tablespoon flour, and fold into the batter.

5. Scrape the batter into the prepared pan, and bake in the center of the oven until a pick inserted in the center comes out clean, 1 hour and 20 minutes.

6. Cool the cake in the pan on a wire rack for 10 minutes. Then run a knife around the sides of the pan to loosen the cake, and turn it out onto the rack. Peel off the paper and allow the cake to cool completely.
Makes 1 loaf

SANTA FE HEAVENLY HOT CHOCOLATE

★ ★ ★

Arriving in Santa Fe on a blustery day in April, I could think of nothing more welcoming than a cup of soothing hot chocolate at the Inn of the Anasazi. After getting over the shock of the cold weather, I began to analyze the flavor of this rich, sensual brew, quite reminiscent of the chocolate I had enjoyed in Mexico. A second cup helped me to identify the hint of cinnamon and the brown sugar, which creates a mellow sweetness.

1½ ounces best-quality bittersweet chocolate, broken into pieces
1½ teaspoons light brown sugar
⅛ teaspoon ground cinnamon
1 cup whole milk

Combine the chocolate, brown sugar, cinnamon, and ¼ cup of the milk in a small heavy saucepan. Whisk constantly over medium heat until the mixture forms a smooth paste. Then slowly add the remaining ¾ cup milk, whisking until well mixed and warmed through. Serve immediately in a large mug.

Serves 1

PART THREE

CAFE
LUNCH

The Salad Plate

For a really substantial lunch, how about a salad? Americans, curiously, call some of their biggest meals "salad." In coffee shops and luncheonettes, most "salad plates" include generous scoops of chicken, egg, tuna, or ham salad, and heaping mounds of mayonnaisey potatoes. Lighter "side salads" made of greens, grains, vegetables, or fruit are of an entirely different species. In this book, they're in a separate chapter, Dinner Side Salads.

Reading through these recipes, you'll notice some unusual combinations: duck with roasted beets in an orange-honey vinaigrette; shrimp and celery root tossed in rémoulade sauce; a tangy mayonnaise made with orange zest and tomato, and more. For brighter picnics, try the fiesta-colored coleslaws, studded with peppers and carrots. And no, I didn't forget the potato salad. How could I, when we adore it so? There are eight versions here, everything from an eggy, pickley Lone Star classic to a creation inspired by my Alaskan sojourn, resplendent with flaked pink salmon and dill. There can *never* be too much of these, so go for big batches!

CHEERY CHERRY CHICKEN SALAD

★ ★ ★

When opulent, ruby red Bing cherries are in season, I can't resist including them in as many recipes as possible. This salad is an experiment that worked particularly well—in fact, it currently tops my list of chicken salads.

Wine: Russian River Valley (CA) Gewürztraminer

3 cups coarsely shredded cooked chicken
3 cups pitted fresh Bing cherries
2 ribs celery, cut into ¼-inch dice
¾ cup walnut halves
Salt and freshly ground black pepper,
*   to taste*
½ cup mayonnaise
½ cup plain nonfat yogurt
2 tablespoons chopped fresh tarragon leaves,
*   or 1 tablespoon dried*

   1. Combine the chicken, cherries, celery, and walnut halves in a large bowl. Sprinkle with salt and pepper, and toss well.
   2. Combine the mayonnaise, yogurt, and tarragon in a small bowl. Using a rubber spatula, fold the dressing gently into the chicken. Adjust the seasonings and serve immediately, or cover and refrigerate for up to 8 hours.
   Serves 6

CHILI CHICKEN SALAD

★ ★ ★

Here's a chili for a sultry summer day—fresh cool chicken salad with a pungent Southwestern feel and a spiced-up dressing. If you like, roll it up in flour tortillas. A burst of juice from the sweet red grapes adds a complementary sweet note.

Wine: Colorado Viognier
Beer: Southwestern amber ale

4 cups coarsely shredded cooked chicken
½ cup diced (¼ inch) red bell pepper
½ cup diced (¼ inch) green bell pepper
¼ cup chopped pitted ripe black olives
2 scallions (3 inches green left on), thinly sliced on
*   the diagonal*
3 tablespoons chopped fresh cilantro leaves
½ cup mayonnaise
½ cup sour cream
2 tablespoons fresh lime juice
1 teaspoon finely minced fresh jalapeño pepper,
*   or to taste*
½ teaspoon finely grated orange zest
¼ teaspoon chili powder
⅛ teaspoon ground cumin
Salt and freshly ground black pepper, to taste
1 ripe avocado
Red lettuce leaves (oak-leaf if possible), for garnish
Small bunches of seedless red grapes, for garnish

   1. Combine the chicken, both bell peppers, the olives, scallions, and 2 tablespoons of the cilantro in a large bowl.
   2. In a separate bowl, combine the mayonnaise, sour cream, 1 tablespoon of the lime juice, the jalapeño, orange zest, chili powder,

cumin, salt, and pepper. Stir together thoroughly. Add to the chicken and vegetables, and toss well.

3. Place the remaining 1 tablespoon lime juice in a small bowl. Cut the avocado in half. Remove the pit, peel the avocado, and cut it into ¼-inch dice. Toss the avocado with the lime juice (to prevent discoloration).

4. To serve, arrange the chicken salad on top of a bed of lettuce leaves. Scatter the avocado over the top, and sprinkle with the remaining 1 tablespoon chopped cilantro. Decorate with small bunches of red grapes.

Serves 6

APRICOT, HAM, AND CHEESE SALAD

★ ★ ★

It's never been my way to leave well enough alone, so it didn't surprise me that while writing this book, some of my most rewarding moments came when spinning American favorites into new recipes. Take, for example, the classic combination of ham and cheese. Always delicious as a salad, with the addition of tart dried apricots, and dressed with a creamy sweet apricot mayonnaise, the combination becomes a guest-worthy luncheon entrée.

Wine: Washington State Riesling

DRESSING
½ cup mayonnaise
½ cup sour cream or plain nonfat yogurt
1½ tablespoons apricot preserves, minced
1½ tablespoons honey mustard

SALAD
6 ounces Gruyère cheese, in one piece
1 pound baked ham, coarsely shredded
2 ribs celery, cut into 1¾ x ¼-inch strips
2 scallions (3 inches green left on), sliced thinly on the diagonal
1 red bell pepper, stemmed, seeded, halved, and cut into thin strips lengthwise (about 2½ inches long)
½ cup plump dried apricots, halved crosswise
2 tablespoons coarsely chopped fresh flat-leaf parsley
Salt and freshly ground black pepper, to taste

1. Prepare the dressing: Combine the mayonnaise, sour cream, apricot preserves, and honey mustard in a small bowl and mix well. Set aside.

2. Prepare the salad: Using a cheese plane or a very sharp knife, cut the cheese into shavings (paper-thin slices) about 3¼ inches long and 2 inches wide.

3. Place the cheese, ham, celery, scallions, bell pepper, dried apricots, and parsley in a large bowl. Add the dressing and toss all the ingredients together gently with a large rubber spatula, being careful that the cheese slices don't stick together. Season with salt and pepper, and serve.

Serves 6 to 8

A Bit About Wine and Beer

★ ★ ★

President and first gastronome Thomas Jefferson was devoted to his country, of that there's no question. But he was equally dedicated to exploring and enjoying everything that was wonderful to eat and drink, both at home and abroad. As America's ambassador to France, he sampled the world's finest wines at the source, then returned determined to establish the U.S. as a winemaking nation. He imported vines and vine tenders and brought European wine technology to his Monticello plantation. And he offered unfailing support for experimental winemaking efforts throughout the colonies.

Jefferson's dream of transforming the United States into a major winemaking force was not realized in his lifetime, but it did eventually happen, and today American-made wines command respect around the world. Versatile and food-friendly, they complement the rich heritage of American cooking.

Although a winemaking tradition existed in some states, it was not until the post-World War II period that Americans really began to understand that wine could and should play an integral role in the pleasures of the American table. American wines have improved in virtually every vintage since then, especially in the last thirty years, a period during which domestic winemaking has been completely revolutionized. Innovative vintners combined a respect for new technology with a love of grapes at a level that made most of us forget that for a long time when Americans thought of domestic wine it was jug wines they envisioned. In the 1960s, as our vineyards became abundant, inspired California winemakers, most notably those in the Napa Valley, began carefully creating fine-quality wines on a small scale and the term "boutique winery" entered our vocabularies. Today California vintners produce almost 90 percent of American-made wine, but equally delightful offerings come from other wine producing states, including: Washington, Oregon, and New York (where French immigrants to the Hudson River Valley first made wine in 1677).

American wines are generally referred to by the name of the principal varietal from which they are made: 75 percent of that grape for a varietally labeled wine, 85 percent if a specific American Viticultural Area (AVA) is on the label. The most important and most widely grown grapes in American vineyards are Chardonnay (the most popular white wine in America), Sauvignon Blanc, Cabernet Sauvignon (the varietal that put domestic winemaking on the map), Pinot Noir, and the widely planted Zinfandel.

As a general rule, a consistent, familiar, reliable California Cabernet Sauvignon is a perfect fit with red meat, game, lamb, and many other full-flavored dishes. A dry, pungent Sauvignon Blanc from Texas complements fish and shellfish, and is also the perfect foil for a handmade goat cheese. Full-bodied California Merlots are well suited to Mediterranean-influenced dishes and dry Rieslings to Pacific Rim–style cooking. A red Zinfandel is more than a match for sweet or spicy barbecue dishes. A California Rhône-style wine brings out the best from poultry and a Washington State Chardonnay matches up to a gumbo.

All-American Beer

Surely there's nothing more American than an icy cold beer on a hot summer day, whether it's keeping company with a ballpark hot dog or tapped from a keg at a backyard barbecue. Even so, most people will probably be surprised to discover that when it comes to volume, the United States brews more beer than any other country in the world.

Our love of beer is practically a patriotic duty. The pilgrims had no sooner landed than they set about homebrewing a regular supply of ale, and in 1777 the Sons of Liberty would plot the Boston Tea Party, conspiring over clandestine tankards of ale rather than cups of tea. A century later more than 4,000 breweries had sprung up, though eventually Prohibition caused thousands of them to cease operations until its repeal in 1933. Small-scale regional beermakers bounced back in the 1940s only to find themselves gobbled up by large breweries over the next several decades. By the 1960s only ten independent breweries were left; small-scale brewing in America was nearly extinct. Then Fritz Maytag bought and saved San Francisco's Anchor Brewing Company, planting the seeds for the renaissance of small-batch, artisanal beermaking and pioneering the microbrewery movement that would bring fresh, hand-crafted beer to its rightful place at the American table—at home and in restaurants. For, like wine, the destiny of these versatile brews is to complement and enhance the flavor of food. Just as there is a wine for every taste, there is a beer. Balance is the key pairing beer with food, so think in terms of light-bodied beers for lighter foods, darker, sweeter beers for rich or heavy dishes, light to amber beers with spicy dishes, and bitter ones with fried foods. For example, velvety, roasty, toasty stouts are perfect partners for game, rich stews, steaks, and grilled mushrooms, while lighter lagers, pilseners, and pale ales are compatible with meals featuring salads, grilled seafood, or chicken dishes.

Unlike many wines which improve with age, most beers should be consumed within six months of their bottling date. Increasingly brewers are indicating dates on their labels, so be sure to look out for them, buying your beer at a store with high turnover so it's more likely to be fresh. Store it upright in the back of the refrigerator where it won't get bumped around. Most beers, especially ales, stouts, and porters, taste best served at near cellar temperature (45°F to 55°F), which allows their aroma and flavors to expand. Allow wheat beers and lagers to warm up for 10 to 15 minutes before serving.

———★———

The wine and beer serving suggestions that accompany many of the recipes here are by no means written in stone. They are broad-stroke recommendations intended to provide you with general guidelines into which wine or beer style is most likely to bring out the best in your cooking. My hope is that they will inspire you to continue pairing American dishes with American-made wines and beers from throughout the country. Whichever accompaniment you choose, it's bound to enhance your enjoyment of a good dish and vice versa.

ORANGE, HAM, AND AVOCADO SALAD

★ ★ ★

Although they may seem like unlikely bedfellows, ham and buttery avocado, combined with tomatoes and basil and served on top of a bed of tart, crispy frisée, makes a succulent warm-weather entrée salad. Serve it with thinly sliced oranges and a dark raisin pumpernickel bread slathered with Maytag Blue cheese.

Wine: California Chardonnay

1 pound honey-baked ham, coarsely shredded
2 ripe plum tomatoes, halved lengthwise and
    cut into lengthwise slivers
½ small red onion, slivered lengthwise
½ cup loosely packed torn fresh basil leaves
2 tablespoons fresh lemon juice
2 ripe avocados, halved, pitted, and peeled
Salt and freshly ground black pepper,
    to taste
½ cup Orange Honey Vinaigrette
    (recipe follows)
1 head frisée lettuce, rinsed and dried

1. Place the ham, tomatoes, red onion, and basil leaves in a large bowl.
2. Place the lemon juice in a small bowl. Turn the avocado halves, pitted side down, and cut lengthwise into coarse slices. Place the slices in the lemon juice and toss gently (this prevents discoloration). Add the avocado, with the lemon juice, to the ham. Season with salt and pepper.
3. Add the vinaigrette, and fold the ingredients together gently with a large rubber spatula.
4. Serve on a bed of frisée lettuce.
Serves 4 to 6

Orange Honey Dressing

——★——

Combining fresh orange juice and garlic creates a dressing both sweet and pungent, appropriate for use on vegetable as well as fruit salads. An intensely fruity extra virgin olive oil would overwhelm these flavors, so for this you should use only pure olive oil.

1 small clove garlic, finely minced
¼ teaspoon coarse salt
1½ teaspoons Dijon mustard
1 teaspoon honey
2 tablespoons fresh orange juice
½ cup pure olive oil
Freshly ground black pepper, to taste

1. Place the garlic, coarse salt, mustard, honey, and orange juice in a bowl. Whisk together.
2. Slowly drizzle in the olive oil, whisking constantly until thickened.
3. Season with pepper. Store, covered, in the refrigerator for up to 2 days. Bring to room temperature before using.
Makes about ⅔ cup

BLT SALAD

★ ★ ★

Almost as American as apple pie, a BLT is the sandwich I weigh against a club sandwich when I make my lunch choice at a luncheonette or diner. At home one day, and not in a sandwich frame of mind, I had a thought—why not use the combination in a salad? Why not lightly dress it in a creamy ranch dressing? And why not toss in a handful of chunky oven-roasted, aromatic croutons? Why not, indeed. Once you lightly dress the salad, pass extra dressing at table for those who might prefer a little more. Follow the salad with a selection of your favorite American cheeses.

Beer: Minnesota light lager

½ pound slab bacon, cut into 1 x ¼-inch pieces
4 cups cubed (1 inch) French bread
1 teaspoon dried thyme
Salt and freshly ground black pepper, to taste
5 cups (6 ounces) mesclun (baby salad greens), rinsed and dried
4 ripe tomatoes, cut into 1-inch cubes
2 tablespoons snipped fresh chives
½ cup Ranch Dressing (recipe follows), plus more for serving

1. Cook the bacon in a nonstick skillet over medium-low heat until golden brown, 15 minutes. Transfer it to paper towels to drain, reserving 2 tablespoons of the bacon fat.
2. Preheat the oven to 350°F.
3. Place the bread cubes in a large bowl and toss with the reserved 2 tablespoons bacon fat, the dried thyme, and salt and pepper. Spread the cubes in a single layer on a baking sheet and toast until golden, 12 to 15 minutes, shaking the pan once or twice.
4. Place the mesclun in a large bowl. Toss it with the bacon, tomatoes, toasted bread cubes, chives, and salt and pepper.

5. Just before serving, toss with the Ranch Dressing. Pass the additional dressing at the table.
Serves 4

Ranch Dressing

———★———

Some say ranch dressing was originally conceived for use on salads, but an opposing group claims it began as a dipping sauce for fried zucchini. Whichever is true, it is, for sure, an American creation. Once you have perfected the basic dressing, you can vary the seasonings with the addition of other fresh herbs or even chopped bacon.

⅓ cup plain nonfat yogurt
⅓ cup mayonnaise
½ cup buttermilk
2 teaspoons finely grated onion
1 small clove garlic, pressed
Salt and coarsely ground black pepper, to taste
1 tablespoon snipped fresh chives

Whisk the yogurt, mayonnaise, and buttermilk together. Stir in the onion and garlic. Season with salt and a generous grinding of pepper, and fold in the chives. Refrigerate, covered, until ready to use, up to 8 hours.
Makes about 1¼ cups

AUTUMN DUCK SALAD

★ ★ ★

Great Long Island duckling highlights this hearty autumnal salad brightened by the sweet taste of ripe mango. It's robust and just right for a weekend supper—a nice reward for raking those piles of leaves or cleaning out the garage.

There is definitely some advance preparation required to pull this sublime salad together, but it is well worth the effort. Roast the duck and the beets the day before you plan to serve the salad. If you prefer, roasted dark-meat chicken or turkey may be substituted for the duck.

Beer: Brooklyn lager

2 large bunches arugula, tough stems removed,
    rinsed and dried (2 cups)
1½ cups diced (½ inch) ripe mango
1 teaspoon plus 2 tablespoons snipped
    fresh chives
Salt and freshly ground black pepper, to taste
10 tablespoons Orange Honey Dressing
    (page 80)
2 cups shredded cooked duck meat from Roasted
    Duck with a Crispy Skin (page 427)
1½ cups cooked or canned black beans,
    rinsed and drained if canned
2 tablespoons chopped fresh flat-leaf parsley
1 cup diced (¼ inch) Oven-Roasted Beets
    (page 279)

1. Place the arugula and 1 cup of the mango in a large bowl. Sprinkle with the 1 teaspoon chives. Season with salt and pepper, and toss with 2 tablespoons of the dressing. Divide among four dinner plates, distributing the mango equally.

2. Place the shredded duck, black beans, chopped parsley, and 1 tablespoon of the chives in the same bowl. Season with salt and pepper, and toss with 6 tablespoons of the dressing. Arrange the mixture on top of the greens.

3. Toss the beets with the remaining 2 tablespoons vinaigrette, and scatter them decoratively over the duck. Sprinkle with the remaining ½ cup diced mango, and garnish with the remaining 1 tablespoon snipped chives. Serve immediately.

Serves 4

★★★★★★★★★★★★★★★★★★★★★★★★★★

PLAYING LESS HARD TO GET

—❦—

There was a time when duck used to be difficult to find fresh, or even frozen, and locating it usually required a trip to Chinatown or a gourmet market. Ordering duck in a restaurant wasn't any easier; many required at least half a day's notice. Well, duck is not as elusive as it was years ago. Today you can buy duck relatively easily at your local market. The variety you are most likely to find is the Pekin duck, also known as the Long Island duck. This breed is raised throughout the United States and has a lovely, mild flavor, well suited for roasting. Other varieties include Muscovy, which has stronger flavored meat than the Pekin, and Moulard, generally used to make foie gras.

★★★★★★★★★★★★★★★★★★★★★★★★★★

DRESSY FRESH TUNA SALAD

★ ★ ★

Tuna salads run the gamut from the mayonnaise-swathed canned variety to delicately prepared steaks fanned over baby garden greens. I've chosen to feature pan-seared fresh tuna for this salad. A light vinaigrette is all that's needed to enhance all the flavors. Chives make a suitable garnish, but for a more aggressive taste, basil would be my herb of choice. A leaf or two of opal basil would be gorgeous!

Wine: Texas Sauvignon Blanc
Beer: Mid-Atlantic pale ale

1 pound fresh tuna steak, cut 1 inch thick
3 tablespoons olive oil
1 tablespoon finely chopped shallots
½ teaspoon coarsely ground black pepper
2 ripe tomatoes
1 cup asparagus tips, lightly blanched
½ pound mesclun (mixed baby salad greens),
    rinsed and dried
½ cup Shallot Mustard Vinaigrette (recipe follows)
Salt and freshly ground black pepper, to taste
2 tablespoons finely chopped fresh chives

1. Cut the tuna steak into four equal portions. In a bowl, lightly toss the tuna with the oil, shallots, and coarsely ground pepper. Let rest for 15 minutes.

2. Place a nonstick skillet over medium-high heat. Sear the tuna on the first side until lightly browned, 5 minutes. Turn it over with a spatula, and sear for 3 minutes or until cooked to desired doneness. Let it rest for about 5 minutes.

3. Halve the tomatoes lengthwise, and then slice them crosswise about ¼ inch thick. In a large bowl, gently toss the tomatoes with the asparagus tips and mesclun. Lightly dress with some of the vinaigrette, reserving any remaining. Sprinkle with salt and pepper.

4. Mound the tomatoes and greens on four plates. Sprinkle with 1 tablespoon of the chives.

5. Thinly slice the tuna and arrange the slices in a fan over the greens. Drizzle about 2 teaspoons of the remaining vinaigrette over the tuna, sprinkle with the remaining 1 tablespoon chives, and serve.
Serves 4

Shallot Mustard Vinaigrette

──★──

Fresh shallots liven up this light and delicate vinaigrette. It's ideal for cold seafood salads as well as spring and summer greens.

1 tablespoon Dijon mustard
1½ teaspoons sugar
Salt and freshly ground black pepper, to taste
¼ cup cider vinegar
½ cup olive oil
2 tablespoons finely chopped shallots

1. Whisk the mustard, sugar, salt, pepper, and vinegar together in a small bowl.

2. Slowly drizzle in the oil, whisking constantly until thickened. Stir in the shallots, and adjust the seasonings to taste. Store, covered, in the refrigerator for up to 2 days. Bring to room temperature and whisk before using.
Makes about 1 cup

GRANNY SMITH TUNA SALAD

★ ★ ★

It's hard to imagine going back to the standard cupboard-variety tuna in salad once you've had a taste of this: fresh tuna cooked to a moist medium rare, combined with crisp, tart apples and crunchy celery. Fresh basil stars in a zesty mayonnaise to bind it all together. I particularly enjoy this salad served open-face on toasted multigrain bread, with sliced ripe tomatoes and whole basil leaves on top.

Wine: Finger Lakes (NY)
dry Riesling
Beer: New York State
amber lager

1 tablespoon olive oil
2 fresh tuna steaks (about ½ pound each)
½ cup finely diced celery
½ cup finely diced unpeeled Granny Smith apple
2 scallions (3 inches green left on), thinly sliced
Salt, to taste
½ cup mayonnaise
2 to 3 tablespoons finely chopped fresh basil leaves

1. Heat the oil in a large nonstick skillet over medium-high heat. Sear the tuna on the first side until lightly browned, 5 minutes. Turn it over with a spatula, and sear for 3 minutes or until cooked to your preference. Let the tuna rest for about 5 minutes.
2. Flake the tuna into pieces about 1 x ½ inch, and place them in a large bowl. Add the celery, apples, and scallions, and toss gently. Season with salt.

3. Stir the mayonnaise and basil together in a small bowl. Using a small spatula, fold this dressing into the tuna.
Serves 4

FRESH GREAT LAKES WHITEFISH SALAD

★ ★ ★

Smoked whitefish is standard fare in delicatessens across the country. After eating the sweet fresh whitefish from Lake Michigan, I thought I'd try my hand at creating a contemporary nonsmoked version of the traditional deli favorite. The result is cleaner, purer, and equally, if not more, appealing, but still meant to be served with pumpernickel or toasted bagels. Quartered tomatoes sprinkled with chopped red onion and chopped fresh dill makes a perfect companion dish. Watch carefully for bones when you're flaking it. Whitefish, from wherever it hails, is a very bony fish!

Wine: Michigan Peninsula Seyval Blanc
Beer: Wisconsin lager

1¼ pounds Poached Whitefish (recipe follows)
½ cup diced (¼ inch) celery
2 scallions (3 inches green left on), thinly sliced on the diagonal
2 tablespoons chopped fresh dill leaves
¼ cup sour cream
¼ cup mayonnaise
Salt and freshly ground black pepper, to taste

1. Remove the head, skin, and bones from the whitefish and coarsely flake it into a bowl. (There should be 1 pound of meat.) Add the celery, scallions, and dill, and toss gently.

2. Combine the sour cream and mayonnaise in a small bowl. Add this dressing to the fish, and gently fold it in with a rubber spatula. Season with salt and pepper.

Serves 6

Poached Whitefish

★

2 cups water
1 cup dry white wine
Few pale green celery leaves
4 sprigs fresh flat-leaf parsley
½ carrot
4 black peppercorns
1¼ pounds whole whitefish,
    scales removed
    and gutted

1. Place the water, wine, celery leaves, parsley, carrot, and peppercorns in a medium-size sauté pan and bring to a boil over medium heat. Reduce the heat and when the liquid is simmering, add the whitefish. Poach the fish, uncovered, until cooked through, about 10 minutes per inch of thickness.

2. Remove the fish from the poaching liquid with a slotted spatula. Cool before proceeding with the recipe.

Serves 6 in a salad

DRESS-UP LOBSTER, FAVA, AND BARLEY SALAD

★ ★ ★

Being a committed barley lover, I feel free to let this simple grain mix it up with the most luxurious foods, even lobster and fava beans. This piquant combination serves either as a substantial entrée or, in smaller portions, as an elegant appetizer for an intimate springtime dinner party. To fill out the menu, Sweet Sweet Pea Soup would be a nonpareil starter and Orange Rhubarb Crumble a sublime dessert.

Wine: Monterey County (CA) Chardonnay
Beer: Washington State India pale ale

½ cup uncooked pearl barley
Water, or defatted chicken broth, preferably
    homemade (page 253)
1 pound fresh fava beans (1 cup shelled)
½ pound cooked lobster meat (from a 1¼-pound
    lobster), cut into 1-inch chunks
2 small ripe tomatoes, seeded and cut into
    ½-inch pieces
2 tablespoons coarsely chopped fresh oregano
    or marjoram leaves
1 tablespoon coarsely chopped fresh
    mint leaves
1 tablespoon finely grated lemon zest
Salt and freshly ground black pepper,
    to taste
½ cup Lemony Dressing (recipe follows)
8 cups mesclun (mixed baby salad greens),
    rinsed and dried
4 small sprigs fresh oregano or marjoram,
    for garnish

1. Place the barley in a strainer and rinse it under cold water. Then place it in a saucepan, add water or chicken broth to cover by 2 inches, and bring to a boil. Reduce the heat to medium and simmer until just tender, 45 minutes. Drain, and transfer the barley to a large bowl.

2. Shell the fava beans. Bring a pot of water to a boil. Drop the beans into the water and cook them for 30 seconds. Then drain and refresh under cold water. Slip the beans out of their skins, and add them to the barley along with the lobster meat, tomatoes, oregano, mint, lemon zest, salt, pepper, and ¼ cup of the dressing. Use a rubber spatula, working from under the barley, to toss all of the ingredients together.

3. To serve, toss the greens with enough of the remaining ¼ cup dressing to coat lightly. Divide the greens among four plates. Top each portion with barley salad, and garnish with an oregano or marjoram sprig.

Serves 4

Lemony Dressing

★

Light, fresh, and smooth, this is the ideal dressing to nap seafood or vegetable salads, or delicate greens. Use a simple pure olive oil, because extra virgin would be too heavy for the light lemon juice. Make up a good-size amount as it will keep, well covered, in the refrigerator for up to 1 week.

6 tablespoons fresh lemon juice
1 tablespoon finely grated lemon zest
1 tablespoon Dijon mustard
1 tablespoon sugar
Salt and freshly ground black pepper, to taste
¾ cup olive oil

1. Place the lemon juice, zest, mustard, sugar, salt, and pepper in a small bowl. Whisk together.

2. Slowly drizzle in the oil, whisking constantly until thickened. Adjust the seasonings. Store, covered, in the refrigerator for up to 1 week. Bring to room temperature and rewhisk before using.

Makes about 1¼ cups

CRAB LOUIS SALAD WITH HARD-COOKED EGGS

★ ★ ★

There is no salad more succulent than one made with the sweet meat of fresh Dungeness crabs from the Pacific Northwest. On San Francisco's Fisherman's Wharf, strollers can buy red-and-white-checked cardboard containers piled high with crabmeat, accompanied by a pleated paper cup filled with the herby, spicy Louis dressing. Sometimes I serve Crab Louis on its own as a first course at dinnertime, and sometimes I turn it into this salad for a special luncheon entrée.

Wine: Willamette Valley (OR) Müller-Thurgau
Beer: San Francisco Anchor Steam Beer

LOUIS DRESSING

½ cup mayonnaise
¼ cup sour cream
2 tablespoons chili sauce
1 tablespoon fresh lemon juice
2 tablespoons diced (¼ inch) green bell pepper
1 to 2 tablespoons chopped green and
*   white part of scallions*
1 tablespoon chopped fresh tarragon leaves or
*   snipped fresh chives*
Salt and freshly ground black pepper, to taste

SALAD

1 pound fresh lump or Dungeness crabmeat,
*   picked over to remove any cartilage*
4 cups mesclun (mixed baby greens), rinsed and dried
⅓ cup Orange Honey Dressing (page 80)
4 hard-cooked eggs, sliced
2 teaspoons chopped fresh tarragon leaves

1. Prepare the Louis dressing: Combine the mayonnaise, sour cream, chili sauce, lemon juice, bell pepper, scallions, and 1 tablespoon tarragon in a bowl. Season with salt and pepper, and set aside.

2. Prepare the salad: Place the crabmeat in a bowl, and gently toss it with ¾ cup of the Louis dressing (save any remainder for another use). Adjust the seasonings.

3. To serve, toss the salad greens with the Orange Honey Dressing in a bowl. Arrange the greens in the center of four dinner plates. Top with the crab salad, and garnish with the eggs. Sprinkle with the 2 teaspoons chopped tarragon.

Serves 4

ORANGE-SCENTED CRAB SALAD

★ ★ ★

Fresh, delicate melons, combined with the assertive tastes of ginger and basil, make up a seafood salad just right for a summer lunch. Add

TO COOK DUNGENESS CRABS

Before cooking live Dungeness crabs, which are large (1 to 3 pounds), chill them on ice or in the freezer for 20 minutes to slow their metabolism. If you throw vigorous crabs into boiling water, they will throw off their legs as they would if they were in a fight.

Begin with a large pot of boiling seawater or salted water. Once you drop in the crabs, begin timing. The rule of thumb is to boil for 10 minutes per pound for small crabs (1½ to 2 pounds) or 8 minutes per pound for larger crabs. Drain and cool the crabs, then pry off the top shell of each. Scrape away the gills and viscera from the cavity, then rinse and drain the crab thoroughly. Twist off the legs and crack them, and the claws, with a nutcracker; remove the meat with a pick. Snap the body in half with your hands, or use a heavy knife; pull out the segmented meat.

the basil shortly before serving so the acid from the vinegar and orange juice doesn't discolor it—you want the bright green contrast to the pastel colors of the fruits. Highlight it all with bitter fuchsia-colored radicchio.

Wine: Russian River Valley (CA) Gewürztraminer
Beer: California lager

1 pound fresh lump crabmeat, picked over to remove any cartilage
1½ cups cantaloupe balls (see Note)
2 cups watermelon balls (see Note)
1 cup seeded and diced (¼ inch) plum tomatoes
1½ teaspoons finely minced fresh ginger
2 tablespoons fresh orange juice
1 tablespoon red wine vinegar
½ teaspoon Dijon mustard
Salt and freshly ground black pepper, to taste
¼ cup extra virgin olive oil
½ teaspoon finely grated orange zest
2 tablespoons chopped fresh basil leaves
2 heads red radicchio lettuce, leaves rinsed and patted dry

1. Place the crabmeat, cantaloupe, watermelon, tomatoes, and ginger in a large bowl. Gently toss together with a rubber spatula. Set aside.

2. Combine the orange juice, vinegar, mustard, salt, and pepper in a small bowl. Whisking constantly, slowly drizzle in the olive oil. Continue whisking until the mixture has thickened slightly. Stir in the orange zest.

3. Shortly before serving, toss the dressing and the basil with the crabmeat mixture. Serve on a decorative platter, surrounded by radicchio leaves.

Serves 6

NOTE: Use the small end of a melon baller to scoop the amount of cantaloupe and watermelon balls desired for the recipe.

SHRIMP REMOULADE PARFAIT

★ ★ ★

In Louisiana, shrimp rémoulade has been a long-standing favorite. When it's layered with ripe papaya, tomatoes, and grapes, it takes on a whole new character. The spirited flavor of the rémoulade sauce is a perfect foil for the sweetness of the fruits.

1 pound cooked large shrimp, peeled and deveined
½ cup diced (¼ inch) celery
2½ tablespoons chopped fresh tarragon leaves
Rémoulade Sauce (recipe follows)
2 cups shredded red-leaf lettuce
1 cup green or red seedless grapes, halved crosswise
4 ripe plum tomatoes, seeded and cut into ¼-inch dice
¾ cup diced (¼ inch) ripe papaya

1. Cut the shrimp in half crosswise, and place them in a bowl with the celery and 2 tablespoons of the tarragon. Fold in ½ cup of the Rémoulade Sauce. Set aside.

2. To assemble the parfaits, place 1 tablespoon of the Rémoulade Sauce in each of four large (12-ounce) wine or water goblets. Place ½ cup of the shredded lettuce in each goblet, and top each with ¼ cup of the grapes. Divide the shrimp mixture evenly among the goblets, and top each with diced tomatoes and papaya. Dollop each with 2 teaspoons of the Rémoulade Sauce, and sprinkle with the remaining ½ tablespoon fresh tarragon. Pass any remaining Rémoulade Sauce at the table, if desired.

Serves 4

Rémoulade Sauce

— ★ —

Originally from France but now deeply entrenched in Louisiana cuisine, courtesy of the French Acadians, this piquant mayonnaise-based mustard sauce stars in many delectable regional specialties. The amount of Tabasco sauce depends solely on the cook's desire to play with fire.

1 cup mayonnaise
1 tablespoon Dijon mustard
2 teaspoons whole-grain mustard
1 teaspoon tarragon vinegar
¼ teaspoon Tabasco sauce, or more
2 teaspoons tiny capers, drained and chopped
1 tablespoon chopped fresh flat-leaf parsley
1 scallion (3 inches green left on), very thinly sliced
Salt and freshly ground black pepper, to taste

Combine all the ingredients in a small bowl. Taste, and add more Tabasco, a drop at a time, if desired. Refrigerate, covered, until ready to use, up to 8 hours.
Makes about 1¼ cups

BAYOU SHRIMP AND CELERY ROOT REMOULADE

★ ★ ★

Celery root, with its intensely vivid celery flavor, is marvelous raw in salads as well as roasted or blanched. This root vegetable, also known as celeriac, is grown primarily for the bulb, so don't expect to find any stalks. It's a bit tedious to prepare—you'll need a wide knife with good balance to speed you along. Both the flavor and the texture offer a nice complement to shrimp. The Rémoulade Sauce, traditional to Louisiana, ties all the elements together for a beautiful salad redolent of a gentle summer clime with a little spice added (see Note).

Wine: Virginia Chardonnay
Beer: Mid-Atlantic lager

2 celery root knobs (about 1 pound each)
2 pounds large shrimp, peeled and deveined
1¼ cups Rémoulade Sauce (this page)
¼ cup chopped fresh flat-leaf parsley
Salt and freshly ground black pepper, to taste

1. Trim the roots and stems off the celery knobs, and peel the bumpy surface carefully. Cut the knobs into very thin crosswise slices, and then cut the slices into very thin shreds (julienne). Drop the celery root into cold water until ready to use to prevent discoloration.

2. Cook the shrimp in boiling water until just tender, 1 to 2 minutes. Drain, rinse under cold water, drain well, and pat dry.

3. Drain the celery root and dry it well. In a large bowl, combine the celery root with the shrimp. Toss well with the Rémoulade Sauce, sprinkle with the parsley, and season with salt and pepper. Chill, covered, until serving time, or at least for 1 hour.
Serves 6

NOTE: If you wish to serve this salad without the shrimp, reduce the sauce to 1 cup. All other instructions remain the same.

CONVENTION GRILL EGG SALAD

★ ★ ★

When touring the U.S. researching recipes for this book, I learned to scan the room as I ate. That way, I could see what other tasty-looking dishes people ordered. I didn't want to miss a trick. At the new deco Convention Grill in Minneapolis, I caught sight of a great egg salad sandwich on wheat coming out of the kitchen. The hand-chunked white and creamy yolk blended together with dill-flecked mayonnaise and garnished with lettuce looked so appealing, I tried it out in my kitchen when I got home. I'm a big fan of egg salad, and a critical one, too, and I found this variation as mouthwatering to eat as it was to look at on the waiter's tray. I like it on a bed of mesclun or on pumpernickel bread topped with mesclun.

8 hard-cooked eggs
¾ cup mayonnaise
1 teaspoon Dijon mustard
Salt and freshly ground white pepper, to taste
2 tablespoons chopped fresh dill leaves

1. Cut the eggs in half lengthwise, and separate the yolks from the whites. Cut each white half into quarters and place them in a bowl.

Coarsely chop the yolks and add them to the whites.

2. Fold together gently with the remaining ingredients. Cover and refrigerate until ready to serve.

Makes about 3 cups; serves 6

SMOKED SALMON EGG SALAD

★ ★ ★

This creamy brunch or lunch egg salad combines some favorite ingredients in an unexpected way. When it's not too salty, smoked salmon marries beautifully with hard-cooked eggs and the other usual trimmings. All the seasoning you'll need is some freshly ground black pepper and a touch of lemon juice to brighten the flavors. Be sure not to add salt—the capers and salmon take care of that. In my house, we eat this while the eggs are still slightly warm, and I serve it with toasted bagels or seven-grain bread, thinly sliced red onion, and ripe tomato.

6 hard-cooked eggs
2 ounces thinly sliced smoked salmon
2 teaspoons finely minced shallots
2 teaspoons tiny capers, drained
2 teaspoons finely chopped fresh dill leaves
Freshly ground black pepper, to taste
¼ cup sour cream
2 tablespoons mayonnaise
Finely grated zest of 1 lemon
1 teaspoon fresh lemon juice

1. Quarter the eggs, then coarsely chop them. Place in a bowl.

2. Shred the salmon. Using a fork, gently mix the salmon into the eggs. Stir in the shallots, capers, dill, and pepper.

3. In a separate bowl, combine the remaining ingredients. Stir this dressing and fold it gently into the salad. Serve immediately, or cover and refrigerate until ready to serve.

Makes about 2 cups; serves 4

BLUE PLATE S·P·E·C·I·A·L

Savannah Cocktail Crab Bites with
Hot Stuff Tartar Sauce

"Ya Ya" Gumbo

Eula Mae Dore's Potato Salad

Zesty Picnic Slaw

New Orleans Praline Ice Cream

Minted Iced Tea

EULA MAE DORE'S POTATO SALAD

★ ★ ★

Eula Mae Dore is chef for the McIlhenny family, proprietors of world-famous Tabasco sauce, and after enjoying one of her beautifully presented luncheons on Avery Island, in Cajun bayou country, I talked with her about the potato salad she traditionally serves with her beguilingly aromatic chicken and andouille gumbo. After a gentle beg or two, I learned her recipe secrets. Red-skinned potatoes are essential, allowing one per person and one hard-cooked egg per potato. Only the celery heart is used—the very pale green, tender center ribs. It's added along with red and green bell pepper, all cut into little pieces for inviting color. The result is a creamy, eggy potato salad—velvety and very Southern. I have served it with cold roasted chicken as well as alongside steamy bowls of gumbo.

*6 red boiling potatoes (about 2 pounds
    total), scrubbed*
Salt
6 hard-cooked eggs
1 cup mayonnaise
¼ cup finely diced celery heart
2 tablespoons finely diced red bell pepper
2 tablespoons finely diced green bell pepper
2 tablespoons finely diced gherkin pickles
Freshly ground black pepper, to taste

1. Place the potatoes in a saucepan, cover with water, and add 1 teaspoon salt. Bring to a boil. Reduce the heat to a simmer and cook the potatoes until nice and tender, about 25 minutes. Drain. Peel the potatoes when they are cool enough to handle.

2. Place the egg yolks in a large bowl and mash them with a fork. Add the mayonnaise and mix well. Coarsely chop the egg whites and add them to the mayonnaise mixture.

3. Cut the potatoes into quarters, and then cut the quarters into ¼-inch-thick slices. Add them to the mayonnaise mixture along with the remaining ingredients, including salt, to taste, and toss gently to combine.

Serves 6

BOARDING HOUSE POTATO SALAD

★ ★ ★

I wish I could say that I just stumbled upon Mrs. Wilkes's Boarding House, but when I was in Savannah, Georgia, I made a beeline for the renowned family-style restaurant, located, as it has been since the 1940s, at 107 West Jones Street at Whitaker. An address is scarcely necessary—just keep an eye out for lines around the block and the seductive aromas emanating from within—home-fried chicken, greens, baked ham, barbecued pork, and on and on. After all of us sat down at tables and the food was served family-style, for the first time I truly understood the term "boarding house reach."

Mrs. Wilkes's potato salad served as an inspiration for this variation. While at first glance the ingredients may seem a little "old hat," I think of them as tried and true. I know that when I serve this salad, everyone around my table has at least one big helping (usually more), and I happily share the kudos with Mrs. Wilkes. I urge you to get this one cooking for your next family get-together or summertime picnic. The recipe easily doubles to feed a crowd.

4 to 5 russet potatoes (2½ pounds total),
    peeled and cut into ½-inch dice
Salt
½ cup diced (¼ inch) celery
½ cup diced (¼ inch) red bell pepper
⅓ cup chopped gherkin pickles
2 tablespoons minced red onion
4 hard-cooked eggs, chopped
1 cup mayonnaise
1 teaspoon Dijon mustard
1 tablespoon red wine vinegar
Freshly ground black pepper,
    to taste

1. Place the potatoes in a saucepan and cover with cold water. Add 1 teaspoon salt. Bring to a boil, reduce the heat slightly, and simmer until tender, about 10 minutes. Drain and transfer to a bowl.

2. Add the celery, bell pepper, gherkins, red onion, and eggs. Toss thoroughly.

3. Combine the mayonnaise, mustard, vinegar, pepper, and salt, to taste, in a small bowl. Blend well, and fold into the potatoes with a large rubber spatula. Cover and refrigerate for 3 to 4 hours, bringing to room temperature to serve.

Serves 6 to 8

LONE STAR CREAMY POTATO SALAD

★ ★ ★

I have an open-ended passion for potato salads, and it was in Texas that my own basic recipe—the one that I've made for years—met its match. I first encountered this version at a restaurant in Houston, but soon found it on other menus throughout the state. I learned that adding hard-cooked eggs and sweet pickle relish is the Texan way with potato salad. When serving a crowd, double the recipe.

3 russet potatoes (1½ pounds total), peeled
3 hard-cooked eggs, coarsely chopped
⅓ cup diced (¼ inch) red bell pepper
¾ cup sour cream
½ cup mayonnaise
¼ cup sweet pickle relish
Coarse salt and coarsely ground black pepper,
*   to taste*

1. Cut the potatoes into large chunks. Place them in a pot of salted water to cover, and bring to a boil. Reduce the heat and simmer until tender, about 15 minutes. Drain.

2. When the potatoes are cool enough to handle, cut them into small pieces, about 1 x 1½ inches, and place them in a bowl. Add the eggs and the bell pepper, and toss together gently with a rubber spatula.

3. In a separate bowl, combine the sour cream, mayonnaise, and relish. Toss this dressing gently with the potatoes, season generously with coarse salt and pepper, and serve.

Serves 4 to 6

RED, WHITE, AND BLUE ROASTED POTATO SALAD

★ ★ ★

This recipe is from my friend Linda Gollober, who buys all of her potatoes on weekly expeditions to San Francisco's fabulous Ferry Plaza farmers' market, which features all kinds of great local produce. The rainbow array of potatoes inspired this patriotic salad. The three varieties provide a contrast in color and texture; the new reds are firm and waxy, the Yukon Golds

creamy, and the Peruvian Blues fluffy. (If you can't find Yukon Golds, small White Rose or Yellow Finn potatoes will be just fine.) The salad is a satisfying accompaniment to a sizzling thick steak or barbecued spareribs.

DRESSING
1 tablespoon Dijon mustard
3 tablespoons white wine
*   vinegar*
1 tablespoon fresh lemon
*   juice*
Pinch of sugar
½ cup extra virgin olive oil

POTATOES
¾ pound small red new potatoes
¾ pound small Yukon Gold or White Rose potatoes
¾ pound small Peruvian Blue potatoes
3 tablespoons extra virgin olive oil
½ teaspoon coarse salt
Salt and freshly ground black pepper, to taste
2 tablespoons chopped shallots
2 tablespoons chopped fresh flat-leaf parsley

1. Preheat the oven to 350°F.

2. Prepare the dressing: Whisk together the mustard, vinegar, lemon juice, and sugar in a small bowl. Whisking constantly, slowly drizzle in the olive oil and continue whisking until the dressing is smooth and creamy. Set aside.

3. Prepare the potatoes: Wash all the potatoes well and pat them dry. Cut the potatoes in half and place them in two bowls: the gold and blue in one, the red in the other. Drizzle all with the olive oil and sprinkle with the coarse salt. Toss well to coat evenly. Place all of the potatoes in one layer on a baking sheet, keeping the red potatoes separate from the others. Roast in the center of the oven until tender, 30 minutes for the Yukon Gold and the Peruvian Blue potatoes, 45 minutes for the red. As they are cooked, transfer the potatoes to a large bowl.

4. Let the potatoes cool for 15 to 20 minutes. Then add the dressing and toss gently. Season with salt and pepper, and sprinkle with the shallots and parsley. Serve the salad at room temperature.

Serves 6

CHIFFON POTATO SALAD

★ ★ ★

Far from the basic down-home potato salad recipe, this elegant, light, garden variety is charming for dressier occasions. Crisp cucumber acts as the foil for velvety avocado, and a lemony vinaigrette holds the sum together without overwhelming it. More composed than tossed, the presentation is as refined as the flavor.

6 tablespoons fresh lemon juice
4 tablespoons white wine vinegar
½ cup olive oil
2 heads Boston lettuce (each about ¾ pound)
6 russet potatoes (about 3 pounds total)
Salt
Coarsely ground black pepper, to taste
1 hothouse (seedless) cucumber, peeled and
*   cut into ½-inch dice*
4 ribs celery, cut into ½-inch dice
6 scallions (3 inches green left on), thinly
*   sliced on the diagonal*
2 ripe avocados
2 tablespoons chopped fresh flat-leaf parsley,
*   for garnish*

1. Place 4 tablespoons of the lemon juice, the vinegar, and oil in a small bowl and whisk together well. Set aside.

2. Separate the lettuce leaves and rinse them. Gently pat them dry and set them aside.

3. Peel the potatoes, cut them in half lengthwise and then cut them into ¼-inch-thick slices. Place the slices in a pot, cover with cold water, add 1 teaspoon salt, and bring to a boil. Reduce the heat to medium and simmer until tender but not mushy, 8 to 10 minutes. Do not overcook. Drain, and transfer to a bowl. While the potatoes are still warm, toss them gently with ½ cup of the dressing. Season with salt, to taste, and pepper, and set aside.

4. Toss the cucumber, celery, and scallions together in a large bowl. Reserving 8 to 10 whole lettuce leaves, tear the remaining lettuce into bite-size pieces and add to the bowl.

5. Shortly before serving, toss the lettuce mixture with the remaining dressing. Add the potatoes and gently toss together.

6. Arrange the whole lettuce leaves decoratively around the rim of a serving platter or large shallow bowl, and mound the potato salad in the center.

7. Place the remaining 2 tablespoons lemon juice in a bowl. Halve, pit, and peel the avocados. Slice them into coarse pieces. Place the slices in the lemon juice to prevent discoloration. Arrange the avocado over the potato salad, sprinkle with the chopped parsley, and serve.

Serves 12

★★★

THE POTATO BIN

—❦—

This book is full of potatoes, prepared every which way. I use them constantly—most cooks do, and for good reasons. I can't think of another food that is altogether so versatile, filling, delicious, inexpensive, and chock full of vitamins, minerals, and complex carbohydrates as the potato. This humblest of vegetables comes with more history than most, too.

The first potatoes to travel from the Americas to Europe ended their journey at the Vatican in 1588—a gift to the Pope from the Spanish sovereign, via the conqueror Pizarro. The Pope's botanist planted them and drew beautiful pictures of the results, which he called "little truffles" (taraturfli). Little did anyone know what effect this curious tuber (which the botanist did not eat) would have on the entire Western world. Within two centuries, it was sustaining millions, from southern Spain to the British Isles. Without it, many would doubtless have starved. After the French Revolution, the Paris Commune declared it Republican and made eating it compulsory. More than a million Irish fled to the United States because of potatoes—the lack of them, in this case. And without those refugees, of course, our story would be a very different one.

Generation after generation, we never tire of potatoes. These days, we can buy many more kinds than our mothers and grandmothers could—dozens of different spuds in a marvelous array of shapes, sizes, and textures. I often spot heirloom varieties at farmers' markets. Though there are far too many kinds to detail here (or for anyone to remember!), some guidelines will help you when you're shopping.

• Starchy potatoes (Idahos or russets) are best for baking or mashing.

• Waxy, low-starch varieties that hold their shape well make the best gratins and non-creamy potato salads. Round Whites and Round Reds work well, as do new (immature) potatoes of any kind. True new potatoes are thin-skinned and highly perishable, available only in spring and early summer.

• Specialty potatoes, such as Bintje, Carole/Carola, Yellow Finn, and Yukon Gold (among others), are golden-hued, low-starch varieties and retain their shape better when cooked. You can roast or steam and slice these; you can also prepare them as you would a baking potato.

• Blue potatoes are showing up in markets more frequently now and are temptingly colorful. I find them bland and mealy, however, with the exception of Peruvian Blues. Try these as homemade potato chips, or toss them together with red-skinned new potatoes to make the eye-catching Red, White, and Blue, Roasted Potato Salad on page 93.

Store potatoes in a paper bag in a cool, dark spot. Keep them out of the refrigerator; the cold will convert their sugars to starch. If for some reason they have been refrigerated, bring them to room temperature before cooking.

★★★

ALASKAN POTATO SALAD

★ ★ ★

For me, there can never be too many potato salads. Whether seasoned with a touch of Louisiana, Texas, or Alaska, each has its own charm. While this version does not require any specifically Alaskan ingredients, I first ate it at The Tutka Bay Lodge in Homer, Alaska. It was prepared for me by owner Nelda Osgood's mother, Mrs. Stone, who is a native of Kodiak Island.

6 red boiling potatoes (about 2 pounds total),
*   scrubbed*
2½ teaspoons salt
4 slices bacon
1 cup chopped onions
2 tablespoons all-purpose flour
2 tablespoons sugar
½ teaspoon celery seeds
Freshly ground black pepper,
*   to taste*
¾ cup water
⅓ cup cider vinegar
¼ cup chopped fresh flat-leaf parsley

1. Place the potatoes in a saucepan, cover with cold water, and add 1 teaspoon of the salt. Bring to a boil. Then reduce the heat and simmer until cooked through, about 25 minutes.

2. While the potatoes are cooking, fry the bacon in a nonstick skillet over medium heat until crisp, about 8 minutes. Using a slotted spoon, transfer the bacon to paper towels to drain. Reserve the skillet with the bacon fat.

3. Drain the potatoes. When they are cool enough to handle, peel them and cut them into ¼-inch-thick slices. Place them in a large bowl. Crumble the bacon and add it to the potatoes.

4. Place the reserved skillet over medium-low heat, add the onions, and cook until golden, about 10 minutes. Stir in the flour, sugar, the remaining 1½ teaspoons salt, the celery seeds, and pepper. Cook over low heat, stirring for 3 minutes.

5. Increase the heat slightly. Add the water and vinegar and bring to a boil, stirring constantly. Boil for 1 minute. Pour this dressing over the potatoes and bacon, and fold together gently with a large rubber spatula. Fold in the parsley, and serve hot or at room temperature.

Serves 6 to 8

ORANGE DUCKY POTATO SALAD

★ ★ ★

Red new potatoes and rich, dark-meated duck make perfect partners when pulled together with summer's first green beans and a refreshing hint of orange zest. The effect is startling, an exotic entrée salad fit for any time of year.

Wine: Long Island (NY) Cabernet Franc
Beer: Montana red ale

4 cups coarsely shredded cooked duck (see Note)
8 medium red new potatoes (about 2 pounds total),
*   quartered*
¼ pound thin green beans or haricots verts, stem
*   ends trimmed, halved crosswise*
Coarse salt and freshly ground black pepper, to taste
Finely grated zest of 1 orange
6 tablespoons Orange Honey Dressing (page 80), or
*   more to taste*
2 tablespoons chopped fresh flat-leaf parsley
1 large bunch arugula or head of frisée, tough stems
*   discarded, rinsed and dried*

1. Place the shredded duck in a bowl.

2. Bring a pot of salted water to a boil. Add the potatoes and cook until tender, 10 minutes. Using a slotted spoon, transfer the potatoes to the bowl containing the duck. Add the beans to the same boiling water and cook until just tender, 3 to 4 minutes. Refresh the beans under cold water, drain well, and add to the duck.

3. Season the salad with coarse salt and pepper. Add the orange zest, dressing, and 1 tablespoon of the parsley. Toss well.

4. Arrange the salad on a bed of arugula, and sprinkle with the remaining 1 tablespoon parsley. If you like, drizzle with extra dressing before serving.

Serves 6

NOTE: This salad is delicious enough to roast a duck for. See page 427 for Roasted Duck with a Crispy Skin, if you wish to start from scratch.

FRESH SALMON POTATO SALAD

★ ★ ★

During my visit to Alaska, I was intrigued by the remnants of Russia's culinary influence. At home, that influence resulted in one of the tastier inspirations of my trip—this lightly dressed salad of potatoes, salmon, and dill. Be very careful when flaking the salmon. Just follow the natural grain of the fish and gently break the pieces off with your fingers.

Wine: Hudson Valley (NY) Seyval Blanc
Beer: Chicago pale ale

3 cups water
1 cup dry white wine
3 sprigs fresh
    flat-leaf
    parsley
1 bay leaf
4 black pepper-
    corns
½ pound salmon
    fillet
2 russet potatoes
    (about 1 pound total), peeled
    and cut into ¼-inch dice
Salt
½ cup diced (¼ inch) celery
3 hard-cooked eggs, coarsely chopped
2 or 3 scallions (3 inches green left on),
    thinly sliced on the diagonal
2 tablespoons chopped dill leaves, or more to taste
Coarsely ground black pepper, to taste
¾ cup Lemon Dill Yogurt Dressing
    (recipe follows)
½ pound mesclun (mixed baby salad greens),
    rinsed and dried
Fresh dill sprigs, for garnish

1. Combine the water, wine, parsley sprigs, bay leaf, and peppercorns in a large wide pot and bring to a boil. Reduce the heat and simmer for 10 minutes. Add the salmon and cook, partially covered, until the flesh flakes easily when tested with a fork, about 5 minutes. Carefully remove the salmon from the cooking liquid and set it aside; discard the cooking liquid.

2. Place the potatoes in a saucepan, cover with water, and add 1 teaspoon salt. Bring to a boil. Then reduce the heat to medium and cook until just tender, 5 to 8 minutes. Drain, transfer to a large bowl, and cool to room temperature.

3. When the potatoes have cooled, add the celery, eggs, scallions, and dill.

4. Pat the salmon dry with paper towels, and carefully break it along the grain into large

flakes, discarding any skin and bones. Add it to the potatoes. Season with salt and pepper.

5. Add ½ cup of the lemon dressing and gently fold all the ingredients together with a rubber spatula.

6. To serve, toss the mesclun with the remaining ¼ cup dressing, then divide it among four dinner plates. Arrange the salad in the center, and garnish with fresh dill sprigs.

Serves 4

Lemon Dill Yogurt Dressing

★

Light and creamy, with the consistency of a rich mayonnaise, this dressing is a healthful yet flavorful alternative to the ordinary dressings used to season potato salads and slaws. I find the yogurt adds a creamy, complementary tang to these salads without taking away any of the nostalgic flavor.

1 cup plain nonfat yogurt, drained for 1 hour
*   in a strainer*
1 tablespoon fresh lemon juice
1 teaspoon finely grated lemon zest
¼ cup extra virgin olive oil
¼ teaspoon coarsely ground black pepper
2 teaspoons chopped fresh dill leaves

1. Mix the yogurt, lemon juice, and zest together in a small bowl. Slowly drizzle in the olive oil, whisking constantly until smooth and slightly thick.

2. Fold in the pepper and the chopped dill. Refrigerate, covered, until ready to use, up to 8 hours.

Makes about 1⅓ cups

BACKYARD MACARONI SALAD

★ ★ ★

There's nothing fancy about macaroni salad. When you're craving one like Mom used to make, no matter where you're from, this is the recipe to turn to. I tried developing the salad with penne and rigatoni, but in the end, only elbows did the trick. Old-fashioned pickle relish adds the final homey touch. For a flash of a little something new, a ripe mango garnish dazzles.

½ pound elbow macaroni
¼ cup milk
¾ cup seeded and diced (¼ inch) ripe plum tomatoes
*   (about 3 tomatoes), with any juices*
¼ cup diced (¼ inch) red bell pepper
¼ cup diced (¼ inch) green bell pepper
¼ cup minced red onion
¼ cup chopped fresh dill leaves
¾ cup mayonnaise
¼ cup sour cream
2 tablespoons sweet pickle relish (do not drain)
Salt and freshly ground black pepper,
*   to taste*
½ cup diced (¼ inch) ripe mango,
*   for garnish*

1. Cook the macaroni in boiling salted water until just tender, stirring occasionally, 6 to 8 minutes. Drain, rinse under cold water, drain again, and place in a large bowl.

2. Toss the macaroni with the milk. Then toss in all of the vegetables, including any tomato juices, and the dill.

3. In a separate bowl, combine the mayonnaise, sour cream, pickle relish, salt, and pepper. Toss with the macaroni. Refrigerate the salad, covered, for at least 4 hours. Before serving, bring it to room temperature, adjust the seasoning, and garnish with the mango.

Serves 6

EAST NORWALK COLESLAW

★ ★ ★

When I was a child, I lived in East Norwalk, Connecticut, where my best friend was Carol Yacklus. Every once in a while her mom would invite me to dinner. I looked forward to these meals—especially because Carol's mother made the best creamy coleslaw. Years later, my mother bumped into Mrs. Yacklus and told her that I still talked about my passion for her coleslaw. She was happy to share her recipe and now, whenever the craving strikes, I can easily satisfy it. This coleslaw matches up well with deli sandwiches, meat loaf, or a backyard barbecue.

1 cup mayonnaise
½ cup sour cream
½ cup corn oil
2 tablespoons milk
1 teaspoon caraway seeds
Salt and freshly ground black pepper,
    to taste
1 head green cabbage (about 2 pounds),
    tough leaves removed, cored, and quartered
1 large carrot, peeled and coarsely grated
1 green bell pepper, stemmed, seeded, and
    grated
1 tablespoon chopped fresh flat-leaf parsley

1. In a small bowl, whisk together the mayonnaise, sour cream, oil, milk, caraway seeds, salt, and pepper.

2. Thinly slice the cabbage, and place it in a large bowl along with the carrot and bell pepper. Using two large forks, toss with the mayonnaise mixture and the parsley. Adjust the seasonings, to taste. Refrigerate, covered, for at least 4 hours, then bring to room temperature before serving.

Serves 6 to 8

CORKY'S MEMPHIS-STYLE COLESLAW

★ ★ ★

When I was on my *All Around the World* book tour, I had the good fortune to visit Memphis, Tennessee. Between interviews, I managed a quick trip to Graceland—of course—followed by some barbecue at Corky's. It was my first time for both, and both are worth return visits, especially Corky's. Besides great barbecue, Corky's, with its wooden walls, red-napped tables, and country music, serves a zesty coleslaw that perfectly complements their peppery tomato-based barbecue sauce. Plates of ribs, sliced brisket on a bun, or tender pork shoulder feel more complete with a side of this slaw.

1 head green cabbage (about 2 pounds), tough
    leaves removed, cored, and shredded
2 carrots, peeled and grated
1 green bell pepper, stemmed, seeded, and
    finely diced
2 tablespoons grated onion
2 cups mayonnaise
¾ cup sugar
¼ cup Dijon mustard
¼ cup cider vinegar
2 tablespoons celery seeds
1 teaspoon salt
⅛ teaspoon freshly ground white pepper

1. Place the cabbage, carrots, bell pepper, and onion in a large bowl. Toss thoroughly and set aside.

2. In another bowl, mix together all the remaining ingredients. Pour this dressing over the vegetables, and toss well to combine.

3. Cover the coleslaw and refrigerate for at least 3 hours, then bring to room temperature before serving.

Serves 6

ZESTY PICNIC SLAW

★ ★ ★

When you'd prefer a non-creamy slaw, this is the one to pick. A sweet, peppery cabbage salad with a vinaigrette dressing, it has an affinity for cold roast pork or a duck sandwich on toasted peasant bread, and it's not bad on burgers either! A frosty beer is the ideal beverage here. Make the slaw at least a few hours before serving to allow the flavors to mellow.

DRESSING
1 small clove garlic
¼ teaspoon coarse salt
1½ teaspoons Dijon mustard
1½ teaspoons finely grated orange zest
2 tablespoon fresh orange juice
1 tablespoon cider vinegar
½ teaspoon sugar
¼ cup extra virgin olive oil
¼ cup olive oil
Salt and freshly ground black pepper,
    to taste

SLAW
4 cups very thinly sliced red cabbage
4 cups very thinly sliced green cabbage
1 red bell pepper, stemmed, seeded,
    and julienned
1 green bell pepper, stemmed, seeded,
    and julienned
1 yellow bell pepper, stemmed, seeded,
    and julienned
2 carrots, peeled and coarsely grated
1 teaspoon caraway seeds
Salt and freshly ground black pepper, to taste
2 tablespoons snipped fresh chives

1. Prepare the dressing: Finely mince the garlic with the coarse salt. Place the garlic and salt in a bowl with the mustard, orange zest, orange juice, vinegar, and sugar. Whisk together.

2. Slowly drizzle in both of the olive oils, whisking constantly until thickened. Season with salt and pepper and set aside.

3. Prepare the slaw: Combine all of the vegetables and the caraway seeds in a large bowl. Toss well with the dressing, cover, and let rest in the refrigerator for at least 3 hours before serving. Just before serving, taste for salt and pepper and toss with the snipped chives.

Serves 6

FOURTH OF JULY HAM AND CABBAGE SLAW

★ ★ ★

Pale green slivers of cabbage combine with pink slivers of baked ham to make an interesting, festive salad. A creamy mustard dressing ties the flavors together. As the slaw sits, it gets creamier, so make it a day ahead if you like.

A great way to complete a menu for a Fourth of July celebration would be to make this slaw an accompaniment to Grilled Barbecued Chicken, Red, White, and Blue Roasted Potato Salad, and Sweet Cherry Pie.

DRESSING
½ cup mayonnaise
½ cup sour cream
¼ cup honey mustard
1 tablespoon Dijon mustard
1 teaspoon celery seeds
¼ cup chopped fresh dill leaves

SLAW
1 head green cabbage (about 2 pounds)
1 pound baked ham in one piece,
*   cut into julienne strips*
*   about 2½ x ⅛ inches*
2 carrots, peeled and coarsely grated
1 green bell pepper, stemmed, seeded,
*   and coarsely grated*
4 scallions (3 inches green left on),
*   thinly sliced on the diagonal*
¼ cup chopped fresh dill leaves
Salt and freshly ground black pepper,
*   to taste*

1. Prepare the dressing: Combine all the ingredients together in a small bowl, stir well, and set aside.

2. Prepare the slaw: Remove the core and any tough outer leaves from the cabbage. Slice the cabbage into fine slivers, and place them in a large bowl. Add the ham, carrots, bell pepper, scallions, and dill. Combine well.

3. Toss the mixture thoroughly with the reserved dressing, and season with salt and pepper. Cover and refrigerate for at least 4 hours, or as long as overnight, before serving. Serve at room temperature.

Serves 8

A RUSSIAN DRESSING TRIO

★ ★ ★

Although Russian dressing is a typical American deli sandwich spread, it probably has its roots in the salad dressings used throughout Russia. Logically, it follows that when Eastern European immigrants opened delicatessens featuring foods from home, this dressing would make an appearance. Apparently, the first written recipe for it appeared in 1922, and contained pimientos and bell peppers.

The trio that follows has something for every taste. It begins with a simple sandwich spread flavored with sweet pickle relish. Then there's a richer salad garnish given more body by the addition of finely chopped hard-cooked egg. Use it on arranged salads and the traditional steak-house hearts of lettuce. Finally, for dollop-ing on a shrimp or crab cocktail, the final variation benefits from the zesty addition of chili sauce and horseradish. The versatility of the elementary mayonnaise and ketchup base makes the dressing a practical one to keep in mind.

Russian Sandwich Dressing

—★—

Use this on white-meat turkey on rye or a roll, cold meat loaf on white, or cold rare roast beef on a roll with lettuce.

½ cup mayonnaise
2 tablespoons ketchup
1½ tablespoons sweet pickle relish

Mix all the ingredients together in a small bowl. Refrigerate, covered, until ready to use, up to 24 hours.
Makes about ¾ cup

Russian Salad Dressing

—★—

Another easy version of the classic dressing, this one is perfect with crab-meat, lobster, or shrimp salad.

¾ cup mayonnaise
3 tablespoons ketchup
1½ tablespoons sweet pickle relish
1 hard-cooked egg, finely chopped

★★★★★★★★★★★★★★★★★★★★★★★★

DRESSING OR VINAIGRETTE?

—❧—

Salad dressings can be made with vinegar, but they don't have to be. Sometimes a mayonnaise or a lemon juice and olive oil base makes for a nice change of pace. On the other hand, a true vinaigrette, a word we've borrowed from the French, must contain some kind of vinegar. If it doesn't, it isn't a vinaigrette—it's a dressing!

★★★★★★★★★★★★★★★★★★★★★★★★

Mix all the ingredients together in a small bowl. Refrigerate, covered, until ready to use, up to 8 hours.

Makes about 1 cup

Russian Seafood Dressing

——— ★ ———

Russian dressing takes on a more complex melding of flavors here for a more refined seafood presentation.

½ cup mayonnaise
2½ tablespoons chili sauce
Dash of Tabasco sauce
¼ teaspoon prepared white horseradish, drained
1 ripe plum tomato, seeded and cut into tiny dice
1 teaspoon capers, drained and lightly chopped
1 teaspoon finely grated lemon zest
1 teaspoon finely chopped fresh dill leaves

Mix all the ingredients together in a small bowl. Refrigerate, covered, until ready to use. Use within 24 hours for the freshest taste.

Makes about ¾ cup

AVOCADO MINT MAYONNAISE

★ ★ ★

No more do we have to bemoan the fact that the traditional fresh uncooked-egg-yolk version of mayonnaise is off-limits. A rich silky mayonnaise made from a perfectly ripe avocado is just the answer. It has just the right consistency for a dollop on Little Beef Pancakes and is also an excellent dip for raw garden vegetables. Fresh basil or tarragon can be substituted for the mint.

2 ripe avocados, halved, pitted and peeled
¼ cup fresh lime juice
¼ cup extra virgin olive oil
¼ cup chopped fresh mint leaves
Salt and freshly ground black pepper, to taste

1. Toss the avocado in a small bowl with the lime juice, mashing it slightly.

2. Transfer the avocado to a food processor, and purée it. With the machine running, slowly drizzle the oil through the feed tube.

3. Transfer the mixture to a bowl, fold in the mint, and season with the salt and pepper. Serve immediately.

Makes about 2 cups

CAESAR DRESSING

★ ★ ★

I'm a glutton for Caesar salad—anchovies, croutons, and all. When I don't want to go to the trouble of making it, I whip up this dressing and toss it onto crisp romaine lettuce for a rich and satisfying salad to serve with grilled or broiled chicken. Shave a bit of fresh Parmesan cheese over the top for a touch of authenticity.

1 small clove garlic
¼ teaspoon coarse salt
1½ teaspoons Dijon mustard
2 tablespoons fresh lemon juice
¼ cup extra virgin olive oil
¼ cup pure olive oil
1 teaspoon sugar
Salt and freshly ground black pepper,
    to taste

1. Finely mince the garlic with the coarse salt. Transfer the garlic and salt to a bowl, add mustard and lemon juice, and whisk together.

2. Slowly drizzle in both olive oils, whisking constantly until thickened. Season with the sugar, salt, and pepper. Store, covered, in the refrigerator up to 2 days. Bring to room temperature before using.

Makes about ⅔ cup

DRESS-UP TOMATO ORANGE MAYONNAISE

★ ★ ★

I was introduced to the combination of tomato and orange with my first taste of an aromatic veal Marengo ages ago. Years later, the memory of that strong affinity served me well when I created this mayonnaise for boiled lobsters. It could also accompany crab-lobster cakes or salmon cakes, or seared salmon.

½ cup mayonnaise
¼ cup sour cream
2 teaspoons tomato paste
¼ cup seeded diced (¼ inch) tomatoes
2 tablespoons chopped fresh tarragon leaves
1½ teaspoons finely grated orange zest
Salt and freshly ground black pepper, to taste

Combine the mayonnaise, sour cream, and tomato paste in a small bowl. Stir in the remaining ingredients, and season to taste.

Makes about 1 cup

Sandwiches

The American sandwich sure has changed, and keeps on changing. There's sandwich art everywhere—coffee shops, delis, upscale restaurants, and our own kitchens. We like to alter the basic elements, flavoring our mayonnaise with garlic and herbs, replacing iceberg lettuce with avocado, arugula, or spinach. And we invent wildly, pairing ingredients that have never met before and boldly accessorizing with salsas, chutneys, savory jellies, roasted vegetables, farmstead cheese. Nobody in the world makes sandwiches as well as we do. Anything goes, as long as it tastes good.

I love to innovate, and you'll find the creations that follow deliciously surprising. Like Gorgeous Smoked Duck and Cashew Butter, which is served on rye with red pepper jelly and caramelized onions. I've also turned traditional salads—Caesar, Cobb, crab Louis—into sandwiches, and taken some creative liberties with the classic Reuben, BLT, and meatball grinder. If you're looking for ham and cheese or cream cheese and smoked salmon, you'll find them in quesadillas. The recipes here, updated or newfangled, are all-American originals.

RICH LITTLE PO' BOY

★ ★ ★

There are many different stories about the origin of the celebrated Louisiana po' boy (for poor boy) sandwich. One thing is for certain: it sprang up in the Depression years. Buddy Stall, a writer who seems to know everything there is to know about New Orleans, says that two brothers, Clovis and Denny Martin, created the sandwich, which could fill a man's belly for a nickel (for a small one) or a dime (larger) and had an instant success. There was one drawback, however: they found that the traditional French bread, with its pointy ends and doughy interior, resulted in too much waste. So they turned to a local baker to create a better loaf, 30 inches long with rounded ends. The po' boy has been a New Orleans institution ever since. It now comes in as many variations as you can imagine, with the classic being made with roast beef. When you order a po' boy, you'll be asked if you want it "dressed." You bet you do—lettuce, tomato, cheese, and mayonnaise! Here is my version.

Beer: Seattle porter

3 small ripe tomatoes, halved
Salt and freshly ground black pepper,
*   to taste*
1 small (12-inch) loaf Italian bread
¼ cup Rémoulade Sauce (page 89)
¼ pound thinly sliced rare roast beef
4 thin slices ripe Brie, chilled
4 to 6 lettuce leaves, rinsed and patted dry

1. Preheat a grill or broiler, setting the rack 3 inches from the heat source.
2. Grill or broil the skin side of the tomato halves until just slightly charred (15 minutes for

the grill, 8 minutes for the broiler). Sprinkle the cut side of the tomatoes with salt and pepper. Set them aside.
3. Halve the bread lengthwise and scoop out the inside, both top and bottom of the loaf. Spread each cut side of the bread with the Rémoulade Sauce. Arrange the roast beef evenly over the bottom half, and lay the cheese diagonally over the meat. Top with the lettuce.
4. Place the reserved grilled tomatoes on the top half of the bread, and mash them just slightly with a fork. Invert the top over the bottom half of the sandwich, cut it in half crosswise, and serve immediately.
Serves 2

PHILLY CHEESE STEAK SANDWICH, SHEILA STYLE

★ ★ ★

Being Philly born, I had to step up to the plate and give my own version of that city's renowned cheese steak sandwich. It's not the one you'll taste at the popular Reading Terminal Market in Center City. It's my own invention, created in my kitchen on Manhattan's Upper West Side. I think it gives the traditional sandwich a run for the money.

FRANCINE MAROUKIAN ON PHILADELPHIA CHEESE STEAKS

—❦—

When Francine Maroukian, a food editor, writer, and caterer, was catering director of the Silver Palate, she regaled me with stories of her weekends in Philadelphia, which always included a rave about the great Philly cheese steaks she'd had. Although I'm a Philadelphia native, I never understood what the big deal was. While researching this book, I visited that city's Reading Terminal Market, and again had one for myself. I liked it, but my passion fell short of Francine's, so I asked her to please explain to me what it was all about. This is what she wrote:

"Cheese steaks belong to Philadelphia. They appear simple enough but are actually impossible to duplicate. There's no sense trying to find one, nevertheless eat one, anywhere else in the country. This constitutes the only cheese steak absolute, the only thing everyone agrees on. The rest is open to discussion, even controversy, and Philadelphians separate into camps over the basic components.

"Cheese steaks must be on a roll with a crusty yet not brittle exterior and a soft but substantial inside. The meat, which can range from thinly sliced to almost shaved, is a less important concern and seems to be a matter of style. The shaved meat is almost chopped while cooking and the cheese is mixed throughout, sort of like scrambled eggs. While this does make it easier and neater to eat, my vote goes to the sliced meat.

"Here comes the part that those who have never tasted a Philadelphia cheese steak must accept on blind faith: there are basically two cheese choices. One is Whiz. That's right, Cheez Whiz. This is served warm and ladled right onto the roll; the cooked meat is placed on top. The other choice is American, pale yellow American. These slices are placed on top of the cooking meat to bubble, melt, and finally ooze. The cheese/meat is laid on the bread by spatula, or the roll is opened and used like a mitt to pick up the melted combination.

"Toppings are offered in self-serve vats, but to retain purity of taste none should be used. The only exception is fried onions. I consider these more an option than a topping because they are ordered from the grill man along with the cheese of choice.

"And that's another sticking point for the out-of-towner. Cheese steaks are primarily sold through windows at stands. They are not served on a plate, but wrapped in insulated foil and brown-bagged. While cheese steaks are not fast food, they are definitely quick eating. As the line in front of you shrinks, you can feel the number of people, hungry people, growing behind you. Pressure builds. You simply cannot waste the window man's time. You must use the ordering code (see box, page 108).

"Finding the best also includes intangible considerations, some too subtle, too subjective, to explain. They have to do with geography, with neighborhood loyalty, with 'roots.' Ultimately it may be impossible to reveal the perfect cheese steaks."

Beer: Pennsylvania Octoberfest

MARINADE
¼ cup olive oil
¼ cup red wine vinegar
1 large clove garlic, finely minced
1 tablespoon Dijon mustard

SANDWICH
1 skirt steak (about 1 pound), trimmed and cut on
*   the diagonal into 3 or 4 pieces*
8 slices (½ inch thick) peasant bread
*   (about 6 x 4½ inches)*
4 teaspoons Dijon mustard
1 recipe Caramelized Onions (page 296)
¼ pound Monterey Jack cheese, grated
*   (about 1 cup)*
2 ounces Vermont Cheddar cheese, grated
*   (about ½ cup)*

1. Prepare the marinade: Combine all the marinade ingredients in a bowl. Add the skirt steak, coating it well with the marinade. Cover loosely and marinate in the refrigerator for at least 3 hours or overnight.

2. Preheat the broiler (see Note).

3. Shortly before serving, remove the meat from the marinade and lightly pat dry, then broil the steak for 3 to 4 minutes per side for medium-rare (adjust the cooking time to your taste). Transfer the meat to a cutting board and let it rest for 10 minutes. Then slice it thinly on the diagonal, cover it loosely with aluminum foil to keep warm, and set it aside. Wash and dry the broiler tray.

4. Lightly toast the bread in the broiler on one side (be careful not to burn it). Spread the toasted side of 4 slices with 1 teaspoon mustard each. Top with about ¼ cup of the cara-melized onions, and cover with the sliced steak.

5. Combine the grated cheeses in a small bowl. Cover the untoasted sides of the other 4 slices of bread evenly with the grated cheese. Place under the broiler until the cheese is melted and bubbly, about 1 minute. Top the steak with the bread, cheese side down. Cut the sandwiches in half and serve immediately.

Serves 4

NOTE: This sandwich may be prepared on the grill. If you wish to do so, don't pretoast either side of the bread. Layer the bread as described in steps 4 and 5. Then place it on the grill. The outside of the bread will toast and the cheese layer will melt at the same time.

★★★★★★★★★★★★★★★★★★★★★★★★★★★★

CHEESE STEAK ORDERING CODE

—❦—

One Whiz: One cheese steak with Cheez Whiz, please

One American: One cheese steak with American, please

One Wit: One cheese steak with onions, please

One Wit Whiz: One cheese steak with onions and Cheez Whiz, please

One Wit American: One cheese steak with onions and American cheese, please

One Works: One cheese steak with onions, peppers, mushrooms, and a little tomato sauce, please

One Works Whiz: You figure it out

★★★★★★★★★★★★★★★★★★★★★★★★★★★★

GOLD'S DELI GRILLED PASTRAMI

★ ★ ★

Once a week, after high school English class, Wendy Posner, my best friend, and I would drive over to Gold's Delicatessen, on the Post Road in Westport, Connecticut, and have a grilled pastrami sandwich. Once in love I never forgot, so to the best of my memory, here is my teenage favorite. With the addition of a little sauerkraut, you would have a Reuben sandwich. For the most authentic flavor, deli rye bread is essential.

Beer: New York State amber ale

2½ teaspoons unsalted butter, at room
    temperature
2 slices rye bread
1½ teaspoons Dijon mustard
4 slices (about 2 ounces) pastrami
2 thin slices white onion
2 slices ripe tomato
2 slices (2 ounces) Swiss cheese

1. Working on a sheet of waxed paper, spread ¾ teaspoon of the butter on one side of each slice of the bread. Turn the slices over, and spread the mustard on the other side.

2. Lay the pastrami on the mustard side of one of the bread slices. Cover with the onion and tomato, then with the Swiss cheese. Top with the remaining slice of bread, buttered side up. Using the waxed paper, press down on the sandwich to flatten it slightly.

3. Heat the remaining 1 teaspoon butter in a nonstick skillet over medium heat. Add the sandwich, and cook, pressing down on it with a spatula, for 3 minutes until golden brown. Turn the sandwich over and cook for 2 minutes longer.

Serves 1

PASTRAMI REUBEN

★ ★ ★

In New York City, there is a restaurant-delicatessen called Reuben's. For over 55 years, beginning in 1935, it ruled the roost on 58th Street off Fifth Avenue, next door to a favorite store of my youth (or anybody's youth!)—FAO Schwarz toy store (now it's a bit farther downtown on Madison Avenue). Fabled in stories of the era, it was said that a politician couldn't be elected if he hadn't been photographed eating one of Reuben's overstuffed sandwiches. The fame of Reuben's spread far beyond New York, with the incredibly popular "Reuben Sandwich" appearing on countless menus across the country. Before long it became a national institution. Originating as "corned beef on rye toast, topped with sauerkraut, and imported Swiss cheese, and grilled to perfection," I have reconstituted this age-old favorite by using pastrami and adding some grilled onions between the layers.

Beer: San Francisco Anchor Steam Beer

2 teaspoons vegetable oil
1 onion, sliced
2 tablespoons unsalted butter, at room temperature
4 slices rye bread
2 tablespoons Thousand Island Dressing
    (recipe follows)
8 slices (about ¼ pound) lean pastrami
¼ cup sauerkraut, drained
4 slices (about ¼ pound) Swiss cheese

1. Heat the oil in a nonstick skillet over medium-low heat. Add the onion and cook, stirring occasionally, until softened and golden brown, 10 to 12 minutes. Set aside.

2. Working on a sheet of waxed paper, spread the butter on one side of each slice of bread. Turn the slices over, and spread the other side with the Thousand Island Dressing.

3. Cover the dressing evenly with the onions, sauerkraut, and cheese. Cover with the remaining slice of bread, dressing side down. Using the waxed paper, press down on the sandwich to flatten it slightly.

4. Remove the sandwiches from the waxed paper and cook them in a nonstick skillet over medium-high heat until the bread is golden brown and the cheese has melted, about 3 minutes per side. Cut in half and serve immediately.
Serves 2

Thousand Island Dressing

This American original falls somewhere between Russian and Louis dressing. According to Craig Claiborne, one explanation has it as the creation of the executive chef at the Drake Hotel in Chicago after he and his wife had returned from a journey through the Thousand Islands near Ontario, New York. Once back in the kitchen, he created a new salad dressing. Upon first seeing it, with its unique bumpy texture, the chef's wife remarked that it reminded her of the Thousand Islands, and so they named it. My version is an excellent condiment for anything from a Pastrami Reuben to a fresh crabmeat cocktail.

¾ cup mayonnaise
¼ cup plain nonfat yogurt
3 tablespoons chili sauce
¼ cup finely diced green bell pepper
2 tablespoons finely diced roasted red
    bell pepper
1 teaspoon grated onion

Mix all the ingredients together in a small bowl. Serve immediately, or refrigerate, covered, up to 8 hours.
Makes about 1¾ cups

MY HERO

★ ★ ★

Depending on where your hero hails from, the stack of fillings between the bread will vary in type and amount. I must say that even though I now call my deli meat sandwich a hero, this girl from Philly will always feel a strong sense of loyalty to the name hoagie.

Beer: New England lager

HERO WORSHIP

—❦—

Americans *love* sandwiches—not only the everyday classics, but larger-than-life regional masterpieces that go by colorful, often interchangeable names: hoagies, submarines, heroes, and so on. I've even heard them called "Dagwoods," after the Bumstead of comics fame who makes his monumental sandwiches in the middle of the night, invariably with a piece of Swiss cheese hanging over the side and an olive on a toothpick spear. They're "hoagies" in my native Philadelphia, supposedly after the Hog Island shipyard, where Italian workers ate big stuffed sandwiches during World War I. "Submarine" was coined in the next war, it is said, at a Connecticut submarine base. A sandwich is a "hero" when it's so huge it takes a hero to eat it—this from food journalist Clementine Paddleford, writing in the 1930s about New York's Manganaro's deli.

Call it what you like, and make what you like of it. Dagwood puts everything but the kitchen sink in his sandwich. Manganaro's still fills its version to the brim with Italian antipasti—meats, cheeses, peppers, lettuce, and tomatoes. In my hometown, everything's optional but the Italian bread, lettuce, tomato, onion, and salad oil. New Englanders eat something called a "grinder," a hero stuffed with hot meatballs, sausage and peppers, veal parmigiana, or the like. These are aptly named and a real workout for the jaw! New Orleans has two big sandwiches: the round muffuletta, dressed in a garlicky green-olive salad, and the warming po' boy, which is often soaked in gravy. Cuban immigrants press ham, roast pork, cheese, and sweet pickles between slabs of French bread in a *plancha,* a kind of sandwich iron. But perhaps you have a better idea. Try it! Give it a jaunty title, and who knows—perhaps both the recipe and its name will live on.

---

1 French or Italian roll, 7 to 8 inches long
1 tablespoon plus 2 teaspoons extra virgin
    olive oil
16 arugula leaves
1 ripe plum tomato
1 tablespoon balsamic vinegar
Salt and freshly ground black pepper,
    to taste
3 slices (4 ounces) mozzarella cheese
    (about ⅛ inch thick)
4 whole fresh basil leaves, rinsed and patted dry
2 thin slices (2 ounces) prosciutto di Parma
4 thin slices (1 ounce) Genoa salami

1. Slice the bread horizontally and scoop out some of the center. Brush each cut side of bread with 1 teaspoon of the olive oil.

2. Remove and discard the tough stems from the arugula. Rinse the leaves, pat them dry, and place them in a bowl.

3. Halve the tomato lengthwise. Scoop out and discard the seeds. Cut the halves lengthwise into ¼-inch strips. Add to the arugula and toss with the remaining tablespoon olive oil and the balsamic vinegar. Season with salt and pepper.

4. Layer the bottom half of the roll with the cheese, basil leaves, prosciutto, and salami. Top with the salad. Cover with the top half of the roll, cut in half on the diagonal, and chow down. Yum!

Serves 1

ROASTED LAMB AND YELLOW PEPPER SANDWICH

★ ★ ★

Thinly sliced lamb from Sunday's roast leg becomes a robust summer meal here. Combined with roasted vegetables and fresh greens, it's summery flavors have a California feel to me. Chopped fresh mint as a final touch livens up the earthy taste of the sandwich.

Wine: California Rhône-style Mourvèdre
Beer: Washington State porter

4 slices (½ inch thick) peasant bread, toasted
¼ cup Roasted Garlic Mayonnaise (recipe follows)
1 large bunch arugula, stems removed, leaves rinsed and patted dry
8 thin slices medium-rare roast lamb
2 yellow bell pepper halves, roasted (see How to Roast a Bell Pepper, page 132)
2 teaspoons finely chopped fresh mint leaves

1. Cover one side of each slice of toast with 1 tablespoon of the mayonnaise. Top 2 of the slices evenly with the arugula, lamb, and roasted peppers.

2. Sprinkle each sandwich with the chopped mint, and cover with the remaining 2 slices of bread, mayonnaise side down. Cut the sandwiches in half and serve immediately.

Serves 2

Roasted Garlic Mayonnaise

——★——

The addition of a clove or two of roasted garlic is a simple trick to enhance plain mayonnaise. Since you don't need to roast an entire head, place one or two unpeeled cloves on a piece of aluminum foil, drizzle with some olive oil, fold up the foil, and bake in a 350°F toaster oven for one hour. Squeeze the soft roasted garlic "jam" out of the skin, and there you are!

¼ cup mayonnaise
1 or 2 cloves roasted garlic (see headnote), to taste
Salt and freshly ground black pepper, to taste

Mix all the ingredients together in a small bowl. Refrigerate, covered, up to 8 hours.

Makes about ¼ cup

OPEN-FACE SANDWICHES

—❦—

I see open-face sandwiches falling into two distinct camps: dainty and delicate, and hot and hearty. While both are unencumbered by a top slice of bread, the former are Scandinavian-inspired and composed of lightly buttered, thinly sliced rye, pumpernickel, or other grain breads topped with attractively arranged smoked fish, meats, and pâtés, and finished with a bright garnish. While they make lovely hors d'oeuvres or a delicious light lunch, it's the latter—a piled-high, hot meaty sandwich moistened with creamy gravy—that Americans really love. Leftover turkey, chicken, roast beef, sliced steak, meat loaf, or even flavorful grilled vegetables are just some possible hot open-face toppings. To create your masterpiece, keep in mind:

• The bread you choose should not impart its own assertive flavor, so use a sturdy white bread (not the soft sandwich variety) or try my White Toasting Loaf (page 202).

• Top the bread, which can be toasted, with a generous helping of sliced meat or poultry and pour a healthy dose of hot gravy on top.

• Accompany your sandwich with mashed potatoes, creamed corn, green beans, or whatever your favorite sopper-upper is.

• This is obviously a knife-and-fork-sandwich, but also be sure to supply lots of napkins. The gravy can get drippy.

THE HOT BROWN

★ ★ ★

Louisville, Kentucky, is home to the Kentucky Derby, the Mint Julep, and the Hot Brown. While the first two may be familiar to you, the Hot Brown gets instant recognition usually only from locals. The Brown Hotel opened in 1925, and the renowned Hot Brown was born three or four years later. The hotel band played from 10 P.M. until 1 A.M., and when they took a mid-

night break, the social set usually ordered ham and eggs. To add some spice to the menu, Fred K. Schmidt, the chef, created an open-face turkey sandwich covered in Mornay sauce, added crisp bacon and a garnish of pimiento for pizzazz, and called it the Hot Brown. It soon became the talk of the town. The Brown Hotel's current executive chef, Franklin Dye, was kind enough to share the famous, and still popular, recipe with me. For a sublime taste sensation, serve it with Fresh Whole-Cranberry Relish on the side.

Beer: American pale ale

½ cup (1 stick) unsalted butter
6 tablespoons all-purpose flour
3 to 3½ cups milk
¾ cup freshly grated Parmesan cheese
1 large egg, lightly beaten
Salt and freshly ground black pepper, to taste
Pinch of cayenne pepper
8 to 12 slices best-quality white bread,
*   lightly toasted*
1½ to 2¼ pounds sliced cooked turkey breast
8 to 12 strips bacon, cooked until crisp

1. Melt the butter in a heavy saucepan over medium heat. Add the flour and cook, whisking, for 2 minutes. Whisking constantly, slowly add 3 cups of milk; continue whisking until smooth. Stir in 6 tablespoons of the Parmesan and the egg, and cook over medium heat until thickened, about 10 minutes. Do not allow the sauce to boil. If it is too thick, add up to ½ cup additional milk. Remove from the heat and season with salt, pepper, and cayenne.

BLUE PLATE

S·P·E·C·I·A·L

**Number One Hot Open Turkey
Sandwich with Scratch White Gravy**

Mashed Yukon Golds

Fresh Whole-Cranberry Relish

Minty Sweet Peas

Cherry Carrot Salad

Big Time Banana Split

2. Preheat the broiler.

3. For each sandwich, place 2 slices of toast on a metal or flameproof dish. Cover the toast with the sliced turkey (about 6 ounces per sandwich), and top with a generous amount of sauce (⅔ to ¾ cup per sandwich). Sprinkle each with a tablespoon of the remaining Parmesan cheese.

4. Cook the sandwiches under the broiler (you will have to do this in batches) until they are speckled brown and bubbly, about 1½ minutes. Remove from the broiler, top each serving with 2 slices of bacon, and serve immediately.

Serves 4 to 6

NUMBER ONE HOT OPEN TURKEY SANDWICH

★ ★ ★

The definitive blue plate special for me is a hot open turkey sandwich. Meat loaf runs a close second. Spilling over a large plate, tender turkey served on warm open inch-thick slices of fresh white bread, next to a mountain of mashed potatoes with everything smothered in rich homemade gravy, is heaven. I'm small, but I always eat every last morsel. Use some of the recipes in this book to create a winning version.

Wine: California light Grenache
Beer: Minnesota lager

2 thick slices fresh white bread, preferably White
*   Toasting Loaf (page 202)*
6 slices (1 ounce each) roast turkey breast from
*   My Thanksgiving Turkey (page 422)*
½ cup Mashed Yukon Golds (page 298), hot
⅓ to ½ cup Scratch White Gravy (recipe follows), hot
Fresh Whole-Cranberry Relish (page 184), for serving

Slightly overlap the bread slices on a warmed dinner plate, and arrange the sliced turkey over the bread. Spoon the mashed potatoes alongside, and ladle the gravy over all. Serve with cranberry relish.

Makes 1 sandwich

Scratch White Gravy

———★———

By cooking the flour for a minute or two, you lose the floury taste and end up with a smoother tasting gravy. The onions add a soupçon of extra flavor, making this the ideal turkey topping. Be sure to spoon enough gravy over the sandwich so that it runs into the potatoes.

3 tablespoons turkey or chicken drippings or
   unsalted butter
¼ cup finely chopped onion
3 tablespoons all-purpose flour
2 cups defatted turkey or chicken broth,
   preferably homemade (page 253)
1 cup milk
Salt and freshly ground black pepper, to taste

1. Heat the drippings or melt the butter in a heavy saucepan. Add the onions and cook over low heat, stirring, until they wilt, 5 to 8 minutes. Sprinkle in the flour and cook, stirring, until the mixture is bubbly, 2 to 3 minutes.

2. Remove the pan from the heat. Whisking constantly, slowly pour in the broth and milk; continue whisking until the mixture is smooth. Return the pan to medium-high heat and cook, whisking, until it comes to a boil. Then cook it 2 minutes more, whisking constantly until the gravy thickens nicely.

3. Season to taste with salt and pepper, and serve.

Makes about 3 cups

★★★★★★★★★★★★★★★★★★★★★★★★★★★

WHAT'S A "BLUE PLATE SPECIAL"?

—❦—

Blue Willow, created in England in 1780, is one of the world's most recognizable china patterns. The pattern recounts a romantic Chinese legend of two lovers running across a bridge to elope, chased by the bride's father. The couple, unfortunately, dies (how they die remains debatable), but their spirit lives on in the two birds that are always featured in the design.

Blue Willow has been imported to America since the 1800s, and by the 1900s the pattern was being mass-marketed by both Sears Roebuck and Woolworth's. During the Depression, heavy Blue Willow grille-style plates, a sectioned dinner plate that separates the meat, potatoes, and vegetables, were so universally used by restaurants that the term "Blue Plate Special" came to mean an inexpensive but hearty restaurant meal. Today Blue Willow is an enormously popular collector's item. But you don't need to own any to enjoy the specials I've sprinkled throughout the book.

★★★★★★★★★★★★★★★★★★★★★★★★★★★

TURKEY MEATBALL GRINDER

★ ★ ★

Neighborhood Italian restaurants are the source for grinders—Italian hero sandwiches filled with meatballs, sausages, and the like. I find them absolutely irresistible. But with lighter eating a priority on many menus, turkey has become the meat of choice for these finger-licking sandwiches. When well spiced and cooked in a highly flavored tomato sauce, ground turkey is a more than satisfying substitute for beef or pork. The turkey meatballs in their lusty sauce are also delicious for an updated version of the old-time favorite, spaghetti and meatballs.

Beer: New England lager

TOMATO SAUCE

3 tablespoons extra virgin olive oil
1 onion, chopped
1 green bell pepper, stemmed, seeded, halved
   lengthwise, and cut into crosswise slivers
1 red bell pepper, stemmed, seeded, halved
   lengthwise, and cut into crosswise slivers
2 cloves garlic, peeled and slightly
   bruised
2 cans (28 ounces each) Italian plum
   tomatoes, drained (reserve
   the juices) and chopped
2 tablespoons tomato paste
2 teaspoons dried oregano
Pinch of sugar
Salt and freshly ground black
   pepper, to taste
¼ cup chopped fresh flat-leaf
   parsley

TURKEY MEATBALLS

2 pounds ground turkey
1 onion, grated
1 tablespoon minced garlic
1 teaspoon dried basil
1 teaspoon dried oregano
1 teaspoon fennel seeds
Salt and coarsely ground black pepper, to taste
1 large egg, lightly beaten (optional)
2 tablespoons olive oil, or more as needed

3 loaves Italian bread (about 15 x 3 inches),
   each cut into 3 pieces, or 8 French rolls
   (about 5 x 3 inches)

1. Prepare the tomato sauce: Heat the oil in a large heavy pot over medium-low heat. Add the onion, both bell peppers, and the garlic and cook until softened, 15 minutes, stirring occasionally. Add the tomatoes along with 1 cup of the reserved juices, the tomato paste, oregano, sugar, salt, and pepper. Cook until thickened, 25 minutes.

2. Adjust the seasonings. Mash the garlic cloves with the back of a spoon, and stir back into the sauce. Stir in the parsley and set the sauce aside.

3. Prepare the turkey meatballs: Place all of the ingredients except the olive oil in a bowl, and mix lightly but thoroughly. Do not overmix. Form the mixture into 24 meatballs, each about 1½ inches in diameter.

4. Heat the 2 tablespoons oil in a medium-size skillet over medium-high heat, and cook the meatballs in batches, shaking the pan occasionally, until browned and cooked through, 10 to 12 minutes. Transfer the meatballs to paper towels to drain. Add more oil, if necessary, as you cook the remaining batches.

5. Place the tomato sauce over medium heat to warm through. Add the meatballs and cook to blend the flavors, 12 minutes.

6. While the sauce is heating, cut the bread in half horizontally, and remove some of the center, both top and bottom, to create a cavity.

7. To serve, spoon about ¼ cup of the sauce into each hollowed-out bread, coating the interior well. Arrange 3 meatballs in each roll, and serve immediately.

Serves 8

REALLY THICK CHICKEN REUBEN

★ ★ ★

My modern version of the classic Reuben is light, delicious, and eminently more attractive than the old-timer, which is heavy on the corned beef, Swiss cheese, and sauerkraut and served on lavishly buttered rye. It's the mere touch of sauerkraut and the fresh Thousand Island Dressing that does the trick. As the sandwich is grilled, the avocado melts along with the cheese, producing a rich, luscious texture. Once you get the feel of making a Reuben, the sky's the limit and creativity is encouraged—how about a thick slice of brisket, Vermont Cheddar, and Zesty Picnic Slaw on grilled sourdough bread?

Beer: Maryland pale ale

1 whole skinless, boneless chicken breast, halved lengthwise
1 tablespoon olive oil
Salt and freshly ground black pepper, to taste
2 tablespoons unsalted butter, at room temperature
4 slices rye or peasant bread
2 tablespoons Thousand Island Dressing (page 110)
¼ cup sauerkraut, drained
½ ripe avocado, peeled, pitted, and sliced lengthwise
2 slices (about 2 ounces) Monterey Jack cheese

1. Preheat the broiler.

2. Lay the chicken breast on one side of a long sheet of waxed paper, spreading out the fillet. Fold the waxed paper over to cover the chicken, and using a rolling pin or the flat side of a chef's knife, flatten the breast to about ¼ inch thick. Brush the chicken with the olive oil and sprinkle with salt and pepper.

3. Broil the chicken breast, about 3 inches from high heat, until cooked through, 2 to 3 minutes on each side. Set aside.

4. Working on a fresh sheet of waxed paper, spread the butter on one side of each slice of bread. Turn the slices over, and spread the other side with the Thousand Island Dressing.

5. Lay the chicken breasts over the dressing on 2 slices of bread. Cover the chicken evenly with the sauerkraut, avocado slices, and then the cheese. Lay the remaining 2 slices of bread over the cheese, dressing side down. Using the waxed paper, press down on the sandwich to flatten it slightly.

6. Remove the sandwiches from the waxed paper and cook them in a nonstick skillet over medium-high heat until the bread is golden brown and the cheese has melted, about 3 minutes per side. Cut in half and serve immediately.

Serves 2

SOUTH-OF-THE-BORDER CHICKEN WITH MANGO

★ ★ ★

When out of my kitchen comes a chicken sandwich on deli slices of raisin pumpernickel, sporting a slice of ripe mango and swathed in chipotle mayonnaise, then you know I'm having a particularly good and creative day. If mangoes are hard to find, this bold sandwich works just as well with avocado.

Beer: Colorado amber ale

1 can (7.6 ounces) chipotle peppers in adobo
½ cup mayonnaise
8 slices (½ inch thick) raisin pumpernickel bread,
    lightly toasted
1 pound sliced cooked white chicken meat
    (about 24 slices)
4 cups mesclun (mixed baby salad greens),
    rinsed and patted dry
4 slices peeled ripe mango or avocado

1. Place the chipotle peppers and its sauce in a food processor and purée until smooth. Scrape this mixture into a small bowl. Place 1 tablespoon of the mixture back in the food processor (freeze the remainder for another use), add the mayonnaise, and blend until smooth.

2. Spread some of the chipotle mayonnaise on one side of each slice of bread.

3. Lay the chicken meat evenly over 4 of the slices. Top with the mesclun and a slice of mango. Cover with the remaining 4 slices of bread, mayonnaise side down. Cut in half and serve immediately.

Serves 4

COBB SALAD "CLUB"

★ ★ ★

Cobb salad has been served in one form or another in restaurants around the nation since 1926, when Bob Cobb, owner of the Brown Derby restaurant in Los Angeles, brought it to life. Each chef adds his or her personal touch to this famous salad, as it is an ingenious way to use up leftovers. There are certain traditional ingredients—lettuce, tomato, chicken, bacon, avocado, hard-cooked egg, chives, and Roquefort cheese—that have set the standard. I've included many of the basics in this club sandwich version. Instead of adding the blue cheese to the sandwich, I've created a blue cheese mayonnaise that holds all the flavor but makes for easier eating.

As for the club sandwich's two-slice/three-slice of toast controversy: While on book tours, I usually arrive late at night in hotels all over the country. Once checked in, I order a room service club sandwich. Some are constructed with three slices of toast, others with two, so it seems either way is correct. At home, make mine on a roll!

Beer: Minnesota ale

BLUE CHEESE MAYONNAISE
¼ cup mayonnaise
¼ cup sour cream
2 ounces blue cheese, crumbled (about ¼ cup)
1 teaspoon snipped fresh chives
Freshly ground black pepper, to taste

SANDWICH
4 slices thick-cut bacon
½ ripe avocado, peeled, pitted, and thinly
    sliced lengthwise
1 tablespoon fresh lemon juice
2 soft wheat or other best-quality rolls
2 hard-cooked eggs, sliced
¼ pound cooked skinless, boneless chicken breast,
    thinly sliced lengthwise
1 ripe plum tomato, thinly sliced lengthwise
1 teaspoon snipped fresh chives
2 large leaves Bibb lettuce, rinsed and
    patted dry
Potato chips, for serving
Pickle spears, for serving

1. Prepare the blue cheese mayonnaise: Combine the mayonnaise and sour cream in a bowl. Add the blue cheese, chives, and pepper, and blend with a fork so the mayonnaise has a slightly chunky texture. Set aside.

2. Prepare the sandwich: Cook the bacon in a nonstick skillet over medium heat until just browned but not too crispy, about 8 minutes on the first side and 3 to 4 minutes on the second. Drain on paper towels, and set aside.

3. Toss the avocado slices gently in the lemon juice to prevent discoloration.

4. Halve the rolls and scoop out some of the interior. Spread both sides of each roll with the mayonnaise. Lay the egg slices over the bottom half. Cover with the avocado slices, and top evenly with the chicken. Cover with the tomato slices and sprinkle with the chives.

5. Arrange the bacon slices and then a lettuce leaf on top, and cover with the top of the roll. Serve with potato chips and pickle spears.

Makes 2 sandwiches

GORGEOUS SMOKED DUCK AND CASHEW BUTTER

★ ★ ★

Lunch at Bayonna, Susan Spicer's inviting restaurant in the heart of New Orleans' French Quarter, is an experience not to be missed. The entrées on the bill of fare are elegant and thor-oughly innovative, but my never-ending search for true American flavors led me to a grilled duck and cashew butter sandwich, which was unbelievably scrumptious. While I didn't get the recipe from Susan, my attempt at duplication pays homage to her extraordinary lunch. If you have any difficulty finding cashew butter, try a health food store. (If peanut butter is inevitable, its Southern overtones will lend intriguing dimensions too.) In any case, once you open the jar, be sure to store it in the refrigerator. For extra zest, serve this sandwich with Robin Lee's Dilly Beans.

Wine: Russian River Valley (CA) Pinot Noir
Beer: Louisiana lager

5 tablespoons olive oil
2 large red onions, halved lengthwise and slivered
2 tablespoons light brown sugar
½ pound smoked duck breast
8 slices (½ inch thick) best-quality rye bread
¼ cup cashew butter or peanut butter
¼ cup red pepper jelly

1. Heat 2 tablespoons of the olive oil in a nonstick skillet. Add the onions and cook over low heat until very soft, 15 minutes. Sprinkle with the brown sugar and cook 5 minutes longer. Set aside.

2. Trim most of the fat off the top of the duck breast, and slice it very thin. Set aside.

3. Brush one side of each slice of rye bread with the remaining 3 tablespoons olive oil. Turn the slices over and spread the other side with the cashew butter.

4. To assemble the sandwiches, spread the onions evenly over the cashew butter on 4 of the slices, and top with the duck. Spread the red pepper jelly over the cashew butter on the remaining 4 slices, and invert over the duck.

5. Place a large nonstick skillet over medium heat, and when it is hot, cook the sand-

wiches until golden, 3 to 4 minutes per side. Cut in half and serve immediately.

Serves 4

GRILLED ALOHA CLUB

★ ★ ★

Lightly grilled ahi (yellowfin tuna) and sweet pineapple, slices of crisp bacon, and rich basil mayonnaise will evoke the gentle breezes of the Hawaiian Islands—well, almost. This contemporary club sandwich is best eaten on a soft summer's night. Just a sprinkle of mesclun makes a perfect topping. Aloha!

Wine: Monterey County (CA) Chardonnay
Beer: California amber lager

BASIL MAYONNAISE
6 tablespoons mayonnaise
1 teaspoon olive oil
1 teaspoon fresh lemon juice
1 tablespoon chopped fresh basil leaves
Salt and freshly ground black pepper, to taste

MARINADE
3 tablespoons olive oil
3 tablespoons rice wine vinegar
1 tablespoon finely minced garlic
2 tablespoons finely chopped fresh basil leaves
Salt and freshly ground black pepper, to taste

SANDWICH
4 slices (¼ inch thick) fresh pineapple, cored
4 ahi (yellowfin tuna) steaks (about 6 ounces each)
8 slices bacon
8 slices (½ inch thick) sourdough bread, lightly toasted
2 cups mesclun (mixed baby salad greens),
  rinsed and dried

1. Prepare the basil mayonnaise: Combine all the mayonnaise ingredients in a small bowl, stir together thoroughly, and set aside, covered, in the refrigerator.

2. Prepare the marinade: Combine all the marinade ingredients in a medium-size bowl. Stir well and set aside.

3. Preheat the grill.

4. While the grill is heating, prepare the sandwich: Soak the pineapple slices in the marinade for 15 minutes.

5. Remove the pineapple from the marinade, shake off any excess, and place the slices on the grill. Cook over high heat until there are nice grill marks, about 1½ minutes per side. Remove and set aside.

6. Place the ahi steaks in the marinade, turning to coat them well, and leave for 15 minutes.

7. Meanwhile, cook the bacon in a nonstick skillet over medium heat until it is just crisp and golden brown, 6 minutes on the first side and 2 minutes on the second. Drain on a paper towel.

8. Oil the grill rack well and grill the ahi steaks over medium heat, 3 inches from the heat source, for 2 to 3 minutes per side or until done to your liking.

9. To assemble the sandwiches, spread one side of each slice of toast with 1½ teaspoons of the basil mayonnaise. Top 4 of the slices with a steak, followed by a pineapple slice, 2 slices of bacon, and ½ cup of the greens. Top with the remaining slices of toast, mayonnaise side down. Cut in half and serve immediately.

Serves 4

HAWAIIAN TUNA MELT

An American standard gets updated with the use of fresh, not canned, tuna. Combined with mangoes, this contemporary melt was inspired by a visit to Hawaii. To make a different base for this lush open-face sandwich, you might want to try one of the exciting new versions of English muffin, such as whole grain, that can be found in upscale markets.

Wine: Napa Valley (CA) Chenin Blanc
Beer: Hawaiian pale ale

1 Seared Tuna Steak (6 ounces; page 463)
1 English muffin, halved and lightly toasted
2 tablespoons Green Goddess Dressing
    (recipe follows)
⅓ cup alfalfa sprouts
½ small ripe avocado, peeled, pitted, and
    thinly sliced
½ small ripe mango or papaya, peeled, pitted
    (or seeded), and thinly sliced
2 slices Monterey Jack cheese
1 teaspoon snipped fresh chives

1. Preheat the broiler.
2. Slice the seared tuna, with the grain, into thin pieces.
3. To assemble the sandwiches, place the toasted muffin halves on a baking sheet. Spread each with 1 tablespoon Green Goddess Dressing, and cover evenly with the tuna slices. Top with the alfalfa sprouts, avocado, mango, and a slice of Monterey Jack.
4. Broil until the cheese is melted and bubbly, about 1 minute. Sprinkle evenly with the chives and serve immediately.
Serves 1 or 2

Green Goddess Dressing

★

In the 1920s when it dressed salads at San Francisco's Sheraton Palace Hotel, this classic was a favorite. But currently Green Goddess seems to be experiencing an undeserved fall from grace. As you'll find, when Green Goddess is homemade, its flavor is delicious. The goddess can once again command culinary kudos, particularly when served on fresh tuna, a salad of Belgian endive and even as a replacement for tartar sauce with crab or salmon cakes.

2 cups mayonnaise
8 anchovy fillets, drained
2 scallions (3 inches green left on), trimmed
¼ cup snipped fresh chives
¼ cup chopped fresh flat-leaf parsley
2 tablespoons chopped fresh tarragon leaves
¼ cup tarragon vinegar

1. Place the mayonnaise in a bowl.
2. Mince the anchovies with the scallions, and combine with the mayonnaise. Mix in all the fresh herbs and the vinegar. Serve immediately, or refrigerate, covered, up to 8 hours.
Makes about 3 cups

BLYTHE'S TUNA FISH SANDWICH

★ ★ ★

My friend Blythe served me the yummiest tuna sandwich on a hot summer afternoon on her deck overlooking an idyllic lake in New York State. Knowing my penchant for adapting recipes to better suit my own taste, she bet me that her Walla Walla onions would stay. And so they have. For the best taste, do try to include them, although Vidalias make a fine substitute. Blythe says you should "cut a thick slice from a tomato right out of the garden to put on the sandwich." For those without gardens, a summer farmers' market tomato should be equally delicious. Serve sparkling cider or grape juice in tall pretty glasses alongside.

2 cans (6 ounces each) solid white tuna packed in
*   water, drained*
1 small Walla Walla or Vidalia onion, cut into
*   ¼-inch dice*
1 hard-cooked egg, coarsely
*   chopped*
¼ cup mayonnaise,
*   or more if*
*   desired*
12 slices best-quality
*   multigrain or rye*
*   bread, toasted*
6 slices (¼ inch thick)
*   ripe tomato*

Flake the tuna into a bowl. Using a fork, mix in the onion and hard-cooked egg. Blend in the mayonnaise. Spread the tuna over 6 slices of the toast, top with the tomato slices, and cover with the remaining toast. Cut in half, and serve immediately.
Serves 6

RED'S EATS LOBSTER ROLLS

★ ★ ★

One glorious summer weekend, on the way to Boothbay Harbor, Maine, I made the traditional stop for the renowned lobster rolls at Red's Eats on Water Street in Wiscasset. Owned by Allen W. Gagnon, this little red caboose always has a line of lobster-hungry souls at its take-out window. I patiently waited my turn for a taste of their famous fare—simple but delectable, a whole piece of mayonnaise-slathered lobster tail meat nestled into a hot dog roll and served in a red-and-white-checkered cardboard holder. In this city-slicker version, I dress up the mayonnaise for added panache and cut up the lobster—one whole tail per roll is an extravagant indulgence.

Wine: Long Island (NY) Chardonnay
Beer: Boston amber lager

ORANGE TARRAGON MAYONNAISE
2 cups fresh orange juice
½ cup mayonnaise
½ cup sour cream
2 teaspoons chopped fresh tarragon,
*   or ¾ teaspoon dried*
Salt, to taste

SANDWICH

1 pound cooked lobster meat (see Note)
1 cup diced (¼ inch) celery
1 tablespoon chopped fresh tarragon
6 top-split hot dog rolls
2 tablespoons unsalted butter, at room temperature
   (optional)

   1. Prepare the orange tarragon mayonnaise: Place the orange juice in a small heavy saucepan over medium heat. Cook, swirling the pan, until the juice is reduced to a thick syrup, about 20 minutes. You should have about 3 tablespoons.

   2. Combine the orange syrup, mayonnaise, sour cream, tarragon, and salt in a bowl. Cover, and refrigerate for at least 2 hours before use.

   3. Prepare the sandwich: Cut the lobster meat into ½-inch pieces and place them in a mixing bowl. Add ¾ cup of the mayonnaise, the celery, and tarragon. Toss well.

   4. Toast the hot dog rolls. Spread them with the butter, if desired, and the remaining ¼ cup of the mayonnaise. Using a small spoon, gently place the lobster in the rolls, being careful not to break them. Serve immediately.
   Serves 6

NOTE: A 1¼-pound lobster yields about ¼ pound meat. See page 482 for How to Boil and Eat a Lobster.

CRAB LOUIS AND AVOCADO MELT

★ ★ ★

Enjoy this melt that is laden with fresh lump crabmeat, and enhanced by just the right amount of Louis dressing. It takes on a creamy consistency when the avocado melts ever-so-slightly under the broiler. Just a second or two is all that is necessary to melt the cheese to perfection. This is rich enough to serve eight, but so delicious there may be enough for only four.

Wine: Monterey County (CA) Riesling
Beer: California extra special bitter

LOUIS DRESSING

¼ cup mayonnaise
2 tablespoons sour cream
1 tablespoon chili sauce
1½ teaspoons fresh lemon juice
1 tablespoon diced (¼ inch) green
   bell pepper
1 tablespoon chopped scallions
   (white and green part)
1½ teaspoons chopped fresh tarragon or
   snipped chives
Salt and freshly ground black pepper,
   to taste

SANDWICH

1 pound fresh lump crabmeat, picked over to
   remove any cartilage
½ cup diced (¼ inch) celery
½ cup diced (¼ inch) seeded ripe plum tomato
1 teaspoon finely grated lemon zest
½ teaspoon dried tarragon
Salt and freshly ground black pepper, to taste
½ cup mayonnaise
8 slices (½ inch thick) sourdough bread
   (4 x 4 inches), lightly toasted
1 ripe avocado, peeled, pitted, and thinly sliced
6 ounces Monterey Jack cheese, grated
   (about 1½ cups)
2 tablespoons snipped fresh chives or
   chopped fresh flat-leaf parsley

   1. Prepare the Louis dressing: Combine the mayonnaise, sour cream, chili sauce, lemon juice, bell pepper, scallions, and tarragon in a bowl. Season with salt and pepper, and set aside.

2. Prepare the sandwich: Gently mix the crabmeat with the celery, tomato, lemon zest, tarragon, salt, pepper, and mayonnaise. Set aside.

3. Preheat the broiler.

4. Spread one side of each slice of the toast generously with the Louis dressing. Top the slices with the crabmeat mixture. Cover evenly with the avocado slices. Spoon the grated cheese over the avocado, and place the sandwiches on a baking sheet.

5. Just before serving, place the sandwiches under the broiler just to melt the cheese. Sprinkle with the chives, and serve immediately.

Serves 8

CAESAR SANDWICH

★ ★ ★

Caesar salad has reemerged of late to become featured restaurant fare, and since it is a favorite of mine, I'm always happy to see it on the menu. At the same time, baskets of bread, always a restaurant staple, have become much more interesting, with the appearance of rustic varieties, often combined with sweet breads or even biscuits. So, with such good pre-entrée offerings,

many times I find myself filled up before I get to the main attraction.

What all this Caesar salading and bread noshing has given me is a good deal of eating pleasure and a good idea for a sandwich. Although the croutons are gone, the anchovies are a major component, and the raw eggs are replaced with a sliced hard-cooked egg. *Et tu, Caesar?*

Beer: California wheat beer

DRESSING
1 tablespoon fresh lemon juice
¾ teaspoon Dijon mustard
½ teaspoon finely minced garlic
1 teaspoon sugar
Salt and freshly ground black pepper,
   to taste
2 tablespoons extra virgin olive oil
2 tablespoons pure olive oil

SANDWICH
4 soft rolls (about 5 x 4 inches), halved
2 tablespoons extra virgin olive oil
2 cloves garlic, halved
1 can (90 grams) anchovies in oil, or
   12 anchovy fillets
4 hard-cooked eggs, sliced
2 tablespoons chopped fresh flat-leaf parsley
Freshly ground black pepper, to taste
2 to 3 ounces Parmesan cheese, shaved
1 head romaine lettuce, large, tough outer
   leaves and stems discarded, rinsed and
   patted dry

1. Prepare the dressing: Combine the lemon juice, mustard, garlic, sugar, salt, and pepper in a bowl and whisk well. Slowly drizzle in both olive oils, whisking constantly until thickened. Set aside.

2. When you are ready to prepare the sandwiches, preheat the broiler.

3. Pull out some of the interior of the rolls. Brush each cut side of the rolls with olive oil and rub with the cut sides of the garlic cloves. Place the rolls on a baking sheet and toast lightly.

4. Lay about 3 anchovy fillets on the bottom half of each roll. Arrange a sliced egg over each. Sprinkle with parsley and pepper. Top with the cheese.

5. Tear the lettuce into smaller pieces, and toss with the dressing. Cover each sandwich evenly with lettuce leaves, stacking them lengthwise. Replace the top half of the roll, cut each one in half, and serve immediately.

Serves 4

MAINE SCALLOP ROLLS

★ ★ ★

I tasted my first scallop roll at the Clam Festival in Yarmouth, and loved it. This just may be the best sandwich Maine has to offer—even better than the famous lobster roll. There are a couple of tricks to making great scallop rolls. Bay scallops are a must, and you should cook only a quarter-pound batch at a time (otherwise they will release too much liquid). Medium-high heat is essential for a quick sauté. Do not sprinkle them with salt until they are cooked, or they will release too much liquid. Fresh tartar sauce is a second must for the complete taste experience. No kidding, these are spectacular.

BAY OR SEA SCALLOPS AND A TIP OR TWO

— ❦ —

Of all of the mollusks, there is no question that the scallop—which is actually the muscle that closes the shell—is the sweetest of them all. These creamy-textured, translucent morsels are both versatile and delicious. But rather than waxing ecstatic, I want to be sure that you know the difference between bay scallops and sea scallops.

• **Bay scallops** are the little ones; about the size of a gum ball. They make for prime, sweet eating as far as I'm concerned. Most would agree. These scallops are more localized than their larger cousins and are most likely to be caught around Nantucket (Massachusetts) and Long Island (New York) during the late fall and winter. If you're longing for them, be ready to pay, as they don't come cheap! They must be cooked quickly over high heat. Don't crowd the pan—and don't add salt until they are finished cooking, as it will bring out too much liquid and the scallops will stew.

• **Sea scallops** are the large ones; they are plentiful and available year round. Ranging anywhere from the size of a golf ball to the size of a small biscuit, they are generally harvested in the North Atlantic. While they must be cooked, don't overcook them!

Wine: Long Island (NY) Pinot Blanc
Beer: Maine pale ale

2 tablespoons unsalted butter
2 teaspoons vegetable oil
1 pound bay scallops
Paprika, to taste
Freshly ground black pepper, to taste
Salt, to taste
4 top-split hot dog rolls, lightly toasted
Tartar Sauce (page 440), for serving

1. Heat 1 tablespoon of the butter and 1 teaspoon of the oil in a nonstick skillet over medium-high heat. Add ¼ pound of the scallops and sauté, shaking the pan often, until golden, 2 minutes, sprinkling them lightly with paprika and pepper. When the scallops are cooked, sprinkle them with salt and spoon them very carefully into a hot dog roll.

2. Add another ¼ pound of the scallops to the skillet and repeat the process.

3. Wipe the skillet out with a paper towel, and add the remaining 1 tablespoon butter and 1 teaspoon oil to the skillet. Proceed with the next two batches.

4. Serve the scallop rolls immediately, with Tartar Sauce for topping.
Serves 4

GARDEN SHOWER SHRIMP ROLLS

★ ★ ★

For an authentic taste of summer on Cape Cod, in Maine, or on the East End of Long Island, no food can compete with a fresh seafood roll. Lobster is a favorite for many, but since fresh lobster is not always easy to obtain, or for that matter, easily affordable, I've made shrimp an all-year-round substitute. I once served this version at a garden bridal shower to rave reviews. Prepared simply or dressed up as it is here, shrimp salad piled high on hot dog buns makes for delicious eating.

Wine: Hudson Valley (NY) Tocai Friulano
Beer: Massachusetts India pale ale

2½ pounds medium shrimp
4 ribs celery, cut into ¼-inch dice
  (reserve the celery leaves)
3 black peppercorns
3 sprigs fresh flat-leaf parsley
2½ cups halved seedless red grapes
2 tablespoons chopped fresh tarragon leaves,
  or 1½ teaspoons dried
1 tablespoon finely grated orange zest
Salt and freshly ground black pepper, to taste
¾ cup mayonnaise
½ cup sour cream
12 top-split hot dog rolls
Small bunches of seedless red grapes, for garnish

1. Peel and devein the shrimp.

2. Add the reserved celery leaves, peppercorns, and parsley sprigs to a medium-size pot of water, and bring to a boil. Add the shrimp, stir, and boil until just cooked through, 3 minutes. Drain, rinse under cold water, and drain again. Pat the shrimp dry with paper towels and halve them crosswise. Place them in a large bowl. (Discard the celery leaves, parsley sprigs, and peppercorns.)

3. Add the diced celery, grapes, tarragon, orange zest, salt, and pepper to the shrimp. Toss well.

4. In a separate bowl, mix the mayonnaise and sour cream together. Set aside ⅓ cup of the mixture and fold the rest into the shrimp salad.

5. Carefully scoop some of the bread out of

the center of the hot dog rolls.

6. Just before serving, lightly spread some of the reserved dressing inside the rolls. Fill the rolls with the shrimp salad. Arrange the rolls attractively on a platter or tray, and garnish with the bunches of grapes.

Serves 12

PAN-SEARED CHIPOTLE-SHRIMP FAJITAS

★ ★ ★

The shrimp in these zesty fajitas marinate to a redolent succulence in a combination of chipotle peppers and other popular Southwestern ingredients. Even when topped with Black Bean Salad and Guacamole, they hold their own, and make a nice change of pace from the more typical beef and chicken versions.

Beer: New Mexico India pale ale with a shot of tequila

8 flour tortillas (7½-inch diameter)
1 can (7.6 ounces) chipotle peppers in adobo
1½ pounds medium shrimp, peeled and deveined
1½ tablespoons olive oil
1½ tablespoons fresh lime juice
1½ tablespoons finely minced garlic
½ teaspoon ground cumin
Salt and freshly ground black pepper, to taste
1 recipe Black Bean Salad (page 338)
1 recipe Guacamole (page 176)
1 ripe papaya, peeled and cut into ¼-inch dice
¼ cup chopped fresh cilantro leaves

1. Preheat the oven to 250°F.

2. Wrap the flour tortillas in aluminum foil and place them in the oven to warm.

3. Place the chipotles with the adobo sauce in a food processor and purée until smooth. Set aside.

4. In a bowl, combine the shrimp with 3 tablespoons of the chipotle purée (save the remainder for another use), the olive oil, lime juice, garlic, cumin, salt, and pepper. Toss, and marinate for 15 minutes.

5. Heat a nonstick skillet over medium-high heat until it is hot. Add half the shrimp and sauté until cooked through, 1 to 2 minutes per side. Repeat with the remaining shrimp.

6. Place the tortillas in a napkin-lined basket. Arrange the shrimp, Black Bean Salad, Guacamole, and papaya on a serving platter or in individual bowls. Let each person fill a tortilla according to taste. Sprinkle with the chopped cilantro, fold or roll the tortillas, and enjoy!

Serves 4

WALLA WALLA TOMATO AND SARDINE SANDWICH

★ ★ ★

Walla Walla onions are not easy to come by, so when I was in Washington, their home state, I carried some back with me to New York. All I could think about was the sandwich I would make. The result was everything I had hoped for. The better the quality of the sardines, the more peasanty the bread, and the riper the tomato, the better the bite. But oh, those Walla Walla sweets! Do try to locate some.

Beer: Seattle India pale ale

4 slices (½ inch thick) peasant bread, toasted or
    grilled
2 tablespoons mayonnaise
4 slices (¼ inch thick) Walla Walla or other
    sweet onion
1 can (about 4¾ ounces) best-quality imported
    sardines, drained
4 slices (¼ inch thick) ripe tomato
Coarsely ground black pepper, to taste

1. Spread one side of each slice of toast with the mayonnaise.
2. Cover 2 of the slices with 2 onion slices each. Top the onions with 2 sardines each, mashing them slightly with a fork. Cover with 2 tomato slices, sprinkle with pepper, and top with the remaining 2 slices of toast. Dig in.
    Serves 2

ROASTED TOMATO SANDWICHES

★ ★ ★

Roasted tomatoes are part and parcel of many contemporary sandwiches. Served atop well-flavored goat cheese that has been spread on toasted bread, their sweetness harmonizes with the cheese's tang and texture. Roasted tomatoes can also be spooned over angel-hair pasta for a quick, light summer meal—especially aromatic when sprinkled with extra-fresh basil.

Wine: Napa Valley (CA) Sangiovese

4 ripe tomatoes, cored
4 tablespoons extra virgin olive oil
Pinch of sugar (see Note)
1 pound soft goat cheese
2 teaspoons finely grated orange zest
2 teaspoons finely chopped fresh
    basil leaves
Salt and freshly ground black
    pepper, to taste
4 slices (½ inch thick)
    crusty peasant bread
8 whole fresh basil leaves

1. Preheat the oven to 250°F.
2. Halve the tomatoes crosswise, and place them on a baking sheet. Drizzle them with 1 tablespoon of the olive oil and sprinkle with the sugar. Bake on the center rack of the oven for 3 hours. Using a spatula, carefully transfer the tomatoes to a plate to cool.
3. While the tomatoes are roasting, gently crumble the goat cheese into a bowl. Add 2 tablespoons of the olive oil, the orange zest, chopped basil, salt, and pepper. Cover and refrigerate until the tomatoes have finished roasting and are cooled.
4. When you are ready to serve the sandwiches, lightly toast the bread. Spread the cheese mixture on one side of each slice. Top with 2 whole basil leaves and 2 tomato halves. Sprinkle with salt and pepper, and drizzle with the remaining 1 tablespoon olive oil. Serve immediately.
    Serves 4

NOTE: Don't omit the sugar—it eliminates any acidic undertaste in the tomatoes.

★★

AT THE WHISTLE STOP CAFE

—❦—

While in Georgia attending the Peach Festival, I discovered that close by, in Juliette, was the actual Whistle Stop Cafe, made famous by Fannie Flagg in her novel *Fried Green Tomatoes at the Whistle Stop Cafe,* and the film based on the book. This was a wonderful discovery, and an opportunity to visit was not to be missed.

The restaurant lies about eight miles off the highway, down a gently rolling country lane. Behind it, just like in the movie, flowed a shallow river, and waders splashed around looking for relief from the 96°F heat. Just beyond, regularly passing trains tooted their horns, the whistles gone with the demise of steam trains.

I arrived to find a large group of folks sitting on rockers awaiting their tables. No hostess there—you just sign in on the clipboard hanging on a nail by the door, and wait your turn for a table. Too excited to wait, I decided to take a seat at the counter. Right under my nose, orders of fried green tomatoes (about eight golden slices per plate) rapidly fired out of the kitchen and onto the tables of all us hungry pilgrims. Ceiling fans whirred overhead, but the heat didn't seem to curb anybody's appetite, certainly not mine. When my order arrived, I downed every single slice, a smile on my face and juice dripping down my chin. I would have had a second order, but the peach cobbler (made with fresh Georgia peaches, of course) was just too tempting. Plenty of refreshing iced tea, drunk from a canning jar, was a must.

If you love fried green tomatoes, think you'll love them if you ever have the opportunity to try them, or even if you just love the movie and think of the cafe as a shrine, pay it a visit. It's on McCrackin Street in Juliette and the phone number there is (912) 994-3670.

★★

BACON, LETTUCE, AND FRIED GREEN TOMATO SANDWICH

★ ★ ★

The end of summer is always bittersweet. I anticipate missing the luscious ripe tomatoes, sweet corn, and long hot days. Once I spy baskets full of green tomatoes, however, I start whistling an autumn tune. Although I'm not a Southerner, I really appreciate them sliced thick, lightly dusted with cornmeal, fried crisp, and served with homemade bread-and-butter pickles. They're not a bad way to cure the end-of-summer blues!

Beer: Southern lager

8 slices thick-cut bacon
¾ cup all-purpose flour
¼ cup stone-ground cornmeal
Salt and freshly ground black pepper, to taste
1 cup milk
¼ cup olive oil, plus more if necessary
8 slices (¼ inch thick) green tomatoes
¼ cup mayonnaise
1 tablespoon chili sauce
8 slices rye bread, lightly toasted
2 large bunches arugula, tough stems removed,
     leaves rinsed and patted dry

1. Cook the bacon in a nonstick skillet over medium heat until just browned and crisp, 6 minutes on the first side and 2 minutes on the second. Transfer the bacon to a paper towel to drain, and set aside. Strain the bacon fat into a cup, and wipe out the skillet with a paper towel.

2. Combine the flour, cornmeal, salt, and pepper in a medium-size bowl. Add the milk and stir well. The mixture should resemble pancake batter.

3. Add the olive oil to the cleaned skillet along with the strained bacon fat, and place it over medium-high heat. Working in batches, dip the tomato slices in the batter, letting the excess drip back into the bowl, and fry them until golden brown, about 3 minutes per side. Add more olive oil to the pan if necessary. Drain the tomatoes on paper towels.

4. Stir the mayonnaise and the chili sauce together in a small bowl.

5. To serve, spread one side of each slice of toast with about 1½ teaspoons of the may-onnaise mixture. Lay 2 slices of bacon over each of 4 slices of toast. Cover the bacon with 2 fried tomato slices, and top evenly with arugula. Cover with the remaining 4 slices of toast, mayonnaise side down. Cut in half and serve immediately.
   Serves 4

A SUMMER TOMATO SANDWICH

★ ★ ★

When my tomatoes ripen, I begin eating them sun-warmed right in the garden, straight off the vine. The first of the season that do make it into the kitchen go right into this sandwich. Some purists prefer their tomato sandwiches without salt and pepper, but I like to spice up the flawless beauties. The choice is yours. Just be sure the tomatoes are really ripe and the bread is fresh and soft. Serve with minty iced tea.

3 tablespoons mayonnaise, or more
    to taste
4 slices best-quality white bread,
    crusts removed
2 ripe garden tomatoes
Coarse salt and freshly ground black pepper,
    to taste

Spread mayonnaise over one side of each of the bread slices. Cut the tomatoes into ¼-inch-thick slices, and arrange them on two of the bread slices. Sprinkle with coarse salt and pepper, and cover with the remaining bread, mayonnaise side down. Cut the sandwiches in half and eat them up as quickly as you can.
   Serves 2

GRILLED TOMATO, BACON, AND CHEDDAR SANDWICH

★ ★ ★

I can't think of anything more satisfying than a properly grilled cheese sandwich, especially one cooked with a little imagination and flair. In this recipe, ripe plum tomatoes are grilled to add an extra dimension to the Vermont aged Cheddar. I find that a drizzle of maple syrup enhances the sweetness of well-cured bacon. The final result is just waiting to sit beside a bowl of Real Cream of Tomato Soup! When preparing these sandwiches, note that the buttered sides of the bread go on the outside.

Beer: Vermont amber ale

2 ripe plum tomatoes, halved lengthwise
Salt and freshly ground black pepper, to taste
6 slices bacon
4 slices rye bread
2 tablespoons unsalted butter, at room temperature
4 thin slices (about 2 ounces) Vermont Cheddar
   cheese
1 tablespoon pure maple syrup

   1. Preheat the broiler.
   2. Sprinkle the cut sides of the tomatoes with salt and pepper. Place the tomatoes on a baking sheet cut side down and broil until slightly charred and easy to mash, about 8 minutes. Set aside.
   3. Fry the bacon slices in a nonstick skillet until just golden brown, 6 minutes on one side and 2 minutes on the second side. Drain on paper towels.

   4. Spread one side of each slice of rye bread with the butter. Lay the cheese over the *un*buttered side of 2 of the slices, then add 3 slices of bacon, and drizzle with the maple syrup. Top each with 2 tomato halves, mashing them down slightly. Top with the remaining 2 slices of bread, buttered side *out*.
   5. Grill the sandwiches in a nonstick skillet over medium heat, occasionally pressing down on them with the back of a spatula, until golden brown, 3 to 4 minutes per side. Cut the sandwiches in half and serve immediately.
   Serves 2

GRILLED VEGETABLE AND INDIANA GOAT CHEESE SANDWICH

★ ★ ★

I received a wonderful selection of farmstead Capriole goat cheese from Indiana and chose the luxuriously spreadable American Alpine version to use in this grilled vegetable sandwich. Just a little brush of oil on some peasant bread was all that was needed to complete the picture. You can easily recreate it with any available fresh goat cheese. If you like, arrange a few crisp arugula leaves on top of the grilled pepper before covering it with the second slice of bread. This greenery will add a peppery freshness.

Wine: California Sauvignon Blanc–Sémillon blend
Beer: Wisconsin brown lager

★★★★★★★★★★★★★★★★★★★★★★★★★

HOW TO ROAST A BELL PEPPER

—❦—

1. Heat the broiler.

2. Cut the bell pepper in half, and remove the core and seeds. Flatten the pepper halves slightly with the palm of your hand. Lay the halves, skin side up, in a single layer on a small baking sheet. Broil about 3 inches from the heat until the skins are charred black, 12 to 15 minutes.

3. Remove the peppers from the broiler and place them in a paper or plastic bag. Close it tight, and let the peppers steam for about 15 minutes. Then slip off the charred skin, and proceed with the recipe.

★★★★★★★★★★★★★★★★★★★★★★★★★

6 slices (½ inch thick) eggplant
3 tablespoons olive oil
Salt and freshly ground black pepper, to taste
4 slices (½ inch thick) red onion
2 ripe tomatoes, cut into ½-inch-thick slices
4 slices (½ inch thick) peasant bread (6 x 3 inches), toasted
2 ounces (about ½ cup) spreadable goat cheese
1 red bell pepper, roasted (see box, above)
Arugula leaves (optional)

1. Preheat the grill or broiler.
2. Brush the eggplant slices generously on both sides with some of the olive oil, and grill or broil for 4 to 5 minutes per side, until browned and tender. Sprinkle with salt and pepper, and set aside.

3. Lightly brush the onion slices on both sides with olive oil, and grill or broil for 6 to 7 minutes per side, until browned and tender. Set aside.
4. Brush the tomato slices with olive oil, and grill or broil for 4 to 5 minutes per side, until browned and tender. Sprinkle with salt and pepper, and set aside.
5. Brush both sides of the bread slices with a little bit of olive oil and toast or grill them until just golden.
6. To assemble the sandwiches, spread the goat cheese over 2 slices of bread. Top with eggplant slices to cover, then tomato slices, onions, and a pepper half, and arugula leaves, if using. Cover with the remaining bread, and cut in half to serve.
Serves 2

PIMIENTO CHEESE WITH CUCUMBER SANDWICH

★ ★ ★

Pimiento cheese is back! This old-time Southern favorite is finding new life during the cocktail hour, at tea parties, and even in bars and diners. I found a bowl of it surrounded by crackers for a happy hour snack in Savannah, and my associate Laurie was the first to order a pimiento cheese sandwich at the Tip Top Diner in San Antonio. I have used homemade roasted red bell peppers instead of the usual jarred pimientos and added mellow-tasting scallions for the sharper grated onions. If you like, spice it up with a dash of Tabasco or Worcestershire sauce. For the best sandwiches, serve this on freshly made white bread and top it with thinly sliced cucumbers.

1 red bell pepper, roasted (see box, facing page)
½ pound sharp Cheddar cheese, coarsely grated
½ cup mayonnaise
1 scallion (3 inches green left on), thinly sliced on
the diagonal
1 tablespoon chopped fresh flat-leaf parsley
Salt and freshly ground black pepper, to taste
8 slices best-quality fresh white bread
Thinly sliced unpeeled hothouse (seedless) cucumber,
to taste

1. Cut the roasted peppers into ¼-inch dice and place in a medium-size bowl. Add the grated cheese, mayonnaise, scallions, and parsley. Combine, then season with salt and pepper.

2. Spread the cheese mixture on 4 slices of the bread. Top with cucumber slices and the remaining bread slices.
Serves 4

INDIAN TACO

★ ★ ★

This was one of the most engaging dishes I tasted on my visit to South Dakota. Traditional Native American fry bread, resembling a fluffy tortilla, is heaped with all the usual Mexican-American taco fillings and served up with a knife and fork. The best I found was at the Woodenknife Cafe in Interior, a small town perched on the edge of the wild, lunar-looking Badlands, where the taco reigns supreme at breakfast time. I prefer my zesty Indian Taco as a luncheon special.

Beer: Colorado lager

1 pound ground beef round
1 cup tomato sauce
1 tablespoon tomato paste
1 tablespoon honey
1 teaspoon ground cumin
Salt and freshly ground black pepper, to taste
4 Indian Fry Breads (page 208)
4 cups shredded lettuce
1 cup diced (¼ inch) ripe tomatoes
1 cup coarsely chopped red onions
½ cup sliced pitted ripe olives
1 cup shredded Vermont Cheddar cheese
⅓ cup sour cream
½ cup Roasted Rosy Salsa (page 196) or your favorite
2 tablespoons chopped fresh cilantro leaves or
flat-leaf parsley, for garnish

1. Sauté the meat in an ungreased nonstick skillet over medium heat, breaking up any clumps, until browned, about 5 minutes. Drain off any fat, and stir in the tomato sauce, tomato paste, honey, cumin, salt, and pepper.

2. To assemble the tacos, place an Indian Fry Bread on each dinner plate, and spoon the beef mixture evenly over them. Top evenly with the lettuce, tomatoes, onions, olives, cheese, a dollop each of sour cream and salsa, and garnish with the cilantro. Serve immediately.
Serves 4

BARBECUED CHICKEN QUESADILLAS

★ ★ ★

These summery quesadillas make good use of leftover chicken. Combining it with barbecue

QUESADILLAS

—❧—

Basically, U.S.A.-style quesadillas are sandwiches—cheese and an array of other ingredients that are layered between two flour tortillas, and then toasted, baked, or skillet fried (my preference). Originally from Mexico (where they are less like sandwiches and more like turnovers), I think the form offers up intriguing possibilities. Open the refrigerator and conjure up combinations—from leftovers like chicken or duck, seafood, or vegetables and herbs. They will all fit deliciously between the two tortillas. Pair your picks with mild or sharp or peppery Monterey Jack and Cheddar. Once they are skillet fried, and the cheese is melted, quesadillas are as suitable for a bite during the cocktail hour as they are for a substantial suppertime entrée. Don't be shy with your flavors. Generous amounts of herbs, vegetables, and cheeses are the secret behind the best!

sauce, two types of cheese, and fresh spinach makes for an unexpected and delicious filling.

Wine: California Pinot Noir
Beer: California pale ale

4 flour tortillas (7½-inch diameter)
2 ounces Monterey Jack cheese, grated (about ½ cup)
½ cup shredded cooked chicken
¼ cup barbecue sauce, preferably
   Backyard Barbecue Sauce (page 355)
2 scallions (3 inches green left on), thinly sliced on
   the diagonal
2 teaspoons chopped fresh cilantro leaves
6 to 8 fresh spinach leaves, tough stems discarded,
   rinsed and patted dry
2 ounces Wisconsin Cheddar, grated (about ½ cup)
Velvety Mango Cream (recipe follows), or Silky
   Papaya Relish or Fresh Pineapple Relish
   (page 182 or 186)

1. Place 2 tortillas on a work surface and sprinkle them evenly with the Monterey Jack.
2. Combine the chicken and the barbecue sauce in a small bowl. Scatter the mixture evenly over the cheese on each tortilla, along with the scallions and chopped cilantro.
3. Lay the spinach leaves flat over both surfaces to cover all the ingredients. Sprinkle with the Cheddar. Place a second tortilla over each, creating a sandwich, and press down with the palm of your hand.
4. Heat a nonstick skillet over medium heat until it is very hot. Using a large spatula, place a quesadilla in the skillet and cook, pressing down with the spatula and turning it once, until the cheese melts and the tortillas brown slightly, 3 to 4 minutes per side. Transfer the quesadilla to a low oven (250°F) to keep warm. Repeat with the remaining quesadilla.
5. Cut each quesadilla into quarters and serve hot, with a bowl of mango cream or papaya or pineapple relish alongside.
Serves 2

Velvety Mango Cream

———★———

Drizzle this sensuous cream atop or beside hot-from-the-pan quesadillas. Make sure you have a lush, ripe mango so that the sweetness will blend with a little Southwestern-style heat. I fill a squeeze bottle with this cream and squiggle it in a decorative pattern on the edge of the plate. I leave the design to your sense of adventure. This cream also goes splendidly with roasted duck.

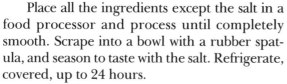

1 ripe mango, peeled, pitted, and cut into
   1-inch pieces
½ cup sour cream
Juice of 1 lime
1 or 2 dashes Tabasco sauce, to taste
¼ teaspoon ground cumin
Salt, to taste

Place all the ingredients except the salt in a food processor and process until completely smooth. Scrape into a bowl with a rubber spatula, and season to taste with the salt. Refrigerate, covered, up to 24 hours.
   Makes about 2 cups

DUCK AND CARAMELIZED ONION QUESADILLAS

★ ★ ★

I enjoy serving these for a light winter luncheon—their rich flavor seems to warm up the weather. You don't have to roast a duck for this dish (it's great when you have leftovers on hand); dark chicken meat substitutes nicely.

Wine: Amador County (CA) Zinfandel
Beer: Rocky Mountain brown ale

2 tablespoons olive oil
1 large red onion, halved lengthwise and slivered
1 tablespoon sugar
Salt and freshly ground black pepper, to taste
1 tablespoon balsamic vinegar
4 flour tortillas (7½-inch diameter)
4 ounces Monterey Jack cheese, grated (about 1 cup)
¼ to ½ cup shredded cooked duck meat
2 tablespoons chopped fresh flat-leaf parsley
Velvety Mango Cream (this page),or
   Fresh Pineapple Relish or Summer Peach
   Relish (page 186 or 183)

1. Place the oil in a nonstick skillet over medium heat. Sauté the onion, shaking the skillet, until wilted, 10 minutes.

2. Sprinkle the sugar, salt, and pepper over the onions and cook for 3 minutes, shaking and stirring the skillet, to caramelize the onions. Drizzle with the vinegar and cook for another 2 minutes. Remove from the heat and set aside.

3. Place 2 tortillas on a work surface, and sprinkle them evenly with half of the cheese. Scatter the duck evenly over the cheese. Top each with half of the caramelized onions. Sprinkle with the chopped parsley and the remaining cheese.

4. Place a second tortilla over each, creating a sandwich, and press down with the palm of your hand.

5. Heat a nonstick skillet over medium heat until it is very hot. Using a large spatula, place a quesadilla in the skillet and cook, pressing down with the spatula and turning it once, until the cheese melts and the tortillas brown slightly, 3 to 4 minutes per side. Transfer the quesadilla to a low oven (250°F) to keep warm. Repeat with the remaining quesadilla.

6. Cut each quesadilla into quarters and serve hot, with a bowl of cream or relish alongside.

Serves 2

NEW AMERICAN HAM AND CHEESE QUESADILLAS

★ ★ ★

I found that even old standard sandwich fillings, like the popular deli ham and cheese combo, take on a new character when served quesadilla style. Freshly sliced mushrooms and scallions spark the texture, and Bread-and-Butter Pickles or crisp Pennsylvania Dutch Chowchow is the perfect foil for this meltingly luscious knife-and-fork sandwich.

Beer: Pennsylvania amber lager

4 flour tortillas (7½-inch diameter)
1 teaspoon Dijon mustard
4 ounces Vermont Cheddar, grated (about 1 cup)
4 thin slices baked Virginia ham
6 very thin slices ripe tomato
1 small white mushroom, cleaned and thinly sliced
2 scallions (white part and 3 inches green),
very thinly sliced
1½ tablespoons chopped fresh flat-leaf parsley
Bread-and-Butter Pickles or Pennsylvania Dutch
Chowchow (page 192 or 187)

1. Place 2 tortillas on a work surface and spread each evenly with the mustard. Sprinkle

evenly with half of the cheese. Top with the ham slices and cover with the tomato slices.

2. Sprinkle the mushrooms, scallions, and parsley over the tomato slices, and then add the remaining cheese. Place a second tortilla over each, creating a sandwich, and press down with the palm of your hand.

3. Heat a nonstick skillet over medium heat until it is very hot. Using a large spatula, place a quesadilla in the skillet and cook, pressing down with the spatula and turning it once, until the cheese melts and the tortillas brown slightly, 3 to 4 minutes per side. Transfer the quesadilla to a low oven (250°F) to keep warm. Repeat with the remaining quesadilla.

4. Cut each quesadilla into quarters and serve hot, with a bowl of bread-and-butter pickles or chowchow alongside.

Serves 2

SHRIMP QUESADILLAS

★ ★ ★

These are light and delicious—a good choice to serve during a hot spell. A homemade Silky Papaya Relish or Fresh Pineapple Relish would make the tastiest accompaniment.

Wine: Santa Barbara County (CA) Sauvignon
Blanc
Beer: Texas lager

¼ pound small shrimp, shelled and deveined
4 flour tortillas (7½-inch diameter)
4 ounces Monterey Jack cheese, grated (about 1 cup)
¼ cup Guacamole (page 176) or mashed avocado
Silky Papaya Relish or Fresh Pineapple Relish
(page 182 or 186)

1. Cook the shrimp in boiling water until cooked through, 1 minute. Drain and set aside. (If you are using regular-size shrimp, cut them into smaller pieces.)

2. Place 2 tortillas on a work surface and sprinkle them evenly with half of the cheese. Scatter the shrimp evenly over the cheese. Top with the Guacamole, and sprinkle with the remaining cheese.

3. Place a second tortilla over each, creating a sandwich, and press down on the ingredients with the palm of your hand.

4. Heat a nonstick skillet over medium heat until it is very hot. Using a large spatula, place a quesadilla in the skillet and cook, pressing down with the spatula and turning it once, until the cheese melts and the tortillas brown slightly, 3 to 4 minutes per side. Transfer the quesadilla to a low oven (250°F) to keep warm. Repeat with the remaining quesadilla.

5. Cut each quesadilla into quarters and serve hot, with a bowl of relish alongside.

Serves 2

SALMON QUESADILLAS WITH A SCHMEAR

★ ★ ★

Until you've had a bagel with lox and cream cheese in one of New York City's famous delis, you haven't had the real thing since a lot of the real thing includes that certain deli ambiance, and waiters the likes of which exist nowhere else. So, rather than trying to recreate a classic, allow me to satisfy your craving with this somewhat unorthodox—but no less delicious—twist. Be sure that the tomatoes are very ripe so they add plenty of juicy sweetness to this creamy, sophisticated quesadilla.

Wine: Washington State Dry Riesling
Beer: New Mexico copper lager

4 flour tortillas (7½-inch diameter)
¼ pound soft goat cheese
¼ cup sour cream
½ cup diced (¼ inch) and seeded tomatoes
    (about 2 small tomatoes)
2 teaspoons capers, drained
1½ teaspoons snipped fresh chives
1 teaspoon finely grated lemon zest
Freshly ground black pepper, to taste
¼ pound smoked salmon, thinly sliced
Pico de Gallo (page 196)

1. Place 2 tortillas on a work surface and sprinkle them evenly with half of the cheese. Slather 1 tablespoon of the sour cream over each.

2. Scatter the tomatoes, capers, chives, lemon zest, and pepper evenly over each. Arrange the salmon over the top.

3. Cover with the remaining cheese and sour cream.

4. Place a second tortilla over each, creating a sandwich, and press down with the palm of your hand.

5. Heat a nonstick skillet over medium heat until it is very hot. Using a large spatula, place a quesadilla in the skillet and cook, pressing down with the spatula and turning it once, until the cheese melts and the tortillas brown slightly, 3 to 4 minutes per side. Transfer the quesadilla to a low oven (250°F) to keep warm. Repeat with the remaining quesadilla.

6. Cut each quesadilla into quarters and serve hot, with a bowl of the Pico de Gallo alongside.

Serves 2

PART FOUR

THE COCKTAIL HOUR

Mixed Drinks

The cocktail hour, as Bernard DeVoto, essayist and author, reverentially referred to it in a treatise he wrote on the martini, is when people from every walk of life lay down the accumulated baggage of their trip through the day and pick up their spirits. The following spirit-raising potables, both alcoholic and nonalcoholic, come from a two-hundred-year-old American tradition that is as beloved a part of our culture as baseball, jazz, and musical comedy.

I invited bar master Dale DeGroff, renowned from Los Angeles's Hotel Bel Air (where he worked from 1978 to 1984) to New York's Rainbow Room (where he's working now), to aid me in selecting the cocktails—including the "virgins"—for this chapter.

THE MARTINI

★ ★ ★

Shaken, stirred, straight up, or on the rocks, with an olive, a twist, or even an oyster, the king of the cocktails is the martini.

Although it is not known for sure when or by whom the drink was invented, or even from whom or from what the name evolved, by the late nineteenth century, a martini was comprised of half gin and half *sweet* vermouth. Just after the turn of the century, at the famous bar of the Knickerbocker Hotel in New York City, the principal bartender, Martini di Arma di Taggia, made martinis using equal parts of gin and *dry* vermouth. (His name may be a coincidence: the actual drink has its roots in a drink traced as far back as the 1860s.)

During Prohibition, the gin was so bad that everything imaginable was added to mask the noxious flavor, and the martini waned in popularity. It wasn't until Prohibition ended, and good gin was again available, that people once again ordered the martini—due in large part to the *Thin Man* movies, featuring the very social Nick and Nora Charles, who drank them in endless quantities. The Nick and Nora recipe called for 3 parts gin to 1 part dry vermouth, but the martini got even drier as America got wetter. By the 1960s, the proportions had evolved to 11 parts gin to 1 part vermouth, and vodka, replac-

ing the gin, had made serious inroads. Today we have the 32-to-1 martini, but remember: It's not a martini if that last trace of vermouth disappears entirely.

This martini is served with both an olive and lemon zest.

Ice cubes
2 dashes dry French vermouth
3 to 4 ounces (6 to 8 tablespoons) gin or vodka
1 pitted green Spanish olive (no pimiento)
Strip of lemon zest, for garnish

1. Place a martini glass in the refrigerator or freezer to chill.

2. Fill a mixing glass with ice cubes.

3. Pour the vermouth, then the gin, over the ice. Stir 30 times if they are little ice cubes, 50 times if they're standard-size.

4. Drop the olive into the chilled martini glass, and strain the martini into the glass. "Flame" the lemon zest (see box, page 144). Then drop it in the drink and serve.

Serves 1

THE MANHATTAN

★ ★ ★

Here's the quintessential rye cocktail—except in Minnesota and Wisconsin, where they prefer brandy Manhattans, and down South, where they prefer bourbon Manhattans (see Note).

Ice cubes
1½ ounces (3 tablespoons) rye whiskey
½ ounce (1 tablespoon) sweet Italian vermouth
  (see Note)
2 dashes Angostura bitters
1 maraschino cherry with stem, for garnish

1. Place a glass in the refrigerator or freezer to chill.
2. Fill a mixing glass with ice cubes.
3. Pour the rye, vermouth, and bitters over the ice, and stir.
4. Strain into the chilled glass, garnish with the cherry, and serve.

Serves 1

NOTE: If you prefer a dry Manhattan, use dry vermouth and garnish with a lemon peel. If you want to use brandy or bourbon, the proportions are the same.

AMERICAN BEAUTY COCKTAIL

★ ★ ★

I do not know which came first, the American Beauty rose or the cocktail. The cocktail is as tasty as the rose is beautiful. In fact, bar master Dale DeGroff calls the taste "ambrosial"—rich and slightly sweet, and refers to the drink as a "cordial cocktail," because it works both before and after dinner.

Ice cubes
1 ounce (2 tablespoons) brandy
1 ounce (2 tablespoons) dry vermouth
1 ounce (2 tablespoons) fresh orange juice
¼ ounce (½ tablespoon) grenadine syrup
¼ ounce (½ tablespoon) ruby port
1 rose petal (organically grown, nonsprayed only),
*   for garnish*

1. Chill a cocktail glass in the refrigerator or freezer.
2. Fill a mixing glass with ice cubes.
3. Pour the brandy, vermouth, orange juice, grenadine, and port over the ice and shake well.
4. Strain into the chilled glass, garnish with the rose petal, and serve.

Serves 1

BETWEEN THE SHEETS

★ ★ ★

This drink is a relative of the classic Sidecar (see the following recipe), with a sexier name.

Ice cubes
1½ ounces (3 tablespoons) brandy
½ ounce (1 tablespoon) Benedictine
½ ounce (1 tablespoon) Cointreau
½ ounce (1 tablespoon) fresh lemon juice
1 strip orange zest (½ inch wide), for garnish

1. Chill a cocktail glass in the refrigerator or freezer.
2. Fill a mixing glass with ice cubes.
3. Pour the brandy, Benedictine, Cointreau, and lemon juice over the ice and shake well. Strain into the chilled cocktail glass.
4. "Flame" the orange zest over the top of the drink (see box, page 144). Then drop the zest in the drink and serve.

Serves 1

NOTE: For a sweeter drink, add a little sugar syrup (see Simple Sugar Syrup for Drinks, page 152).

★ ★

HOW TO "FLAME" CITRUS ZEST

—❧—

This trick is fun and adds some drama while contributing a burst of orange or lemon flavor to a drink.

Cut a strip of peel 2 inches long and ½ inch wide from a firm fresh orange or lemon. Remove as much of the white pith as possible. Light a long kitchen match, and holding it and the strip over the surface of the drink, warm the strip so that it exudes a bit of oil before you drop it onto the surface of the drink.

★ ★

SIDECAR

★ ★ ★

This drink was invented at Harry's American Bar in Paris during the 1940s. It was named after the motorcycle sidecar in which the person for whom it was created always arrived. It's a very sophisticated brandy-based cocktail with a hint of citrus and sweetness.

1 lemon wedge
Superfine sugar
Ice cubes
1 ounce (2 tablespoons) brandy
1 ounce (2 tablespoons) Cointreau
¾ ounce (1½ tablespoons) fresh lemon juice
1 strip (1 x ½ inch) orange zest, for garnish

1. Rub the rim of a cocktail glass with the cut side of the lemon wedge. Spread some superfine sugar in a saucer, then dip the wet rim of the glass into the sugar to coat. Chill the sugar-rimmed glass in the refrigerator or freezer.

2. Fill a mixing glass with ice cubes.

3. Pour the brandy, Cointreau, and lemon juice over the ice and shake well.

4. Strain into the chilled glass. Twist the strip of orange zest over the drink, drop it in, and serve.

Serves 1

COSMOPOLITAN

★ ★ ★

Dale DeGroff did not invent this drink, and when *New York* Magazine gave him the credit, he set out to find the true inventor. While the Fog City Diner in San Francisco had it on their menu for years, his best sources said it came from Miami Beach and was created by a woman named Cheryl Cook. Where are you, Cheryl Cook? Today, it is considered the hottest drink in the country!

Ice cubes
1 ounce (2 tablespoons) Absolut Citron vodka
1 ounce (2 tablespoons) Cointreau
½ ounce (1 tablespoon) fresh lime juice
2 ounces (¼ cup) cranberry juice
Strip of lemon zest, for garnish

1. Chill a large martini glass in the refrigerator or freezer.

2. Fill a mixing glass with ice cubes.

3. Pour the vodka, Cointreau, and both the juices over the ice, and shake well.

4. Strain into the chilled glass, "flame" the lemon zest over the top (see box, facing page), and drop the zest into the drink. Serve.

Serves 1

BRONX COCKTAIL

★ ★ ★

The Bronx Cocktail is a nineteenth-century classic from the Big Brass Rail, a gentlemen's bar in the old Waldorf Hotel (before the Astoria wing), when the hotel was located on the present site of the Empire State Building. It was created by the principal bartender, Johnny Solon, after, it is said, a trip to the Bronx Zoo. Still popular today, the drink is always on the Rainbow Room menu.

Ice cubes
1½ ounces (3 tablespoons) gin
½ ounce (1 tablespoon) sweet vermouth
½ ounce (1 tablespoon) dry vermouth
2 ounces (¼ cup) fresh orange juice
1 dash Angostura bitters
Strip of orange zest (½ inch wide), for garnish

1. Chill a large martini glass in the refrigerator or freezer.

2. Fill a mixing glass with ice cubes.

3. Pour the gin, both vermouths, the orange juice, and bitters over the ice, and shake well.

4. Strain into the chilled glass, "flame" the orange zest over the top (see box, facing page), and serve.

Serves 1

THE FITZGERALD

★ ★ ★

A modern classic from the Rainbow Room, this drink was named by a member of the *New Yorker* magazine staff. Invented by Dale DeGroff, it was first called The Gin Thing, but the *New Yorker* staffer, noting that the menu had a drink called The Hemingway, suggested that the Rainbow Room give F. Scott Fitzgerald equal time—hence the name change. It's a good summer gin drink, with its golden color and lemonade flavors.

Ice cubes
2 ounces (¼ cup) gin
1 ounce (2 tablespoons) fresh lemon juice
1 ounce (2 tablespoons) Simple Sugar Syrup for
    Drinks (page 152)
4 dashes Angostura bitters
1 slice of lemon, for garnish

1. Fill an Old Fashioned glass with ice cubes.

2. Fill a mixing glass with ice cubes. Add the gin, lemon juice, sugar syrup, and bitters, and shake well.

3. Strain into the Old Fashioned glass, garnish with the lemon slice, and serve.

Serves 1

MY MAI TAI

★ ★ ★

A Mai Tai is one island drink that doesn't include the expected tropical fruit juices. Instead it combines rum with a delicately flavored orange liqueur and a creamy almond syrup. A little extra time put into garnish and decoration is worth the effort. Now, where's that breathtaking Hawaiian sunset to complete the picture?

Ice cubes
Juice of 1 lime
2 ounces (¼ cup) rum
¾ ounce (1½ tablespoons) Curaçao
3 dashes orgeat syrup (see Note, page 152)
Shaved or crushed ice, for serving
1 fresh pineapple spear
1 maraschino cherry
1 paper umbrella (optional)

1. Fill a mixing glass with ice cubes.
2. Pour the lime juice, rum, Curaçao, and orgeat syrup over the ice and shake well.
3. Strain into a highball glass half full with shaved or crushed ice.
4. Garnish with the pineapple spear and cherry. The paper umbrella is optional, but in my opinion, it does add to the Mai Tai experience.
Serves 1

AUNT MARE'S BLOODY MARY

★ ★ ★

Anyone who specializes in great "Bloody's" has his or her own style and recipe, and my friend Wende Sasse's Aunt Mare and Uncle Manny are no different. Whenever we visit, this is the drink they make, and is it ever bloody good.

About ¼ cup coarse salt
Wedge of lime
Ice cubes
2 ounces (¼ cup) vodka
6 ounces (¾ cup) tomato juice
Dash of Tabasco sauce
Dash of Worcestershire sauce
Pinch of ground white pepper
1 to 2 fresh dill sprigs, for garnish

1. Place the salt on a small plate. Moisten the rim of an 8-ounce balloon wine glass by running the lime wedge around it. Dip the rim in the salt, making sure it is well coated.
2. Fill a small pitcher with ice cubes. Add the vodka, tomato juice, Tabasco sauce, Worcestershire sauce, and pepper to the pitcher. Stir and strain into the glass. Garnish with dill and serve.
Serves 1

BLOODY BULL

★ ★ ★

Wende Sasse gave me her Bloody Mary recipe for the *New Basics Cookbook,* and her aunt and uncle's recipe for this book (see facing page). When Wende met her husband, Steedie, a Bloody Bull was the first drink he made for her, and it certainly helped win her heart. It also helps on a rough Sunday morning, if you happen to need it.

Ice cubes
1 ounce (2 tablespoons) vodka
2 ounces (¼ cup) beef bouillon or broth (canned is okay here), chilled
2 ounces (¼ cup) tomato juice
Juice of ½ lemon
Salt and freshly ground black pepper, to taste
1 thin lemon slice

1. Fill an Old Fashioned glass with ice cubes.

2. Pour the vodka over the ice, and stir to chill. Add the beef bouillon, tomato juice, and lemon juice and stir again. Top with a sprinkling of salt and pepper and a slice of lemon. Down the hatch.

Serves 1

KENTUCKY COLONEL

★ ★ ★

The Kentucky Colonel is a special drink at the Hotel Bel Air in Los Angeles. The head bartender during the 1940s and '50s, Spence, probably created the drink for Joseph Drowne, the former owner of the hotel, who was from Texas (not Kentucky) and a real bourbon fan.

Ice cubes
2 ounces (¼ cup) bourbon
1 ounce (2 tablespoons) Benedictine

1. Fill an Old Fashioned glass with ice cubes.

2. Fill a mixing glass with ice cubes. Add the bourbon and Benedictine, and shake well.

3. Strain into the Old Fashioned glass, and serve.

Serves 1

DALE'S MINT JULEP

★ ★ ★

According to Irena Chalmers, author and publisher, there are over 3,000 herbs in the mint family. Just think of the possibilities for julep recipes! The julep is one of the earliest American libations, and embraces a host of ingredients. Although nonalcoholic versions can be traced back to Persia as early as A.D. 1400, it is definitely the American South that has laid claim to this potent classic. Juleps have long been made with brandy (regular or peach), bourbon, rye, or rum, depending on which state you come from, and they have also been the cause of considerable commotion when it comes to the topic of garnish, everyone having very strong opinions. For instance, Virginians never bruise their mint, and they believe their brethren in Kentucky are heathens for doing so. Some old recipes even call for pineapple and peach along with mint! No other American drink seems to arouse such passion; this is Dale DeGroff's version.

2 large sprigs fresh mint
1 ounce (2 tablespoons) Southern Comfort
¼ teaspoon superfine sugar
Crushed ice
1½ ounces (3 tablespoons) bourbon

THE ALL-AMERICAN SPIRIT

Bourbon was William Faulkner's drink, and maybe your grandmother's, too. It's the most civil of spirits—smooth, sweet, and old-fashioned. But not passé. In fact, this classic Southern whiskey (most of it is from Kentucky and Tennessee) is making something of a comeback, and not only because homegrown is in. Bourbon is deeply satisfying, with a big, generous flavor that mixes genially with fruit brandies, liqueurs, bitters, fruit juice, and sparkling mixers. It's classy in ham or turkey glaze, and it's divine in chocolate cake. Connoisseurs take their bourbon neat, of course. I like it best in a traditional Mint Julep.

Bourbon is a type of whiskey, which means, among other things, that it's made from a mash of fermented grain, and aged in new charred oak barrels for two or more years. When a whiskey mash is at least 51 percent corn, then the resulting liquor qualifies as straight bourbon. Most bourbons are much more than half corn;

that's why they're so richly flavored. The term "sour mash" that you see on many bourbons refers to previously fermented mash that's used as starter for new fermentation. Virtually all bourbon makers use sour mash, though not all choose to say so on their labels.

With the surge of interest has come a bouquet of new, premium types: "single barrel" bourbons, which are the most admired; distinctive "small batch" bourbons, from select barrels; unfiltered bourbons; and "wheated" bourbons, made from mash that's part wheat. Each is unique, due to subtle but significant differences in distilling and aging. Tasters typically use words like "caramel," "maple," "oak," and "nutmeg" when describing fine bourbons; for high notes, they might say "lemon," "clover," or "new-mown hay." This is fancy talk for what was once a frontiersman's drink, but Faulkner would have understood.

1. Remove several leaves from 1 mint sprig and place them in a highball glass or silver mint julep cup.

2. Add the Southern Comfort and the superfine sugar. Using a spoon, muddle (see Note) to bruise or mash the mint.

3. Pack the glass full of crushed ice and pour in the bourbon. Agitate the mixture to frost the outside of the glass, garnish with the remaining mint sprig, and serve immediately.
Serves 1

NOTE: "Muddle" means to mash or crush; it's a term closely associated with the preparation of such classic drinks as a Mint Julep or Old Fashioned.

WISCONSIN CHERRY BOUNCE

★ ★ ★

A "bounce" is a drink, dating from Colonial times, made by pouring spirits over fruit and beefing up the result with sugar and, usually, spices; the name could very well indicate the effect the drink had on its imbibers. This particular libation was invented by descendants of the Scandinavians who settled in Door County, Wisconsin (the northern part of the peninsula, above Green Bay) where tart cherries are bountiful. Make this in the summer when sour cherries are in season—mid-July to early August—and then tuck it away for a special Christmas treat. Serve in delicate cordial glasses to ring in the holiday season.

2 cups ripe sour cherries with pits, stems removed
½ cup sugar
1 bottle (1 fifth) vodka

1. Place the cherries in a 1-liter sterilized bottle.

2. Combine the sugar and vodka in a small saucepan, and heat, stirring, over medium heat, until the sugar is completely dissolved, about 5 minutes. Let cool slightly, then, using a funnel if necessary, pour the mixture into the bottle.

3. Cap the bottle and place it in a cool dark place for at least 1 month, ideally 4 to 6 months. Discard the cherries when serving.

Makes about twenty-four 1-ounce servings

RAINBOW PUNCH

★ ★ ★

Rainbow Punch is the most popular nonalcoholic cocktail at New York's famous Rainbow Room.

Get festive with the garnish for this drink. Buy a citrus stripper from a gourmet kitchen store, make a spiral of orange zest and a spiral of lime zest, and wrap them around a wedge of pineapple. It's great that wacky tropical drinks have made a comeback! Maybe you can even find the little paper umbrellas.

Ice cubes
3 ounces (6 tablespoons) fresh orange juice
3 ounces (6 tablespoons) pineapple juice
½ ounce (1 tablespoon) fresh lime juice
½ ounce (1 tablespoon) Simple Sugar Syrup for Drinks (page 152)
2 dashes grenadine syrup
2 dashes Angostura bitters
Splash of club soda

Fill a mixing glass with ice cubes, and add all the ingredients except the club soda. Shake well. Strain into a large goblet, top with the club soda, and serve (add an exotic garnish if you like—see the headnote).

Serves 1

LIME RICKEY

★ ★ ★

This is the drinking man's nonalcoholic drink. Not that it's completely nonalcoholic—Angostura bitters, used in place of the more typical rickey ingredient of gin or whiskey, has, like vanilla extract, an alcoholic base.

1 ounce (2 tablespoons) fresh lime
*   juice*
1 ounce (2 tablespoons) Simple Sugar Syrup
*   for Drinks (page 152)*
3 dashes Angostura bitters
Ice cubes
4 ounces (½ cup) sparkling water
2 thin slices of lime, for garnish

1. Pour the lime juice, syrup, and bitters over ice cubes in a highball glass and stir.
2. Top with the sparkling water, garnish with the lime, and serve.
Serves 1

CITRUS CREAM

★ ★ ★

To me this always seems like an adult version of the orange ice pop with the vanilla ice cream center. It's delicious. (Don't forget, the juices must be fresh.)

Ice cubes
2 ounces (¼ cup) fresh orange juice
1 ounce (2 tablespoons) fresh
*   grapefruit juice*
1 ounce (2 tablespoons) Simple Sugar Syrup for
*   Drinks (page 152)*
¼ ounce (½ tablespoon) grenadine syrup
2 ounces (¼ cup) half-and-half or heavy
*   (or whipping) cream*
Pinch of ground cinnamon, for garnish

1. Chill a large cocktail glass in the refrigerator or freezer.
2. Fill a mixing glass with ice cubes. Add the juices, syrup, Grenadine, and half-and-half, and shake well.
3. Strain into the chilled cocktail glass, garnish with the pinch of cinnamon, and serve.
Serves 1

RAMOS FIZZ

★ ★ ★

Dale DeGroff told me that during his years at the Hotel Bel Air in Los Angeles, he cured thousands of hangovers with this soothing, creamy drink—the citrus provides vitamin C, yet the acid is low, and so is the alcohol content.

Ice cubes
1½ ounces (3 tablespoons) gin
½ ounce (1 tablespoon) fresh lemon juice
½ ounce (1 tablespoon) fresh lime juice
1 small egg white
1 ounce (2 tablespoons) milk
2 ounces (¼ cup) Simple Sugar Syrup for Drinks
*   (page 152)*
1 dash orange-flower water
1 ounce (2 tablespoons) club soda

1. Fill a cocktail shaker with ice cubes. Add all the ingredients except the club soda, and shake until you think your arms will fall off.

2. Strain into a small highball or Fizz glass, top with the club soda, and serve.

Serves 1

VIRGIN KIR ROYALE

★ ★ ★

There are many still and sparkling nonalcoholic wines on the market. Although many of them do not taste very good alone, they are excellent as a base for nonalcoholic cocktails.

1 ounce (2 tablespoons) raspberry syrup
5 ounces (½ cup plus 2 tablespoons) nonalcoholic
 sparkling wine, cold
1 strip lemon zest, for garnish
1 fresh raspberry, for garnish

Pour the raspberry syrup into a champagne flute, and fill it slowly with the sparkling wine. Garnish with the lemon zest and raspberry, and serve.

Serves 1

VIRGIN MELON DAIQUIRI

★ ★ ★

When melons are sweet, make pitchers of this ambrosia. For the drinkers in the party, just add a shot of rum.

½ cup cubed honeydew and muskmelon,
 mixed
3 ounces (6 tablespoons) nonalcoholic
 white wine, cold
2 ounces (¼ cup) Simple Sugar Syrup for Drinks
 (page 152)
1 ounce (2 tablespoons) fresh lemon juice
¾ cup cracked or crushed ice
1 small piece fresh melon, for garnish
1 ripe strawberry, for garnish

Place the cubed melon, the wine, syrup, and lemon juice in a blender. Add the ice, and purée. Pour into a large goblet, garnish with the melon and strawberry, and serve.

Serves 1

VIRGIN ROYAL HAWAIIAN

★ ★ ★

The original gin-based Royal Hawaiian was *the* drink at the Royal Hawaiian Hotel in Honolulu many years ago, and it's still popular today, enjoying its part in the revival of classic cocktails all over the U.S. To recreate the original, just add a shot of gin.

Ice cubes
3 ounces (6 tablespoons) pineapple juice
1 ounce (2 tablespoons) orgeat syrup (see Note)
1 ounce (2 tablespoons) fresh lemon juice
½ ounce (1 tablespoon) Simple Sugar Syrup for
    Drinks (this page)

1. Chill a cocktail glass in the refrigerator or freezer.
2. Fill a mixing glass with ice cubes and add all the ingredients. Shake well, strain into the chilled glass, and serve.
Serves 1

NOTE: Orgeat syrup is a creamy almond syrup. You'll find it with the Italian specialties in better food stores.

GINGER SPICE COOLER

★ ★ ★

Adding bitters and ginger beer to nonalcoholic wine gives it zing and fizz and makes the drink both special and fun.

Ice cubes
4 ounces (½ cup) nonalcoholic white wine, cold
2 dashes Angostura bitters
3 ounces (6 tablespoons) Jamaican ginger beer soda,
    cold
1 strip fresh sugar cane or seasonal fruit,
    for garnish

1. Fill a large goblet with ice cubes. Stir in the wine and the bitters, and top with the ginger beer.
2. Garnish with a strip of sugar cane or a small piece of fruit, and serve.
Serves 1

SIMPLE SUGAR SYRUP FOR DRINKS

★ ★ ★

2 cups water
1 cup sugar

1. Combine the water and sugar in a saucepan. Bring to a simmer, and continue simmering, stirring occasionally, until the sugar dissolves, 3 to 4 minutes.
2. Cool, and refrigerate in a closed container. Use as needed. The syrup will keep for up to 3 months.
Makes about 2½ cups

Complements

I find that parties go best when guests are warmed up by more than just drinks. Cocktail foods heighten an evening's fun. They titillate palates, calm hunger, and help break the ice among guests. Miniature fritters, pancakes, and club sandwiches can even act as conversation starters. They designate an occasion as special, something outside the ordinary.

Pass around Deep South Crab Dollop before sitting your friends down for a Mardi Gras supper. If you're cooking Southwestern, whet their appetites with Crispy Shrimp Nestled in a Blanket, liberally seasoned with lime and jalapeño. You'll find pickled shrimp from the Florida Panhandle, smoked salmon spread from Seattle, and Pacific Rim–inspired chicken kebabs from San Francisco. And the pride of Buffalo's Anchor Bar, Buffalo Chicken Wings, which nowadays are made in all fifty states. What better way to preface an all-American meal?

CONFETTI CORN FRITTERS

★ ★ ★

Invite everyone into the kitchen so these fritters can be fried to order and served piping hot. The small dice of red pepper and the corn kernels not only add flavor, but give the fritters a lighter, more interesting texture. Drain the fritters well to ensure that they are greaseless. If your kitchen isn't big enough to hold a crowd, serve them in a basket lined with a linen napkin to keep them nice and toasty.

1 cup fresh or frozen corn kernels
1 red bell pepper, stemmed, seeded, and
  cut into ⅛-inch dice
1½ cups all-purpose flour
½ cup yellow cornmeal
1 tablespoon baking powder
1 tablespoon sugar
2 teaspoons chili powder
1½ teaspoons ground cumin
1 teaspoon salt
½ teaspoon freshly ground black pepper
⅛ teaspoon cayenne pepper
2 large eggs, lightly beaten
1 cup milk
2 tablespoons snipped fresh chives
Vegetable or corn oil, for frying
Hot Stuff Tartar Sauce (recipe follows),
  for serving

1. Bring a pot of lightly salted water to a boil, and blanch the corn for 2 minutes. Remove with a slotted spoon and drain. Repeat with the bell pepper. Drain and reserve.

2. Sift the flour, cornmeal, baking powder, sugar, chili powder, cumin, salt, black pepper, and cayenne together into a large mixing bowl.

3. In a separate bowl, mix together the eggs, milk, chives, and the reserved corn and red bell pepper. Add to the flour mixture and stir to combine. Let rest, covered, in the refrigerator for 30 minutes.

4. Pour oil to a depth of 1 inch in a deep, heavy pot and heat it over medium heat to 370°F. Using a ½-teaspoon measuring spoon, drop 5 to 6 spoonfuls of the batter into the oil, being careful not to splatter. Do not crowd the pot. Use a slotted spoon to turn the fritters as needed to brown them evenly.

5. Cook the fritters until they are golden brown, about 1 minute, and remove from the oil with the slotted spoon. Drain well on paper towels. Serve immediately, along with a bowl of Hot Stuff Tartar Sauce for dipping.

Makes about 100 fritters

Hot Stuff Tartar Sauce

—★—

When you want to add some spice to Confetti Corn Fritters or Hot Time Party Shrimp, whip up some Hot Stuff. Serve it in a snazzy bowl alongside, but warn dippers to go a little easy—

this can be a powerful sauce. If you prefer less heat, check page 440 for a milder Tartar Sauce.

1 cup mayonnaise
1 teaspoon Dijon mustard
1 teaspoon tomato paste
1 teaspoon finely grated lemon zest
1 tablespoon fresh lemon juice
2 dashes Tabasco sauce, or to taste
2 tablespoons very finely chopped sweet pickle
2 tablespoons finely minced shallots
2 tablespoons chopped fresh flat-leaf parsley
1 teaspoon finely minced and seeded fresh
  jalapeño pepper
1 tablespoon tiny capers, drained
Salt and freshly ground black pepper,
  to taste

Combine the mayonnaise, mustard, tomato paste, lemon zest, lemon juice, Tabasco sauce, and pickles in a bowl. Stir in the shallots, parsley, jalapeño, capers, and salt and pepper. Refrigerate, covered, for at least 1 hour for the flavors to blend, and for up to 2 days.
  Makes about 1¼ cups

COCKTAIL CORN CAKES

★ ★ ★

These little corn cakes are delightful canapes, topped with any number of garnishes, such as a tiny dollop of finely mashed avocado, a few grains of fresh salmon caviar, or a sprinkle of snipped chives.

2 cups cooked corn kernels
⅔ cup heavy (or whipping) cream
⅔ cup yellow cornmeal
⅔ cup all-purpose flour
1 teaspoon baking powder
½ teaspoon salt
⅛ teaspoon freshly ground black pepper
3 large eggs, lightly beaten
⅓ cup unsalted butter, melted
¼ cup vegetable oil, or more if necessary

1. Combine the corn and cream in a food processor or blender, and purée. Transfer the mixture to a bowl.

2. Stir the cornmeal, flour, baking powder, salt, and pepper into the purée. Add the eggs and melted butter, and combine well.

3. Place about 2 teaspoons of the oil in a nonstick skillet over medium-high heat. Add the batter to the pan in teaspoonfuls, about 6 at a time. Cook until golden brown, about 1 minute per side. Drain on paper towels. Continue until all of the batter is used, adding more oil to the skillet as necessary. Serve on a pretty tray with little cocktail napkins.
  Makes about 100 cakes

ZUCCHINI HERB PANCAKES

★ ★ ★

This mixture of grated zucchini and potatoes makes some of the lightest little pancakes I know. They're original enough to serve as an hors d'oeuvre, topped with a dot of Velvety Mango Cream, at the most elegant cocktail party. They also make a flavorful base for a mini-spoonful of caviar. Serve with cocktail napkins.

2 peeled zucchini (1 pound), coarsely grated
1 teaspoon coarse salt
1 russet potato, peeled
1 tablespoon chopped fresh tarragon, or
   1 teaspoon dried
2 tablespoons all-purpose flour
Salt and coarsely ground black pepper, to taste
1 large egg, beaten
2 tablespoons olive oil
2 tablespoons unsalted butter
½ cup Velvety Mango Cream (page 135), for serving

1. Place the grated zucchini in a colander, sprinkle with the coarse salt, and let drain for 30 minutes. Rinse and drain well, squeezing out as much liquid as possible in a kitchen towel. Pat dry again with a paper towel, and place in a bowl.

2. Coarsely grate the potato, working quickly to avoid discoloration, and add it to the zucchini, along with any liquid given off. Toss together with the tarragon, flour, salt, and pepper. Add the egg and combine well.

3. Heat 1 tablespoon each of the olive oil and the butter in a large nonstick skillet over medium-high heat until slightly foamy.

4. Spoon 1 level tablespoon of the vegetable mixture into the skillet for each pancake (cook about 5 at a time), and press with the back of a spatula to flatten them—they should be about 2 inches across. Cook until golden, 3 minutes per side, adding the remaining tablespoon each of oil and butter as necessary.

5. Drain on paper towels. Serve immediately, or make ahead, and 15 minutes before serving time, place on a baking sheet, cover loosely with aluminum foil, and heat in a low (250°F) oven. Top each pancake with a tiny dollop of Velvety Mango Cream, and serve.

Makes about 25 pancakes

LITTLE CARROT GINGER PANCAKES

★ ★ ★

These are some wild little cakes, with their touch of ginger. If you decide to make them in a larger size as a main course or side dish, serve applesauce alongside for a winner accompaniment; the recipe will make about fifteen 3-inch pancakes.

6 carrots (¾ pound), peeled and coarsely grated
1 russet potato, peeled
3 tablespoons snipped fresh chives
1 tablespoon grated fresh ginger
2 teaspoons finely grated orange zest
2 tablespoons all-purpose flour
Salt and coarsely ground black pepper, to taste
1 large egg, beaten
2 tablespoons olive oil
2 tablespoons unsalted butter

1. Place the carrots in a bowl. Coarsely grate the potato, working quickly to avoid discoloration, and add it to the carrots, along with any liquid given off. Add the chives, ginger, and orange zest, and toss to combine. Sprinkle with the flour, salt, and pepper, and mix. Add the egg and combine well.

2. Heat 1 tablespoon each of the olive oil and the butter in a large nonstick skillet over medium-high heat until slightly foamy.

3. Spoon 1 level tablespoon of the vegetable mixture into the skillet for each pancake (cook about 5 at a time), and press with the back of a spatula to flatten them—they should be about 2 inches across. Cook until golden, 3 minutes per side, adding the remaining tablespoons of oil and butter as necessary.

4. Drain on paper towels. Serve immediately, or make ahead and, 15 minutes before serving time, place on a baking sheet, cover with aluminum foil, and heat in a low (250°F) oven.

Makes about 30 pancakes

LITTLE BEET HORSERADISH PANCAKES

★ ★ ★

Diminutive pancakes served with a flavorful mayonnaise are light and colorful, and satisfy a range of appetites. I am partial to these because I find the sweet taste of beets countered by the subtle bite of horseradish a particularly compelling combination. While I enjoy serving them on their own, as I do all the vegetable pancakes, a variety—these plus the Zucchini Herb and Little Carrot Ginger—arranged on a tray decorated with fresh flowers, makes a spectacular presentation. All three can be made in advance, then reheated in a 250°F oven for 15 minutes before serving.

1 pound beets, peeled and grated
½ pound russet potatoes, peeled and grated
1 large egg, lightly beaten
2 tablespoons all-purpose flour
1 tablespoon prepared horseradish, drained
Salt and freshly ground black
*   pepper, to taste*
3 tablespoons olive oil
3 tablespoons unsalted butter
Avocado Mint Mayonnaise
*   (page 103), for serving*

1. Place the grated beets and potatoes in a bowl. Add the egg and mix well. Add the flour and toss to combine. Stir in the horseradish, salt, and pepper.

2. Heat 1 tablespoon each of the olive oil and the butter in a large nonstick skillet over medium-high heat until slightly foamy.

3. Spoon a tablespoon of the beet mixture into the skillet for each pancake (cook about 5 at a time), and press with the back of a spatula to flatten them—they should be about 2 inches across. Cook until browned, 3 to 4 minutes per side, adding the remaining oil and butter as necessary. Drain on paper towels. Top each pancake with a tiny dollop of Avocado Mint Mayonnaise, and serve.

Makes about 30 pancakes

CAJUN SPICED PECANS

★ ★ ★

I find pecans, the quintessential Southern nut, irresistible. Here I've spiced them up with the zydeco flavors of the Bayou towns of Abbeyville and New Iberia and the Cajun Deep South. Pop some into your mouth while you're enjoying lots of good talk and good music. Plan to make these

★★★★★★★★★★★★★★★★★★★★★★★★★★

ZYDECO

—❦—

How did the lively rural music, heard throughout southwestern Louisiana, but particularly on the bayous and prairies, come to be called "zydeco"? Glad you asked. As I've heard it, there are a couple of theories. The music—generally played by a band consisting of a piano accordion, washboard, lead and bass guitars, and a drum—was originally called (and also still is) "la la" music. Then, in 1950, Clifton Chenier, the king of la la, had a hit song entitled, "Les Haricots ne Sont pas Salés," which translates as "The Beans Are Not Salted." The Cajun pronunciation of the words *les haricots* is thought to have evolved into the word "zydeco" and became tied to that style of music. And that's theory number one.

The other ties the derivation into the phrase *fais do-do*, the Cajun term for putting on a dance. When slurred just right, that too could easily evolve into zydeco.

And there you have it. Either way, it is impossible *not* to dance to this zesty music—unless you've stopped briefly to eat equally irresistible Cajun cuisine.

★★★★★★★★★★★★★★★★★★★★★★★★★★

on a day when the humidity is low so they will dry thoroughly. This recipe can be doubled—just use two baking sheets.

2 tablespoons unsalted butter
1 tablespoon olive oil
1 tablespoon Worcestershire sauce
½ teaspoon Tabasco sauce
¾ teaspoon ground cumin
½ teaspoon sweet paprika
½ teaspoon garlic powder
2 cups pecan halves
2 teaspoons coarse salt

1. Preheat the oven to 325°F.
2. Heat the butter and the oil in a medium-size heavy saucepan over low heat. Add the Worcestershire, Tabasco, cumin, paprika, and garlic powder. Stir, and simmer gently over low heat to blend the flavors, 2 to 3 minutes.
3. Add the nuts and toss them to coat. Spread the nuts in a single layer on a baking sheet, and bake for 15 minutes, shaking the pan occasionally.
4. Pour the hot nuts into a bowl and toss with the coarse salt. Spread them out on the baking sheet again, and let cool to room temperature. Store in an airtight container.

Makes about 2 cups

TINY TOMATO SURPRISES

★ ★ ★

When I was growing up, lunch at Schrafft's was my idea of heaven on earth. Schrafft's was a chain of marvelous luncheon restaurants beloved by women. Perfect sandwiches, salads, and other fare was served with meticulous care by Irish waitresses in trim black uniforms and white aprons and caps. My favorite Schrafft's lunch was the "Tomato Surprise," a zigzag-edged tomato shell stuffed with tuna, chicken, crab, shrimp, or egg salad and garnished with a small sprig of curly parsley. My memories have carried me right into the cocktail hour with this one-bite hors d'oeuvre—cherry tomatoes stuffed with shrimp salad napped in a creamy, herb-spiked avocado mayonnaise.

100 tiny cherry tomatoes (about 2 pints)
1 pound medium shrimp, peeled and
*   deveined*
⅓ cup mayonnaise
⅓ cup sour cream
1 tablespoon fresh lime juice
½ small avocado, peeled
2 tablespoons snipped fresh chives
1 tablespoon chopped fresh dill
Salt and freshly ground black pepper,
*   to taste*

1. With a small paring knife, cut a small slice off the tops of the cherry tomatoes and use a small spoon, like a demitasse spoon, to carefully hollow them out. Discard the pulp and set the tomato shells aside.

2. Bring a pot of water to a boil. Add the shrimp, reduce the heat to a simmer, and cook until cooked through, 1 minute. Drain, and allow to cool. Cut the shrimp into very tiny dice.

3. Place the mayonnaise, sour cream, lime juice, and avocado in a bowl and mash together with a fork. Stir in 1 tablespoon of the chives and the dill, and season with salt and pepper. Add the shrimp, and stir well.

4. With the small spoon, carefully stuff the shrimp salad into the tomatoes. Make sure to stuff them all the way to the bottom to prevent the tomatoes from rolling over. Place on baking sheets, cover with plastic wrap, and refrigerate

for up to 30 minutes before serving. Arrange decoratively on a platter, sprinkle with the remaining 1 tablespoon chives, and serve.
Makes 100 pieces

MORE COCKTAIL TOMATO SURPRISES

★ ★ ★

A refreshing one-bite surprise to serve with a chilled glass of California Riesling or frothy American lager. Light as a feather, these crab curry–stuffed tomatoes will make a nice beginning to a party on a festive summer evening.

100 cherry tomatoes (about 2 pints)
½ cup mayonnaise
2 teaspoons finely chopped mango chutney
2 teaspoons curry powder
½ pound fresh lump crabmeat, picked over
*   for shell and cartilage*
3 tablespoons dried currants
2 tablespoons very finely minced celery
2 tablespoons very finely minced Granny Smith
*   apple*
Salt, to taste
2 tablespoons snipped fresh chives, for
*   garnish*

1. With a small paring knife, cut a small slice off the tops of the cherry tomatoes and use a small spoon, like a demitasse spoon, to carefully hollow them out. Discard the pulp and set the tomato shells aside.

2. In a bowl, combine the mayonnaise, chutney, and curry powder. Add the crabmeat, breaking it up into smaller pieces with a fork, along with the currants, celery, and apple. Season with salt and toss well.

3. With the small spoon, carefully stuff the crab salad into the tomatoes. Make sure to stuff them all the way to the bottom to prevent them from rolling over. Place on baking sheets, cover with plastic wrap, and refrigerate for up to 30 minutes before serving. Arrange decoratively on a platter, sprinkle with the chives, and serve.

Makes 100 pieces

ALL-AMERICAN DEVILED EGGS

★ ★ ★

While they might seem passé, whenever I ask someone what they think of as a typical American cocktail food, without taking a breath they answer "deviled eggs." So how could I resist including them in my U.S.A. book? Great deviled eggs require perfectly hard-cooked eggs and just the right proportion of spices. A dollop of salmon caviar on each egg would put these front and center on a swanky cocktail tray.

6 large eggs
1 teaspoon Dijon mustard
1 to 2 dashes Tabasco sauce
Salt, to taste
¼ teaspoon freshly ground black pepper
1 tablespoon snipped fresh chives
3 tablespoons mayonnaise
Paprika, for garnish
Whole fresh chives, for garnish

1. Place the eggs in a saucepan. Gently rinse them with warm water and drain them. Cover the eggs with cold water, place the pan over medium-high heat, and bring to a boil. Reduce the heat to a gentle simmer and cook for exactly 13 minutes. Drain the eggs, rinse under cold water, and peel. Let them cool in the refrigerator, loosely covered, for 15 minutes.

2. Halve the eggs lengthwise, and carefully scoop out the yolks. Place the yolks in a bowl and mash them with a fork. Add the mustard, Tabasco, salt, pepper, and chives. Stir in the mayonnaise.

WHAT THE DEVIL'S A DEVIL?

— ❧ —

We Americans credit the devil for some of our zingiest fare, including Devils on Horseback (oysters wrapped in bacon and seasoned with lemon juice and hot pepper sauce), deviled crab (crabmeat in cream, mustard, and cayenne), and deviled almonds (tossed with butter, chutney, pickles, Worcestershire sauce, salt, and cayenne). The devil shows up in the name of a dish as the result of one of two possibilities: When a dish is prepared with mustard, hot pepper sauce, or cayenne pepper, making it hot or spicy; or when it is sinfully, temptingly, devilishly dark and rich—devil's food cake, for example. But clearly you can enjoy a little devil's fare and still keep the faith.

3. Fill the whites with the egg yolk mixture, and dust the tops with paprika. Arrange the eggs in a spoke design on a decorative platter garnished with whole chives.
Makes 12 halves

OYSTERS ROCKEFELLER

★ ★ ★

Oysters Rockefeller, one of America's classic grand recipes, is steeped in tradition going back to its invention in the late 1800s. Jules Alciatore, of Antoine's Restaurant in New Orleans, created the deluxe dish and named it after one of the richest men in the United States, John D. Rockefeller. While the story of its origin has remained pretty much intact through the years, the recipe has evolved chef by chef (including in my kitchen), until only a few of the original ingredients remain as formulated. The formula for the greens atop the oysters remains an Antoine's secret. I've tried my hand with Swiss chard, fennel, and tarragon to enhance the original anise-flavored cordial that was included. I have followed the traditional cooking method—on a bed of rock salt, which not only holds the oysters steady but holds in the heat as well. If you choose not to cook them on the rock salt, simply place the oysters on a baking sheet. They will still be plenty hot and very delicious. I figure on four oysters per person.

Wine: Napa Valley (CA) sparkling wine

1 large bunch green Swiss chard (about 1 pound), well rinsed
6 tablespoons (¾ stick) unsalted butter
¼ cup finely chopped shallots
¼ cup finely chopped fennel bulb
1 tablespoon chopped fresh tarragon, or 1½ teaspoons dried
2 tablespoons Pernod liqueur
Salt and freshly ground black pepper, to taste
¼ cup fine dry bread crumbs
24 oysters on the half shell
6 cups rock salt

1. Preheat the broiler.
2. Cut out the large white stems from the Swiss chard, and coarsely chop the leaves.
3. Melt the butter in a nonstick skillet over low heat. Add the shallots and fennel, and wilt, covered, for 5 minutes, stirring once or twice. Add the Swiss chard and tarragon. Stir to combine. Cover, and cook over medium-low heat for 5 minutes. Stir in the Pernod, and season with salt and pepper. Let the mixture cool slightly.
4. Place the greens and the bread crumbs in a blender and blend for about 1 minute. Turn the motor off and scrape down the sides.
5. Using a small sharp knife, carefully cut from underneath each oyster to free it from its shell. Hold the oyster level to retain the liquor.
6. Spoon a teaspoon of the vegetable mixture on top of each oyster, patting it down lightly with the tines of a fork. Place a 1-inch layer of rock salt in an attractive 12-inch round oven-to-table dish. Place the oysters on the rock salt, pushing the shells down into the salt to anchor them. Place the dish under the broiler, 3 inches from the heat source, and broil for 2 to 3 minutes. Remove, and serve immediately.
Serves 8

The Art of Oyster Eating

★ ★ ★

I first met Jon Rowley, the renowned Seattle-based seafood consultant years ago at a Columbia River spring chinook salmon and Oregon Pinot Noir dinner he arranged at the New York restaurant, Sign of the Dove. Now, whenever I have a seafood question, I always give him a call.

I'm passionate about oysters, as are so many people, and love to listen to Jon talk about these favorite bivalves. I don't believe there is anyone more knowledgeable on the subject, so when I was writing this book, I asked him to tell me his thoughts on the mystique involved in eating an oyster. Here's what he had to say.

From Jon:

The oyster, perhaps more than any other food, is a feast for all the senses. A feast for your eyes first of all. Raw oysters are traditionally served on a platter of shaved ice in a symmetrical circular pattern with bills (fronts) outward, like the petals of a flower. If of good quality and opened well, oysters served icy cold, glistening brightly in their own juices, are beautiful unto themselves, needing no garnish to attract the eye or the imagination. Forgo the fork and pick up a shell. When you feel the cold damp roughness of the oyster shell, your salivary glands perk up in anticipation. You are already starting to "taste" the oyster. As you lift the oyster to your mouth, pause momentarily to smell the sea. The sooner the oyster is off the shucking knife, the more compelling the oceanic fragrance. Now tilt your head back, close your eyes, and slurp in the oyster and its juices together. If the oyster has been iced down before opening and is minutes or less off the shucking knife, the oyster is as cold and vibrant as an icy gust of wind at low tide.

Before concentrating on what you taste, experience the sensation of the oyster. M.F.K. Fisher, the doyenne of American oyster poets, referred adoringly to the oyster's "strange, cold succulence." Novelist Tom Robbins, whose Thanksgiving dinner consists of oysters, caviar, and very good Champagne, likens this sensation to "French-kissing a mermaid."

As you carefully chew the oyster, your palate becomes inundated with a variety of distinct tastes that come in succession. If the oyster is well fed, plump, and firm, the first taste is sweetness from the glycogen, which the warmth of your mouth is already breaking down into sugars. The sweet taste dissipates quickly, then comes a succession of brine, various mineral, algal, and other mollusk flavors on the tip, sides, and finally on the back of your tongue and the soft palate at the back of your mouth. Each oyster has a unique lineup of flavors. The most intriguing, most difficult to describe, and certainly the most important taste when it comes to combining with wine or ale, is the aftertaste, or finish—those flavors that linger after the oyster is swallowed. Some of the aftertaste is actually sensation—an enlivening of the tongue, cheeks, and the roof of your mouth.

When you have swallowed the oyster and its juices, invigorate the mouth with a brisk dry white wine, or a malty porter or stout. Take a bite of a crusty light rye bread, like a French seigle, to neutralize the tastebuds, and then go to the next oyster.

Oysters are always a beginning, a prelude to a life-enriching experience yet to come.

Aw Shucks!

Earlier I mention that for oysters to be a feast for the eyes, they must be opened well. Oyster shucking is an art. On top of species differences, each individual oyster is uniquely formed and uniquely challenging to open. No one has yet been able to invent a mechanical oyster opener that will out-perform the hand of a skilled human shucker. There are many styles of oyster knives, and regional as well as individual shucking techniques. Some commercial shuckers go through the bill, of the oyster; some go through the side. Most restaurant shuckers open from the hinge or the back of the oyster to avoid shell fragments.

In the time it takes to pick up an oyster and position it cup side down, an expert oyster opener has already devised the plan of attack. With amazing skill and speed, the shucker finds the invisible soft area in the hinge, "pops" the shell with a twist of the knife, then darts the knife deftly forward over the top of the meat to sever the adductor muscle that holds the two shells, or valves, together. After the top shell is flicked away, the shucker goes under the meat with the knife to sever the adductor on the bottom shell so the oyster can be properly slurped. (In France, the bottom adductor is left attached to the shell to show freshness.)

A well-shucked oyster presents itself firm, plump, glistening in its own juices, contentedly unaware of what has just taken place so artfully at its expense. The meat and mantle are free from grit and unscathed by the shucker's knife work. Most half-shell oysters are eaten in restaurants. The task of opening oysters is too daunting for most people. Actually, it is easier than it seems if you have the right tool and a little guidance in technique.

1. Wash the oysters, especially the notch at the hinge, with cold running water to remove grit and sand. You may need a stiff brush.

2. Before opening, place the oysters in ice for 1 hour so they are well chilled when served.

3. You should not shuck bare-handed. Instead, use a thick glove or a folded kitchen towel to cushion the oyster and protect your hand. Holding the oyster in one hand cup side down, hinge toward you, use the other hand to insert the oyster knife into the hinge. Twist and rock the knife and oyster together, applying gentle pressure. As soon as you feel the point of the knife penetrate the hinge, twist the blade to pop the shell, and run the point of the blade forward over the meat along the inside of the top shell to sever the adductor muscle.

4. Discard the top shell. Cut under the oyster meat to release it from the bottom shell, being careful to retain as much liquid as possible.

5. Place the opened oyster in its bottom shell on a bed of crushed ice. The desired result is a perfect oyster meat untouched by the knife. If you did nick the meat, flip it over. Nobody will know but you. In fact, some professional shuckers routinely flip oyster meats, believing bottoms up is a better look.

PANHANDLE PICKLED SHRIMP

★ ★ ★

A fine Jacksonville cook and author of the *Seasonal Florida* cookbook, Jo Manning has graciously shared her recipe for these delicious pickled shrimp. Bright pink in color, with glimpses of pale yellow peeking through, these shrimp are so pretty that I recommend serving them in the jar to showcase their natural beauty. They would be a perfect picnic starter or late summer hors d'oeuvre. One important tip: Be sure not to overcook the shrimp, or they will end up tough and stringy. One minute is enough because they will continue to "cook" in the marinade.

¾ cup water
½ cup olive oil
½ cup vegetable oil
⅓ cup fresh lemon juice
2 lemons, cut into ⅛-inch-thick
  slices
10 black peppercorns
3 small bay leaves
1½ teaspoons sugar
1½ teaspoons salt
½ teaspoon dill seeds
½ teaspoon mustard seeds
¼ teaspoon celery seeds
⅛ teaspoon freshly ground black pepper
2½ pounds medium shrimp, peeled and deveined
1 medium onion, cut into ¼-inch-thick slices and
  separated into rings
¼ cup chopped fresh flat-leaf parsley

1. Place all of the ingredients except the shrimp, onion, and parsley in a large, deep nonreactive pot. Bring to a boil and simmer, uncovered, for 10 minutes.

2. Add the shrimp and simmer briefly, until they just turn pink, about 1 minute. Do not overcook. Using a slotted spoon, transfer the shrimp to a bowl. Set the cooking liquid aside to cool.

3. In a large wide-mouthed glass jar with a screw top, arrange a layer of some of the shrimp, then some of the onion rings, and some parsley; repeat the layers until all the ingredients are used, covering each layer as you go with the cooking liquid. Cover, and refrigerate for 24 hours before serving. The shrimp will keep in the refrigerator for 1 week. Serve with toothpicks and paper cocktail napkins to catch the drips.
Serves 10 to 12

CILANTRO PESTO GRILLED SHRIMP

★ ★ ★

The best shrimp-off-the-grill that I have ever tasted were at Rosario's in San Antonio. They're swathed in luxurious cilantro pesto, the buttery smoothness of pine nuts (also called piñon nuts or pignoli) mellowing the bite of garlic. They inspired me to create this recipe. Leave the tails on the shrimp so they're easy to pick up.

Wine: Finger Lakes (NY) dry Riesling
Beer: Texas Belgian-style white beer

1½ pounds (about 36) large shrimp, peeled,
  deveined, tails left on
¾ cup San Antonio Cilantro Piñon Pesto (recipe follows)

1. Place the shrimp in a bowl, and toss them with 6 tablespoons of the pesto. Set aside to marinate for 30 minutes.

2. Preheat a grill to high heat, or preheat the broiler.

3. Thread the shrimp crosswise onto long metal skewers, about five to six to a skewer. Grill or broil the skewers in batches, 3 inches from the coals or heating element, for 3 minutes per side.

4. Remove the shrimp from the skewers and place them in bowl. Toss with the remaining 6 tablespoons pesto, and serve immediately.

Serves 6 to 8

San Antonio Cilantro Piñon Pesto

———★———

In the melting pot of American cuisine, pesto doesn't necessarily mean basil anymore. Here I give it a Southwest twang, using cilantro leaves as the herb of choice to liven up grilled shrimp or add punch to grilled salmon or poultry.

3 cups (loosely packed) fresh cilantro leaves,
*   rinsed and patted thoroughly dry*
2 tablespoons pine (piñon) nuts
1 teaspoon minced garlic
Pinch of ground cumin
Salt and freshly ground black pepper,
*   to taste*
½ cup extra virgin olive oil

1. Place the cilantro leaves in the bowl of a food processor and pulse the machine on and off until the leaves are coarsely chopped. Add the pine nuts, garlic, cumin, and salt and pepper and pulse the machine on and off until the mixture is well chopped but not puréed.

2. With the machine running, slowly drizzle in the olive oil through the feed tube and process until the mixture is smooth and well combined. Transfer to a glass jar with a lid and refrigerate, covered, up to 3 days.

Makes about ¾ cup

CRISPY SHRIMP NESTLED IN A BLANKET

★ ★ ★

Infused with the spices of the Southwest, these crispy cocktail shrimp are at home anywhere in the country that there's a party is going on. Serve them in a straw basket, offer Sweet Jalapeño Sauce as a dip, and watch them disappear. Be sure to leave the tails on the shrimp to serve as natural handles—it makes eating so much tidier! But do remember to have a little bowl or dish handy for guests to dispose of the leftover tails.

2 tablespoons fresh lime juice
1 teaspoon finely grated lime zest
1 teaspoon finely chopped seeded fresh jalapeño
  pepper
½ teaspoon ground cumin
½ teaspoon chili powder
Pinch of ground cinnamon
Pinch of cayenne pepper
Salt, to taste
32 large shrimp (about 1⅓ pounds), peeled
  and deveined, tails left on
4 sheets (approximately 17 x 12 inches each)
  frozen phyllo pastry, thawed
½ cup (1 stick) unsalted butter, melted
2 to 3 tablespoons vegetable oil
Sweet Jalapeño Sauce (recipe follows),
  for serving

1. Combine the lime juice, lime zest, jalapeño pepper, cumin, chili powder, cinnamon, cayenne, and salt in a medium-size bowl.

2. Add the shrimp and toss well to coat with the marinade. Let rest, loosely covered, at room temperature for 1 hour.

3. Lay the thawed phyllo pastry sheets on a dish towel. Cover the pastry with a sheet of waxed paper and then a slightly dampened dish towel and set aside until ready to use.

4. Place 1 sheet of phyllo lengthwise in front of you on a clean work surface. Brush it all over with melted butter. Cover with a second sheet of phyllo and brush it with butter. Cut the phyllo crosswise into eight 2-inch-wide strips. Then cut it in half lengthwise. You should have sixteen 6 x 2-inch rectangles. Drain the shrimp. Place one shrimp at the bottom of a strip so the tail will be exposed when the shrimp is rolled up in the pastry. Roll it up neatly, then brush the phyllo roll all over with melted butter, and set aside. Repeat with more shrimp until the phyllo strips are used up, then repeat the procedure with the last 2 sheets of phyllo and remaining shrimp.

5. Heat 1 tablespoon of the oil in a nonstick skillet over medium-high heat. Cook the shrimp, about 8 to a batch until brown, 30 seconds per side. Drain on paper towels, and serve immediately with the Sweet Jalapeño Sauce for dipping.

Makes 32 pieces

Sweet Jalapeño Sauce

★

Sweet, rich, and just the right flavor for dipping well-spiced Crispy Shrimp, serve this sauce in a small bowl in the center of a colorful tray with the shrimp arranged around it. Sweet Jalapeño Sauce also has just the right zest for dipping San Fran Chicken Kebabs.

¾ cup jalapeño jelly
¾ cup apple juice
¼ cup (packed) dark brown sugar
1 tablespoon cider vinegar
1 tablespoon minced garlic
1 teaspoon finely grated lime zest
½ teaspoon salt

1. Combine all of the ingredients in a heavy saucepan. Simmer gently over medium-low heat, uncovered, stirring occasionally, until the sauce thickens and has reduced to a jam-like consistency, 30 minutes.

2. Cool to room temperature and refrigerate, covered, until the sauce thickens, or up to 1 week. Remove the sauce from the refrigerator 20 minutes before use.

Makes about 1 cup

HOT TIME PARTY SHRIMP

★ ★ ★

Add some zing and some zip to your usual party fare with fried shrimp coated in hot Cajun-inspired spices, and crowned with Hot Stuff Tartar Sauce. Rock shrimp, fished off the coast of Maine and the east coast of Florida, are perfect for these zesty bites. The meat is firm and sweet and very similar in taste to lobster. Buy rock shrimp shelled if you can. If not, peel them carefully—wearing rubber gloves will prevent scrapes caused by working with the tough shells. Cut along the outer curve of the tail with scissors, then pull the shell away to release the meat. Remove the vein, rinse off, and pat dry with paper towels. Rock shrimp should be eaten on the day they are purchased

because they do not keep well. If you can't find rock shrimp, large shrimp will do.

1 pound rock shrimp, peeled, or large shrimp,
*   peeled and cut into thirds*
1 cup yellow cornmeal
2 teaspoons chili powder
1 teaspoon ground cumin
1 teaspoon salt
½ teaspoon cayenne pepper
1 cup milk
1 cup corn oil
Hot Stuff Tartar Sauce (page 154)

1. Devein and rinse the shrimp. Pat dry on paper towels.

2. Combine the cornmeal, chili powder, cumin, salt, and cayenne in a pie plate. Stir together well.

3. Place the milk in a bowl. Dip the shrimp in the milk, and using a slotted spoon, transfer them to the cornmeal mixture. Dredge them in the cornmeal, shaking off any excess.

4. Place the oil in a heavy skillet over medium-high heat.

5. When the oil is hot, fry the shrimp in small batches until golden brown and crisp, 3 minutes. Lift them out with a slotted spoon and drain them on several layers of paper towels. Serve immediately in a basket lined with a linen napkin, with Hot Stuff Tartar Sauce for dipping.

Serves 8

SIMPLY SUPER SHRIMP NACHOS

★ ★ ★

Rosario's, in San Antonio, serves some of the most delicious Tex-Mex food in the Southwest, and as soon as I tasted the restaurant's shrimp nachos, I knew that I would have to include a version of them in this book. They're as easy as can be to make. The only tip is to try to find larger-than-normal tortilla chips. But if you can only find the average size, they'll do just fine.

Beer: Arizona ale

24 medium (about ¾ pound) shrimp,
    peeled and deveined
1 tablespoon extra virgin olive oil
2 teaspoons fresh lime juice
¼ teaspoon chili powder
¼ teaspoon ground cumin
Pinch of salt
2 cloves garlic, peeled and pressed
48 large flat nacho corn chips
1½ cups Guacamole (page 176)
2 ripe plum tomatoes, seeded and cut into ¼-inch
    dice
2 to 3 ounces Monterey Jack cheese, grated
    (½ to ¾ cup)
48 small (bottled) jalapeño
    slices, drained
2 tablespoons chopped
    fresh cilantro or
    fresh flat-leaf parsley

1. Rinse the shrimp and drain them well. Pat dry and place in a bowl.

2. In a small bowl, combine the oil, lime juice, chili powder, cumin, salt, and garlic. Add to the shrimp, toss well to combine, and marinate for 15 minutes.

3. Preheat a nonstick skillet over medium-high heat for 2 minutes. Remove the shrimp from the marinade and sauté until cooked through, 2 minutes per side. Cut them in half lengthwise, and refrigerate, covered, until ready to continue.

4. When you are ready to prepare the nachos, preheat the broiler.

5. Lay the nacho chips on two baking sheets. Place half a shrimp, cut side down, in the center of each.

6. Place 1 teaspoon of guacamole on top of each shrimp, and sprinkle with a little chopped tomato. Next, top with grated cheese. Place a jalapeño slice in the center of each, pressing down slightly. Sprinkle with cilantro.

7. Just before serving, place the nachos under the broiler, 3 inches from the heat source, just to melt the cheese, 1 minute only. Leave the oven door open so that you can keep an eye on them. Serve immediately.

Makes 48 nachos

SAVANNAH COCKTAIL CRAB BITES

★ ★ ★

These mini crab cakes seem to me to be rooted deeper into the South than into Maryland. They are quite delicate, with only a small amount of cracker crumbs in the binding. Embellished with honey-baked Virginia ham and dipped into Hot Stuff Tartar Sauce, they are the perfect pique to the pre-dinner appetite. Be sure to chill the crab cakes before frying them so they will hold together as they cook.

*½ pound fresh lump crabmeat, picked over for
    shell and cartilage*
*¼ cup very finely diced honey-baked
    Virginia ham*
¼ cup very finely diced green bell pepper
2 tablespoons snipped fresh chives
1 tablespoon coarsely grated onion
1 teaspoon finely grated orange zest
½ cup mayonnaise
2½ tablespoons Dijon mustard
Pinch of cayenne pepper
Salt and freshly ground black pepper, to taste
1 large egg, lightly beaten
*1¼ cups saltine cracker crumbs
    (about 25 crackers)*
¼ cup vegetable oil
*Hot Stuff Tartar Sauce (page 154),
    for serving*

1. In a bowl, gently combine the crab, ham, bell pepper, chives, onion, and orange zest.

2. In a separate bowl, combine the mayonnaise, mustard, cayenne, salt, and pepper. Using a rubber spatula, fold this into the crab mixture. Add the beaten egg, and fold in ¼ cup of the cracker crumbs.

3. Form the crab mixture into 1-inch cakes about ½ inch thick. Dredge them in the remaining cup of cracker crumbs and place on a plate. Chill, very loosely covered, for 1 hour.

4. Heat 2 tablespoons of the oil in a nonstick skillet over medium heat. Cook the crab bites until golden, about 1½ minutes per side. Serve immediately, with Hot Stuff Tartar Sauce for dipping.

Makes about 30 crab bites

SAN FRAN CHICKEN KEBABS

★ ★ ★

An Asian-influenced marinade flavors this crisp and succulent cocktail kebab, which is further enhanced by a dip in Sweet Jalapeño Sauce.

Wine: Monterey County (CA) Riesling

MARINADE
¼ cup hoisin sauce
¼ cup rice wine vinegar
2 tablespoons peanut oil
2 tablespoons Asian sesame oil
3 tablespoons finely minced fresh ginger

KEBABS
*2 whole skinless, boneless chicken breasts
    (about 1 pound each), cut into
    ¾-inch cubes*
*80 snow peas (about 1 pound),
    lightly blanched*
*Sweet Jalapeño Sauce (page 166),
    for serving*

1. Prepare the marinade: Combine all of the ingredients in a medium-size bowl. Add the cubed chicken and toss well. Cover, and let rest at room temperature for 2 hours.

2. Soak 40 bamboo skewers (6 inches long) in water 30 minutes to 1 hour.

3. Shortly before serving, preheat the oven to 450°F.

4. Thread one snow pea, carefully folded in half, onto a skewer. Next, skewer two pieces of chicken, being careful that they do not touch, and finish with another snow pea. Repeat with the remaining skewers.

5. Place the kebabs on a baking sheet and bake until the chicken is cooked through, 5 to 7 minutes.

6. Serve immediately, with a small bowl of Sweet Jalapeño Sauce for dipping.

Makes 40 skewers

BUFFALO CHICKEN WINGS

★ ★ ★

It was 1940 when Frank and Teresa Bellissimo started "winging" it at their Anchor Bar in Buffalo, New York. The story goes that one Friday night the Bellissimos' son Dominic asked for a snack for himself and his friends. Teresa had mistakenly received a delivery of too many chicken wings, so she fried up a batch, bathed them in hot sauce and margarine, and served them to the boys with the house blue cheese dressing for dipping. And the rest is history! After fifty-five years, the brick landmark on the corner of Main and North is still home to their famous chicken wings.

Beer: Your current favorite

THE ANCHOR BAR

—❦—

The rustic dark wood interior hasn't changed much in all this time, except for the ever-expanding collection of memorabilia that graces the original wooden bar at the Anchor. Out-of-state devotees send license plates from all over the country to decorate the bar, and celebrity fans sign 8 x 10-inch glossies for the dining room wall. The deep-fried fiery wings are what it's all about. They are served with carrot and celery sticks and blue cheese dipping sauce. Edie Bellissimo, Dominic's wife, now tends the roost of this great American shrine, where the only change is the addition of jazz on Friday and Saturday nights. By the way, the Bellissimo recipes for wings and dip are closely held secrets, so after eating them, I created my own homage.

4 large ribs celery, trimmed
4 large carrots, peeled
4 pounds chicken wings (about 24), tips removed, rinsed and patted dry
½ cup (1 stick) unsalted butter
2 tablespoons Tabasco sauce, or more to taste
1 cup peanut oil
1 cup vegetable oil
Coarse salt and freshly ground black pepper, to taste
Maytag Blue Dip (recipe follows)

1. Cut the celery and carrots into sticks, and set aside for serving.

2. Using a sharp knife, separate the chicken wings at the joint so you have a "drumstick" and a "thigh." Set aside.

3. Melt the butter with the Tabasco in a small saucepan. Transfer it to a large bowl and set aside.

4. Heat the peanut and vegetable oils in a deep heavy pot over medium-high heat. Once the oil is 375°F, cook the thighs and drumsticks, in small batches, until they are golden brown and cooked through, about 10 minutes. As they finish cooking, remove them with tongs and place them on paper towels to drain. Then place the wings in the bowl and toss them with the Tabasco mixture to coat. Season with coarse salt and pepper.

5. Serve the wings immediately, with the celery and carrot sticks and Maytag Blue Dip alongside.

Serves 4 to 6

Maytag Blue Dip

---★---

This is *the* one for Buffalo Chicken Wings. However, it is also a scrumptious dip for fresh vegetables and can be used as a salad dressing over tart greens or even on top of a hamburger. While Roquefort is traditionally called for, I love mellow, crumbly Maytag Blue from Iowa. Don't blend in the cheese—just fold the ingredients together (otherwise the dressing takes on a peculiar grayish color).

1 cup sour cream
1 cup mayonnaise
¾ cup coarsely crumbled Maytag Blue cheese
1 tablespoon cider vinegar
1 tablespoon fresh lemon juice
2 dashes Tabasco sauce
1 tablespoon grated onion
½ teaspoon very finely minced garlic
2 tablespoons chopped fresh flat-leaf parsley
Salt and freshly ground black pepper, to taste

Fold the sour cream and mayonnaise together in a bowl. Add the blue cheese and fold gently. Fold in the remaining ingredients, and adjust the seasonings to taste. Refrigerate, covered, until ready to use. The sauce will keep about a week.

Makes about 2 cups

NORTH CAROLINA TACOS AL PASTOR

★ ★ ★

When you're cooking barbecued pork, no matter the style, be sure to make plenty. And hope that you've made enough to freeze the extra, along with lots of zesty sauce. That way, you'll have some on hand for these cocktail Tacos al Pastor, lushly topped with a fruit relish. Make

sure the corn tortillas are very fresh so that they remain soft and pliable. Otherwise, they will break and the sauce will drip. Keep lots of cocktail napkins handy.

24 fresh corn tortillas (4-inch diameter; see Note)
2 cups North Carolina–Style Pulled Pork Barbecue (page 376) or other barbecued pork meat, warmed
½ cup very finely grated Monterey Jack cheese (optional)
1 cup Fresh Pineapple Relish (page 186) or Summer Peach Relish (page 183)
4 scallions (3 inches green left on), thinly sliced on the diagonal
¼ cup chopped fresh cilantro leaves

1. Preheat the oven to 350°F.

2. Wrap the tortillas in aluminum foil and heat them in the oven until warmed through, 10 to 15 minutes.

3. Assemble the tacos: Place a warm tortilla in the palm of your hand and curl the sides up gently. Fill with a tablespoon of the barbecued pork followed by a teaspoon of the grated cheese, if desired, and about 2 teaspoons of the relish. Sprinkle with scallions and cilantro, roll closed and arrange on a serving platter seam-side down, being careful that the taco doesn't open up and spill. Repeat with the remaining tacos, working quickly so they remain warm for serving. Serve immediately.

Makes 24 tacos

NOTE: If you are unable to find 4-inch corn tortillas, you can use larger ones and cut out 4-inch circles with scissors.

SPICED MAPLE COCKTAIL RIBS

★ ★ ★

There's some of Vermont and a touch of the Southwest here. Together they do their stuff as a coating for finger-licking riblets, which are bound to be popular at any party. They are the type of tidbit you just can't get enough of. All you need to finish the picture is a great Midwestern beer and lots of small paper napkins.

Beer: Wisconsin nut brown ale

2 pounds cocktail spareribs, cut into 2-inch pieces
Salt and freshly ground black pepper, to taste
⅓ cup pure maple syrup
⅓ cup Dijon mustard
2 tablespoons unsulfured molasses
2 tablespoons cider vinegar
1 teaspoon ground cumin

1. Preheat the oven to 350°F.

2. Place the ribs in a shallow roasting pan and sprinkle with salt and pepper. Bake for 45 minutes.

3. While the ribs are cooking, combine the remaining ingredients in a small bowl. Stir well and set aside.

4. Remove the pan from the oven and drain off any fat. Toss the ribs with ½ cup of the marinade. Return them to the oven and bake, turning the ribs and basting them occasionally (if needed) with the remaining ¼ cup marinade, for 30 minutes. Serve immediately.

Serves 10

NOTE: This recipe is easily doubled.

THE COCKTAIL CLUB

★ ★ ★

Like many folks, I crave a good club sandwich from time to time. But I don't think they have to be confined to lunchtime fare. While I might be tempted to eat one for dinner, if I'm dining solo, a club is not appropriate as the main event at a dinner party. That's not to say they can't be around company altogether. I've come up with a diminutive version—perfect little clubs to serve as cocktail accompaniments.

Wine: Sonoma Valley (CA) Gewürztraminer
Beer: Wisconsin nut brown ale

6 strips bacon
¼ pound Swiss cheese, grated (about 1 cup)
¼ pound baked Virginia ham, cut into
    ¼-inch dice
2 tablespoons chopped fresh flat-leaf
    parsley
¾ cup plus 1 tablespoon mayonnaise
Salt and freshly ground black pepper,
    to taste
40 slices round cocktail-size rye bread
2 cups mesclun (mixed baby salad greens),
    rinsed and patted dry
20 slices Slowly Roasted Plum Tomatoes
    (page 307)

1. Fry the bacon in a large skillet over medium heat until it is very crisp, 6 minutes on the first side and about 3 minutes on the second. Drain on paper towels.

2. Place the cheese and ham in a bowl. Crumble the bacon well, and add it to the bowl along with the parsley, 6 tablespoons of the mayonnaise, and the salt and pepper. Toss well to combine.

3. Spread ½ teaspoon of the remaining mayonnaise over one side of each bread slice. Distribute the cheese mixture evenly over half of the slices, spreading it out to the edges. Top each with a few mesclun leaves and a tomato slice. Cover with the remaining bread slices, mayonnaise side down.

4. To serve, cut the sandwiches in half on the diagonal.

Makes 40 pieces

SUMMER COCKTAIL QUESADILLAS

★ ★ ★

Layer two of summer's best flavors onto flour tortillas that have been spread with a spicy New Orleans mix and you've got unexpected sultry-weather cocktail fare. I find these mini quesadillas just right at a glorious sunset gathering during July or August. If you have strips of tortilla left over, fry them crisp and use them to garnish Guacamole Soup.

7 flour tortillas (9-inch diameter)
½ cup Muffuletta Slather (page 175)
48 slices Slowly Roasted Plum Tomatoes (page 307)
48 tiny whole fresh basil leaves
1 cup finely shredded Monterey Jack cheese

1. Use a 2-inch round cookie cutter to cut 96 rounds from the flour tortillas.

2. Arrange 48 tortilla rounds on two baking sheets. Spread ½ teaspoon of the Muffuletta Slather over each round. Top with a roasted tomato slice and a basil leaf. Sprinkle 1 teaspoon of the shredded cheese over each, and top with the remaining tortilla rounds. Press each one down gently with the palm of your hand to compact them slightly.

3. Heat a nonstick skillet over medium heat until very hot. Cook the quesadillas in batches, pressing them down slightly with the back of a metal spatula, until the tortillas are golden and the cheese has melted, about 1½ minutes per side. Place them in a low oven (250°F) to keep warm while you cook the remainder.

Makes 48 quesadillas

DEEP SOUTH CRAB DOLLOP

★ ★ ★

Iwas looking for a luscious bite to enhance my benne wafers, and naturally, Cajun and Creole flavors came to mind. From there, it was no reach to think of crab, but this recipe, with the addition of allspice and cumin, gives a new twist to a favorite combination.

2 cups fresh lump crabmeat, picked over
*   for shell and cartilage*
3 scallions (3 inches green left on), thinly sliced
½ cup mayonnaise
¼ cup sour cream
¼ cup grated green bell pepper
2 dashes Tabasco sauce
1½ teaspoons snipped fresh chives
½ teaspoon finely grated lemon zest
¼ teaspoon ground cumin
⅛ teaspoon ground allspice
Salt and freshly ground black pepper, to taste
Dixie Benne Wafers (recipe follows)

1. Toss the crabmeat and the scallions together in a bowl.

2. In a smaller bowl, combine the mayonnaise, sour cream, bell pepper, Tabasco, chives, lemon zest, cumin, and allspice. Using a rubber spatula, gently fold the mixture into the crabmeat. Season with salt and pepper, and adjust the other seasonings to taste. Cover and refrigerate until ready to use, up to 24 hours.

3. Serve atop Dixie Benne Wafers.

Makes about 2 cups

Dixie Benne Wafers

───★───

When I owned The Silver Palate, I sold tins and tins of benne wafers and felt so elegant having a true gourmet product from the South on the shelves. They just flew out the door. Today, I bake my own version. The benne, or sesame seed, was first introduced in the South by slaves who sowed it around their quarters for good luck. Plantation cooks turned the tiny seeds into candy, cakes, and pastes. These savory benne wafers, with their mild sesame flavor, are just the right bite during cocktail hour when you want to offer a little something to take the edge off hunger.

2 cups all-purpose flour
2 tablespoons sugar
1 teaspoon salt, plus more for sprinkling
¼ teaspoon ground cumin
⅛ teaspoon cayenne pepper, or more to taste
½ cup solid vegetable shortening, cold
¼ cup (½ stick) unsalted butter, cold,
  cut into small pieces
⅔ cup sesame seeds, toasted (see Note)
½ cup cold milk

1. Preheat the oven to 350°F.
2. Sift the flour, sugar, 1 teaspoon salt, cumin, and cayenne together into a bowl.
3. With a pastry cutter or two knives, cut the shortening and the butter into the dry ingredients until uniformly distributed. Mix in the sesame seeds until they are evenly distributed.
4. Gradually pour in the milk, mixing until the dough just begins to hold together. With your hands, form the dough into a ball.
5. Roll the dough out to ⅛-inch thickness on a lightly floured surface. Cut the dough into 2-inch circles with a biscuit cutter. Using a spatula, transfer the wafers to ungreased baking sheets.
6. Bake in the center of the oven until light gold and crispy, 20 minutes. While the wafers are hot and still on the baking sheets, sprinkle them lightly with salt to taste. Let them cool completely on the baking sheets. Store in airtight containers up to 1 week.
Makes about 75 wafers

NOTE: To toast sesame seeds, place them in a nonstick skillet and stir constantly over medium heat until golden brown, 2 to 3 minutes.

MUFFULETTA SLATHER

In New Orleans, an immense round muffuletta sandwich, overflowing with a pungent olive salad on top of Italian deli meats and cheeses, is a popular favorite. I've simply pulled out the olive salad and embellished it with lots of other good tastes to make a great slather for thinly sliced grilled or toasted peasant bread.

¾ cup pitted green California or Spanish
  Manzanilla olives
¾ cup pitted ripe California or Greek
  Kalamata olives
1 clove garlic, finely chopped
1 teaspoon tiny capers, drained
¼ cup extra virgin olive oil
1 teaspoon fresh lemon juice
2 tablespoons chopped fresh basil leaves
Freshly ground black pepper, to taste

1. In a food processor, combine both the olives, the garlic, and capers. Process until just smooth, scraping down the sides of the bowl if necessary. With the machine running, slowly drizzle in the oil and lemon juice through the feed tube and process until well combined.

2. Transfer the mixture to a bowl, and fold in the basil and pepper. Let rest at room temperature for 1 hour for the flavors to come out. The slather will keep 3 to 5 days if stored in a tightly covered container in the refrigerator.

Makes about 1 cup

SEATTLE SLATHER

★ ★ ★

I was inspired by the delicious Pacific Northwest salmon and the pure Nordic flavors that appear in the area's cuisine when I mixed up this slather. Spread it on thin toasted rounds of Boston Brown Bread for a transcontinental taste sensation.

Wine: Yakima Valley (WA) Riesling
Beer: Seattle pale ale

½ pound mild soft chèvre, at room temperature
¼ cup sour cream
1 tablespoon vodka
3 tablespoons snipped fresh chives
2 tablespoons very finely diced sweet gherkin pickles
1 tablespoon tiny capers, drained and lightly chopped
1 tablespoon finely grated orange zest
Freshly ground black pepper, to taste
2 ounces thinly sliced smoked salmon, cut into ¼-inch dice (about ⅔ cup)

1. Combine the cheese with the sour cream and vodka in a medium-size bowl.

2. Using a rubber spatula, fold in the chives, gherkins, capers, orange zest, and pepper. Combine well. Taste for seasoning, and fold in the salmon.

3. Scrape the mixture into a serving bowl, and refrigerate for 1 to 2 hours for the flavors to blend. Remove 15 minutes before serving.

Makes about 1½ cups

GUACAMOLE

★ ★ ★

I like my guacamole a combination of smooth and chunky, so I purée one avocado and mash the others before combining them. If you don't care for lime juice or cilantro, substitute lemon juice and parsley or fresh basil.

For the best results, make as close to serving time as possible, as the avocado will discolor rapidly. Some people feel that putting the seed into the guacamole (removing it, of course,

SO GOOD, SO GREEN

The avocado is a New World delicacy, first tasted by a European—a certain Hernandez de Oviredo—in 1526, in what is now Colombia. Spanish colonists soon grew to love the buttery green fruit as much as the Mayas and Aztecs did, and began cultivating it wherever the climate allowed. Today, avocados grow in the Caribbean, Africa, the Middle East, Central and South America, Florida, and California. Of all the species cultivated today, I love the pear-shaped Hass (often called "California avocado") best. Its smooth, nutty taste works well in Guacamole and recipes such as Orange, Ham, and Avocado Salad. It's delicious plain, too. Think of it as a firm custard, and eat it with a spoon, sprinkled with salt and a little lime juice.

A Hass is ready to eat when its pebbly skin is purplish black. It should yield slightly to the touch. Slice it in half, pit it, and stuff it with seafood or ripe, dressed melon balls. Dice it into quesadilla fillings and slip it under the cheese in seafood-melt sandwiches. I also enjoy it puréed into dressings as a mayonnaise substitute.

An avocado is best eaten as soon as it's opened, as exposure to air dulls its flavor and browns its flesh. A sprinkling of lemon or lime juice helps maintain freshness somewhat. Sour cream, salsa, and mayonnaise do the same for mashed avocado. You should also seal up tightly whatever you can't serve right away. If the surface flesh browns, gently scrape it off with a spoon.

---

before serving!) will keep it from discoloring. In any case, cover tightly with plastic wrap and refrigerate for up to 4 hours, no longer. Serve with a bowl of tortilla chips.

3 ripe avocados, peeled and pitted
3 tablespoons fresh lime juice
1 teaspoon finely minced garlic
½ cup seeded diced (¼ inch) ripe tomatoes
2 tablespoons chopped fresh cilantro leaves
Salt, to taste

1. Place one of the avocados, the lime juice, and the garlic in a food processor and process until smooth.

2. Using a fork, coarsely mash the 2 remaining avocados in a bowl.

3. Add the puréed avocado, the diced tomato, and the cilantro. Stir to combine. Season with salt. Serve, preferably immediately (see headnote).

Makes 2 generous cups

PART FIVE

DINNER TIME

The Relish Tray

To relish something is to enjoy it, which is exactly how I feel about relish. Pickles, chutneys, salsas, fruit butters, and ketchups—relishes all—lend their tingle to recipes throughout this book. Indeed, I would be hard pressed to cook without them, and in my travels for this book, I found dozens of new ideas.

At the Dog Team Tavern in Middlebury, Vermont, I sat before a spinning relish wheel, big as myself, hung with copper buckets of pickled beets, piccalilli, white beans, pot cheese, and apple butter, all meant as garnish for the huge sticky bun on our table—pizza-sized, divided eight ways. In Lancaster, Pennsylvania, I lost my heart to Pennsylvania Dutch chowchow. The cherry chutneys of Northwestern Michigan were a revelation, as was a mango chutney barbecue sauce that I sampled on Maui. Southwestern salsas were big and brilliant. And everywhere I went I found bold native ingredients—peppers, peaches, cranberries, and more—to fire my imagination. I hope this chapter will fire yours, too.

SILKY PAPAYA RELISH

★ ★ ★

I find this relish silky, refreshing, and the ideal complement to any Southwestern dish. Ripe papaya, highlighted by flecks of jalapeños, sets off black bean salads, quesadillas, western omelets, and pan-fried skirt steaks. For nonpareil taste, make it up shortly before you serve it.

1 ripe papaya (about 1 pound)
1½ teaspoons seeded, finely chopped
  jalapeño pepper
¼ cup finely chopped red onion
2 tablespoons chopped fresh cilantro leaves
Finely grated zest of 1 lime
¼ cup fresh lime juice

1. Peel and seed the papaya, and cut it into ¼-inch dice. Place in a medium-size bowl.

2. Gently fold the jalapeño, red onion, cilantro, and lime zest into the papaya. Toss in the lime juice. Refrigerate, covered, until ready to use, no longer than 4 hours.

Makes about 2 cups

MACCAN FAMILY ZUCCHINI RELISH

★ ★ ★

R oe Maccan Griffith, from Kansas City, who is my associate Laurie's mom, gave me her family's favorite zucchini relish recipe. I make it all

summer long and use it as a topping for burgers, sandwiches, and cold meats. This relish is so yummy and easy to make, you'll want to keep some on hand all year round for a great fresh-tasting condiment.

5 cups grated zucchini (4 medium zucchini)
2 cups grated onions (2 large onions)
6½ teaspoons salt
1 cup diced (⅛ inch) green bell pepper
1 cup diced (⅛ inch) red bell pepper
2¼ cups sugar
1¼ cups white vinegar
2 teaspoons ground nutmeg
2 teaspoons dry mustard
1½ teaspoons ground turmeric
1½ teaspoons cornstarch
1 teaspoon celery salt
¼ teaspoon freshly ground black pepper

1. Place the zucchini, onions, and salt in a large bowl. Mix well, cover, and refrigerate overnight.

2. The following day, place the mixture in a fine-mesh strainer. Drain well, rinse under cold water, and then drain again for 1 hour.

3. Prepare four 1-pint canning jars and lids by sterilizing them in boiling water according to the manufacturer's instructions.

4. Place the zucchini mixture in a heavy pot, and add all the remaining ingredients. Bring to a boil. Reduce the heat and simmer, stirring occasionally, for 30 minutes.

5. Spoon the hot mixture into the jars, leaving ¼ inch head space, and seal and process according to the manufacturer's instructions. Or if you prefer, simply refrigerate, covered, for up to 3 weeks.

Makes about 5 cups

NOTE: This recipe can be doubled.

SUMMER PEACH RELISH

★ ★ ★

Cookout side dishes do deserve a freshening up now and then, and this recipe is a worthwhile place to start. Once I discovered how good peach relish is, I spread it on everything, from

QUICK POINTERS ON PEACHES

—❦—

Whether you put up preserves and relish, add them to ice cream, or eat them out of hand with the tasty juices dripping to your elbow, you want to select the best peaches of the season at your local produce stand or farmers' market.

• The red or "blush" on a peach is not an indication of ripeness; look for creamy gold to yellow undertones to know your peach was picked when it was ripe.

• Smell the fruit: A peach is a member of the rose family and should have a pleasingly sweet fragrance.

• Avoid any peaches with a greenish skin tone. It means the peach was picked too early and will not ripen any further or soften.

• Peaches bruise easily, so be careful not to squeeze them. They should be soft to the touch, but not mushy.

• If your peaches feel hard, place them on the kitchen counter for a day or two. They will ripen more and soften at room temperature.

• Once peaches are ripe, keep them refrigerated. Eat within a week of purchasing them.

• To peel a peach, dip it into boiling water for 30 seconds, then plunge it into an ice water bath. The skin should slip off easily.

• To prevent sliced fresh peaches from browning, sprinkle them with a little lemon juice.

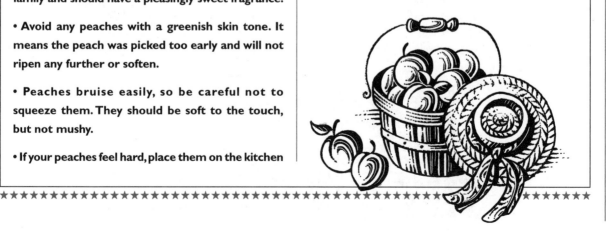

grilled picnic favorites to a cold turkey sandwich. The possibilities are endless, so be sure to make some in July, when peaches are in season. A final dash of lemon juice brightens the flavors as the relish cools.

6 to 8 ripe peaches, peeled, pitted, and
   cut into ½-inch dice (6 cups)
3 tablespoons fresh lemon juice
1 red bell pepper, stemmed, seeded, and
   cut into ¼-inch dice
¼ cup diced (¼ inch) red onion
2 teaspoons finely minced green jalapeño
   pepper, or more to taste
1 tablespoon finely minced fresh ginger
1 tablespoon finely minced crystallized
   ginger
1 teaspoon salt
¼ teaspoon ground mace
1 cup golden raisins
1 cup cider vinegar

1. Place the peaches in a large heavy saucepan, and stir in 2 tablespoons of the lemon juice. Add all the remaining ingredients and toss well. Bring to a boil, stirring once. Reduce the heat to medium and simmer for 30 minutes.

2. Remove the pan from the heat and let the relish cool to room temperature. Stir in the remaining 1 tablespoon lemon juice. The relish will thicken as it cools. Refrigerate it, covered, until ready to use, up to 4 weeks.

   Makes about 5 cups

FRESH WHOLE-CRANBERRY RELISH

★ ★ ★

No matter how many combinations I've tried, this remains my favorite whole-cranberry relish. I make it every year, as soon as fresh cranberries come into the market in the fall. Most bags are packed in 12-ounce portions, so you will need to buy two for this recipe, freezing the unused portion of the second bag for another recipe (cranberries freeze beautifully).

4 cups (about 1 pound) fresh cranberries,
   picked over and rinsed
2 cups sugar
½ cup cranberry juice
½ cup fresh orange juice
1 tablespoon finely grated orange zest

1. Combine all the ingredients in a heavy saucepan and stir well. Place the pan over medium heat, and boil until the berries pop open, about 10 minutes.

2. Skim the foam off the surface with a metal spoon, and let the relish cool to room temperature. Refrigerate, covered, up to 2 months.

   Serves 10

★★

CRANBERRIES: A NORTH AMERICAN NATIVE

— ❧ —

A cranberry bog in harvest season is a dazzling sight—a sea of vivid scarlet rimmed by flaming autumn trees. I paid an unforgettable visit to one, on a crisp and brilliant October afternoon. I was in South Carver, Massachusetts, just east of Plymouth Rock. This is cranberry country. Southeastern Massachusetts is home to more than 13,000 acres of bogs, most of which supply to Ocean Spray, Inc. Cranberries have been cultivated here since the early nineteenth century; today, they're the state's largest food crop.

The bog had been flooded the night before, then worked that morning by a machine called an "egg beater," which churned up the low-lying plants and shook the berries loose. Millions were afloat at one end when I arrived, as they waited for a machine called a "vacuum" to suck them up a conveyor belt and into a truck. Berries harvested this way are used mostly for juices, prepared sauces, and relishes. Those we buy fresh are picked up by a huge, lawn mower–type vehicle that combs them off the vines with metal teeth.

One of three fruits native to North America (along with the blueberry and Concord grape), the cranberry was growing wild long before the Pilgrims arrived in 1620. They named it "crane berry," after its drooping, crane-like stem and pink blossom. The Native Americans had long used it as food, dye, and medicine, and the settlers quickly learned to do the same. Experience also taught the newcomers that the berries made an excellent scurvy preventative at sea (we now know why: They're rich in vitamin C).

Today, more than one hundred varieties of cranberries grow in Europe, Asia, and the Americas, in places with a favorable, temperate climate and moist, acid soil. In the United States, some grow on century-old vines. These will continue to flourish, as far as anyone knows, for as long as they go undamaged. Commercial production in this country is largely limited to four varieties:

Early Black: Small dark berries, which were first cultivated on Cape Cod in 1850.

McFarlin: An egg-shaped berry popular with Washington and Oregon growers.

Searles: Deep red, from Wisconsin.

Howes: Large, oval, and the most common type, grown principally in Massachusetts and New Jersey.

I use cranberries year-round, in meat sauces and glazes, breads, pies, and fruit compotes. Cranberry sauce needn't be restricted to roast turkey—try it alongside a curry, on a tuna salad sandwich, or with any other dish that would benefit from a bright-tasting, tart-sweet relish. Keeping cranberries on hand is easy: Just buy them fresh during their fall season and store them in your freezer. Try dried cranberries, too; they're especially good in stuffing.

★★

FRESH PINEAPPLE RELISH

★ ★ ★

When pickle relish out of a jar is just not special enough, this pineapple relish, made from sweet, juicy fresh pineapple, is easy to cook up. It's colorful and crunchingly delicious served along with baked ham, fried chicken, and thick, juicy burgers. I also love a dollop on a tuna sandwich.

4 cups diced (½ inch) fresh ripe pineapple
   (about 1 medium pineapple)
2 onions, cut into ¼-inch dice
1 red bell pepper, stemmed, seeded, and
   cut into ¼-inch dice
4 cloves garlic, minced
2 tablespoons finely minced fresh ginger
1 cup golden raisins
1 small dried red chile pepper, crushed
1 teaspoon salt
¼ teaspoon ground cinnamon
1 cup (packed) light brown sugar
½ cup cider vinegar

1. Place all of the ingredients in a heavy saucepan and bring to a boil. Reduce the heat to medium and simmer, stirring occasionally, for 30 minutes.

2. Let the relish cool to room temperature, and then refrigerate it, covered, until ready to use. Serve at room temperature with pork, fish, or poultry.
Makes about 4 cups

PICCALILLI CORN SALAD

★ ★ ★

Wait till you try this revitalization of an American classic. Piccalilli combined with pickled fresh corn salad results in a delicious salad that can be eaten as a side dish, topping, even on its own. I'm particularly fond of the unexpected jolt that comes from the addition of curry powder. While parsley is used in this recipe, slivered basil or chopped cilantro would make a good substitute. I always add the herbs just before serving so the vinaigrette doesn't darken them and sap their fresh flavor.

6 ears fresh corn
1 cup diced (¼ inch) hothouse (seedless)
   cucumber
1 cup diced (¼ inch) green bell pepper
1 tomato, cored, seeded, and cut into ¼-inch dice
¼ cup finely chopped red onion
1 scallion (3 inches green left on), thinly sliced
   on the diagonal
3 tablespoons olive oil
2 tablespoons cider vinegar
½ teaspoon Dijon mustard
½ teaspoon minced garlic
½ teaspoon sugar
Pinch of curry powder
Salt and freshly ground black pepper, to taste
2 tablespoons chopped fresh flat-leaf parsley

1. Shuck the ears of corn, and trim off the stem ends. Using a small sharp paring knife, stand each ear upright on its end, and holding the top of the ear with one hand, run the knife carefully down the cob, just under the kernels, pressing against the cob, to cut them off. Cook the kernels in a pot of boiling salted water for 2 to 3 minutes, and then refresh them under cold water. Drain well.

2. In a bowl, combine the corn with the cucumber, bell pepper, tomato, red onion, and scallion.

3. Whisk the olive oil, vinegar, mustard, garlic, sugar, curry powder, salt, and pepper together in a small bowl. Pour this dressing over the salad and stir well. Before serving, toss with the parsley.

Serves 8

PENNSYLVANIA DUTCH CHOWCHOW

★ ★ ★

Of all the foods I tasted in Lancaster County, Pennsylvania, nothing was more delicious than chowchow, the traditional Pennsylvania Dutch mixture of pickled vegetables that is so integral to the family table that the Mennonite and Amish cooks I met had a year's supply stored in their cellars.

Ruth Fox is a charming Mennonite woman who was kind enough to invite me to dinner one Friday night when I was visiting Mennonite friends in Lancaster for the weekend. That night she served the best chowchow I've ever tasted. Hers is no less than a quilt in a jar, each container resplendent with cauliflower, cucumbers, yellow and green beans, dark red kidney beans, and scarlet bell peppers.

According to my research, the word "chowchow" may have derived—surprisingly—from the Mandarin word *cha*, meaning "mixed," and is thought to have originally referred to an orange peel and ginger condiment brought to this country by the Chinese laborers who worked on the railroads during the nineteenth century.

1 head cauliflower, broken into florets and trimmed
2 cups green beans, stem ends trimmed, cut into 1-inch lengths
2 cups yellow wax beans, stem ends trimmed, cut into 1-inch lengths
2 cups peeled and diced (½ inch) carrots
2 cups diced (½ inch) celery
2 cups diced (½ inch) hothouse (seedless) cucumber
2 cups fresh lima beans
2 cups corn kernels
1 red bell pepper, stemmed, seeded, and cut into ¼-inch dice
1 green bell pepper, stemmed, seeded, and cut into ¼-inch dice
1 cup white pearl onions
1 can (16 ounces) dark red kidney beans, drained and rinsed
6 cups cider vinegar
6 cups sugar
2 tablespoons coarse salt

1. Prepare four 1-quart canning jars and lids by sterilizing them in boiling water according to the manufacturer's instructions.

2. Bring a large pot of water to a boil, and cook all the vegetables, separately, until just tender: 2 minutes for the cauliflower, 1 minute for the green and the wax beans, 1 minute for the carrots and the celery, 30 seconds for the cucumber, 1 to 2 minutes for the lima beans, 1 minute for the corn, 1 minute for both the bell peppers, and 1 to 2 minutes for the onions.

3. As each vegetable is done, remove it from the boiling water with a slotted spoon and place it in a large nonreactive pot. Peel the onions after draining, then add them to the pot.

4. Add the kidney beans to the vegetables, then stir in the vinegar, sugar, and coarse salt. Place the pot over high heat, and bring to a boil. As soon as the mixture boils, remove the pot from the heat.

5. Pack the hot vegetables into the jars, and cover with the syrup. Leaving ¼ inch head space, seal and process according to the manufacturer's instructions.

6. Leave in a cool, dark place for 6 weeks before serving; refrigerate after opening.

Makes 4 quarts

SWEETLY PICKLED BEETS

★ ★ ★

The Patricia Murphy's Candlelight Room in Westchester County, New York, was my family's favorite place to go for celebratory meals. Always crowded, the inevitable wait for a table was made much easier to endure by taking a stroll through the restaurant's pretty gardens and making a visit to the gift shop.

Patricia Murphy's country decor was charming, but for me the special lures were the pre-dinner dishes that arrived as soon as you were shown to your table. Huge steamy popovers, nestled under linen napkins, were universally adored. Everyone always said I ate too many. That was probably true . . . but, oh! they were just so ethereal, I couldn't help it. These were followed by a superlative relish tray filled with pickled crab apples, watermelon rind, corn, herbed cottage cheese, and scrumptious pickled beets. These memories were really the inspiration for this chapter, so it was imperative that I include a recipe that emulated those glorious beets. Serve them with cold poultry as well as meat, and of course, cottage cheese.

6 to 8 beets (about 2 pounds)
1 teaspoon celery seeds
1 cup sugar
4 teaspoons dry mustard
Salt, to taste
1½ cups cider vinegar

1. Rinse and trim the beets, leaving 1 inch of stem and root. Place them in a pot, cover with water, and bring to a boil. Reduce heat to medium and cook until just tender, 45 to 50 minutes. Reserve 1 cup of the cooking liquid, and drain the beets. When they are cool enough to handle, slip off the skins. Trim the ends and cut the beets into ¼-inch-thick slices. Place them in a bowl.

2. Place the celery seeds in a cheesecloth bag. Mix the sugar, mustard, and salt together in a small bowl.

3. In a small saucepan, combine the vinegar, reserved beet cooking liquid, and spice bag. Bring to a boil. Add the sugar mixture, stir, and bring to a boil again. Reduce the heat to low and cook for 5 minutes. Remove and discard the spice bag. Pour the hot liquid over the beets, and let rest, covered, at room temperature for at least 24 hours. (If there are any mustard pieces they will dissolve.) Refrigerate in a covered container for up to 1 month.

Serves 8

A MARKET WITH A HEART

—❦—

*T*he Lancaster Central Market, in the heart of Pennsylvania Dutch country, is a living, thriving artifact, a modern commercial hub with an antique style. Get there at dawn any Tuesday, Friday, or Saturday, and you'll see the region's celebrated bounty trundled out of cars, trucks, and buggies and into market stalls. There's always an impressive array of homemade favorites: cured meats, pickles, preserves, cheeses, and pies, sold alongside handcrafted Amish and Mennonite quilts, furniture, and toys. Fruits and vegetables come directly from nearby farms, fresh picked; and butchers' stands offer superb local poultry, pork, and beef. This is how it's been here, more or less, since 1742. The Victorian-era market building (a handsome Romanesque structure), the motor vehicles, and the tourists have changed the look, but not the spirit, of this very traditional place. It's a center for a self-sufficient, agrarian society—a rare and wonderful thing in the modern age.

The Amish of Lancaster County (Lancaster is the seat) are tenacious people, determined to remain plain in their ways and separate from the outside world. Although they live not to far west of Philadelphia, they've succumbed very little to its influence. Many still speak their ancestral Pennsylvania Dutch (a German dialect) among themselves and wear sturdy, unadorned nineteenth-century-style clothes.

The Mennonite lifestyle is less strict, but equally focused in its devotion to God and its respect for the land. The food traditions of both groups are the same. I'm fond of their wholesome, hearty cooking, which reflects so much about their way of life. I find it impossible to visit the market without picking up some chowchow, which is a pickled sweet-and-sour vegetable medley in the bright hues of autumn. I usually buy some bags of thick, square-cut noodles for Amish-style pot pies, some hand-twisted thick pretzels, apple butter, and earthy, brown-sugar shoofly pie, too. One needn't be fancy to create full flavor, after all.

If you're interested in a visit to Lancaster, the main number for tourist information is (800) PADUTCH!

ROBIN LEE'S DILLY BEANS

★ ★ ★

I first tasted Robin's perfect dilly beans during a dinner at the James Beard House in New York City. Her husband, Frank Lee, chef-owner of Slightly North of Broad, in Charleston, South Carolina, was the guest chef there. Robin was kind enough to share the recipe with me, and here it is. The beans are packed standing upright in the jar. When summer comes around and green beans are in their prime, these are the pickles to make!

2 pounds fresh green beans, stem ends trimmed
4 cloves garlic, peeled
1 teaspoon cayenne pepper, or more to taste
4 large sprigs fresh dill
2½ cups cider vinegar
2½ cups water
¼ cup coarse salt

1. Prepare four 1-pint canning jars and lids by sterilizing them in boiling water according to the manufacturer's instructions.

2. Bring a large pot of water to a boil, add the green beans, and cook until they are tender but still crunchy, 4 to 5 minutes. Drain the beans well.

3. Place 1 clove of garlic into each of the jars, along with ¼ teaspoon cayenne and a sprig of dill. Pack the green beans upright in the jars, to fit within ¼ inch of the top rim.

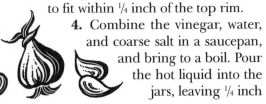

4. Combine the vinegar, water, and coarse salt in a saucepan, and bring to a boil. Pour the hot liquid into the jars, leaving ¼ inch

head space. Seal and process according to the manufacturer's instructions.

5. Store the beans in a cool dark place for at least 2 weeks before eating. Serve cold.

Makes 4 pints

PICKLED WATERMELON RIND

★ ★ ★

I fondly remember watermelon pickles served up on some of the relish trays I enjoyed as a child. That memory was pleasantly jogged recently, by the visits I paid to summer state fairs while researching this book. Inevitably, homey jars of them were part of the lineup of pickles and preserves proudly exhibited, and I longed to cook up some of my own.

Although I never actually thought I'd get down to making watermelon pickles, I did indeed succumb to those summer longings, and here is the result. They do take some time to prepare, but are not difficult to make. And, boy, are they good. Only the white section of the rind is used, which means that you will have lots of juicy red melon to nibble on while you work. The pickle is a great condiment to serve all winter long, especially on the holiday table—it is dazzling alongside turkey and baked ham.

1 watermelon (about 20 pounds)
2 quarts water
½ cup coarse salt
1½ teaspoons whole cloves
1½ teaspoons whole allspice
¼ teaspoon mustard seeds
1 cinnamon stick (3 inches long)
3½ cups sugar
1 cup cider vinegar
1 lemon, thinly sliced

1. Cut the watermelon in half lengthwise, and then into 1-inch-thick slices. Carefully remove the dark green outer rind with a small sharp knife. Then remove the pink flesh and reserve it for another use. All that should remain is the white rind. Cut the rind into 1-inch pieces and set them aside.

2. Combine the water and coarse salt in a large heavy pot, and heat over medium heat, stirring, just until the salt has dissolved, about 5 minutes. Remove the pot from the heat, and add the watermelon rind. Stir, and set aside at room temperature for at least 6 hours or as long as overnight.

3. Prepare three 1-pint canning jars and lids by sterilizing them in boiling water according to the manufacturer's instructions.

4. Drain the watermelon rind, rinse it well, and drain again. Place it in a large heavy pot, and cover with cold water. Bring the water to a boil, reduce the heat, and simmer for 20 minutes. Drain and set aside.

5. Tie the cloves, allspice, mustard seeds, and cinnamon stick together in a cheesecloth bag. Place the bag in a large heavy pot along with the sugar, vinegar, and lemon slices. Bring the mixture to a boil, reduce the heat slightly, and simmer for 10 minutes.

6. Add the watermelon rind and simmer until transparent, 8 to 10 minutes. Remove and discard the spice bag.

7. Pack the hot pickles and the syrup into jars, leaving ¼ inch head space. Seal and process according to the manufacturer's instructions if you like. If not, the pickles, well covered, will keep in the refrigerator for 6 months. Store processed pickles in a cool, dark place; refrigerate after opening.

Makes 3 pints

SPICED CANTALOUPE PICKLES

★ ★ ★

Succulent and delicious, this unique, well-textured pickled fruit is an ideal condiment to serve with roast pork, turkey, or baked ham. To really enjoy the fruits of your labor, select cantaloupes that are very firm (but not green)—a ripe melon will make a mushy pickle. If you have only seen these at specialty food shops and think they must be difficult to make, let me assure you they aren't. And just wait till you taste the results.

3 large, firm cantaloupes
¼ cup pickling spices
1 cinnamon stick
  (2 inches long)
3 cups cider vinegar
2 cups water
4 cups sugar

1. Seed and peel the cantaloupes, and cut the fruit into 1-inch cubes (you should have about 12 cups).

2. Tie the pickling spices and the cinnamon stick together in a cheesecloth bag. Place the bag in a large nonreactive pot along with the vinegar and water. Bring to a boil, reduce the heat to medium, and simmer for 5 minutes. Remove the pot from the heat, add the melon, and let stand for 1½ to 2 hours, tossing occasionally.

3. Prepare four 1-pint canning jars and lids by sterilizing them in boiling water according to the manufacturer's instructions.

4. Add the sugar to the melon, stirring well to combine, and bring to a boil. Reduce the heat to a simmer and cook, stirring occasionally, until the cantaloupe is slightly translucent, 45 minutes. The fruit should have a gemlike quality.

5. Pack the melon into the jars. Cover with the hot syrup, making sure there are no air pockets; leave ¼ inch head space. Seal and process according to the manufacturer's instructions. Store the jars in a cool, dark place; refrigerate after opening.

Makes 4 pints

BREAD-AND-BUTTER PICKLES

★ ★ ★

I used to buy my bread-and-butter pickles from Harriet Tanner, whose husband grows the best corn in northwestern Connecticut, but I never seemed to buy enough. So, I worked up a recipe that I'm particularly happy with, and now I make my own. As far as I'm concerned, bread-and-butters, America's favorite home-canned pickles, go well with almost everything. At lunchtime I like to put a jar on the table and then watch as it empties; it's hard to eat just a few.

4 pounds Kirby (pickling) cucumbers (about 6 inches long), ends trimmed, cut into ¼-inch-thick slices
2 pounds small onions, thinly sliced
⅓ cup coarse salt
Ice cubes
3 cups cider vinegar
2 cups sugar
2 tablespoons mustard seeds
2 teaspoons ground turmeric
2 teaspoons celery seeds
1 teaspoon ground ginger
1 teaspoon black peppercorns

1. Place the cucumbers, onions, and coarse salt in a large bowl and toss well to combine. Cover the surface with ice cubes and let stand for 2 hours. Drain, rinse, and drain again.

2. Prepare six 1-pint canning jars and lids by sterilizing them in boiling water according to the manufacturer's instructions.

3. Combine the vinegar, sugar, and all of the spices in a large heavy nonreactive pot and bring to a boil. Add the cucumbers and onions and return the mixture to a boil. Cook for 1 minute and remove from the heat.

4. Pack the hot pickles into the jars. Cover with the hot syrup, making sure there are no air pockets, leave ¼ inch head space. Seal and process according to the manufacturer's instructions. Store the pickles in a cool, dark place for at least 2 weeks before using; refrigerate after opening.

Makes 6 pints

ERV NUSSBAUM'S DILL PICKLES

★ ★ ★

My brother-in-law, Donald Yanell, taunts me every year while I impatiently wait for him to put up these pickles following a recipe developed by his great friend, artist and gardener Erv Nussbaum. Once the pickles are in the jar, fermentation begins as the yeast in the rye bread does its work. No cooking necessary! August is the ideal time to put these up, when cukes are bountiful and dill flowers are abundant.

★★★★★★★★★★★★★★★★★★★★★★★★★★

TO DRY FRESH DILL

—❧—

*I*t is in the summer that dill flourishes in my garden, and while the graceful flowers seem to exist solely for their beauty, when dried they become a forceful flavoring agent. The best way to dry dill is to gather it in small bunches and fasten the stems together at the bottom with a rubber band. Hang the bunches upside down in a cool, dark place until they are fairly dry; for use in pickling, they should still be flexible. (If you're just after the weed or seed, they can be completely dry.) The taste is intense.

★★★★★★★★★★★★★★★★★★★★★★★★★★

6 cups cold water
½ cup coarse salt
8 cloves garlic, very coarsely chopped
2 teaspoons dill seeds
1 teaspoon pickling spices
7 pounds Kirby (pickling) cucumbers, rinsed
1 large bunch dried dill flowers (see box) or fresh dill
½ slice rye bread

1. Mix the water and coarse salt together in a 1-gallon jar with a good seal. Add the garlic, dill seeds, and pickling spices, stirring until the salt has dissolved.

2. Pack the jar tightly with the cucumbers. Add more cold water if necessary to fill the jar within ½ inch of the rim.

3. Place a clump of dried dill flowers on top of the cucumbers. Then place the bread on top of the dill flowers, pressing down. Close the lid tightly. Turn the jar upside down so all the ingredients mix around the cucumbers.

4. Place the jar, right side up, in a cool, dark location for 3 weeks. Do not refrigerate, but make sure the jar stays cool.

5. After 3 weeks, remove the bread and the dill flowers. Replace the lid. Refrigerate. The pickles will keep for up to 1 year.

Makes 1 gallon

BING CHERRY CHUTNEY

★ ★ ★

My affection for both sweet and savory is highlighted in this ruby chutney. Easily put together once the cherries are pitted, this completely American condiment is the consummate choice to accent game birds, roasted pork loin, or

Thanksgiving turkey. If you prefer a more astringent taste, use red wine vinegar instead of mellow cider vinegar.

4 cups fresh Bing cherries, pitted
1 red bell pepper, stemmed, seeded, and
    cut into ¼-inch dice
½ cup diced (¼ inch) red onion
2 tablespoons finely minced fresh ginger
2 teaspoons finely minced garlic
1 cup golden raisins
1 small dried red chile pepper,
    crushed
1 teaspoon salt
¼ teaspoon ground cinnamon
1 cup sugar
½ cup cider vinegar

1. Place all the ingredients in a heavy saucepan and bring to a boil. Reduce the heat to medium and simmer, uncovered, stirring often, for 30 minutes.

2. Remove the pan from the heat and let the chutney cool to room temperature. Refrigerate, covered, until ready to use. This will keep in the refrigerator in a covered container for up to 6 weeks.

Makes about 4 cups

PAPAYA CONFETTI SAUCE

★ ★ ★

This refreshing salsa-like relish, with its gently spicy taste, gives a marvelous punch dolloped on a shrimp quesadilla or a crab cake or a grilled chicken paillard.

1 very ripe papaya, halved, seeded, and peeled
¼ cup fresh lime juice
1 ripe plum tomato, seeded and cut into
    ¼-inch dice (2 tablespoons)
1 to 2 teaspoons finely minced seeded
    green jalapeño pepper
1 teaspoon coarsely chopped fresh cilantro leaves
Salt, to taste

1. Cut the papaya halves in half again. Cut one of these pieces into ¼-inch dice (enough to measure ¼ cup). Set aside.

2. Purée the remaining papaya with the lime juice in a food processor until smooth. Transfer the purée to a bowl.

3. Add the reserved diced papaya and the tomato, jalapeño, and cilantro. Season with the salt. Refrigerate, covered, until ready to use, for up to 24 hours.

Makes about 1 cup

PETOSKEY SOUR CHERRY SALSA

★ ★ ★

When I was in Michigan during sour cherry season, I had the good fortune one day to go cherry picking in an extraordinary orchard on the edge of Lake Charlevoix. The fairytale setting of restored blue-trimmed white barns and trees heavy with fruit was made even more magical by the rich, deep color of the sky. It is a wonderful memory.

The season for ripe sour cherries is fleeting, so start inquiring at a farmers' market or greengrocer at the beginning of July for the exact date that the cherries will arrive. Believe me, this is one of the few times when it's okay to be a pest. Serve your bounty with roast pork, venison, and all game birds.

2 cups fresh sour cherries, pitted and
  coarsely chopped
½ cup finely diced red bell pepper
⅓ cup finely diced red onion
1 teaspoon finely minced garlic
1 teaspoon finely minced seeded green jalapeño
  or other chile pepper, or more to taste
¼ cup cider vinegar
3 tablespoons sugar
1 tablespoon fresh lemon juice
1 to 2 tablespoons coarsely chopped fresh
  cilantro leaves (optional)
Salt, to taste

   1. Combine the cherries, bell pepper, onion, garlic, jalapeño, vinegar, sugar, and lemon juice in a large saucepan. Simmer, partially covered, over medium heat, stirring occasionally, until the vegetables have softened, 10 minutes.
   2. Uncover and cook for 5 minutes longer. Reduce the heat if the salsa boils.
   3. Transfer the salsa to a bowl and let it cool to room temperature. Stir in the cilantro, if desired, and season with salt. If not serving immediately, refrigerate, covered, up to 24 hours.
   Makes about 2 cups

CREAMY SALSA VERDE

★ ★ ★

The heat of this salsa echoes the warmth of the trendy Liberty Bar in San Antonio, Texas, during Saturday lunch at the time of the annual Fiesta. It was all I could do to keep from ordering everything on the menu because it all just sounded so appealing. The dish I decided to order, grilled quail atop a pool of salsa verde, was irresistible. When I returned home from my trip, I cooked up my version of each. In addition to being a beautiful sauce for quail, it makes a wonderful dip for tortilla chips, and complements Hot and Smooth Breakfast Burritos, Duck and Caramelized Onion Quesadillas, San Fran Chicken Kebabs, as well as roast pork.

2 green jalapeño peppers, halved
  and seeded
2 pounds tomatillos, husks removed
3 scallions (3 inches green left on),
  trimmed and sliced
¾ cup chopped fresh cilantro leaves
1½ teaspoons finely chopped garlic
½ cup defatted chicken broth,
  preferably homemade (page 253)
1 teaspoon cornstarch
1½ tablespoons unsalted butter
¼ cup fresh lime juice
½ teaspoon sugar
¼ cup heavy (or whipping) cream

   1. Preheat the broiler.
   2. Place the jalapeños, cut side down, on a baking sheet and broil until charred, 12 to 15 minutes. Place the peppers in a paper bag, seal the bag, and allow them to steam for 10 minutes. Then slip off the skins, coarsely chop, and set aside. (Wear rubber gloves to prevent irritation.)

3. Coarsely chop the tomatillos, and place them in a heavy pot along with the jalapeños, scallions, ½ cup of the cilantro, garlic, and chicken broth. Partially cover and cook over medium heat, stirring once or twice, for 10 minutes. Set aside ¼ cup of the cooking liquid, and let the tomatillos cool to room temperature. Then purée the mixture in a food processor, and return to the pot.

4. Mix the reserved liquid with the cornstarch, and add it to the pot. Cook, stirring, over medium heat until the sauce thickens, 5 minutes. Stir in the butter, lime juice, and sugar, and let cool slightly.

5. Put the salsa through a strainer to remove most of the seeds. Return it to the food processor, add the cream and the remaining ¼ cup cilantro, and process until it is smooth with little flecks of cilantro showing. Refrigerate the salsa until ready to use. When serving it as a dip, bring the salsa to room temperature; or serve it warm.

Makes about 2 cups

PICO DE GALLO

★ ★ ★

This Southwestern salsa is named for a rooster's "peck," or "beak," because at one time it was eaten with the fingers in sort of a pecking fashion. Although a salsa can be cooked, this one is made of raw vegetables and can top every-

thing from fish to poultry. I still think that there is nothing better as a dip for chips.

3 tomatoes, cored, seeded and cut into ¼-inch dice (1½ cups)
¼ cup finely minced shallots
2 tablespoons chopped fresh cilantro leaves
2 tablespoons fresh lime juice
Salt and freshly ground black pepper, to taste
1 tablespoon finely chopped jalapeño pepper, or to taste (optional)

Toss all of the ingredients together in a bowl, and let rest for up to 1 hour before serving, but not too much longer. The fresher the better.

Makes about 1 cup

ROASTED ROSY SALSA

★ ★ ★

With its deep-roasted flavors and a few charred flecks from the grill, this is a true Southwestern salsa, found on tables throughout San Antonio and Santa Fe. It is an excellent condiment as well as a dip for corn tortillas, and can be made somewhat more piquant with the addition of another chile or two.

2 red bell peppers, stemmed, halved, and seeded
1 red jalapeño pepper, halved and seeded
1 green jalapeño pepper, halved and seeded
2 onions, peeled and halved
2 large tomatoes, cored and halved
1 clove garlic, peeled
2 tablespoons extra virgin olive oil
½ teaspoon ground cumin
Juice of 1 lime

1. Preheat the broiler.

2. Place the bell peppers, both jalepeños, and the onions, cut side down, on a baking sheet, and broil 3 inches from the heat source, until blackened, 12 to 15 minutes. Place the peppers in a paper bag, seal the bag, and allow them to steam for 10 minutes. Set the onions aside.

3. Place the tomatoes and garlic on the baking sheet, and broil on both sides until blackened and soft, 12 to 15 minutes.

4. Peel the charred skin from all of the unpeeled vegetables. (Wear rubber gloves to prevent irritation from the jalapeños.) Chop them coarsely and place them in a heavy saucepan.

5. Add 1 tablespoon of the olive oil and the cumin to the vegetables, and cook, uncovered, stirring, over high heat for the flavors to blend, about 3 minutes. Remove from the heat and allow to cool slightly.

6. Place the mixture in a food processor and pulse until it is finely and evenly chopped but not a purée.

7. Transfer the salsa to a bowl, and stir in the remaining 1 tablespoon of olive oil and the lime juice. Adjust the seasonings, and serve at room temperature. If not using immediately, refrigerate, covered, up to 2 days.

Makes about 1½ cups

GARDEN CHILI SAUCE

V ibrant summer vegetables, spiced up to your liking, are the basic ingredients in this typically American sauce. It peps up hot dogs and hamburgers, and I like it as a change from the traditional ketchup and mustard. If you prefer a powerful kick, add two red chiles instead of one. I also enjoy this sauce on a grilled cheese sandwich or as an accompaniment to a western omelet.

6 pounds plum tomatoes, peeled, cored,
  and coarsely chopped
2 cups diced (¼ inch) red bell peppers
2 cups coarsely chopped onions
1 to 2 hot red chile peppers, seeded and
  finely minced (1 to 2 tablespoons)
1 cup (packed) dark brown sugar
3 tablespoons coarse salt
3 tablespoons pickling spices
1 tablespoon mustard seeds
1 tablespoon celery seeds
2½ cups cider vinegar
2 tablespoons fresh lemon juice

1. Prepare four 1-pint canning jars and lids by sterilizing them in boiling water according to the manufacturer's instructions.

2. Combine the tomatoes, bell peppers, onions, hot peppers, brown sugar, and coarse salt in a heavy nonreactive pot. Cook gently over medium heat for 45 minutes.

3. Tie the pickling spices, mustard seeds, and celery seeds in a cheesecloth bag. Add this to the vegetables and cook over medium-low heat until reduced by half, stirring occasionally to prevent sticking, for 45 minutes.

4. Add the vinegar and cook over low heat for 40 minutes longer. Then stir in the lemon juice.

5. Pack the hot sauce into the jars, leaving ¼ inch head space. Seal and process according to the manufacturer's instructions. Store the sauce in a cool, dry place; refrigerate after opening.

Makes 4 pints

MAUI MANGO BARBECUE SAUCE

★ ★ ★

The first time I had a taste of this sweet, rich, and spicy sauce over some grilled fish was on Maui; I went wild with enthusiasm. I couldn't wait to come home and do my best to reproduce it. This is pretty close and pretty delicious! It complements salmon, ono, and duck as well as lamb, and blends well into the brilliant cuisines of the Pacific Rim. Use it liberally!

1 ripe mango, peeled, pitted, and cut into
small cubes
1 cup prepared mango chutney
½ cup finely chopped onion
1 tablespoon finely minced garlic
1 can (28 ounces) peeled plum tomatoes,
crushed, with their juices
2 tablespoons cider vinegar
1 tablespoon unsulfured molasses
1 teaspoon Tabasco sauce

1. Combine all the ingredients in a heavy saucepan. Simmer, covered, over low heat until the ingredients are blended and the sauce has thickened, 15 minutes. Set it aside to cool slightly.

2. Purée the sauce until smooth in a food processor or blender. Refrigerate, covered, up to 3 days.

Makes about 5 cups

SPICED TOMATO KETCHUP

★ ★ ★

In the seventeenth century it could have meant fermented walnuts, mushrooms, or berries. But now, centuries later, there is nothing that says "ketchup" more to Americans than the bottle of lush, perfectly spiced tomato purée. Deriving from the Chinese word *ket-tsiap* (which referred to pickled fish sauce), the condiment as we know it was first introduced by the H.J. Heinz Company of Pennsylvania in the late nineteenth century. Because ketchup making is such an arduous process, few home cooks bring out the pots and devise their own, but as I discovered, some patience and effort are well worth the reward.

After buying bushels of ripe Jersey tomatoes, I began the process. I'm here to tell you that I wasn't able to match the bottled magic on my first try. Not only were the tomatoes wrong (they were too watery), too much allspice made the sauce bitter. So I began anew, with a lighter hand in spicing and ripe plum tomatoes instead. I found that firm, small tomatoes produce the ideal texture. A heavy nonreactive pot is also essential because 3 hours of cooking is necessary. Be ready for a marvelous surprise! You'll find this ketchup has a lighter texture and finer flavor than you've experienced with others.

8 whole cloves
8 black peppercorns
4 whole allspice
1 cinnamon stick (about 3 inches long)
¼ teaspoon mustard seeds
10 pounds ripe plum tomatoes, cored and
    quartered
2 large onions, coarsely chopped
2 cloves garlic, peeled and crushed
⅓ cup cider vinegar
1 tablespoon dark brown sugar
1 tablespoon fresh lemon juice
Salt, to taste

1. Tie all the spices up in a cheesecloth bag.

2. Place the tomatoes, onions, garlic, and the spice bag in a large heavy nonreactive pot. Bring to a boil, reduce the heat to medium, and simmer, uncovered, stirring occasionally, for 1 hour.

3. Strain the mixture through a sieve in small batches, pressing down on the tomatoes with a spoon to extract all but the skins. Return the strained liquid and the spice bag to the pot. Add the vinegar and the brown sugar. Simmer, uncovered, over medium-low heat, stirring occasionally, for 2 hours. Remove from the heat and discard the spice bag.

4. Allow the mixture to cool slightly, and then purée in a food processor until completely smooth. Transfer the ketchup to a bowl, stir in the lemon juice, and season to taste with salt. Refrigerate, covered, for up to 3 weeks.

Makes about 4 cups

LANCASTER APPLE BUTTER

★ ★ ★

Until I spent a weekend in Lancaster County, Pennsylvania, I had always thought of apple butter as one of those elusive foods that was sold in jars or served on relish trays at quaint country inns. But visiting with Mennonite and Amish families, I was treated to the most delicious, perfectly spiced apple butter imaginable. I knew the time had come for me to have a lesson in this all-American spread. To begin with, I learned that any old apple won't do. For the perfect consistency, it has to be a mealy-textured cooking apple, such as Gravenstein, McIntosh, or Rome Beauty. Cooked with cider, then baked with a touch of cinnamon and a splash of vinegar, this apple butter is thick, dark, and deeply aromatic. Although this recipe may be more work than a trip to the supermarket, it is eminently worthwhile, and the apple butter will keep for up to 3 weeks—if you don't eat it all at the first taste!

6 pounds mealy apples (Gravenstein,
    McIntosh, Rome Beauty)
1 cup apple cider
1 tablespoon ground cinnamon
¼ cup cider vinegar
2 cups (packed) dark brown sugar

1. Peel and core the apples, then quarter them. Place the apples in a heavy ovenproof pot, add the cider, and bring to a boil over medium heat. Reduce the heat to a simmer, cover, and cook until the apples are soft, about 30 minutes.

2. Preheat the oven to 350°F.

3. Press the apples, along with any liquid, through a strainer into a bowl. Return the mixture to the pot and add the cinnamon, vinegar, and brown sugar. Bake, uncovered, for 3 hours, stirring occasionally. Cool to room temperature and refrigerate, covered, for up to 3 weeks.

Makes about 5 cups

SHAKER APPLESAUCE

★ ★ ★

At the Shaker Village in Hancock, Massachusetts, dinner is prepared for visitors every Saturday during the summer months. In the Great Cook Room, a large basement kitchen reflecting traditional Shaker style, the best of Shaker cookery is recreated in simple, homey dishes such as pot roast baked in cranberry sauce. At one of the meals, I enjoyed a golden applesauce that was served as an accompaniment. The cook told me that she began by boiling up a syrup of apple cider and then "threw" the apples in. I proceeded a bit more cautiously in my kitchen. The sweet flavor of the cider underlines the distinctive fall taste of the combination of McIntosh, Golden Delicious, Red Delicious, and Granny Smith apples. A cinnamon stick and lemon zest brighten the flavor of this super-chunky sauce.

8 apples (a combination of McIntosh,
   Golden Delicious, Red Delicious,
   and Granny Smith)
1 tablespoon fresh lemon juice
1 cup apple cider
½ cup sugar
1 teaspoon finely grated lemon zest
1 cinnamon stick (1 inch long)

1. Core, peel, and cut the apples into large chunks, tossing them with the lemon juice to prevent discoloration.

2. Place the apples and all the remaining ingredients in a large heavy pot, and bring to a boil. Reduce the heat to a simmer, cover partially, and cook until the apples are very tender, 15 minutes.

3. Uncover the pot and cook 5 minutes more.

4. Remove the pot from the heat and discard the cinnamon stick. Cool to room temperature and then refrigerate, covered, until ready to use, up to 5 days.

Makes about 4 cups

SAVORY HERBED FARMER CHEESE

★ ★ ★

When I stretched my memory looking for childhood relish tray favorites, I recalled that I always put a spoonful or two of cottage cheese on my plate—the perfect companion to those tart relishes and pickled foods. This herbed cheese is an adult variation, enlivened with lemon zest and chives.

24 ounces farmer cheese
3 tablespoons snipped fresh chives
1½ teaspoons finely grated lemon zest
Salt and freshly ground black pepper,
   to taste

Place the cheese in a bowl and gently stir in the remaining ingredients, being careful not to break up the curds too much. Serve at room temperature.

Serves 8 to 10

DINNERTIME

Breads

What accompanies a soul-enriching soup best? What makes a good sandwich great? What's the sop of choice for gravy? Fragrantly fresh, excellent bread, of course! And bread in the oven emits the sweetest of kitchen aromas. If you haven't gotten a whiff recently, I suggest you roll up your sleeves and start kneading. This is deeply satisfying work.

But it's not *much* work. Recipes calling for dough that needs to rise or starters that must be made a day ahead require some planning, but don't add up to much more labor than batter bread. Those American classics don't require yeast and can be made more quickly. You'll find some of the best known and loved of them here, including steamed Boston Brown Bread, Country Cornbread, and Southern-style biscuits. But for real satisfaction, do bake up the White Toasting Loaf, the Whole-Wheat Wheat Berry Bread, and the Raisin Pumpernickel Bread.

WHITE TOASTING LOAF

★ ★ ★

This basic all-purpose bread, with a bit of a buttermilk tang, is great for grilled sandwiches, hot open-face sandwiches such as meat loaf, and morning toast. It's so easy to make that you might find yourself routinely baking bread. Besides that, it keeps well—just wrap it in plastic wrap and refrigerate it once you've enjoyed the first fresh, warm slices with lots of butter. Be sure to use a serrated knife for slicing so that the bread doesn't tear.

¼ cup warm water
1 tablespoon sugar
1 package active dry yeast
4½ to 5 cups unbleached all-purpose flour
2 teaspoons salt
*6 tablespoons (¾ stick) unsalted butter, melted and
    cooled to room temperature*
1½ cups buttermilk, at room temperature

1. Combine the warm water with the sugar in a small bowl. Add the yeast, stir well, and set aside until foamy, about 5 minutes.

2. Mix 4½ cups of the flour and the salt in a large bowl. In another large bowl, combine the melted butter, buttermilk, and the yeast mixture. Add the flour mixture, 1 cup at a time, to the liquid ingredients, combining it with your hands until the mixture is a stiff dough.

3. Turn the dough onto a lightly floured work surface, and knead it for 10 minutes. Add the remaining ½ cup flour while you're kneading if the dough seems too sticky. Shape the dough into a ball.

4. Generously grease a bowl with butter. Add the dough and roll it around in the bowl to coat. Cover the bowl loosely with plastic wrap, and set it in a warm place until the dough has doubled in volume, about 1½ hours.

5. Punch the dough down. Turn the dough out onto a lightly floured work surface and knead it 5 times. Return the dough to the greased bowl, and roll it around to coat it well with butter. Cover the bowl loosely, and set it aside until the dough has doubled in volume, about 1 hour.

6. Grease two 9 x 5 x 2¾-inch loaf pans.

7. Divide the dough in half. Flatten each half to form a rectangle about 9 x 6 inches, and roll them up lengthwise. Pinch the seam and ends closed, and tuck the ends under. Place the dough in the prepared pans, cover loosely with plastic wrap, and set aside in a warm place until doubled in volume, about 1¼ hours.

8. Preheat the oven to 400°F.

9. Place the pans in the oven and reduce the temperature to 375°F. Bake for 15 minutes and then reduce the temperature to 350°F. Bake until the loaves are golden brown and sound hollow when tapped on the bottom, 45 to 50 minutes longer. (If the bread is browning too quickly, cover it with aluminum foil.)

10. Remove the loaves from the pans and set them on a wire rack to cool.

Makes 2 loaves

WHOLE-WHEAT WHEAT BERRY BREAD

★ ★ ★

Full of flavor and texture, and easy to make—a requirement for me when baking bread—this loaf longs to be toasted and makes any sandwich more exciting. The wheat berries, pumpkin seeds, and sunflower seeds that enrich it can be found in health food stores and even in some well-stocked supermarkets. (Note that the wheat berries need an overnight soaking.)

When setting bread dough aside to rise in a warm place, I like to put it in my gas oven, which is the older type with an ever-burning pilot light, leaving the door slightly ajar. But any warm draft-free spot is fine.

You can easily make rolls out of this recipe (see box, this page). They make a stunning presentation, richly encrusted in seeds.

1 cup wheat berries
3½ cups water
1 package active
    dry yeast
1½ cups warm water
3 cups unbleached
    all-purpose flour
2 cups whole-wheat
    flour
1 tablespoon salt
1 cup honey
1 cup pumpkin seeds,
    toasted (see Note)
1 cup coarsely chopped pecans, lightly
    toasted (see Note)
½ cup sunflower seeds

1. Soak the berries in water to cover overnight.

2. Drain the berries and place them in a saucepan with the 3½ cups water. Bring to a boil, reduce the heat, and simmer, partially covered, until tender, 1 hour. Drain, and set aside to cool to room temperature.

3. Combine the yeast and the warm water

WHEAT BERRY ROLLS

—❦—

*T*o make rolls, instead of shaping the dough into loaves, pat the dough out to a 7½-inch square that's about 1 inch thick. Cut the dough into squares (irregular shapes are fine) approximately 1½ x 1½ inches. Whisk together 1 egg and ¼ cup water, and brush this wash over the rolls. Mix together 1 cup sunflower seeds and 1 cup pumpkin seeds, and scatter them over a work surface. Roll the rolls in the seeds (they should be rough looking). Line a baking sheet with parchment paper, or sprinkle it with cornmeal, and place the rolls on it, 1 inch apart. Cover loosely with plastic wrap and set aside to rise until doubled in volume, 30 minutes to 1 hour. Bake in a preheated 375°F oven until deep golden brown and crusty, about 30 minutes. Break one in half to test for doneness. Remove the rolls from the baking sheet and set them on a rack to cool.

Makes about 24 rolls.

in a small bowl, and set aside until foamy, about 5 minutes.

4. Stir the all-purpose flour, whole-wheat flour, and salt together in a bowl and set aside.

5. Place the yeast mixture and the honey in a large bowl, and stir to combine. Add the flour mixture, and stir until it forms a dough. Turn the dough out onto a lightly floured work surface, and knead it for 10 minutes. The dough will be very sticky. Lightly dust your hands with all-purpose flour, if the bread is too sticky to knead.

6. In a bowl, stir together the wheat berries, pumpkin seeds, pecans, and sunflower seeds. Knead this mixture into the dough until well dispersed, 2 to 3 minutes. Form the dough into a ball.

7. Generously grease a large bowl with butter. Add the dough and roll it around in the bowl to coat. Cover the bowl loosely with plastic wrap, and set it aside in a warm place until the dough has doubled in volume, about 1½ hours.

8. Grease two 9 x 5 x 2¾-inch loaf pans.

9. Knead the dough slightly. Divide it in half, form it into 2 loaf shapes, and slip them into the prepared pans.

10. Cover the pans loosely with plastic wrap, and set them aside in a warm place until the dough has doubled in volume, about 1½ hours.

11. Preheat the oven to 400°F.

12. Bake the bread in the center of the oven for 30 minutes. Then reduce the temperature to 350°F and bake until the loaves are a deep golden brown, 45 minutes to 1 hour. (Cover the loaves with aluminum foil if they are browning too quickly.) When they're done, the loaves will sound hollow when tapped on the bottom. Remove the loaves from the pans and set them on a wire rack to cool.

Makes 2 loaves

NOTE: To toast pumpkin seeds: Place them in a single layer on a baking sheet, and bake for 7 to 15 minutes in a preheated 350°F oven, shaking the pan once or twice. Begin checking the seeds after 5 minutes to ensure that they don't burn.

To lightly toast pecans: Place them in a single layer on a baking sheet, and bake for 5 to 7 minutes in a preheated 350°F oven.

NEW DELI RYE BREAD

★ ★ ★

To make this bread, you'll need to prepare the sourdough starter one day in advance, so be sure to plan accordingly. It's the starter that makes this bread so special, and only a little commercial yeast is used to get it going. Once you master it, you'll find that this is a great all-purpose loaf—wonderful anytime. It is superb for grilled cheese and ham, and even better simply toasted and spread with raspberry jam. Corned beef and pastrami layered on it are pretty terrific, too! Freeze the second loaf until the first is eaten.

SOURDOUGH STARTER
¼ teaspoon active dry yeast
1 cup warm water
1½ cups unbleached all-
*   purpose flour*
½ cup rye flour

DOUGH
2 teaspoons active dry yeast
1 cup warm water
1 tablespoon salt
3 tablespoons vegetable oil
2 tablespoons sugar
3 tablespoons caraway seeds
2½ cups unbleached all-
*   purpose flour*
1½ cups rye flour,
*   or more as needed*
Yellow cornmeal, for the baking sheet

1. Prepare the sourdough starter the day before you plan to bake the bread: Stir the yeast into the warm water in a medium-size bowl. Set it aside until foamy, 5 minutes. Then add both

YEAST BREAD BASICS

—❦—

• I use active dry yeast for my breads. I find it reliable and easy to store in a cool, dry place.

• Proofing yeast—dissolving yeast in warm water, sometimes with a little sugar—was once an essential step in baking bread, thereby showing "proof" the yeast was still alive. Since yeast now comes well wrapped with an expiration date on the packaging, much of the guesswork is eliminated. I still like to proof my yeast, though, just to be sure.

• Heat kills yeast, so make sure the water used to dissolve it does not exceed 110°F. If the water is lukewarm to the touch, that is about right.

• Kneading the dough produces gluten, which gives the bread its fine texture. You will know the bread has been kneaded enough when it is soft, elastic, and springs back when you touch it.

• Generously grease, with butter or vegetable oil, the bowl the dough will rise in. When greasing the baking pans, always use butter.

• Let your bread rise in a warm, draft-free area. A gas oven with a pilot light is perfect. If you don't have a gas oven, a bowl of hot tap water placed in the bottom of the oven also does the trick.

• When baking bread the heat from the oven causes the dough to have a final growth spurt before the yeast dies. So, when baking bread in a loaf pan, place it in the oven when the dough has risen just level with the top of the pan.

• To double-check that a loaf that looks done is really done, it's best to give it a light tap on the bottom with your finger. If it sounds hollow, the bread is cooked through. If your bread is in a loaf pan, turn it partially out onto a kitchen towel to give it a tap. If it still sounds too solid, return it to the oven for a bit more time.

flours, and mix them into the yeast mixture with your hands until incorporated. Cover the bowl loosely with plastic wrap and set it aside in a warm place overnight.

2. The next day, prepare the dough: Stir the yeast into the warm water in a large bowl, and set it aside until foamy, 5 minutes. Then add the reserved sourdough starter, and stir to dissolve. Add the salt, 2 tablespoons of the vegetable oil, the sugar, and caraway seeds, and mix well. Gradually add the all-purpose flour and 1½ cups of the rye flour, mixing it

with your hands until a stiff dough is formed.

3. Turn the dough out onto a lightly floured work surface, and knead until it is smooth and elastic, about 10 minutes, adding additional rye flour as necessary.

4. Generously grease a large bowl with the 1 remaining tablespoon of vegetable oil. Scrape the dough into a ball and add it to the bowl, rolling the dough around to coat. Cover the bowl loosely with plastic wrap, and set it aside in a warm place until the dough has doubled in volume, about 1 hour.

5. Turn the dough onto a work surface and divide it in half. Shape each half into an elongated loaf, about 8 inches long, pushing the dough away from you and tapering the ends.

6. Sprinkle a large baking sheet with the cornmeal. Place the 2 loaves on the sheet and cover it loosely with plastic wrap. Set it aside in a warm place until the loaves have doubled in volume, 30 minutes.

7. Meanwhile, preheat the oven to 425°F. Fifteen minutes before baking time, fill an 8-inch square baking pan with boiling water and place it on the bottom oven rack to create steam.

8. Using a razor blade or a small sharp knife, slash the loaves diagonally, about ¼ inch deep, in four places. Bake the loaves in the center of the oven until a deep golden brown, 40 minutes. (Cover the loaves with aluminum foil if they are browning too quickly.) When they are done, the loaves will sound hollow when tapped on the bottom. Cool the loaves on a wire rack.

Makes 2 loaves

RAISIN PUMPERNICKEL BREAD

★ ★ ★

Rye flour, having very little gluten, forms a nice dense loaf, and density is what you strive for in pumpernickel. The finished result is made more complex and hearty with the addition of cocoa powder and coffee, and slightly sweet with the addition of molasses and brown sugar. It keeps well and mellows with age. This flecked pumpernickel is perfection when sliced thin and served with delicate slices of baked ham and a coarse, grainy mustard. It also lends itself beautifully to grilled sandwiches.

STARTER
⅛ *teaspoon active dry yeast*
½ *cup plus 2 tablespoons warm water*
1 *cup unbleached all-purpose flour*
⅓ *cup rye flour*

DOUGH
1½ *cups raisins*
1 *package active dry yeast*
1 *cup brewed coffee, at room temperature*
½ *cup unsulfured molasses*
1 *cup coarse wheat bran*
½ *cup rye flour*
⅓ *cup unsweetened cocoa powder*
¼ *cup (packed) dark brown sugar*
6 *to 6¼ cups whole-wheat flour*
1 *tablespoon salt*
Yellow cornmeal, for the baking sheet

1. Make the starter the day before you plan to bake the bread: Stir the yeast into the warm water in a medium-size bowl, and set it aside until foamy, 5 minutes. Then add both flours and stir until combined. Cover the bowl with plastic wrap and allow to sit at room temperature overnight.

2. The following day, prepare the dough: Place the raisins in a small bowl and cover with warm water by 2 inches (about 2 cups). Set aside for 1 hour.

3. Drain the raisins, reserving the soaking liquid. Set the raisins aside.

4. Heat 1¼ cups of the raisin soaking liquid in a small saucepan until it is just warm to the touch. Place the warm liquid in a large bowl, and stir the yeast into it. Add the reserved starter along with with the coffee, molasses, wheat bran, rye flour, cocoa powder, and brown sugar. Mix well.

5. Add 6 cups of the whole-wheat flour and the salt, and continue mixing until a stiff dough is formed.

6. Turn the dough out onto a lightly floured work surface, and knead until a smooth dough is formed, about 10 minutes. Knead in the reserved raisins, and the remaining ¼ cup whole-wheat flour if the dough is too sticky. Form the dough into a ball.

7. Generously grease a large bowl. Add the dough and roll it around in the bowl to coat. Cover the bowl loosely with plastic wrap and set it aside in a warm place until the dough has doubled in volume, 1 hour.

8. Sprinkle a large baking sheet generously with cornmeal. Divide the dough in half, and form each half into a round. Place the rounds on the prepared baking sheet, cover loosely with plastic wrap, and let rise for 1 hour in a warm place.

9. Meanwhile, preheat the oven to 375°F. Fifteen minutes before baking time, fill an 8-inch square baking dish with boiling water, and place it on the bottom oven rack to create steam.

10. Using a razor blade or a small sharp knife, slash the loaves diagonally, about ¼ inch deep, in four places. Bake the bread in the center of the oven until it sounds hollow when tapped on the bottom, 1 hour 10 minutes to 1 hour 15 minutes. Cool the loaves on a wire rack.

Makes 2 small round loaves

PARKER HOUSE ROLLS

★ ★ ★

One of America's favorite rolls was created at the Parker House Hotel in Boston in the mid-1800s by, it is said, a baker provoked by the actions of a hostile guest. Maybe the guest was impatient to get a basket of bread or maybe he didn't like the bread that had been brought to his table. Whatever the reason, the annoyed baker hurried some unfinished dough into the oven, and what came out were light, puffy rolls with the famous off-center crease. Serve the rolls nestled in a linen napkin–lined basket, with a pot of sweet butter alongside, and say a quiet thanks to that angry diner, whoever he may be.

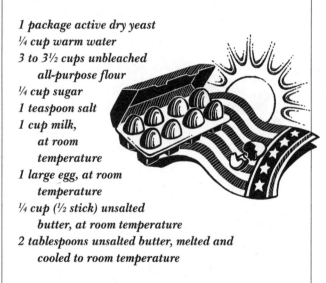

1 package active dry yeast
¼ cup warm water
3 to 3½ cups unbleached
*   all-purpose flour*
¼ cup sugar
1 teaspoon salt
1 cup milk,
*   at room*
*   temperature*
1 large egg, at room
*   temperature*
¼ cup (½ stick) unsalted
*   butter, at room temperature*
2 tablespoons unsalted butter, melted and
*   cooled to room temperature*

1. The day before you plan to bake the rolls, prepare the dough: Stir the yeast into the warm water in a small bowl. Set it aside until foamy, about 5 minutes.

2. Combine 3 cups of the flour, the sugar, and salt in a large bowl and set aside.

3. Mix the milk and egg together in a medium-size bowl. Add the ¼ cup butter, and mix. (Don't worry if the butter is not completely incorporated—it will be further incorporated in the next step.)

4. Make a well in the dry ingredients, and add the liquid ingredients and the yeast. Using your hands, gradually incorporate the dry ingredients into the liquid to form a sticky dough.

5. Turn the dough out onto a lightly floured work surface, and knead, incorporating the remaining ½ cup flour, until the dough is smooth and elastic, about 7 minutes.

6. Generously grease a large bowl with butter. Add the dough and roll it around in the bowl to coat. Cover the bowl loosely with plastic wrap, and set it aside in a warm place until the dough has doubled in volume, about 1 hour.

7. Punch down the dough and knead it briefly (2 or 3 times). Butter the bowl again, and turn the dough in it to coat. Cover, and refrigerate overnight.

8. The next day, turn the dough out onto a lightly floured work surface. Divide it in half. Press each half out to form an 8 x 5½-inch rectangle (½ inch thick). Cut each rectangle into 4 pieces crosswise and in half lengthwise, so that you have 8 rectangles (16 total). Brush the dough evenly with the melted butter. Fold each rectangle in half but do not press down on it (you want the crease).

9. Grease two 9 x 5 x 2¾-inch loaf pans. Arrange the rolls, seam side up and facing in the same direction, in two rows in each pan (8 rolls per pan). Cover the pans loosely with plastic wrap, and set aside in a warm place until the rolls have doubled in volume, about 1½ hours.

10. Preheat the oven to 350°F.

11. Remove the wrap, and bake the rolls in the center of the oven until golden brown, 25 to 30 minutes. Remove the pans from the oven and cool the rolls slightly, in the pans, on a wire rack. Break the rolls apart, and serve warm.

Makes 16 rolls

INDIAN FRY BREAD

★ ★ ★

There are endless regional variations of this Native American flatbread—each tribe, and each family within a tribe, has its own special recipe for it. One of many uses for fry bread, and my favorite to date, is as a base for a marvelous Indian Taco that I first feasted on in South Dakota. It can also be topped with a favorite chili recipe and garnished with Guacamole and Pico de Gallo for a quick and tasty dinner. Or, what better after-school snack than warm fry bread drizzled with honey or lavishly sprinkled with confectioners' sugar?

3 cups all-purpose flour
1 tablespoon baking powder
½ teaspoon salt
1½ cups warm water
4 cups vegetable oil

1. Sift the flour, baking powder, and salt together into a large bowl. Add the warm water and stir with a wooden spoon until the mixture begins to gather into a ball. Knead the dough on a lightly floured surface with your hands until it is just smooth, 1 to 2 minutes. Do not overwork it. The dough will be sticky. Place in a bowl and cover loosely with plastic wrap. Refrigerate for 1 hour.

2. Heat the oil to 350°F in a heavy pot (about 9 inches in diameter and 4 inches deep).

3. Lightly flour a clean work surface. Pull off egg-size portions of the dough and roll them into ball shapes. Using a floured rolling pin, roll the balls out to form 6-inch rounds. Pierce the center of each one with a knife, and then prick it several times with the tines of a fork.

4. Fry the rounds, one at a time, in the hot oil until golden brown, about 1½ minutes per side. They will have a slightly crispy exterior and a soft interior. Drain them on paper towels.

5. For best results, serve immediately (fry bread does not keep).

Makes 12 rounds

JALAPEÑO CHEESE BREAD

★ ★ ★

Semolina flour adds a buttery yellow color and good body to this bread, which is enhanced with flecks of jalapeño for an authentic taste of the Southwest. I first sampled a slice at Goode Company BBQ, a restaurant in Houston, Texas (see page 349 for A Great Pit Master Barbecues Up a Storm), and I knew I had to have the recipe. It makes a great sandwich bread, stuffed with grilled veggies or meat, and it's also perfect to tote on a picnic. Serve Jalapeño Cheese Bread with Brisket BBQ with Goode's Mop, Barbecued Spare Ribs, or Super-Crispy Buttermilk Fried Chicken and all the fixin's, and you'll have a meal to remember.

1 tablespoon unsalted butter
¼ cup finely minced green jalapeño pepper
  (seeds and ribs removed)
1 package active dry yeast
¼ cup warm water
1 cup milk, at room temperature
3 tablespoons unsalted butter, melted and
  cooled to room temperature
1 large egg, lightly beaten, at room
  temperature
2½ to 3 cups unbleached all-purpose flour
1½ cups plus 1 tablespoon semolina flour
2 tablespoons sugar
1 teaspoon salt
½ pound white Cheddar cheese, grated
  (about 2 cups)

1. Melt the butter in a small skillet over low heat. Add the jalapeños and sauté until softened, 5 minutes. Cool to room temperature.

2. In a large bowl, stir the yeast into the warm water, and set aside until foamy, about 5 minutes. Then add the milk, melted butter, and egg, and mix well.

3. In a medium-size bowl, combine 2½ cups of the all-purpose flour, 1½ cups of the semolina flour, and the sugar and salt. Gradually add the dry ingredients to the liquid ingredients, mixing until a stiff dough is formed.

4. Turn the dough out onto a lightly floured surface, and knead it until smooth, about 10 minutes, adding the remaining ½ cup all-purpose flour as necessary. Form the dough into a ball.

5. Generously grease a large bowl with butter. Add the dough and roll it around in the bowl to coat. Cover the bowl loosely with plastic wrap, and set it aside in a warm place until the dough has doubled in volume, 1 hour.

6. Turn the dough out onto a lightly floured work surface, and knead the cheese and the reserved jalapeños into it, about 2 minutes. Form the dough into a rectangular loaf.

7. Grease a 9 x 5 x 2¾-inch baking pan. Dust the pan with the remaining 1 tablespoon semolina flour.

8. Place the dough in the pan and cover it loosely with plastic wrap. Set it aside in a warm place until doubled in volume, 1 hour.

9. Preheat the oven to 350°F.

10. Remove the plastic wrap, and bake the bread in the center of the oven until it is golden on top and sounds hollow when tapped on the bottom, 1 hour. Cool the loaf in the pan on a wire rack for 10 minutes, then remove the bread from the pan and cool completely on the rack.

Makes 1 loaf

BOSTON BROWN BREAD

★ ★ ★

Dense, savory, and rich, Boston brown bread is a steamed quick bread that was popular among eighteenth-century Puritans, who typically served it on the Sabbath along with Boston baked beans. Still popular today, it is easy to make and delicious eaten warm with cold unsalted butter. In the autumn, it is heavenly served with homemade Lancaster Apple Butter and sharp aged Vermont Cheddar cheese or Summer Peach Chutney. I bake mine in clean one-pound coffee cans to achieve the classic cylindrical shape. At a Fannie Farmer one-hundredth anniversary celebration, Boston chef Jasper White toasted thin slices of Boston brown bread, buttered them, and draped smoked salmon on top. What a good idea, resulting in a wonderful layering of rich tastes!

½ cup golden raisins
½ cup plus 2 tablespoons apple cider
½ cup yellow cornmeal
½ cup whole-wheat flour
6 tablespoons rye flour
2 tablespoons coarse wheat bran
1 teaspoon baking soda
½ teaspoon salt
1 cup buttermilk
⅓ cup unsulfured molasses
2 tablespoons honey
*½ cup coarsely grated carrots (about 2
    medium carrots)*

1. Soak the raisins in the ½ cup apple cider for 15 minutes.

2. In a large bowl, stir together the cornmeal, whole-wheat flour, rye flour, wheat bran, baking soda, and salt.

3. Combine the buttermilk, molasses, honey, and remaining 2 tablespoons apple cider in a small bowl. Stir well. Add this to the dry ingredients and stir well.

4. Stir in the reserved raisins with their soaking liquid and the grated carrots.

5. Generously grease a clean 1-pound coffee can. Pour the batter into the can, and cover it tightly with a double thickness of aluminum foil. Place the can in a deep saucepan (you could use two saucepans, using one as the cover). Add boiling water to reach halfway up the sides of the can. Cover, and steam over medium-low heat (the water should be at a gentle simmer) until a tester inserted in the center comes out clean, about 1½ hours. Keep an eye on the water level and add more, if necessary; it should stay at about halfway up the can.

6. Cool on a wire rack for at least 10 minutes before unmolding and slicing into rounds. The bread will keep, cooled and sealed in a plastic bag, up to about a week in the refrigerator.

Makes 1 loaf

CONFETTI SPOONBREAD

★ ★ ★

This "soufflé" cornbread, traditionally made with either white or yellow cornmeal, was originally thought to have gotten its name because you eat it with a spoon. But, according to noted food authority John Mariani, the word may be derived from *suppawn*, a Native American word for porridge. Be sure not to overcook it, because you want spoonbread nice and fluffy!

¼ cup fresh or frozen corn kernels
¼ cup finely diced red bell pepper
1 cup yellow cornmeal
3 cups milk
1 teaspoon salt
1 teaspoon baking powder
2 tablespoons unsalted butter, melted
3 large eggs, separated

1. Preheat the oven to 375°F. Lightly grease a 2-quart ovenproof soufflé or casserole dish.

2. Bring a saucepan of water to a boil, and lightly blanch the corn for about 2 minutes. Remove the corn from the water with a slotted spoon, then rinse under cold water. Drain and pat dry.

3. Add the bell pepper to the boiling water and blanch for 2 minutes, then drain, rinse, drain again, and pat dry.

4. Combine the cornmeal and 2 cups of milk in a heavy pot, and cook over medium-high heat, stirring constantly, until stiff, about 5 minutes. Be careful not to burn the mixture. Remove from the heat.

5. Add the salt, baking powder, melted butter, and the remaining 1 cup milk. Stir well to combine.

6. Beat the egg yolks and add them to the cornmeal mixture, then stir in the corn and bell peppers. Beat the egg whites until stiff, and using a rubber spatula, gently fold them into the cornmeal mixture until just incorporated. Do not overmix.

7. Scrape the mixture into the prepared soufflé dish, and bake until the top is golden brown, 35 to 45 minutes. Serve immediately.

Serves 4 to 6

Praise the Bread & Pass the Cheese

★ ★ ★

Americans love cheese. Just saying the word brings a smile to our face. We're not only the world's biggest producer of cheese, we also import more of this delectable treat than any other country. Mild or pungent, buttery or sharp, creamy as can be or hard enough to grate, cheese is the perfect companion for crusty breads and good wines, a satisfying finale to a special meal, and a quick, tasty choice for a family snack.

Cheesemaking in America

Although cheese was known to the ancient Sumerians as early as 4,000 years before the birth of Christ, in the timeline of food history America's cheese tradition is relatively recent.

Early settlers brought a taste for cheese with them to these shores. Luckily they also brought along with them the treasured hand-written recipes and ancient techniques for making the Old World favorites that would become New World traditions. That's why almost all cheese in America is a variation on a classic from another country. The exceptions are these three original American cheeses: Monterey Jack, Colby, and Brick.

For generations, cheese in America was made by hand in small quantities, using intuition and milk from the farm or dairy where it was produced. No two batches were alike, though the best cheesemakers achieved levels of welcome consistency. In the nineteenth century, American cheesemaking moved from farm to factory production, then eventually and inevitably to mass-production and standardization. The romance of cheese became lost in the shuffle as made-in-the-U.S.A. cheeses began to lose their personalities, growing blander by the decade.

Artisanal Cheesemakers

The best things to eat in life are handmade, and luckily for us in the past two decades there has been a renaissance in artisanal cheesemaking in America. On small farms and dairies across the country, cheesemakers have begun producing handmade cheeses with the depth of flavor and unique character that set them apart from anything you'll find at the local grocery store. Real Cheddar, Brie and Camembert, blue cheese and goat cheese, are being made with real flavor and real care.

As I traveled across the United States, I visited local cheesemakers, sampling their wares and delighting in my discoveries. The cheesemakers below all sell their cheese mail-order, but some are also distributed nationwide, so you just might discover that their fine cheese is a short journey from your kitchen.

Coach Farm
Pine Plains, New York
(518) 398-5325

Once the makers of famous fine leather products, Miles and Lillian Cahn, and their daughter Susan, now produce some of the most superb goat cheese available, along with Yo-goat, a thick goat milk/yogurt drink. During my visit, their luscious fresh white cheese with its tangy finish won me over; its texture was incredibly creamy, moist, and flaky.

Shelburne Farms
Shelburne, Vermont
(802) 985-8686

Shelburne Farms, located on scenic Lake Champlain, produces a world-class raw milk farmhouse Cheddar. The raw milk (rather than pasteurized milk) from their herd of sixty purebred Swiss cows gives this cheese more complexity and depth of flavor than any factory-produced one. Cheddar far and wide is an American favorite; one taste of Shelburne's deep, rich version will have you thinking maybe you have never really tasted Cheddar before.

Cabot Creamery Cooperative
Cabot, Vermont
(802) 563-2231; (802) 563-2604

Founded in 1919, and committed to quality, this creamery puts out an award-winning Cheddar the likes of which I had not tasted before visiting. They also produce butter and a variety of other dairy products, including other cheeses. My visit led me to sample delicious, blue ribbon mild, sharp, and extra-sharp creamy Cheddars. The longer a cheese is allowed to age, the greater the piquancy it acquires. Their "private" (aged over 18 months) and "vintage" (aged over 30 months) versions are superb, with that distinctive Cheddar bite that everyone should try.

Capriole, Inc.
Greenville, Indiana
(800) 448-4628

Judy Schad and her husband produce a variety of outstanding prize-winning goat cheeses, which are distributed nationwide to specialty cheese shops and also sold mail-order. The hand-ladling technique produces the finest texture. If you have never tried goat cheese, I suggest their Banon—mild, creamy, and simply delightful. For goat-cheese lovers, sample the award-winning Wabash Cannonball or Mont St. Francis for more of a tangy kick.

Maytag Blue Cheese
Newton, Iowa
(800) 247-2458

Maytag Dairy Farm was founded by Elmer H. Maytag, the appliance king's son, and it produces one of America's finest blue cheeses. On my visit to the beautiful town of Newton, I found out that Elmer's hobby was raising Maytag Holsteins, which produced especially high quality milk. With little prospect of making money in the milking industry, Elmer set out to find a use for his product; he enlisted the opinion of the Iowa State University dairy department, who suggested he try their new process for making blue cheese, and Maytag Blue was born. And solely through word of mouth, this little cheese made it big!

Laura Chenel's Chèvre
Sonoma, California
(707) 996-4477

Laura Chenel has been supplying San Francisco Bay area restaurants and local farmers' markets with her extraordinarily delicious chèvre since 1981. A pioneer in the American goat cheese industry, she began making cheese from her farm's abundance of fresh goat milk in the early 1970s. Her latest variety of fresh and aged cheeses, include a fromage blanc, cabécou, crottin, and taupinière.

COUNTRY CORNBREAD

★ ★ ★

Cornbread comes in many sizes and forms. The batter can be baked in a square pan (my choice), in little tea loaves, in a skillet or muffin tins, or in the form of johnnycake or spoonbread. I like my cornbread slightly sweet and moist, and this recipe meets both those needs. The addition of yogurt and creamed corn makes for a particularly good bread.

1½ cups yellow cornmeal
½ cup all-purpose flour
3 tablespoons sugar
1 tablespoon baking powder
½ teaspoon salt
½ cup milk
½ cup plain nonfat yogurt
2 tablespoons unsalted butter, melted
2 tablespoons vegetable oil
2 large eggs, lightly beaten
1 cup creamed corn, canned or homemade
   (page 285)

1. Preheat the oven to 400°F. Grease an 8-inch square baking pan.

2. Combine the cornmeal, flour, sugar, baking powder, and salt in a mixing bowl. Stir well.

3. In another bowl, combine the milk, yogurt, melted butter, oil, and eggs. Add this to the cornmeal mixture and stir until just combined. Then stir in the creamed corn.

4. Scrape the batter into the prepared pan, and bake in the center of the oven until the top is golden brown and a toothpick inserted in the center comes out just clean, 45 minutes.

5. Cool in the pan on a rack for 15 to 20 minutes. Then remove the cornbread from the pan and let it cool completely on a wire rack. Cut it into squares to serve.

Serves 6

ROLLED BAKING POWDER BISCUITS

★ ★ ★

Steaming hot from the oven, then split and loaded with butter and strawberry jam, there's nothing quite like these little biscuits. Baking them with the sides touching results in a soft white biscuit. If you want a crisper, crunchier biscuit, place them an inch apart on the baking sheet. Using a shiny baking sheet (that is, not a nonstick one) will produce the desired lightly browned bottom. To make a savory biscuit, herbs, shredded meats, and/or cheese can be added after cutting in the shortening and butter. These are perfect to serve along with fried chicken, breakfast sausage and eggs, or the way they do in Savannah, Georgia—hot, with a little orange marmalade, before dinner.

2 cups sifted all-purpose flour
1 tablespoon baking powder
1 teaspoon salt
2 tablespoons solid vegetable shortening,
   cold
2 tablespoons unsalted butter, cold
⅔ cup plus 2 tablespoons milk

★★★

GOLDEN BISCUITS

—❦—

*T*o make tender, fluffy, ultra-light biscuits, less handling, not more, is the golden rule here. Think of the dough as pie pastry with leavener and less fat, and apply the same minimal touch you would use for crust. Knead just long enough to get all ingredients combined (about 30 seconds), then pat or roll it out for cutting as deftly as you can. You can also "drop" the dough onto baking sheets by altering it with additional milk, as specified for Dropped Ham Biscuits, page 216.

What fat you use, and how much, will affect lightness as well. Less produces an airier biscuit, more a richer one. Butter renders terrific flavor, but not necessarily the best texture, while vegetable shortening makes for a fluffier but less tasty biscuit. That's why many recipes call for both. Many recipes call for buttermilk, too; Southerners have always relished the pleasant tang it gives a biscuit. Sweet cream biscuits are a traditional favorite, also suitable for breakfast or strawberry shortcake.

★★★

1. Preheat the oven to 450°F.

2. Sift the flour, baking powder, and salt together into a bowl. Using a pastry cutter, cut the shortening and the butter into the dry ingredients until the mixture resembles a coarse meal. Pour in the milk, and toss the ingredients together with your fingertips until they can be gathered up into a ball.

3. Turn the dough out onto a lightly floured surface and knead it for not more than 12 to 15 strokes. Roll the dough out ¾ inch thick. Using a 2-inch biscuit cutter, cut it into rounds. Gather up the scraps, reroll, and cut out as many more biscuits as possible. Arrange the biscuits, edges touching, on an ungreased shiny (not nonstick) baking sheet and bake until lightly browned, 10 to 12 minutes. Serve hot.

Makes 9 biscuits

ROLLED BUTTERMILK BISCUITS

★ ★ ★

I love these biscuits because the buttermilk gives them a moist texture and a subtle, tangy flavor. To keep them light, take care not to knead the dough more than twelve to fifteen strokes. Cut the biscuits with a sharp pastry cutter (a dull one will seal the edges and keep the biscuits from rising). I like to serve these piping hot from the oven in a small straw basket lined with a linen napkin.

2 cups sifted all-purpose flour
1 teaspoon baking powder
½ teaspoon salt
2 tablespoons solid vegetable shortening, cold
2 tablespoons unsalted butter, cold
1 cup buttermilk

1. Preheat the oven to 450°F.

2. Sift the flour, baking powder, and salt together into a bowl. Using a pastry cutter, cut the shortening and butter into the dry ingredients until the mixture resembles coarse meal. Pour in the buttermilk, and toss the ingredients together with your fingertips until they can be gathered up into a ball.

3. Turn the dough out onto a lightly floured surface, and knead it for not more than 12 to 15 strokes. Roll the dough out ¾ inch thick. Using a 2-inch biscuit cutter, cut it into rounds. Gather up the scraps, reroll, and cut out as many more biscuits as possible. Arrange the biscuits, edges touching, on an ungreased shiny (not nonstick) baking sheet and bake until lightly browned, 10 to 12 minutes. Serve hot.

Makes 9 biscuits

DROPPED HAM BISCUITS

★ ★ ★

Dropped biscuits resemble rolled biscuits except that they have just enough extra milk to make the dough light enough to fall off the spoon—hence the name. I use a wooden spoon to do the job and drop about ¼ cup of dough per biscuit onto the baking sheet. I have studded these large and fluffy gems with ham for an inviting savory flavor.

2 cups sifted all-purpose flour
1 tablespoon baking powder
1 teaspoon salt
2 tablespoons solid vegetable
shortening, cold
2 tablespoons unsalted butter, cold
2 ounces Smithfield or Black Forest
ham, cut into tiny dice
1½ cups milk

1. Preheat the oven to 450°F. Lightly grease a shiny (not nonstick) baking sheet.

2. Sift the flour, baking powder, and salt together into a bowl. Using a pastry cutter, cut the shortening and the butter into the dry ingredients until the mixture resembles coarse meal. Stir in the ham. Then pour in the milk and stir the ingredients together with a wooden spoon until just mixed; you should be able to drop the dough from the spoon.

3. Drop the dough by large spoonfuls (about ¼ cup) onto the prepared baking sheet, leaving about 1 inch space between the biscuits. Bake until lightly browned, 10 to 12 minutes. Serve hot.

Makes 12 biscuits

Soups

I stir maternal passions into soups. They're watched over, carefully nurtured as their flavors meld. And good soups are nurturing in turn—healthy and deeply satisfying.

I begin by gathering vegetables and herbs, and fish, poultry, or meat. I spread everything out on my kitchen table and ponder: What will awaken my senses this time? I usually decide on an initial flavor burst from onions, leeks, shallots, and/or garlic. I sometimes add herbs and spices early on, to draw their aromatic oils deep in the soup. Fresh vegetables often take a starring role, as they do in Garden Broccoli Vegetable Soup, or they can be used to complement meat or poultry. My fish and shellfish soups are brimming with ocean plenty, thick with oysters, crabs, halibut, clams. There's less filling fare here, too—Light and Spicy Tomato Soup, Celery Apple Soup, and more. All these recipes use homegrown American ingredients only. Indeed, I'd have trouble thinking of any American food that I *couldn't* put to use in a fine pot of soup.

GUACAMOLE SOUP

★ ★ ★

Whether it's served in Sante Fe with blue corn chips or in Tucson or Wyoming or anywhere else in the United States, I've never seen a drop of guacamole left in a bowl. Everyone seems to love it. So, I thought, why not create a guacamole-based summer soup? I can't think of anything better to pour into decorative mugs as a prelude to a dinner of spicy fajitas and quesadillas. Garden-fresh herbs, such as chives complete with their lavender blossoms or nasturtium blossoms nodding on their stems, would make a beautiful garnish. Serve some toasted Jalapeño Cheese Bread or Country Cornbread alongside.

4 ripe avocados
4 tablespoons fresh lime juice
3 cups plain nonfat yogurt, chilled
3 cups defatted chicken broth, preferably
*   homemade (page 253), chilled*
2 teaspoons salt
¼ teaspoon freshly ground black pepper
5 ripe plum tomatoes, seeded and cut into
*   ¼-inch dice (1½ cups)*
2 tablespoons snipped fresh chives,
*   for garnish*

   1. Peel and pit 2 of the avocados. Chop the flesh coarsely and place it in a large bowl. Toss with 2 tablespoons of the lime juice.
   2. Combine the yogurt, broth, and chopped avocado in a blender or food processor, and purée until smooth. Return the purée to the bowl and stir in the salt and pepper.
   3. Peel, pit, and chop the remaining 2 avocados into ¼-inch dice. Toss with the remaining 2 tablespoons lime juice, and add to the puréed

soup along with the tomatoes. Refrigerate for 1 to 2 hours before serving. Serve chilled, garnished with the snipped chives.
   Serves 6

ROASTED AND FRESH VEGETABLE GAZPACHO

★ ★ ★

Although I've devised many different gazpachos over the years, these days I've been adding roasted vegetables to the mix. I find that their deep flavor adds a welcome dimension to the traditionally uncooked version of this zesty concoction.

ROASTING VEGETABLES
2 red bell peppers, stemmed, seeded, and
*   coarsely chopped*
2 red onions, coarsely chopped
3 ripe tomatoes, cored and coarsely chopped
¼ cup chopped fresh flat-leaf parsley
¼ cup extra virgin olive oil
Salt and freshly ground black pepper,
*   to taste*

FRESH VEGETABLES

1 hothouse (seedless) cucumber, peeled and
    coarsely chopped
2 ripe tomatoes, cored and coarsely chopped
1 red bell pepper, stemmed, seeded, and
    coarsely chopped
2 shallots, coarsely chopped

TO FINISH

2 cups tomato juice
½ cup red wine vinegar
⅓ cup extra virgin olive oil
2 dashes Tabasco sauce
Salt and freshly ground black pepper, to taste
1 to 1½ ripe avocados, peeled, pitted, and
    cut into ¼-inch dice, for garnish
2 tablespoons fresh lemon juice
¼ cup chopped fresh flat-leaf parsley
1 hothouse (seedless) cucumber, peeled and
    cut into ¼-inch dice, for garnish

    1. Preheat the oven to 400°F.

    2. Prepare the roasted vegetables: Toss all of the roasting vegetable ingredients together and place them in a shallow roasting pan. Roast, stirring once or twice, for 30 minutes. Transfer them to a large bowl, add all the fresh vegetables along with 1 cup of the tomato juice. Set aside.

    3. In a bowl, whisk the remaining 1 cup tomato juice with the vinegar, olive oil, Tabasco sauce, salt, and pepper. Stir this into the vegetable mixture.

    4. Working in batches, place the mixture in a blender or food processor and pulse 6 to 8 times, until it is blended but still a little chunky. Transfer the soup to a large bowl, season with salt and pepper, and chill, covered, for at least 6, but no longer than 24, hours before serving.

    5. Toss the diced avocado with the lemon juice to prevent discoloration. Stir the parsley into the soup, and serve chilled, in bright mugs or bowls, garnished with the avocados and cucumbers.

Serves 6 to 8

INDIAN SUMMER BORSCHT

★ ★ ★

I used to make summer borscht with both milk and eggs to ensure the rich texture I enjoyed. But in these days of light and low-fat, I wanted to find a way to keep the lushness without sacrificing the flavor and texture of one of my favorite soups. Now I slow-roast the beets and then cook them in apple juice. The nonfat yogurt adds just the right tang and a surprisingly creaminess. Altogether a perfect sweet-and-sour blend that says traditional borscht.

3 pounds beets (about 12 medium)
4 cups apple juice
4 cups water
6 tablespoons fresh
    lemon juice
Pinch of salt
2½ cups plain nonfat yogurt
6 large red radishes, cut into small dice, for garnish
½ cup diced (¼ inch) hothouse (seedless) cucumber,
    for garnish

    1. Preheat the oven to 350°F.

    2. Rinse the beets well, and trim off the stem and root, leaving 1 inch of each. Wrap the beets individually in aluminum foil and place them on a baking sheet. Bake until tender, 1½ hours. Remove the beets from the oven, and set them aside briefly, in the foil, to cool. When they are cool enough to handle, put on rubber gloves and slip off the skins. Coarsely grate the beets.

    3. Place the grated beets in a heavy pot. Add the apple juice, water, lemon juice, and salt, and bring to a boil. Reduce the heat to a simmer and cook, partially covered, skimming off any foam that rises to the top, for 15 minutes. Remove the soup from the heat and let it cool to room temperature.

4. Place 2 cups of the yogurt in a bowl and whisk in about 3 cups of the soup. Gradually whisk this mixture back into the soup until thoroughly combined. Chill the soup completely in the refrigerator.

5. Divide the soup among eight bowls, and garnish each one with 1 tablespoon of the remaining yogurt and a sprinkling of diced radish and cucumber.

Serves 8

DRESS-UP CUCUMBER DILL SOUP

★ ★ ★

Elegant and light, this smooth cucumber soup is enhanced by the "gritty" taste and distinct saltiness of golden whitefish roe from the Great Lakes and Pacific Northwest. It could easily be served at any black tie dinner party. This type of caviar is reasonably priced and is usually available in specialty food and caviar shops.

2 tablespoons olive oil
1 onion, coarsely chopped
3 hothouse (seedless) cucumbers, unpeeled,
   coarsely chopped
1 large bunch fresh dill, ferns chopped
   (about ½ cup), stems reserved
6 cups defatted vegetable broth or chicken broth,
   preferably homemade (page 255 or 253)
½ cup heavy (or whipping) cream
1 cup finely diced peeled hothouse (seedless)
   cucumber
2 to 4 ounces American golden or fresh
   salmon caviar

1. Heat the oil in a large heavy pot over medium-low heat. Add the onion and cook until wilted, 5 to 7 minutes. Add the chopped cucumbers and cook, stirring, for 5 minutes more.

2. Tie the dill stems together with kitchen string, and add them to the pot along with the broth. Bring to a boil. Reduce the heat to medium and simmer, partially covered, until the cucumbers are tender, 15 minutes. Stir in ¼ cup of the chopped dill, and let the soup cool to room temperature. Remove and discard the dill stems.

3. Purée the soup, in batches, in a blender or food processor until smooth. Transfer it to a bowl, and stir in the cream, 2 tablespoons of the chopped dill, and the finely diced cucumber. Chill the soup for at least 4 hours.

4. Serve the soup in small portions, dolloped with the caviar (the amount depending on how much of a sport you are). Garnish the soup with any remaining chopped dill.

Serves 4 to 6

PEAR AND WATERCRESS SOUP

★ ★ ★

Pear lovers will really appreciate the subtle flavor of this autumnal soup. Juicy Anjous combined with zucchini and the peppery bite of watercress makes for a lovely first course, especially served before a main course of small feathered game or roast pork. Garnish each serving with a vibrant orange or yellow nasturtium blossom for a splash of color.

2 tablespoons unsalted butter

1 onion, chopped

4 ripe Anjou pears, peeled, cored, and cut into
   ½-inch dice

2 zucchini, trimmed and cut into ½-inch dice

5 cups defatted chicken broth, preferably
   homemade (page 253)

2 bunches watercress, well rinsed,
   tough stems removed (4 cups of
   delicate stems and leaves)

1 cup heavy (or whipping) cream

Salt and freshly ground white pepper,
   to taste

1. Melt the butter over low heat in a large heavy pot. Add the onion and cook, stirring, for 10 minutes.

2. Add the pears, zucchini, and 4 cups of the chicken broth. Bring to a boil. Reduce the heat to a simmer and cook, partially covered, for 40 minutes.

3. Remove the soup from the heat and stir in the watercress. Cover the soup and let it stand for 5 minutes to wilt the watercress leaves.

4. Purée the soup in batches, in a blender or food processor, until very smooth. Return the soup to the pot, and stir in the remaining 1 cup broth and the cream. Season to taste with salt and white pepper. Heat the soup through, without boiling, and serve immediately.

Serves 6 to 8

CELERY APPLE SOUP

★ ★ ★

When making celery soup, I always include the leaves atop the celery ribs because they impart an intense flavor that I like. The blending of celery and apple makes for a pleasant starter that won't leave everyone too full for the rest of the meal. Always wash celery very well, especially toward the bottom of the ribs, as that area can hold a lot of dirt.

2 teaspoons vegetable oil

2 cups coarsely chopped onion

1 tablespoon minced garlic

8 ribs celery, with leaves, rinsed and
   coarsely chopped

2 Granny Smith apples, peeled, cored, and
   coarsely chopped

1 tablespoon dried tarragon

6 cups defatted vegetable broth or chicken broth,
   preferably homemade (page 255 or 253)

1 cup apple juice

½ cup plus 2 tablespoons coarsely chopped
   fresh flat-leaf parsley

Salt and freshly ground black pepper, to taste

1. Heat the oil in a large heavy pot over medium-low heat. Add the onions, garlic, celery, apples, and tarragon. Cook, stirring occasionally, until the vegetables have wilted, 15 minutes.

2. Add the broth and apple juice. Raise the heat and bring the soup to a boil. Then reduce the heat to a simmer and cook until the celery is tender, 40 minutes. Stir in the ½ cup parsley and allow the soup to cool slightly.

3. Purée the soup, in batches, in a blender or food processor until very smooth. Return it to the pot and heat it through gently. Season with salt and pepper, garnish with the remaining 2 tablespoons parsley, and serve.

Serves 6

CHIPPEWA WILD RICE SOUP

★ ★ ★

It was a cold, cold day in Bemidji, Minnesota, when I first ate a bowl of wild rice soup on the Chippewa Indian reservation (see page 323 for Wild Rice). Back home, on a cold January day in New York, I relived my trip by cooking up my own variation of this soup, which is popular throughout America's heartland. Most local cookbooks call for a little bit of sherry to be added to wild rice soup, but while I did decide to leave that as an option, I prefer this soup in its pure form, chock-full of winter vegetables, wild rice, and chicken. For an intense broth, don't overfill the pot with water—8 cups is plenty. Once it has cooked and the chicken has done its job, shred it up and return it to the soup.

½ cup wild rice
12 cups water
Salt
1 chicken (approximately 3 pounds), cut into pieces
4 ribs celery, with leaves, cut into ½-inch pieces
4 carrots, peeled and cut into ½-inch pieces
3 parsnips, peeled and cut into ½-inch pieces
2 onions, cut into ½-inch pieces
3 cloves garlic, lightly bruised
1 small bunch fresh dill, tied with kitchen string
¼ cup dry sherry (optional)
¼ cup chopped fresh flat-leaf parsley

1. Rinse the wild rice well in a strainer under cold water; drain.

2. Bring 4 cups of the water to a boil, and add 2 teaspoons salt. Stir in the rice and simmer over medium heat until just tender, 40 minutes. Drain. Set aside 1½ cups of the cooked rice.

3. While the rice is cooking, rinse the chicken, and remove any excess fat. Place the chicken in a large stockpot, and add the remaining 8 cups water and 1 tablespoon salt. Cover, and bring to a boil. Uncover, and skim off any foam that has risen to the surface.

4. Add all of the vegetables and the dill. Cover, and simmer over medium heat until the chicken is tender, 45 minutes.

5. Remove the chicken from the pot and allow it to cool. When it is cool enough to handle, discard the skin and bones and shred the meat into large pieces. Return the meat to the pot. Remove and discard the dill.

6. Add the reserved wild rice and the sherry, if using, to the soup. Simmer over medium heat, uncovered, for 15 minutes. Adjust the seasonings and stir in the chopped parsley. Serve immediately.

Serves 6 to 8

BLUE RIBBON SPLIT PEA SOUP

★ ★ ★

Next time you have a leftover ham bone, use it to make this soup. I find there is nothing more satisfying on a cold Sunday night than split pea soup, a slice of pumpernickel topped with a hunk of Vermont Cheddar and some cranberry relish. Add a bay leaf, some thyme, and a pinch of tarragon to the pot to turn this soup from ordinary to extraordinary.

1 meaty ham bone, or 1 large ham hock
1 pound dried green split peas
2 carrots, peeled
2 ribs celery
1 onion
1 parsnip
1 leek (3 inches green left on), trimmed of root,
    split lengthwise, and well washed and
    patted dry
2 tablespoons olive oil
1 bay leaf
4 sprigs fresh thyme, or 1 teaspoon dried
1 teaspoon dried tarragon
4 cups defatted chicken broth, preferably
    homemade (page 253)
4 cups water
Salt and freshly ground black pepper, to taste
2 tablespoons chopped fresh flat-leaf parsley

1. Trim any fat off the ham bone, and set the ham bone aside. Pick over the split peas and discard any stones; rinse, drain, and set aside.

2. Cut the carrots, celery, onion, parsnip, and leek into small dice. Heat the oil in a large heavy pot over low heat, add all of the vegetables, and cook until wilted, 10 to 12 minutes.

3. Add the split peas and cook for 1 minute. Then add all the herbs, the ham bone, broth, and water. Bring the mixture to a boil, reduce the heat to a simmer, cover partially, and cook, stirring occasionally, until the peas are cooked, 45 minutes.

4. Remove the ham bone, bay leaf, and thyme sprigs. When it is cool enough to handle, shred any meat from the bone and return the meat to the pot. Reheat the soup, season to taste with salt and pepper, and stir in the parsley. Serve immediately.

Serves 6

VEGETABLE SPLIT PEA SOUP

★ ★ ★

A pot full of vegetables thickened with a moderate amount of split peas makes for a soup that has both ample body and a subtle sweetness. If I don't have a ham bone on hand, I buy a large ham hock, which imparts the same rich depth to the broth. A large bowl of this soup is a complete meal when served with crusty bread and a green salad.

¾ cup dried green split peas
8 cups defatted chicken broth, preferably
    homemade (page 253)
1 meaty ham bone, or 1 large ham hock
    (see headnote)
2 ribs celery, coarsely chopped
1 bay leaf
½ cup chopped fresh flat-leaf parsley
½ teaspoon dried tarragon
½ teaspoon dried thyme
2 tablespoons olive oil
1 tablespoon unsalted butter
6 carrots, peeled, halved lengthwise,
    and cut crosswise into ½-inch pieces
3 onions, coarsely chopped
2 leeks (3 inches green left on), trimmed of roots,
    well washed, patted dry, and cut into ½-inch
    dice
3 cloves garlic, minced
2 zucchini, trimmed and cut into
    ½-inch dice
10 ounces fresh spinach, rinsed, tough stems
    removed, and cut crosswise into
    1-inch strips
4 ripe tomatoes, cored, seeded, and cut into
    ½-inch dice
Salt and freshly ground black pepper,
    to taste

1. Pick through the split peas and discard any stones; rinse and drain.

2. Combine the split peas and the broth in a large heavy pot and bring to a boil. Add the ham bone, celery, bay leaf, ¼ cup of the parsley, the tarragon, and the thyme. Reduce the heat and simmer, partially covered, for about 45 minutes.

3. Meanwhile, heat the olive oil and butter in a separate pot over medium-low heat. Add the carrots, onions, leeks, and garlic. Cook, partially covered, stirring occasionally, until the vegetables are tender, about 20 minutes. Add them to the soup (after it's cooked for 45 minutes) and simmer, partially covered, stirring once or twice, for 30 minutes more. Remove the ham bone and set it aside. Remove and discard the bay leaf.

4. Add the zucchini to the soup and cook 15 minutes longer, stirring from the bottom.

5. Add the spinach and simmer for 10 minutes. Stir in the tomatoes and the remaining ¼ cup parsley. Remove from the heat, and season with salt and pepper. When the ham bone is cool enough to handle, shred the meat from the bone and stir it into the soup. Heat through and serve.

Serves 6 to 8

SWEET SWEET PEA SOUP

★ ★ ★

At a spring wedding in the garden or a light luncheon for friends, this fresh sweet pea soup is sure to be a hit. It is delicate and delicious, served either hot or cold. An open-face shrimp or chicken salad sandwich makes a charming accompaniment. If you serve the soup cold, it's essential to use defatted broth so that no fat will rise to the top. Besides the radishes, you can garnish with some finely diced cucumbers and snipped fresh chives or even a lavender chive blossom or two.

¼ cup (½ stick) unsalted butter
2 cups coarsely chopped onions
8 cups defatted chicken broth, preferably homemade (page 253)
4 packages (10 ounces each) frozen peas, defrosted
1 cup coarsely chopped fresh mint leaves
1 cup heavy (or whipping) cream
Salt and freshly ground white pepper, to taste
8 red radishes, cut into ⅛-inch dice, for garnish

1. Melt the butter in a large heavy pot over low heat. Add the onions and cook, stirring occasionally, until wilted, 10 to 12 minutes.

2. Add the chicken broth and peas. Bring to a boil, reduce the heat to a simmer, and cook, partially covered, for 15 minutes. Then stir in the mint and allow to cool slightly.

3. Purée the soup, in batches, in a blender or food processor until completely smooth. As each batch is puréed, pour it through a strainer into a bowl to remove the skins from the peas. Use the back of a wooden spoon to mash the solids gently, extracting as much liquid as possible.

4. Stir in the cream, and season to taste with salt and white pepper. If serving cold, cover and chill well in the refrigerator until serving time. If serving hot, return to the pot and heat, stirring, over low heat until warmed through; do not allow to boil.

5. To serve, ladle small portions into demitasse cups. Garnish each portion with diced radish.

Serves 6 to 8

SUNSET RED LENTIL SOUP

★ ★ ★

The subtle suggestion of fresh orange adds an unusual twist to this lentil soup. The color of the soup—reminiscent of a vibrant Southwestern sunset—makes it pleasing to the eye as well as the palate. As an added bonus, you have the pleasure of hearty indulgence with barely any fat.

1 navel orange
2 tablespoons olive oil
3 onions, halved lengthwise and slivered
4 carrots, peeled and grated
½ teaspoon salt
¼ teaspoon freshly ground black pepper
2 teaspoons dried marjoram
1 can (28 ounces) peeled plum tomatoes, crushed, with their juices
1 generous tablespoon tomato paste
1 teaspoon dark or light brown sugar
6 cups defatted chicken broth or vegetable broth, preferably homemade (pages 253 or 255)
1 cup dried red lentils, rinsed and drained
¼ cup coarsely chopped fresh flat-leaf parsley

1. Peel the rind off the orange with a paring knife, in one long strip, if possible. Scrape all the excess pith off the back of the peel, and set it aside. Halve the orange and squeeze the juice from it. Set the juice aside.

2. Heat the olive oil in a large heavy pot over low heat. Add the onions and carrots and cook, stirring occasionally, until wilted, about 15 minutes. Sprinkle with the salt, pepper, and marjoram during the last 2 minutes.

3. Add the tomatoes, tomato paste, brown sugar, broth, reserved orange peel and juice, and the lentils. Bring the mixture to a boil. Reduce the heat to medium and simmer, partially covered, stirring occasionally, for 30 minutes.

4. Discard the orange peel, adjust the seasonings, and stir in the parsley. Serve hot.
Serves 6

MAUD ABRAMS SCHOOL LIMA BEAN SOUP

★ ★ ★

At the Lima Bean Festival in Cape May, New Jersey, the Transitional First Grade of the Maud Abrams School served up cups of their first-prize soup. After a tiring three-hour drive from Manhattan to attend the festival, this was the soup that rejuvenated me—it was delicious. I've created a smoother texture for my version by puréeing a small amount of the soup with half-and-half before finishing it off. I'd serve this for any wintery Sunday lunch with well-grilled sausages and a Bibb lettuce salad.

LIMAS AT THE SOURCE

—🍎—

Just-picked limas are one of summer's great treats—sweet and meaty enough to eat *al dente*, adorned with just a little butter, salt, and pepper. They're well suited to more imaginative preparations, too, as I learned on my pilgrimage to West Cape May, New Jersey, home of the giant Fordhook lima (cousin of the smaller "baby" lima). Each September, this tiny southern Jersey town rolls out the red carpet for its beloved bean, celebrating it with games, live music, and, of course, plenty of hearty home-cooking.

This was my first research expedition for the *U.S.A. Cookbook*, so I was very excited. Hungry, too. I moved from booth to booth, eating my way from one end of Wilbraham Park to the other. First-graders from the Maud Abrams School got me started with a paper cup brimming with their blue-ribbon soup, resplendent with plump limas and seasoned with sweet marjoram and oregano. One taste of the barbecued, baked, and buttered lima beans served up by members of the Allen African Methodist Episcopal Church wouldn't do—I required a whole plateful of those. And I was just getting started. There were lima, ham, and tomato casseroles, limas with thick-cut vegetables, limas with pork barbecue, even a whole roasted suckling pig, carved up for sandwiches. I downed fresh lemonade—the perfect accompaniment—between helpings.

West Cape May's mayor, the Honorable John Vasser, Jr., made me the guest of honor, which meant I was to choose that year's Lima Bean Queen. No judging required, thank heavens: I just reached in a box and drew out the name of nine-year-old Ashley Rupert. She donned her royal mantle, an oversized green sweatshirt, and the crowd applauded in approval. The fair began to wind down then, so Mayor Vasser whisked me off for a tour of a local lima field. The vines, which have dark green, heart-shaped leaves, were heavy with beans—the last of the season, Mayor Vasser said. Harvesting machines were advancing from the next field, tempting me to pluck and eat on the spot, before these beauties were gone for good.

Fresh lima beans are usually sold in their pods, which should be firm and dark green. Buy Fordhooks if you can, as they're fuller-flavored than baby limas. Don't shell them until you're ready to cook. Unshelled, they'll keep in your refrigerator for up to a week. Cook them alone in boiling salted water (about 15 minutes or until tender) or check the Index for recipes, all of which were inspired by my visit to West Cape May.

¾ *pound dried lima beans*
¼ *pound slab bacon, rind removed,*
   cut into ¼-inch dice
1 *tablespoon unsalted butter*
4 *carrots, peeled and coarsely*
   chopped
2 *ribs celery, coarsely chopped*
1 *onion, coarsely chopped*
1 *teaspoon dried marjoram*
1 *teaspoon dried oregano*
7 *cups defatted chicken broth, preferably*
   homemade (page 253)
1 *small boiling potato, peeled and coarsely*
   chopped
½ *cup half-and-half*
¼ *cup chopped fresh flat-leaf parsley*
Salt and freshly ground black pepper,
   to taste

1. Pick over the lima beans, discarding any stones. Soak them overnight in cold water to cover by 2 inches (or see page 336 for How to Quick-Soak Beans).

2. Drain the lima beans, rinse in several changes of cold water, and drain again.

3. Sauté the bacon in a heavy pot over low heat until the fat has been rendered, 3 to 5 minutes. Add the butter, carrots, celery, and onion, and cook over low heat until wilted, about 10 minutes. Stir in the marjoram and oregano.

4. Add the drained lima beans, 6 cups of the broth, and the potato to the pot. Bring to a boil. Skim the foam from the top, reduce the heat to medium-low, and cook, partially covered, stirring the soup occasionally from the bottom, for 45 minutes.

5. Combine the half-and-half and ½ cup of the soup in a blender, and purée. Stir the purée back into the soup along with the remaining 1 cup broth and the parsley. Season with salt and pepper. Serve hot.

Serves 6 to 8

SHEILA'S BLACK BEAN SOUP

★ ★ ★

Whether drizzled with sherry and garnished with a thin slice of lime, South Carolina style, or spiced up with the flavors of Cuba, the way they do it in Miami, black bean soup has increased in popularity on the American dinner table. My recipe combines a little of each variation, with a hint of the Southwest thrown in.

1 *pound dried black beans*
1 *ham hock*
2 *tablespoons extra virgin olive oil*
1 *large onion, cut into ½-inch dice*
4 *large cloves garlic, lightly crushed*
3 *quarts water*
2 *bay leaves*
1 *small dried red chile pepper*
2 *tablespoons ground cumin*
1 *tablespoon dried oregano*
1 *bunch fresh cilantro, with roots if possible,*
   well rinsed
4 *tablespoons chopped fresh flat-leaf parsley*
Salt and freshly ground black pepper,
   to taste
1 *red bell pepper, stemmed, seeded, and cut*
   into ¼-inch dice
1 *tablespoon dark brown sugar*
2 *tablespoons dry sherry*
2 *teaspoons fresh lime juice*
1 *cup sour cream or ½ cup dry sherry,*
   for garnish
Thin lime slices, for garnish

1. Pick over the beans, discarding any stones. Soak them overnight in cold water to cover by 2 inches (or see page 336 for How to

Quick-Soak Beans). Drain the beans and rinse them several times in cold water. Set them aside.

2. Place the ham hock in a large saucepan, add water to cover, and bring to a boil. Cook for 10 minutes; then drain.

3. Heat the oil in a large heavy pot over medium-low heat. Add the onion and cook until almost wilted, 10 minutes. Add the garlic and cook for another 5 minutes.

4. Add the ham hock, beans, water, bay leaves, dried chile, cumin, and oregano. Gently bruise the stems and roots of 4 large sprigs of cilantro. Tie them together with kitchen string. Chop the remaining cilantro leaves and set them aside (you need ¼ cup). Add the stems to the pot along with 2 tablespoons of the chopped parsley.

5. Bring the soup to a boil. Then reduce the heat to medium and simmer, uncovered, for 1½ hours. You may have to reduce the heat periodically. Skim off any foam that rises to the surface.

6. Remove the ham hock and set it aside. When it is cool enough to handle, shred any meat and add it to the pot. Remove and discard the cilantro stems.

7. Remove the garlic cloves and 2 cups of the soup, and purée in a blender or food processor. Stir the purée back into the soup. Season with salt and pepper.

8. Add the bell pepper, brown sugar, sherry, lime juice, the chopped cilantro, and the remaining 2 tablespoons parsley. Cook for another 30 minutes. Remove and discard the bay leaves, and serve the soup, garnishing each bowl with a dollop of sour cream and a slice of lime, or with a drizzle of sherry and a lime slice.

Serves 6

EAST COAST ASPARAGUS HERB SOUP

★ ★ ★

Every year, at the end of April, the asparagus wake up in their beds on the East Coast. For a month or so, while the bright green stalks are at their best, I cook them in every way imaginable. Their vibrant flavor seems to me to be the essence of the season. This soup, with its velvety consistency, is so rich and satisfying that only a small helping is necessary. I use a garnish of delicate, lightly blanched tips to enhance the garden freshness of each serving. The soup is an ideal start to a meal of Blushing Pink Shrimp and Peas.

When you're shopping for asparagus, look for crisp, bright green stalks with small, tight tips that haven't started to flower. And make sure you choose a deep green bunch of dill.

1½ pounds fresh asparagus
1 tablespoon unsalted butter
1 tablespoon olive oil
1 onion, chopped
2 ripe tomatoes
4 cups vegetable or defatted chicken broth,
*   preferably homemade (page 255 or 253)*
6 tablespoons chopped fresh dill
½ teaspoon dried tarragon, crushed
Pinch of cayenne pepper
½ cup heavy (or whipping) cream

1. Snap or cut the tough bottom off the asparagus stems. Cut off and reserve the asparagus tips. Cut the remaining asparagus stalks into 1-inch lengths.

2. Heat the butter and the oil in a large heavy saucepan over low heat. Add the onion and cook, stirring occasionally, until wilted, 10 minutes.

3. Chop 1 of the tomatoes and add it to the pan along with the asparagus pieces (not the tips). Stir to mix all the vegetables. Add the broth, 4 tablespoons of the dill, the tarragon, and the cayenne. Bring to a boil. Reduce the heat to medium, and cook until the asparagus is tender, 15 minutes. Cool to room temperature.

4. Meanwhile, blanch the reserved asparagus tips in a small pot of boiling water until just tender, 2 to 3 minutes. Rinse them under cold water and set them aside. Seed the remaining tomato, cut it into ¼-inch dice, and set it aside.

5. Purée the soup, in batches, in a blender or food processor gradually adding the cream, until smooth. Return the soup to the pot.

6. To serve, heat the soup through over low heat. Ladle it into bowls, and garnish with the asparagus tips and the diced tomato. Sprinkle with the remaining 2 tablespoons of dill.

Serves 4

LEMON BASIL ARTICHOKE SOUP

★ ★ ★

I've always considered homemade artichoke soup a luxury because it takes a good amount of work for a small return on your investment—in terms of quantity, not quality. The taste is delicate, and once you get it, you're addicted. The secret is to not only chop up the artichoke hearts but also to scrape

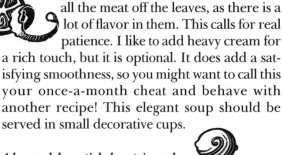

all the meat off the leaves, as there is a lot of flavor in them. This calls for real patience. I like to add heavy cream for a rich touch, but it is optional. It does add a satisfying smoothness, so you might want to call this your once-a-month cheat and behave with another recipe! This elegant soup should be served in small decorative cups.

4 large globe artichokes, trimmed
 (see box, page 230)
Salt
2 tablespoons olive oil
1 tablespoon unsalted butter
2 onions, coarsely chopped
2 ribs celery, cut into ¼-inch dice
1 russet potato, cut into ½-inch dice
5½ to 6 cups defatted chicken broth,
 preferably homemade (page 253)
¼ cup fresh lemon juice
1 cup whole fresh basil leaves, coarsely chopped
1 cup heavy (or whipping) cream (optional)
2 ripe plum tomatoes, seeded and cut into tiny dice,
 for garnish
¼ cup slivered fresh basil leaves, for garnish

1. Bring a large pot of water to a boil. Add salt, and cook the artichokes until tender, about 40 minutes. Drain the artichokes and let them cool to room temperature.

2. Remove all the large leaves from the artichokes, scraping off the meat and setting it aside. Remove and discard the purple-tipped small center leaves and the hairy chokes. Cut the artichoke hearts into small pieces and add them to the reserved meat.

3. Heat the oil and the butter in a large heavy pot over low heat, and cook the onions and celery until wilted, stirring occasionally, about 10 minutes. Add the artichoke meat, potato, broth, and lemon juice. Bring to a boil, reduce the heat, and simmer, partially covered, for 20 minutes.

ARTICHOKES: A BEAUTIFUL THISTLE

—❦—

Artichokes are a flower—a heavenly flower, delicious as a bud and lovely as a huge, violet-blue thistle. In Monterey County, California, just east of the coastal drama at Big Sur, they grow in breathtaking profusion, in sunny green fields that are painstakingly worked by hundreds of hand-pickers. Seventy-five percent of the nation's artichokes come from here; the rest come from adjoining counties. Castroville, the nearest town for most of the farmers in these parts, has declared itself the "Artichoke Center of the World," and celebrates this status in an annual artichoke blowout that's presided over by an Artichoke Queen. The first queen, crowned in 1948, was Marilyn Monroe. She made an effective monarch, they say; apparently more people than ever before tried artichokes that year.

Don't be put off by the spiky armor; artichokes aren't nearly as difficult to prepare as they look. Just cut off the stems at the base and snap off the small, tough bottom leaves. Trim 1 inch off the top of the artichoke with a knife, and trim the tips off any other leaves with scissors. Rub the artichokes all over with lemon, to prevent discoloration, and put them in a nonreactive pot with enough water to cover halfway. For each quart of water used, add 1 teaspoon salt and 2 tablespoons each of lemon juice and olive oil. (I like to throw in some parsley sprigs and chopped onion and carrot, too.) Bring the liquid to a boil, cover, and simmer for 30 to 45 minutes, until the bases can be easily pierced with a fork. Carefully lift out the artichokes and drain them upside down on paper towels.

Eating an artichoke leaf by leaf is a sensual experience. Dunk the bottom of each leaf in a vinaigrette, a simple mayonnaise, or a vegetable dip. Draw it through your teeth to scrape off the fleshy underside, then discard the rest. Throw out the purple-tipped, light-colored center leaves, as well (you can loosen these with a gentle twist), then use a small spoon or knife to remove and discard the hairy choke. Cut the heart into smaller pieces before eating.

Baby artichokes are less fussy. You can simply sauté them whole, halved, or quartered. Be vigilant about freshness in all artichokes. Buy only those that are tight and glossy, with no spreading or yellowed leaves. Store them unwashed in a plastic bag in your refrigerator.

---

4. Add the chopped basil and stir well. Let the soup cool slightly.

5. Purée the soup, in batches, in a blender or food processor until it is completely smooth. Return the purée to the pot, and add the cream, if desired. Heat through over very low heat, adjusting the seasonings. Serve immediately, garnished with the diced tomatoes and slivered basil.

Serves 4 to 6

AUGUST CONFETTI CORN CHOWDER

★ ★ ★

When the corn is high and sweet and the market is bursting with zucchini and basil, it's time for the chowder pot to hit the stove. In this recipe, I add the corncobs to the broth for their rich flavor. Instead of the usual butter and flour thickener, I purée some of the corn and potatoes and use that to give body to the soup. Basil, dill, and scallions add a dash of flavor when stirred in just before serving.

8 ears fresh Silver Queen or other sweet corn,
  shucked
6 cups defatted chicken or vegetable broth,
  preferably homemade (pages 253 and 255)
1 red bell pepper, stemmed, seeded, and cut into
  ¼-inch dice
1 russet potato, peeled and cubed
1 quart milk
¼ pound slab bacon, rind removed, cut into
  ¼-inch pieces
1 onion, cut into ¼-inch dice
Salt and freshly ground black pepper,
  to taste
1 small zucchini, trimmed and cut into
  very small dice
6 tablespoons chopped fresh flat-leaf parsley
½ cup slivered fresh basil leaves, for garnish
2 tablespoons coarsely chopped fresh dill,
  for garnish
2 scallions (3 inches green left on), thinly
  sliced, for garnish

1. Remove the kernels from the cobs, and set them aside. Cut the cobs in half and place them in a heavy soup pot.

2. Add the broth to the pot, bring it to a boil, and then reduce the heat to low. Cover the pot and simmer for 20 minutes.

3. While the broth is cooking, blanch the bell pepper in a small pot of boiling water for 1 minute. (This keeps them from "bleeding" and turning the soup a pink color.) Drain and set them aside.

4. Remove and discard the corncobs, and add the potato cubes and half of the reserved corn kernels to the broth. Bring to a boil, reduce the heat to medium, and cook, covered, until the potatoes are tender, 10 to 12 minutes. Remove from the heat and allow to cool slightly.

5. Purée the soup, in batches, in a blender or food processor until just smooth (do not overblend). Transfer the soup to a large bowl, stir in the milk, and set aside.

6. In the same soup pot, sauté the bacon over low heat just until the fat has been rendered, about 5 minutes. Add the onion and continue to cook, stirring constantly, until wilted, 10 minutes. Add the puréed soup, season with salt and pepper, and cook over low heat until very hot.

7. Add the zucchini and the remaining corn kernels. Cook over medium heat for 5 to 8 minutes (do not boil).

8. Before serving, stir in the blanched bell pepper and 4 tablespoons of the parsley. Garnish with the basil, dill, scallions, and the remaining parsley, and serve piping hot.

Serves 6 to 8

CORN AND LIMA CHOWDER

★ ★ ★

When I think of chowders, Northeastern clam and fresh corn come immediately to mind. Yet the term *chowder* finds its roots on quite another coast. Most historical accounts of this hearty soup trace it back to seaside villages of Brittany and to the French word *chaudière,* a large cauldron. When the boats came into port after long days of fishing, the sailors all added some of their catch to the soup pot, and *voilà,* chowder was born. Via French settlers in Nova Scotia, this tradition worked its way down to the shores of New England. But it doesn't stop there. As summer draws to an end and New Jersey offers up crops of corn and limas, I use them in this bewitching succotash-like soup. The spike of licorice-flavored basil leaves brightens all the chowder ingredients. Keep this Jersey chowder nice and chunky!

2 onions
1 red bell pepper, stemmed and seeded
2 russet potatoes, peeled
¼ pound slab bacon, rind removed, cut into
    ¼-inch dice
2 tablespoons unsalted butter
2 tablespoons all-purpose flour
4 cups defatted chicken broth, preferably
    homemade (page 253)
1 cup heavy (or whipping) cream
3 cups cooked corn
1 cup cooked baby lima beans
Salt and freshly ground black pepper,
    to taste
3 scallions (3 inches green left on), thinly sliced
    on the diagonal
1 tablespoon thinly slivered fresh basil leaves,
    for garnish

1. Cut the onions, and bell pepper into ¼-inch dice and set them aside separately. Cut the potatoes into ¼-inch dice, place them in a bowl, and cover with cold water.

2. Cook the bacon in a heavy soup pot over low heat until the fat is rendered, about 5 minutes. Add the butter and stir to melt it.

3. Add the onions and cook, stirring, until wilted, 10 minutes. Add the flour and cook, stirring, another 5 minutes.

4. Add the broth and potatoes. Cook over medium-low heat until the potatoes are tender but not mushy, 10 to 12 minutes. Add the cream, corn, lima beans, salt, and pepper, and cook, stirring once or twice, for 7 minutes.

5. Add the bell pepper and scallions. Adjust the seasonings and cook another 5 minutes. Serve immediately, garnished with the basil.

Serves 6

GARDEN BROCCOLI VEGETABLE SOUP

★ ★ ★

I found that I was bored with the usual broccoli soup, creamy and pale green, so I experimented a bit and came up with this variation. The sweetness of carrots and the complex acidity of tomatoes counters the strong cabbage flavor of cooked broccoli. The addition of fresh basil just before the soup is puréed adds an appealing emerald hue to the bowl.

2 heads broccoli (about 1½ pounds each), trimmed
2 tablespoons unsalted butter
2 tablespoons extra virgin olive oil
2 cups finely chopped well-washed leeks
   (white plus 3 inches of green),
      patted dry
2 carrots, peeled and finely chopped
1 tablespoon finely minced garlic
6 cups defatted chicken broth, preferably
   homemade (page 253)
2 ripe plum tomatoes, seeded and chopped
1 teaspoon finely grated lemon zest
2 cups whole fresh basil leaves, rinsed
Salt and freshly ground black pepper,
   to taste

1. Trim off the tough stem ends of the broccoli, and using a vegetable peeler, remove the tough outer layer of the stems. Cut the stems into small pieces. Cut the head into small florets, setting aside the smallest for garnish.

2. In a heavy pot, heat the butter and the oil over low heat. Add the leeks and the carrots, and cook, stirring, until wilted, 10 to 12 minutes. Add the garlic and cook, stirring, another 2 to 3 minutes.

3. Add the broth and bring it to a boil. Stir in the broccoli, tomatoes, and lemon zest, and return to a boil. Cover, reduce the heat to medium, and simmer until the broccoli is tender, 20 to 25 minutes.

4. Meanwhile, bring a small pot of water to a boil and blanch the reserved broccoli florets for 2 minutes. Rinse under cold water, drain, and pat dry. Set aside for garnish.

5. Remove the soup from the heat. Stir in the basil, cover, and let rest for 5 minutes. Then purée the soup, in batches, in a blender or food processor. Return it to the pot and reheat it. Season with salt and pepper.

6. Serve piping hot, garnished with the reserved broccoli florets.

Serves 4

CREAMY FIDDLEHEAD FERN SOUP

★ ★ ★

Norman Legace, a great outdoorsman who lives in northwestern Connecticut, surprised me one fine day in May with a sack full of fiddlehead ferns—his latest find from along the shores of Sandy Brook in Pittsfield, Massachusetts. Grateful for such a lovely gift, I prepared this soup. It is a delightful way to begin a meal of Baked Salmon on a Bed of Leeks. Snipped chives will lend a savory dash. Or if you can find chive blossoms, lay one or two across the soup before serving.

2 tablespoons unsalted butter
2 tablespoons olive oil
2 onions, chopped
1 tablespoon chopped garlic
¼ teaspoon ground mace
Pinch of cayenne pepper
1¼ pounds fresh fiddlehead ferns, ends
   trimmed to 1 inch from the spiral,
   rinsed
5 cups defatted vegetable or
   chicken broth, preferably homemade
   (page 255 or 253)
Salt and freshly ground black pepper, to taste
¾ cup heavy (or whipping) cream
2 tablespoons snipped fresh chives, for garnish

1. Heat the butter and the oil in a heavy pot. Add the onions and cook, stirring, over low heat until wilted, 10 minutes. Add the garlic and cook until the onions are soft and translucent, about 5 minutes more. Sprinkle in the mace and cayenne, and stir until the spices have been absorbed by the oil.

2. Set aside 12 of the smallest ferns. Add the remaining fiddleheads and the broth to the pot. Bring to a boil; then reduce the heat to medium-low. Simmer, partially covered, until the fiddle-heads are tender, 10 minutes. Season with salt and pepper. Let the soup cool to room temperature.

3. Meanwhile, bring a small pot of water to a boil. Cook the 12 reserved fiddleheads for 4 minutes. Drain, refresh in a bowl of ice water, and drain again.

4. Purée the soup, in batches, in a blender or food processor until smooth, gradually adding the cream through the feed tube.

5. Before serving, reheat the soup over very low heat. Ladle the soup into 4 small bowls, garnish each with a sprinkling of chives and 3 of the ferns, and serve.

Serves 4

YUKON GOLD AND LEEK SOUP

Carolyn Maxwell, from Lewistown, Pennsylvania, my first and best friend in New York, always made the ultimate vichyssoise, never stinting on the butter and cream. Ordinarily I hate to mess with perfection, but, the appearance of beautiful Yukon Gold potatoes in the market has allowed me to cut back on the amount of cream in the original recipe somewhat. The creamy texture of the potato's golden flesh adds a natural buttery flavor to the soup, so that massive amounts of the real thing are not necessary to add rich taste. This soup is made extra-special with its garnish of golden caviar, snipped chives, and sour cream. Carolyn now owns a bed-and-breakfast, Country Country, in Quakertown, Pennsylvania. Whenever I visit, I'm delighted when she brings a tureen of her vichyssoise to the table.

4 large leeks (white bulbs only)
2 tablespoons cider vinegar
¼ cup (½ stick) unsalted butter
1 onion, thinly sliced
4 Yukon Gold potatoes (about ½ pound each), peeled and thinly sliced
4 cups defatted chicken broth, preferably homemade (page 253)
2 teaspoons fresh lemon juice
1½ cups milk
2¼ cups heavy (or whipping) cream
Salt and freshly ground black pepper, to taste
6 teaspoons American golden caviar, for garnish
1 bunch fresh chives, snipped, for garnish
½ cup sour cream, for garnish

1. Trim the roots from the leeks, and cut a 1½-inch-deep "X" through the top and bottom ends of each bulb. Place the leeks in a bowl, add the vinegar, and cover with cold water. Let soak for 20 minutes to remove any sand from the leeks. Drain, and rinse well under cold water. Thinly slice the leeks crosswise.

2. Melt the butter in a heavy soup pot over medium-low heat. Add the leeks and onion. Cook, stirring occasionally, until wilted, about 15 minutes. Add the potatoes, chicken broth, and lemon juice, and bring to a boil. Then reduce the heat to medium and simmer for 20 minutes. Partially cover the pot and simmer, stirring occasionally, 20 minutes more. If the soup boils, further reduce the heat. Remove it from the heat and let it cool to room temperature.

3. Process the soup, in batches, in a blender or food processor, pulsing the machine on and off so that some texture remains. Return it to the pot, and add the milk and 1½ cups of the cream. Season generously with salt and pepper, and heat over medium heat just to a simmer. Do not boil. Remove from the heat and cool to room temperature. Refrigerate, covered, overnight.

4. The following day, stir in the remaining ¾ cup cream. Cover and return to the refrigerator until ready to use. Serve chilled or hot, garnished with caviar, chives, and a dollop of sour cream.

Serves 6

CREAMY FRESH MOREL SOUP

★ ★ ★

I visited Boyne City, Michigan, during morel season so that I could participate in my first-ever mushroom hunt (see page 294 for The Morel—and More—of the Story). Although it didn't result in my finding a whole lot of mushrooms, it did inspire me to create this creamy, intensely flavored soup.

10 ounces fresh morels, wiped or brushed clean
½ pound white mushrooms, stems trimmed
3 tablespoons unsalted butter
1 tablespoon olive oil
2 onions, coarsely chopped
Salt and freshly ground black pepper, to taste
4 cups defatted chicken broth, preferably
    homemade (page 253)
½ cup heavy (or whipping) cream
2 teaspoons snipped fresh chives, for garnish

1. Choose 2 ounces of the smaller morels, and set them aside. Halve the remaining morels lengthwise, and wipe or brush them again to make sure that they are clean inside. Slice them again crosswise. Wipe the white mushroom caps clean with a damp paper towel. Slice the mushrooms and set aside.

2. Heat 2 tablespoons of the butter and the oil in a heavy pot over medium-low heat. Add the onions and cook, stirring, until wilted, 15 minutes. Add the sliced morels and the white mushrooms. Cook, stirring occasionally, until wilted, 2 to 3 minutes. Season with salt and pepper.

3. Add the chicken broth and bring it to a boil. Reduce the heat to a simmer, cover, and cook, stirring occasionally, for 20 minutes.

4. Meanwhile, sauté the reserved whole morels in the remaining 1 tablespoon butter over medium heat until just tender, about 5 minutes. Using a slotted spoon, transfer them to a small bowl and set aside.

5. With a slotted spoon, remove the solids from the soup and transfer them to a food processor.

6. Line a strainer with cheesecloth or a paper towel, and place over a bowl. Pour the broth through it to remove any sand. Wipe out the soup pot.

7. Add 1 cup of the strained broth to the mushroom mixture in the processor, and purée until smooth. Return the purée to the pot along with the remaining strained broth and the cream. Adjust the seasonings.

8. Before serving, heat the soup through over low heat. Divide it among four bowls, and garnish each bowl with some of the whole morels and snipped chives. Serve immediately.

Serves 4

CREAM OF MUSHROOM SOUP

★ ★ ★

Being a fierce wild-mushroom lover, I am always tempted to add some to soups for extra flavor, but truth be told, you can draw a different but equally satisfying flavor from the nice white domestic variety as you can from the woody wilds. A hint of thyme or marjoram will impart a beautiful herbaceous perfume to the delicate mushrooms in this rich, creamy, and comforting soup.

2 pounds white mushrooms, stems
*   trimmed off*
2 tablespoons olive oil
2 tablespoons unsalted butter
1 large onion, coarsely chopped
1½ tablespoons minced garlic
½ teaspoon dried thyme
Pinch of ground nutmeg
Salt and freshly ground black pepper,
*   to taste*
4½ cups defatted chicken broth,
*   preferably homemade (page 253)*
½ cup heavy (or whipping) cream
2 tablespoons snipped fresh chives,
*   for garnish*

1. Wipe the mushroom caps clean with a damp paper towel. Slice the mushrooms and set them aside.

2. Heat the oil and the butter in a large heavy pot over low heat. Add the onion and cook until wilted, stirring occasionally, 10 to 12 minutes. Add the garlic and cook 2 minutes more.

3. Add the mushrooms and cook, uncovered, stirring frequently, for 15 minutes. Season with the thyme, nutmeg, salt, and pepper.

4. Add the chicken broth and bring to a boil. Reduce the heat to medium, cover, and simmer for 30 minutes. Remove the pot from the heat and let cool to room temperature.

5. Purée the soup, in batches, in a food processor until smooth, adding the cream gradually through the feed tube. Return the soup to the pot and adjust the seasonings to taste. Before serving, heat the soup through over very low heat (do not boil). Garnish with the chives, and serve piping hot.
Serves 6

HOME-STYLE MUSHROOM BARLEY SOUP

★ ★ ★

A traditional New York City Jewish deli offering, thick mushroom barley soup is also the essence of good home cooking. At least, my gang thinks so. Whenever I prepare it, I remind myself not to overcook the barley. A little "bite" to it is good.

2 quarts defatted chicken broth, preferably
*   homemade (page 253)*
½ cup uncooked pearl barley, rinsed and drained
2 carrots, peeled and cut into ¼-inch dice
1 tablespoon chopped fresh sage leaves,
*   or ½ teaspoon dried*
1 tablespoon unsalted butter
1 tablespoon olive oil
1 onion, chopped
10 ounces white mushrooms, wiped clean
*   and cut into quarters*
2 cloves garlic, finely chopped
Salt and freshly ground black pepper, to taste
¼ cup chopped fresh flat-leaf parsley

1. Combine the broth, barley, carrots, and sage in a large heavy pot. Bring to a boil. Then stir, cover, and simmer for 40 minutes.

2. Meanwhile, heat the butter and the oil in a nonstick skillet over medium-low heat. Add the onion and cook, stirring, until softened, 10 minutes. Add the mushrooms, raise the heat to medium-high, and cook, stirring, for 5 minutes. Add the garlic and cook 5 minutes more. Stir the mushroom mixture into the soup, and season with salt and pepper.

3. Cook the soup, partially covered, for 20 minutes longer. Stir in the parsley and serve.

Serves 4

SUNNY ROASTED RED PEPPER SOUP

★ ★ ★

A swirl of vibrant Velvety Mango Cream will enliven the deep, comforting flavors that fuse within a bowl of this roasted pepper soup. Diced avocado adds some Southwestern razzle-dazzle.

6 red bell peppers, stemmed, seeded,
   and halved lengthwise
1 leek (2 inches green left on)
1 tablespoon white vinegar
3 tablespoons unsalted butter
2 tablespoons olive oil
1 onion, coarsely chopped
½ teaspoon salt
¼ teaspoon freshly ground black pepper
1 teaspoon sugar
1 russet potato (½ pound), thinly sliced
6 cups defatted chicken broth, preferably
   homemade (page 253)
½ cup Velvety Mango Cream
   (page 135)
½ ripe avocado, peeled and cut into
   ¼-inch dice, for garnish

1. Preheat the broiler or a grill.

2. Broil or grill 6 of the pepper halves until the skins are blackened (or see page 132 How to Roast a Bell Pepper). Place them in a paper or plastic bag and let them steam for 10 minutes. Slip off the skins, coarsely chop, and set aside. Coarsely chop the remaining 6 pepper halves and set them aside.

3. Trim the root end off the leek, and cut a 1½-inch "X" in both ends. Place the leek in a bowl. Add the vinegar and water to cover; soak for 15 minutes. Drain, and rinse well to remove all the dirt. Dry, then coarsely chop the leek.

4. Heat the butter and the oil in a heavy soup pot over medium-low heat. Add the leeks, onion, salt, and pepper, and cook, stirring, until the vegetables have wilted, 10 minutes. Add the uncooked red bell peppers, sprinkle with the sugar, and cook for 5 minutes.

5. Add the roasted red bell peppers, the potato, and the chicken broth. Bring the soup to a boil. Reduce the heat to medium and simmer, partially covered, until the vegetables are tender, about 30 minutes. Remove from the heat and allow to cool slightly.

6. Purée the soup, in batches, in a blender or food processor, allowing some slight texture to remain. Return the soup to the pot and heat it through, adjusting the seasonings. Serve in shallow bowls, drizzled with the Mango Cream and garnished with diced avocado.

Serves 6

SORREL SOUP

★ ★ ★

I've always enjoyed cooking with sorrel, and in fact, was once given a packet of seeds from France that produced a yearly crop in my Connecticut garden until an onslaught of mint took over. I'm hoping that with the increasing popularity and availability of arugula, cilantro, and lemongrass, Americans will continue to develop an interest in tangy herbs and greens, and that long-underutilized sorrel will become more available. Seek out this perennial herb in the early spring—you can often find it at farmers' markets—and turn it into a pleasant tangy soup. In this recipe I've balanced sorrel's sourish flavor with a touch of mace and complemented it with the addition of yogurt. Scatter snipped fresh chives on top for a lovely touch of color—if you can find them with their beautiful lavender blossoms early in the season you'll have a dazzling presentation.

2 tablespoons unsalted butter
4 leeks (3 inches green left on), well washed, dried, and thinly sliced
2 cloves garlic, minced
10 cups tightly packed fresh sorrel leaves (washed, stems removed)
4 cups vegetable broth, preferably homemade (page 255)
Salt and freshly ground black pepper, to taste
½ teaspoon ground mace
2 cups plain nonfat yogurt
3 tablespoons snipped fresh chives, for garnish
6 chives with blossoms, for garnish (optional)

1. Melt the butter in a large heavy pot. Add the leeks and garlic, and cook over medium-low heat until wilted, 10 to 12 minutes.

2. Add the sorrel, cover, and cook until wilted, 5 minutes.

3. Add the vegetable broth, salt, pepper, and mace. Bring to a boil, reduce the heat slightly, and simmer, uncovered, for 20 minutes. Cool to room temperature.

4. Purée the soup, in batches, in a blender or food processor until completely smooth, gradually adding 1½ cups of the yogurt.

5. To serve cold, chill the soup completely for 4 hours or overnight. To serve it hot, heat it through gently over medium-low heat. Serve in shallow bowls, dolloped with a generous tablespoon of the remaining yogurt and sprinkled with snipped chives. Lay a chive blossom across the top, if desired.

Serves 4

VELVET SQUASH SOUP

★ ★ ★

On those late summer days when yellow squash is running rampant in the garden, you might want to make a batch of this light and delicate hot soup. A hint of fresh basil nicely complements the mellow curry flavor. Serve a bowl of Velvet Squash Soup before Orange Blossom Butterflied Leg of Lamb.

2 tablespoons unsalted butter
2 tablespoons olive oil
2 cups thinly sliced well-washed leeks
*   (white plus 3 inches green)*
2 teaspoons best-quality curry powder
6 cups defatted chicken broth, preferably
*   homemade (page 253)*
1½ pounds yellow summer squash,
*   ends trimmed, coarsely chopped*
2 cups coarsely chopped seeded ripe plum
*   tomatoes*
Salt and freshly ground black pepper, to taste
¼ cup shredded fresh basil leaves, for garnish

  1. In a heavy pot, heat the butter and the oil over low heat. Pat the leeks dry, add them to the pot. Cook, stirring, until wilted, 10 to 12 minutes, sprinkling with the curry powder during the last 2 minutes.
  2. Add the broth and bring it to a boil. Add the squash and the tomatoes. Return to a boil, reduce the heat to medium, cover, and simmer until the vegetables have softened, 20 minutes. Let the soup cool slightly.
  3. Purée the soup, in batches, in a blender or food processor. Return the purée to the pot, season with salt and pepper, and serve garnished with the shredded basil.
  Serves 4

LIGHT AND SPICY TOMATO SOUP

★ ★ ★

In this book, there are two creamy tomato soups: the traditional one, enriched with heavy cream, and this one, the lighter variation, with nothing more than an illusion of richness. For this, I slice some potatoes, lay them in the bottom of the bowl, and then ladle in the soup. The potatoes add a bit of thickness, as well as a slightly creamy texture, as they "melt," resulting in creamy tomato soup without the cream.

2 tablespoons vegetable oil
2 cups coarsely chopped onions
1 tablespoon minced garlic
2 cups defatted chicken broth or vegetable broth,
*   preferably homemade (page 253 or 255)*
2 cans (28 ounces each) plum tomatoes, undrained
Finely grated zest of 2 oranges
Juice of 2 oranges
2 tablespoons honey
2 cinnamon sticks (each 3 inches long)
½ teaspoon ground allspice
¼ teaspoon ground nutmeg
2 russet potatoes, peeled and cut into ¼-inch-thick
*   slices*
Salt and coarsely ground black pepper, to taste
2 tablespoons snipped fresh chives, for garnish

1. Heat the oil in a large heavy pot over low heat. Add the onions and cook, stirring occasionally, for 5 minutes. Add the garlic and cook for 5 minutes more.

2. Add the broth, tomatoes plus their juices, orange zest, orange juice, honey, and all of the spices, breaking up the tomatoes with the back of a large spoon as they are added. Raise the heat and bring the soup to a boil. Then reduce the heat to medium and simmer, stirring occasionally, for 30 minutes.

3. While the soup is simmering, place the potatoes in a saucepan, cover with water, and add a pinch of salt. Bring to a boil and simmer until the potatoes are just tender, 8 minutes. Drain and set aside.

4. Remove and discard the cinnamon sticks. Purée the soup, in batches, in a blender or food processor until very smooth. Return it to the pot and season with salt and pepper.

5. Before serving, warm the soup gently. Divide the potato slices among 8 soup bowls, ladle the soup over the potatoes, and sprinkle with the chives. Serve immediately.

Serves 8

REAL CREAM OF TOMATO SOUP

★ ★ ★

For an easy Sunday night supper, I can think of nothing more delicious than classic cream of tomato soup (the genuine article) and grilled cheese sandwiches. To me, there is nothing more American. When I was young, I was a real Campbell's connoisseur—I loved their version (still do), and my mother kept cans of it in the pantry. Interestingly, when Campbell's began making their cream of tomato soup, they grew fields of tomatoes in Camden, New Jersey, near their plant so they could pick, cook, and can, with no time wasted. Here I've gently spiced up meaty Romas (plum tomatoes) with some allspice and tarragon, and then smoothed it all out with heavy cream. The soup is luscious served hot or cold—you make the choice. For a touch of green color, add fresh chives.

2 tablespoons unsalted butter
1 large onion, coarsely chopped
1 large clove garlic, finely minced
2 tablespoons chopped fresh tarragon leaves, or 1½ teaspoons dried
½ teaspoon ground allspice
½ teaspoon sugar
6 cups defatted chicken broth, preferably homemade (page 253)
3 pounds ripe plum tomatoes, peeled and coarsely chopped
1 tablespoon tomato paste
1 tablespoon finely grated orange zest
1 cup heavy (or whipping) cream
2 tablespoons snipped fresh chives, for garnish

1. Melt the butter in a large heavy pot over medium-low heat. Add the onions and cook until softened, 10 minutes. Add the garlic, tarragon, allspice, and sugar, and cook, stirring, for 1 minute more.

2. Add the chicken broth, tomatoes, and tomato paste to the pot. Bring to a boil. Then reduce the heat to medium, partially cover, and simmer for 30 minutes. Stir in the orange zest and allow to cool to room temperature.

3. Purée the soup, in batches, in a blender or food processor. Return it to the pot, stir in the cream, and heat through over very low heat. Do not boil. Garnish with the chives, and serve.

Serves 6 to 8

ZUCCHINI AND SWISS CHARD SOUP

★ ★ ★

The vegetables in this soup blend so enigmatically, don't be surprised when family members or guests are unable to identify its savory flavors. Zucchini makes a light base, leeks add a mellow oniony sweetness, and Swiss chard releases just a hint of a lemony bite, complementing the mint-like taste of the basil. The embellishment of a

fresh nasturtium blossom makes the perfect-style garnish.

2 tablespoons unsalted butter
2 tablespoons extra virgin olive oil
2 cups finely chopped well-washed leeks
4 cups defatted chicken broth, preferably
*   homemade (page 253)*
2 pounds zucchini, ends trimmed, coarsely
*   chopped*
½ pound green Swiss chard, rinsed
1 cup whole fresh basil leaves
Salt and freshly ground black pepper, to taste

1. Heat the butter and the oil in a heavy pot over low heat. Add the leeks and cook, stirring, until wilted, 10 to 12 minutes.

2. Add the broth and bring to a boil. Add the zucchini, return to a boil, and then reduce the heat to medium. Simmer, covered, for 20 minutes.

3. Meanwhile, cut out the large stems from the Swiss chard. Stack the leaves and cut them crosswise into 1-inch strips. Set them aside.

CHOOSING SWISS CHARD

— ❧ —

Leafy greens have moved into the spotlight in recent years, heralded as being inexpensive, highly nutritious, and easy to prepare. One of my favorites, Swiss chard, is no exception. With its rich green color and wonderful flavor, it provides delicious eating.

Swiss chard is almost two vegetables in one: The spectacular long curly leaves can be prepared in the same manner as spinach; the white or ruby red broad, succulent ribs take longer to cook and can be sautéed or braised much the way you would celery. Both the leaves and ribs can be eaten raw in salads, as well. I enhance chard with a squeeze of lemon, a grinding of nutmeg, chopped garlic or, as I do in my soup recipe, with fresh basil.

When choosing chard, look for crinkly, dark green leaves void of any yellow spots; the smaller the leaf, the more tender the vegetable. Swiss chard can be stored for up to 5 days, unwashed, in the vegetable crisper.

4. Remove the soup from the heat. Add the Swiss chard and basil, and cover the pot. Let it rest for 5 minutes to wilt the greens.

5. Purée the soup, in batches, in a blender or a food processor. Return it to the pot and season with salt and pepper. Heat through to serve.

Serves 4 to 6

BAR CHEESE SOUP

★ ★ ★

My vague memories of "bar cheese" evoke a crock filled with pale yellow stuff, usually found in bars and served next to a plastic basket filled with crackers. Yet the name just seemed to suit this robust heartland soup. It is appropriate to use a sharp Wisconsin Cheddar here, but I do prefer the subtle coloring you get from a good pale Vermont Cheddar.

¼ pound slab bacon, rind removed, cut into
*   ¼-inch dice*
2 tablespoons olive oil
1 tablespoon unsalted butter
1 large onion, coarsely chopped
2 carrots, peeled and coarsely chopped
1 rib celery, coarsely chopped
1 tablespoon all-purpose flour
2 Yukon Gold potatoes (6 ounces each), peeled
*   and coarsely chopped*
4 cups defatted chicken broth, preferably
*   homemade (page 253)*
1 bottle (12 ounces) lager
2 cups grated Vermont Cheddar cheese
2 tablespoons snipped fresh chives,
*   for garnish*

1. Sauté the bacon in a nonstick skillet over low heat until golden brown, about 5 minutes. Using a slotted spoon, transfer the bacon to a paper towel to drain.

2. Heat the olive oil and the butter in a large heavy pot over low heat. Add the onion, carrots, and celery, and cook, stirring, until wilted, about 20 minutes.

3. Sprinkle the flour over the vegetables, and stir to combine. Add the potatoes, broth, and beer. Bring to a boil, reduce the heat to medium, and simmer, covered, until the potatoes are tender, about 20 minutes. Remove from the heat and allow to cool slightly.

4. Strain the soup, reserving the broth. Combine the strained vegetables and 1 cup of the reserved broth in a food processor, and process until just smooth.

5. Return the puréed soup to the pot along with the remaining reserved broth. Bring the soup to a gentle simmer over medium heat. Gradually add the cheese, stirring constantly until it melts. Stir in the reserved bacon. Garnish the soup with the chives, and serve.

Serves 4

ROASTED WINTER VEGETABLE SOUP

★ ★ ★

Well spiced and soothing, a puréed soup of winter vegetables is a comforting way to bring some warmth to those bone-chilling days. A little brown sugar brings out the natural sweetness of the vegetables and the pine nuts adds a nice textural contrast to the smoothness of the purée.

2 butternut squash (about 2 pounds each)
4 carrots, peeled
½ pound parsnips, peeled
1 large onion, thinly sliced
¼ cup (packed) light brown sugar
¼ cup (½ stick) unsalted butter
9 cups defatted chicken broth, plus 1 cup as needed,
    preferably homemade (page 253)
½ teaspoon ground mace
2 teaspoons finely chopped crystallized ginger
Pinch of cayenne pepper
Salt, to taste
½ cup toasted pine nuts (see box, this page), for
    garnish
3 tablespoons chopped fresh flat-leaf parsley,
    for garnish

1. Preheat the oven to 350°F.
2. Halve the squash lengthwise and scoop out the seeds. Place the squash cut side up in a large roasting pan. Cut the carrots and parsnips into small pieces, and scatter them, along with the onion, around the squash. Sprinkle the cut surfaces of the squash with the brown sugar and dot all over with the butter. Pour 2½ cups of the broth into the pan, and cover it tightly with aluminum foil. Bake until all the vegetables are very soft, 2 hours.

★★★★★★★★★★★★★★★★★★★★★★★★★★

TO TOAST PINE NUTS

—❦—

*P*reheat the oven to 350°F. Spread the nuts in a single layer on a baking sheet and toast until golden and fragrant, 3 to 5 minutes. Check after 3 minutes, as pine nuts burn easily.

★★★★★★★★★★★★★★★★★★★★★★★★★★

3. Carefully remove the foil and let the vegetables cool slightly. Scoop the squash out of the skins, and place it in a heavy soup pot. Add the other vegetables and the remaining 6½ cups broth. Season with the mace, crystallized ginger, cayenne, and salt. Stir together and bring to a boil. Reduce the heat to a simmer and cook, covered, for the flavors to combine, 10 minutes.
4. Purée the soup, in batches, in a blender or food processor until it is very smooth. Return the soup to the pot and add extra broth if necessary to thin it to the desired consistency. Heat it through. Serve the soup in large shallow soup bowls, garnished with the pine nuts and parsley.
Serves 10

Winter Vegetables

★ ★ ★

Winter, for most of us, is the season to take shelter and seek solace. We need more comfort in the cold months, especially when it comes to food. If it's gray and sleety outside, we seem to instinctively crave winter squashes, roots, and tubers. They're earthier, more filling, and appropriately mellow-tasting, great in warming soups, stews, sautés, and purées. They're also an important source of vitamins and minerals. The following, all favorites of mine, are widely available during the winter months, and sometimes year-round (check the Index under individual vegetables for a selection of recipes):

Parsnip: This carrot relative is sweet, nutty, and rich in potassium and magnesium. Parsnips grow best in the cold, so they're in their prime in the dead of winter. Buy crisp, small ones (large parsnips can be woody) and use them as you would carrots. I especially like them diced and glazed in a skillet with butter, sugar, and lemon juice or roasted with other root vegetables. Fresh parsnips keep in the refrigerator for up to 3 weeks.

Carrot: We all know carrots—the average American eats 10 pounds of them a year. But have you ever tried them steamed and tossed in maple syrup and butter, or with ginger, brown sugar, butter, and caraway seed? Grated carrot mixed with dried cherries and yogurt makes a refreshing salad. Carrots are a leading source of vitamin A (which means your mother was right when she said they were good for your eyes!).

Turnip: Fresh turnips have a creamy, mildly sweet flesh that absorbs the flavor of the broth or seasoning you're cooking with. Whichever type you're buying— they range from the grapefruit-size Macomber to the tiny "baby"variety—should be smooth-skinned and heavy for its size. Calcium-rich turnips can be steamed, boiled, sautéed, baked, braised, or glazed. Try them roasted in lamb stew. And don't throw out the delicious greens. Cut them off the turnips as soon as you get them home (they tend to leach out flavor), and cook them as you would spinach.

Rutabaga: This round turnip relative is usually sold waxed. If you don't remove its rind until you're ready to cook, the rutabaga will keep in your refrigerator for weeks. Its orange-yellow flesh tastes like a cross between turnip and cabbage. Purée with carrots for an appealingly sweet dish, or prepare them alone with a little butter and brown sugar. They have even more calcium than turnips and double the vitamin C.

Celeriac (celery root): Celeriac is brown, knobby, and hairy outside and white and quite firm inside. I *love* it! Cut it open (be careful, using a sturdy, very sharp knife), and you'll get a heady celery perfume that matches its fine, intense flavor. Try it blanched and julienned in salad. Toss it alone or with shrimp in a rémoulade sauce. It's heavenly puréed with potatoes or pears. Buy the smallest celeriac you can find; these, like most root vegetables, get tougher as they grow bigger.

Leek: Although I love this onion relative all year round, I find its subtle sweetness especially well suited to cold-weather dishes. Use it with onion in soups and stews, and you'll get added dimension. It's superb braised (a classic preparation), roasted, grilled, or sautéed. Refrigerated leeks keep up to 5 days. They can be very sandy on the inside, so you'll need to soak and/or rinse very thoroughly. To remove sand from a leek you're cooking whole, trim the root base and all but 3 inches of the dark green portion, cut a 1- or 2-inch vertical slit at each end, and soak in water with a little vinegar for an hour. Leeks are even more nourishing than onions, higher in calcium, iron, potassium, and vitamin C.

Winter Squash: Most of us are familiar with just a few varieties. Visit a farmers' market in season, however, and you may encounter a dozen new ones, including some heirlooms, in a riot of autumn colors. This selection of

so-called winter squashes narrows once winter really hits, to a half-dozen or fewer types, all of which have an excellent balance of minerals, vitamins, and cancer-fighting carotene. They usually include the *acorn* squash, popular for its moist, rich orange flesh, and the large, pear-shaped *butternut* squash, which is very similar to acorn in flavor and consistency. You're also likely to come across the odd-shaped *buttercup* and *turban* squashes, both orange-fleshed and exceptionally sweet. Look for *sugar pumpkins* (the small, edible kind) or *golden nugget* squash, which makes a great substitute when pumpkins aren't available. Huge *Hubbard*

squashes, sometimes cut up and sold in wedges, are tasty but a bit mealy (the right recipe can correct this). For something completely different, try the oblong *spaghetti* squash, which has mild yellow flesh that can be pulled out in pasta-like strands after it's been cooked.

Prepare most winter squashes in a way that will concentrate their flesh and flavor. Baking is easiest—just cut the squash in two, scoop out the seeds, and put the halves cut side down in a flat pan or oven dish. Bake in a preheated 350° to 375°F oven until tender, 1 to 1½ hours, depending on the type and size of squash. Grilling and sautéing produce great results, although cutting and peeling the raw squash can be time-consuming. Cooked flesh can be mashed, puréed into soups, or used in pie filling. Winter squash pairs well with the other vegetables of the season—Roasted Winter Vegetable Soup (page 242) is a particularly savory union.

BEEF AND VEGETABLE BARLEY SOUP

★ ★ ★

Hearty and deep-flavored—that's this soup! I always make it with short ribs of beef because I love the rich flavor they impart, and I mix beef broth with the cooking water for a more satisfying base. Vegetables are added in two stages: the first infuse the broth as it cooks with good vegetable essence; the second batch is added to the strained broth and cooked just before the soup is served. That way they are full of taste instead of boiled out and limp. Another Sheila secret: Rather than adding uncooked barley to the soup, I cook it ahead of time and add it shortly before serving. This way I can add the perfect amount and it won't absorb too much of the broth. This soup should be accompanied by slices of fresh rye bread.

3½ pounds short ribs of beef
3 carrots
3 ribs celery, with leaves
2 onions
4 whole cloves
4 cloves garlic
6 cups water
2 to 4 cups defatted beef broth,
    preferably homemade (page 252)
½ ounce dried porcini mushrooms
4 large fresh flat-leaf parsley sprigs
3 carrots, peeled and cut into
    ¼-inch dice
3 ribs celery, cut into ¼-inch dice
1 cup cooked pearl barley
Salt and freshly ground black pepper,
    to taste
2 tablespoons chopped fresh flat-leaf parsley

1. Wipe the short ribs with a damp paper towel, and place them in a large heavy soup pot along with the whole carrots and celery.

2. Stud the onions with the cloves, and add them to the pot along with the garlic. Add the water and 2 cups of the beef broth (the liquid should cover the meat by at least 1½ inches). Bring to a boil, and then reduce the heat to medium. Cover the pot and simmer, occasionally skimming the foam that rises to the surface, for about 1 hour.

3. Add the porcini mushrooms and parsley sprigs and simmer, covered, until the meat is very tender, 1 hour. The meat should easily fall off the bones.

4. Transfer the meat to a bowl, discarding the bones, and allow to cool to room temperature. When cool enough to handle, trim off and discard any fat and shred the meat into medium-size pieces. Set it aside, covered.

5. Strain the broth through a strainer into a large bowl. Then strain it again through a strainer lined with a double layer of cheesecloth. Chill the broth, uncovered, in the refrigerator, until the fat rises to the top, at least 4 hours or overnight.

6. Remove the fat by skimming it off with a metal spoon or by pouring the broth through a gravy separator. Return the defatted broth to the soup pot.

7. Add the cut-up carrots and celery to the broth and bring to a boil. Reduce the heat to medium and simmer, covered, until the vegetables are tender, about 10 minutes. Add the cooked barley, reserved beef, and the remaining 2 cups of beef broth, if necessary. Heat through, season with salt and pepper, stir in the chopped parsley, and serve immediately, in soup bowls, piping hot.

Serves 4 to 6

BERTA'S CHICKEN VEGETABLE SOUP

★ ★ ★

My mother, Berta, has a knack for making a good, perfectly balanced pot of soup. She seems to know instinctively the right ratio of vegetables to broth to herbs. I like the combination of split peas and barley used to thicken this soup, but I have taken some liberties with this recipe. Berta uses water alone; the base of my soup is a mixture of chicken broth and water, which results in a more intense flavor.

½ cup uncooked pearl barley
½ cup dried green or yellow split peas
1 chicken (2 to 2½ pounds), cut into quarters
4 cups defatted chicken broth, preferably
*   homemade (page 253)*
2 cups water
2 large onions, cut into ½-inch pieces
3 carrots, peeled and cut into ¼-inch rounds
3 parsnips, peeled and cut into ½-inch rounds
3 ribs celery, cut into ½-inch slices
6 mushrooms, each cut into 6 pieces
Salt and freshly ground black pepper,
*   to taste*
2 teaspoons chopped fresh dill

1. Rinse the barley and soak it in cold water for 30 minutes. Drain and set aside. Pick over the split peas and discard any stones; rinse, drain, and set aside.

2. Clean the chicken well, and place it in a large heavy soup pot. Add the chicken broth and water (the chicken should be covered), and bring to a boil over high heat. When the soup starts to boil, add all the vegetables, split peas, and barley, and stir. When the soup returns to a boil, reduce the heat to low, and simmer gently, partially covered, skimming any foam and stirring occasionally, until the chicken is cooked through and the vegetables are tender, 1 hour.

3. Remove the chicken from the pot. When it is cool enough to handle, discard the skin and shred the meat into large pieces. Return about a third of the meat to the pot (save the remaining meat for another use, such as a salad), and reheat. Just before serving, season with salt and pepper and stir in the dill.

Serves 6

NATHALIE'S SHE-CRAB SOUP

★ ★ ★

My deepest thanks go to Atlanta star cook Nathalie Dupree for sharing her recipe for this traditional Southern favorite. The best time to make this richly delicious soup is in the spring, when the blue she-crabs are in season and full of the pungent roe that lends its unique, tangy flavor to the pot. But it can be made off-season by substituting lump crabmeat for the she-crab, and hard-cooked egg yolks for the roe. If you can get hold of she-crabs, then by all means use them. A touch of sherry or Madeira is traditionally added just before serving.

2 tablespoons unsalted butter

1 scallion (3 inches green left on), finely
   chopped

1 rib celery, finely chopped

2 tablespoons all-purpose flour

1 quart milk

2½ cups heavy (or whipping) cream

3 cups cooked she-crab or other lump crabmeat,
   picked over to remove cartilage

½ cup she-crab roe or 2 hard-cooked egg yolks,
   crumbled

Salt and freshly ground white pepper,
   to taste

Tabasco sauce, to taste

⅓ cup dry Madeira

Paprika, to taste

1. Melt the butter in a heavy saucepan over low heat. Add the scallions and celery, and cook, stirring, until the scallions are soft but not browned, 7 to 10 minutes. Stir in the flour; then add the milk and 2 cups of the cream. Raise the heat to medium and bring to a boil, stirring constantly. Remove the pan from the heat and allow the mixture to cool slightly before adding the crabmeat and the roe.

2. Before serving, warm the soup over low heat, stirring, just to heat it through. Season with salt, white pepper, and Tabasco sauce.

3. While the soup is reheating, whip the remaining ½ cup cream until soft peaks form.

4. To serve, place a scant tablespoon of Madeira in each soup bowl. Add the soup, and dollop with the whipped cream. Sprinkle lightly with paprika, and serve immediately.

Serves 6

CALIFORNIA SHELLFISH SOUP

★ ★ ★

When we were working on the *Silver Palate Cookbook*, Michael McLaughlin made a delicious shellfish soup based on San Francisco's renowned fish stew called cioppino. His key to the blending of unusual flavors is to add a good-quality California Zinfandel to the well-seasoned tomato sauce base. This is the wine to drink with the robust soup as well. I like to serve shellfish soup over a bed of fluffy couscous—pasta bowls are ideal. A hot, crusty, dense bread is the perfect accompaniment for sopping up any extra broth.

¼ cup olive oil

2 cups finely chopped onions

2 red bell peppers, stemmed, seeded,
   and coarsely diced

1 green bell pepper, stemmed, seeded,
   and coarsely diced

6 to 8 cloves garlic, finely chopped

2 cups fish broth, preferably homemade
   (page 254)

2 cups California red Zinfandel wine

1 can (35 ounces) peeled plum tomatoes,
   drained and coarsely chopped

1½ tablespoons dried basil

1 teaspoon dried thyme

1 bay leaf

Salt and freshly ground black pepper,
   to taste

Crushed red pepper flakes, to taste

8 mussels

8 small clams, such as littlenecks or cherrystones

8 large shrimp, peeled and deveined

¾ pound bay scallops

1 cup chopped fresh flat-leaf parsley

1 box (10 ounces) couscous, cooked and
   hot, for serving (optional)

1. Heat the oil in a large heavy pot over low heat. Add the onions, red and green bell peppers, and garlic, and cook, covered, stirring occasionally, until the vegetables are soft, about 15 minutes.

2. Add the broth, wine, and tomatoes. Raise the heat to high.

3. Stir in the basil, thyme, and bay leaf. Season with the salt, pepper, and red pepper flakes.

4. Bring the soup to a boil. Then reduce the heat and simmer, partially covered, for 30 minutes. Stir occasionally, crushing the tomatoes with the back of the spoon. Correct the seasonings. (You can prepare the soup through this step the day before serving; it will keep and improve, covered, in the refrigerator.)

5. Scrub the mussels and clams well, and debeard the mussels just before cooking them. Place the mussels and clams in a heavy kettle, add an inch of water, cover, and set over high heat. As they steam open, remove them with a slotted spoon and set them aside. Discard any shellfish that don't open.

6. Rinse the shrimp and scallops in cool tap water, and pat in them dry.

7. Before serving time, bring the soup to a boil. Drop in the shrimp and scallops, and cook for 3 minutes. Add the clams and mussels (in their shells). Add the parsley, stir well, and remove from the heat. Let stand, covered, for 1 minute.

8. Ladle the soup into heated bowls, over cooked couscous, if using, dividing the seafood equally. Serve immediately.

Serves 4 to 6

NEW ENGLAND CLAM CHOWDER

★ ★ ★

Many versions of this New England favorite are heavily thickened with flour. I find that this dulls the flavors and makes for an unappealing texture. In my chowder, the potatoes add just the right amount of thickening, keeping the chowder lighter and fresh-tasting. Quahogs (hard-shelled clams) are the best choice for chowder. Their well-flavored steaming liquid gives depth to the soup's broth, and the slab bacon adds the traditional smoky taste. No salt should be necessary once the bacon is added. The cream, of course, is irresistible!

6 pounds cherrystone clams or other
    quahogs
1 rib celery, with leaves, cut into
    2-inch pieces
1 carrot, halved
2 bay leaves
3 sprigs fresh thyme
3 onions, coarsely chopped
2 cups water
½ cup bottled clam juice
½ pound slab bacon, rind removed,
    cut into ¼-inch dice
1 tablespoon chopped fresh thyme leaves
2 tablespoons unsalted butter
8 small white new potatoes, cut into
    ¼-inch dice
2 cups heavy (or whipping) cream
Freshly ground black pepper, to taste
2 tablespoons chopped fresh flat-leaf parsley

1. Wash the clams well in cold water and put them in a heavy soup pot. Add the celery, carrot, 1 bay leaf, the thyme sprigs, and one third of the chopped onions.

2. Add the water and clam juice. Cover the pot and bring to a boil over high heat. Cook, shaking the pot occasionally, until the clams open, about 5 minutes. Remove the clams from the shells, pouring any broth in the shells into the pot. Discard the shells and any clams that haven't opened. Cover the clams and set aside. Strain the broth through a fine sieve and set it aside.

3. Wipe out the pot, then add the bacon, and cook over low heat until the fat is rendered and the bacon is slightly crisp, about 10 minutes. Add the remaining chopped onions, the remaining bay leaf, the chopped thyme, and the butter. Cook, stirring, until the onions have wilted, 15 minutes.

4. Add the potatoes and the strained broth. Simmer, partially covered, over medium heat until the potatoes are cooked through, 10 to 12 minutes. Skim off any foam that rises to the surface.

5. Meanwhile, coarsely chop the reserved clams.

6. Add the clams and the cream, and simmer over medium heat until the clams are just cooked through, 5 to 7 minutes. Do not overcook them.

7. Remove and discard the bay leaf. Season the chowder generously with pepper, stir in the parsley, and serve immediately.

Serves 6 to 8

CLAM CHOWDER: MAKE MINE THICK

— 🍲 —

The debate has simmered for years: white or red? I'm not talking wine here, but clam chowder. The tomato-based "Manhattan" variety gets little respect in New England, where the filling cream soup reigns supreme. The mouthwatering New Bedford chowder so lovingly lionized in *Moby Dick* was certainly white, and thick with ship biscuit and butter—real sustenance for real men of the sea!

Red chowder seems to be a twentieth-century innovation, perhaps introduced by Italian immigrants as a New York version of Neapolitan clam and vegetable soup. Or perhaps tomatoes were simply a poor man's substitute for cream. Whatever its origin, it's a fine idea. But, sadly, this soup is rarely made hearty enough to rival its venerable cousin. I like to enrich my Manhattan chowder with slab bacon and butter; I use chicken broth and reserved clam liquor instead of fish stock. I make it robust, not thin, with plenty of tomatoes, vegetables, clams, and fresh herbs—a dish worthy of the hungriest harpooner. And I never forget to serve the Oysterettes!

OLD INN ON THE GREEN SEAFOOD BISQUE

★ ★ ★

Leslie Miller, a friend of long standing, and her husband, Brad Wagstaff, have done a lovely job in restoring the Old Inn on the Green in New Marlborough, Massachusetts. On a midsummer night, dinner there was made particularly memorable by chef Christopher Capstick's heavenly seafood bisque. While not exactly a classic bisque, it has the expected opulent, creamy texture and full-bodied depth of flavor. I often present this extravagant soup garnished with fresh nasturtiums, using a different-colored flower on each serving.

2 tablespoons unsalted butter
4 large shallots, finely chopped (½ cup)
3 cloves garlic, finely chopped
    (1 tablespoon)
2 tablespoons cognac
2 tablespoons all-purpose flour
3 tablespoons tomato paste
4 cups fish broth, preferably homemade
    (page 254)
4 cups bottled clam juice
Pinch of saffron, crumbled
¼ pound sole fillet, cut into ½-inch dice
¼ pound halibut fillet, cut into ½-inch dice
¼ pound sea scallops, cut into ½-inch dice
¼ pound medium shrimp, peeled and deveined,
    cut into ½-inch dice
4 cups heavy (or whipping) cream
1 tablespoon chopped fresh thyme leaves
Fresh nasturtium flowers, for garnish
    (optional)
Fresh thyme sprigs, for garnish
    (optional)

FLAMING LIQUOR

—❦—

Use care when flaming (flambéeing) alcohol. Roll up your sleeves and keep the pan at a safe distance from your face. Always flame off the heat and never lean over the pan during flaming.

To flame, add the liquor or liqueur to the food in the pan and warm it over medium-low or low heat. Remove the pan from the heat. Light a long kitchen match, tilt the pan slightly so that the liquid gathers in a pool, then ignite it, and return the pan to an upright position. Allow the alcohol to burn off completely before returning the pan to the heat. The flame will subside by itself fairly quickly.

1. Melt the butter in a large heavy pot over medium-low heat. Add the shallots and the garlic, and cook, stirring, until softened and lightly browned, about 8 minutes.

2. Add the cognac and warm slightly. Remove the pan from the heat and flame the alcohol (see box, this page).

3. When the flame subsides, stir in the flour, tomato paste, and 1 cup of the fish broth. Cook the mixture over medium heat until it forms a thick, bubbly paste, about 5 minutes.

4. Add the remaining 3 cups fish broth, the clam juice, and the saffron. Stir to combine well. Combine the diced sole, halibut, scallops, and shrimp in a bowl, and add half of this mixture to the soup (refrigerate the rest). Bring to a boil, reduce the heat to a gentle boil, and cook until the soup has reduced by a third, 45 minutes.

5. Stir in the cream and simmer for 1 hour more.

6. Add the remaining diced fish and the thyme, and cook for 10 minutes longer.

7. Serve in shallow soup bowls, garnished with fresh nasturtium flowers and small sprigs of thyme, if using.

Serves 6

OYSTER STEW

★ ★ ★

In New England and the mid-Atlantic states, oyster stew is traditionally served at either Thanksgiving or Christmas. Steeped in tradition, it is a very simple blending of the freshest oysters, their liquor, milk, and cream. As it is extremely rich, small bowls will suffice as a preface to an elegant holiday feast.

2 pints shucked oysters with their liquor
2 cups heavy (or whipping) cream
1 cup milk
1 or 2 dashes Tabasco sauce
Salt and freshly ground black pepper,
  to taste
6 tablespoons (¾ stick) unsalted butter
2 tablespoons snipped fresh chives,
  for garnish

1. Drain the oysters, reserving their liquor.

2. In a small heavy saucepan, combine the cream, milk, and reserved oyster liquor. Bring just to the boiling point. Season with the Tabasco sauce, salt, and pepper.

3. Melt the butter in a nonstick skillet over medium-low heat. Add the oysters and cook just until the edges curl, 2 to 4 minutes. Add them to the hot cream mixture and adjust the seasonings. Divide the stew among small bowls and serve immediately, garnished with the chives.

Serves 6 to 8

BEEF BROTH

★ ★ ★

Homemade beef broth is so far superior to any prepared version that it's well worth the effort to make it. Roasting the vegetables and the bones is the key to bringing out the deepest flavor and richest color. Herbs and spices all contribute to the final result. Don't add salt at the beginning, because as the broth cooks, it reduces and concentrates the salty flavor. Your final steps of straining, cooling, defatting, pack-

ing up, and freezing will ensure that you have a great base for soups, stews, and sauces always within reach.

4 onions, unpeeled
4 ribs celery with leaves
4 carrots, unpeeled
4 tomatoes
3 parsnips, unpeeled
3 leeks, trimmed (3 inches of green left on),
*   well washed, and patted dry*
4 cloves garlic, unpeeled
3 pounds beef flanken with bones
3 pounds beef bones
4 quarts water
8 black peppercorns
6 whole cloves
4 large sprigs fresh thyme
1 bay leaf
Coarse salt, to taste

1. Preheat the oven to 450°F.

2. Rinse and coarsely chop all of the vegetables. Place them in a flameproof roasting pan, add the garlic, and arrange the meat and bones on the top. Roast, uncovered, for 1 hour.

3. Transfer the meat, bones, and vegetables to a very large soup pot.

4. Pour 1 quart of the water into the roasting pan and bring it to a hard boil over high heat, scraping up any brown bits on the bottom of the pan. Pour this into the soup pot, and add the remaining 3 quarts of water.

5. Add the peppercorns, cloves, thyme sprigs, and bay leaf. Bring to a boil, skimming off any foam that rises to the surface. Reduce the heat to medium-low and simmer, partially covered, for 2 hours. Then uncover and simmer 1 hour more, adding salt to taste after 30 minutes.

6. Remove and discard the meat and bones. Strain the broth through a sieve into a bowl, then line the sieve with a double thickness of dampened cheesecloth and strain again. Cool to room temperature.

7. If the broth is to be used immediately, allow the fat to rise to the surface; then degrease the broth completely by skimming off the fat with a metal spoon or by pouring the broth through a gravy separator. If it is not for immediate use, transfer the cooled broth to a storage container, and refrigerate it, covered, for 4 hours or overnight. Remove and discard the hardened layer of fat from the top.

8. Use the defatted broth within 3 or 4 days, or transfer it to freezer containers and freeze it for up to 3 months.

Makes about 6 cups

CHICKEN BROTH

★ ★ ★

This is it! The miracle cure for any illness and the most important broth in your culinary repertoire. Early on in the cooking game, my mother, Berta, taught me how to make her chicken broth: not too much water, plenty of chicken pieces, parsnips for sweetness, skins left on the veggies for color, no strong boiling for clarity, and defatting for purity and health. Make enough for the freezer so you'll always have some on hand.

6 pounds chicken backs and wings

4 ribs celery with leaves

4 carrots, unpeeled, halved

2 onions, unpeeled, halved

2 parsnips, unpeeled, halved

1 large ripe tomato or 3 ripe plum tomatoes,
*   halved*

4 cloves garlic, unpeeled, lightly bruised

8 sprigs fresh flat-leaf parsley, stems lightly bruised

4 sprigs fresh dill, stems lightly bruised (optional)

1 large bunch fresh thyme

6 black peppercorns

4 whole cloves

1 bay leaf

1 tablespoon coarse salt, or to taste

4 quarts water

1. Rinse the chicken pieces well, removing all excess fat. Place the chicken in a large soup pot, and add all the remaining ingredients.

2. Bring to a boil over medium-high heat. Reduce the heat to medium and simmer gently, partially covered, for 1½ hours, carefully skimming off any foam that rises to the surface. Adjust the seasonings and cook 30 minutes longer. Remove the pot from the heat, and let the broth cool slightly.

3. Strain the broth through a sieve into a bowl, then line the sieve with a double thickness of dampened cheesecloth and pour through again. Cool to room temperature.

4. If the broth is to be used immediately, allow the fat to rise to the surface; then degrease the broth completely by skimming off the fat with a metal spoon or by pouring the broth through a gravy separator. If it is not for immediate use, transfer the cooled broth to a storage container and refrigerate it, covered, for 4 hours or overnight. Remove the hardened layer of fat from the top before using. Use the defatted broth within 4 days, or transfer it to freezer containers and freeze it for up to 3 months.

Makes about 4 quarts

FISH BROTH

★ ★ ★

Fish broth, or stock, is something that is rarely commercially produced, so it is almost always necessary to make your own. Cook up a batch or two and freeze some to have on hand. Bottled clam juice can be an adequate substitute on some occasions, but there is nothing as flavorful as a well-made broth. Most fish markets will be happy to sell trimmings, even if you haven't made another fish purchase. When flavoring the broth, fresh herbs and vegetables are essential. Be sure to use those celery leaves and thyme for a rich, beautiful flavor.

2 to 2½ pounds fish trimmings
*   (heads, tails, and bones)*

2 onions, quartered

2 carrots, coarsely chopped

2 ribs celery with leaves, coarsely chopped

4 white mushrooms, stems trimmed,
*   wiped clean and quartered*

6 fresh flat-leaf parsley sprigs, stems bruised

2 sprigs fresh thyme

6 black peppercorns

6 cups water

2 cups dry white wine

A FEW BROTH TIPS

—❦—

• A good supply of vegetables add important depth to the flavor of a broth. Onions, carrots, celery, and parsnips are all good choices. More assertive vegetables, such as broccoli, cabbage, Brussels sprouts, cauliflower, and beets are not; their flavors will overpower a broth.

• I like my beef broth deeply colored and so I roast the vegetables and bones before simmering them. It takes extra time, but the rich look and taste the roasting adds to the final result is worth the effort.

• Don't rush a broth. Gently simmering the liquid for the correct amount of time, will give you a clearer, cleaner flavor.

• The easiest way to degrease broth is to refrigerate it for several hours. The fat will harden on the top of the liquid and will be simple to just scoop off.

---

1. Rinse the fish trimmings well in several changes of water or until the water runs clear. Place the trimmings and all of the remaining ingredients in a large heavy pot. Bring to a boil, reduce the heat, and simmer, uncovered, for 25 minutes.

2. Remove the fish trimmings and the vegetables with a slotted spoon; discard them. Let the broth cool slightly, and then strain it into a bowl, through a strainer lined with a double thickness of dampened cheesecloth.

3. Cool the broth to room temperature. Refrigerate, covered, for up to 2 days, or transfer to freezer containers and freeze for up to 3 months.
Makes about 6 cups

VEGETABLE BROTH

★ ★ ★

As more and more people demand vegetable broths, they are becoming available commercially—but the prepared ones will never be as good as one you make at home. I find that most commercial broths have too much salt in them. For the very best flavor and color, just wash the vegetables—don't peel them. Don't forget the mushrooms, as they add immense flavor.

1 onion, unpeeled
2 cloves garlic, unpeeled, lightly bruised
2 ribs celery with leaves, cut into large chunks
2 carrots, unpeeled, cut into large chunks
2 leeks, trimmed, well washed, and cut into
    large chunks
8 white mushrooms, halved
2 tomatoes, quartered
4 new potatoes, halved
4 whole cloves
8 sprigs fresh flat-leaf parsley
2 sprigs fresh dill
1 bay leaf
8 black peppercorns
1 teaspoon coarse salt
10 cups water

1. Rinse all of the vegetables well. Stud the onion with the cloves.

2. Place all of the ingredients in a large heavy pot and bring to a boil. Reduce the heat and simmer, uncovered, for 1 hour. Adjust the seasonings to taste and simmer for 30 minutes more.

3. Strain the broth, reserving the vegetables for another use if desired.

4. Cool the broth to room temperature. Then refrigerate it, covered, or freeze it. Refrigerated, it will keep for up to 4 days; frozen, for up to 3 months.

Makes about 4 cups

NOTE: This recipe is easily doubled.

Dinner Side Salads

Americans like their salads raw and cooked, and completely green, flecked with green, and not at all green. We eat light ones as side dishes, substantial ones as entrées (see The Salad Plate chapter for more on these). If it's refreshing, and if there's color or crunch, it's okay to call it salad. In this chapter, only a portion of the recipes involve salad greens. But what greens—tender baby spinach, peppery arugula, handfuls of slivered fresh basil. Mesclun fascinates the palate most of all with a lively flavor dance of tart, bitter, and sweet.

How about a salad of raw Walla Walla onions or one of vivid roasted bell peppers strewn with edible flowers? In summer, vine-ripened farmstand tomatoes play the starring role! A winter salad of fennel, grapefruit, and pomegranate seeds can brighten up the shortest of days. And when the days get longer, fiddleheads, asparagus, and crisp sugar snaps say "spring."

LIBERTY SPINACH SALAD

★ ★ ★

A visit to the trendy Liberty Bar in San Antonio, Texas, is a treat, especially on a Saturday during the annual Fiesta, held in April. Luxurious "haute" Southwestern food, like grilled quail served atop salsa verde, is feasted on by the brunch crowd, and it was a happy day for me when I discovered the salad below. It is a flawless presentation of caramelized sweet pears, arranged on top of tender baby spinach leaves and highlighted by a bite of fresh chèvre. Look no farther for a way to begin a meal featuring a succulent roast leg of lamb.

CUMIN DRESSING
2 tablespoons fresh lime juice
1 teaspoon Dijon mustard
1 teaspoon finely minced garlic
1 teaspoon ground cumin
1 teaspoon sugar
Salt and coarsely ground black pepper, to taste
½ cup olive oil

SALAD
4 ripe Bosc pears
1½ pounds baby spinach or tender young
*   leaves, stems removed, well rinsed*
*   and dried*
Salt and freshly ground black pepper, to taste
¼ pound creamy chèvre, crumbled
1 generous tablespoon snipped fresh chives

1. Prepare the cumin dressing: Place the lime juice, mustard, garlic, cumin, sugar, salt, and pepper in a small bowl and whisk to combine. Slowly drizzle in the oil, whisking constantly until thickened. Set aside.

2. Preheat a stove-top grill (see Note) to high.

3. Prepare the salad: Cut the pears into quarters and remove the cores. Cut the quarters lengthwise into ¼-inch-thick slices. Place the pears in a bowl and toss well with 3 tablespoons of the dressing. Make sure the pear slices are all coated with the dressing.

4. Place some of the pear slices diagonally on the grill, 3 inches from the heat source, and grill until they are nicely colored (good grill marks), about 3 minutes per side. Remove to a plate and set aside. Repeat with the remaining pears.

5. Place the spinach in a large bowl, sprinkle with salt and pepper, and toss with the remaining dressing. Divide the salad among six plates. Arrange 6 or 7 pear slices over the spinach in a star pattern, top decoratively with the goat cheese, and sprinkle evenly with the snipped chives. Serve immediately.

Serves 6

NOTE: If you don't have a stove-top grill, you could use an iron skillet with raised grill marks on the bottom (heat over medium-high heat

BLUE PLATE
S·P·E·C·I·A·L

Dress-Up Cucumber Dill Soup

Seared Fresh Tuna and Noodles

Liberty Spinach Salad

Grilled Scallions

Laurie's Winter Lemon Ice Cream

after you put the pear slices in the dressing). Use the broiler as a last resort; you'll have to watch the pears carefully.

A VEGETABLE SPRING SALAD

★ ★ ★

Fiddlehead ferns herald spring and give an unusual woodsy flavor to this salad. When preparing fiddleheads, clean them well under cold running water, removing any brown papery skin. Trim the stems to within 1 inch of the spirals. For salads and sautés, precook the ferns in boiling salted water for 10 minutes. Drain, drop into a bowl of ice water, drain again, and pat dry before continuing with the recipe.

1 pound medium-thick asparagus
½ pound fiddlehead ferns, cleaned and
*   trimmed (see headnote)*
4 cups mesclun (mixed baby salad greens),
*   rinsed and dried*
2 tablespoons chopped fresh flat-leaf parsley
1 tablespoon snipped fresh chives
Coarse salt and coarsely ground black pepper,
*   to taste*
¼ cup Shallot Mustard Vinaigrette
*   (page 83)*
Edible flowers, such as violets (optional)

1. Trim the tips from the asparagus, reserving the stems for another use.
2. Bring a small pot of salted water to a boil, and blanch the asparagus tips until bright green, 1 to 2 minutes, depending on their size. Drain, refresh under cold water, drain again, and pat dry. Set aside, well wrapped in plastic wrap, in

★ ★

MESCLUN

—❦—

Mesclun, that mix of young, tender salad greens, is grown by specialty farmers, and often includes arugula, chervil, frisée, dandelion, and oak leaf lettuce.

When shopping for mesclun, beware: Not all markets that list it for sale are actually selling mesclun, confusing any toss of lettuces with the real thing. While the mix may be tasty, it probably doesn't warrant the high price.

★ ★

the refrigerator crisper until serving time. Bring another small pot of salted water to a boil, and cook the fiddleheads for 10 minutes; they should still have their green color. Drain, plunge into ice water, drain again, and pat dry.

3. In a large bowl, combine the greens, fiddleheads, and asparagus tips. Sprinkle with the chopped parsley, chives, and coarse salt and pepper. Toss with the vinaigrette. Garnish with edible flowers, if desired.

Serves 6

EARLY GARDEN SALAD

★ ★ ★

In late April, my garden is ready with some of the best vegetables of the year. When tossed with a fresh lemony dressing, this crisp, verdant salad

★ ★

HOW TO COOK FRESH FAVA BEANS

—❦—

*F*ava beans are at their most tender in the early spring when the season first starts. As the season progresses, they form an outer skin that becomes tough when cooked. It's important to remove this skin before proceeding with my recipes.

Remove the beans from the pods (3 pounds of unshelled fava beans will yield 1 pound of shelled). Drop the beans in a pot of boiling water for 30 seconds, then drain and refresh in icy-cold water. The beans are then cooked enough for crisp salads. Slip the skins off and proceed with the recipe.

★ ★

shows them all off to perfection. A garnish of tiny violets, sweet pea tendrils, and lavender chive blossoms adds a sweet-as-spring touch.

1 pound medium-thick asparagus, tough ends removed, cut into 1-inch pieces
½ pound sugar snap peas, strings removed
1½ pounds fava beans, shelled
1 cup sweet peas, preferably fresh
2 tablespoons snipped fresh chives
¼ cup Lemony Dressing (page 86)
Salt and freshly ground black pepper, to taste
1 bunch (about 6 ounces) fresh spinach or arugula, tough stems removed, rinsed and patted dry
4 large red radishes, finely diced

1. Bring a large saucepan of water to a boil, and lightly blanch the asparagus, 2 to 3 minutes. Drain, and rinse under cold water. Repeat with the sugar snap peas (2 to 3 minutes), fava beans (30 seconds), and sweet peas (5 to 10 minutes, depending on size; see Note). Peel the heavy outer skin from the fava beans (see box, this page), and pat all the vegetables very dry with a paper towel. Place them in a bowl and sprinkle with the chives.

2. Just before serving, toss the vegetables with the Lemony Dressing, salt, and pepper. Arrange the spinach leaves on six plates, and place the salad in the center of the greens. Sprinkle with the diced radishes, and serve.

Serves 6

NOTE: To save time, the sugar snaps, favas, and sweet peas can be blanched in the same water; just remove the sugar snaps with a slotted spoon before adding the favas, and the favas before adding the sweet peas. The asparagus have to be cooked in separate water because their flavor is so strong.

MARDI GRAS SALAD

★ ★ ★

Inspired by the colors of the New Orleans pre-Lenten celebration—purple, green, and gold—I created this salad as a delightful appetizer. The crisp greens are enhanced by the rich flavor of roasted beets, and the olive and pepper confetti is a tasty topper. While shopping in my local cheese shop, I came upon a New York State feta cheese made with pure goat's milk produced by the Lively Run Dairy. Aged for sixty days, it has just the right tang to pull all of the salad flavors together. Of course, if you can't find a domestic feta, a fresh Greek feta is an acceptable substitute.

6 cups frisée lettuce or mesclun (mixed baby lettuce greens), rinsed and dried
Coarse salt and freshly ground black pepper, to taste
5 tablespoons Ruby Grapefruit Shallot Dressing (recipe follows)
2 cups cubed (1 inch) Oven-Roasted Beets (page 279)
¼ cup finely diced red bell pepper
¼ cup finely diced yellow bell pepper
¼ cup finely diced green bell pepper
¼ cup finely diced pitted black olives
½ cup finely crumbled fresh feta cheese

1. Place the greens in a bowl, sprinkle with the coarse salt and pepper, and toss with 4 tablespoons of the dressing. Divide the greens among four salad plates.
2. Toss the beets with the remaining 1 tablespoon dressing, and distribute them evenly over the greens.
3. Sprinkle all of the diced bell peppers and the olives evenly over each of the salads. Top with the cheese, and serve immediately.

Serves 4

Ruby Grapefruit Shallot Dressing

———★———

When red grapefruits are in the market, stock up. Deeply pink and sweetly delicious, they are wonderful for breakfast, as dessert, or in salads. Be sure to save one for this unusual dressing, which will make a vegetable salad very special, indeed.

¼ cup fresh red grapefruit juice
1 tablespoon finely chopped shallots
1 teaspoon Dijon mustard
1 teaspoon sugar
Salt and freshly ground black pepper, to taste
½ cup olive oil

In a small bowl, whisk together the grapefruit juice, shallots, mustard, sugar, salt, and pepper. Slowly drizzle in the oil, whisking constantly until thickened. Adjust the seasonings to taste. Store, covered, in the refrigerator for up to 2 days. Bring to room temperature before using.
Makes about ¾ cup

RAINBOW ROASTED PEPPER SALAD

★ ★ ★

Healthful, delicious, and glorious to look at, roasted peppers are perfect at both casual and dress-up meals—terrific in salads, unbeatable on grilled bread, and the ideal substitute for winter tomatoes. This salad will dazzle a buffet all year long. . . and don't forget it when you're rolling up those fajitas!

4 large bell peppers, a mixture of red,
yellow, and orange
1 to 2 teaspoons minced garlic, to taste
2 tablespoons extra virgin olive oil
1 tablespoon fresh lemon juice
Coarse salt and coarsely ground black
pepper, to taste
¼ cup finely slivered fresh basil leaves
Fresh nasturtium blossoms or other
edible flowers, for garnish

1. Preheat the broiler.

2. Stem, seed, and halve the bell peppers lengthwise. Flatten each half slightly with the palm of your hand. Arrange the peppers, skin side up, on a baking sheet lined with aluminum foil. Place under the broiler, about 3 inches from the heat source, and broil until the skins are charred black, 12 to 15 minutes.

3. Transfer the peppers to a paper or plastic bag, close it tightly, and let them steam for 10 to 15 minutes. Then slip off and discard the charred skins. Arrange the peppers attractively on a decorative serving platter.

4. Sprinkle the garlic evenly over the peppers, and drizzle with the olive oil and lemon juice. Sprinkle with coarse salt and pepper. Let the vegetables rest for 15 minutes to mellow the flavors. Just before serving, sprinkle with the basil and garnish with the nasturtium flowers.

Serves 4

CHERRY CARROT SALAD

★ ★ ★

Light and delicate with the subtle tang of yogurt and dried cherries, this salad is the answer when you are looking for that extra side dish that can stand on its own. I find the hint of caraway blends beautifully with pork or game.

¼ cup mayonnaise
¼ cup plain nonfat yogurt or regular sour cream
1 tablespoon fresh lemon juice
1 teaspoon sugar
Salt and freshly ground black pepper, to taste
6 carrots, peeled
½ cup dried cherries
½ teaspoon caraway seeds

1. Combine the mayonnaise, yogurt, lemon juice, sugar, salt, and pepper in a small bowl. Stir well.

2. Coarsely grate the carrots into a bowl, and toss with the cherries and caraway seeds. Stir in the dressing. Serve immediately, or refrigerate, covered, until ready to serve.

Serves 4 to 6

SIMPLY ASPARAGUS SALAD

★ ★ ★

Sometimes the simplest things are the best. This rule is golden when asparagus comes into season. One of my pet peeves is overcooked vegetables; asparagus needs no more than 2 to 3 minutes in boiling water. A sprinkle of chopped eggs and parsley enhances the freshness of spring's harbinger, and a drizzle of a light dressing is all that is necessary to complete this delicate starter or side salad.

36 medium-thick asparagus, tough ends
    removed
2 tablespoons fresh lemon juice
1 teaspoon finely grated lemon zest
1 teaspoon Dijon mustard
1 teaspoon sugar
Salt and freshly ground black pepper,
    to taste
¼ cup olive oil
2 hard-cooked eggs, finely chopped
2 tablespoons chopped fresh flat-leaf parsley

1. Bring a pot of water to a boil, add the asparagus, and cook for 2 to 3 minutes. Drain and run under cold water to refresh. Pat the asparagus dry with a kitchen towel.

2. Place the lemon juice, lemon zest, mustard, sugar, salt, and pepper in a small bowl. Slowly drizzle in the olive oil, whisking constantly until slightly thickened. Set it aside.

3. Gently combine the chopped eggs with the parsley. Arrange 6 asparagus in the center of each salad plate, and sprinkle each with the egg and parsley mixture. Just before serving, drizzle each portion with 1 tablespoon of the dressing.

Serves 6

SUMMER BEAN, SUGAR SNAP, AND TOMATO SALAD

★ ★ ★

When summer's vegetables are at their very best, my rule of thumb is to keep the preparation as simple as possible. I have learned—the hard way—that too much jazzing around masks the just-picked essence. Vibrant colors and flavors dominate this salad, and a simple garlic vinaigrette ties all the goodness together. Toss the vinaigrette into the salad just before serving so that you don't lose the bright green of the beans and peas.

VINAIGRETTE
1 small clove garlic
¼ teaspoon coarse salt
2 tablespoons red wine vinegar
2 teaspoons Dijon mustard
Pinch of sugar
¼ cup extra virgin olive oil
Coarsely ground black pepper, to taste

SALAD
½ pound tender green beans, stem ends
    trimmed
½ pound tender wax beans, stem ends
    trimmed
¼ pound sugar snap peas, strings removed
1 large shallot
3 large ripe tomatoes, cored
¾ cup whole fresh basil leaves, rinsed and
    patted dry
Salt and freshly ground black pepper,
    to taste

1. Prepare the vinaigrette: Finely mince the garlic with the salt, and place it in a small bowl

CALIFORNIA OLIVE OIL

—❦—

Think olive oil, and you'll probably think Italy and Spain, and perhaps France, Portugal, Greece, and the Middle East. But it's made here, too, in our own California. I've been watching the U.S. olive oil industry with interest for some years. The boom started in the 1980s, when cholesterol-conscious Americans began their love affair with olive oil because it has a wonderful intense flavor and no saturated fat. Today, exciting new producers are emerging, and like the California vintners of the late 1960s and early 1970s, they are on the cusp of success. I expect it won't be long before their oils are counted among the world's best.

Franciscans began growing olives at their southern California missions in the late eighteenth century. From there, the American olive oil business took off, at least by nineteenth-century standards. By 1910, a million trees flourished statewide, supplying some of the finest oil available at that time. The next seventy years weren't so kind to olive farmers, however, as Americans began buying less expensive imports.

Sales increased during the world wars, when European exporting slowed, but they plummeted again in the 1950s. What chance was there during the decade of meat loaf, mashed potatoes, and TV dinners? Most California-grown olives wound up in cans—and most still do.

California oil is still pricier than its European competitors, due to limited production and high start-up costs. The most popular types of olives used to make California oil are:

Manzanillo, for oil that is sweet, intense, and hearty.

Sevillano, for oil that is strong and grassy.

Mission, for oil that is mild, fruity, and peppery.

Picholine, for oil that is sweet and mild.

Lucques, for oil that is tart and peppery.

Though the oils of each olive-growing region have much in common, every brand is distinct. But before you begin sampling from the many varieties produced in the U.S.A. and elsewhere, it's essential that you understand how they're graded. Here are the terms to remember:

Extra virgin refers to green or green-gold oils of the highest, most flavorful grade, made from the first "cold" (all natural) pressing of perfectly ripe, undamaged fruit.

★★★★★★★★★★★★★★★★★★★★★★★★★★★★★★★★★★★★★★

Virgin oil is a first pressing, extracted from olives that are slightly blemished or not quite ripe.

Fine (fino) virgin is a blend of extra virgin and virgin.

Pure oil comes from pulp left over from the first pressing.

Light and **extra light** varieties have been filtered to make a delicate, almost flavorless product that is interchangeable with vegetable oil. They are not lower in calories than other grades.

The top grades are lowest in acid: extra virgin is less than 1 percent acid, while pure can be as much as 4 percent.

When deciding which grade to buy, consider how much olive taste you want in your food. If you want just a hint, you might opt for pure. For vinaigrettes and robust sauces, I usually use extra virgin. For pronounced olive taste in a sautéed dish, I sometimes use a mixture of virgin and extra virgin olive oil to cook in.

Whichever oil you settle on should be fresh, bottled within the last two years. Once opened, oil should be stored in an airtight bottle in a cool, dark place and used up within 4 months. Refrigeration extends its life somewhat. It gets cloudy when chilled but will clear up again when returned to room temperature.

★★★★★★★★★★★★★★★★★★★★★★★★★★★★★★★★★★★★★★

along with the vinegar, mustard, and sugar. Mix well. Slowly drizzle in the olive oil, whisking constantly. Season with pepper and set aside.

2. Prepare the salad: Bring a saucepan of salted water to a boil, and cook the green beans until just tender, 3 to 5 minutes. Remove with a slotted spoon, drain well, rinse under cold water, and drain again. Repeat with the wax beans (3 to 5 minutes) and the sugar snaps (2 to 3 minutes). Pat all the vegetables dry. Place in a large bowl.

3. Halve the shallot lengthwise and cut it into slivers. Add to the beans. Then cut the tomatoes into 1-inch cubes and add them to the beans.

4. Stack the basil leaves, roll them up together, and slice them very thinly on the diagonal. Add the basil to the salad, season with salt and pepper, and toss well. Just before serving, toss with the vinaigrette. Serve at room temperature.

Serves 4 to 6

TOMATO SALAD IN A BREAD BOWL

★ ★ ★

Here the juiciest of the summer tomatoes are turned into an edible centerpiece. This salad is a good choice to serve with burgers at a backyard cookout. It's also easily transported to a picnic. Just pack the salad up in plastic containers, leaving the toasted bread out until serving time. Wrap the bread "bowl" in a large brown paper bag. At mealtime, toss the toasted bread into the salad and fill the bowl.

*1 large round crusty peasant bread
    (about 1½ pounds)*
1 large hothouse (seedless) cucumber
8 large ripe plum tomatoes, each cut into 8 pieces
*1 large yellow bell pepper, stemmed, seeded,
    and cut into ¼-inch dice*
1 cup pitted black olives, coarsely chopped
*1 small red onion, halved lengthwise and
    thinly slivered*
1 teaspoon finely minced garlic
*1 cup fresh basil leaves, rinsed, patted dry, and
    slivered*
*Coarse salt and coarsely ground black pepper,
    to taste*
¼ cup extra virgin olive oil, or less to taste
2 tablespoons red wine vinegar

1. Preheat the broiler.
2. Cut a thin slice off the top of the peasant bread. Set aside for another use.
3. Carefully cut or pull out most of the inside of the bread, making a shell; the wall of the shell should be ½ to ¾ inch thick. Tear the bread you've removed into large irregular pieces, approximately 2½ inches square. Place the bread pieces on a baking sheet and lightly toast them under the broiler, shaking the pan often so they don't burn, about 3 minutes. Set them aside.
4. Halve the cucumbers lengthwise, and then halve them lengthwise again. Cut them into ½-inch chunks and place them in a bowl. Add the tomatoes, bell pepper, olives, red onion, garlic, and basil. Season with salt and pepper and toss well. Just before serving, add the reserved toasted bread.

5. Drizzle the olive oil and vinegar over the salad and toss gently.
6. Carefully fill the hollowed bread bowl with salad, and serve. Replenish the bowl with salad as necessary.
Serves 8

SUMMER FARM STAND TOMATO SALAD

★ ★ ★

When visiting friends on the eastern end of Long Island during tomato season, I harken to the irresistible call of the farm stands that dot the tree-lined roads. I always wind up buying way too many tomatoes and eating way too many juicy tomato sandwiches (well, I'm not sure I can actually ever get enough!). But there are always plenty of tomatoes left to create new salads, and this is one of the highlights.

*½ cup Tomato Balsamic Vinaigrette, or more if
    needed (recipe follows)*
*2 bunches (6 ounces each) arugula,
    tough stems removed, rinsed and
    patted dry*
*3 pounds ripe tomatoes in assorted colors
    (red, orange, and yellow, if possible),
    sliced ¼ inch thick*
2 to 4 ounces ricotta salata cheese
½ teaspoon cracked black peppercorns
4 red cherry tomatoes, halved
4 small yellow pear tomatoes, halved
*18 whole fresh basil leaves, rinsed, patted dry,
    and finely slivered*

1. Make the Tomato Balsamic Vinaigrette at

least 2 hours ahead, to allow the flavors to develop.

2. Wrap the washed arugula in a kitchen towel and place in the crisper drawer of the refrigerator for 30 minutes to an hour before use.

3. To serve the salad, arrange the arugula leaves around the edge of a large serving platter,

★★

A PASSION FOR TOMATOES

—🍅—

Although tomatoes are native to the Americas (they first grew in what is now coastal Peru), it was the Italians who showed Americans how to eat them. In fact, it was Italians who showed Americans they *could* eat them. Before the late 1800s, the so-called "love apple" was widely feared, believed by many to be poisonous or at least too passion-provoking to be consumed by the morally upright. (This despite the fact that many respected citizen-gardeners, Thomas Jefferson among them, ate them without suffering any ill effects.) Even when tomato sauces and tomato ketchup became acceptable, suspicion of the raw fruit lingered. Today, of course, they're considered one of the most wholesome and all-American of foods.

We now grow more than 175 different types. The smallest are smaller than blueberries, while beefsteaks often weigh in at 1½ pounds or more. Hard-to-find heirloom varieties such as Brandywine and Rutgers are often superior to hybrid beefsteaks and slicers. Look for them at farmers' markets and farm stands in season.

The tastiest, juiciest summer tomatoes are best served in a simple salad, with fresh basil, extra virgin olive oil, salt, and freshly ground pepper. Yellow tomatoes are pretty, but milder than red.

In winter, when a good local tomato is hard to find, try substituting sweet Israeli imports; they're often loaded with sunny flavor. Plum tomatoes, the best choice for sauce, are good year-round—and fine canned, in a pinch.

Tomatoes are low in calories and high in potassium, iron, carotene, and vitamins A and C. Always buy the ripest fruit you can, unless preparing a green tomato dish—of course. If you must buy them green, ripen them at room temperature, out of the sun. Avoid refrigeration, whatever your plans are, for flavor stops developing in a tomato that's been chilled below 50°F.

★★

scattering some leaves in the center. Arrange the tomato slices decoratively in the middle, overlapping the colors. Spoon the vinaigrette over the tomatoes.

4. Coarsely grate the ricotta salata over the top, and sprinkle with the cracked pepper. Scatter the small tomato halves around the edge, sprinkle evenly with the basil, and serve.

Serves 6 to 8

Tomato Balsamic Vinaigrette

— ★ —

Chef Dennis Terczak, of the Sole Mio Restaurant in Chicago, was kind enough to share his delicious summer salad vinaigrette with me. He serves it drizzled on top of grilled mozzarella with perfectly sautéed spinach on either side of the cheese. I first tasted it when I was working on the *New Basics Cookbook*, and it remains one of my favorites; it's perfect tossed with arugula and is a great way to infuse winter tomatoes with extra flavor.

1 large ripe tomato, peeled, seeded, and
*   chopped*
1 tablespoon minced shallots
½ teaspoon minced garlic
½ cup canned tomato juice
¼ cup balsamic vinegar
¼ cup extra virgin olive oil
Salt and freshly ground black pepper,
*   to taste*

1. Place the chopped tomato in a heavy saucepan, and cook it over low heat until all the liquid has evaporated, about 5 minutes. Transfer it to a bowl and set it aside to cool.

2. Add the remaining ingredients and mix well. Let stand at least 2 hours before using, so the flavors can blend.

Makes about 1½ cups

SCINTILLATING SCALLIONS AND RIPE TOMATOES

★ ★ ★

Here's a star turn for the scallion. No longer just a lowly garnish or flavoring ingredient, scallions today are broiled, baked, grilled, knotted, tied into a bow, and heaven only knows what else. How appropriate, then, to enhance ripe garden tomatoes with a hearty helping. The dressing—a flavorful combination of garlic and lemon juice—is all that's needed to round out the salad. Serve it in the center of a little mound of mesclun, garnished with a sprinkle of parsley.

8 ripe plum tomatoes, each cut into 8 pieces
4 scallions (3 inches green left on),
*   thinly sliced on the diagonal*
⅓ cup plus 1 tablespoon coarsely chopped
*   fresh flat-leaf parsley*
¼ cup Lemony Dressing (page 86)
4 cups mesclun (mixed baby salad greens),
*   rinsed and patted dry*

Combine the tomatoes, scallions, ⅓ cup parsley, and the Lemony Dressing in a bowl.

Divide the mesclun among four salad plates and top with the salad. Sprinkle with the 1 tablespoon parsley, and serve immediately at room temperature.

Serves 4

★★★★★★★★★★★★★★★★★★★★★★★★★★

CHOOSING CAULIFLOWER

—❦—

*T*o choose the best cauliflower, look for a firm white head cradled in bright green leaves, without any dark blemishes. To separate it into florets, core the cauliflower, and with a small knife, make a little slit into the stem of each cluster. Gently break the cluster into bite sizes, working from the stem toward the top. Cook in boiling salted water, with a squeeze of lemon juice to keep the florets white, until each floret is tender but not too soft, 4 to 5 minutes.

★★★★★★★★★★★★★★★★★★★★★★★★★★

DELICATE CAULIFLOWER SALAD

★ ★ ★

When tossed with an assertive dressing flecked with fresh herbs, this lily-white member of the cabbage family puts its best flower forward in a salad that can balance the rich flavor of pork or roast duck.

1 head cauliflower (2½ to 3 pounds)
1 tablespoon fresh lemon juice
1 cup mayonnaise
1 tablespoon Dijon mustard
1 tablespoon grainy mustard
1 tablespoon drained tiny capers
3 tablespoons chopped fresh flat-leaf parsley
2 tablespoons chopped fresh tarragon,
*   or 1 teaspoon dried, crumbled*
1½ teaspoons finely grated lemon zest
Salt and freshly ground black pepper,
*   to taste*
1 hard-cooked egg, coarsely chopped,
*   for garnish*
½ cup seeded diced tomato, for garnish

1. Remove the leaves and core from the cauliflower, and separate the head into small florets.

2. Bring a pot of salted water to a boil, and add the lemon juice. Add the cauliflower and cook until just tender, 4 to 5 minutes. Drain, and refresh under cold water. Drain again and pat dry. Place in a bowl.

3. In a separate bowl, combine the mayonnaise, both mustards, capers, 2 tablespoons of the parsley, tarragon, lemon zest, salt, and pepper. Using a rubber spatula, fold this dressing into the cauliflower. Cover and refrigerate for 2 to 4 hours before serving so that the flavors blend. Serve at room temperature, garnished with the chopped eggs, the remaining 1 tablespoon parsley, and the diced tomatoes.

Serves 6

WALLA WALLA ONION SALAD

★ ★ ★

When Washington's Walla Wallas arrive in the market in June it's time to make this salad. While Vidalia onions are sweeter, they are huge in comparison to these little jewels—true Walla Wallas are diminutive onions. So although you can substitute other sweet onions for the Walla Wallas, do look for them in season. Gently grilled sourdough bread is ideal for absorbing the juices.

ONIONS: SWEET AND PUNGENT

—❦—

Vidalias, Walla Wallas, and Mauis are America's onion sweeties—white-fleshed beauties so low in sulfur that they're practically fruity. Chop them up, and no tears! Chomp on one raw, and you'll taste something that's creamy and delicate, yet still very much an onion. Once hard to find, they're turning up in supermarkets all over the nation. They get their winning names from the places they're grown: Vidalia, Georgia; Walla Walla, Washington; and the Hawaiian island of Maui. Of the three, Vidalias (available May and June) are probably easiest to find outside their growing area, but the others do show up, or if not, can be mail-ordered. Look for Walla Wallas from June to September and Mauis from April to July.

I prefer to use sweet onions in recipes that call for little or no cooking—mostly relishes and salads. They're terrific on sandwiches (such as Blythe's Tuna Fish Sandwich) and burgers, and in salads. Try them on toasted peasant bread slathered with mayonnaise and topped with sardines and ripe tomatoes, or in an onion salad. Purchase and store with care, as their high water content makes them bruise and spoil easily. Look for dry, paper-thin skin when buying, and store them in a cool, dry place, preferably not touching one another. A friend of mine hangs her Vidalias from the rafters of her basement, in the legs of old panty hose. She ties a knot between the onions, and cuts them free when she's ready to use them.

Bermuda, Spanish, and red onions, while not quite as sweet, are also mild enough to eat raw. The pungent yellow type is still my staple onion—the backbone for most of my soups, sauces, and sautés. I like to keep shallots in the kitchen at all times, too; their hearty, nutty flavor (sharper than onion, but not as potent as garlic) is ideal for vinaigrettes and many sauces. The small globe onion is interchangeable with the yellow—a good choice when you want a very assertive onion taste (as in onion soup or confit). Tiny pearl onions (cherry size) and boiling onions (slightly bigger) are best cooked whole, in a cream sauce or stew.

2 small Walla Walla onions
2 tablespoons extra virgin olive oil
2 tablespoons fresh lemon juice
¼ teaspoon caraway seeds
Coarse salt and freshly ground black pepper, to taste
4 thick slices crusty sourdough bread, grilled or
    toasted

Slice the onions very thin. Arrange them on a dinner plate, overlapping slightly. Drizzle the olive oil and lemon juice all over the onions, and sprinkle with the caraway seeds, coarse salt, and pepper. Set aside, loosely covered, at room temperature for up to 1 hour before serving. Serve atop the grilled sourdough bread.

Serves 4

AMERICAN BEAN SALAD

★ ★ ★

In the early springtime, when fresh cranberry beans are in season, put this salad together. Bursting with daffodil freshness and enticing hues, it should grace every meal where spring lamb is on the menu. If you happen to find fresh fava beans, buy a couple of pounds, shell them and blanch them (see box, page 260) and then add the beans to the salad.

½ pound green beans, stem ends trimmed
½ pound wax beans, stem ends trimmed
1½ pounds shelled fresh cranberry beans
1 can (15½ ounces) dark red kidney beans,
    rinsed and drained
4 scallions (3 inches green left on), thinly sliced
    on the diagonal
5 tablespoons chopped fresh flat-leaf
    parsley
6 tablespoons Lemony Dressing (page 86)
Salt and freshly ground black pepper,
    to taste

1. Bring a large pot of water to a boil, add the green beans and wax beans, and cook until just tender, 3 to 5 minutes. Drain, and refresh under cold water. Drain well, pat dry, and place in a large bowl.

2. Meanwhile, bring a saucepan of water to a boil and cook the cranberry beans until tender, 15 minutes. Drain, rinse under cold water, drain well, and add to the green beans along with the kidney beans, scallions, and 4 tablespoons of the parsley.

3. Just before serving, toss the dressing with the salad. Season with salt and pepper, and sprinkle with the remaining 1 tablespoon chopped parsley.

Serves 6

FABULOUS FENNEL BREAD SALAD

★ ★ ★

Crisp and refreshing, this fennel bread salad hits the spot at a summer picnic. It's an ideal traveler because there is no mayonnaise to worry about. Once you have the croutons toasted and the vegetables prepared, it's simply a matter of tossing them together in the right order. Be sure to hold the basil until the end, because it will discolor as soon as it's tossed with the vinegar.

4 cups French bread cubes (1 inch)
½ cup extra virgin olive oil
Salt and freshly ground black pepper, to taste
1 fennel bulb (about 1½ pounds), ferns trimmed off
1 large red bell pepper, stemmed and seeded
1 small red onion, halved lengthwise and slivered
4 ripe plum tomatoes, each cut into 8 pieces
1 cup pitted imported black olives, such as Niçoise or Gaeta
2 tablespoons red wine vinegar
1 cup finely slivered fresh basil leaves

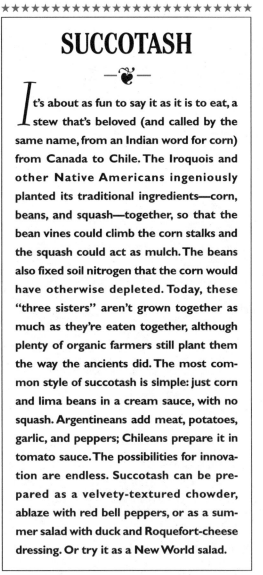

1. Preheat the oven to 350°F.

2. Place the bread cubes in a bowl and toss with 2 tablespoons of the olive oil and the salt and pepper. Spread the cubes in a single layer on a baking sheet, and bake, shaking the pan once or twice, until golden, 20 minutes. Set aside, covered loosely with a cloth towel.

3. Trim off the base of the fennel bulb, and slice the fennel into thin lengthwise slivers. Cut the bell pepper into thin lengthwise slivers. Place them in a large bowl and toss with the onion, tomatoes, and olives.

4. Just before serving, transfer the vegetables to a decorative serving bowl. Sprinkle with salt and pepper. Toss with the remaining 6 tablespoons olive oil and the vinegar. Add the basil and toss gently. Add the toasted bread cubes, toss, and serve immediately.

Serves 6 to 8

SUCCOTASH

—❦—

*I*t's about as fun to say it as it is to eat, a stew that's beloved (and called by the same name, from an Indian word for corn) from Canada to Chile. The Iroquois and other Native Americans ingeniously planted its traditional ingredients—corn, beans, and squash—together, so that the bean vines could climb the corn stalks and the squash could act as mulch. The beans also fixed soil nitrogen that the corn would have otherwise depleted. Today, these "three sisters" aren't grown together as much as they're eaten together, although plenty of organic farmers still plant them the way the ancients did. The most common style of succotash is simple: just corn and lima beans in a cream sauce, with no squash. Argentineans add meat, potatoes, garlic, and peppers; Chileans prepare it in tomato sauce. The possibilities for innovation are endless. Succotash can be prepared as a velvety-textured chowder, ablaze with red bell peppers, or as a summer salad with duck and Roquefort-cheese dressing. Or try it as a New World salad.

NEW WORLD SUCCOTASH SALAD

★ ★ ★

Ijust tossed caution to the wind when it came to revising this classic American combination of corn and limas, traditionally served warm as a comfy side dish, and turned it into a zesty salad. The crunch of cucumbers and scallions, as well as a splash of curry vinaigrette flecked with cilantro, counterbalances the mild and softer vegetables. The result is festive enough for a party. Serve it at an Indian summer family cookout.

2 cups cooked baby lima beans
2 cups cooked corn kernels, preferably fresh
*2 cups cooked thin green beans, cut into
    ½-inch lengths*
*2 ripe plum tomatoes, seeded and cut into
    ¼-inch dice*
*1 red bell pepper, stemmed, seeded, and cut into
    ¼ -inch dice*
*1 scallion (3 inches green left on), thinly sliced
    on the diagonal*
*2 tablespoons finely chopped
    red onion*
3 tablespoons olive oil
2 tablespoons cider vinegar
½ teaspoon Dijon mustard
1 small clove garlic
¼ teaspoon curry powder
¼ teaspoon salt
½ teaspoon sugar

Freshly ground black pepper, to taste
*3 tablespoons chopped fresh
    cilantro or flat-leaf parsley*

1. Combine all the vegetables in a large bowl.

2. In a small bowl, stir together the oil, vinegar, and mustard. Mince the garlic with the curry powder and salt, and whisk this into the dressing along with the sugar. Season with pepper, and add to the vegetables. Sprinkle with the cilantro, toss well, and serve.
    Serves 6 to 8

GARDEN ORZO SALAD

★ ★ ★

This sunny pasta salad is another appealing side dish to serve at a cookout, or with a spring-time leg of lamb. For a deeper, richer flavor, toss the vinaigrette into the orzo while it's still warm. Other fresh herbs, such as slivered basil or chopped dill, may be substituted for the parsley to elicit a more pungent tang.

VINAIGRETTE
⅓ cup red wine vinegar
1½ teaspoons Dijon mustard
1½ teaspoons sugar
Salt and freshly ground black pepper, to taste
⅔ cup olive oil

SALAD
3 cups orzo
*1 red bell pepper, stemmed, seeded, and cut into
    ¼-inch dice*
*1 yellow bell pepper, stemmed, seeded, and cut
    into ¼-inch dice*
10 ounces fresh or frozen sweet peas, cooked
1 cup coarsely chopped pitted black olives
½ cup diced (¼ inch) red onion
1 cup golden raisins
½ cup coarsely chopped fresh flat-leaf parsley
Salt and freshly ground black pepper, to taste

1. Prepare the vinaigrette: Combine the vinegar, mustard, sugar, salt, and pepper in a bowl and whisk well. Slowly drizzle in the oil, whisking constantly until the vinaigrette is slightly thick. Set aside.

2. Prepare the salad: Cook the orzo in boiling salted water until just tender, 8 to 10 minutes. Drain, rinse under warm water, and drain again. Transfer the orzo to a large bowl, and toss it immediately with the vinaigrette.

3. Add the remaining ingredients and toss well. Serve at room temperature.

Serves 10 to 12

AN AMERICAN CHRISTMAS SALAD

★ ★ ★

There are those moments when timing is everything, and the coming together of the ingredients in this salad is one of them. It happens to fall just around the Christmas holiday season. Juicy pink Texas grapefruits are at their prime, and rosy pomegranates from the South overflow from market bins, as do fern-topped, anise-flavored fennel. Composed with holiday spirit, this vibrantly colored and flavored salad is delightful as either a first course or a side dish.

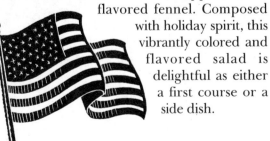

1 fennel bulb (about 1 pound)
2 red or pink grapefruit
¾ cup unpitted ripe California olives or
*   imported olives, such as Gaeta*
½ cup Ruby Grapefruit Shallot Dressing,
*   (page 261)*
Freshly ground black pepper
*   (optional)*
½ cup pomegranate seeds (1 pomegranate)

1. Remove the ferns from the fennel; coarsely chop and set them aside. Trim off the bottom of the bulb, and then cut the bulb into very thin lengthwise slices. Place them in a bowl.

2. Section the grapefruit (reserve the juices to make the dressing).

3. Arrange the fennel slices decoratively in the center of six salad plates. Place 3 grapefruit sections, in the form of a flower, in the center of the fennel. Divide the olives equally among the salads, and drizzle each salad lightly with the dressing. Top with a generous grinding of black pepper, if desired. Sprinkle each plate with a few pomegranate seeds and the reserved fennel ferns. Serve immediately.

Serves 6

ANNE ROSENZWEIG'S WATERMELON SALAD

★ ★ ★

Anne Rosenzweig, chef of the three-star New York City restaurant Arcadia (as well as the popular Lobster Club), is forever creating magical new dishes. This recipe, which she uses as a bed for soft-shell crabs, is no exception. Salty and dense, feta is the perfect foil for summer's juicy sweet melon and the crisp peppery flavor of mint. Try your best to find fresh feta for the salad. It is available in most cheese shops and Greek food stores.

8 cups diced (¾ inch) and seeded watermelon,
    very cold
4 cups diced (¾ inch) fresh feta cheese,
    at room temperature
2 cups chopped fresh mint leaves
¾ cup fruity extra virgin olive oil, or more
    if desired
Juice of 2 limes
Freshly ground black pepper, to taste

Just before serving, toss all of the ingredients together in a large bowl. (If you do this ahead of time, the watermelon will release a lot of its own juices and the salad will be too liquidy.)
Serves 12

VIRGINIA WALDORF SALAD

★ ★ ★

When I went down to Wakefield, Virginia, for the annual shad planking, I had no idea that I'd be in the center of peanut farm country. But once there, I caught on pretty quickly, even enjoying a visit to a tiny peanut museum that had been built in 1890.

In celebration of that local crop, I had great fun creating this recipe—a nonclassic Waldorf salad showcasing plenty of peanut flavor. A touch of peanut butter subtly seasons the light dressing, bringing all of the ingredients together.

3 Anjou pears, cored and cut into
    ½-inch pieces
1 cup diced (½ inch) celery
1 cup seedless red grapes, halved
¼-pound piece of smoked turkey,
    cut into ½-inch pieces
½ cup dried cherries
½ cup unsalted roasted peanuts
¾ cup plain nonfat yogurt
¼ cup mayonnaise
1 tablespoon smooth peanut butter
¼ cup chopped fresh flat-leaf
    parsley
Salt and freshly ground black pepper,
    to taste

1. Combine the pears, celery, grapes, turkey, dried cherries, and peanuts in a large bowl. Toss thoroughly.
2. In a separate bowl, whisk together the yogurt, mayonnaise, peanut butter, and all but 2 teaspoons of the parsley. Fold the dressing into the salad, and season with salt and pepper. Serve garnished with the remaining chopped parsley.
Serves 6

BASIL SAUCE

★ ★ ★

During summer's basil season, I like to keep a jar of this fresh, light sauce to use to "spike" an already prepared salad dressing or to toss over pasta. If you're as much a fan of the herb as I am, you'll find countless ways to use it.

2 cups fresh basil leaves, rinsed and
*   patted dry*
¼ cup plus 1 tablespoon olive oil
Salt and freshly ground black pepper,
*   to taste*

1. Place the basil leaves in a food processor and chop the leaves fine.

2. With the motor running, slowly drizzle in the ¼ cup olive oil and process until the sauce is thick. Season with salt and pepper.

3. Use immediately, or place in a small jar and cover with the remaining 1 tablespoon oil before putting on the lid. Refrigerate and use within 3 to 4 days.

Makes about 6 tablespoons

The Farmers' Market

Americans grow some of the world's sweetest, brightest vegetables—a splendid, vitamin-packed variety of greens, bulbs, tubers, roots, and squashes. A visit to a market—if we're lucky, a farmers' market—allows us to choose the freshest the season has to offer: maybe baby peas, asparagus, and new potatoes if it's spring, or pumpkin, cauliflower, and kale if it's fall. Summer finds the market spilling over with plenty. Winter's offerings are less colorful, but no less delicious. In this chapter, I'll show you how to roast vegetables, sauté and glaze them, and whip them into silky purées.

Here, I've paired carrots with maple butter, red cabbage with dried cherries, and acorn squash with fennel. Familiar favorites include mashed potatoes, creamed spinach, fried green tomatoes, collard greens, and Harvard beets. The vegetarian chili and jambalaya recipes, both inspired by my travels, are rich with spice and hearty enough to serve as entrées. So here's to your health *and* enjoyment!

ROASTED ASPARAGUS

★ ★ ★

Recently I've taken a shine to the deep, lusty character of roasted asparagus. A squeeze of fresh lemon juice and a sprinkle of fresh herbs are all you need to pop the flavors. These roasted vegetables stand out in particular when served with an Herb-Crusted Rack of Lamb.

1 pound medium asparagus, tough ends removed
2 tablespoons extra virgin olive oil
Coarse salt and freshly ground black pepper,
*   to taste*
1 tablespoon chopped fresh flat-leaf parsley
2 lemons, halved, for garnish

1. Preheat the oven to 400°F.

2. Place the asparagus, facing in one direction, in a baking dish to fit. Toss to coat very well with the olive oil, coarse salt, and pepper, then pat into a single layer. Cover with aluminum foil, and roast in the center of the oven for 10 minutes. Remove the foil and roast for 10 minutes longer. Sprinkle with the parsley, and serve immediately with lemon halves for squeezing.

Serves 4

WELL-DRESSED ASPARAGUS

★ ★ ★

When asparagus is plentiful in the spring, I eat it as often and in as many ways as possible. My inspiration for this zesty dish was the visits I

made to the many Little Italy communities around the United States. Often, restaurants will serve asparagus embellished with an easy sauce that's made just before the dish is served. A quick sprinkle of parsley finishes it off.

6 tablespoons extra virgin olive oil
½ cup fresh lemon juice
2 cloves garlic, finely minced
3 tablespoons drained tiny capers
1 teaspoon finely grated lemon zest
2 tablespoons chopped fresh flat-leaf parsley
Freshly ground black pepper, to taste
1 pound medium-thick asparagus, tough ends
*   removed*

1. Combine the oil, lemon juice, garlic, capers, and lemon zest in a small saucepan. Place over low heat and cook, swirling the pan, to heat through, 2 to 3 minutes. Stir in 1 tablespoon of the parsley and a generous grinding of black pepper. Remove from the heat.

2. Bring a saucepan of salted water to a boil, and cook the asparagus until just tender, 2 to 3 minutes. Drain, pat dry, and arrange on a serving platter. Spoon the sauce over the asparagus, sprinkle with the remaining 1 tablespoon parsley, and serve immediately.

Serves 4

ALL-AMERICAN HARVARD BEETS

★ ★ ★

One story goes that the original "Harvard" beets made their debut at an English tavern called Harwood's. One of its frequent customers, a Russian émigré, moved to Boston, opened a restaurant there, and named it after the English tavern. He mispronounced the name of his new place, so that it sounded more like "Harvard"—ironic, given its location. So the dish he brought from England was soon known as Harvard beets! Another theory has it that the name comes from the similarity of the dish's deep crimson color to the Harvard football team's jerseys. No matter the origin, the really important thing is the beet's themselves.

As many variations as I've made of these sweet-and-sour beets (and I've made a lot—my apron is proof), this one is still my favorite. I love the sweet bite the crystallized ginger adds.

1 recipe Oven-Roasted Beets (recipe follows)
½ cup sugar
1 tablespoon finely chopped crystallized
*   ginger*
5 tablespoons red wine vinegar
¼ cup fresh orange juice
1½ tablespoons cornstarch
Salt and freshly ground black pepper,
*   to taste*
1 tablespoon unsalted butter
Grated zest of 2 oranges

1. Prepare the Oven-Roasted Beets through removing the skins in step 3. Cut the beets into ¼-inch dice; you should have 4 cups. Set them aside.

2. Combine the sugar, crystallized ginger, vinegar, orange juice, cornstarch, salt, and pepper in a heavy saucepan. Whisk well and bring to a boil over medium heat, whisking constantly until the mixture is clear and thickened, 4 to 5 minutes. Whisk in the butter and zest, and cook just until the butter has melted.

3. Remove the pan from the heat and pour the sauce over the beets. Toss gently and let cool completely before serving.
Serves 4 to 6

Oven-Roasted Beets

★

Once you've roasted beets, you may never boil them again. The flavor and the extraordinary color are mouth-watering. Simple as one, two, three to prepare, roasted beets keep beautifully for up to a week in the refrigerator crisper. Use them to liven up composed salads, such as Autumn Duck Salad or Mardi Gras Salad, side dishes, such as Morels and Butterflies, or as condiments. Or slice and drizzle them with extra virgin olive oil and lemon or orange juice, and a sprinkling of salt, pepper, and fresh chives for a perfect stand-alone salad.

2 pounds beets (about 8)

1. Preheat the oven to 350°F.

2. Rinse the beets well and trim the stems and roots, leaving 1 inch of each.

3. Wrap the beets individually in aluminum foil. Place them on a baking sheet and roast until tender, about 1 hour (about 1½ hours if they're large) . Remove the beets from the oven and set aside until they are cool enough to handle. Then unwrap the beets and slip the skins off. Wear rubber gloves if you don't want to dye your fingers. Cover, and store in the refrigerator until ready to use.

Serves 4 to 6

THUMBS-UP BROCCOLI

★ ★ ★

Bored with broccoli? Try this—I guarantee you won't be disappointed. The cold tomato sauce is easy to make ahead of time, as is the fruity orange-infused gremolata garnish. Just refrigerate both, covered, until ready to use. Blanch the broccoli right before serving, and artfully arrange the plate for an enticing dish.

2 pounds broccoli

TOMATO SAUCE
4 cups diced (½ inch) ripe tomatoes
2 tablespoons finely minced shallots
2 tablespoons extra virgin olive oil
1 teaspoon fresh orange juice
Pinch of sugar
2 tablespoons chopped fresh flat-leaf parsley

GREMOLATA
Finely grated zest of 1 orange
1 clove garlic, finely minced
2 tablespoons chopped fresh flat-leaf parsley

1. Trim the ends of the broccoli stems so that each spear is 6 inches from the crown to the bottom. Scrape off the tough outer fibers with a vegetable peeler. Set aside.

2. Prepare the sauce: Toss the ingredients together in a bowl and set aside.

3. Prepare the gremolata: Chop the ingredients together in a small bowl to combine well. Set aside.

4. Just before serving, bring a pot of salted water to a boil, and cook the broccoli until just tender, about 3 minutes. Drain, and arrange in the center of a serving platter. Spoon the tomato sauce over the top, sprinkle with the gremolata, and serve immediately.

Serves 6 to 8

THE BEST BRUSSELS SPROUTS EVER

★ ★ ★

I was confabbing with chef Anne Rosenzweig on things to do with vegetables and she suggested this dish, which she serves at her restaurant, The Lobster Club. When I tried it, she asked, "Aren't they the best Brussels sprouts ever?" And they are! The bacon gives them a deep, rich flavor and marries well with the vegetables' unexpected crunch; the sprinkling of chives makes its own contribution to what is simply a great combination of tastes. Don't overcook the sprouts. In the Chinese fashion, they should be cooked until just crisp-tender.

1¼ *pounds fresh Brussels sprouts*
1 *tablespoon olive oil*
1 *tablespoon unsalted butter*
½ *pound lean slab bacon, rind removed,*
    cut into ¼*-inch dice*
3 *carrots, peeled and cut into small dice*
2 *teaspoons snipped fresh chives*

1. Trim the stem ends off the Brussels sprouts, and remove any tough outer leaves. Halve the sprouts lengthwise, and then cut them into julienne strips.

2. Heat the oil and butter together in a heavy pot. Add the bacon and cook over medium-low heat until it renders its fat and turns golden, 5 to 6 minutes. Add the carrots and cook, stirring constantly, until they begin to soften, about 5 minutes.

3. Add the sprouts to the pot, toss well, and cook, stirring, until they are crisp-tender, 5 minutes. Sprinkle with the chives and serve immediately.

Serves 4 to 6

CREAMY CARAWAY CABBAGE

★ ★ ★

As a creamy, smooth accompaniment to ham and pork, cabbage is one of America's most often-cooked vegetables. The delicate, curly, loose leaves of the Savoy variety create a delectable dish, far different from the heavier, more

typical head of cabbage. Fresh dill, added just as the dish finishes cooking, piques the vibrant green vegetable.

1 *head (2 pounds) Savoy cabbage*
½ *pound lean slab bacon, rind removed,*
    cut into ½*-inch cubes*
1 *teaspoon caraway seeds*
Salt and freshly ground black pepper, to taste
½ *cup sour cream*
2 *teaspoons Dijon mustard*
2 *tablespoons chopped fresh dill*

1. Remove any tough outer leaves from the cabbage. Cut it in half lengthwise, remove the core, and finely shred the cabbage.

2. Bring a large saucepan of salted water to a boil, add the cabbage, and cook until wilted, 2 to 3 minutes. Drain well.

3. In a heavy pot, cook the bacon over medium-low heat until it renders its fat and turns golden, 6 to 8 minutes. Add the wilted cabbage, the caraway seeds, and the salt and pepper. Combine the sour cream and mustard in a small bowl, and stir this into the cabbage. Warm gently over low heat, toss with the chopped dill, and serve.

Serves 6

SMOTHERED RED, RED CABBAGE

★ ★ ★

Although I love red cabbage when it's cooked in bacon fat and nestled up to a roast goose, the time has come for a lighter approach. This version is spicy, with the added bite of Cajun sausage. The result, with tart dried cherries filling the role more often given raisins, is a fault-less complement to game birds such as roasted partridge and grouse.

1 head (2 pounds) red cabbage
2 Granny Smith apples
½ pound andouille sausage, cut into
    ½-inch dice
2 tablespoons olive oil
2 red onions, thinly sliced
½ cup dry red wine
½ cup red wine vinegar
½ cup defatted chicken broth, preferably
    homemade (page 253)
¼ cup (packed) dark brown sugar
1 teaspoon dried thyme
Salt and freshly ground black pepper,
    to taste
½ cup dried cherries

   1. Remove the tough outer leaves from the cabbage. Cut it in half lengthwise, remove the core, and finely shred the cabbage.
   2. Core and peel the apples, and cut them into 1-inch cubes.
   3. In a large heavy pot, brown the sausage over medium-low heat for 10 minutes. Add the olive oil and the onions, and cook, stirring until wilted, 5 minutes. Add all the remaining ingredients except the dried cherries, and combine well. Cover, and cook over medium heat, stirring occasionally, for 30 minutes.
   4. Add the dried cherries, re-cover, and continue to cook, stirring occasionally, until fragrant and well blended, 30 minutes more. Serve hot.
   Serves 6 to 8

MAPLE BUTTER CARROTS

★ ★ ★

I would guess there are few refrigerators that are carrotless, with so many of us depending on this easy-to-find year-round vegetables, but you may be looking for a new way to prepare them. If so, stock up on some maple butter soon after the fresh syrup comes in (you'll find it, in jars, in gourmet shops). Tossed into the hot carrots, it will melt and sweetly glaze them.

12 carrots, peeled and cut into 1½-inch lengths
2 tablespoons pure maple butter
Salt and freshly ground black pepper, to taste
Pinch of ground nutmeg

   1. Bring salted water to a boil in a medium saucepan. Add the carrots and cook until tender, 10 to 12 minutes. Drain the carrots thoroughly and return them to the pot. Immediately toss them with the maple butter and season with salt and pepper.
   2. Transfer to a pretty bowl, sprinkle the nutmeg over the carrots, and serve.
   Serves 4 to 6

CAULIFLOWER "RAREBIT"

★ ★ ★

Cauliflower is one of those winter vegetables that flourish when given the proper attention. Prepared as a gratin, with just a hint of the devilish flavors that give Welsh rarebit its kick, cauliflower is assertive enough to serve with a roast leg of lamb or a peppery rib-eye steak. I think you will love the blending of the flavors.

1 large head (about 3 pounds) cauliflower
2 tablespoons fresh lemon juice
¼ cup (½ stick) unsalted butter
¼ cup all-purpose flour
1 teaspoon dry mustard
2 cups milk
1 cup grated sharp Vermont Cheddar cheese
½ teaspoon Worcestershire sauce
2 dashes Tabasco sauce
2 tablespoons snipped fresh chives
¼ cup dried bread crumbs

1. Preheat the oven to 350°F. Lightly butter a 12 x 9 x 2-inch baking dish.

2. Trim the green leaves from the cauliflower, and cut the head into small florets, removing the core. Bring a pot of salted water to a boil, and add the lemon juice. Add the cauliflower and simmer until just tender, about 10 minutes. Drain well and pat dry.

3. Melt the butter in a heavy saucepan over low heat. Whisk in the flour and mustard until it forms a paste. Pour the milk in slowly, whisking until the mixture is smooth. Continue to cook over low heat, whisking, until the sauce is thick, 4 to 5 minutes. Then stir in the grated cheese, Worcestershire, and Tabasco, and remove from the heat. Fold in the chives.

4. Arrange the cauliflower florets in the baking dish so they are standing heads up in an even layer. Pour the sauce evenly over the top, and dust with the bread crumbs. Bake until golden brown, 40 to 45 minutes.

5. Just before serving, if you wish, run the cauliflower under the broiler, 3 inches from the heat source, to deepen the brown top slightly, 1 to 2 minutes. Be careful that it doesn't burn! Serve immediately.

Serves 6

BRAISED AND GLAZED CELERY

★ ★ ★

Simple braised celery, finished with a delicate sweet-and-sour sauce, is an ideal dish to serve with wintry roasted game birds or a rich venison stew.

2 bunches celery, washed, leaves and tough
*   bottoms removed*
⅓ cup defatted chicken or vegetable broth,
*   preferably homemade (page 253 or 255)*
3 tablespoons fresh lemon juice
5 tablespoons unsalted
*   butter*
1 teaspoon sugar
1 teaspoon salt
1 tablespoon
*   chopped fresh*
*   flat-leaf parsley*

1. Cut the celery ribs into 4-inch lengths, on the diagonal. Place them in a large heavy pot along with the broth, lemon juice, 2 tablespoons of the butter, sugar, and salt. Bring to a boil. Reduce the heat to medium-low, cover, and cook, shaking the pan occasionally, until the celery is tender, 30 minutes.

2. Add the remaining 3 tablespoons butter to the pot and cook the celery, uncovered, over medium-high heat, shaking the pan often, until lightly browned, about 10 minutes. Transfer it to a serving dish, sprinkle with the parsley, and serve immediately.

Serves 4 to 6

SILKY CORN PUDDING

★ ★ ★

I am one of the purists who are devoted to unadorned corn pudding—prepared simply, full of August's sweetest, with no infringement from peppers or bacon. I do, however, melt down some onions and

caramelize them with a sprinkling of sugar for added body. I particularly love to serve this with a richly roasted meat or North Carolina–Style Pulled Pork or other barbecue. However, in Alaska I had a great corn pudding served alongside grilled teriyaki halibut—so now I prepare it to accompany fish dishes as well.

SWEET SUMMER CORN

—❧—

Every year, toward the end of July, I stake out my nearby farmers' market, impatient for corn. Only the fresh-picked, local stuff will do. By "fresh-picked" I mean *same day*, if possible. Same hour would be best, but that's usually asking too much. I'm not being precious here—it does matter. Corn sugar begins to turn to starch the minute an ear leaves the stalk. Two days later, the sweetness is mostly gone. So get that corn home and eat it, and for goodness sake don't husk it until you're ready to cook!

If you're not sure if corn is fresh, ask. If you don't trust the answer, check the husks (they should be bright, tight, and perhaps damp), the silk at the top (dry is okay, brittle is not), and the stem (it should be moist). Sneak a poke at a top kernel. If a milky liquid spurts out, the corn is in good shape.

"Sweet corn" comes in many varieties: Quickie, Athos, Butter and Sugar, Merit, Seneca, and Chief, among others, I'm particularly fond of Country

Gentleman, a small heirloom corn. And who doesn't love the late-season Kandy Korn and the sweetest of the sweet, Silver Queen? The "field corns"—flour, flint, and dent—used for meal, oil, syrup, liquor, starch, and more are quite different—not at all suitable for eating off the cob. Popcorn, too, is in a class by itself.

I boil sweet corn for 2 to 4 minutes in lightly sugared water (1 teaspoon per quart). I don't feel it's necessary to boil in the husk, although many chefs do. However, I do recommend that you roast and grill in the husk. To grill, peel back the husks, leaving them attached at the base, extract the silk from each ear, then rewrap and tie the husks at the top with kitchen string. Soak the rewrapped ears in cold water for 10 minutes (they'll incinerate if you don't!), then place them over hot coals for 15 to 30 minutes, turning frequently. Serve still in the husks, letting eaters remove their own. And don't forget the butter or the salt and pepper shakers.

3 cups fresh corn kernels (4 ears)
2 tablespoons unsalted butter
1 tablespoon olive oil
¾ cup diced (¼ inch) onion
1 teaspoon sugar
3 tablespoons snipped fresh chives
4 large egg yolks
2 cups heavy (or whipping) cream
1 teaspoon Dijon mustard
1 or 2 dashes Tabasco sauce
Salt and freshly ground black pepper, to taste

1. Bring a saucepan of water to a boil, add the corn, and cook over medium-high heat for 5 minutes. Drain well, and set aside.

2. Heat the butter and the oil in a heavy pot over low heat, and add the onions. Cook, stirring often, until they are very soft, 15 minutes. Sprinkle the sugar over the onions, and stir with a fork. Let rest off the heat, 5 minutes.

3. Meanwhile, preheat the oven to 350°F, and put the tea kettle on to boil.

4. Combine the corn, onions, and chives in a 9 x 9 x 2-inch oven-to-table baking dish.

5. Whisk together the egg yolks, cream, mustard, Tabasco, salt, and pepper. Pour this over the corn. Place the baking dish in a larger pan, and pour boiling water in the larger pan to reach about halfway up the baking dish. Carefully place it in the oven, and bake until set and lightly golden, 1 hour. Serve immediately.

Serves 6

CREAMED CORN

★ ★ ★

I grew up on canned cream corn, which I adored . . . until I learned there was something even better: homemade! During the last week in August, with the kernels so sweet, my childhood choice is easy to recreate. The luscious silkiness comes from well-puréed corn instead of a butter-flour thickener. The last-minute addition of whole kernels adds a nice corn texture. Creamed corn is great with meat loaf and mashed potatoes—a total-comfort meal.

8 ears sweet corn
6 cups defatted chicken broth, preferably
*   homemade (page 253)*
3 tablespoons sugar
½ cup half-and-half
Salt and freshly ground white pepper, to taste

1. Shuck the ears of corn, and carefully cut the kernels off the cobs, reserving the cobs. Set aside.

2. Pour the broth into a large heavy pot and bring it to a boil. Reduce the heat, add the corncobs, cover, and simmer for 20 minutes to flavor the broth. Remove and discard the cobs.

3. Add the corn kernels and sugar to the broth, and bring to a boil. Reduce the heat, partially cover, and simmer until very tender, 15 to 20 minutes. Using a slotted spoon, remove 1 cup of the corn from the broth and set it aside.

4. Purée the remaining corn and broth, in batches, in a blender or food processor until nearly smooth (a bit of texture should remain). Transfer the purée to a bowl, add the reserved whole kernels and the half-and-half, and season with salt and white pepper. Serve hot.

Serves 6

SOUTHWESTERN GRILLED CORN WITH A FLAIR

★ ★ ★

To me, late July, August, and early September are blessed months because nature's gifts of corn and tomatoes are available to grace the garden and table. While both can't be beat in their purest form, I enjoy dressing them up as well. For a backyard cookout, this is an easy way to prepare corn without having to run into the kitchen to steam it. You'll find the texture a little softer when grilled, yet the flavor will be deep and satisfying. The nice thing about this corn is that all the preparation can be done ahead of time—then you just grill it and eat!

6 tablespoons (¾ stick) unsalted butter,
    at room temperature
1 tablespoon chopped fresh cilantro leaves
¼ teaspoon chili powder
⅛ teaspoon ground cumin
8 ears sweet corn

1. Prepare a barbecue grill with medium-hot coals.

2. In a small bowl, combine the butter with the cilantro, chili powder, and cumin. Set aside.

3. Carefully peel back the cornhusks to about 1 inch from the bottom of the cob. Remove and discard the silks.

4. Rub the ears of corn evenly with the flavored butter, and then rewrap the corn in the husks. Tie the husks at the top with a piece of kitchen string. Soak the husks in a bowl of cold water to cover for 20 minutes (this keeps them from burning on the grill).

5. Grill the corn, about 5 inches from the heat source, turning them occasionally, until the husks are charred, about 15 minutes. Remove from the heat and serve with the husks unopened. Keep a good supply of napkins close by.
Serves 4

EGGPLANT-ZUCCHINI COMPOTE

★ ★ ★

Indian-summer vegetables are made for stewing. This compote, inspired by my adoration for the classic French *ratatouille*, is rich in both herbs and fruity olive oil. The stronger and deeper the flavor, the better.

2 eggplants (about 2 pounds), unpeeled, cut into
    1-inch cubes
2 teaspoons coarse salt
Olive oil for frying
¼ cup extra virgin olive oil
2 onions, coarsely chopped
1 tablespoon minced garlic
4 zucchini (about ½ pound each), ends
    trimmed, cut into ½-inch dice
1 red bell pepper, stemmed, seeded,
    and cut into ½-inch dice
1 can (35 ounces) Italian plum
    tomatoes, chopped, with
    their juices
1 tablespoon tomato paste
1 teaspoon sugar
1 cup torn fresh basil leaves
1 tablespoon fresh thyme leaves, or
    1 teaspoon dried
Salt and freshly ground black pepper, to taste

1. Place the eggplant in a colander and sprinkle with the coarse salt. Weight the eggplant down with a heavy pot lid, or with a plate with a heavy can on top, for 1 hour. Then rinse the eggplant lightly, drain it, and pat it thoroughly dry.

2. Pour olive oil to a depth of ¼ inch in a skillet, and heat over medium heat. Cook the eggplant, in batches, adding more oil as necessary, until golden, 3 to 5 minutes. Using a slotted spoon, transfer the cooked eggplant to a bowl lined with paper towels.

3. Heat the extra virgin olive oil in a large heavy pot over low heat. Add the onions and cook, stirring, until almost wilted, 13 minutes. Stir in the garlic and cook for 2 minutes.

4. Add the zucchini and bell pepper, and cook over medium heat to soften, stirring often, for 10 minutes. Add the eggplant.

5. Stir in the tomatoes with their juices, the tomato paste, sugar, basil, and thyme. Season with salt and pepper. Simmer over medium heat for 15 minutes. Reduce the heat to medium-low and cook, stirring often, for another 15 minutes. Serve hot or at room temperature.

Serves 8

GOLDEN EGGPLANT CURRY

★ ★ ★

Eggplant, simmered in a luxurious curry-cream sauce and set off by a sprinkling of fresh basil, is a substantial dish that can stand on its own as a main course as well as blend into a meal. As an entrée, it can be served over white rice or fluffy couscous. It is also a splendid complement to pork loin, roast chicken, leg of lamb, or a sizzling grilled steak. I always mellow curry

powder by cooking it for a couple of minutes before adding liquids, thereby releasing its sensual aroma.

Wine: Russian River Valley (CA) Zinfandel
Beer: Boston amber lager

2 eggplants (about 2 pounds), unpeeled, cut into
 ½-inch cubes
2 teaspoons coarse salt
Vegetable oil for frying
2 tablespoons olive oil
2 onions, cut into ½-inch dice
1 tablespoon minced fresh ginger
1 tablespoon minced garlic
2 tablespoons best-quality curry powder
4 large ripe tomatoes (about 2 pounds), peeled
 and cut into ½-inch dice, juices reserved
1 tablespoon all-purpose flour
1½ cups defatted chicken or vegetable broth,
 preferably homemade (page 253)
¼ cup heavy (or whipping) cream
1 tablespoon chopped mango chutney
Salt, to taste
½ cup slivered fresh basil leaves

1. Place the eggplant in a colander and sprinkle with the coarse salt. Weight the eggplant down with a heavy pot lid, or with a plate with a heavy can on top, for 1 hour. Then rinse the eggplant lightly, drain it, and pat it thoroughly dry.

2. Pour vegetable oil to a depth of ¼ inch into a nonstick skillet and heat over medium heat. Sauté the eggplant, in batches, adding more oil as necessary, until golden, 3 to 5 minutes. Using a slotted spoon, transfer the cooked eggplant to a bowl lined with paper towels.

3. Heat the olive oil in a large heavy pot over medium-low heat. Add the onions and cook, stirring, until wilted, 12 minutes. Add the ginger and garlic and cook, stirring, for 2 minutes. Sprinkle with the curry powder and cook, stirring, for 2 minutes more.

4. Add the tomatoes with their juices and bring to a boil. Reduce the heat and simmer for 1 minute. Then sprinkle with the flour and cook, stirring, for 2 minutes. Add the broth, bring it to a boil, and reduce the heat to low. Simmer gently, without boiling, for 10 minutes.

5. Add the cream and chutney, season with salt, and simmer, stirring, for 2 minutes. Fold in the eggplant and simmer over low heat until cooked through, 5 minutes. Sprinkle with the slivered basil and serve immediately.

Serves 4 to 6

FENNEL AND ACORN SQUASH WHIP

★ ★ ★

Fennel and acorn squash have a surprising affinity for each other. Although sugary winter squash is delicious on its own, the sweet licorice flavor of the fennel brightens the taste and makes for a more interesting side dish.

1 acorn squash (about 1 pound)
1 fennel bulb (about 1½ pounds), ferns trimmed off, chopped into 1- to 2-inch pieces
¼ cup (½ stick) unsalted butter
½ cup fresh orange juice
Salt and freshly ground black pepper, to taste
1 tablespoon snipped fresh chives, chopped fresh flat-leaf parsley, or slivered fresh basil leaves, for garnish

1. Bring a saucepan of water to a boil.

2. Cut the acorn squash in half lengthwise. Remove the seeds and then cut the squash into large chunks. Cook the squash in the boiling water until tender, 10 minutes. Drain. When the squash is cool enough to handle, remove the skin with a paring knife. Cut it into ½-inch cubes and set aside.

3. Meanwhile, bring another pot of water to a boil. Add the fennel and cook until tender, 12 to 15 minutes. Drain and set aside.

4. Melt the butter with the orange juice in a large skillet over medium-low heat, and cook for 2 minutes. Add the vegetables and cook, stirring, for 10 minutes.

5. Transfer the vegetables to a food processor and purée until smooth. Serve warm, garnished with the chives.

Serves 4

SAUTEED FIDDLEHEAD FERNS

★ ★ ★

These marvelous green spirals are the young, tight coils of the ostrich fern, which show up in vegetable markets for about two weeks in the early spring. When sautéed as I suggest here, they make a nice accompaniment to simply prepared fish fillets.

½ *pound fiddlehead ferns, well washed*
2 tablespoons olive oil
2 large shallots, slivered lengthwise
1 tablespoon unsalted butter
1 teaspoon finely minced garlic
2 tablespoons drained tiny capers
2 teaspoons finely grated lemon zest
2 tablespoons fresh lemon juice
2 tablespoons chopped fresh flat-leaf parsley

1. Prepare a bowl of ice water. Trim the tails of the ferns to about 1 inch beyond the spirals, removing any brown covering.

2. Bring a pot of salted water to a boil, and cook the fiddleheads until tender, 5 minutes. Drain them and then plunge them immediately into the bowl of ice water. Drain again and pat dry. Set aside.

3. Heat the oil in a skillet over low heat. Add the shallots and cook for 3 minutes. Then add the butter, garlic, capers, and lemon zest, and cook until the shallots are wilted, 2 minutes. Add the fiddleheads and cook over medium heat, shaking the pan constantly, until bright green and slightly softened, 5 minutes. Serve immediately, sprinkled with lemon juice and the chopped parsley.

Serves 4

FIDDLEHEADS

— ❦ —

Why don't more people eat fiddlehead ferns? They're so *good*—a gift in spring, from the woods. But they don't look like food. Shaped like the scrolled end of a violin, they're odder-looking than the most squiggly pasta—a vegetable from planet Venus, it seems! Sauté them in olive oil and butter, however, and you'll find them eminently edible, tasting something like a grassy, artichoke-asparagus cross. Or try them in Creamy Fiddlehead Fern Soup.

Longtime fiddlehead enthusiasts love to hunt theirs in the wild. This is fine if you're experienced, but watch out if you're not—some varieties can make you quite nauseous. Even store-bought ferns are potentially toxic if not thoroughly cooked for 10 minutes or more.

Fresh fiddleheads are bright green, firm, and tightly coiled (those coils, when not harvested, unfurl into gorgeous, feathery semaphores). Blackened ends are no problem—just snip them off before cooking. Ferns don't keep well, so eat them right away if you can. Otherwise, wrap them tightly and refrigerate for no more than 2 days.

ROASTED GARLIC

★ ★ ★

When garlic is roasted, its usual biting flavor is transformed to a mellow sweetness and the cloves take on a jam-like consistency. Separate the roasted cloves and squeeze the meltingly soft nectar onto toasted country bread, or use it to add some real zest to mayonnaise or mashed potatoes.

1 head garlic
3 tablespoons dry white wine
1 to 2 teaspoons olive oil
½ teaspoon dried thyme
Salt and freshly ground black pepper, to taste

1. Preheat the oven to 350°F.
2. Remove the papery exterior from the head of garlic, but do not separate or peel the cloves. Cut a ¼-inch slice off the top of the head.
3. Place the garlic in an oven-proof 4-ounce ramekin. Drizzle the wine and olive oil over it, and sprinkle with the thyme, salt, and pepper. Cover the ramekin with aluminum foil and bake, basting occasionally, until soft, about 1 hour.

Makes 1 head

DOWN-HOME GREENS

★ ★ ★

If ever there was a dish to save your country ham bone for, this is it! I had a lot of people working over these greens to make them as good as they are. First, Lula Mae Green, from South Carolina, helped me tell when they were cooked. Second, my associate, Laurie Griffith, advised that "they'd be real good with a splash of vinegar." And third, me, who brought a real Smithfield country ham back from Virginia, and bossed around everyone else who was helping out that day. Remember, if you use a bone from a Smithfield country ham, don't add salt to the greens because the bone still has lots of salty meat on it.

2 pounds collard greens, well rinsed
2 tablespoons olive oil
3 cloves garlic, cut into thin lengthwise slices
1 meaty ham bone, preferably Smithfield
½ cup defatted chicken broth, preferably homemade (page 253)
Freshly ground black pepper, to taste
Salt, to taste (optional)
1 tablespoon cider vinegar

1. Remove the tough stems from the collard greens. Stack about 10 leaves in a pile and roll them up from stem to tip. Cut the roll crosswise into 1-inch strips. Set them aside, and repeat with the remaining leaves.
2. Place the oil in a large heavy pot over low heat. Add the garlic and cook, stirring, until it begins to color slightly, 5 minutes.
3. Add the greens to the pot, raise the heat to medium-high, and toss until they wilt slightly, about 5 minutes. Add the ham bone and drizzle in the chicken broth. When the broth begins to boil, cover the pot, reduce the heat to medium, and cook, shaking the pan occasionally, until the greens are tender but still slightly crunchy, about 12 to 15 minutes.
4. Remove the ham bone and set it aside to cool slightly. Season the greens with pepper.

When the ham bone is cool enough to handle, shred any meat from the bone and add it to the greens. Season with salt, if necessary. Just before serving, reheat the greens, sprinkle with the vinegar, and toss to combine. Serve immediately.

Serves 4 to 6

GINGERED SUNCHOKES AND PEARS

★ ★ ★

The Jerusalem artichoke, more poetically known as "sunchoke," is one of North America's few indigenous foods. (Others include cranberries, wild rice, Concord grapes, and blueberries.) They are graced with a pristine white flesh and distinctive nutty flavor that combines impeccably with apples and pears. Whipped up light and fluffy, Jerusalem artichokes are an intriguing substitute for heavier mashed potatoes. They are small and somewhat gnarled, so peeling is a bit labor-intensive, but I prefer to do it rather than leave them unpeeled. I urge you to try this all-American vegetable.

1½ pounds Jerusalem artichokes, peeled
3 tablespoons unsalted butter
2 Anjou pears, peeled, cored, cut into ½-inch
  pieces, and tossed with 2 tablespoons
  fresh lemon juice
2 tablespoons dry sherry
Pinch of ground ginger
¼ cup sour cream
Salt and freshly ground black pepper, to taste
2 tablespoons coarsely chopped crystallized
  ginger, for garnish

1. Cut the Jerusalem artichokes into 1½-inch pieces, place them in a saucepan, and cover with water. Bring to a boil, reduce the heat slightly, and simmer over medium heat until very are tender, 20 minutes. Drain well and set aside.

2. Meanwhile, melt the butter in a nonstick skillet over medium heat. Add the pears and sauté until lightly colored, 5 minutes. Add the sherry and ginger and cook, stirring frequently until very soft, 15 minutes.

3. Place the Jerusalem artichokes and the pears in a food processor and process until smooth. Add the sour cream, salt, and pepper and process just to blend. Serve immediately, or set aside and then warm gently over low heat just before serving. Sprinkle with the crystallized ginger, and serve.

Serves 6

CREAMY LEEK RIBBONS

★ ★ ★

Delicate in flavor, silky in texture, this is an elegant presentation for the noblest member of the lily family—enchanting with roast loin of pork or roasted game birds. A soaking in water mixed with vinegar helps leach out any sand in the leeks.

4 large leeks, root ends trimmed, 3½ inches
   green left on
2 tablespoons white vinegar
1 chicken or vegetable bouillon cube
   (optional)
2 teaspoons finely grated orange zest
Pinch of ground nutmeg
Salt and freshly ground black pepper,
   to taste
1 cup heavy (or whipping) cream
1 tablespoon snipped fresh chives

1. Cut a 2-inch "X" through the bulb end of each leek. Place the leeks in a bowl, add the vinegar, and cover with water. Let rest for 30 minutes to remove the dirt. Drain, and rinse well under running water.

2. Bring a pot of water to a boil, adding the bouillon cube for flavor if you like. Add the leeks, reduce the heat to medium, and simmer until softened, 3 to 5 minutes. Drain, run under cold water, and carefully separate the layers. Pat dry. Place in a nonstick skillet.

3. Sprinkle the orange zest, nutmeg, salt, and pepper over the leeks. Pour the cream over all, and cook over medium heat, shaking the skillet, until the cream thickens and coats the leeks well (spoon some on top if necessary), 10 minutes. Serve immediately, sprinkled with the chives.

Serves 4 to 6

NAPA WILD WILD MUSHROOMS

★ ★ ★

Dinner at Mustard's in the Napa Valley is always a great meal. On one of my visits I had a delicious appetizer of wild mushrooms served on grilled peasant bread and topped with Laura Chenel's Cabécou goat cheese. That fabulous appetizer inspired this dish.

3 tablespoons unsalted butter
3 tablespoons extra virgin olive oil
½ pound fresh shiitake mushrooms,
   stems trimmed off, caps wiped clean
¼ pound fresh cremini mushrooms,
   stems trimmed off, caps wiped clean
¼ pound fresh chanterelle mushrooms,
   stems trimmed off, caps wiped clean
3 cloves garlic, finely chopped
1 shallot, finely chopped
Salt and freshly ground black pepper,
   to taste
1 tablespoon chopped fresh flat-leaf parsley
4 small slices toasted or grilled peasant bread
2 ounces Cabécou or other creamy goat cheese
1 tablespoon snipped fresh chives

1. Heat the butter and the oil in a large skillet over low heat. Stir in all the mushrooms. Raise the heat to medium and cook, stirring and shaking the pan constantly, until lightly colored, 3 minutes. Then add the garlic and shallot and cook for 2 minutes more. Season with salt and pepper, and toss with the parsley.

2. Arrange one piece of toast in the center of each of four small plates. Spoon the mushrooms evenly over the toast, and top with a small dollop of cheese. Sprinkle each serving with chives, and serve immediately.

Serves 4

PORTOBELLOS IN TOMATO SAUCE

The powerhouse combination of woodsy portobellos and sweet tomato sauce atop a bed of creamy polenta is, to my mind, a vegetarian dream dish. It's hearty enough to easily satisfy any appetite on a cold winter night. The idea for the dish was shared with me by Katharine Kagel, chef-owner of Cafe Pasqual in Santa Fe, New Mexico. Katharine urges anyone recreating her sauce to make it with fresh herbs, and I concur, since they are now more readily available, and make the dish as good as it is. You may do a double take on the amounts of two such strong herbs as thyme and oregano, but they are correct. If you're feeling a bit timid, then reduce the oregano to ¼ cup. Katharine cooks it up full strength for her customers!

Wine: Washington State Merlot
Beer: San Francisco Anchor Steam Beer

MUSHROOMS
4 cloves garlic, minced
2 tablespoons fresh thyme leaves
½ teaspoon ground nutmeg
1 teaspoon freshly ground black pepper
Juice and grated zest of 2 lemons
⅓ cup balsamic vinegar
½ cup olive oil
6 large fresh portobello mushrooms, stems trimmed off, caps wiped clean

TOMATO SAUCE
2 tablespoons olive oil
2 red bell peppers, roasted (see How to Roast a Bell Pepper, page 132) and coarsely chopped
1 red onion, sliced
4 cloves garlic, minced
½ cup (loosely packed) chopped fresh oregano leaves
¼ cup (loosely packed) chopped fresh thyme leaves
10 ripe plum tomatoes, cut into quarters
1 cup red wine, preferably Merlot or Zinfandel
2 bay leaves
1 cup water
Salt and freshly ground black pepper, to taste
Polenta with Mascarpone (page 321), hot

1. Prepare the mushrooms: Combine all the ingredients except the mushrooms in a bowl and whisk together. Add the mushrooms, turning to coat them, and marinate, loosely covered, at room temperature for 2 hours.

2. Meanwhile, prepare the tomato sauce: Heat the olive oil in a large nonreactive sauté pan over medium heat. Add the bell peppers, onion, and garlic and sauté until soft, 7 to 10 minutes. Stir in the oregano, thyme, tomatoes, wine, bay leaves, water, salt, and pepper. Cook, uncovered, until reduced by half, 35 minutes.

3. Working in batches, transfer the sauce to a blender and purée until smooth. Then pass the purée through a fine-mesh strainer. Season to taste with salt and pepper.

4. Prepare a barbecue grill with medium-hot coals.

5. Reheat the tomato sauce in a saucepan and cover to keep warm.

6. Arrange the mushrooms on the grill rack over the hot coals, and grill, turning once, until heated through, 3 to 5 minutes on each side.

7. To serve, mound the polenta in the center of a shallow bowl and spoon the tomato sauce over the top. Cover with a grilled mushroom.

Serves 6

The Morel (& More) of the Story

★ ★ ★

*I*n Boyne City, Michigan, the self-proclaimed "Mushroom Capital of the World," spring is heralded each year by morels, which emerge in spongy clumps in aspen groves and mixed stands of other trees in the forests around town. These cone-shaped fungi are prized not only for their earthy, nutty taste but for the fun people have foraging for them. The high point of morel season, which runs just a few weeks in May, is the National Mushroom Hunting Championship, as important to Boyne City's civic identity as Mardi Gras is to New Orleans'.

Mushroom enthusiasts ("shroomers") come from all over the nation to compete in this ninety-minute scramble for a little fame and a lot of flavor. Competitors meet in a local park and are bussed to secret gathering spots. Locals, who know the terrain, can bag eighty or more in this time. Outsiders, who compete in a separate category, can't hope to do as well. On my first try, I collected just eight, along with generous bouquets of ramps (wild leeks), fiddlehead ferns, and wildflowers. I harvested the mushrooms in the nick of time, minutes before a distant siren signaled the hunt's close.

Although morels grow all over the Americas, they're best known and loved in the northern Midwest and Pacific Northwest, where the damp and fertile woods are especially rich in mushrooms. The people of these regions have known for generations that morels, and many other wild fungi, are sublime food. The rest of us are catching on. Mushrooming is increasingly popular, as is home cultivation of a host of varieties, native and foreign, on logs and in sawdust, straw and sterile compost. I prefer to shop at farmers' markets and gourmet stores, where I'm guaranteed a better yield than I got in Boyne City. Mail order can be even easier, and a boon to cooks who can't buy exotics where they live. Some varieties dry well; rehydrated, they yield hearty brown stock.

Marketing for Mushrooms

When buying fresh mushrooms, inspect carefully. They should be dry (as opposed to damp or slimy), firm, and solid-colored (not blotchy). Spread them out in your refrigerator, unstacked, in a paper bag or open container covered loosely with a lightly dampened cloth or paper towel. Use them within a few days—they're highly perishable. Clean them gingerly, right before cooking. I usually just wipe them off with a damp paper towel. If that doesn't work, I loosen the dirt with a soft mushroom brush, then wipe with a moist cloth and dry gently between paper towels. This can be tedious, but it's well worth the effort.

Worldwide, over 1,800 species of mushrooms and fungi are considered edible; the rest range from mildly poisonous to lethal. (One inedible kind, the "false morel," appears in the same places as the true morel, and looks much like it. Inexperienced shroomers, beware!) The following glossary describes some popular "wild" types, many of which are now grown commercially.

Black trumpet (black chanterelle): A close relative of the golden-hued chanterelle (see below), this brown-black, highly fragrant variety is often used as a "false truffle." Diced into scrambled eggs, it certainly looks like the part, but has a deep buttery taste.

Chanterelle: This species' bright color has an apricot-like flavor to match. Try chanterelles lightly sautéed in olive oil and garlic, mounded on grilled peasant bread, topped with a dollop of chèvre. You can also use them with poultry, and eggs and in creamy pasta sauces.

Coral: The delicate, pinkish fingers of this odd-looking variety are tastiest when baked at high heat. A little butter, lemon juice, parsley, and pepper can enhance its refined, almost seafood-like flavor.

Cremini: A member of the genus *Agaricus*—that is, a close relative of the common supermarket mushroom. At their best, mushrooms in this group are creamy-textured when raw. This is a durable type which produces lots of flavorful liquid when cooked. It's also versatile, excellent stuffed, sautéed, roasted, and grilled.

Enoki: I eat these bean sprout–like mushrooms raw, stir-fried, or lightly sautéed in bunches. The Japanese often foil-wrap them for grilling with fish or poultry. Although quite mild, their crunchy texture and unusual appearance (the tiny caps, like pinheads, top long white stems) can add interest to many dishes.

Morel: There are several species of morels ranging from under an inch to 5 inches tall, the most popular being the yellow type, which has recently been successfully domesticated. Just as tasty are white morels, a smaller variety, and black morels, which are more difficult to spot, if you're out hunting. All morels

are best sautéed in garlic and butter or added to simple cream sauces. They're also great for stuffing, since they're hollow. Dried morels reconstitute well and produce an especially savory broth.

Oyster: This fan-shaped "wood mushroom" has a silky, mild character that works best in cream sauces and gratins. Although dried oysters are widely available, they have little flavor.

Porcini (cèpe): The meaty character of this wide-capped (1 to 10 inches), light brown mushroom has made it the favorite of many aficionados. Often used dried in soups, American-grown fresh porcini caps can be consumed grilled, braised, broiled, or sautéed.

Portobello: Like the cremini (see above), the portobello is closely related to the domestic white mushroom. Its meatiness, however, calls to mind the porcini. Portobellos are large and hardy, and caps are delicious grilled or roasted.

Shiitake: Americans love this steaky, smoky Japanese import. It's adaptable, excellent raw, sautéed, and baked. Shiitake are extensively cultivated here and thus widely available fresh. Dried, they yield a rich broth when reconstituted.

WILD MOREL SAUTE

★ ★ ★

Mid-May is when fresh morels begin entering the specialty vegetable markets, so save this recipe for a celebratory occasion during the season. They're absolutely delicious prepared this way, but they do cook down a lot. If you want to give a few of your favorite friends a real treat, just serve tiny portions in the center of pretty plates—or be selfish and just invite one other person to splurge on two sybaritic portions. When I hunted for mine in Boyne City, Michigan, the world's wild morel capital, I ate them all myself! However you bring them home, this quick sauté is all they need.

½ pound fresh morels
2 tablespoons unsalted butter
2 tablespoons finely chopped shallots
1 teaspoon finely chopped garlic
1 tablespoon chopped fresh flat-leaf parsley or
*   snipped fresh chives*

1. Halve the morels lengthwise, brushing out any visible dirt. Do not wash them.
2. Melt the butter in a nonstick skillet over low heat. Add the shallots and garlic, and cook over medium-low heat until wilted, stirring constantly, 3 minutes. Do no let them burn. Add the mushrooms and stir together. Continue cooking until the mushrooms are just tender, 4 to 5 minutes. Serve immediately, sprinkled with the parsley.
Serves 2 to 4

CARAMELIZED ONIONS

★ ★ ★

When you're looking for a topping for a Philly Cheese Steak Sandwich or a grilled porterhouse, these onions will do the trick. A little sugar caramelizes them just the right amount.

6 onions
2 tablespoons unsalted butter
2 tablespoons olive oil
2 tablespoons sugar
Salt and freshly ground black pepper, to taste

1. Cut the onions in half crosswise and then into thin slivers.
2. Heat the butter and the olive oil in a large skillet over medium heat. Add the onions and cook, stirring occasionally, until they are wilted, 5 minutes.
3. Sprinkle with sugar and continue to cook, stirring occasionally, until carmelized, 30 minutes. Season with salt and pepper, and serve.
Makes 4 portions

SONNY BRYAN'S ONION RINGS

★ ★ ★

In Dallas, my favorite barbecue haunt is Sonny Bryan's, where the best onion rings in the world are served daily. Pit master Charlie Riddle has his own special recipe that has been keeping the

customers coming for years. A little flattery went just far enough to catch Charlie's secret: the taste comes from a beer batter, and the unexcelled crispness from double dipping. His rings are deliciously crusty and I wouldn't try to one-up him on a bet, but no need—I think this recipe comes close to perfection!

4 large eggs, beaten
1 cup milk
1 cup beer
4 cups all-purpose flour
2 teaspoons baking powder
Vegetable oil or solid vegetable shortening,
*   for frying*
4 extra-large yellow onions, sliced ½ inch
*   thick and separated into rings*
Coarse salt, to taste

1. Mix the eggs, milk, and beer together in a bowl.

2. Mix 2 cups of the flour and 1 teaspoon of the baking powder together in each of two bowls.

3. Pour oil to a depth of 3 inches in a large heavy pot, and heat over medium heat until it is very hot (375° to 400°F).

4. Dip the onion rings into the egg mixture and then into the first bowl of flour. Redip into the egg mixture and then into the second bowl of flour. Carefully, add the onion rings to the hot oil in small batches.

5. Cook the onion rings, turning once, until golden brown, about 3 minutes. Using a slotted spoon or a long-handled fork, transfer the onions to paper towels to drain. Sprinkle with coarse salt to taste, and serve immediately.
Serves 8

PARSNIP AND APPLE WHIP

★ ★ ★

The flavor of autumn's apples permeates this lighter-than-feathers whip, which could easily replace mashed potatoes with the next pork roast you pop in the oven. Parsnips' comforting sweetness and succulent texture reach far beyond their ordinary soup-pot role in this flavorful dish.

1½ pounds parsnips, peeled and coarsely
*   chopped*
2 Granny Smith apples, peeled, cored
*   and coarsely chopped*
3 tablespoons unsalted butter
1 teaspoon sugar
Pinch of ground cardamom
Pinch of ground cinnamon
¼ cup sour cream
Salt, to taste
1 tablespoon snipped fresh chives,
*   for garnish*

1. Place the parsnips in a saucepan and cover with cold water. Bring to a boil, cover, and cook until very tender, 20 minutes. Drain, and place in a food processor.

2. Meanwhile, melt the butter over medium heat in a nonstick skillet. Add the apples and cook, shaking the pan occasionally, for 10 minutes. Add the sugar, cardamom, and cinnamon, and cook until the apples are very soft and lightly colored, 10 minutes. Place them in the food processor, add the sour cream, and process until the mixture is very smooth.

3. Transfer the purée to a serving bowl and season with salt. Serve immediately, sprinkled with the chives.

Serves 4 to 6

MINTY SWEET PEAS

★ ★ ★

It is said that Thomas Jefferson took great pride in the sweet peas grown at Monticello and enjoyed serving the first crop to his closest friends. Whether this is apocryphal or not, there are certain truths about peas: One pound in the pod yields one cup of loose peas—enough for two people. The most delectable, tender fresh peas will be found in the springtime. If you have a craving any other time of the year, frozen sweet peas do the job nicely. Just be sure to use lots of fresh mint—it's available all year round to spruce up these little green gems.

1/2 teaspoon sugar
2 cups shelled fresh peas (2 pounds unshelled)
2 tablespoons unsalted butter
Salt and freshly ground black pepper, to taste
2 tablespoons chopped fresh mint leaves

1. Fill a small saucepan with lightly salted water to a depth of 1/2 inch. Bring to a boil, and

add the sugar and the peas. Reduce the heat to low, cover, and simmer until the peas are bright green and tender, 5 to 10 minutes, depending on size. Drain, and place in a serving bowl.

2. Toss the peas with the butter, salt, pepper, and chopped mint. Serve immediately.

Serves 4

MASHED YUKON GOLDS

★ ★ ★

Homey, fluffy, buttery, and delicious—that's what mashed potatoes should be. Because Yukon Golds already have a buttery flavor and a creamy texture, when cooked, they are without question, at least to my mind, the best potatoes to use. In this recipe I've hedged a bit on the amounts of milk and butter because I know everyone has their texture preferences. Some like mashed potatoes smooth, others want them a little lumpy, and some even like them stiff. This is how I like them: drizzled with Fresh Basil Oil. They are sublime! The best method for reheating mashed potatoes is in the microwave oven on full power, covered with waxed paper. Enjoy them with roast chicken, steak, and your favorite fried chicken and gravy!

2 pounds Yukon Gold potatoes
1/2 to 3/4 cup milk
2 to 4 tablespoons unsalted
*   butter, at room*
*   temperature*
Salt and freshly ground black
*   pepper, to taste*
1/4 cup Fresh Basil Oil (recipe
*   follows)*

1. Bring a pot of salted water to a boil.

2. Wash the potatoes and cut them in half. Place them in the boiling water and cook until tender, about 25 minutes. Drain them well and return them to the pot over very low heat. Shake the pot for about 10 seconds to remove any remaining moisture. When cool enough to handle, remove and discard the potato skins.

3. Mash the potatoes in a bowl, or push them through a potato ricer. Warm the milk with the butter in a small saucepan, and mix into the potatoes. Season generously with salt and pepper, and fluff with a fork. Serve immediately, drizzled with Fresh Basil Oil.

Serves 4

Fresh Basil Oil

---★---

Emerald colored and pungent flavored, this oil should be made in the summer when basil is plentiful. It can be drizzled into vegetable soups or over fluffy mashed potatoes, or used as a garnish for seared fish. Refrigerate the oil, because it will quickly spoil if left at room temperature.

1 cup fresh basil leaves, rinsed
1¼ cups extra virgin olive oil

1. Trim the stems off the basil leaves. Bring a saucepan of water to a boil, and blanch the leaves in it for 30 seconds. Drain and dry thoroughly between paper towels.

2. Place the basil and ¼ cup of the olive oil in a food processor. Process until smooth. With the motor running, slowly drizzle in the remaining 1 cup oil through the feed tube. Transfer to a glass jar with a lid and store, covered, in the refrigerator for up to 5 days. Bring to room temperature before using. Use the oil as is, flecked with fresh basil, or strain it through a fine sieve if you prefer.

Makes 1¼ cups

GARLICKY RED-JACKET MASHED POTATOES

★ ★ ★

There are all types of mashed-potato aficionados: proponents of including the skins, advocates of leaving some lumps, and fans of the super-smooth. I don't know who originated this version, but it has a natural affinity for collard greens, barbecue, and all manifestations of pork. Be sure to start with a thin-skinned

red boiling potato. I add a touch of cider vinegar to brighten the flavors when I've almost finished mashing. The amount of vinegar is up to your taste.

6 red-skinned boiling potatoes (about 2 pounds),
  unpeeled, cut into quarters
2 tablespoons olive oil
2 cloves garlic, finely minced
½ cup sour cream
½ cup milk, warmed
1 tablespoon cider vinegar, or
  more to taste
Salt and freshly ground black pepper,
  to taste

1. Place the quartered potatoes in a saucepan, cover with cold water, and bring to a boil. Reduce the heat to a simmer and cook until tender, 25 minutes. Drain well.

2. Meanwhile, heat the olive oil in a skillet over low heat. Add the garlic and cook, stirring occasionally, until pale golden, 2 minutes. Place the garlic in a mixing bowl and add the drained potatoes.

3. Mash the potatoes and the garlic with a fork or a potato masher. Add the sour cream. Slowly pour in the warm milk and continue to mash. Add the vinegar, and season with salt and pepper. Serve immediately.
Serves 4 to 6

PAN-ROASTED BABY WHITES

★ ★ ★

On Long Island in the summer, the potato fields are dotted with harvesters draped with burlap bags digging up small white new potatoes.

About the same size as baby reds but with a much finer flavor and more delicate skin, they are some of the world's best. Fresh herbs and garlic are ideal pan-roasting partners to make a crisp and savory side dish for roasted meats and poultry, or for a thick steak right off the grill.

3 tablespoons olive oil
1¾ pounds very small white new potatoes,
  unpeeled, washed (see Note)
1 teaspoon finely minced garlic
1 tablespoon chopped fresh thyme leaves
1 tablespoon chopped fresh rosemary leaves
1 teaspoon coarse salt

1. Heat the olive oil in a nonstick skillet over medium-low heat. Add the potatoes and cook, shaking the pan occasionally, until they are tender and browned, 25 to 30 minutes.

2. Add the remaining ingredients, toss well, and serve immediately.
Serves 4 to 6

NOTE: If anything other than very small new potatoes are used, parboil them in salted water for 10 minutes, until just tender. Proceed with step 1.

MINTY NEW POTATOES AND FENNEL

★ ★ ★

By combining the star ingredient with other interesting vegetables, contemporary potato salads have matured into more sophisticated dishes. In this one, fennel and the aromatic flavors of mint and garlic turn potato salad into a hearty winter dish that's assertive enough to accompany the most substantial roast. A fruity olive oil and generous grindings of black pepper tie these flavors together perfectly.

1 fennel bulb (about 1½ pounds)
1 pound small white new potatoes, unpeeled, washed
¼ cup fruity extra virgin olive oil, or more if desired
Coarse salt and coarsely ground black pepper,
    to taste
1 teaspoon finely minced garlic
¼ cup chopped fresh mint leaves

1. Preheat the oven to 350°F.

2. Halve the fennel bulb lengthwise. Chop and reserve some of the ferns if desired. Remove the bottom of the bulb, and slice the bulb lengthwise into ½-inch pieces. Combine the fennel and the potatoes in a mixing bowl.

3. Toss the vegetables with the ¼ cup oil and a generous amount of coarse salt and pepper. Lay them in a single layer on a baking sheet, and roast in the oven until the vegetables are tender, 1¼ hours.

4. When the potatoes are cool enough to handle, cut them in half and place in a serving bowl with the fennel. Add extra olive oil if desired. Toss with the garlic, mint, and salt and pepper to taste. Sprinkle on the reserved ferns, if using, and serve warm or at room temperature.

Serves 6

PERFECT BAKED POTATOES

★ ★ ★

To create this all-time American favorite, begin with firm russet potatoes with no eyes or green patches. Once they're baked—soft inside with a crispy skin—they're ready to serve steaming hot. They're delicious as is with just a bit of salt and pepper, or cut open and topped with the toppings as described in the recipe or with a dollop of crème fraîche and a teaspoon of black caviar. Or for another winning topper, try plain yogurt, shredded Monterey Jack cheese, and minced fresh cilantro.

4 to 6 russet potatoes
    (about ½ pound each)
Salt and freshly ground black
    pepper, to taste
Optional toppings: Extra virgin olive oil or unsalted
    butter or sour cream and snipped fresh chives

1. Preheat the oven to 375°F.

2. Scrub the potatoes under cold water and pat them dry. Prick the potatoes all over with the tines of a fork. Bake on the middle rack of the oven until the skin is crispy and the insides are cooked through, 1¼ hours.

3. Make a 2- to 2½-inch slit down the center of each potato, and squeeze the ends together to pop them open.

4. Serve hot, sprinkled with salt and pepper and topped with a drizzle of oil, a pat of butter, or a dollop of sour cream and a sprinkling of chives.

Serves 4 to 6

WHIPPED SWEET POTATOES

★ ★ ★

Here's my recipe for some really good, fluffy whipped sweet potatoes. Easily prepared ahead for reheating at serving time, think of this delicious accompaniment often throughout the fall and winter, not just for Thanksgiving dinner.

3 pounds sweet potatoes (about 6 medium),
    peeled and cut into 1-inch pieces
4 carrots (about 1 pound) peeled and
    cut into 1-inch pieces
2 chicken bouillon cubes
6 tablespoons (¾ stick) unsalted butter,
    cut into small pieces
¼ cup (packed) light brown sugar
2 tablespoons fresh orange juice
1 tablespoon ground nutmeg
Salt, to taste

A SWEET POTATO BY ANY NAME

—❦—

Few Americans have ever tasted yams, though most think they have. What we believe to be a yam is actually an orange-fleshed sweet potato. True yams are tubers, fleshy swellings on the underground portion of the stem, not even related to the sweet potato, which is a root. The most common type of yam is huge (one to two feet long) with white, starchy flesh. It grows in the tropics, and is particularly popular in the West Indies. To find one in the United States, you'd have to visit a Latin or Caribbean market.

How the two became confused is unclear. Some Southern slaves, it seems, may have called the American sweet potato by their word for the similar tasting, more familiar (to them) yam. And since the mix-up seems to originate in the South, where most sweet potatoes are grown, voilà—a ready, if unscientific, explanation.

Sweet potatoes in some form are a holiday must. In my mother's kitchen they were sweetened and mashed, topped with a layer of marshmallows, and baked to a golden brown. The marshmallow crust atop the puréed sweets said "Happy Thanksgiving" to us as much as the turkey did. But I don't relegate sweet potatoes to just special occasions. I serve them throughout the winter mashed, braised in stews, cooked in pies, or just plain baked to eat on a cold, blustery day. They cheer up simple poultry and pork dishes, and baked, make an easy accompaniment to a suppertime plate of scrambled eggs.

Choose sweet potatoes that are small to medium in size and firm, with no cuts or bruises. Watch out for knobs (they make peeling difficult), but don't worry about little hairs. The yellow variety isn't nearly as dense or sweet as the orange kind. Not all orange potatoes taste alike, either; darker ones are usually sweeter.

1. Place the sweet potatoes, carrots, and bouillon cubes in a large heavy pot and cover with cold water. Bring to a boil. Then reduce the heat and simmer until the vegetables are very tender, 15 to 20 minutes. Drain, reserving 6 tablespoons of the cooking liquid, and place in a bowl.

2. Using a mixer, whip the vegetables with the reserved cooking liquid and the remaining ingredients. Serve immediately, or reheat in a double boiler or, covered, in a 350°F oven for 15 to 20 minutes.

Serves 6 to 8

OCTOBER 31ST PUMPKIN PUREE

★ ★ ★

Once we're deep into winter, a search through the markets for fresh pumpkin is futile, and I end up making dishes with butternut squash and sweet potatoes. But during a recent October, I remembered to buy extra pumpkins, and finally, with four put aside, I had a winter's supply. Cooking with fresh pumpkin can be a bit touch-and-go. The first time out, I boiled pumpkin

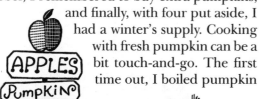

and found that since it is such a watery vegetable, this method just didn't work at all. On the second go around, I baked it, with excellent results. This pumpkin purée is light and would be splendid served alongside pork, any game, or Devilishly Good Chicken. You could even make up extra during the fall and freeze it so you won't have to go through the winter without this specialty.

2 pumpkins (about 4 pounds each)
¼ cup (½ stick) unsalted butter, cut into
*   small pieces*
¼ cup (packed) light brown sugar
½ teaspoon ground ginger
¼ teaspoon ground mace
¼ teaspoon ground nutmeg
Pinch of cayenne pepper
¼ teaspoon salt, or to taste
¼ cup sour cream

1. Preheat the oven to 375°F.

2. Halve the pumpkins, remove the seeds and fibers, and cut into wedges. Place the wedges, skin side down, in shallow roasting pans to fit. Cover tightly with aluminum foil and bake until tender, 1½ hours. Lower the oven heat to 350°F.

3. When the pumpkin is cool enough to handle, remove and discard the skin. Place the pulp in a bowl and toss with the butter, brown sugar, spices, and salt.

4. Purée, in batches, in a food processor until just smooth. Transfer the purée to a bowl, fold in the sour cream, and adjust the seasonings to taste. To reheat, place in an ovenproof serving dish, cover, and heat in the oven for 15 to 20 minutes.

Serves 8

GRILLED SCALLIONS

★ ★ ★

Besides being super served along with roasted peppers for any Southwestern dish, these svelte onions make a beautiful garnish. Once the scallions are ready for cooking, be sure to place them across the grates so they don't fall through the cracks.

18 scallions of equal size
2 tablespoons extra virgin olive oil
1 tablespoon fresh lemon juice
½ teaspoon finely chopped garlic
Salt and freshly ground black pepper,
    to taste

   1. Prepare a barbecue grill with medium-hot coals.
   2. Trim the root end off the scallions, and trim off all but 3 inches of the green ends.
   3. Combine the olive oil, lemon juice, garlic, salt, and pepper in a shallow flat dish. Add the scallions and coat well with the mixture.
   4. Lay the scallions on the grill, and cook, 3 inches from the heat source, for 3 minutes per side. Serve immediately.
   Serves 4 to 6

PAN-FRIED SCALLIONS

★ ★ ★

In 1995, one of the food fashions of the year was—of all things—the scallion. Suddenly this favorite flavor enhancer was given a star turn, and showed up center plate in every form imaginable. Well, I would like to keep scallions in the limelight. They are particularly enjoyable quickly pan-fried, and add some flair to a humble piece of fish or a grilled chicken cutlet. Just a squeeze of lemon juice and some parsley or cilantro is all the decoration needed to make them shine.

18 scallions of equal size
¼ cup extra virgin olive oil
Salt and freshly ground black pepper,
    to taste
1 tablespoon chopped fresh flat-leaf parsley or
    cilantro leaves
4 to 6 lemon quarters, for garnish

   1. Trim the root ends off the scallions, and trim off all but 3 inches of the green ends.
   2. Place the olive oil in a nonstick skillet over medium-low heat. Add half of the scallions and cook, turning once, until wilted and lightly browned, 5 minutes. Season with salt and pepper and transfer to a serving platter. Repeat with the remaining scallions. Sprinkle with the parsley and serve immediately, with the lemon alongside.
   Serve 4 to 6

MELTING GOLDEN SQUASH IN A SKILLET

★ ★ ★

I was inspired to create this recipe by a squash dish I ate at Savannah's own Mrs. Wilkes's

Boarding House, a favorite breakfast and lunchtime restaurant. Meltingly smooth, these vegetables were served in a large bowl family-style, enough to feed a table full of hungry guests. I hold back a bit on the butter in my version, but I can assure you that Mrs. Wilkes doesn't. Any which way, this is an ambrosial side dish.

¼ cup (½ stick) unsalted butter
4 cups thinly sliced (about ⅛ inch) yellow
   summer squash
1 large onion, slivered
¼ cup defatted chicken broth, preferably
   homemade (page 253)
1 teaspoon sugar
1 teaspoon salt
¼ teaspoon freshly ground black pepper,
   or more to taste
1 tablespoon chopped fresh flat-leaf parsley

   Melt the butter in a large skillet over medium-low heat. Add the squash, onions, broth, and sugar. Stir well and cook, covered, stirring occasionally, until the squash and onions are meltingly tender, about 20 minutes. Season with the salt and pepper, sprinkle with the chopped parsley, and serve immediately.
   Serves 4

SUNNY SUMMER SQUASH BAKE

★ ★ ★

In the summertime, you'll find plenty of thin-skinned yellow squashes bursting with seasonal sweetness. When choosing squash at the farm stand, stay away from the very large ones because they will be loaded with seeds. Those that are medium-size and thinner tend to be less seedy. Once you give them a tender roasting, an extra drizzle of fruity olive oil will tie the dish together and the basil will add a scent of assertive vibrancy. This dish nicely sets off grilled lamb or skirt steak fajitas.

3 pounds yellow squash, rinsed, ends trimmed
2 large onions, cut into 1-inch pieces
1 tablespoon finely minced garlic
Coarse salt and freshly ground black pepper,
   to taste
¼ cup fruity extra virgin olive oil, plus
   more if desired
¾ cup thinly slivered fresh basil leaves

   1. Preheat the oven to 350°F.
   2. Cut the squash into 1-inch cubes and place them in a large bowl. Toss with the onions, garlic, coarse salt, pepper, and ¼ cup olive oil.
   3. Place the vegetables in a shallow baking

pan to fit, and bake until tender, tossing once or twice, 1¼ hours. Transfer the mixture to a large bowl, season generously with more salt and pepper, and drizzle with a little extra olive oil if you like. Toss with the basil, and serve immediately.

Serves 4 to 6

BLUE PLATE CREAMED SPINACH

★ ★ ★

Whether served in a small Blue Willow bowl, a nod to the blue plate of blue plate special fame, or beside a generous slice of meat loaf or fried ham steak, there's no food more soothing or memory-evoking than creamed spinach. Today a pinch or two from the spice cupboard and a recess from our usual cholesterol watch is all that's needed to return to Mom's kitchen.

2 pounds fresh spinach
1 tablespoon unsalted butter
1 tablespoon finely minced garlic
¾ cup heavy (or whipping) cream
⅛ teaspoon ground nutmeg
Pinch of cayenne pepper
Salt and freshly ground black pepper, to taste

1. Rinse the spinach thoroughly and shake the excess water off. Remove and discard the stems, then pat the leaves dry and coarsely chop them.

2. Melt the butter in a heavy saucepan over low heat. Add the garlic and cook, stirring, until slightly softened, 2 to 3 minutes. Add the cream, nutmeg, and cayenne. Cook over medium heat until thickened, 5 minutes. Stir in the spinach, season with salt and pepper, cover, and wilt for 3 minutes. Uncover and cook, stirring occasionally, until the cream slightly thickens, 3 to 4 minutes more. Serve immediately.

Serves 4

SCALLOPED GREEN TOMATOES

★ ★ ★

To me, buttery, crisp, tart green tomatoes have a flavor that is reminiscent of a New England autumn day. When sliced and baked in a classic shallow French gratin dish until they develop a crunchy golden brown crust, they are delectable!

6 green tomatoes (about 2 pounds)
¼ cup (½ stick) unsalted butter
1 cup dried bread crumbs
1 tablespoon sugar
Salt and freshly ground black pepper,
*   to taste*
4 slices bacon, for garnish
1 lemon half
1 tablespoon chopped fresh flat-leaf parsley,
*   for garnish*

1. Preheat the oven to 350°F. Butter a 9-inch-square oven-to-table baking dish.

2. Slice the tomatoes ¼ inch thick.

3. Melt the butter in a small saucepan over low heat. Remove it from the heat and stir in the bread crumbs, sugar, salt, and pepper.

4. Line the bottom of the prepared baking dish with a layer of sliced tomatoes, and sprinkle with some of the bread crumb mixture. Repeat with more tomato slices and bread crumbs until the dish is filled, finishing with the bread crumbs.

5. Bake in the center of the oven until the tomatoes are tender, 1 hour.

6. Meanwhile, cook the bacon in a nonstick skillet until crisp, 6 to 8 minutes. Drain the slices on a paper towel, and then crumble. Set aside.

7. Just before serving, squeeze the lemon half over the top of the baked tomatoes. Sprinkle with the chopped parsley and then with the crumbled bacon.

Serves 4 to 6

SLOWLY ROASTED PLUM TOMATOES

★ ★ ★

Once the tomatoes in my garden begin to ripen, there are moments when it is close to impossible for me to see beyond eating anything but these juicy red orbs. So I make salads, sandwiches, sauces, soups, and anything else I can conjure up. My obsession has led me to roasting the ripest of the Romas (plums). Just a sprinkling of sugar begins to caramelize their natural sweetness as they dry during a long, slow roasting. Arrange them on a platter and serve them as a spread for slices of grilled peasant bread. If you have a garden, fresh nasturtium blossoms, along with a few of their leaves, make a beautiful garnish.

24 ripe plum tomatoes (about 4 pounds)
2 tablespoons extra virgin olive oil
2 to 3 teaspoons sugar
Salt and freshly ground black pepper, to taste
3 tablespoons fresh thyme leaves, or 2 teaspoons dried

1. Preheat the oven to 250°F. Line 2 baking sheets with parchment paper or aluminum foil.

2. Trim a thin slice off the end of each tomato, and cut each one into 3 thick crosswise slices. Arrange the slices in a single layer on the prepared baking sheets.

3. Brush the tops of the tomato slices with the oil. Sprinkle with sugar, salt, pepper, and 2 tablespoons of the fresh thyme or 1½ teaspoons of the dried. Bake until reduced in size and velvety soft, 2 hours.

4. Using a spatula, carefully transfer the tomatoes to a serving platter. Sprinkle the remaining thyme over them, and serve atop grilled or toasted peasant bread.

Serves 6

FRESH HERBED TOMATO SAUCE

★ ★ ★

I like my tomato sauces to have a rich, fresh, herby taste, and I get it all in this mix that begins with fruity olive oil and garlic for zest. Plum, or

Roma, tomatoes always make the meatiest sauce; most other varieties are too watery. The bit of sugar counters the inherent acid quality of the tomatoes and brings out their sweetness.

6 pounds ripe plum tomatoes
¼ cup extra virgin olive oil
4 cloves garlic
2 tablespoons tomato paste
½ cup dry red wine
½ cup coarsely torn basil leaves
½ cup coarsely chopped fresh flat-leaf parsley
2 teaspoons dried oregano
1 teaspoon sugar
Salt and freshly ground black pepper, to taste

HOW TO PEEL AND SEED TOMATOES

—❧—

Working with one tomato at a time, cut an "X" just through the skin on the stem end. Drop it into a pot of boiling water for 30 seconds, then remove to a bowl of ice water to stop the cooking. Slip off the skin and cut the tomato in half, crosswise. Holding it over a strainer that has been set over a bowl, scoop out the seeds with a thumb or forefinger, or squeeze gently and shake out the seeds, catching the seeds in the strainer and the juices in the bowl. Tap the strainer against the side of the bowl to release any remaining juice. Discard the seeds and proceed according to recipe.

1. Peel and seed the tomatoes (see box, this page) and chop them coarsely. Set them aside.

2. Heat the oil in a large heavy pot over medium heat. Add the garlic and cook, stirring, until it colors slightly, 3 to 4 minutes.

3. Carefully add the tomatoes (making sure the hot oil doesn't splatter). Stir in the remaining ingredients and simmer uncovered, stirring occasionally, until the tomatoes have melted to form a sauce, 30 minutes.

4. Serve immediately over pasta, or cool to room temperature and refrigerate, covered, for up to 2 days. The sauce may also be frozen for later use.

Makes about 8 cups

SUMMER STEWED TOMATOES

★ ★ ★

Don't let a sour memory of watery and not-quite-fresh-tasting canned stewed tomatoes prevent you from trying this recipe. For me, the dish is familiar, comforting, and very American. In my updated version, celery and onions, slow cooking, and a pinch of brown sugar and fresh herbs put stewed tomatoes right up there with the best vegetable dishes.

8 meaty ripe tomatoes (about ½ pound each)
1 tablespoon unsalted butter
1 tablespoon olive oil
4 ribs celery, cut into ½-inch dice
1 onion, cut into ½-inch dice
2 cloves garlic, finely minced
1 tablespoon dark brown sugar
Pinch of ground allspice
1 tablespoon thinly slivered fresh basil or
    tarragon leaves
2 teaspoons fresh lemon juice
Salt and freshly ground black pepper, to taste

1. Peel and seed the tomatoes (see box, facing page). Cut them into large chunks, reserving the juice separately.

2. Heat the butter and oil in a large heavy pot over low heat. Add the celery, onion, and garlic and cook, stirring, until wilted, 10 minutes. Add the reserved tomato juice along with the brown sugar. Cook over low heat until the sugar dissolves, 2 minutes. Add the tomatoes, allspice, and basil, and cook over low heat, partially covered, stirring occasionally, for 30 minutes. Uncover and cook until the tomatoes are stewed, 15 minutes. Season with the lemon juice, salt, and pepper. Serve hot.

Serves 6

GLAZED TURNIPS

★ ★ ★

One of our underutilized vegetables, the white turnip appears more often in dishes in Europe than it does in this country. In this recipe, I've tempered the turnips' basic sharp flavor slightly by glazing them with butter and sugar—a won-

derfully easy enhancement that makes the vegetable very pleasing to the palate.

6 white turnips (about ¼ pound each)
2 tablespoons unsalted butter
1 tablespoon fresh lemon juice
2 teaspoons sugar
2 tablespoons snipped fresh chives

1. Bring a large saucepan of salted water to a boil.

2. Trim off the root and stem ends, then peel the turnips and cut them into quarters. Cook them in the boiling water until tender, 10 minutes. Drain and pat dry.

3. Melt the butter in a large nonstick skillet. Add the turnips and the lemon juice, and toss well to coat. Sprinkle with the sugar and cook over medium heat, shaking the pan and occasionally turning the turnips with a spatula, until the turnips are glazed and just golden brown, 10 to 12 minutes. Sprinkle with the chives and serve immediately.

Serves 4

ROASTED ROOT VEGETABLES

★ ★ ★

When it's February and all the vegetables are looking heavy and gloomy, brighten them up with a roast in a hot oven. But first give them a tenderizing steam. The beets will then hold their color and the softened vegetables will drink up the seasonings as they roast. Pulled from the oven, these vegetables will have luscious flavor and a jewel-like glow. Piled in the center of a crown roast of pork, they'll take some of the edge off those winter doldrums.

6 carrots, peeled, then halved lengthwise and
  crosswise
6 parsnips, peeled, then halved lengthwise and
  crosswise
4 sweet potatoes, peeled and cut into 1-inch dice
4 turnips, peeled and cut into 1-inch dice
4 beets, peeled and cut into 1-inch dice
¼ cup olive oil
2 teaspoons dried thyme
Salt and freshly ground black pepper, to taste

1. Preheat the oven to 450°F. Bring water to a boil in a saucepan fitted with a steamer basket.

2. Steam the vegetables separately, doing the beets last, until tender, about 10 minutes for each. As they are steamed, use a slotted spoon to transfer them to a large bowl.

3. Toss the vegetables with the olive oil, thyme, salt, and pepper.

4. Arrange the vegetables in a single layer on two large baking sheets, and roast, shaking the baking sheets occasionally, until they are nicely colored and fork-tender, 30 minutes. Serve immediately.

Serves 8 to 10

MAQUE CHOUX

★ ★ ★

Traditionally, the Southern rural dish, maque choux, is made with corn, onions, bell peppers, and milk, but there are endless regional variations. On St. Helena's Island, South Carolina, for instance, okra and cream are added to the basic recipe. Because I love succotash, I've

replaced the peppers with limas, substituted broth for the milk, and added tomatoes and fresh thyme and parsley. My maque choux wound up somewhat unrecognizable, but is it ever delicious.

¼ cup (½ stick) unsalted butter
1 cup coarsely chopped onion
2 cloves garlic, minced
¼ cup defatted chicken broth, preferably
  homemade (page 253)
2 cups cooked corn kernels, fresh or frozen
1 cup cooked baby lima beans
1 cup diced (¼ inch) seeded plum tomatoes
  (about 4 tomatoes)
1 teaspoon sugar
2 tablespoons chopped fresh flat-leaf parsley
2 teaspoons finely chopped fresh thyme leaves,
  or ¾ teaspoon dried
Salt and freshly ground black pepper, to taste

BLUE PLATE
S·P·E·C·I·A·L

**Mrs. Green's Southern Fried Chicken
with Fried Chicken Gravy**

Confetti Spoon Bread

Red Rice

Maque Choux

Harvest Sweet Potato Pie

Homey Vanilla Ice Cream

Old-Fashioned Lemonade

1. Melt the butter in a nonstick skillet over medium-low heat. Add the onions and cook until wilted, stirring occasionally, 10 minutes. Add the garlic and cook 2 minutes more.

2. Add the broth and corn, and cook for 8 minutes. Add the lima beans and the tomatoes, sprinkle with the sugar, and cook until the tomatoes have softened, 5 minutes, stirring. Then add the parsley and thyme, and season with salt and pepper. Serve immediately.

Serves 6

VEGETABLE CHILI

★ ★ ★

I adore this chili—the vegetables give plenty of chili kick without using any meat. I serve mine in deep bowls on a base of Vegetable-Studded Barley, and garnish it with yogurt, grated Monterey Jack cheese, and a few golden raisins. You can also serve it over plain rice or barley—something to soak up the flavorful sauce.

Wine: Dry Creek Valley (CA) Zinfandel
Beer: California pale ale

2 tablespoons olive oil
2 tablespoons extra virgin olive oil
4 onions, coarsely chopped
4 carrots, peeled and cut into ½-inch pieces
2 tablespoons minced garlic
2 tablespoons chili powder
2 tablespoons ground cumin
½ pound red new potatoes, cut into ½-inch pieces
1 red bell pepper, stemmed, seeded, and cut into ½-inch pieces
1 green bell pepper, stemmed, seeded, and cut into ½-inch pieces
1 yellow bell pepper, stemmed, seeded, and cut into ½-inch pieces
2 cans (28 ounces each) peeled plum tomatoes, chopped, with the juices
1 tablespoon tomato paste
1 tablespoon dark brown sugar
2 teaspoons dried oregano
1 teaspoon fennel seeds
2 yellow squash, halved lengthwise and cut into ½-inch pieces
2 zucchini, trimmed and cut into ½-inch pieces
¼ cup chopped fresh flat-leaf parsley
¼ cup chopped fresh cilantro leaves
Salt and coarsely ground black pepper, to taste
1 can (15½ ounces) chickpeas (garbanzo beans), drained
2 tablespoons fresh lemon juice
Chopped fresh flat-leaf parsley, for garnish (optional)
Chopped fresh cilantro leaves, for garnish (optional)

1. Heat both olive oils in a large heavy pot over medium heat. Add the onions and carrots and cook until the onions are wilted, stirring, 10 minutes. Add the garlic and cook for another 2 minutes. Reduce the heat to low, and stir in the chili powder and cumin. Cook 1 minute more.

2. Stir in the potatoes, all of the bell peppers, the tomatoes with their juices, the tomato paste, brown sugar, oregano, and fennel seeds. Bring to a boil. Reduce the heat and simmer, partially covered, stirring occasionally, for 25 minutes.

3. Add the squash, zucchini, parsley, and cilantro. Season with salt and pepper, and adjust the other seasonings. Stir in the chickpeas. Simmer uncovered, stirring occasionally, until the vegetables are tender, 20 minutes.

4. Stir in the lemon juice. Sprinkle with extra parsley and cilantro, if desired, and serve.

Serves 8 to 10

VEGETABLE JAMBALAYA

★ ★ ★

Jambalaya is a beloved Louisiana Creole one-pot meal that originated out of practicality and convenience. At one time, it was made up of a healthy amount of cooked rice and whatever else was available in the kitchen, be it meat, fish, or vegetables. My vegetable version tastes great on the day it's made and the next day, too, if you're lucky enough to have any leftovers.

Wine: Central Coast (CA) Rhône-style blend
Beer: Wisconsin brown lager

3 tablespoons vegetable oil
1 cup diced (½ inch) onion
2 large garlic cloves, minced
¾ cup diced (½ inch) celery
½ cup diced (¼ inch) carrots
1 teaspoon dried thyme
2 teaspoons paprika
½ teaspoon salt
Pinch of cayenne pepper
1 bay leaf
2 green bell peppers, stemmed, seeded, and
*   cut into ½-inch dice*
2 red bell peppers, stemmed, seeded, and
*   cut into ½-inch dice*
1 cup cooked black-eyed peas
1 can (28 ounces) plum tomatoes, chopped,
*   with the juices*
3½ cups vegetable broth, preferably homemade
*   (page 255)*
2 zucchini, cut into ½-inch dice
1¼ cups long-grain white rice
¼ cup chopped fresh flat-leaf parsley

1. Heat the oil in a large heavy pot over low heat. Add the onions and cook, stirring, until wilted, 10 minutes. Add the garlic, celery, and carrots. Cook, stirring, 1 minute longer.

2. Mix in the thyme, paprika, salt, cayenne, and bay leaf. Add both of the bell peppers, the black-eyed peas, tomatoes with their juices, and broth. Bring to a boil. Reduce the heat to medium-low and cook, partially covered, for 10 minutes for the flavors to blend. Adjust the seasonings. Remove and discard the bay leaf. (You can set the jambalaya aside at this point, to be finished later.)

3. Add the zucchini and bring the sauce to a boil. Stir in the rice, cover, reduce the heat to low, and cook until the rice is tender, 20 minutes. Adjust the seasonings, stir in the parsley, and serve immediately.

Serves 6

Noodles, Grains & Beans

Before 1980, who would have predicted that legumes, noodles, and grains would become some of America's most popular foods? A few visionaries—very few. These foods are so newly front and center that we tend to forget how much Americans have always relished them, both with and without poultry, meat, or fish.

Some of the dishes in this chapter go back a century or more, others are based on traditional preparations. I open with macaroni and cheese— I wouldn't dream of calling this book "American" without it!—and close with a bright black-bean salad. In between, there's hearty Louisiana "dirty rice," replete with chopped chicken livers, a barley risotto, venison-sauced spaghetti from the Broken Arrow Ranch in Ingram, Texas, and more. Beans are especially good for you—rich in fiber, low in fat, and loaded with protein, vitamins, and minerals. And they're delicious! Enjoy Austin Baked Beans, Charro Pintos, or any other bean dish here!

AMERICAN MACARONI AND CHEESE

★ ★ ★

As big a fan as I am of the classic American creamy, bubbling casserole of macaroni and cheese, this old-fashioned comfort food is ripe for rethinking. For my updated version, I have combined two cheeses, letting a mild, straw-hued Cheddar from Shelburne Farms in Vermont melt together with a buttery jalapeño-flavored Monterey Jack from California. Adding sautéed sweet red peppers both tames and complements the small sparks of the Jack. Since the traditional elbow macaroni is no longer *de rigueur*, a little creativity is encouraged in your choice of pasta tubes to complete the dish.

Beer: American lager

2 tablespoons vegetable oil

1 pound ziti pasta

1 cup cold water

1 red bell pepper, stemmed, seeded, and cut into ¼-inch dice

1 green bell pepper, stemmed, seeded, and cut into ¼-inch dice

4 cups milk

¼ cup (½ stick) unsalted butter

6 tablespoons all-purpose flour

1 teaspoon paprika

½ teaspoon salt, or more to taste

6 ounces Monterey Jack cheese with jalapeños, grated (about 1½ cups)

6 ounces Vermont Cheddar cheese, grated (about 1½ cups)

1 tablespoon chopped fresh flat-leaf parsley

1. Bring a large pot of salted water to a boil with 1 tablespoon of the vegetable oil. Add the ziti, stir, and return to a boil. Cook until the pasta is just tender, about 10 minutes. Drain the pasta. Run under cold water and drain again. Place in a large bowl.

2. Heat the remaining 1 tablespoon vegetable oil in a nonstick skillet over low heat. Add both of the bell peppers and cook, stirring, until wilted, 10 minutes. Remove them with a slotted spoon and add them to the ziti. Stir to combine and set aside.

3. Preheat the oven to 350°F. Lightly oil or butter a 13 x 9 x 2-inch baking dish.

4. Bring the milk just to a boil in a heavy saucepan. Set aside.

5. Melt the butter in another heavy saucepan over low heat. Add the flour and ½ teaspoon of the paprika, and whisk the mixture over medium-low heat for 5 minutes. Do not let the flour burn. Remove the pan from the heat.

6. Whisking constantly, slowly add the hot milk to the flour mixture. Return the pan to the heat and cook over medium heat, whisking constantly, until slightly thickened, 5 minutes. The mixture should coat the back of a spoon, and a finger run through it should leave a trail. Season with the salt.

7. Combine both of the grated cheeses and set aside 1 cup. Stir the remaining cheese into the hot sauce. Toss the sauce with the ziti, and spread the mixture evenly in the prepared baking dish. Sprinkle the top evenly with the remaining 1 cup grated cheese and ½ teaspoon paprika. Bake until bubbly and golden 25 to 30 minutes. Serve immediately, sprinkled with the parsley.

Serves 8

NOODLES, GRAINS & BEANS

315

****

HOW TO COOK DRIED PASTA

—🍃—

Bring salted water (1 teaspoon salt per quart of water) to a rolling boil in a large pot (at least a 5-quart capacity; figure on 1 gallon of water per pound of pasta). If desired, add 1 tablespoon vegetable oil per gallon of water. Add the noodles to the water, stir, allow the water to return to a boil, and then start timing. Cook until the noodles are *al dente* (tender but still firm to the bite). The cooking time will depend on the size and shape of the pasta. Drain immediately, and continue with the recipe. If I'm making a cold pasta salad, I rinse the starch off under cold water. However, this should be a personal preference when using hot pasta.

****

MORELS AND BUTTERFLIES

★ ★ ★

A trek through the Michigan woods to gather morels (see page 294 for The Morel—& More—of the Story) inspired more dishes than number of mushrooms gathered, but even for this one

alone, it was worth it. Remember not to add any salt until the very end, as it will draw the water out of the mushrooms. A vegetable salad of tomatoes, Oven-Roasted Beets, green beans, and cucumbers is all you need to make a complete, light meal! Warm crusty bread tops it off.

Wine: Central Coast (CA) Syrah
Beer: Colorado brown ale

¾ *pound butterfly (farfalle or bowtie) pasta*
½ *pound fresh morel mushrooms,*
    brushed clean
3 *tablespoons extra virgin olive oil*
2 *tablespoons unsalted butter*
2 *cloves garlic, finely chopped*
2 *tablespoons chopped fresh flat-leaf parsley*
2 *tablespoons finely slivered fresh basil*
    leaves
2 *teaspoons finely grated lemon zest*
Salt and coarsely ground black pepper,
    to taste
Freshly grated Parmesan cheese, for serving

1. Bring a large pot of salted water to a boil. Add the pasta and cook until just tender, about 10 minutes.

2. Meanwhile, trim the stems from the morels and slice the large heads crosswise, leaving any small ones whole.

3. In a large nonstick skillet, heat 2 tablespoons of the olive oil and the butter over medium-high heat. Add the mushrooms and garlic. Cook quickly, shaking the pan or stirring, and adding both of the herbs as the mushrooms cook, until they are just tender, 3 to 5 minutes. Sprinkle them with the lemon zest, salt, and pepper as they finish cooking.

4. Drain the pasta and place it in a large shallow bowl. Toss in the mushrooms, and drizzle with the remaining 1 tablespoon olive oil. Serve immediately, with the cheese alongside.

Serves 4

PENNE WITH SUMMERTIME RED AND YELLOW PEPPERS

★ ★ ★

The sweet flavors of the peppers and tomatoes make a nice light sauce for an easy summer pasta dish. A green salad with some arugula for bite makes an ideal accompaniment. Toasted peasant bread brushed with extra virgin olive oil, rubbed with garlic, and sprinkled with pepper fills out the meal.

Wine: Santa Barbara County (CA) Nebbiolo
Beer: San Francisco amber ale

¼ cup olive oil
2 cloves garlic, thinly sliced
2 onions, coarsely chopped
4 yellow bell peppers, stemmed, seeded, and
   each cut into 8 lengthwise strips
4 red bell peppers, stemmed, seeded, and
   each cut into 8 lengthwise strips
½ cup dry white wine
1 cup fresh basil leaves, slivered
4 ripe plum tomatoes, seeded and each cut
   into 4 pieces
Salt and freshly ground black pepper, to taste
½ pound dried penne or other tube-shaped pasta
¼ pound ricotta salata cheese (see Note)

1. Bring a large pot of salted water to a boil.
2. Meanwhile, heat the oil in a large heavy pot over low heat. Add the garlic and cook, stirring, for 2 minutes. Do not let the garlic brown. Add the onions and cook, stirring occasionally, until wilted, 5 to 7 minutes.
3. Add the yellow and red bell peppers and cook, stirring, over medium heat, for 10 minutes. Add the wine and ¾ cup of the basil. Cook, stirring, until the peppers are very soft, 7 to 10 minutes.
4. Add the tomatoes and cook to soften, 5 minutes; season with salt and pepper. Remove from the heat and transfer to a large shallow bowl.
5. While the tomatoes are cooking, cook the pasta in the boiling water until just tender, 8 to 12 minutes. Drain the pasta.
6. Toss the pasta over the sauce. Add the remaining ¼ cup basil and toss again to combine. Coarsely grate the ricotta salata over all, and toss lightly. Serve immediately.

Serves 4 to 6

NOTE: Italy's ricotta salata is not like the familiar soft-curd ricotta cheese, but rather a pressed and dried sheep's milk that is just firm enough for grating and soft enough to crumble. I love its mild nutty flavor. It is available in Italian markets, and better cheese departments in both speicalty food stores and supermarkets.

RIGATONI WITH EGGPLANT AND TOMATO SAUCE

★ ★ ★

An abundance of olive oil gives this substantial vegetable sauce its lushness. Rigatoni is the pasta shape of choice—it will hold the sauce in its grooves. The addition of torn basil leaves at the end lends a garden-fresh flavor.

Wine: Sonoma County (CA) Cabernet Franc

4 eggplants (about 2 pounds), cut into
    1-inch cubes
2 teaspoons coarse salt
Olive oil
4 cloves garlic
2 onions, cut into ½-inch dice
2 cans (28 ounces each) peeled Italian tomatoes,
    coarsely chopped, with their juices
2 tablespoons tomato paste
2 teaspoons dried oregano
10 whole fresh basil leaves
¼ cup chopped fresh flat-leaf parsley
1 teaspoon sugar
Salt and freshly ground black pepper,
    to taste
1 cup torn fresh basil leaves
6 ripe plum tomatoes, each cut into 8 pieces
1 pound dried rigatoni pasta

1. Place the eggplant in a colander and sprinkle the coarse salt over it. Weight it down with a heavy pot lid, or with a plate with a heavy can on top, and set it aside for 1 hour. Then rinse the eggplant, drain, and pat dry.

2. Pour olive oil to a depth of ¼ inch in a nonstick skillet and heat it over medium heat. Sauté the eggplant, in batches, until golden, 3 to 5 minutes. Using a slotted spoon, transfer the cooked eggplant to a bowl lined with paper towels. Set aside.

3. Pour ¼ cup olive oil into a large heavy pot. Add the garlic cloves and cook over medium heat until golden, 3 to 5 minutes. Do not burn them. Remove

and discard the garlic. Reduce the heat to low, add the onions, and cook, stirring occasionally, until wilted, about 10 minutes.

4. Add the chopped tomatoes with their juices, the tomato paste, and the eggplant. Stir in the oregano, whole basil leaves, parsley, sugar, salt, and pepper. Bring to a boil. Reduce the heat to medium-low and simmer, stirring, for 15 minutes. Then stir in the torn basil and the fresh tomatoes. Set the sauce aside. (At this point, if not using immediately, the sauce may be refrigerated, covered, for up to 4 days, or it may be frozen. If frozen, defrost before proceeding with the recipe.)

5. Shortly before serving, bring a large pot of salted water to a boil. Cook the rigatoni until just tender, 10 minutes. While the pasta is cooking, heat the sauce through over low heat. Drain the pasta and return it to the pot. Add 1 cup of the sauce and toss to coat. Serve in shallow bowls, topped with the remaining sauce.

Serves 4 as an entrée or 8 as a side dish

HUGHES'S SPAGHETTI WITH VENISON

★ ★ ★

Elizabeth and Mike Hughes, owners of the marvelous Broken Arrow Ranch in Ingram, Texas, are renowned not only for Mike's unrivaled game (available by mail order; see On the Road at the back of the book), but Elizabeth's recipes using Broken Arrow's venison. One of my favorites is this simple venison spaghetti sauce. There is something very homey about it that suits an old-fashioned bowl of spaghetti.

Wine: Texas Merlot
Beer: Colorado porter

3 tablespoons olive oil
1½ cups diced (¼ inch) onions
1 large clove garlic, finely minced
1 pound ground venison
¾ cup defatted chicken or vegetable broth,
*   preferably homemade (page 253 or 255)*
1 can (14 ounces) Italian plum tomatoes,
*   crushed*
1 can (8 ounces) prepared tomato sauce
½ cup tomato paste
1½ cups diced (¼ inch) green bell pepper
¼ pound white mushrooms, cleaned, trimmed,
*   and sliced ¼ inch thick*
1½ cups chopped fresh flat-leaf parsley
2 teaspoons Worcestershire sauce
2 teaspoons red wine vinegar
1 teaspoon Tabasco sauce
1½ teaspoons dried oregano
1½ teaspoons chili powder
1½ teaspoons paprika
1½ teaspoons sugar
½ teaspoon dried basil
1½ teaspoons chopped fresh rosemary, or
*   ½ teaspoon dried*
½ teaspoon dried marjoram
1 bay leaf
Salt and freshly ground black pepper, to taste
¾ pound dried spaghetti

1. Heat 2 tablespoons of the oil in a large heavy pot over low heat. Add the onions and cook, stirring, until almost wilted, 8 minutes. Add the garlic and cook for 2 minutes more.

2. Crumble in the venison, raise the heat to medium, and brown well, stirring often to break up the clumps, about 10 minutes. Remove the pot from the heat.

3. Add all the remaining ingredients, (except the spaghetti and the remaining oil), to the meat. Return the pot to the heat and simmer, uncovered, over low heat, stirring occasionally, until the flavors are well blended, 40 to 45 minutes.

4. Just before serving, bring a large pot of salted water to a boil. Add the remaining 1 tablespoon olive oil and cook the spaghetti until just tender, 10 to 12 minutes. Drain, and place in a large pasta bowl. Remove the bay leaf from the sauce, then toss the pasta with some of the sauce. Divide the spaghetti among individual pasta bowls, and top evenly with the remaining sauce. Serve immediately.

Serves 4

SUMMER GARDEN NOODLES

★ ★ ★

When the days are hot and you want to keep stovetime to a minimum, a dinner of raw vegetables served over linguine makes a quick, tasty entrée. The addition of goat cheese just before serving makes the sauce thicker and helps it to cling to the noodles. Make up a pitcher of Old-Fashioned Lemonade to drink with this salad.

4 ripe plum tomatoes, seeded and cut into small dice
1 hothouse (seedless) cucumber, peeled and
   cut into small dice
1 large red bell pepper, stemmed, seeded,
   and cut into small dice
1 small yellow squash, trimmed and
   cut into small dice
1 zucchini, trimmed and cut into small dice
3 scallions (3 inches green left on), thinly sliced
½ cup golden raisins
Finely grated zest and juice of 1 lemon
1 ripe avocado, peeled, pitted, and
   cut into ½-inch dice
⅓ cup olive oil
Salt and freshly ground pepper, to taste
¾ pound dried linguine
1 cup shredded fresh basil leaves
¼ pound soft goat cheese, crumbled

1. Bring a large pot of salted water to a boil.
2. Meanwhile, combine the tomatoes, cucumber, bell pepper, squash, zucchini, scallions, raisins, and lemon zest in a large serving bowl. Toss the lemon juice and avocado together, and then add to the other vegetables along with the olive oil. Season with salt and pepper.
3. Add the pasta to the boiling water and cook until just tender, 10 minutes. Drain well and toss with the vegetables and the basil. Sprinkle with the crumbled goat cheese and serve immediately.

Serves 8

PORTOBELLO BARLEY RISOTTO

★ ★ ★

Substituting hearty, rustic barley for the classic Italian Arborio rice results in a risotto-style dish that's as satisfying as the original. In this recipe, the sweet wine and golden raisins make an interesting foil for the assertive flavor of rosemary. If you prefer a creamier risotto, add a bit more hot broth just before serving. Served in shallow bowls and sprinkled with Parmesan cheese, this is just the right dish for a luncheon or light dinner entrée. A salad of arugula and tomatoes, and a loaf of hot crusty bread, is all you'll need to complete this meal.

Wine: Central Coast (CA) Rhône-style blend
Beer: San Francisco Anchor Steam Beer

½ pound portobello mushrooms
4 tablespoons olive oil
1 onion, coarsely chopped
4½ cups defatted chicken broth,
   preferably homemade (page 253)
1 cup pearl barley, rinsed
½ teaspoon ground allspice
1 tablespoon chopped fresh rosemary, or
   1 teaspoon crumbled dried
½ cup sweet white wine, such as Riesling
½ cup golden raisins
Salt and freshly ground black pepper,
   to taste
2 tablespoons chopped fresh flat-leaf parsley,
   for garnish

1. Trim off the mushroom stems and clean the caps with a damp cloth. Cut them into 1-inch chunks.
2. Heat 2 tablespoons of the oil in a large heavy pot over medium-high heat. Add the mushrooms and cook, stirring often, until

lightly browned and softened, 5 to 7 minutes. Remove the mushrooms from the pan and set them aside.

3. Reduce the heat to medium-low, and add the remaining 2 tablespoons oil and the onions. Cook, stirring, until they soften, 10 minutes.

4. While the onions are cooking, bring the broth to a boil in a medium-size saucepan. Reduce the heat to a gentle simmer.

5. Add the barley, allspice, and rosemary to the onions. Raise the heat to medium-high and cook, stirring, for 1 minute, to ensure that the barley is evenly coated with oil. Add the wine and cook until it has nearly evaporated, about 5 minutes.

6. Add ½ cup of the hot broth to the barley mixture and cook, stirring frequently, over medium heat until it has been absorbed into the barley. Repeat, making sure each addition has been absorbed before adding the next, until the barley is tender and nearly all the broth has been absorbed, about 45 minutes.

7. Stir in the reserved mushrooms and the raisins. Cook for a few minutes longer, until the risotto reaches the desired consistency. Then season with salt and pepper and serve immediately, sprinkling each portion with some of the chopped parsley.

Serves 4

VEGETABLE-STUDDED BARLEY

★ ★ ★

Barley, a grain of the grass family, is one of my favorite accompaniments for chilis and stews. But in this dish, barley stands proudly on its own, with all the integrity of the grain intact.

I cook barley until just tender, usually about 45 minutes. Watch the cooking time carefully or the grains will quickly become too soft.

2 cups diced (¼ inch) carrots
10 ounces white mushrooms
1 cup pearl barley
4 cups defatted chicken broth, preferably
    homemade (page 253)
1 cup water
1 tablespoon chopped fresh thyme, or
    ½ teaspoon dried
2 tablespoons chopped fresh flat-leaf parsley
Salt and freshly ground black pepper, to taste

1. Bring a saucepan of water to a boil, add the carrots, and cook until tender, about 10 minutes. Drain and set aside.

2. Trim, wipe clean, and quarter the mushrooms.

3. Rinse the barley in a strainer, and then place it in a large heavy pot. Add the broth, water, thyme, and mushrooms. Bring to a boil. Reduce the heat to medium and simmer, uncovered, until the barley is tender and the liquid has been absorbed, 40 to 50 minutes.

4. Stir in the carrots and the chopped parsley. Season with salt and pepper to taste, and serve immediately.

Serves 6

POLENTA WITH MASCARPONE

★ ★ ★

When I visited Sante Fe, I quickly discovered that chiles and salsa weren't a given at every meal. Not that I really expected them to be, but this dish, served at Cafe Pasqual, was a surprise. Chef-owner Katharine Kagel serves her irresistible polenta enriched with sinfully creamy Italian triple-cream mascarpone cheese. One important note: no instant polenta here—you'll have to stir for your supper! Try it as a bed for her Grilled Portobellos in Tomato Sauce.

8 cups water
¾ teaspoon saffron threads
2 teaspoons salt
2 cups polenta (stone-ground cornmeal)
½ pound mascarpone cheese
1 cup freshly grated Asiago or Parmesan
*   cheese*

Place the water in a heavy saucepan and add the saffron and salt. Bring to a rolling boil over high heat. Slowly add the polenta, stirring constantly, and cook until the raw taste disappears and the polenta begins to come away from the sides of the pan, about 10 to 15 minutes. Add both of the cheeses, stirring well. Keep warm in a covered double boiler over the lowest possible heat.

Serves 4 to 6

LENTIL BARLEY VEGETABLE STEW

★ ★ ★

Colorful and healthful, this is a stew tailored for the '90s, brimming with vegetables, legumes, and grains. You won't hear any complaints about missing the meat—this will satisfy the heartiest of appetites. Serve it in bowls, with some warm crusty peasant bread and a green salad.

Wine: Oregon Pinot Noir
Beer: California ale

¼ cup olive oil
4 carrots, peeled and cut into ¼-inch dice
2 leeks (3 inches green left on), well washed
*   and cut into ¼-inch dice*
2 ribs celery, cut into ¼-inch dice
2 zucchini, trimmed and cut into
*   ¼-inch dice*
1 large onion, cut into ¼-inch dice
1 tablespoon minced garlic
1 tablespoon fresh thyme leaves, or
*   1 teaspoon dried*
1 cup dried lentils, rinsed
½ cup pearl barley, rinsed
6 to 7 cups vegetable broth, preferably
*   homemade (page 255)*
2 cups diced (½ inch) seeded ripe tomatoes
1 cup torn fresh basil leaves
½ cup coarsely chopped fresh flat-leaf parsley
Salt and freshly ground black pepper, to taste

1. Place the olive oil in a large heavy pot and add the carrots, leeks, celery, zucchini, onion, and garlic. Cook over low heat, stirring, until the vegetables are wilted, 15 minutes. Stir in the thyme.

2. Add the lentils, barley, and 6 cups of the vegetable broth. Bring to a boil. Reduce the heat to medium, and simmer uncovered, stirring often, for 30 minutes. Then add the tomatoes, basil, and parsley, season with salt and pepper, and cook until the lentils and barley are tender, 10 minutes more. If the stew seems a bit dry, add the remaining cup of broth.

3. If not serving immediately, refrigerate, covered, for up to 6 hours, and reheat slowly at serving time.

Serves 6

WILD RICE AND AUTUMNAL FRUITS

★ ★ ★

Deliciously nutty and invitingly chewy, wild rice, one of America's few indigenous crops, is harvested by hand, which is the reason it is so expensive. I've mixed it with long-grain white rice to stretch the dollars—and because the white rice helps the wild rice play off the sweet dried fruits, crunchy pecans, and plenty of strongly flavored herbs. This is an extraordinary dish. Be sure you don't overcook the rice(s), or you will lose the appealing texture.

4 cups water
1 cup wild rice, rinsed and drained
4½ cups defatted chicken broth, preferably homemade (page 253)
2 cups long-grain white rice
2 tablespoons olive oil
1 cup diced (¼ inch) onions
1 cup diced (½ inch) celery
1 cup dried cherries
Grated zest of 2 oranges
2 tablespoons fresh thyme leaves, or 2 teaspoons dried
2 teaspoons dried marjoram
1 tablespoon chopped fresh sage leaves, or 1 teaspoon dried sage, crumbled
Salt and freshly ground black pepper
1 cup pecan halves
1 cup pitted prunes, quartered

1. Bring the water to a boil in a heavy saucepan. Add the wild rice, reduce the heat to medium-low, and cook at a gentle simmer, uncovered, until the rice is just tender, 30 to 45 minutes. Do not overcook. Place the rice in a strainer to drain off any liquid, transfer it to a large bowl, and set aside.

2. Pour the broth into another heavy saucepan and bring it to a boil. Stir in the white rice, and return to a boil. Reduce the heat to low, cover, and simmer, covered, until the rice is just tender, 20 minutes. Fluff with a fork and add to the wild rice.

3. Heat the oil in a heavy pan over low heat. Add the onions, celery, and cherries and cook to wilt the vegetables, stirring occasionally, about 8 to 10 minutes. Add to the rice and toss.

4. Add the orange zest, all of the herbs, the salt, and pepper. Fold in the pecans and prunes. Serve warm.

Serves 8 to 10

NOODLES, GRAINS & BEANS

WILD RICE TABBOULEH

★ ★ ★

This recipe was created with wild rice given to me as a gift from the Chippewa Indians when I visited their Leech Lake reservation in Bemidji, Minnesota. Among the Chippewa people, the gathering of wild rice, or *mahnomin*, is one of the year's most important activities, both socially and economically. To the Chippewa, wild rice is considered a gift of the Great Spirit. I've always enjoyed creating interesting recipes with this unique grass, and was particularly grateful for such a welcome gift. Here I mix it with ingredients usually found in Middle Eastern tabbouleh. The fresh lemon juice and cucumber crunch add a sparkling

WILD RICE

—❦—

To be a part of a real wild-rice harvest, I had to fly in a tiny commuter plane to Bemidji, Minnesota, a ruggedly beautiful, heavily forested region some 250 miles north of Minneapolis. Native Americans have been gathering wild rice here the same way for hundreds of years, in the glacier-carved wetlands where it grows in dense groves. My Chippewa (Ojibwa) guides and I traveled in wooden canoes. They, like their ancestors, worked in pairs: one person poled from the stern while the other used cedar sticks to deftly pull the tall stalks over the boat and knock the ripe grains loose. Back on the shore, they dried the grains in the sun first, then in an iron kettle over a roaring wood fire. Hulling and winnowing, once accomplished more or less by hand, is now done by machine.

True wild rice must be harvested manually. It's the tradition here, and the law. To protect the environment and ancient practice, only local Native Americans are permitted to take rice. Others grow it in flooded paddies, in this region and elsewhere—hence the oxymoron "cultivated wild rice." Actually, wild rice isn't really rice. It's the seed of an aquatic grass, more flavorful and nutritious than rice. Connoisseurs prefer Native American "lake rice" and can easily distinguish it from machine-harvested "paddy rice." They find lake rice muskier and nuttier, which is due in part to how it's "parched" over an open fire. True enough, but paddy rice is plenty good, and less costly.

Rinse wild rice before cooking. It requires more water or broth than true rice—I use 4 cups for every 1 cup of grain. Timing is a little tricky: some varieties cook in half an hour, while others take up to 45 minutes. Check frequently, and turn off the heat when your rice is still a little chewy. Overcook it, and the grains will split open and turn mushy. Wild rice is delicious plain or fancy. If you want to dress it up, try the recipe for Wild Rice and Autumnal Fruits on the facing page.

brightness to the underlying earthy flavor. There is one very important thing to know about cooking wild rice: Don't overdo it! The cooking time varies, so start checking the texture after 30 minutes. You want to make sure that it is just tender, not at all gummy.

4 cups water
Salt
1 cup wild rice, rinsed and drained
¼ cup olive oil
2 tablespoons fresh lemon juice
4 ripe plum tomatoes, seeded and
    cut into ½-inch dice
1 cup peeled and diced (½ inch) hothouse
    (seedless) cucumber
¼ cup minced red onion
½ cup chopped fresh flat-leaf parsley
½ cup chopped fresh mint leaves
Freshly ground black pepper, to taste

1. Bring the water, with 1 tablespoon salt, to a boil in a heavy saucepan. Add the wild rice, reduce the heat to medium-low, and cook, uncovered, until it is tender, 30 to 45 minutes. Do not overcook. Drain it well and place it in a large bowl.

2. While it is still warm, toss the rice with the oil and lemon juice. Let the mixture cool to room temperature.

3. Add the remaining ingredients to the rice and toss well with a fork. Serve at room temperature.

Serves 6

DOWN-AND-DIRTY RICE

★ ★ ★

"**D**irty rice" is a real soul food of Louisiana Cajun origin, served as a side dish. The name refers to the color of the rice, created when chopped-up chicken gizzards and livers are added to it, and has nothing to do with the marvelous, pungent flavor, which is far from dirty. A toss of fresh parsley will give nice color to the plate.

½ pound chicken livers, rinsed and patted dry
½ pound chicken gizzards, trimmed, rinsed,
    and patted dry
6 ounces slab bacon, rind removed,
    cut into ¼-inch dice
½ cup diced (¼ inch) onion
½ cup diced (¼ inch) green bell pepper
3 garlic cloves, minced
1 teaspoon cumin
1 teaspoon coarse salt, or to taste
Freshly ground black pepper, to taste
½ teaspoon Tabasco sauce, or more
    to taste
1 cup long-grain white rice
1 tablespoon olive oil
2½ cups defatted chicken broth,
    preferably homemade (page 253)
2 scallions (3 inches green left on),
    thinly sliced on the diagonal
2 to 3 tablespoons chopped fresh flat-leaf
    parsley

1. Coarsely chop the livers with a sharp knife. Set aside.

2. Chop the gizzards fine in a food processor, pulsing the machine on and off. Set aside.

3. In a large heavy pot, cook the bacon over medium heat until it is just browned and crispy and the fat is rendered, 6 to 8 minutes. Add the liver and gizzards and cook, stirring, for 5 minutes.

4. Add the onions and green pepper and cook, strirring, until wilted, 8 minutes. Add the garlic and cook for another 2 minutes. Add the cumin, coarse salt, pepper, and Tabasco sauce; cook, stirring, for 2 minutes more.

5. Stir in the rice and the oil and cook, stirring, for 2 minutes.

6. Add the broth, stir, and bring to a boil. Reduce the heat to medium-low and simmer, covered, until the rice is tender and the liquid has been absorbed, 20 minutes. Fluff with a fork. Stir in the scallions and parsley, and serve.

Serves 6

RED RICE

★ ★ ★

I've tried red rice in every form and combination all over South Carolina's low country and into Savannah, Georgia. Traditionally a mixture of rice and tomatoes, it is a favorite of the locals and of more than a few transplanted North-

erners—at home, in mom-and-pop diners, and even in the most elegant dining spots.

Miss Daisy Mae, in her cafe at the BP gas station on Edisto Island, south of Charleston, South Carolina, feeds hundreds of folks a day from the batches she cooks up in her huge roasting pans. She invited me to watch as she mixed her magic together. Miss Daisy Mae didn't add too many ingredients other than ripe tomatoes, a little bacon, and, of course, rice. She keeps her specialty on the drier side of wet.

At the other end of the scale, at elegant Elizabeth's on 37th, a highly regarded, award-winning restaurant in Savannah, I was served a delicious, highly spiced red rice—moist, resembling risotto, resplendent with a tiny dice of ham, onions, and fresh tomatoes.

The following version is my own creation (creative license seems to be the trick in the Southern kitchen). I've filled it with bacon, baked ham, and lots of tomatoes. Since I prefer my red rice moist, I've used the juice from the tomatoes as well as chicken broth. Old Bay Seasoning is the spice of choice in this kitchen, but a cautious amount of mixed Cajun spice would be an appropriate substitute.

¼ pound slab bacon, rind removed, cut into
  ¼-inch dice
1 onion, cut into ¼-inch dice
1 red bell pepper, stemmed, seeded, and
  cut into ¼-inch dice
2 cups long-grain white rice
½ pound baked ham, cut into ¼-inch dice
½ teaspoon Old Bay Seasoning, or more
  to taste
1 can (14 ounces) plum tomatoes, chopped,
  with their juices
4 tomatoes, seeded and cut into ½-inch dice,
  juices saved
1 teaspoon sugar
4 cups defatted chicken broth, preferably
  homemade (page 253)

1. Cook the bacon in a large heavy pot over low heat until the fat is rendered and the bacon crisps slightly, 6 to 8 minutes. Using a slotted spoon, transfer the bacon to paper towels to drain. Discard all but 2 tablespoons of the fat in the pot.

2. Add the onion and pepper to the fat and cook over low heat, stirring, until wilted, 10 minutes. Add the rice and cook, stirring, 2 minutes. Add the reserved bacon, ham, and Old Bay Seasoning.

3. Add the canned and fresh tomatoes with their juices, the sugar, and chicken broth. Increase the heat and bring the mixture to a boil. Reduce the heat to medium-low, cover, and simmer gently, stirring once or twice, until most of the liquid has been absorbed and the rice is tender, 20 minutes. Serve piping hot.

Serves 8

A RISOTTO FOR SPRING

★ ★ ★

Garden asparagus, crisp peas, and woodsy morels combine with Arborio rice to make a meal that sings of spring. If fresh morels aren't available, try chanterelles or other wild mushrooms. It's the freshness of the dish that makes it so special. Serve this as an entrée or in small portions as an appetizer. It even works as a side dish with a roasted leg of lamb.

Wine: Willamette Valley (OR) Pinot Noir
Beer: Wisconsin brown lager

½ *pound medium-thick asparagus, tough ends removed*
1 *cup fresh or frozen peas*
6 *ounces fresh morels or other fresh wild mushrooms*
3 *tablespoons olive oil*
1 *onion, chopped*
1 *large clove garlic, finely minced*
5 *cups defatted chicken broth, preferably homemade (page 253)*
1½ *cups Arborio rice*
½ *cup dry white wine*
1 *tablespoon snipped fresh chives or chopped fresh flat-leaf parsley*
1 *tablespoon unsalted butter*
Salt and freshly ground black pepper, to taste
Freshly grated Parmesan cheese, for serving

1. Cut the asparagus on the diagonal into 1-inch pieces. Bring a saucepan of water to a boil, and cook the asparagus until bright green, 2 to 3 minutes. Drain, refresh under cold water, drain again, and set aside.

2. If you are using fresh peas, cook them in a pan of boiling water until bright green, 5 to 7 minutes. If you are using frozen peas, place them in a strainer to thaw. Set aside.

3. Halve the morels lengthwise and brush out any dirt. Heat 1 tablespoon of the olive oil in a nonstick skillet over medium heat. Add the mushrooms and sauté, shaking the pan, until they are just tender, 5 minutes. Set them aside.

4. Heat the remaining 2 tablespoons olive oil in a large heavy pot over low heat. Add the onion and cook, stirring occasionally, until wilted, 8 to 10 minutes. Add the garlic and cook 1 minute more.

5. While the onion is cooking, bring the chicken broth to a boil in a medium-size saucepan. Reduce the heat to a gentle simmer.

6. Raise the heat under the onion to medium-low, add the rice, and stir well with a

wooden spoon so that all the grains are evenly coated with oil. Add the wine and cook, stirring, until it has been absorbed by the rice, 3 to 4 minutes.

7. Add about ½ cup of the hot broth to the rice mixture and cook, stirring frequently, over medium heat until the broth has been absorbed. Repeat, making sure each addition has been absorbed before adding the next, until the rice is tender and nearly all the broth has been absorbed, 35 to 45 minutes. Stir in the asparagus, mushrooms, peas, and chives.

8. When all the broth has been absorbed but the risotto is still creamy, add the butter and season with salt and pepper. Serve immediately, passing a bowl of grated Parmesan cheese alongside.

Serves 4 to 6

COWBOY RICE SALAD

★ ★ ★

The cowboys of yore near the Mexico border loved their chili seasonings, and so do I, whether in steaming bowls of stick-to-your-bones red or in lighter dishes filled with nourishing vegetables and beans. While, this salad certainly wasn't chuck wagon fare, I created it for hearty outdoorsmen appetites. Serve it as a luncheon entrée or as a substantial accompaniment to a grilled salmon cookout in the backyard.

½ *pound sugar snap peas, strings removed*
1 *small onion, cut into ¼-inch dice*
1 *tablespoon olive oil*
1 *cup long-grain white rice*
¼ *teaspoon chili powder*
⅛ *teaspoon ground turmeric*
1 *piece (½ inch) of cinnamon stick*
3½ *cups defatted chicken broth, preferably homemade (page 253)*
Salt and freshly ground black pepper, to taste
2 *teaspoons finely grated lime zest*
½ *cup diced (¼ inch) red bell pepper*
¾ *cup cooked baby lima beans*
¾ *cup cooked dark red kidney beans*
½ *skinless, boneless chicken breast (about ¼ pound), cooked and shredded*
1 *small spicy smoked sausage (turkey or Cajun), cooked and cut into small pieces (optional)*
2 *tablespoons chopped fresh cilantro or fresh flat-leaf parsley*
½ *cup Luscious Lime Dressing (page 330)*
Lime wedges, for serving

1. Bring a saucepan of water to a boil, add the snap peas, and cook until bright green, 2 minutes. Drain, refresh under cold water, drain again, and set aside.

2. Place the onion and olive oil in a heavy saucepan. Cook over low heat, stirring, until the onion is wilted, 10 minutes. Stir in the rice, chili powder, turmeric, and cinnamon stick. Add the chicken broth and bring to a boil. Stir, reduce the heat, and simmer, covered, until the rice is tender, 20 minutes.

3. Fluff the rice with a fork and transfer it to a large bowl. Season with salt, pepper, and lime zest. Toss in the sugar snap peas, red bell pepper, limas, and kidney beans. Add the shredded chicken, the sausage, if using, the cilantro, and the vinaigrette, tossing gently. Adjust the seasonings. Serve at room temperature, with lime wedges, for squeezing.

Serves 6

Amber Waves

	RICE	STARTERS &, VEGETABLES	FLAVOR ENHANCERS
NEW ENGLAND	Long-grain white	Bacon fat, shallots, onions, carrots, corn, limas, broth	Bacon, salt pork, ham bone, maple syrup, molasses, clams
MID ATLANTIC	Long-grain white, short-grain white	Lard, onions, celery, carrots, corn, limas, broth	Baked ham, navy beans, molasses, sauerkraut, oysters, clams, crab
SOUTH	Long-grain white, brown, Texmati, Carolina gold	Vegetable oil, bacon fat, onions, green bell peppers, garlic, tomatoes, broth	Bacon, ham, salt pork, andouille, chicken livers, shrimp, black-eyed peas, red beans, greens
HEARTLAND	Long-grain white, wild	Butter, onions, red bell peppers, garlic, cabbage, corn, broth	Slab bacon, ham bone, sausage, shredded pork, wild mushrooms, cheese
CALIFORNIA	Brown , short-grain white, Calmati, jasmine	Olive oil, onions, garlic, artichokes, broth	Prosciutto, chicken, sun-dried tomatoes, olives, wine
PACIFIC NORTHWEST	Long-grain white, wild	Olive oil, Walla Walla onions, shallots, leeks, mushrooms, broth	Mussels, oysters, crab, wine, lentils
SOUTHWEST	Long-grain white, Texmati	Lard, onions, garlic, chili peppers, bell peppers, tomatoes, broth	Chorizo
HAWAII	Medium-grain white, long-grain brown, jasmine	Vegetable oil, onions, garlic, ginger, broth	Scallops, tuna, duck, coconut milk, soy sauce

# of Grain

SPICES	SIZZLERS	HERBS	SPARKLERS	GARNISHES
Bay leaves, cinnamon sticks, curry powder		Parsley, tarragon, chives	Cranberries, apple brandy, orange zest, red onion, peas	Chives, tarragon, lobster
Old Bay Seasoning		Mint, dill	Dill pickles, asparagus tips	Peanuts, pecans, watercress
Old Bay Seasoning, bay leaves, red pepper flakes, mace, curry powder	Tabasco sauce	Parsley, oregano, thyme		Scallions, citrus sections, peaches, flaked catfish, pecans
		Parsley, dill, mint	Brandy	Pecans, sunflower seeds, grated Cheddar cheese, dried cherries
Saffron	Chiles	Basil, sage, thyme, rosemary, oregano	Citrus juice, vinegar, soy sauce, capers	Bean sprouts, basil, avocado, edible flowers, yogurt, grated Monterey Jack, crumbled goat cheese, almonds, pine nuts
Caraway seeds	Hot Asian chili oil	Mint, chives, dill	Diced cucumber, dried blueberries, vodka	Caviar, smoked salmon or smoked trout, asparagus tips, grated Tillamook cheese, hazelnuts
Chili powder, cumin, cinnamon, vanilla	Cayenne, chili sauce, Tabasco sauce, chiles in adobo, chili peppers	Cilantro, chives	Salsa, lime zest	Cilantro, roasted bell peppers, grated Cheddar cheese, grated Monterey Jack, guacamole, sour cream
Curry powder	Hot Asian chili oil	Lemongrass, mint, cilantro, chives	Pineapple, mango, papaya, banana, coconut, lime juice, rice wine vinegar	Coconut, macadamia nuts, cashews, sesame seeds, bean sprouts, scallions

Luscious Lime Dressing

★

Fresh, light, and bursting with astringent lime flavor, this dressing enhances fresh vegetables, fruit, and even more robust entrée salads, like Cowboy Rice Salad or San Antonio Chicken Fiesta.

¼ cup fresh lime juice
1 teaspoon honey
2 teaspoons finely grated lime zest
1 teaspoon finely minced garlic
Salt and freshly ground black pepper, to taste
½ cup olive oil

1. Place the lime juice, honey, lime zest, garlic, salt, and pepper in a bowl. Whisk together.
2. Slowly drizzle in the olive oil, whisking constantly until thickened. Store, covered, in the refrigerator for up to 1 week. Bring to room temperature before using.
Makes about ¾ cup

MONDAY RED BEANS AND RICE

★ ★ ★

Once upon a time, everyone in New Orleans cooked red beans and rice on Mondays. The traditional recipe called for the beans to be simmered all day long, with lots of seasoning and pork hocks or spicy andouille sausage, which allowed the home cook to get the laundry done in the meantime. Fluffy rice and a good length of sausage completed the standard dish. It remains a New Orleans favorite. Don't add salt to the beans until they have finished cooking, as it will prevent them from softening. And don't substitute bouillon cubes for the broth—they are too salty for this dish.

Wine: Dry Creek Valley (CA) Zinfandel
Beer: Louisiana lager

1 cup dried red kidney beans
1¾ cups unsalted beef broth or chicken broth, preferably homemade (page 253)
¾ cup water
1 cup canned tomatoes, drained and crushed
1 teaspoon Tabasco sauce
2 bay leaves
½ pound slab bacon, rind removed, cut into ½-inch pieces
2 carrots, peeled and cut into ½-inch pieces
2 ribs celery, cut into ½-inch pieces
1 large onion, coarsely chopped
4 cloves garlic, finely minced
1 pound smoked andouille sausage, in large pieces
Salt and freshly ground black pepper, to taste
Cooked white rice, for serving

1. Pick over the beans, discarding any stones. Soak them overnight in cold water to cover by 2 inches (or see How to Quick-Soak Beans, page 336).

2. Drain the beans, rinse in several changes of cold water, and drain. Set them aside.

3. Preheat the oven to 350°F.

4. Combine the broth, water, crushed tomatoes, Tabasco sauce, and bay leaves in a large heavy ovenproof pot. Bring to a boil and remove from the heat.

5. Add the beans to the hot liquid. Stir in the bacon, carrots, celery, onion, and garlic. Bury the sausage in the center, cover, and bake in the oven for 1½ hours. Uncover and cook for 30 minutes more.

6. Remove and discard the bay leaf. Season with salt and pepper, and serve over rice.

Serves 6

BLUE PLATE

S·P·E·C·I·A·L

**Baked Cider-Glazed Apricot Ham
with Raisin Sauce**

Creamy Caraway Cabbage

Denver-Style Baked Beans

Shaker Applesauce

Boston Brown Bread

Lemon Chess Pie

DENVER-STYLE BAKED BEANS

★ ★ ★

I met Marion Staples several years ago while I was on one of my book tours. We have kept in touch and I was delighted when she sent me her lima bean recipe along with the following note: "Having lived in the West for so long, I've developed a spicier palate, tending to add more herbs, 'western seasonings,' peppers, and other 'hot stuff' to give my standard recipes a kick." I get a great kick out of her baked lima beans, too. The luxurious consistency makes this dish a perfect choice to serve along with honey-dipped fried chicken, potato salad, piccalilli, coleslaw, and biscuits.

1 pound dried lima beans
6 cups water
2 bay leaves
6 slices bacon
1 cup coarsely chopped celery
⅔ cup minced onion
½ cup diced (¼ inch) green bell pepper
2 teaspoons minced fresh cilantro leaves
1 clove garlic, minced
1 cup ketchup
⅔ cup light molasses
1 teaspoon dry mustard
1 teaspoon chili powder
1 teaspoon ground cumin
Pinch of freshly ground black pepper
Pinch of cayenne pepper
Salt, to taste

1. Pick over the limas, discarding any stones. Rinse the lima beans well, place them in a bowl with cold water to cover by 2 inches, and soak them overnight (or see How to Quick Soak Beans, page 336).

2. Preheat the oven to 350°F.

3. Drain the lima beans, rinse in several changes of cold water, and drain again. Place them in a large heavy pot with the 6 cups water and the bay leaves. Bring to a boil, reduce the heat, and simmer until the beans are slightly softened 30 minutes. While they are cooking, skim off any foam that rises to the surface.

4. Meanwhile, in a nonstick skillet over medium heat, cook 2 slices of the bacon until browned, 6 to 8 minutes. Remove them from the skillet, drain on paper towels, crumble and set aside. Add the celery, onion, bell pepper, cilantro, and garlic to the skillet and cook over medium heat, stirring occasionally, until wilted, about 10 minutes. Set aside.

5. Drain the lima beans, reserving 1½ cups of the cooking liquid, and place the beans and reserved liquid in a bowl. Discard the bay leaves. Stir in the cooked vegetables and bacon, the ketchup, molasses, mustard, chili powder, cumin, pepper, and cayenne.

6. Place the mixture in a shallow baking dish, and cover with the remaining 4 slices bacon. Bake, uncovered, until the beans are very tender, 1½ hours. Remove from the oven and season with salt. Once removed from the oven, the beans and sauce will thicken as they sit.

Serves 6 to 8

AUSTIN BAKED BEANS

★ ★ ★

Rhapsodizing over baked beans might seem silly, but the beans I ate at Jim Goode's Barbecue in Houston, Texas, justify the excess. I not only devoured his luscious beans at lunch, I had four

quarts sent up to New York to make the moment last a little longer. Here's my version: The beans are enriched with honey-baked ham and smoky bacon, with large chunks of apples added to sweeten the sauce, Texas style. Adding salt during cooking prevents the beans from softening, so hold off on the salt until the beans are cooked to your liking.

1 pound dried navy beans
6 ounces slab bacon, rind removed, cut into
    ½-inch dice
1 large onion, coarsely chopped
1 green bell pepper, stemmed, seeded, and
    cut into ¼-inch dice
1 red bell pepper, stemmed, seeded, and
    cut into ¼-inch dice
1 can (28 ounces) plum tomatoes, coarsely
    chopped, with their juices
½ pound honey-baked ham, cut into ¼-inch dice
1 smoked pork chop (about ½ pound), cut into
    ¼-inch dice
1 cup ketchup
¾ cup (packed) dark brown sugar
¼ cup honey
¼ cup dark molasses
1 tablespoon Worcestershire sauce
1 teaspoon dry mustard
2 Granny Smith apples, peeled, cored, and
    cut into 1-inch cubes
Salt, to taste

1. Pick over the beans, discarding any stones. Soak them overnight in cold water to cover by 2 inches (or see How to Quick-Soak Beans, page 336).

2. Drain the beans, rinse in several changes of cold water, and drain again.

3. Place the beans in a large heavy pot and add water to cover by 2 inches. Bring to a boil, reduce the heat to medium, and simmer until the beans are just tender but not mushy, 45 minutes. While they are cooking, skim off any foam that rises to the top. Drain and set aside.

4. Preheat the oven to 350°F.

5. Place the bacon in a heavy ovenproof pot. Cook over low heat until the fat is just rendered (do not brown the bacon), 5 to 6 minutes. Remove the bacon with a slotted spoon and set it aside. Add the onion to the pot and cook over low heat until wilted, 10 minutes. Add both bell peppers and cook, stirring, for another 5 minutes. Add the beans, reserved bacon, and the tomatoes (reserve the juices). Then add the remaining ingredients except the reserved tomato juices, apples, and salt, and fold together gently. Cover, transfer to the oven, and bake for 2 hours.

6. Add the apples and ½ cup of the reserved tomato juices, and bake, uncovered, until thick and fragrant, 2 hours. Season with salt, and serve hot and bubbly.

Serves 6 to 8

STEWED WHITE BEANS

★ ★ ★

I like my beans a little bit soupy—cooked until just tender but not at all mushy. If you like yours the same way, test a bean by squeezing it between your thumb and forefinger. A little resistance, then squish, means the beans are cooked perfectly. At that point I could eat them right out of the pot, but it's preferable to serve them in a shallow soup bowl with crusty bread, some Maytag Blue cheese, and an Oregon Pinot Noir.

1 pound dried white kidney beans
3 tablespoons extra virgin olive oil
1 onion, cut into ¼-inch dice
4 whole garlic cloves
4 whole allspice
4 carrots, peeled and cut into ½-inch dice
2 ribs celery, cut into ½-inch dice
3 large sprigs fresh thyme, or 1 teaspoon dried
2 bay leaves
6 cups unsalted defatted chicken broth,
*   preferably homemade (page 253)*
Finely grated zest of 1 lemon
Salt and freshly ground black pepper,
*   to taste*

1. Pick over the beans, discarding any stones. Rinse the beans, place them in a large bowl with cold water to cover by 2 inches, and soak overnight (or see How to Quick-Soak Beans, page 336).

2. Drain the beans, rinse them in several changes of cold water, and drain again.

3. Heat the oil in a large heavy pot over low heat. Add the onion and cook until wilted, 10 minutes, stirring occasionally. Add the garlic and allspice and cook for 5 minutes more.

4. Add the beans, carrots, celery, thyme, bay leaves, and broth. Bring to a boil. Then reduce the heat to a simmer, cover, and cook for 30 minutes. Uncover and cook until the beans are just tender but not mushy, 15 minutes.

5. Discard the garlic cloves, thyme sprigs, bay leaves, and allspice berries. Add the lemon zest, and season with salt and pepper. The beans will absorb most of the extra liquid as they cool down. Serve at room temperature.

Serves 6 to 8

The American

	BEANS	STARTERS & VEGETABLES	FLAVOR ENHANCERS
NEW ENGLAND	White kidney, navy, lima, cranberry	Bacon fat, onions, carrots, celery, corn, leeks, butternut squash	Bacon, salt pork, ham bone, barley, brown sugar, molasses, maple syrup, ketchup, Dijon mustard
MID ATLANTIC	White kidney, navy, lima	Peanut oil, onions, corn, cabbage	Salt pork, crab, Smithfield ham, sausage, duck, mustard, molasses
SOUTH	Black-eyed peas, black, red, red kidney, lima, pink	Bacon fat, salt pork, Vidalia onions, garlic, yams, collards, bell peppers	Bacon, ham hock, salt pork, Smithfield or country ham, andouille
HEARTLAND	Lima, Great Northern, white kidney, red kidney, navy, soy	Vegetable oil, bacon fat, salt pork, onions, garlic, celery, carrots, cabbage, spinach	Ham bone, kielbasa, bacon, brown sugar, tomato paste
CALIFORNIA	Garbanzo, fava, black, mung, lentils	Olive oil, onions, garlic, bell peppers, eggplant, tomatoes, olives	Lamb, roasted garlic, pasta
PACIFIC NORTHWEST	White kidney, lentils	Vegetable oil, onions, garlic, celery, ginger, apples	Salmon, crab, wild mushrooms, cranberries
SOUTHWEST	Anasazi, Appaloosa, pinto, pink	Olive oil, onions, garlic, bell peppers	Chorizo sausage, cocoa powder
HAWAII	Black, red kidney, black-eyed peas, adzuki, mung	Peanut oil, onions, garlic	Suckling pig

Bean Pot

SPICES	SIZZLERS	HERBS	SPARKLERS	GARNISHES
Bay leaves, cloves, dry mustard		Parsley, dill, thyme, tarragon, chives	Apple cider, cider vinegar	Chopped onions, grated Cheddar cheese, dried cranberries, pumpkin seeds
Bay leaves, Old Bay Seasoning		Chives, dill, chervil	Dry sherry, orange marmalade, roasted tomatoes	Tomatoes, julienned scallions, crab, candied orange
Bay leaves, cloves, peppercorns, curry powder	Cayenne, Tabasco sauce	Parsley, marjoram	Lemon juice, lime juice, sherry vinegar, orange zest	Mango, Vidalia onions, fried plantains, scallions, rice
Fennel seeds, bay leaves, allspice	Chili powder, BBQ sauce, chili sauce, red pepper flakes	Parsley, chives	Cider vinegar	Fried scallions, shredded endive, crystallized ginger
Saffron	Chili oil	Thyme, oregano, rosemary, basil, mint, sage, cilantro	Red wine vinegar, lemon juice, lime juice, citrus zest	Avocado, sun-dried tomatoes, mesclun, dried apricots, pesto, pine nuts, Monterey Jack, sour cream
Caraway seeds, coriander		Dill, chives, basil, mint	Cider vinegar	Scallions, radishes, Walla Walla onions, red onions, alfalfa sprouts, cucumber, beets, hard-cooked eggs
Cumin, cinnamon, allspice	Chili powder, chiles, chili sauce	Cilantro, oregano	Lime juice	Scallions, corn, pineapple, cilantro pesto, guacamole, sour cream, pine nuts, tortilla chips
Curry powder, ginger, lemongrass	Chili sauce, chiles chili oil	Basil, cilantro	Soy sauce, lime juice, rice vinegar	Pineapple, scallions, shredded coconut, peanuts, raisins, sesame seeds, mint

JAZZED-UP LIMAS AND BLACK-EYED PEAS

★ ★ ★

Among the dishes I sampled on my visit to Georgia was a particularly memorable one that combined limas and black-eyed peas. Never able to leave a recipe as I found it, I've jazzed up my beans 'n' peas with smoked pork chops and collards, making a robust one-dish meal. If you serve it alongside honey-dipped fried chicken and sweet potatoes, a Southern-style feast will be yours for the eating.

Wine: Sonoma County (CA) Cabernet Sauvignon
Beer: Colorado brown ale

½ pound dried black-eyed peas
½ pound dried baby lima beans
¼ pound slab bacon, rind removed,
    cut into ¼-inch dice
1 onion, chopped
4 whole garlic cloves
2 smoked pork chops (½ pound each),
    cut into ¼-inch dice
3 sprigs fresh thyme, or 1 teaspoon dried
1 bay leaf
6 cups unsalted defatted chicken
    broth, preferably homemade
    (page 253)
1 pound collard greens, washed,
    tough stems removed, coarsely
    chopped
1 teaspoon finely grated lemon
    zest
Coarsely ground black pepper,
    to taste

1. Pick over the peas and lima beans, discarding any stones. Soak them overnight in cold water to cover by 2 inches (or see box, below).

2. Drain the peas and beans, rinse in several changes of cold water, and drain again.

3. Place the bacon in a large heavy pot over low heat, and cook until the fat is rendered and the bacon has browned slightly, about 8 minutes. Add the onion, garlic, and pork, and cook, stirring, until the onions wilt slightly, 5 minutes.

4. Add the drained peas and beans along with the thyme, bay leaf, and broth. Bring to a boil, skimming off any foam that rises to the top. Reduce the heat to medium-low and simmer, covered, for 30 minutes.

5. Add the collards and lemon zest and return to a boil. Reduce the heat and cook, uncovered, until the beans are tender but not mushy and the collards are tender, 8 minutes. Season with black pepper and serve hot.

Serves 6 to 8

★★★★★★★★★★★★★★★★★★★★★★★

HOW TO QUICK-SOAK BEANS

—❧—

Place the picked-over beans in a large heavy pot with cold water to cover by 2 inches. Bring to a boil over medium-high heat and boil for 2 minutes. Remove from the heat and let stand for 1 hour, covered. Drain the beans, rinse in several changes of cold water, and drain again.

The beans are now ready to use in recipes.

★★★★★★★★★★★★★★★★★★★★★★★

CHARRO PINTOS

★ ★ ★

This dish will give you a little "Tex" and an equal dose of "Mex." The "Tex" part is the pinto beans, cooked, ranch style, while "Mex" comes from the spicing, echoing the savory zing of the Mexican *charro's comidas*, or cowboy's dinner.

Serve this dish as you would chili, in a bowl by itself or over rice or barley.

½ pound dried pinto beans
¼ pound slab bacon, rind removed, cut into
*   ¼-inch pieces*
1 tablespoon olive oil
1 large onion, cut into ½-inch dice
4 cloves garlic, finely minced
3 carrots, peeled and cut into ½-inch pieces
2 ribs celery, cut into ½-inch pieces
1 can (28 ounces) plum tomatoes, chopped,
*   drained (reserve juices)*
6 cups water
2 large sprigs fresh cilantro, stems lightly
*   bruised*
2 sprigs fresh thyme, or ½ teaspoon dried
½ teaspoon dried oregano
¼ cup chopped fresh cilantro leaves
Salt and freshly ground black pepper,
*   to taste*

1. Pick over the beans, discarding any stones. Soak them overnight in cold water to cover by 2 inches (or see box, facing).

2. Drain the beans, rinse in several changes of cold water, and drain again. Set them aside.

3. Place the bacon and oil in a large heavy pot over low heat, and cook until the fat is rendered and the bacon has browned slightly, about 8 minutes. Pour off all but 2 to 3 tablespoons of the fat. Add the onion and cook, stirring, until almost wilted, 8 minutes. Add the garlic and

cook stirring occasionally, for 2 minutes. Then add the carrots, celery, and the beans. Add the chopped tomatoes with ½ cup of reserved juices, and the water. Stir in the cilantro sprigs, thyme, and oregano. Bring to a boil. Reduce the heat to medium and simmer, uncovered, until the beans are tender but not mushy, about 1½ hours. While they are cooking, skim off any foam that rises to the surface.

4. Stir in the chopped cilantro, and season with salt and pepper. Serve immediately.
Serves 6

SUCCULENT WHITE BEANS

★ ★ ★

Riad Aamar, former chef-owner of the first-rate restaurant Doc's, on Lake Waramaug in New Preston, Connecticut, made more people happy with his beans than with any other dish. To make them as lush as Riad's, the trick is to add a little broth after they've finished cooking. I love to cook some penne pasta and serve these right over the top. But they are truly perfect on their own.

¾ pound white (Great Northern) beans
8 cups water
2 bay leaves
2 tablespoons extra virgin olive oil
2 large cloves garlic, sliced
4 sprigs fresh sage or thyme, or 1 teaspoon dried
3 ripe plum tomatoes, quartered lengthwise
2 cups defatted chicken broth, preferably
*   homemade (page 253)*
Salt and freshly ground black pepper, to taste
2 tablespoons chopped fresh flat-leaf parsley

1. Pick over the beans, discarding any stones. Soak them overnight in cold water to cover by 2 inches (or see How to Quick-Soak Beans, page 336).

2. Drain the beans, rinse in several changes of cold water, and drain again. Place the beans in a large heavy pot, and add the 8 cups water along with the bay leaves. Bring to a boil over high heat. Reduce the heat to medium and simmer until the beans are tender but not mushy, 40 to 45 minutes. While they are cooking, skim off any foam that rises to the surface. Remove the pot from the heat.

3. In another heavy pot, heat the olive oil over medium-low heat. Add the garlic and cook until lightly browned, 4 to 5 minutes. Add the beans, sage, tomatoes, and broth, and cook over medium heat for 5 minutes. Season with salt and pepper, garnish with parsley, and serve immediately.

Serves 4 to 6

BLACK BEAN SALAD

★ ★ ★

I find that you get the most flavor into your bean salad if you toss them with a vinaigrette or other dressing while they are still warm.

DRESSING
2 tablespoons fresh orange juice
1 teaspoon finely minced garlic
1 teaspoon finely grated orange zest
¼ teaspoon ground cumin
Salt and freshly ground black pepper,
*   to taste*
¼ cup extra virgin olive oil
2 tablespoons chopped fresh cilantro leaves

SALAD
½ pound dried black beans
4 cups water
2 garlic cloves, bruised
1 onion, halved
6 sprigs fresh flat-leaf parsley
2 ripe tomatoes, seeded and cut into
*   ¼-inch dice*
½ cup diced (¼ inch) red bell pepper
2 scallions (3 inches green left on),
*   thinly sliced on the diagonal*
½ teaspoon finely minced garlic
2 tablespoons chopped fresh cilantro leaves

1. Prepare the dressing: Combine the orange juice, garlic, orange zest, cumin, salt, and pepper in a bowl and whisk together well. Whisking constantly, drizzle in the olive oil. Continue whisking until the dressing is slightly thick. Stir in the chopped cilantro and set aside.

2. Prepare the salad: Pick over the beans, discarding any stones. Use the quick-soak method to prepare the beans (page 336). Place the drained beans in a heavy pot and add the 4 cups water.

3. Add the garlic, onion, and parsley sprigs. Bring to a boil, skim off the foam, and reduce the heat to medium. Simmer, uncovered, over medium heat until the beans are tender but not mushy, 30 to 40 minutes. Drain any excess liquid and transfer the beans to a bowl.

4. While they are still warm, toss the beans with the reserved dressing. Shortly before serving, add the tomatoes, red bell pepper, scallions, garlic, and cilantro, and stir well. Let rest at room temperature if serving immediately. If not, refrigerate, covered, until ready to use, bringing the dish to room temperature before serving.

Serves 4

Beef

For decades, we've been regarded as a nation of beef eaters. And we are. Our steakhouses are the world's best; our barbecued brisket is legendary. Our children are crazy about burgers. And meat loaf, for many of us, is Comfort Food Number One.

This wasn't always so. Although cattle arrived with the Spanish colonials, beef didn't outpace pork until the 1920s. That's surprising to read now, since most of us can picture in our minds the celebrated Texas longhorn drives of the mid-to-late nineteenth century that helped bring beef to Midwest railheads; for years, animals arrived via rail from Kansas City. Today's Texans and Kansans are fiercely proud of their beef cookery, which includes dishes like my juicy Skirt Steak Fajitas Party and smoky Barbecued Short Ribs of Beef. Northeasterners, who for years ate mostly corned beef, created slow-simmered dishes for it like New England Boiled Dinner.

You'll find venison and buffalo in this chapter, too. Once upon a time, these were much more common than beef. Enterprising ranchers are now raising the animals our forebears hunted. If your butcher doesn't carry them yet, pester him a bit!

ROASTED TENDERLOIN OF BEEF

★ ★ ★

An elegant tenderloin of beef is an entrée long associated with special occasions. Butter-soft and priced accordingly, this is one meat whose flavor you don't want to mask. Slivers of garlic, and salt, and pepper are about all you need. Tenderloin is best started at a high oven temperature to sear in the juices and then finished at a lower heat to hold them in. In summer, I serve slices of the beef at room temperature with tomatoes and basil leaves alternating between the slices. It is a slightly unusual presentation that helps to lighten the dish and make it appropriate for warm-weather parties.

Wine: Napa Valley (CA) Cabernet Sauvignon
Beer: New York State stout

1 tenderloin of beef (about 3¾ pounds)
3 cloves garlic, thinly slivered
1 tablespoon olive oil
Coarse salt and coarsely ground black pepper,
*   to taste*
5 to 6 ripe tomatoes, sliced ¼ inch thick
Leaves from 1 large bunch fresh basil

   1. Preheat the oven to 425°F.

   2. With the point of a small sharp knife, cut small slits into the meat and insert the garlic slivers into them. Brush the meat with the olive oil, and rub it with coarse salt and pepper.

   3. Place the meat on a rack in a shallow roasting pan and roast it for 15 minutes. Then reduce the temperature to 350°F and roast for another 20 minutes for medium rare, 5 minutes longer for medium. Let the roast rest at room temperature for 20 minutes before slicing.

   4. Slice the tenderloin about ½ inch thick, and arrange the slices on a platter, placing 1 slice of tomato and 1 basil leaf between each slice of meat.

Serves 12

PAUL McILHENNY'S TABASCO-SEARED STEAK

★ ★ ★

I was fortunate to be able to visit Tabasco's Paul McIlhenny, a prominent member of the family that has given the world the famous Avery Island, Louisiana, hot sauce. While I was there, this excellent avocational chef waxed ecstatic about his recipe for a zesty rib-eye steak. I had some trepidation about trying it, wondering if I'd burn up from the combination of Tabasco and cracked pepper that he had liberally used to coat the meat. Well, it was quite the contrary. Together those two fiery ingredients complemented rather than overpowered the meat, and I whole-heartedly recommend you try it next time you're firing up the grill. Serve it with Eula Mae Dore's Potato Salad, Celery Root Rémoulade, and corn on the cob.

Wine: Napa Valley (CA) Syrah
Beer: Maine porter

1 rib-eye steak, 1½ inches thick (about 1 pound)
Tabasco sauce, to taste
Cracked black pepper, to taste

1. Prepare a barbecue grill with medium-hot coals.

2. Sprinkle one side of the steak with several dashes of Tabasco sauce, and smear the Tabasco around well with the back of a spoon. Then sprinkle the same side generously with cracked pepper. Grill the steak, prepared side down, for 3 to 5 minutes.

3. Sprinkle the uncooked side of the steak with Tabasco, spreading it with the back of the spoon, and sprinkle it with cracked pepper. Turn the steak over and grill for 3 to 5 minutes for medium-rare.

4. Let the steak rest for 5 minutes before cutting it into thin slices on the diagonal. Serve immediately.
Serves 2

BARBECUED STEAK

★ ★ ★

A porterhouse is a great cut of beef containing just about everything you would want in a steak: a piece of succulent loin divided by a T-bone (great for gnawing on) from a piece of tender fillet. The fat that surrounds the meat adds flavor to the steak, so leave it on for cooking. Once grilled, trim it off. For the best result I choose a thick cut, which I then thinly slice as I serve it.

Wine: Texas Cabernet Sauvignon
Beer: Texas Belgian-style ale

½ cup Goode's BBQ Beef Rub (recipe follows)
1 porterhouse steak, 2 inches thick (about 2¾ pounds)

1. Rub the steak well all over with the BBQ Rub. Wrap it tightly in plastic wrap and let it rest in the refrigerator overnight.

2. Prepare a barbecue grill with medium-hot coals.

3. Grill the steak for 10 to 12 minutes per side for medium-rare meat, or more or less to your taste.

4. Let the steak rest for 5 to 10 minutes before slicing it thin. Serve immediately.
Serves 4

Goode's BBQ Beef Rub

★

R ubs are dry herb and spice combinations that are applied, before cooking, to meat, poultry, and fish, to deeply flavor and season them. This is the concoction of Houston's barbecue master Jim Goode, whose superior BBQ Mop appears on page 348.

A VISIT TO AVERY ISLAND

—❦—

Tabasco sauce, with its well-deserved capital "T," has been an American pantry staple for decades. Almost every kind of restaurant uses it, too—Tex-Mex, Cajun, Cuban, Caribbean, you name it! It's the mother of all pepper sauces, made by the descendants of Edmund McIlhenny, the man who created it a century and a half ago. Tabasco production hasn't left McIlhenny's farm, either; today it's still brewed and bottled on his 2,500-acre Avery Island (actually a hill on an ancient salt deposit), in the Louisiana Gulf Coast marshlands. Over the years, his progeny have turned the place into a paradise, with a water-bird sanctuary, a botanical garden, fields of sugar cane and bright peppers, and roadways lined with moss-swagged live oaks.

The McIlhenny clan didn't start out so fortunate. Union invasion forced Edmund and his brood to flee the island during the Civil War; and the aftermath wasn't pretty. Their once-lucrative salt mines were flooded and their sugar-cane crop destroyed. But fiery little Mexican capsicums planted just before the war flourished. McIlhenny ground them with local salt, aged them thirty days in crockery jars, and added vinegar. The result was liquid gold. By 1868, he was selling hundreds of bottles. In 1870 he got a patent and named his product "Tabasco," from a Central American Indian word meaning "land where the soil is humid."

Today's recipe doesn't differ much from the original. Peppers are mashed together with Avery Island salt (at which point their aroma can clear sinuses), then fermented in oak barrels for three years. The aged pulp is inspected for color, smell, and moisture level before it's pumped into vats and blended with distilled white vinegar. This mixture is stirred for several weeks and strained before it goes into McIlhenny's distinctive slim bottles with red caps, green-foil neckbands, and diamond-shaped labels.

When I visited Avery Island, I'd been adding Tabasco's sweet, smoky heat to deviled lamb chops, buffalo chicken wings, and Bloody Marys for years. It was great fun to see at last where it comes from. I also got to observe how the makers themselves use it when I lunched with Paul McIlhenny, Edmund's great-grandson, in his executive dining room. Eula Mae Dore, a retired employee and old family friend, had done the cooking; I was soon to find out why Paul called her "Avery Island's great treasure."

She started us out with tall, mint-garnished glasses of iced tea and plates of eggy potato salad. Paul doused his salad with Tabasco jalapeño sauce and I followed suit. Steaming bowls of gumbo followed, spiced with onions, garlic, peppers, and, of course, Tabasco. Dessert, a moist chocolate bread pudding, was heavenly. But no recipes! Like many great cooks, Eula Mae never uses one. She did tell me how to make her delicious potato salad, however, and I've included it in this book. And check out Paul's Tabasco-laden recipe for seared steak, on page 340.

2½ tablespoons dark brown sugar
2 tablespoons paprika
2 teaspoons dry mustard
2 teaspoons onion powder
2 teaspoons garlic powder
1½ teaspoons dried basil
1 teaspoon ground bay leaf
    (about 1 leaf; see Note)
¾ teaspoon ground coriander
¾ teaspoon ground savory
¾ teaspoon dried thyme
¾ teaspoon freshly ground
    black pepper
¾ teaspoon freshly ground
    white pepper
⅛ teaspoon ground cumin
Salt, to taste

   Mix all the ingredients together in a small bowl. Store in an airtight container for up to 4 months.
   Makes ¾ cup

NOTE: To grind bay leaves, crumble them and place in a clean spice or coffee grinder. Grind to a fine powder.

SPEARFISH CANYON BUFFALO STEAK

★ ★ ★

I visited buffalo farms in the Black Hills of South Dakota while developing recipes for this book and had the opportunity to see regenerated herds dotting much of the landscape there. As the demand for leaner meat grows in America, buffalo is increasing in popularity, and no wonder. The rich, tender meat produced by the buffalo is lean, and free of any hormones, steroids, and antibiotics. At the Cheyenne Crossing Cafe, outside of Deadwood, I sampled both buffalo steak and buffalo burger. They were mouthwatering.

   Once back in New York, I was able to find buffalo meat available in a local butcher shop, so I prepared it at home. I invite you to do the same, but first a couple of pointers. One, you must be prepared to eat your steak rare. This succulent meat is very lean and therefore should not be overcooked. And two, it must also be cooked quickly over high heat. That said, eat and enjoy.

Wine: Colorado Merlot
Beer: Massachusetts porter

1 buffalo steak, cut 1½ inches thick
    (about ¾ pound)
1 teaspoon olive oil
Coarse salt and coarsely ground black pepper,
    to taste

   1. Prepare a barbecue grill with very hot coals.
   2. Brush the steak on both sides with the olive oil, and sprinkle with coarse salt and pepper.
   3. Grill the steak over high heat for 3 minutes per side (it must be rare because it has no fat to add tenderness). Let the meat rest for 2 to 3 minutes.
   4. Cut the steak into thin slices on the diagonal, and serve immediately.
   Serves 1 to 2

SKIRT STEAK FAJITA PARTY

★ ★ ★

Relatively inexpensive, yet one of the juiciest cuts of beef, skirt steak is a perfect choice for beef fajitas. Most people like to assemble their own, so I set out the meat and toppings, along with a basket of warm tortillas, and let them have that pleasure. Since fajitas are eaten handheld and can be drippy, supply plenty of napkins.

Wine: Monterey County (CA) Petite-Sirah
Beer: New York State porter

MARINADE
2 tablespoons extra virgin olive oil
1½ tablespoons fresh lime juice
½ teaspoon chili powder
½ teaspoon ground cumin
¼ teaspoon salt
2 dashes Tabasco sauce, or more to taste
4 cloves garlic, pressed

FAJITAS
1 skirt steak (about 1½ pounds), cut in half crosswise
2 tablespoons olive oil
2 red bell peppers, stemmed, seeded, and cut into ¼-inch strips
1 green bell pepper, stemmed, seeded, and cut into ¼-inch strips
1 red onion, halved lengthwise and cut into ¼-inch slivers
Salt and freshly ground black pepper, to taste
12 flour tortillas (7½-inch diameter), warmed
1½ cups Pico de Gallo (page 196)
1½ cups Guacamole (page 176)
¼ cup chopped fresh cilantro leaves

1. Combine the marinade ingredients and pour the mixture over the meat in a medium-size bowl. Cover loosely and marinate in the refrigerator for 2 hours.

2. Thirty minutes before you are ready to cook, prepare a barbecue grill with hot coals.

3. Grill the skirt steak for 3 to 4 minutes per side (depending on the thickness) for medium-rare meat. Transfer the steak to a cutting board and let it rest for 10 minutes.

4. While the steak is resting, heat the olive oil in a nonstick skillet over medium-high heat. Sauté both bell peppers and the red onion, stirring occasionally, until wilted, 8 to 10 minutes. Season with salt and pepper and transfer to a serving bowl.

5. Slice the steak against the grain into ¼-inch-thick diagonal strips. Place the steak on a serving platter.

6. Set out the steak, peppers and onion mixture, a basket of tortillas, and bowls of Pico de Gallo, Guacamole, and the chopped cilantro. To assemble the fajitas, place a few strips of the steak in the middle of a tortilla. Top with some pepper and onion strips, a spoonful of Pico de Gallo, a dollop of Guacamole, and a sprinkling of chopped cilantro. Fold the tortilla sides in toward the middle, pick up, eat, and enjoy.

Serves 6

NEW ENGLAND BOILED DINNER

★ ★ ★

Similar to the French *pot au feu*, the Italian *bollito misto*, and the Irish corned beef and cabbage, this robust one-dish meal combines slowly cooked meat with hearty winter vegetables.

While the assertive cabbage, Brussels sprouts, and rutabagas are sometimes cooked along with the meat, I prefer to cook them separately. I add the leeks, carrots, and parsnips during the last half hour to get maximum flavor in the meat and broth. Be sure to boil the beets by themselves or they will color everything red. My recipe calls for a fresh brisket, but if you prefer, a corned brisket may be substituted. With either, the final result is delicious, especially when accompanied by Horseradish Mustard Tarragon Sauce and Fresh Whole-Cranberry Relish.

Wine: Long Island (NY) Merlot
Beer: New Hampshire porter

1 beef brisket (4½ to 5 pounds; not first-cut)
2 onions
8 whole cloves
6 cloves garlic
6 black peppercorns
2 teaspoons coarse salt, or more to taste
6 cups defatted beef broth, preferably homemade (page 252), or more if needed
8 small beets, trimmed of all but 1 inch of stems, root left intact
4 white turnips (½ pound each), peeled and halved
8 small red-skinned new potatoes, scrubbed
1 rutabaga (1½ pounds), peeled and cut into large chunks
1 pint Brussels sprouts
1 head green cabbage (2 pounds), cored and quartered
8 small or 4 large parsnips, peeled and halved lengthwise if large
8 medium-small leeks (3 inches green left on), trimmed and well rinsed
8 carrots, peeled and halved lengthwise if large
6 cups water
2 tablespoons chopped fresh flat-leaf parsley
Horseradish Mustard Tarragon Sauce (recipe follows), for serving
Fresh Whole-Cranberry Relish (page 184), for serving

1. Place the brisket in a large heavy pot. Stud each onion with 4 whole cloves and add them to the pot along with the garlic, peppercorns, and coarse salt. Add the broth and bring to a boil. Then reduce the heat to a simmer and cook, partially covered, until just tender, 2½ hours. Check the liquid level every 30 minutes, adding more broth if it's getting low.

2. While the meat is cooking, prepare the vegetables: Place the beets in a medium-size saucepan, add water to cover, and bring to a boil; cook until tender, 30 to 40 minutes. Let cool until easy to handle, then trim, peel, halve, and set aside, keeping the beets separate from the other vegetables.

3. Bring a large pot of salted water to a boil. Add the turnips, potatoes, and rutabaga. Bring back to a boil and cook until tender: 20 to 25 minutes for the turnips, 25 to 30 minutes for the potatoes, and 40 to 45 minutes for the rutabaga. As the vegetables are done, remove them from the pot with a slotted spoon and set them aside.

4. While the vegetables are cooking, trim the stems and coarse leaves off the Brussels sprouts, and cut an "X" in the stem end of each one.

5. Once all of the first vegetables are done, add the Brussels sprouts and cabbage to the pot, and cook until tender: 7 minutes for the Brussels sprouts and 15 minutes for the cabbage. Remove with a slotted spoon and set aside.

6. When the brisket is ready, transfer it to a plate and strain the broth into another pot that is large enough to hold the meat and the vegetables. Place the meat in the strained broth, and add the parsnips, leeks, and carrots. Add the water (or enough to cover) and bring to a boil. Reduce the heat to a simmer and cook, partially covered, until the meat is fork-tender and the vegetables are cooked through, 30 minutes. Remove the meat from the broth, allowing the vegetables to sit in the broth, off the heat, until ready to serve.

7. Trim any excess fat off the meat and let the meat rest at least 15 minutes before slicing. Just before slicing, heat the broth (with the parsnips, leeks, and carrots) over low heat. Add all the reserved vegetables except the beets to the broth to warm through. Remove all the vegetables to the platter for serving, then add the beets to the broth to warm through.

8. Cut the brisket into thin diagonal slices against the grain. Transfer to a large serving platter and surround the meat with all the vegetables. Just before bringing it to the table, drizzle with some hot broth and sprinkle parsley over all. Fill a gravy boat with hot broth and serve it alongside, along with a pot of mustard, a bowl of Horseradish Tarragon Sauce, and a bowl of Fresh Whole-Cranberry Relish.

Serves 8

Horseradish Mustard Tarragon Sauce

★

Light and flavorful, this sauce is the classic complement to the renowned New England boiled dinner or a standing rib roast. If you can't find fresh tarragon, I recommend using fresh chives, which are usually available all year round, instead of the dried herb.

1 cup mayonnaise
2 tablespoons Dijon mustard
3 tablespoons drained prepared
    white horseradish
1 tablespoon chopped fresh tarragon or
    snipped fresh chives
1 cup heavy (or whipping) cream,
    whipped

In a small bowl, mix the mayonnaise, mustard, horseradish, and tarragon together. Using a rubber spatula, fold in the whipped cream. Cover and refrigerate before use. (Serve within 6 hours for the freshest flavor and best texture.)

Makes about 2 cups

SHAKER CRANBERRY BRISKET

★ ★ ★

When I spent time at the Shaker Village in Hancock, Massachusetts, I not only learned about the religious beliefs and customs of this communal sect, but also enjoyed a firsthand taste of their culinary legacy. Relying on local and home-grown foods, the Shaker sisters of the eighteenth and nineteenth centuries prepared meals for the entire community. One of their specialties was a brisket made sweet and savory by the addition of cranberry sauce. I'm a lover of meat dishes that incorporate fruit, and although this one wasn't on the menu during my visit, the combination sounded so intriguing, I developed my own recipe using the two ingredients. It may not be the official version, but it is delicious. Serve it with Creamy Leek Ribbons and Whipped Sweet Potatoes.

Wine: Santa Barbara County (CA) Pinot Noir
Beer: Rhode Island stout

1 first-cut beef brisket (4½ to 5 pounds)
Coarsely ground black pepper, to taste
3 tablespoons olive oil
4 carrots, peeled and cut into 1-inch lengths
2 onions, halved lengthwise and slivered
2 cloves garlic, lightly bruised
6 whole cloves
2 cups Fresh Whole-Cranberry Relish
  (page 184)
Salt, to taste

1. Preheat the oven to 350°F.

2. Sprinkle the meat generously with pepper, pressing it in slightly.

3. Heat the oil in a large heavy ovenproof pot over low heat. Add the meat, raise the heat to medium-high, and brown well on all sides, 8 to 10 minutes per side. Transfer the meat to a plate.

4. Add the carrots, onions, garlic, and cloves to the pot, and cook, stirring, over medium heat until wilted, 5 minutes. Turn off the heat and add the cranberry relish. Stir to mix it into the vegetables.

5. Place the meat on top of the vegetables, and pour in any accumulated juices. Cover and bake in the center of the oven for 2 hours.

6. Remove the pot from the oven, but leave the oven heat on. Scrape the sauce off the brisket, transfer it to a cutting board, and let it rest for 15 minutes. Cut the brisket into thin diagonal slices against the grain. Gather the slices back together and return them to the pot.

Cover the meat completely with the sauce, and season with salt and pepper.

7. Bake, uncovered, basting the meat occasionally with the sauce, until it is tender, about 1½ to 2 hours. Serve hot, with lots of sauce on top or alongside.
Serves 8

BRISKET BBQ WITH GOODE'S MOP

★ ★ ★

When I visited Houston, Jim Goode, that city's premiere pit master, invited me to watch as he created the barbecued beef for which he is famous. As is traditional, he liberally applied a spicy vinegar sauce to huge sides of fire-cooked meat with a clean rag mop. Each of the sauce's twenty-one ingredients contributes to the extraordinary flavor, and it's well worth adding to your barbecue-basting repertoire. My version calls for the meat to be baked in the oven in the sauce. A small dish-washing mop—or kitchen spoon—will be more to the scale of the meats you'll be barbecuing at home. Serve this with Lone Star Creamy Potato Salad and Corky's Memphis-Style Cole Slaw.

Wine: California Zinfandel
Beer: Texas lager

1 first-cut beef brisket (4½ to 5 pounds)
½ cup Goode's BBQ Beef Rub (page 341)
2 tablespoons olive oil
8 carrots, peeled and halved
    crosswise
3 cups Goode's BBQ Mop
    (recipe follows)

1. The night before you plan to serve the brisket, rub it well all over with the BBQ Beef Rub. Wrap it well in plastic wrap, and refrigerate it overnight for the meat to absorb the flavor of the rub.

2. Preheat the oven to 350°F.

3. Heat the olive oil in a large heavy pot over medium-high heat, and brown the brisket well on both sides, 8 to 10 minutes per side (see Note). Add the carrots and the BBQ Mop. Cover, and bake in the oven for 2 hours.

4. Remove the pot from the oven, but leave the oven on. Scrape the sauce off the brisket, transfer it to a cutting board, and let it rest for 15 minutes. Cut the brisket, across the grain, into ¼-inch-thick slices. Gather the slices together, return them to the pot, and spoon or mop the sauce over them. Cover and cook, basting occasionally with the sauce, until the meat is fork tender, 1½ hours.

Serves 8

NOTE: For the most authentic barbecue flavor, the meat should be browned on an outdoor grill over medium-hot coals for 10 minutes per side before baking it. If you want to enhance the meat further, begin the fire on the grill with mesquite chips—or for a more subtle effect, hickory chips—instead of charcoal.

Goode's BBQ Mop

— ★ —

Adding a couple of tablespoons of Jim Goode's beef rub to his mop gives the mop a ready-made flavorful boost of herbs and spices. To further enhance the mopping process, if fresh thyme is available, tie a bundle of it together with kitchen string and use it to mop the meat with the sauce.

4 cups defatted beef broth, preferably
    homemade (page 252)
2 bay leaves
1 teaspoon dried oregano
2 tablespoons unsalted butter
¼ cup chopped onion
¼ cup chopped celery
¼ cup chopped green bell pepper
¼ cup minced garlic
2 tablespoons Goode's BBQ Beef Rub
    (page 341)
½ teaspoon dry mustard
½ teaspoon salt
½ teaspoon freshly ground white pepper
½ teaspoon freshly ground black pepper
¼ teaspoon cayenne pepper
Finely grated zest of 2 lemons
Juice of 2 lemons
2 tablespoons soy sauce
2 tablespoons white
    wine vinegar
1 tablespoon olive oil
1 tablespoon sesame oil
1 pound smoked bacon,
    finely chopped

1. Place the beef broth in a saucepan and bring it to a boil. Reduce the heat to a simmer and add the bay leaves and oregano.

2. Meanwhile, melt the butter in a nonstick skillet over medium-high heat. Add the onion, celery, bell peppers, garlic, Beef Rub, mustard, salt, white and black peppers, and cayenne. Cook until browned, 5 to 7 minutes. Then add this to the beef broth and stir to combine.

3. Add the lemon zest, lemon juice, soy sauce, vinegar, olive oil, and sesame oil to the simmering broth.

4. Cook the bacon in a nonstick skillet until soft but not crisp, about 6 minutes. Add the bacon and any rendered fat to the beef broth mixture. Continue simmering until the mixture has reduced by one fourth, 45 minutes to 1 hour. Adjust the seasonings, and baste away! Any unused sauce will keep, covered, in the refrigerator for up to 3 days. Or it may be frozen.

Makes about 6 cups

A GREAT PIT MASTER BARBECUES UP A STORM

Houston's barbecue great, Jim Goode, eases languidly into his day. I found him outside the original Goode's Barbecue (there are two), on Kirby Drive, washing his car before the lunchtime onslaught. Jim does brisket—and honey-smoked ham, Czech sausage, jalapeño pork sausage, and spicy pork. He serves up barbecue po' boys, a jalapeño corn bread that critics rave about, and a pecan pie that I rave about. I came for lunch with a big appetite, but I couldn't sample everything; there was too much! So I opted for brisket and ribs, with some pickle-laced potato salad and tangy Austin-style baked beans on the side. Dining was *al fresco*, at long picnic tables set with salt, pepper, and Tabasco. Although there were many seats, I still had to fight for a place.

Tourists love Goode because he's a showman. He cut a dramatic figure the day we met, sporting a flowing, jet-black beard and black ten-gallon hat. He's decked out both his barbecue houses with buffalo heads, snakeskins, and stuffed armadillos; and each has a "Hall of Flame" that's chockablock with souvenirs—barbecue sauces, marinades, salsas, seasonings, dried peppers, cookbooks, and wood for smoking. Houstonians love him, too, because he's an inspired, indigenous barbecue wizard. His craft is pure Texas and he is a state treasure.

Goode Company BBQ is located at 5109 Kirby Drive, two blocks south of Highway 59, Houston, Texas 77098; (713) 522-2530 and at 8911 Katy Freeway, Houston, Texas 77024; (713) 464-1901. The hours at both locations are 11 AM to 10 PM.

SUMPTUOUS SOUTHWESTERN BRISKET

★ ★ ★

My niece, who usually makes brisket for our Rosh Hashanah meal, passed the job on to me while I was working on this book. In the past, both my niece and I have cooked this family-occasion meat pretty traditionally with onions, carrots, and tomatoes. But, for a change of pace, I decided to try something different. A recent visit through the Southwest inspired me to add cinnamon, olives, capers, raisins, and chile to the pot. It was a stretch for Rosh Hashanah, but one my family loved—the flavor combination was so delicious and the gravy so festive—that I urge you to try it for your next family get-together. Meanwhile, I think I've earned the Rosh Hashanah job for life.

Wine: California Zinfandel
Beer: Texas lager

1 first-cut beef brisket (4½ to 5 pounds)
Coarsely ground black pepper,
    to taste
2 tablespoons olive oil
2 onions, halved lengthwise and slivered
6 carrots, peeled and cut into 1-inch lengths
    on the diagonal
2 tablespoons minced garlic
1 teaspoon ground cinnamon
2 cans (28 ounces each) plum tomatoes
1 cup small pitted green Spanish olives
½ cup golden raisins
2 tablespoons drained tiny capers
1 tablespoon dark brown sugar
1 small dried hot chile, or to taste
Salt, to taste

1. Preheat the oven to 350°F.

2. Sprinkle the brisket all over with the pepper, pressing it in slightly.

3. Heat the oil in a large ovenproof pot over medium-high heat. Add the peppered brisket and brown it well on both sides, 8 to 10 minutes per side. Transfer the meat to a large plate.

4. Pour off most of the fat in the pot. Add the onions and carrots and cook over medium heat, stirring and scraping up any brown bits on the bottom, until the onions are golden, about 10 minutes. Then stir in the garlic and cinnamon and cook, stirring constantly, for 1 minute more.

5. Drain the tomatoes, reserving 1 cup of the juices. Crush the tomatoes and add them to the pot along with the reserved juices, olives, raisins, capers, brown sugar, chile, and salt.

6. Return the meat to the pot, placing it on top of the vegetables, and spoon some sauce over it. Cover, and bake for 2 hours.

7. Remove the pot from the oven, but leave the oven on. Scrape the sauce off the brisket, transfer it to a cutting board, and let it rest for 15 minutes. Cut the brisket into thin diagonal slices against the grain. Gather the slices back together and return them to the pot, covering them completely with the sauce. Season with salt and pepper.

8. Bake uncovered, basting occasionally, until the meat is fork-tender, 1½ to 2 hours. Serve with the sauce on top or alongside, removing the chile before serving.

Serves 8

SMOTHERED BEEF SHANKS

★ ★ ★

Beef shanks are easy to make and perfect for feeding a hungry crowd on a wintry day. There will be plenty of meat, but be sure to portion out the marrow bones (the marrow is delicious, and scoopable with a teaspoon). Go heavy on the pepper as the meat is browning—the end result will be all the more flavorful.

Wine: Washington State Cabernet Sauvignon
Beer: Oregon stout

2 tablespoons olive oil
6 pieces of beef shank (from the hind shank)
    2 inches thick (about 1½ pounds each)
Salt and freshly ground black pepper,
    to taste
2 onions, halved lengthwise and slivered
6 cloves garlic
1 cup defatted beef broth, preferably homemade
    (page 252)
½ cup dry red wine
4 large sprigs fresh thyme, or 1 teaspoon dried
1 to 2 tablespoons chopped fresh flat-leaf parsley,
    for garnish
Hot cooked egg noodles, for serving

1. Preheat the oven to 350°F.
2. Heat the oil in a large heavy ovenproof pot. Add the beef shanks and brown them well over medium-high heat, in batches if necessary, about 15 minutes per side, sprinkling them with salt and a generous grinding of pepper. Remove the meat from the pot and set aside.
3. Reduce the heat to medium-low, add the onions, and sauté, stirring, for 5 minutes. Add the garlic and cook for 2 minutes more.
4. Add the broth, wine, and thyme and bring to a boil. Return the meat to the pot. Cover, and bake in the oven until the meat is fork-tender, 3 hours (see Note). Sprinkle with the parsley, and serve in shallow bowls filled with egg noodles. Don't forget to supply spoons for the marrow.
Serves 6

NOTE: When you take the pot out of the oven, it may be a good idea to remove the meat from it and pour the sauce through a gravy separator to remove the fat. This can also be done by careful skimming.

ALL-AMERICAN FIREPOT

★ ★ ★

A cold March night found me in the country, wanting to cook dinner over an open fire. I had just had an old brass pot retinned, and it was the perfect size to hang on the iron crane in the fireplace. When the local supermarket had no short ribs for this hearty dish, the butcher suggested beef shanks instead. They were delicious and meaty, and had the bonus of a large, flavorful marrow bone. To duplicate this earthy meal, you must use a variety of hardwoods that will give you a good bed of warm red coals. You'll also have to add logs to the fire throughout the cooking to keep the fire hot and steady for three or four hours. The amount of broth may seem excessive, but much will evaporate during the long simmer. Although not as dramatic, the meal can be easily prepared on top of the stove as well. You do lose the smoky flavor the wood provides (see Note). A good bread, a fine cheese, and a nice bottle of red wine are all that is necessary to complete a spectacular meal.

Wine: Sonoma County (CA) Merlot
Beer: California porter

6 pieces of beef shank (from the hind shank)
   1½ inches thick (about 1 pound each)
6 cloves garlic
6 carrots, cut into 1-inch lengths
4 ribs celery, cut into 1-inch lengths
12 sprigs fresh flat-leaf parsley
4 onions, halved
6 whole cloves
4 black peppercorns
Pinch of salt
4 sprigs fresh thyme, or 1½ teaspoons
   dried
1 bay leaf
4 quarts water
1 pound white mushrooms, wiped clean with
   a damp cloth
2 chickens (about 2½ pounds each),
   each cut into 8 pieces
⅓ cup pearl barley, rinsed
¼ cup chopped fresh flat-leaf parsley

1. Prepare a fireplace with a good hot fire using two types of hardwood, if possible.

2. Place the beef shanks, garlic, carrots, celery, and parsley in a large cast-iron Dutch oven with a metal handle. Stud the onions with the cloves, and add them to the pot along with the peppercorns, salt, thyme, and bay leaf.

3. Hang the pot on the crane in the fireplace, 5 to 6 inches from the logs, and add the water to the pot (it must cover the ingredients). Bring to a boil over the hot fire, using a long-handled spoon to skim off any foam that rises to the top. Continue to cook, skimming, for 1½ hours. Make sure the meat is always covered with liquid.

4. Meanwhile, quarter the mushroom caps and coarsely chop the stems.

5. Add the chicken legs and thighs, and the chopped mushroom stems, to the pot and cook for another 1½ hours.

6. Add the chicken breasts and cook for 45 minutes. Add the barley, stir, and cook for 15 minutes, skimming off any foam. Add the mushroom caps and cook through, 15 minutes more.

7. Test the meat—it should be tender and almost falling off the bones. Adjust the seasonings, and serve in large shallow bowls, sprinkled with parsley. Each person should get some beef and chicken—and provide spoons for all that good marrow in the beef bones.

Serves 6 to 8

NOTE: If you are preparing your firepot on top of the stove, in step 3 bring the ingredients to a boil over high heat. Then lower the heat and simmer, skimming, for 2 hours. Follow the directions for adding ingredients as given for the fireplace method, cooking the chicken legs and thighs for 30 minutes before adding the breasts. Cook the breasts for 30 minutes, add the barley, cook for 15 minutes, then add the mushrooms and cook 15 minutes more. Test the barley for doneness before serving.

MEAT-AND-POTATOES POT PIE

★ ★ ★

The basis for this dish is a beef stew with a rich gravy. I always add a bit of tomato paste and red currant jelly to the mix because I find that it takes the edge off the sauce and rounds it out with luscious results. The crust for this pot pie is made from sliced potatoes that bake up into a nice crisp covering.

Wine: Washington State Cabernet Sauvignon
Beer: Boston amber lager

*½ pound slab bacon, rind removed, cut into
    ¼-inch dice*
2 tablespoons olive oil, or more as needed
*2½ pounds boneless beef round, cut into
    1½-inch cubes*
1 onion, cut into ¼-inch dice
1 tablespoon finely chopped garlic
1 tablespoon all-purpose flour
*1 can (28 ounces) plum tomatoes, crushed,
    with their juices*
*1¼ cups defatted chicken broth, preferably
    homemade (page 253)*
½ cup dry red wine
1 tablespoon tomato paste
1 tablespoon red currant jelly
3 to 4 sprigs fresh thyme, or 1 teaspoon dried
2 bay leaves
1 long strip orange zest
3 carrots, peeled and cut into 1-inch pieces
*10 ounces white mushrooms, trimmed and
    cut into quarters*
1 cup cooked white kidney beans
Salt and coarsely ground black pepper, to taste
2 russet potatoes, peeled and thinly sliced
¼ cup chopped fresh flat-leaf parsley
2 tablespoons unsalted butter, melted

1. Preheat the oven to 350°F.

2. In a heavy ovenproof pot, cook the bacon over medium-low heat until golden brown and the fat is rendered, 8 to 10 minutes. Using a slotted spoon, set the bacon aside. Add the olive oil to the drippings in the pot.

3. Brown the meat in two batches over medium-high heat, adding additional oil as necessary. Transfer the meat to a bowl.

4. Add the onion to the pot and cook over low heat, stirring occasionally, until wilted, 8 to 10 minutes. Add the garlic and cook for 2 minutes. Sprinkle with the flour and cook, stirring, 1 minute more.

5. Add the remaining ingredients to the pot, except for the potatoes, parsley, and butter. Return the meat, along with any accumulated juices, and the bacon to the pot. Bring to a simmer over medium heat, and then transfer the pot to the oven. Bake, covered, for 1 hour.

6. Remove the cover, adjust the seasoning, and bake, uncovered, until the beef is tender, 1 hour more.

7. About 30 minutes before the stew is finished, bring a small pot of water to a boil. Add the potatoes, return to a boil, and cook for 4 minutes. Drain and dry the potatoes well on paper towels.

8. Stir the parsley into the stew. Using a slotted spoon, transfer the stew to a 2- to 2½-quart round soufflé dish or other ovenproof casserole. Pour enough sauce over the meat to just cover. Arrange the potatoes in an overlapping spiral over the stew. Brush with the melted butter and sprinkle generously with salt and pepper. Bake until the potatoes are golden and tender, 45 minutes. Serve immediately.

Serves 6

SHORT RIBS BAKED IN BEER

★ ★ ★

I based this recipe on a Belgian classic—carbonnades of beef—substituting meaty beef short ribs, one of my favorite cuts, for the more typical boneless chuck or top round. The key to a great carbonnade is to sprinkle the meat generously with black pepper as it browns, and to add the right amount of brown sugar. The beer and onions cook into a lush gravy that blankets the meat. Noodles tossed with tarragon-flecked butter make a tasty bed for the tender ribs.

Wine: Washington State Merlot
Beer: Oregon Belgian-style ale

2 tablespoons vegetable oil
6 short ribs of beef (½ pound each)
Freshly ground black pepper, to taste
6 onions, halved lengthwise and slivered
4 whole cloves garlic
½ teaspoon dried thyme
1 tablespoon all-purpose flour
3 tablespoons dark brown sugar
12 ounces (1½ cups) dark ale
2 tablespoons chopped fresh flat-leaf parsley

1. Preheat the oven to 350°F.

2. Heat the oil in a large heavy ovenproof pot over medium-high heat. Brown the ribs in batches, sprinkling them generously with a good grinding of pepper on both sides, 4 to 5 minutes per side. Remove the ribs and set them aside.

3. Reduce the heat to medium and add the onions, garlic, and thyme. Cook, stirring, for 5 minutes. Then sprinkle the flour and brown sugar over the onions, and cook, stirring occasionally, for 10 minutes longer.

4. Return the short ribs to the pot, along with any accumulated juices. Add the ale and bring to a boil. Cover, and bake in the oven for 2½ hours. Uncover and bake until the meat is tender, 30 minutes more.

5. Transfer the short ribs to a platter, discarding any loose bones. Remove the onions with a slotted spoon and arrange them on top of the meat. Skim the fat from the gravy with a metal spoon, or pour it through a gravy separator. Pour the gravy over the meat and onions, sprinkle with parsley, and serve immediately.

Serves 6

BARBECUED SHORT RIBS OF BEEF

★ ★ ★

When you're in the mood for really succulent ribs, these "shorts" fill the bill. I bake them first, basting every so often with a homemade tomato-rich Kansas City–style barbecue sauce. Then, I finish them on the grill. This is a never-fail cooking method that keeps the ribs from drying out. You can either serve one rib per person for extra-hearty appetites or remove the tender meat from the bone and slice it thin crosswise. Six meaty ribs, when sliced, will feed six people.

Whichever way you serve them, be sure to have extra sauce on the side.

Wine: Central Coast (CA) Nebbiolo
Beer: Pennsylvania marzen-style lager

6 pounds (about 6 ribs) short ribs of beef
Salt and freshly ground black pepper, to taste
2 cups Backyard Barbecue Sauce
(recipe follows), plus more for dipping
(see Note)

1. Preheat the oven to 350°F.
2. Lay the ribs, meaty side up, in a baking pan to fit. Sprinkle all over with salt and pepper, and bake for 15 minutes. Then brush them with barbecue sauce and bake for 1¾ hours, basting generously every 15 to 20 minutes. Turn once or twice during baking.
3. Meanwhile, prepare a barbecue grill with medium-hot coals.
4. Remove the ribs from the pan and place them on the hot grill, meaty side up, 3 to 4 inches from the heat source. Cook for 10 minutes, then turn them over and cook on the meaty side, basting often with barbecue sauce, for 8 to 10 minutes. They should have a nice grilled char when ready.
5. Serve 1 rib per person, or remove the meat from the bone, slice, and serve. Each person should have a small bowl of barbecue sauce for dipping.
   Serves 6

NOTE: Keep the sauce used for dipping the finished meat separate from the sauce used for basting. Discard any leftover basting sauce.

Backyard Barbecue Sauce

——★——

Everyone has their favorite barbecue sauce, as well as an opinion as to whether it should be five-alarm or milder. Mine is tomato-based and on the mild side, but it includes lots of ingredients, resulting in a deep rich taste. I like a smoky flavor in my barbecue sauce, so have added some liquid smoke. It's purely optional and may be left out.

2 tablespoons vegetable oil
1 onion, halved lengthwise, and slivered
4 whole cloves garlic, halved
1 can (28 ounces) Italian plum tomatoes, crushed, with their juices
1½ cups ketchup
1 cup fresh orange juice
6 tablespoons fresh lemon juice
6 tablespoons red wine vinegar
½ cup water
2 tablespoons all-natural liquid smoke (optional)
¼ cup honey
¼ cup (packed) dark brown sugar
3 tablespoons finely chopped crystallized ginger
2 tablespoons dark molasses
1 tablespoon Worcestershire sauce
¼ teaspoon Tabasco sauce
2 tablespoons chili powder
1 tablespoon ground coriander
1 tablespoon dry mustard
1 teaspoon salt

1. Heat the oil in a heavy medium-size saucepan over medium heat. Add the onion and cook, stirring occasionally, until golden

brown, 5 minutes. Add the garlic and cook for 1 minute more.

2. Add the remaining ingredients and stir well to mix. Bring the mixture to a boil, then reduce the heat to very low and cook, uncovered, stirring often, until the sauce thickens and has a smooth texture, 45 minutes to 1 hour.

3. Remove the onion and garlic with a slotted spoon and discard. Adjust seasonings to taste, and then, if the sauce is too thick, add a small amount of water. Cook to blend the seasonings for 2 minutes. Cool to room temperature and refrigerate in covered containers for up to 1 week.

Makes about 5 cups

AROMATIC MEAT LOAF

★ ★ ★

For this meat loaf I combined three types of ground meat with plenty of pungent spices and a little bit of heat. The aromatic perfume exuded by this loaf is indescribably sensuous and the taste—exotic.

Wine: California Rhône-style blend
Beer: Vermont brown ale

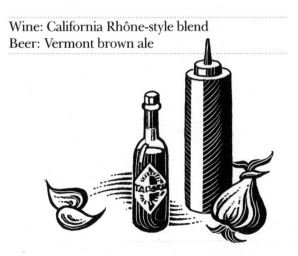

1 onion
1 rib celery
1 carrot, peeled
1 green bell pepper, stemmed and seeded
1 large clove garlic
2 tablespoons vegetable oil
1 tablespoon dried basil
1 teaspoon chili powder
1 teaspoon ground cinnamon
1 teaspoon ground nutmeg
½ teaspoon ground allspice
Salt and freshly ground black pepper, to taste
1½ pounds ground pork
1 pound ground beef round
½ pound ground veal
½ cup heavy (or whipping) cream
¼ cup ketchup
2 teaspoons A.1. steak sauce
½ teaspoon Tabasco sauce
1 large egg, lightly beaten
1½ cups bread crumbs, preferably fresh
½ pound bacon strips

1. Preheat the oven to 350°F.

2. Finely chop the onion, celery, carrot, bell pepper, and garlic.

3. Heat the oil in a nonstick skillet over medium heat, and add all of the chopped vegetables. Cook, stirring, until soft, 10 to 12 minutes. Add the basil, chili powder, cinnamon, nutmeg, allspice, salt, and pepper, and stir well to combine.

4. Place all of the ground meats in a large bowl. Add the vegetables and mix into the meat thoroughly with your hands.

5. In a separate bowl, mix together the cream, ketchup, A.1. sauce, Tabasco, and egg. Add this to the meat and stir well to combine. Add the bread crumbs and mix well.

6. Form the meat into a large oval loaf, and place it in a 12 x 9-inch glass baking dish. Cover the top with the bacon strips. Bake until cooked through, 1 hour. Slice and serve immediately.

Serves 8

SUNDAY SOUTHWEST MEAT LOAF

★ ★ ★

During the 1980s, when comfort foods were making a strong statement on the menus of young American chefs, meat loaf became one of the revisited favorites. And I found myself unable to resist ordering these moist, well-seasoned loaves, particularly when they were served with great mashed potatoes. I took my inspiration for this meat loaf from the Southwest. It is more than fine enough to serve to company with Piccalilli Corn Salad—and don't forget those accompanying mashed potatoes.

THE GREAT AMERICAN MEAT LOAF

—❦—

Had I wanted to, I could have filled this entire volume with meat loaf recipes, collected from hundreds of starred restaurants, as well as diners and private recipe files from across the United States. Every American family, it seems, does meat loaf in its own way, and meat loaf allegiances can run deep. So perhaps few readers would be interested in such a book. If your grandmother's version won your heart years ago, why would you need to look farther?

We've been eating meat loaf since colonial times. It began turning up at nickel lunch counters in the mid-nineteenth century; and it's been a primary-school staple for as long as anyone alive today can remember. Once upon a time, it was made mostly with veal; today, beef usually dominates. Many recipes call for some veal and/or pork, too, for flavor and texture. Turkey loaf, a relative newcomer, is the comfort food of choice for those who don't care for red meat.

A good meat loaf is very well seasoned. Be liberal with your spices, since their flavors will diminish when your loaf is baked. Start with chopped onion, plenty of garlic, and fresh herbs when you can get them. Turkey requires even higher spice than red meat. Moisture is also key. Add plenty of wet ingredients (ketchup or tomato sauce, cream, egg, or broth) and use as little "filler" (bread crumbs) as possible. Don't overmix or overbake. I like my meat loaf just firm enough to slice neatly when it's fresh, yet tender enough to keep well a few days in the refrigerator, so I can use the leftovers as filling for the world's *best* sandwiches.

Wine: Amador County (CA) Zinfandel
Beer: Minnesota pale ale

2 cups cubed (1 inch) bread
4 tablespoons olive oil
1 tablespoon plus 2 teaspoons ground cumin
1 tablespoon plus 1 teaspoon ground nutmeg
1 onion, finely chopped
½ cup finely chopped red bell pepper
½ cup finely chopped green bell pepper
½ cup finely chopped scallions (white and
*   green parts)*
1 tablespoon finely minced garlic
1 pound ground beef chuck
1 pound ground pork
2 large eggs
⅓ cup heavy (or whipping) cream
⅓ cup ketchup
Salt and freshly ground black pepper, to taste

1. Preheat the oven to 350°F.

2. Toss the bread cubes with 2 tablespoons of the oil and 1 tablespoon each of the cumin and nutmeg in a large bowl. Place the cubes on a baking sheet and bake, turning them once, until toasted, 15 minutes. Cool to room temperature.

3. Place the cubes in a food processor (reserve the bowl they cooled in) and process to form medium-fine crumbs. Transfer them to a bowl and let rest for 30 minutes.

4. Heat the remaining 2 tablespoons oil in a nonstick skillet over low heat. Add the onion, both bell peppers, and the scallions. Cook, stirring, until almost wilted, 8 minutes. Add the garlic and cook for 5 minutes. Place the vegetables in the bowl that the bread cubes were tossed in, and let cool to room temperature. Add the ground beef and pork, and stir well to combine.

5. Lightly beat the eggs in a small bowl. Add the cream, ketchup, the remaining 2 teaspoons cumin and 1 teaspoon nutmeg, and the salt, and pepper. Add this to the meat and vegetables, and

mix all together lightly with your hands. Add enough of the seasoned bread crumbs to bind everything together.

6. Form the mixture into an oval loaf and place it in a baking dish to fit. Bake until cooked through, 35 to 40 minutes. Do not overcook it, or the loaf will be dry. After it comes out of the oven, use a small spoon to carefully remove any foam that forms around the bottom of the loaf.

7. Let the meat loaf rest for at least 10 minutes before slicing it. Serve hot or at room temperature.

Serves 6

PICADILLO MEAT LOAF

★ ★ ★

The sweet and savory spicing associated with this classic Southwestern dish has always titillated my taste buds, be it a stew, Sloppy Joe, or in a new-fangled meat loaf. I speculate that this highly seasoned, moist loaf—flavored with raisins and cinnamon—will soon become a weeknight favorite. If time is tight, prepare it on a Sunday to enjoy throughout the week. Leftovers are particularly savory. Serve it with Black Bean Salad, roasted red bell peppers, and warm Country Cornbread.

Wine: Sonoma County
    (CA) Zinfandel
Beer: New England
    oatmeal stout

2 teaspoons olive oil

1 onion, cut into ¼-inch dice

1 red bell pepper, stemmed, seeded, and cut into
  ¼-inch dice

4 cloves garlic, minced

4 ripe plum tomatoes, seeded and cut into
  ¼-inch dice

½ cup golden raisins

½ cup coarsely chopped stuffed green olives

2 tablespoons drained tiny capers

1½ teaspoons dried thyme leaves

½ teaspoon ground cumin

¼ teaspoon ground allspice

¼ teaspoon cinnamon

½ cup prepared chili sauce or ketchup

1 large egg, lightly beaten

Salt and freshly ground black pepper, to taste

1 pound ground beef

1 pound ground pork

1. Preheat the oven to 350°F.

2. Heat the oil in a nonstick skillet over low heat. Add the onion and bell pepper and cook, stirring, until almost wilted, 8 minutes. Add the garlic and cook for 2 minutes more. Transfer the mixture to a bowl and cool to room temperature.

3. Add the tomatoes, raisins, olives, capers, thyme, cumin, allspice, and cinnamon to the onion and pepper.

4. In a separate bowl, combine the chili sauce, egg, salt, and pepper. Mix well and set aside.

5. Add the ground beef and pork to the onion and pepper mixture, and mix just to combine. Add the reserved chili sauce mixture and combine all of the ingredients gently with your hands until well blended.

6. Form the meat into a 12 x 6 x 2-inch loaf and place it in a baking dish to fit. Bake in the center of the oven until cooked through, 1 hour.

7. Let rest for 10 minutes before slicing.

Serves 6

COUNTRY MEAT LOAF WITH MUSHROOM GRAVY

★ ★ ★

Michael McLaughlin, chef, cookbook author, and good friend, makes a moist and luxurious meat loaf, that is featured in his book *The Mushroom Book*. The gravy, made from fresh, woodsy shiitakes, makes the dish elegant enough to serve the most discerning diners.

Wine: Central Coast (CA) Pinot Noir
Beer: California porter

1 pound fresh cremini mushrooms, wiped
  clean

6 tablespoons olive oil

2 cups chopped onions

1 large red bell pepper, stemmed, seeded,
  and finely diced

6 cloves garlic, minced

3 tablespoons minced fresh marjoram, or
  1 tablespoon dried, crumbled

1 pound ground beef chuck

1 pound ground veal

1 pound Italian sweet sausage with fennel,
  removed from the casing

3 large eggs, lightly beaten

¾ cup dried bread crumbs

3½ cups defatted chicken broth, preferably
  homemade (page 253)

3 teaspoons salt, or to taste

¾ teaspoon freshly ground black pepper

¼ teaspoon crushed red pepper flakes

1 pound fresh shiitake mushrooms, stems trimmed,
  caps wiped clean and thickly sliced

¼ cup all-purpose flour

1. Preheat the oven to 350°F.

2. Remove the stems from the cremini mushrooms. Finely chop the stems and thickly slice the caps.

3. Heat 3 tablespoons of the olive oil in a large skillet over low heat. Add the chopped cremini stems, onions, bell pepper, half of the garlic, and 2 tablespoons of the marjoram. Cover and cook to soften the vegetables, 10 minutes, stirring once or twice. Remove from the heat and cool to room temperature.

4. Crumble together the ground chuck, veal, and the sausage in a large bowl. Add the onion mixture, eggs, bread crumbs, ½ cup of the chicken broth, 2 teaspoons of the salt, and the pepper, and mix until just combined. Transfer to a flameproof roasting pan and form into a loaf measuring about 12 x 6 x 2 inches.

5. Bake the meat loaf in the center of the oven until cooked through, for 1 hour and 10 minutes. Remove it from the oven and let it rest in the pan on a rack for 5 minutes. Then carefully transfer the meat loaf to a platter, using two spatulas. Do not wash the roasting pan.

6. Heat the remaining 3 tablespoons olive oil in a large skillet over medium heat. Add the remaining garlic, the remaining 1 tablespoon marjoram, and the red pepper flakes. Cover and cook, for 1 minute, stirring once or twice. Add the sliced cremini caps and the shiitakes, and season with the remaining 1 teaspoon salt. Cover and cook, tossing and stirring once or twice, until the mushrooms begin to render their juices, about 5 minutes. Remove from the heat.

7. Place the roasting pan with the meat loaf drippings over low heat. Whisk in the flour and cook, stirring and loosening any brown bits left in the pan, until well combined and golden brown, about 4 minutes. Remove the pan from the heat and slowly whisk in the remaining 3 cups chicken broth. Add the mushroom mixture to the broth mixture in the roasting pan. Set the pan over medium heat and bring to a simmer. Cook until the gravy has thickened slightly and the mushrooms are tender, about 4 minutes. Adjust the seasonings.

8. Cut the meat loaf into thick slices and serve hot, accompanied by the mushroom gravy.

Serves 8

BEST-TIME CHILI

★ ★ ★

For me, any time is a good time to eat chili, but I have to admit that one of the best times is at a Super Bowl party. This recipe cooks up into an easy crowd-pleaser that calls for traditional and creative toppings. I've suggested some to get you started, but don't hesitate to vary them. For example, golden raisins and diced avocado would be nice additions to the ones I've suggested in the ingredients list.

Wine: California Zinfandel
Beer: Texas lager

3 tablespoons olive oil

1 large onion, coarsely chopped

*1 green bell pepper, stemmed, seeded, and
    cut into ¼-inch dice*

*1 red bell pepper, stemmed, seeded, and
    cut into ¼-inch dice*

2 tablespoons finely chopped garlic

*1 pound sweet Italian sausage, removed
    from casing*

2 pounds ground beef round

¼ cup tomato paste

1½ tablespoons unsweetened cocoa powder

¼ cup chili powder

2 tablespoons ground cumin

½ teaspoon ground cinnamon

2 teaspoons dried oregano

*½ teaspoon crushed red pepper flakes, or
    more to taste*

¼ teaspoon freshly ground black pepper

*2 cans (28 ounces each) Italian plum tomatoes,
    drained, with their juices*

½ cup dry red wine

*2 cans (15½ ounces each) dark red kidney
    beans, drained*

1 teaspoon salt, or to taste

*½ cup chopped flat-leaf parsley or
    fresh cilantro leaves*

Plain nonfat yogurt, for garnish

Grated Monterey Jack cheese, for garnish

Diced seeded ripe plum tomatoes, for garnish

*Thinly sliced scallions (white and green parts),
    for garnish*

1. Heat the oil in a large heavy pot over medium-low heat. Add the onion and both bell peppers. Cook, stirring occasionally, until soft, about 10 minutes. Add the garlic and cook 2 minutes longer.

2. Crumble the sausage meat into the pot, and brown well, stirring often to break up the clumps, 10 to 15 minutes. Add the beef and cook, continuing to stir, until browned, 15 minutes more. Drain off most of the fat.

3. Add the tomato paste, cocoa powder, chili powder, cumin, cinnamon, oregano, red pepper flakes, and black pepper. Cook over low heat for 2 minutes, stirring to blend.

4. Add the tomatoes along with 1 cup of reserved juices and the red wine. Simmer, uncovered, over medium meat for 15 minutes. Add the kidney beans and cook to blend the flavors, 15 minutes. Stir in the salt and parsley. Serve immediately in deep bowls, with the garnishes alongside.

Serves 6 to 8

HOG NECK CHILI

★ ★ ★

This robust beef and pork chili is based on Raymond Fair's blue-ribbon winner of the early 1990s Washington State Chili Championship. Three kinds of chiles impart both heat and distinctive flavor and the whole concoction, complete with a shot of bourbon, cooks into a mysterious savory complexity. It's easy to see why this "bowl of red" walked home with the prize.

HOT, HOT, HOT

— ❦ —

Southwestern cooking is for those who can take the heat, be it a suggestive tingle, a luscious slow burn, or an all-out assault on the palate. In my travels through Texas and New Mexico, I found chile peppers smoldering everywhere, in classic fajitas and chili con carne, and in salsas, barbecue, and marinades. The food of Santa Fe was the hottest of all. Dishes there are typically napped in boldly flavored red or green sauce—sometimes both, in a style the locals call "Christmas."

In New Mexico, I loved seeing "ristras," flamboyant strings of red Anaheim chiles, drying in the sun on doorways and sides of buildings. Drying makes them hotter, roasting over a wood fire makes them sweeter. New Mexicans eat them both ways, and myriad other ways, too, and always more as a food than a seasoning. This sets them apart from Texans and Arizonans, who often prefer chili powder—ground chiles mixed with other seasonings—to fresh, cooked, or dried chiles.

All peppers, sweet and hot, are actually berries (genus *Capsicum*). In Mexico, all capsicums are called *chile*; here, only the hot ones are. Like the potato and tomato, they're a New World food that transformed Old World cuisine. We call them peppers because Spanish explorers compared the first they tasted (hot ones) to black pepper, or *pimienta,* and named them a masculine version of the word—*pimiento*—because they were stronger-tasting. Why people like chile peppers so much is a mystery. The pleasure they give is pain; for some reason, we like to irritate our taste buds. Some scientists have suggested that chiles, like aerobic exercise and sex, may stimulate endorphin production.

Not all chiles are created alike. While differences tend to be subtle, heat differences are not. A *habanero* is so much hotter than a *jalapeño* (up to 1,000 times hotter!) that you could never successfully substitute one for another in a recipe. *Anaheims,* when roasted, are mild enough to mound onto peasant bread and eat as a sandwich. Other popular varieties include the versatile, medium-hot *poblano* (*ancho* when dried); the hot *serrano,* first choice among Mexican chefs; and the *chipotle,* a mesquite-smoked jalapeño that's spectacular in barbecue sauce.

If you're not sure about what you've got, add less than the amount specified in a recipe. And always handle any chile with care: When working with chiles, cover your hands with rubber gloves or plastic sandwich bags, and keep them away from your eyes and face. If you find your skin or eyes burning from chile contact, act immediately. Apply yogurt, milk, or mayonnaise to the skin, and flush the eyes with cold water.

To tame a pepper that's too hot, carefully cut out the seeds and central ribs (that's where most of the heat of any pepper lives) and use just the flesh.

Beer: Colorado pale ale

1 pound boneless beef chuck
1 pound boneless pork shoulder
1 pound boneless beef bottom round
2 tablespoons vegetable oil
8 cloves garlic, finely minced
2 onions, coarsely chopped
¼ cup bourbon
4 dried ancho chile peppers, stems and
    seeds discarded
1 bottle (12 ounces) ale
2 cans (28 ounces each) Italian plum tomatoes,
    drained and coarsely chopped
1 cup dry red wine
1 red bell pepper, stemmed, seeded, and
    finely chopped
4 white mushrooms, wiped clean, trimmed
    and finely chopped
⅓ cup pitted ripe olives, finely chopped
1 tablespoon ground cumin
1 tablespoon dried oregano
Salt and freshly ground black pepper,
    to taste
1 serrano chile pepper, stem and seeds
    discarded
1 can (4 ounces) chopped jalapeño
    chile peppers
Hot cooked white rice, for serving

1. Trim and reserve the fat from all the meat. Cut the meat into ½-inch cubes and set aside. Cut the reserved fat into 1-inch pieces and place in a large heavy pot. Cook over low heat to render the fat, 15 to 20 minutes. Once the fat is rendered, remove the solids from the pot with a slotted spoon and discard them.

2. Place the oil in the pot and heat over medium heat. Add the garlic and onions, and cook, stirring often, until lightly browned, about 5 minutes. Add all of the reserved meat and the bourbon. Simmer uncovered, stirring occasionally, for 1 hour.

3. While the meat is simmering, prepare the ancho chiles: Place the chile peppers and the ale in a small saucepan and bring to a boil over medium heat. Reduce the heat and simmer, uncovered, for 30 minutes.

4. Strain the ale into the meat. Place the ancho chile peppers in a blender or food processor and process until completely smooth. Stir the purée, the chopped tomatoes, and the red wine into the meat mixture. Add all the remaining ingredients (except for the rice) and stir well.

5. Simmer the chili uncovered, over low heat, stirring occasionally, until the flavors are well blended, 2 hours. Serve hot, over rice.

Serves 6 to 8

SAVORY VENISON CHILI

★ ★ ★

Venison used to be considered too gamey for most palates, but now much of the meat available in markets is mellow because it is farm-raised. Venison has retained a certain inherent lusty flavor, though, making it an ideal choice for chili because it blends so well with the strong flavors of cumin, oregano, and chili powder. This version, with its beans and carrots, is more stew-like than the one that follows it. Serve it over barley for a light, contemporary touch.

Wine: California Rhône-style blend
Beer: Washington State pale ale

*¼ pound slab bacon, rind removed, cut into
    ¼-inch dice*
1 onion, coarsely chopped
*6 carrots, peeled, halved lengthwise, and
    cut into 1-inch pieces*
2 teaspoons chili powder
2 teaspoons ground cumin
1 teaspoon dried marjoram or oregano
¼ teaspoon crushed red pepper flakes
*2 pounds boneless venison shoulder,
    cut into ½-inch cubes*
*1 can (28 ounces) Italian plum tomatoes,
    crushed*
*1½ cups defatted beef or chicken broth,
    preferably homemade (page 252 or 253)*
½ cup dry red wine
¼ cup tomato paste
*1 can (19 ounces) dark red kidney beans,
    drained*
1 cup baby lima beans, thawed if frozen
*Hot cooked white rice or barley,
    for serving*

1. Cook the bacon in a large nonstick skillet over medium heat until golden brown and the fat is rendered, 6 to 8 minutes. Remove with a slotted spoon and set aside. Don't clean out the skillet.

2. Place 2 tablespoons of the bacon fat in a large heavy pot and heat over medium heat. Add the onion and carrots, sprinkle them with

the chili powder, cumin, marjoram, and red pepper flakes, and cook, stirring, until slightly softened, 5 minutes. Add the reserved bacon.

3. Remove and discard all but 1 tablespoon of the fat from the skillet and heat it over medium-high heat. Add the venison, in small batches, and brown it, transferring the pieces to the pot with a slotted spoon as they are done. (The meat should be browned quickly, so raise the heat to high if necessary.)

4. Add the tomatoes, broth, wine, and tomato paste to the pot. Bring to a simmer and cook, uncovered, for 40 minutes, stirring occasionally. Do not let it boil, or the meat will dry out.

5. Add both beans and adjust the seasonings. Simmer until the meat is tender, 10 minutes. Serve hot, over rice or barley.

Serves 6

NICE AND HOT VENISON CHILI

★ ★ ★

I think of this elegant recipe for venison chili as more of an uptown version of the dish. The lean meat, fired up by the addition of a spoonful or two of chipotle chiles in adobo sauce, needs no support from beans. The sweet Italian sausage is a nice complement to the venison, adding its flavorful texture to the final result. Because venison cooks quickly, this chili takes no more than an hour and a half. Don't let it boil, or the meat will dry out.

Wine: Texas Merlot
Beer: Wisconsin dark lager

4 tablespoons olive oil
1 large onion, cut into ½-inch dice
1 pound sweet Italian sausage, removed
  from casing
2 teaspoons chili powder
2 teaspoons ground cumin
1 teaspoon dried oregano
½ teaspoon crushed red pepper flakes
2 pounds boneless venison shoulder, cut into
  1½-inch cubes
2 cups canned Italian plum tomatoes,
  crushed
2 cups defatted beef broth, preferably homemade
  (page 252)
¼ cup tomato paste
1 tablespoon chipotles in adobo sauce, or
  more to taste
1 tablespoon dark brown sugar
1 red bell pepper, stemmed, seeded, and
  cut into ½-inch dice
Salt and freshly ground black pepper,
  to taste
¼ cup chopped fresh flat-leaf parsley
Hot cooked white rice, for serving

1. Heat 2 tablespoons of the oil in a large heavy pot over low heat. Add the onion and cook, stirring, until soft, about 10 minutes.

2. Crumble the sausage meat into the pot, raise the heat to medium-high, and brown well, stirring often to break up the clumps, 10 minutes. As the sausage cooks, sprinkle it with the chili powder, cumin, oregano, and red pepper flakes.

3. Add the remaining 2 tablespoons oil to a large nonstick skillet. Brown the venison in small batches over medium-high heat, about 5 minutes per batch, adding the venison as it is browned to the pot. (The meat should be browned quickly, so raise the heat to high if necessary.) Add the tomatoes, broth, tomato paste, chipotles, and brown sugar to the pot. Simmer, uncovered, over medium heat, stirring occa-

sionally, for 1 hour. Add the bell pepper and simmer until the venison is tender, 30 minutes. Be sure that the chili does not boil. Season with salt and pepper, and stir in the parsley. Serve over rice.

Serves 4 to 6

BLUE PLATE
S · P · E · C · I · A · L

Neat Sloppy Joes

Cowboy Rice Salad

Piccalilli Corn Salad

Maccan Family Zucchini Relish

Liberty Bar's Chocolate Cake

NEAT SLOPPY JOES

★ ★ ★

Made with chuck plus onion, celery, green pepper, and some basic pantry staples, this dish is ripe for jazzing up with a scent of cinnamon and chili powder. I have also tried it with lean beefalo (see box, page 366) and found it works well. While my associate Laurie and I were working on this dish, she told me that in Kansas, before serving it, they first spread mayonnaise on the buns. So we tried it and, I have to admit, it was a pretty delicious match. There wasn't a bun left in the pantry or a drop of meat left in the pot. Bread-and-butter pickles, potato chips, and a cold glass of root beer complete the meal.

2 tablespoons olive oil
1 cup coarsely chopped onions
2 ribs celery, cut into ¼-inch dice
1 green bell pepper, stemmed, seeded, and cut into ¼-inch dice
2 cloves garlic, finely minced
2 pounds ground beef chuck or beefalo
1 teaspoon chili powder
½ teaspoon ground cinnamon
2 cups Fresh Herbed Tomato Sauce (page 307)
½ cup ketchup
2 tablespoons tomato paste
2 teaspoons Worcestershire sauce
¼ teaspoon Tabasco sauce
Salt and freshly ground black pepper, to taste
6 hamburger buns, toasted, for serving
Mayonnaise, for serving (optional)

1. Heat the oil in a large heavy skillet over medium heat. Add the onions, celery, and bell pepper. Cook, stirring, until soft, about 10 minutes. Add the garlic and cook for another 2 minutes.

2. Raise the heat to medium-high and crumble in the beef. Cook until well browned, stirring to break up the clumps, about 10 minutes. Sprinkle with the chili powder and cinnamon and stir to blend into the meat.

3. Reduce the heat to medium. Add the remaining ingredients through the salt and pepper, and cook, stirring, until the mixture has thickened, 20 minutes. Adjust the seasonings.

4. Serve immediately over hamburger buns. Spread the buns with mayonnaise first, if you wish.
Serves 6

★★★★★★★★★★★★★★★★★★★★★★★★★

DID YOU SAY BEEFALO?

—❦—

Coming soon to a butcher's counter near you: a unique new American meat that tastes like lean beef but is lower in cholesterol than skinless chicken and many kinds of fish. It's called "beefalo" (or "beefalo beef"), after the bison-bovine cross that produces it. The first fertile beefalo was born in 1957, but it's taken this long for the breed to become a viable meat source. They're handsome beasts—big and stocky, with a face and body more like a cow's than a buffalo's.

These hearty animals have lots to recommend them. They're raised on open-range pasture, without steroids or growth hormones and with a shaggy pelt rather than a layer of fat to protect them against the cold. They rarely require antibiotics. They eat little more than grass and hay, which keeps their meat tender and juicy. And because the meat is so low in fat, it cooks in just half the time (more or less) required by beef. If you can find it, try it out in the Neat Sloppy Joes on this page.

★★★★★★★★★★★★★★★★★★★★★★★★★

THE MAYTAG BLUE CHEESEBURGER

★ ★ ★

Maytag Blue, made in Iowa, is one of America's premier cheeses. Made by hand and aged for six months, it's creamy tang makes for a delicious melted surprise when you bite into this burger. I like these burgers dinner size, so I make them extra-big. Topped with Fresh Pineapple Relish and ketchup, and served with Pan-Roasted Baby Whites, what burger could be better?

3 pounds ground beef round
1 small onion, grated
Ketchup
2 teaspoons Worcestershire sauce
2 teaspoons chopped fresh thyme, or ½ teaspoon dried
Salt and freshly ground black pepper, to taste
¼ pound Maytag Blue cheese, divided into 6 chunks
1 teaspoon vegetable oil
6 hamburger rolls, toasted, for serving
Fresh Pineapple Relish (page 186), for serving

1. Place the meat in a bowl. Add the onion, 1 tablespoon ketchup, Worcestershire sauce, thyme, salt, and pepper and mix lightly with your hands.

2. Form the meat into 6 thick patties, about 3 inches across and 1½ inches thick. To stuff the burgers, remove some of the meat from the top center of each patty, insert a chunk of the blue cheese (flattened slightly with the palm of your hand if necessary), and re-cover with the meat.

3. Heat the oil in a nonstick skillet over medium-high heat. Cook the burgers, in batches if necessary, for 5 minutes on the first side; then turn and cook for 3 minutes on the second side for a crusty outside and medium-rare interior. Cook longer if you prefer your burger well done. Place the burgers on the toasted rolls, and serve with ketchup and the relish.

Makes 6 burgers

CHILI BURGERS

★ ★ ★

Chili seasonings spice up these burgers and chopped tomato in the mixture adds succulence to the meat. To garnish the hamburgers, set out bowls filled with your favorite chili toppers: sour cream, scallions, chopped tomatoes, and grated Monterey Jack cheese. Serve the burgers on good grilled multigrain rolls.

Beer: American lager

1 pound ground beef round

1 ripe tomato, seeded and cut into ¼-inch dice

½ cup pitted black olives, chopped

1 teaspoon finely minced garlic

½ teaspoon Dijon mustard

1 tablespoon chili powder

¼ teaspoon dried basil

¼ teaspoon dried oregano

Finely grated zest of 1 lemon

2 tablespoons chopped fresh dill or
*   fresh flat-leaf parsley*

Salt and freshly ground black pepper, to taste

4 hamburger buns, preferably whole-grain,
*   toasted*

⅓ cup sour cream, for garnish (optional)

3 scallions (3 inches green left on), thinly sliced,
*   for garnish (optional)*

1 cup chopped fresh, ripe tomatoes,
*   for garnish (optional)*

½ cup grated Monterey Jack cheese,
*   for garnish (optional)*

1. Prepare a barbecue grill with hot coals.

2. Place the beef in a bowl and mix well with the diced tomato, olives, garlic, mustard, chili powder, basil, oregano, lemon zest, and dill. Season to taste with salt and pepper. Gently form the mixture into 4 patties.

3. Grill the burgers 3 inches from heat, for 3 to 4 minutes per side for medium-rare meat, and 1 to 2 minutes more per side for medium or well done.

4. Serve immediately on toasted buns, and pass the sour cream, scallions, tomatoes, and grated cheese, if using.

Makes 4 burgers

Pork & Ham

America grew up on pork. Well into the twentieth century, we ate more pork than any other meat. Once upon a time there were pigs everywhere—even in the streets of major cities, where many roamed free, snacking on scraps they found lying about. Pioneers heading west trundled huge stores of salt pork; without it, they might have starved. Eventually, beef outstripped pork in popularity. But our pork is still the finest in the world, and we still eat plenty of it, especially in the South and the Heartland, home of a whole lot of magnificent pork barbecue.

Pork is marvelously succulent. It marries graciously with whatever seasoning or sauce you introduce. And the possibilities are endless. I've prepared it with pineapple, dried cranberries, dried cherries, apricots, and prunes, apple juice, orange juice . . . I love pork with fruit! But that's not all. Pork is braised alongside carrots and squash and barbecued slowly until lusciously tender. If you've a hankering for old-fashioned ham, try Glazed Country Ham or the lavish Cider-Glazed Apricot Ham with Raisin Sauce, bristling with cloves and festive attitude.

PINEAPPLE-SMOTHERED PORK LOIN

★ ★ ★

Between visits to the beautiful beaches and drives through dramatically lush scenic spots that punctuate the beauty of Hawaii, a trip there also afforded me a chance to spend time on a pineapple plantation. A sun-sweetened pineapple eaten fresh-picked at the source was a much appreciated perk from the visit. Now, that's a fruit nature truly got right!

Pineapple and pork are wonderful in partnership, especially in this Island-inspired roast. The pineapple slowly cooks into a thick marmalade to use first as a marinade and then as a foundation for the roasting meat. The taste of the moist, sweet-tart pork makes this dish well worth the wait.

Wine: Sonoma County (CA) Pinot Noir
Beer: Oregon porter

1 ripe pineapple
2½ cups sugar
2 cups water
⅓ cup light soy sauce, preferably a
*   Japanese brand*
Cloves from 1 large head garlic, peeled and
**   slightly crushed**
1 boneless pork loin (about 2½ pounds)

1. Peel, core, and cut the pineapple into ½-inch pieces (there should be approximately 5 cups—reserve any extra for a salad).

2. Place the pineapple, sugar, and water in a heavy saucepan and bring the mixture to a boil. Reduce the heat to a simmer and cook, uncovered, stirring occasionally, until the pineapple reaches a marmalade consistency, 40 minutes to 1 hour. Cool to room temperature.

3. Combine the pineapple marmalade, soy sauce, and garlic in a baking dish. Add the pork loin and coat it well with the sauce. Cover and marinate overnight in the refrigerator, turning it once or twice.

4. Preheat the oven to 350°F.

5. Bake the pork loin, still in the marinade, covered, for 20 minutes. Reduce the heat to 325°F, uncover the baking dish, and cook, basting occasionally, for 45 minutes. The internal temperature should reach 150°F to 160°F. Let the pork rest for 10 minutes. Remove the garlic cloves from the sauce and discard them.

6. Thinly slice the pork loin, and spoon the pineapple sauce atop. Serve any extra sauce alongside in a gravy boat.

Serves 6

CIDER-SPLASHED ROASTED PORK LOIN

★ ★ ★

A roast loin of pork basted with apple cider is ideal fare for both elegant and casual dining since it can easily be dressed up or down. With pork being bred so lean these days, I find it necessary to add a little fat to this dish, and to roast it in liquid, basting often. The result served hot makes a lovely Sunday dinner accompanied by

Garlicky Red-Jacket Mashed Potatoes and Down-Home Greens or steamed spinach. At room temperature it goes well with fruit relishes or chutneys and your favorite salads.

Wine: Russian River Valley (CA) Pinot Noir
Beer: California stout

1 boneless pork loin (about 4 pounds)
2 cloves garlic, cut into thin slivers
2 tablespoons unsalted butter, at room temperature
1 teaspoon dried thyme leaves
Salt and freshly ground black pepper, to taste
½ to ¾ cup apple cider

1. Preheat the oven to 350°F.
2. Make small slits all over the pork with the tip of a sharp knife and insert the garlic slivers in them. Place the pork in a shallow roasting pan, and spread the butter all over the top.
3. Sprinkle the meat with the thyme, salt, and pepper. Pour ½ cup of the apple cider in the bottom of the pan, and roast, basting occasionally, until the pork is cooked through (150°F to 160°F on a meat thermometer), 1½ hours. Add the remaining cider to the pan while the pork is roasting, if the basting liquid gets too low. Let the meat rest for at least 10 minutes before slicing.
Serves 8

ASIAN-STYLE BARBECUED PORK TENDERLOIN

★ ★ ★

When tenderized and flavored with Rich Davis's Asian-influenced marinade, a grilled pork loin remains moist throughout the long cooking over hot coals or wood. Rich Davis, from Kansas City, is a barbecue enthusiast and restaurateur who created the commercially successful K.C. Masterpiece barbecue sauce—a sauce that is made in the Kansas City barbecue style, with molasses, tomatoes, and spices. The pungent barbecue sauce of his that is given here shows his creative juices flowing in a different direction, but with equally mouthwatering results. The proof is in this recipe. Enjoy it with a glass of red wine.

Wine: Napa Valley (CA) Gamay Beaujolais
Beer: New York State lager

MARINADE
½ cup soy sauce
2½ tablespoons sesame oil
1½ tablespoons minced garlic
2 teaspoons fresh lime juice
2 teaspoons rice wine vinegar
1½ teaspoons ground ginger
½ teaspoon sugar

1 boneless pork loin (3 pounds)
Asian-Style Barbecue Sauce (recipe follows)

1. Mix all the marinade ingredients together in a small bowl. Place the pork tenderloin in a large glass baking dish, and pour the marinade over it, turning the meat several times to coat it well. Cover loosely with plastic wrap and

refrigerate for approximately 3 hours.

2. Prepare a barbecue grill with medium-hot coals.

3. Grill the tenderloin, turning it occasionally, until it is cooked through. The internal temperature should reach 150°F to 160°F, 45 minutes to 1 hour.

4. Let the tenderloin stand for at least 10 minutes before slicing. Then slice it thinly on the diagonal, and arrange the slices on a serving platter. Pour some of the barbecue sauce over the meat, and serve immediately. Pass extra sauce on the side.

Serves 6 to 8

Asian-Style Barbecue Sauce

★

Rich Davis's Asian-Style Barbecue Sauce is a piquant glaze that results in a deep lacquer coating. Use it on pork tenderloin, as well as ribs or chicken. In deference to Rich, you may want to use his K.C. Masterpiece sauce as the basis, but my Backyard Barbecue Sauce (page 355) will also do the job.

¾ cup prepared barbecue sauce (see headnote)
2 tablespoons soy sauce
1 tablespoon peanut oil
1 tablespoon rice wine vinegar
½ teaspoon finely minced garlic
½ teaspoon freshly ground anise seeds
½ teaspoon ground ginger

Mix all the ingredients together in a small saucepan, and simmer gently for 5 minutes.

Remove the sauce from the heat and cool to room temperature.

Makes 1 cup

NOTE: This recipe doubles easily, and will keep in the refrigerator for up to 3 weeks.

CROWN ROAST OF PORK

★ ★ ★

A crown roast makes a marvelous centerpiece, particularly on the holiday table. Created by tying two sides of pork loin together, with the ends of the rib bones "frenched" (scraped clean of any meat or fat), it is truly magnificent fare. Trimmings from the roast are usually ground up and placed in its center by the butcher. Many cooks use the ground meat to make a savory stuffing, but I prefer to freeze it to use at another time. Instead, I fill the center with roasted vegetables. Wrap the cleaned bones with aluminum foil to keep them from burning while the meat roasts. Before serving, remove the foil and decorate the tips with paper frills.

Wine: Willamette Valley (OR) Pinot Noir
Beer: Connecticut oatmeal stout

1 crown roast of pork (15 to 16 chops,
    about 8½ pounds), bones frenched (see
        To French a Rack of Lamb, page 391)
2 cloves garlic, cut into slivers
1 to 2 tablespoons olive oil
Salt and freshly ground black pepper, to taste
1 cup apple juice or cider
Roasted Root Vegetables (page 309)
8 long rosemary sprigs, for garnish

1. Preheat the oven to 350°F.

2. Using the tip of a small sharp knife, make small slits around the bottom of the chops near the bone. Insert the garlic slivers in the slits.

3. Brush the chops lightly with the oil, and sprinkle all over with salt and pepper. Place the roast on a rack in a shallow roasting pan. Cover the tops of the bones with small pieces of aluminum foil to keep them from burning. Pour the apple juice in the bottom of the pan.

4. Bake, basting occasionally with the pan juices, until a meat thermometer reads 150°F to 160°F when inserted in the thickest part of the chop, 2¼ to 2½ hours (15 to 18 minutes per pound). Since pork is bred so lean these days, check the temperature and doneness after 2 hours.

5. When the roast is finished, transfer it to a large serving platter and fill the center with Roasted Root Vegetables (serve any extra vegetables in a bowl on the side). Entwine long sprigs of fresh rosemary around the tops of bones. Top the bones with decorative paper frills, if desired.

6. To serve, first dish out the vegetables. Then secure the roast with a carving fork and slice downward on both sides of the bone along each chop.

Serves 8

BRAISED PORK

★ ★ ★

Braised pork shoulder (commonly known as a picnic roast) is both a succulent and full-flavored cut. Slow braising brings out these qualities, and the addition of autumnal fruits and vegetables make it a cold-weather favorite in my house.

Wine: Washington State Riesling

1 boneless shoulder of pork (about 5 pounds)
1 teaspoon dried oregano
1 teaspoon dried thyme leaves
1 teaspoon coarse salt
½ teaspoon ground mace
½ teaspoon coarsely ground black pepper
2 tablespoons olive oil
2 large onions, halved lengthwise and slivered
⅔ cup dried cranberries
2 cups apple juice
1 cup Riesling wine
3 whole allspice
1 bay leaf
1 tablespoon red currant jelly
1½ pounds butternut squash, peeled and
*   cut into ½-inch cubes*
4 carrots, peeled and cut into ½-inch pieces
1 tablespoon cornstarch

1. Preheat the oven to 325°F. Wipe the pork clean with a damp paper towel.

2. In a small bowl, combine the oregano, thyme, coarse salt, mace, and pepper. Rub the mixture all over the pork.

3. Heat the oil in a large ovenproof pot over medium-high heat, and brown the pork well on all sides, 8 to 10 minutes per side. Transfer the meat to a plate. Reduce the heat to medium-low, and add the onions and cranberries to the pot. Cook, stirring, for 5 minutes.

4. Add the apple juice, wine, allspice, bay leaf, red currant jelly, squash, and carrots. Bring to a boil, stirring to scrape up any brown bits from the bottom of the pot.

Place the pork on top of the vegetables, and pour in any accumulated juices. Cover and bake, turning the pork over twice, for 2½ hours. It should be nice and tender. Remove from the oven and let rest for a few minutes before transferring to a cutting board. Using a slotted spoon, carefully remove the vegetables from the cooking liquid and reserve them in a bowl.

5. Place ½ cup of the cooking liquid in a small bowl. Add the cornstarch and whisk to combine. Slowly pour it back into the pot, whisking constantly over medium-low heat. Cook, whisking, for 5 minutes. Return the vegetables to the pot and heat to warm through, 1 minute more. Remove the pot from the heat and discard the allspice and bay leaf.

6. Carve the meat into ½-inch-thick slices, and serve the sauce and vegetables in a bowl alongside.

Serves 6 to 8

GENTLEMAN JACK COUNTRY PORK RIBS

★ ★ ★

Country-style pork ribs come from the shoulder end of the pork loin and are also called the end chops. Ask the butcher to completely remove the back blade bone (also called the short bone) and the blade cap and to also cut the piece into individual ribs. You should end up with nice meaty pieces. Unlike spareribs, one of these well-marinated ribs per person is plenty.

Beer: Midwestern lager

6 country-style pork ribs (½ pound each)
⅓ cup Kentucky bourbon
⅓ cup orange marmalade, melted
2 cloves garlic, very finely minced
2 tablespoons fresh orange juice
2 tablespoons dark brown sugar
4 whole cloves
Freshly ground
*   black pepper,*
*   to taste*

1. Place the pork ribs in a large bowl.

2. In another bowl, combine the bourbon, marmalade, garlic, orange juice, brown sugar, cloves, and pepper. Pour the mixture over the ribs, cover loosely with plastic wrap, and refrigerate for 6 to 8 hours or overnight. Bring to room temperature before cooking.

3. Preheat the oven to 350°F, and prepare a barbecue grill with medium-hot coals.

4. Remove the ribs from the marinade and place them in a 13 x 9-inch baking dish, reserving the marinade. Bake for 35 minutes, basting occasionally with the marinade.

5. Place the remaining marinade in a small saucepan. Bring it to a boil, reduce the heat to a simmer, and cook until slightly thickened, about 10 minutes.

6. To finish the ribs, place them on the grill, 3 to 4 inches from the heat source. Grill, brushing them well with the thickened marinade and turning them once or twice, until browned, glazed, and fork-tender, 8 to 10 minutes.

Serves 6

SOUTHERN BARBECUE

—🌶—

While I do not claim to be an expert, I do know that barbecue is serious business in the South. And when Southerners talk about barbecue, you can be sure they are not speaking about little backyard cookouts. The smoky, slow-roasted meats of Southern barbecue range from a whole hog to pork shoulders, ribs, beef brisket, mutton, chicken, and even goat. It comes chopped, sliced, minced, pulled, or clinging to the ribs, and is enjoyed on soft white bread or buns, cornbread, or just piled high with nothing underneath it. Barbecue accompaniments include coleslaw, onions, pickles, baked beans, potato salad, sliced tomatoes, corn on the cob, French fries, and even other substantial entrées like hash on rice, Brunswick stew, or burgoo! Whew! And for all its many combinations, shapes, and tastes, it's called just one thing: barbecue.

So, with such a broad spectrum of definition, you can imagine that when barbecue is the topic, it is a catalyst for great discussion. In fact, it can be regarded as its own category of Southern cuisine. But in all the debate, there are a few things great pit masters—artists who watch over the meat, tenderly basting and monitoring its progress—do agree on: The meat has to be cooked slowly, up to 12 hours, over a low fire (never exceeding 250°F) built of hardwood, such as hickory, apple, oak, or even pecan. No charcoal and no propane is permitted for a genuine barbecue. The meat emerges flavorfully smoked, incredibly tender, moist, and downright delicious.

Along with the slow cooking temperature, the real secret of barbecue is in the sauce. While the meat cooks, the basting sauce keeps the exterior moist. A finishing sauce is applied after the meat is cooked, just before it is served. Sauces are generally "secret," touted to be the chef's treasure. Each has at least one secret ingredient, undivulgeable cooking techniques, a few special incantations that are murmured over the pot, and who knows—maybe even fancy hand movements and footwork that go along with the stirring. The sauce types vary from state to state, even region to region. For example, North Carolina is a state divided by U.S. Highway 1. The western half enjoys a sharp vinegar-and-pepper sauce, while "down east" their finishing sauce is more mild, with a touch of tomato. Sauces from other regions include mustard, tomato, and ketchup as bases, with a vast array of additional seasonings, producing any variation of sweet, tangy, or tart; thick or thin; mild to fire-breathing hot. Sauces can be applied sparingly or used to smother the meat and soak the bread.

If you have a hankering for barbecue, try my recipe for North Carolina–Style Pulled Pork Barbecue (page 376). To help you become master of your own pit—your oven—I invite you to recreate my sauce with my blessings. Of course, my secret incantation over the sauce will go with me to the grave!

BARBECUED SPARERIBS

★ ★ ★

Racks of pork ribs need careful cooking so that they remain succulent and full of flavor without drying out. Unlike most traditional grill cooks, I don't sear them directly on the grill, then watch them cook to a char. My method is to bake and baste them, and then finish them off on the grill. Try it my way—I bet you'll be happy with the results.

Wine: Dry Creek Valley (CA) Zinfandel
Beer: Wisconsin lager

2 racks pork ribs (about 3½ pounds each)
Salt and freshly ground black pepper, to taste
1½ cups Backyard Barbecue Sauce (page 355), plus
more for dipping (keep separately)

1. Preheat the oven to 350°F.
2. Lay the ribs on baking sheets, meaty side up, and sprinkle all over with salt and pepper. Bake for 15 minutes.
3. Brush the ribs all over with barbecue sauce and bake, basting frequently, for 45 minutes more. Remove from the oven.
4. Thirty minutes before the ribs are finished baking, prepare a barbecue grill with medium-hot coals.
5. Place the ribs on the grill, meat side up, 3 to 4 inches from the heat source. Cook for 10 minutes, basting often. Turn the ribs over and cook, basting, for 5 minutes. Cut the ribs apart, and serve them with extra barbecue sauce on the side for dipping.
    Serves 8

NORTH CAROLINA-STYLE PULLED PORK BARBECUE

★ ★ ★

Even though I was born and bred in the Northeast, I've been known to discourse on Southern barbecue. Well, why not? I've eaten plenty of it throughout the South and I do have my own barbecue opinions, though they're not worth getting into a fight over. Better to just offer up my version. When it came to creating my own I looked to North Carolina, a state that's divided into two camps. The idea for the sauce's tomato base comes from the eastern portion of the state, the addition of vinegar from the western portion. The rest is my method of making it all work as a compatible whole. Cooking the meat covered, at a slightly higher temperature than is usual for this dish, yields perfect results in less time.

Wine: Amador County (CA) Barbera
Beer: Pennsylvania double bock

BARBECUE SAUCE
2 cans (32 ounces each) Italian plum tomatoes,
  chopped, with their juices
½ cup unsulfured molasses
½ cup honey
¼ cup tomato paste
2 tablespoons coarsely chopped garlic
2 bay leaves
2 tablespoons ground cumin
1 teaspoon cracked black pepper
1½ teaspoons crushed red pepper flakes,
  or to taste
6 cups water
1⅓ cups cider vinegar
Salt, to taste

2 tablespoons olive oil
4 pounds pork butt (Boston butt)
Soft rolls or sliced white bread,
  for serving
Zesty Picnic Slaw or Corky's Memphis-Style
  Coleslaw (page 100 or 101), for serving
Bread-and-Butter Pickles (page 192),
  for serving

1. The day before you plan to cook the meat, prepare the barbecue sauce: Place the tomatoes, molasses, honey, tomato paste, garlic, bay leaves, cumin, black pepper, and red pepper flakes in a large heavy pot. Bring the mixture to a boil. Reduce the heat and simmer gently, uncovered, over medium-low heat, stirring occasionally, until the mixture is very thick, 1½ hours.

2. Add the water and vinegar, and return the mixture to a boil. Reduce the heat and simmer gently, uncovered, over medium-low heat, for 1½ hours more. Remove and discard the bay leaves, season with salt, and set the sauce aside to cool. You'll have about 6 cups sauce. Cover and refrigerate overnight.

3. Preheat the oven to 275°F.

4. Heat the oil over medium-high heat in an ovenproof casserole or flameproof roasting pan. Add the meat and turn to brown on all sides, 8 minutes per side. Remove the meat and wipe out the casserole.

5. Place a rack in the bottom of the casserole. Place the meat on the rack and cover with 2½ cups barbecue sauce. Cook, covered, basting, until the meat is cooked through and the internal temperature on an instant-read thermometer placed in the thickest part of the meat reads, 150°F to 180°F, 4 hours. Remove the meat from the oven and set aside to cool.

6. Meanwhile, gently heat the reserved barbecue sauce.

7. When the meat is cool enough to handle, trim off and discard the fat. Shred the meat coarsely with your fingers, or pull it with two forks. Place the shredded meat in a large bowl, and toss it with the warmed sauce. Serve the pork on the rolls or bread, with either of the slaws and the pickles on top or on the side. Pass any extra barbecue sauce at table.
Serves 8

TACO POLISH-STYLE

★ ★ ★

On a trip to Texas to attend San Antonio's big April Fiesta, I was surprised to discover that the city has a significant Polish population. This was most evident when my nose led me to the pungent, mouthwatering smell of grilled kielbasa. Served, topped with Guacamole and Pico de Gallo, in a flour tortilla, this was for me, a real cross-cultural culinary find.

A NIGHT IN OLD SAN ANTONIO

The flavors of Texas are as big and diverse as the state itself. To sample them all, you'd need to eat there for years. Or you can go to San Antonio during the April Fiesta, when the city throws the biggest, tastiest block party west of New Orleans. One hundred thousand people come to eat, and there's plenty to go around: a vast selection of foods representing the Lone Star State's mix of cultures, Mexican, German, Cajun, Irish, Polish, African-American, and more. You can start off your evening with a kielbasa taco and finish with baklava or Black Forest cake. For the hours in between, there's barbecue, gumbo, catfish, tamales, corn dogs, wurst, shish kebab… get the idea? Arrive *hungry*.

The feast event, called "A Night in Old San Antonio," actually lasts four nights. It's a centerpiece to a century-old, city-wide celebration of music, art, history, and sport, held in commemoration of Texas's independence from Mexico. Local women stage a vivid "battle" to get things going, pelting one another with fresh flowers in a glittering parade led by marching bands and fantastically garbed "royals" and their entourages. More than 150 events, including costume balls, pops concerts, and track meets, follow in the next nine days. And it's all fueled by the bounty from some 240 vendors packed into the city's 250-year-old "La Villita" district, on the southern bank of the San Antonio River (and right on the famed River Walk).

I entered this food extravaganza a little dazed. A hundred aromas lured me in a hundred directions, it seemed; and a riot of brilliant paper camellias, streamers, and lace-cut banners beckoned my eyes every which way. La Villita's historic adobe buildings slowed my pace, too—I wanted to see them all. Fortunately, I had local food maven Betsy Schultz at my side to get me from place to place; without her, I might have gorged myself on the first chile con carne I happened on. She steered me first to the "Mexican Village," one of more than a dozen distinct areas, where a tejano band serenaded us as we snacked on *gorditas*—chicken or beef in a fluffy corn tortilla that's been grilled and split open. I had mine garnished with guacamole, shredded lettuce, and *pico de gallo*. At the "Texas Village," I sampled homestyle stage-coach barbecue, steer-on-a-stick (marinated beef kebab), Texas caviar (spicy black-eyed pea salad), ranch steak (tenderized beef with ketchup in a flour tortilla), Texas bird legs (succulent barbecued turkey legs), Texas toothpicks (skewered, breaded, and fried jalapeños), and shypoke eggs (grilled cheese and jalapeño, cut to look like fried eggs). Enough already!

Stuffed, we wandered in and out of the other areas, hearing plenty more live music—mariachi, Western swing, country, and jazz—along the way. Betsy broke a few colored, confetti-filled eggs over my head (another time-honored Fiesta tradition), but I was too sated to retaliate. Next time I'll try some brisket biscuit, fried dill pickles, and crawfish etouffée, too. I'll check out those rope dancers and clowns, dance that Chicken Dance, and stroll lovely River Walk when I'm through. Next time I'll come for all four nights.

Beer: Texas lager

*1 fresh or packaged kielbasa sausage (about
    1 pound), cut into quarters crosswise and
    halved lengthwise*
4 flour tortillas (7-inch diameter)
½ cup Pico de Gallo (page 196)
½ cup Guacamole (page 176)
1½ tablespoons chopped fresh cilantro leaves

1. Prepare a barbecue grill with hot coals.

2. Grill the sausage pieces 3 inches from the heat source, until well browned, about 5 minutes per side.

3. Meanwhile, wrap the flour tortillas in aluminum foil and warm them for a few minutes on the outside edge of the grill.

4. To serve, place 2 sausage halves in the center of a flour tortilla and dollop with 2 tablespoons each of Pico de Gallo and Guacamole. Sprinkle with chopped cilantro, fold in half, and serve immediately.

Serves 4

LARRY SMITH'S MOTHER'S PORK CHOPS

★ ★ ★

My good friend and colleague Larry Smith, born and bred in northern Michigan farm country, has long regaled me with tales of his mom's bean soup and her skillet pork chops, which were a once-a-week staple in the Smith family kitchen during his formative years. I think it's the sage and onions that make the chops so memorable. Thanks, Mom, and thanks, Larry, for passing along some really good home cooking! Serve the chops with buttered egg noodles and Shaker Applesauce.

Wine: Washington State Merlot
Beer: Midwestern pale ale

*4 pork loin chops, 1 inch thick
    (about ½ pound each)*
Salt and freshly ground black pepper, to taste
1 tablespoon dried sage leaves, crumbled
2 tablespoons olive oil
4 large onions, halved lengthwise and slivered
¼ cup dry white wine
2 tablespoons chopped fresh sage

1. Sprinkle the pork chops on both sides with salt and pepper. Rub well with the dried sage.

2. Heat the olive oil in a large cast-iron skillet over medium-high heat, and brown the pork chops on both sides, 3 to 4 minutes per side. Reduce the heat to low and cook the chops uncovered, turning once, until cooked through, 20 minutes. Transfer the chops to a plate and set aside.

3. Add the onions to the skillet, raise the heat to medium-high, and cook, stirring, or until wilted, 10 minutes. Add the wine and cook 5 minutes more, scraping up the browned bits

on the bottom of the skillet. Season with salt and pepper, and stir in the chopped fresh sage. Return the chops to the skillet and bury them in the onions. Cook until warmed through, about 5 minutes. Serve immediately.

Serves 4

IOWA FRUIT-STUFFED PORK CHOPS

★ ★ ★

It's not often I think to dedicate a recipe to meat producers, but I do this one. Iowa, our greatest pork-producing state, has led the way in making us a nation with the best pork in the world. Quality pork is what helps make these chops—as well as all the pork recipes in this book—as flavorful as they are. Dressed up with dried fruits and baked, they emerge from the oven aromatic and ready for family or company. Thanks, Iowa.

Wine: Dry Creek Valley (CA) Zinfandel
Beer: California porter

½ cup dried sour cherries
½ cup pitted prunes, halved
½ cup dried apricots, quartered
1¼ cups defatted chicken broth, preferably homemade (page 253)
½ cup bourbon
4 center-cut pork chops, 1½ inches thick (¾ pound each), with a pocket cut in each for stuffing
2 tablespoons olive oil
1 teaspoon dried thyme leaves
Salt and freshly ground black pepper, to taste
4 tablespoons (½ stick) unsalted butter

1. In a mixing bowl, combine all of the dried fruits with ¾ cup of the chicken broth and the bourbon. Set aside for 1 hour to macerate.

2. Preheat the oven to 350°F.

3. Drain the fruit, reserving the liquid. Stuff the pockets of the pork chops equally with the fruit. Close the pockets with toothpicks.

4. Heat the olive oil in a large skillet over medium-high heat, and brown the pork chops for 5 minutes per side. Transfer them to a shallow roasting pan, and sprinkle them with the thyme, salt, and pepper. Dot with 2 tablespoons of the butter. Pour the reserved fruit soaking liquid into the pan.

5. Bake, basting twice, until the chops are cooked through, 30 minutes.

6. Transfer the chops to a plate and cover it loosely with aluminum foil to keep warm. Discard any foam from the roasting pan. Add the remaining ½ cup broth to the pan, and cook over medium-high heat, stirring and scraping up any brown bits on the bottom of the pan, for 2 minutes. Swirl the remaining 2 tablespoons butter into the sauce, adjust the seasonings, and serve in a sauceboat with the pork chops.

Serves 4 hearty appetites

CIDER-GLAZED APRICOT HAM WITH RAISIN SAUCE

★ ★ ★

Festive occasions like Easter, Christmas, or Thanksgiving call for festive eating and a big baked ham is often the choice. When I served up this delicious version, everyone in my house enjoyed it for days, first feasting on luscious dinner slices laced with spiced cider-raisin sauce, and later enjoying leftovers in breakfast ham and eggs and lunchtime mile-high Dagwood-style sandwiches.

Wine: Oregon Pinot Gris
Beer: Missouri lager

1 ready-to-eat Virginia ham, bone in
  (14 to 16 pounds)
Approximately 35 whole cloves
¼ cup apricot preserves
3 tablespoons Dijon mustard
1¼ cups (packed) light brown sugar
4 cups apple cider, or more to taste
1 pound dried apricots
½ cup golden raisins
Pinch of salt
1 cinnamon stick (3 inches long)
1½ tablespoons cornstarch
3 tablespoons water

1. Preheat the oven to 350°F.
2. Carefully cut the thick rind and most of the excess fat off the top of the ham, being careful not to cut through to the meat. Using a sharp knife, score a diamond pattern on the surface.
3. Set the ham in a shallow roasting pan. Set aside 8 cloves and use the rest to stud the ham at the crossed point of each diamond.
4. Melt the apricot preserves slightly in a small saucepan over low heat. Brush the preserves all over the top and sides of the ham, and then brush the mustard all over. Pat 1 cup of the brown sugar all over.
5. Pour 2 cups of the apple cider into the bottom of the pan, and bake the ham, basting frequently, for 45 minutes. Then add the apricots to the basting liquid and bake until the ham is glazed and brown, another 45 minutes.
6. While the ham is baking, place the remaining 2 cups apple cider (or more for a thinner sauce), remaining ¼ cup brown sugar, the golden raisins, and the salt in the top of a double boiler. Cook over simmering water until the sugar has dissolved and the sauce is hot, about 10 minutes.
7. Tie the reserved 8 cloves and the cinnamon stick into a piece of cheesecloth. In a bowl, whisk together the cornstarch and water until smooth. Whisk this into the cider mixture, add the spice bag, cover, and cook the sauce, stirring occasionally, until slightly thickened, 20 minutes.
8. When the ham has finished baking, place it on a serving platter. Remove the apricots from the pan and decorate the top of the ham with them, securing an apricot in each diamond pattern with a toothpick. Defat the hot pan sauce in a gravy separator, and serve it alongside the ham. Remove the spice bag from the raisin sauce and pass the sauce at table.

Serves 20 to 25

COUNTRY HAM

—❦—

Curious about Virginia's formidable ham, I made my way to the picturesque tidewater town of Smithfield, renowned for its style of drying and smoking hams. Paying a visit to a smokehouse was as informative as I expected, and as I toured the site, the mighty hams were ever present: There were hundreds of them—240,000 pounds of them—watchfully suspended over my head, like surrealistic stalactites. Somewhat nervously—were the hams as secured as they looked?—I learned about this famous commodity.

Smithfield ham is one of a group of hams referred to as country or Southern-style ham. It is dry-cured (rather than the more common wet-cured) in a mixture of salt, sugar, and preservatives, then smoked over a selection of hardwoods, such as hickory, oak, plum, and apple. Hams cured this way dehydrate and lose a considerable amount of their original weight. The Smithfield process takes a minimum of 6 months, and the resulting ham has a silky texture, a musky aroma, and a strong, characteristically salty flavor. It is considerably different from the wet-cured versions.

Only hams dry-cured to exact specification for 180 days in Smithfield, Virginia, may be called Genuine Smithfield Hams. But they are not the only country hams, even in Virginia. Others are aged for more time or less time. Although less time results in a ham that is milder and moister than longer-aged hams, they are still delicious. Like wine, hams also vary in taste and flavor from company to company, and even year to year. It is important to find a company whose hams suit your taste.

When preparing a country ham, it is easier and customary to first saw off the large hock, if your ham has one. A hacksaw can handle this, but a local butcher may be a better choice. Call before bringing him your ham. You don't want to lug it over just to find out he won't do it. Before soaking a country ham, you will first need to scrub off the unsightly, but harmless, mold that covers it. Once cleaned, the ham can be soaked. Figure about 2 days to soak if it's aged under a year, 3 days if over. Soaking the ham in unseasoned water, changed daily, causes it to lose some of its saltiness, and to soften in texture, and it also prevents excess dryness.

Country ham offers a challenge when carving. I learned it should be savored in thin, delicate slices, no more than $\frac{1}{8}$ inch thick, for the most tender bite. You will need a good sharp edge on your carving knife to attain these thin slices. To carve, place the ham on a cutting board with the lean side up.

★★★★★★★★★★★★★★★★★★★★★★★★★★★★★★★★★★

Cut several slices from this side, giving the ham a good base to rest on. Turn the ham over and place it on its base. Beginning at the hock end, remove a small wedge. Carve thin slices perpendicular to the bone, always slicing on the same angle as the visible bone, to ensure tender slices. Release the slices by cutting horizontally along the center bone.

Serve the ham with my Rolled Buttermilk Biscuits and the gravy from Traditional Fried Ham and Real Redeye Gravy for true Southern flavor. A cooked country ham will keep, well wrapped, in the refrigerator for about 6 weeks. Like other meats, it will keep longer if taken off the bone in large pieces and not sliced before wrapping, or it can also be frozen.

If you can't find country hams locally, they can easily be mail-ordered. Allow 3 to 4 days for delivery, and remember you will need an additional 2 days for soaking, so plan accordingly.

GWALTNEY GENUINE SMITHFIELD HAMS
Smithfield, Virginia
(800) 292-2773

FINCHVILLE FARMS
Finchville, Kentucky
(502) 834-7952

GATTON FARMS FATHER'S COUNTRY HAM
Bremen, Kentucky
(502) 525-3437

S. WALLACE EDWARDS & SONS
Surry, Virginia
(800) 222-4267

STADLER'S COUNTRY HAM
Elon College, North Carolina
(910) 584-1396

BROADBENT'S B & B FOOD PRODUCTS
Cadiz, Kentucky
(800) 841-2202

★★★★★★★★★★★★★★★★★★★★★★★★★★★★★★★★★★

GLAZED COUNTRY HAM

★ ★ ★

For this recipe, I prefer to use a country ham that has been aged for about 90 days making it less salty than one aged longer. It is also smaller than a Genuine Smithfield Ham, since it has its long hock sawed off. I found a ham this size to be more manageable and just right for my needs. Once the boiling process is complete, and the skin and excess fat is removed, I glaze my ham by baking it. Once glazed, I use a very sharp knife to cut the ham into tissue-paper-thin slices. Remember, this is a cured ham, much like a prosciutto—and should be savored in thin slices.

Serve country ham in the same way you would prosciutto—draped over thin wedges of cantaloupe or honeydew melon—or layer it over muffins with Eggs Benedict. Or serve it Southern style, with warm biscuits slathered with orange marmalade.

Wine: Sonoma County (CA) white Zinfandel
Beer: Mid-Atlantic pilsener

1 aged country ham (about 14 pounds)
3 to 4 tablespoons Dijon mustard
½ cup (lightly packed) dark brown sugar
1½ to 2 cups apple juice

1. Remove the ham from its bag and scrub it well under running water, using a stiff brush to remove the (harmless) surface mold. Soak it, covered in cold water, for 48 hours, changing the water twice.

2. Drain the ham and place it in a deep roasting pan on top of the stove. Cover with water. Bring to a boil, reduce the heat to medium, and simmer, uncovered or partially covered, for about 3½ hours (15 minutes per pound). You will have to keep adding water to the pan to keep the ham well covered. The ham is finished cooking when an instant-read meat thermometer inserted in the thickest part of the meat reads 140°F for moist, tender ham, 155°F if you prefer your ham less juicy.

3. Cool the ham to room temperature, and remove all the skin and excess fat.

4. Preheat the oven to 350°F.

5. Place the ham in a shallow roasting pan and brush it all over with the mustard. Pat it all over with the brown sugar. Pour the apple juice into the bottom of the pan.

6. Bake the ham, basting frequently, until well glazed, 45 minutes.

7. Cut the ham into very thin slices—tissue-paper thin—and serve.

Serves 25 to 30

TRADITIONAL FRIED HAM AND REAL REDEYE GRAVY

★ ★ ★

Earlier in the book, I have a recipe for ham with my own version of redeye gravy. Now, it's dinnertime and time to make the real thing. Serve up the fried ham slices topped with gravy, and Creamy Grits and Down-Home Greens alongside.

2 slices country ham, preferably Smithfield,
*   each ¼ inch thick, skin trimmed off*
½ cup water
½ cup strong brewed coffee

1. Heat a nonstick skillet over medium-high heat. Add the ham slices and fry until browned on both sides and heated through, about 3 minutes per side. Remove the ham to a plate and keep warm. Pour off all but 2 tablespoons of the ham drippings.

2. Place the skillet with the drippings over high heat and stir in the water and coffee. Bring to a boil, scraping up the browned bits on the bottom of the skillet, about 2 minutes. Pour the gravy over the ham and serve.

Serves 2

Lamb

Lamb is lush, the most elegant of meats, and its rich, deep flavor is attracting more American fans all the time. Since lamb has such an assertive taste, I like to prepare it with equally assertive ingredients. Some of the most surprising dishes here involve bright, contrasting elements. The Deviled Lamb Chops have a spicy tingle; the San Francisco Chinatown Lamb Chops are spiked with ginger and soy. The Light Lemony Lamb Salad is cool and refreshing, an excellent choice for a summer dinner party. And the Santa Fe Lamb Stew has a vivid flavor base of onions and garlic, chile, cumin, cinnamon, and orange zest.

I like lamb just as well when it's earthy and warming—stewed with beans and vegetables, or cooked up in a pot of chili. Sometimes the simplest of recipes wins the day—there's something almost voluptuous about a garlicky roast done to a turn.

NAPA VALLEY LEG OF LAMB

★ ★ ★

Visits to the Napa Valley always remind me of the time I spent in Provence. I guess it's their similar climates, crops—from grapes and herbs to olives and figs—and a certain way of life that is in step with the rhythm of the seasons. This simply prepared roast leg of lamb with its earthy herb flavor would feel at home in either place. Enjoy it at a backyard luncheon with Stewed White Beans and Liberty Spinach Salad or for an elegant dinner party with Pan-Roasted Baby Whites.

Wine: Napa Valley (CA) Cabernet Sauvignon

1 leg of lamb (6½ to 7 pounds)
4 large garlic cloves, thinly slivered
3 tablespoons extra virgin olive oil
1 tablespoon cracked black pepper
2 teaspoons dried oregano
2 teaspoons dried tarragon
2 teaspoons dried thyme
2 teaspoons dried rosemary
2 bunches fresh rosemary, for garnish

1. Preheat the oven to 400°F.
2. Cut small slits all over the lamb with the tip of a sharp paring knife, and insert the garlic slivers in them.

3. Place the lamb in a shallow roasting pan and brush it all over with the olive oil. Combine the pepper and all of the dried herbs in a small bowl, and pat the mixture all over the lamb. Place the lamb in the oven and immediately reduce the temperature to 350°F. Roast for about 1½ hours, or until the temperature registers 135°F for rare meat, or 140°F for medium-rare, when an instant-reading thermometer is inserted in the thickest part of the leg. Let the lamb rest for 10 minutes before carving. (The internal temperature will rise slightly as the lamb rests. If you prefer the lamb more well done, roast it for another 10 minutes or so.)

4. Place the lamb on a serving platter and garnish with the rosemary sprigs. Cut into thin slices to serve.

Serves 8

BUTTERFLIED LEG OF LAMB MOSAIC

★ ★ ★

Cooking a boned leg of lamb can be tricky because the meat is so irregular in thickness. But I've devised an oven-roasting method that yields perfect results. And everyone's doneness preference is taken into account. The outer layer of the rolled-up meat is more well done, and toward the center the meat is rare to medium-rare (the slices at the end are done all the way through, of course). Since the thickness varies, a meat thermometer is useless. Just cook the roast exactly as described in the recipe. If your oven temperature is true, it will work every time!

Wine: Central Coast (CA) Cabernet Sauvignon
Beer: San Francisco porter

2 heads garlic
2 tablespoons olive oil
Salt and freshly ground black pepper, to taste
1 butterflied leg of lamb (about 4 pounds;
    see Note, page 388)
6 ounces sun-dried tomatoes packed in oil,
    drained, oil reserved
1 cup (packed) whole fresh basil leaves
3 roasted red bell peppers (see How to Roast a Bell
    Pepper, page 132)

1. Preheat the oven to 350°F.

2. Remove the outer papery skin from the garlic heads, and slice ½ inch off the tops. Place the heads in a small baking dish, drizzle with the olive oil, and sprinkle with salt and pepper. Cover loosely with aluminum foil and bake for 1 hour. Remove the foil and bake for an additional 15 minutes. The garlic should be soft and spreadable. Set aside to cool. Raise the oven temperature to 375°F.

3. Spread the butterflied leg of lamb on a flat surface. If necessary, open up the thicker pieces of lamb with a long, sharp knife to achieve a more uniform piece of meat for stuffing.

4. Squeeze the softened garlic pulp into a small bowl. Stir to make a paste.

5. Spread the garlic paste all over the surface of the lamb, then sprinkle salt and pepper over it. Lay the sun-dried tomatoes evenly over the lamb, and cover with the basil leaves. Top with the roasted red bell pepper halves.

6. Roll the lamb up lengthwise, jelly-roll style, and tie it at intervals with kitchen string.

7. Place the lamb in a shallow roasting pan, and brush it with the reserved sun-dried-tomato oil. Sprinkle with salt and pepper, and roast in the center of the oven for 1 hour. Let rest for 10 to 15 minutes before slicing.

Serves 6 to 8

ORANGE BLOSSOM BUTTERFLIED LEG OF LAMB

★ ★ ★

Abutterflied leg of lamb makes an impressive entrée, but because of the uneven thickness of the meat, when grilled flat, as is done here, you will need to test the meat frequently so that the thinner parts don't overcook. For this dish, I moved away from the more predictable soy sauce or red wine marinade and tried a fruitier approach. The marmalade in the marinade caramelizes the lamb beautifully as it sizzles on the grill.

Wine: Napa Valley (CA) Rhône-style blend
Beer: Massachusetts cream stout

MARINADE
6 tablespoons extra virgin olive oil
6 tablespoons fresh orange juice
3 tablespoons orange marmalade
2 tablespoons finely grated orange zest
2 tablespoons finely minced garlic
Salt and freshly ground black pepper, to taste

1 butterflied leg of lamb (about 4 pounds;
    see Note)
2 scallions (3 inches green left on), thinly sliced
    on the diagonal, for garnish

1. Prepare the marinade: Combine all the marinade ingredients in a small, heavy nonreactive saucepan, and cook over low heat, stirring, until the marmalade has melted, 2 to 3 minutes.

2. Place the lamb in a large bowl and coat it with the marinade. Cover and refrigerate for 6 to 8 hours, or overnight, turning the meat occasionally so that it is well coated.

3. Prepare a barbecue grill with medium-hot coals. Oil the rack well to prevent the marinade from sticking.

4. Grill the lamb flat, 4 inches from the heat source, turning it every 15 minutes and brushing it often with the marinade, until done to your liking, 40 to 50 minutes for medium-rare.

5. Transfer the lamb to a carving board and let it rest for 10 minutes. Then thinly slice the meat on the diagonal, and arrange the slices on a serving platter. Sprinkle with the scallions, and serve immediately.

Serves 6 to 8

NOTE: Have your butcher bone the leg of lamb, then slit the leg lengthwise and spread it flat.

LIGHT LEMONY LAMB SALAD

★ ★ ★

If you are lucky enough to have leftover meat from a roasted leg or grilled butterflied leg of lamb you can do nothing better with it than to put together this salad. The delicate mesclun makes a lovely bed for the string beans and beets, and sweetly complements the meat's complex flavor. The sprinkling of crunchy pecans and pungent basil are, perhaps, unexpected, but just right. Accompanied by fresh crusty bread, it makes a delicious dinner entrée.

NOTES ON LAMB

The delicate flavor and succulent tenderness of lamb makes it a favorite for a wide variety of meals, and an ideal choice for just about any preparation. Although all lamb is highly versatile, some cuts lend themselves especially well to certain kinds of cooking.

A butterflied leg or individual chops are great choices for grilling or broiling, and should be served rare to medium. I prefer loin chops for their tender little noisettes. For the most satisfying eating, get the chops cut at least 1 to 1½ inches thick.

A leg of lamb is well suited to roasting and dry oven heat because it is so tender. A roast rack of lamb (rib chops), with long frenched bones capped by paper frills, makes an instant celebratory meal, a perfect choice for any special occasion. Lamb foreshanks are ideal for braising, resulting in a meltingly tender meat when simmered for 1½ to 2 hours. Ground lamb makes great-tasting burgers and can be substituted for beef in chili recipes.

Lamb takes well to a variety of herbs and spices, including rosemary, basil, bay leaves, cinnamon, curry, garlic, oregano, and freshly ground pepper. Rub a mixture of seasonings on the lamb before broiling or roasting, or mix the herbs into ground lamb for redolent patties.

When selecting fresh lamb, look for meat that is pinkish-red. The lighter the color, the lighter-tasting the meat. Choose deeper-hued cuts if you want a more assertive, meatier flavor.

Wine: Virginia Rhône-style blend
Beer: Pennsylvania double bock

*½ pound thin string beans, stem ends
    snapped*
*4 generous cups mesclun (mixed baby
    lettuce greens)*
2 tablespoons finely chopped shallots
½ cup Lemony Dressing (page 86)
Salt and freshly ground black pepper, to taste
1 cup diced (¼ inch) Oven-Roasted Beets (page 279)
½ cup pecan halves
12 thin slices cooked lamb, all fat removed
¼ cup finely slivered fresh basil leaves

1. Bring a pot of lightly salted water to a boil. Add the green beans and cook until just crisp-tender, 4 to 5 minutes. Drain, rinse under cold running water, and drain again. Set aside.

2. Wash the greens gently and pat them dry. Divide the greens evenly among four dinner plates, piling them in the center.

3. In a bowl, mix the green beans with the shallots. Just before serving, toss the beans with 2 tablespoons of the dressing. Season with salt and pepper. Arrange the beans in the center of the greens.

4. Place the beets in a small bowl and toss them with 2 tablespoons of the dressing. Arrange them decoratively on top of the green beans, and scatter the pecans on top. Lay 3 slices of the lamb, slightly overlapping, in the center of each salad.

5. Drizzle each salad with 2 to 3 teaspoons of the remaining dressing. Sprinkle the slivered basil over the lamb, and serve.

Serves 4

GARDEN LAMB CHOPS

★ ★ ★

Grilled lamb chops are delicious served crudité-style, with lightly cooked, chilled vegetables and a garlicky mayonnaise-style sauce. Arrange all the ingredients attractively on a large decorative platter and make it the centerpiece of a spring buffet.

Wine: Santa Barbara County (CA) Pinot Noir
Beer: American pale ale

MARINADE AND LAMB
½ cup extra virgin olive oil
⅓ cup fresh lime juice
3 large cloves garlic, minced
¼ cup chopped fresh cilantro leaves
1 teaspoon ground cumin
*16 rib lamb chops, 1 inch thick,
    bones frenched (page 391)*

VEGETABLES
*1 pound sugar snap peas,
    strings removed*
*16 baby carrots, preferably with
    1 inch stem left on, peeled*
*½ pound very thin string beans,
    stem ends snapped*
*1 pound thin asparagus,
    tough ends removed*

TO FINISH
Garlic Sauce (recipe follows)
*½ pint yellow or red pear or cherry
    tomatoes*
6 hard-cooked eggs, halved
*3 to 4 tablespoons chopped fresh
    mint leaves, for garnish*
6 to 8 fresh mint sprigs, for garnish

1. Prepare the marinade: Combine all the marinade ingredients through the cumin in a large rectangular glass baking dish and stir well. Add the lamb chops and turn to coat them with the marinade. Cover, and marinate in the refrigerator for 6 to 8 hours.

2. Prepare a barbecue grill with medium-hot coals. Prepare a bowl of ice water and place it by the stove.

3. Prepare the vegetables: Bring a pot of salted water to a boil, and separately blanch the sugar snap peas, carrots, strings beans, and asparagus until just crisp-tender; 2 to 3 minutes for the snap peas, 7 to 8 minutes for the carrots, 5 minutes for the beans, and 2 to 3 minutes for the asparagus. As each vegetable is ready, remove it with a slotted spoon and plunge it into the ice water to stop the cooking. Pat the vegetables dry, and set them aside.

4. Grill the lamb chops, 3 inches from the heat source, brushing them with the marinade, for 5 minutes per side for medium-rare, or to the desired doneness.

5. Place the Garlic Sauce in a pretty serving bowl in the center of a large, attractive platter. Arrange the lamb chops, blanched vegetables, tomatoes, and eggs decoratively around the bowl. Sprinkle with the chopped mint, garnish with the mint sprigs, and serve.

Serves 8

Garlic Sauce

---★---

A spicy version of my Roasted Garlic Mayonnaise, serve this with cold meat sandwiches or as a dip for crudités.

8 cloves garlic, unpeeled
1 tablespoon olive oil
1 cup mayonnaise
Tabasco sauce, to taste
Salt and freshly ground black pepper, to taste

1. Preheat the oven to 350°F.

2. Place the garlic cloves in a small ovenproof dish and drizzle the olive oil over them. Cover with aluminum foil, and bake for 1 hour. Uncover and bake for 15 minutes more. Set aside to cool.

3. When the garlic is cool enough to handle, squeeze the pulp out of the skins into a small bowl. Mash the garlic to form a smooth paste. Add the mayonnaise, Tabasco, salt, and pepper, and stir to combine. Refrigerate, covered, up to 5 days.

Makes about 1 cup

HERB-CRUSTED RACK OF LAMB

★ ★ ★

Ernie's was one of San Francisco's top restaurants in the 1950s and '60s. At dinner any night of the week, you could count on recognizing a good portion of the clientele—anybody who was anybody ate there. I remember, years ago, having to make a reservation at Ernie's weeks ahead of my arrival in town from New York. I didn't want to miss out on their rack of lamb and Grand Marnier soufflé. Thoroughly delicious, the lamb was the best. Ernie's is gone now, but even today, when I prepare a rack, those taste memories come flooding back.

You'll need rib chops for this dish. Ask the butcher to prepare the rack so that the bones are properly "frenched" and the chops are perfectly trimmed. (If you'd prefer to french the chops yourself, see the box below). I've timed the rack for medium-rare chops, remembering that they still cook a little bit once they're out of the oven. Follow this timing unless you prefer your lamb well done, which I personally consider a terrible waste of an expensive cut of meat. Since each chop is small, allow four per person. To feed six comfortably, you'll probably need three racks.

TO FRENCH A RACK OF LAMB

— ❦ —

To french the rib bones of a rack of lamb, place the rack, fat side down, on a flat surface. Using a very sharp knife (a boning knife works well), make a cut across the rack, down to the bone, about 2 inches from the tip of the ribs. From this point, cut out all the meat from between the ends of the bones, then scrape the bones clean. If desired, save the meat scraps to be ground for use in a stuffing for a crown roast or for any other ground lamb dish.

Wine: Long Island (NY) Cabernet Sauvignon
Beer: Texas Belgian-style ale

2 tablespoons fresh bread crumbs
2 cloves garlic, peeled
¼ teaspoon coarse salt
2 tablespoons chopped fresh rosemary or thyme
*   leaves, or ½ teaspoon dried*
1 teaspoon coarsely ground black pepper
3 tablespoons extra virgin olive oil
1 rack of rib lamb chops (8 chops), bones frenched

1 Preheat the oven to 400°F.

2. Place the bread crumbs in a bowl.

3. Mince the garlic together with the salt. Add this to the bread crumbs along with the rosemary and the pepper. Mix in 2 tablespoons of the olive oil.

4. Cut the rack in half, so there are 4 chops to each side. Brush the lamb on the fat side with the remaining 1 tablespoon oil. Coat the rack and the end chops, except for the underside, with the crumb mixture, patting it on well.

5. Arrange the rack on a baking dish to fit, and roast until medium-rare (140°F on an instant-reading thermometer), 20 to 25 minutes. Slice the chops and serve immediately. If desired, decorate the ends of the bones with paper frills before serving.

Serves 2 to 3

CHINATOWN LAMB CHOPS

★ ★ ★

Although most of us don't think to order lamb in Chinese restaurants (if we even see it on the menu), it does have an affinity for the assertive flavors of Chinese cooking. I think you'll find the combination of an Asian-inspired marinade and lamb chops a delightful surprise.

Wine: Napa Valley (CA) Cabernet Sauvignon
Beer: Colorado brown ale

MARINADE
3 tablespoons light soy sauce
3 tablespoons clover honey
2 tablespoons Asian chili sauce (available in
  Asian markets)
1 tablespoon minced fresh ginger
1 tablespoon minced garlic
Juice and finely grated zest of 1 lime

6 loin lamb chops, 1½ inches thick

1. Prepare the marinade: Combine all the marinade ingredients in a large bowl.

2. Add the lamb chops and toss to coat them thoroughly in the marinade. Let them marinate, covered, turning them a few times, in the refrigerator for 2 to 3 hours.

3. Prepare a barbecue grill with medium-hot coals, or preheat the broiler.

4. Grill or broil the lamb chops, 3 inches from the heat source, for 4 to 5 minutes per side for medium-rare meat.

Serves 4 to 6

DEVILED LAMB CHOPS

★ ★ ★

Wait till you taste these little devils. They're just nicely spiced, not searingly so, but they do pack a surprise because most folks, I've found, don't expect to have their lamb served with a little heat. Pile the chops on one half of a large platter with grilled corn piled on the other. If you're not in the mood for wine or beer, an icy pitcher of iced tea is the drink of choice.

Wine: Sonoma County (CA) Cabernet Sauvignon
Beer: Pennsylvania double bock

MARINADE
¼ cup extra virgin olive oil
2½ tablespoons Dijon mustard
2 tablespoons fresh lemon juice
1 tablespoon Worcestershire sauce
1 tablespoon finely minced garlic
1½ teaspoons Tabasco sauce
½ teaspoon paprika
Salt, to taste

8 rib lamb chops, cut 1 inch thick, bones frenched
  (see To French a Rack of Lamb, page 391)

1. Prepare the marinade: Combine all the marinade ingredients in a large bowl.

2. Add the lamb chops and coat them well with the marinade. Cover and refrigerate for 6 to 8 hours, turning them occasionally.

3. Prepare a barbecue grill with medium-hot coals or preheat a broiler.

4. Grill or broil the lamb chops, 3 inches from the heat source, brushing them with the marinade, for 4 to 5 minutes per side for medium-rare meat.

Serves 3 to 4

SOUR CHERRY LAMB SHANKS

★ ★ ★

The slightly tart flavor of northern Michigan's wonderful dried sour cherries is just the right foil for lamb's richest flavor. The added carrots and tomatoes round out the stew, which I scoop over couscous and serve with plenty of crusty bread to mop up all the delicious juices. When shopping for lamb, be sure to buy the fore-shanks (front), not the short (hind) osso buco cut for this dish.

Wine: California Grenache
Beer: Washington State India pale ale

4 lamb foreshanks (about 1 pound each)
1 teaspoon coarsely ground black pepper
Salt, to taste
3 tablespoons olive oil
6 carrots, peeled and cut into ½-inch pieces
1 onion, halved lengthwise and slivered
1 cup defatted chicken broth, preferably
   homemade (page 253)
1 cup dry white wine
2 tablespoons clover honey
4 cloves garlic, lightly crushed
2 cinnamon sticks (each 3 inches long)
4 fresh sage leaves
Pinch of ground allspice
1 cup chopped seeded ripe plum tomatoes
1½ cups dried sour cherries
¼ cup chopped fresh flat-leaf parsley
Cooked couscous or white rice, for serving

1. Preheat the oven to 350°F.
2. Sprinkle the lamb well with the pepper and salt.
3. Heat 2 tablespoons of the olive oil in an ovenproof pot over medium heat. Add 2 of the shanks and brown them well on all sides, about 8 minutes per side. Transfer the browned shanks to a plate, and repeat with the remaining 2 shanks.
4. Pour off all the fat in the pot and add the remaining 1 tablespoon olive oil. Add the carrots and onion, and cook over medium-low heat, stirring occasionally, until wilted, 10 to 12 minutes.
5. Return the lamb shanks to the pot, along with any accumulated juices. Add the chicken broth, wine, honey, garlic, cinnamon sticks, sage, and allspice. Bring to a boil, cover, and transfer to the oven. Roast until the meat is tender, 1 hour.
6. Add the tomatoes and cherries, and cook uncovered for 45 minutes.
7. Remove the cinnamon stick, stir in the parsley, and serve over couscous or rice.
Serves 4

LAMB STEW WITH BEANS AND ESCAROLE, TOO

★ ★ ★

I owe the inspiration for this peasant-style stew, thickened with cannellini beans, to the wonderful Basque community I discovered on a trip to Idaho. Early Basque immigrants came to this country looking for shepherding work and a good many of them settled in Idaho's Snake River Plain. Today, in fact, Boise is home to the largest community of Basque people outside of Europe. This dish is not hot and peppery like Basque cuisine can be, just nourishing and hearty.

Wine: Columbia Valley (WA) Merlot
Beer: Seattle porter

3 tablespoons extra virgin olive oil
3 pounds boneless lamb shoulder, cut into
    1½-inch pieces
Coarsely ground black pepper, to taste
1 large onion, cut into ¼-inch dice
1 tablespoon minced garlic
1 can (28 ounces) peeled Italian plum tomatoes,
    chopped, ½ cup of the juices reserved
1½ cups defatted beef broth, preferably
    homemade (page 252)
1 cup dry red wine
2 tablespoons tomato paste
1 teaspoon sugar
1 tablespoon fresh thyme leaves, or
    1 teaspoon dried
3 cups cooked or rinsed, canned cannellini beans
4 cups coarsely chopped escarole
Salt, to taste

1. Heat the olive oil in a large heavy pot over medium-high heat. Brown the lamb pieces, in small batches, sprinkling them generously with the black pepper, 8 to 10 minutes per batch. Transfer the browned lamb to a bowl.

2. Pour any accumulated meat juices from the bowl into the pot, and add the onion. Cook the onion over low heat, stirring, until almost wilted, about 8 minutes. Add the garlic and cook for 2 minutes more.

3. Add the tomatoes and the reserved juices, the broth, wine, tomato paste, sugar, and thyme. Return the lamb to the pot. Bring the mixture to a boil, reduce the heat to a simmer, cover, and cook over medium heat for 1 hour. Do not let it boil (reduce the heat if necessary).

4. Stir in the beans and escarole, and simmer, uncovered, until the lamb is tender and cooked through, 15 minutes. Season with salt and pepper, and serve in shallow bowls.
Serves 6

MOVE OVER, SPINACH, MAKE ROOM FOR ESCAROLE

— ❦ —

Escarole, a familiar ingredient in Italian cooking, has been growing more popular of late, and is becoming as easy to spot in the produce aisle as it is on a restaurant menu. This mild-tasting variety of endive can be tossed raw into salads or prepared the Italian way, lightly sautéed in olive oil with garlic and a squeeze of lemon. Escarole lends a wonderfully delicate flavor when stirred into soups as a finishing touch, and makes an interesting addition to stews, matching up well with lamb.

When selecting escarole, look for broad, pale green leaves with a fresh, firm texture. As far as nutrition is concerned, this green is hard to beat. Escarole is rich in beta-carotene and vitamin C, potassium, calcium, fiber, and iron, and it's low in calories. To top it off, fresh escarole is in good supply throughout the year, with the peak season being spring through fall.

SPRINGTIME LAMB STEW

★ ★ ★

When spring lamb is at its most tender and sugar snap peas are ready to harvest, seize the culinary moment. Replace the heavier stews of winter with one that warms a chilly evening but hints at the light summer nights to come. Caramelized shallots, which I've added instead of onions, highlight the sweetness of this combination of tastes. I serve this stew in shallow bowls, over noodles or a grain to absorb the sauce.

Wine: Central Coast (CA) Rhône-style blend
Beer: Wisconsin dark lager

4 lamb foreshanks (about 1 pound each)
Coarse salt and freshly ground black pepper, to taste
3 tablespoons olive oil
2 tablespoons unsalted butter
6 shallots, peeled and split into sections if large
2 teaspoons sugar
4 cloves garlic, bruised
2 tablespoons potato starch or all-purpose flour
2 tablespoons tomato paste
1 tablespoon red currant jelly
*2½ cups defatted chicken broth, preferably
    homemade (page 253)*
1 cup dry red wine
1 teaspoon dried thyme
*4 small white turnips, peeled, halved, and
    cut into quarters*
½ pound baby carrots, peeled
*4 tablespoons chopped fresh tarragon leaves, or
    1 tablespoon dried*
1 cup green peas (fresh or frozen), thawed if frozen
1 pound sugar snap peas
¼ cup chopped fresh flat-leaf parsley
*Buttered hot, cooked orzo, couscous, or medium-wide
    egg noodles, for serving*

1. Sprinkle the lamb shanks with salt and pepper. Heat the oil in a nonstick skillet over medium-high heat, and brown the lamb well, 2 shanks at a time, on all sides, about 8 minutes per side. Place them in an ovenproof casserole. Pour the oil out of the skillet and wipe it out with a paper towel.

2. Preheat the oven to 350°F.

3. Melt the butter in the same skillet over low heat. Increase the heat to medium-low. Add the shallots and cook, stirring, until they are softened and browned, 8 to 10 minutes. Sprinkle with the sugar and cook, shaking the skillet, for 5 minutes more. Using a slotted spoon, transfer the shallots to the casserole. Add the garlic cloves to the casserole.

4. Whisk the potato starch into the skillet you used for the shallots along with the tomato paste, red currant jelly, chicken broth, wine, and thyme. Stir well, and bring to a boil. Reduce the heat to medium and cook, stirring constantly, until the sauce thickens slightly, 4 to 5 minutes. Add this mixture to the lamb and stir well to combine.

5. Bring a pot of salted water to a boil, add the turnips and carrots, and cook until tender, about 10 minutes. Remove the vegetables with a slotted spoon, and add to the lamb, along with 2 tablespoons of the tarragon. Stir, cover the casserole, and transfer it to the oven. Bake for 1¼ hours. Remove the casserole cover and bake the lamb until tender, stirring occasionally, 30 minutes more.

6. As the lamb finishes baking, bring a fresh pot of water to a boil. Add the green peas, if fresh, to the boiling water and cook until just tender, 7 to 10 minutes (if using thawed

frozen peas, cook for 1 to 2 minutes, just to heat through). Remove to a bowl with a slotted spoon and keep warm. Add the sugar snaps to the boiling water and cook until bright green, 2 minutes. Drain and add to the bowl with the peas. Set aside until the lamb has finished cooking.

7. Remove the lamb from the oven, stir in the green peas, the sugar snaps, and the remaining 2 tablespoons tarragon. Adjust the seasonings and stir in the parsley. Serve immediately in shallow bowls over orzo, couscous, or egg noodles.

Serves 4

SANTA FE LAMB STEW

★ ★ ★

You may not have thought about combining sweet potatoes with lamb before, but just wait till you try them together in this stew that cooks up in an easy hour. It is delectable sprinkled with toasted pine nuts and served over Polenta with Mascarpone.

Wine: Dry Creek Valley (CA) Zinfandel
Beer: California extra-special bitter

¼ cup olive oil
1 large onion, grated
2 tablespoons finely minced garlic
1 teaspoon chili powder
1 teaspoon ground cumin
½ teaspoon ground cinnamon
Salt and freshly ground black pepper,
*   to taste*
3 pounds boneless lamb shoulder, cut into
*   1½-inch pieces*
2½ cups defatted chicken broth, preferably
*   homemade (page 253)*
1 dried ancho chile, stem and seeds removed
Zest of 1 orange, in wide strips
4 carrots, peeled, halved lengthwise, and
*   cut into 1-inch pieces*
2 sweet potatoes, peeled and cut into
*   1-inch pieces*
2 roasted red bell peppers (see How to Roast
*   a Bell Pepper, page 132), cut into 1-inch*
*   pieces*
½ cup dried apricot halves
Polenta with Mascarpone (page 321),
*   for serving*
¼ cup toasted pine nuts (see To Toast Pine Nuts,
*   page 243), for garnish*
2 tablespoons chopped fresh cilantro leaves,
*   for garnish*

1. Combine the oil, onion, garlic, chili powder, cumin, cinnamon, salt, and pepper in a large heavy pot. Stir well, and then add the meat. Toss the meat with the spice mixture to coat it well.

2. Add the broth, chile, orange zest, carrots, and sweet potatoes. Bring to a boil over high heat. Then reduce the heat and simmer gently, partially covered, over medium heat for 30 minutes. Add the roasted peppers and dried apricots, and cook, partially covered, until the lamb and vegetables are tender, 30 minutes more. Remove and discard the chile and orange zest.

3. Spoon the stew over the polenta in shallow bowls, and sprinkle with the pine nuts and cilantro. Serve immediately.

Serves 4 to 6

BOWL OF RED WITH HEIRLOOM BEANS

★ ★ ★

One of the most popular heirloom beans available today, purple-and-cream-colored Anasazis, also known as Jacob's cattle beans, are related to kidney beans and were cultivated by the Anasazi

HEIRLOOMS

—❦—

If you've got a home garden, chances are you know what I'm talking about when I praise "heirloom" fruits, beans, and vegetables. These are the ancestors of the hybrid varieties cultivated for mass consumption, prized by chefs because they come in such a cornucopia of sizes, shapes, colors, and flavors. To get a sense of the diversity, skim the pages of an heirloom seed catalog, such as the one produced by Seeds Blüm, in Boise, Idaho. It lists twenty-two different kinds of cucumbers, twenty-nine distinct lettuces, thirty-seven potatoes, and much more—it's a breathtaking selection.

Southmeadow Fruit Gardens, a nursery in Baroda, Michigan, grows five hundred different kinds of heirloom fruit trees—apples, pears, nectarines, peaches, plums, cherries, berries, and quinces. Many of these trees produce fruit that tastes far superior to what's commonly available, since they come from trees not bred for the dura-bility and uniformity that supermarket chains require.

But people aren't growing heirlooms just because they look and taste good. Keeping old seed lines active protects our food supply by promoting biodiversity. Organic farmers like to grow heirlooms in their native habitats, where they're usually well adapted enough to thrive without pesticides or other unnatural intervention. The heirloom movement, spearheaded by nonprofit seedbanks and seed-swapping exchanges, is really about sustainable agriculture—the future of food, and the earth that feeds us.

SEEDS BLÜM
HC33 Box 2057, Boise ID 83706
(800) 742-1423

SOUTHMEADOW FRUIT GARDENS
PO Box 211, 10603 Cleveland Avenue,
Baroda, MI 49101
(616) 469-2865 ; Fax (616) 422-1464

Indians in the Southwest one thousand years ago. Today Elizabeth Berry, Santa Fe's renowned bean maven and grower, raises her own version of heirloom Anasazis under another name, New Mexico Red Appaloosa Beans, on her Abiquiu Farm. Look for Anasazis in specialty food shops; if you can't find them, kidney beans make an easy substitute. Serve this chili with warm Country Cornbread.

Beer: Your favorite American lager

½ pound dried Anasazi or kidney beans
1 dried ancho chile
3 tablespoons olive oil
2 red bell peppers, stemmed, seeded, and cut into
    ½-inch dice
1 large onion, coarsely chopped
2 pounds boneless lamb shoulder,
    cut into ½-inch cubes
2 tablespoons minced garlic
2 tablespoons chili powder
2 teaspoons ground cumin
2 teaspoons dried oregano
2 tablespoons unsulfured molasses
1 can (28 ounces) peeled Italian plum tomatoes,
    chopped, with their juices
2 tablespoons tomato paste
1 bottle (12 ounces) lager beer
Salt, to taste
Cooked rice or other grain, for serving
Guacamole (page 176), for serving
½ cup plain nonfat yogurt, for serving
½ cup thinly sliced scallions, for serving

1. Pick over the beans, discarding any stones. Soak them overnight in cold water to cover by 2 inches (or see page 336 for How to Quick-Soak Beans).

2. Drain the beans, rinse in several changes of cold water, and drain again.

3. Place the beans in a saucepan, cover with water, and bring to a boil. Reduce the heat to medium and simmer, uncovered, for 1 hour. Drain, and set aside.

4. While the beans are cooking, soak the ancho chile in hot water to soften it, 30 minutes. Remove the chile from the water, remove the stem and seeds, and purée it in a blender or food processor with 2 tablespoons of the soaking liquid. Set aside.

5. Heat the olive oil in a large heavy pot over low heat. Add the bell peppers and the onion, and cook, stirring occasionally, until wilted, 10 minutes. Add the lamb, raise the heat to medium-high, and brown, stirring constantly, for 5 minutes. Reduce the heat to medium-low.

6. Stir in the garlic, chili powder, cumin, oregano, molasses, tomatoes and their juices, tomato paste, and beer. Add the beans and 1 to 2 tablespoons (depending on taste) of the puréed chile. Bring to a boil, reduce the heat to medium, partially cover, and simmer until the meat and beans are tender, 1¼ hours. Adjust the seasonings and add salt to taste. Serve in bowls over rice, and pass the Guacamole, yogurt, and scallions at the table.

Serves 4 to 6

NEW YORK-STYLE CINCINNATI CHILI

★ ★ ★

Cincinnati has its own way with chili. The renowned slightly sweet, meaty concoction, with spices reminiscent of Greek cuisine, is served over . . . noodles! Two prominent families vie for the distinction of having introduced this chili to

Cincinnati. Nicholas Lambrinides staked his claim in 1949 by opening Skyline Chili, now a chain of wildly popular restaurants that has spread outside of Cincinnati. Before him, though, in 1922, Bulgarian immigrant Athanas Kiradjieff, proprietor of the Empress Hot Dog Stand, introduced a version of chili seasoned with his native spices. Just as meat dishes were served back home, Kiradjieff piled his mixture of finely ground lamb and beef on top of noodles. He, too, expanded into a currently popular chain of restaurants.

Putting aside the debate as to who originated the idea, Cincinnati chili can be enjoyed two way (chili and spaghetti), three way (with Cheddar cheese), four way (with beans or onions under the cheese), or five way (with both onions and beans under the cheese). The chili is also served with plenty of oyster crackers for crumbling on the top. The meat in my version isn't as finely ground as you'll find in typical Cincinnati chili, but it sure is good. Besides the suggested wine and beer, this chili goes down easily with an ice-cold cola.

Wine: Napa Valley (CA) Rhône-style blend
Beer: Midwestern lager

2 tablespoons olive oil
1 cup chopped onions
2 cloves garlic, finely chopped
1 pound ground lamb
1 pound ground beef
2 tablespoons unsweetened cocoa powder
2 tablespoons chili powder
2 teaspoons ground cumin
¼ teaspoon ground cinnamon
¼ teaspoon ground allspice
¼ teaspoon ground coriander
¼ teaspoon ground cardamom
1 can (28 ounces) plum tomatoes, crushed,
    with their juices
2 tablespoons tomato paste
2 tablespoons red wine vinegar
2 tablespoons honey
Salt and freshly ground black pepper,
    to taste
1 pound dried linguine noodles
2 cans (15½ ounces each) dark red kidney beans,
    rinsed and drained, for garnish
4 to 6 scallions (3 inches green left on), thinly
    sliced on the diagonal, for garnish
½ pound grated Monterey Jack cheese,
    for garnish

1. Place the oil and the onions in a heavy pot over low heat, and cook, stirring, until wilted, 10 minutes. Add the garlic and cook for 2 minutes, stirring often. Crumble in the lamb and beef and raise the heat to medium. Brown well, stirring often to break up the clumps, 10 minutes. Remove any excess fat from the pot.

2. Add the cocoa and all of the spices to the meat and cook, stirring, for 1 minute. Add the tomatoes and their juices, the tomato paste, vinegar, and honey. Bring to a simmer and cook, uncovered, until the flavors are well blended, 20 to 30 minutes. Adjust the seasonings, then season generously with salt and pepper.

3. Shortly before serving, bring a large pot of salted water to a boil. Cook the linguine until just tender, 10 to 12 minutes. Heat the beans in a covered saucepan over low heat.

4. Drain the linguine thoroughly. Divide the pasta among six to eight shallow pasta bowls. Top with the chili, then the kidney beans, scallions, and grated cheese. Serve immediately.

Serves 6 to 8

LOS ANGELES LAMB BURGERS

★ ★ ★

To me, avocado, tomatoes, and alfalfa sprouts are a dead giveaway of a Los Angeles–style sandwich. Add lamb to the California equation and you get this juicy and flavorful burger. Be sure you have a really ripe, juicy tomato to slice!

Beer: California pale ale

1 pound lean ground lamb
2 tablespoons coarsely grated onion
2 tablespoons coarsely chopped fresh flat-leaf parsley
½ teaspoon finely grated lemon zest
Salt and freshly ground black pepper, to taste
1 small ripe avocado, peeled and pitted
2 teaspoons fresh lime juice
2 tablespoons plain nonfat yogurt
4 best-quality whole-grain rolls, lightly toasted
1 large ripe tomato, cut into 4 thick slices
½ cup alfalfa sprouts

1. If you will be broiling the burgers, preheat the broiler.

2. In a bowl, lightly mix the lamb with the onion, parsley, lemon zest, salt, and pepper. Form the mixture into 4 patties, each 3 inches across and 1 inch thick.

3. In a separate bowl, mash the avocado with the lime juice and yogurt. Season with salt and pepper.

4. Broil the burgers (3 inches from the heat source) or pan-fry them (over medium heat in a nonstick skillet) until cooked through, 5 minutes per side.

5. Place the burgers on the rolls, and top each one with the avocado mixture, a tomato slice, and alfalfa sprouts. Serve immediately.

Serves 4

Poultry & Game

Had our Founding Fathers agreed with Benjamin Franklin, we'd all now have turkeys embossed on our passports. For turkey, he felt, should be our national bird. But, then, why not honor the pheasant, duck, and partridge as well? The Founding Fathers were no strangers to these birds at table, either. These days, chicken rules the roost, but we still eat other fowl. This chapter is dedicated to them, and to rabbit, too.

I open with the most beloved dishes: roast chicken, Southern-fried chicken, chicken pot pie, and kin. I've also got chicken in curry, jambalaya, gumbo . . . this is not a food one can tire of easily! But if you enjoy chicken, you'll relish the other poultry recipes, too: dark, rich squab simmered in sweet-and-sour sauce or partridge baked under bacon with an elixir-like gravy of bourbon, honey, and butter.

Naturally, I've included a Thanksgiving turkey—not just any recipe, mind you, but my family's favorite. The two rabbit dishes—one savory, the other sweet and sour—demonstrate this mild, moist meat's wonderful versatility.

ROSEMARY-ROASTED CHICKEN

★ ★ ★

My mother, Berta, always prepared roasted chicken on Friday night when I was growing up, and now when I visit, I still look forward to her making it for me. Although I use her roasting method, I have added garlic and fresh herbs to make the preparation my own. She says she doesn't mind. Rosemary has an affinity for chicken, but tarragon or sage is a lovely choice too, and can easily be substituted.

Wine: Central Coast (CA) Rhône-style blend
Beer: Wisconsin lager

1 roasting chicken (4 to 4½ pounds)
2 small oranges, halved
Salt and freshly ground black pepper, to taste
6 sprigs fresh rosemary
2 tablespoons olive oil
2 tablespoons unsalted butter
8 cloves garlic, unpeeled
1 large onion, halved lengthwise and slivered
1 cup defatted chicken broth, preferably
    homemade (page 253)

1. Preheat the oven to 350°F.
2. Remove any giblets from the chicken, and reserve them for another use, if desired. Rinse the chicken well inside and out. Pat it thoroughly dry. Squeeze the juice of one of the oranges all over the chicken. Sprinkle the cavity with salt and pepper. Carefully slip 2 small rosemary sprigs under the skin across the breast. Place 2 rosemary sprigs and the remaining 2 orange halves in the cavity. Tie the legs together with kitchen string.

3. Heat the oil and butter in a nonstick flameproof casserole or Dutch oven over medium heat. Beginning with the breast, carefully brown the chicken all over to a pale golden color, trying not to break the skin, 12 to 15 minutes total. Remove the chicken from the casserole and set it aside, reserving any juices.
4. Combine the garlic cloves and onion in a small shallow roasting pan. Place the chicken on top, and pour the reserved juices over all. Add the broth and cover with aluminum foil. Bake in the center of the oven for 30 minutes.
5. Remove the foil and stir the onion and garlic. Bake uncovered, basting every 15 minutes, until the juices run clear when a sharp knife is inserted into the thickest part of the thigh, 1 hour more.
6. Remove the chicken from the pan. Let rest for 10 minutes, then remove the string, and discard the oranges and rosemary from the cavity. Carve the chicken, and arrange the meat on a serving platter. Spoon the pan juices over the meat. Arrange the onion and garlic around the chicken, and garnish with the 2 remaining rosemary sprigs.
Serves 4

DEVILISHLY GOOD ROASTED CHICKEN

★ ★ ★

An overnight rest in a spicy marinade results in a chicken that is true to its name. When roasted, it releases flavorful juices to serve with mashed white or whipped sweet potatoes. Sheila's Black

Bean Soup makes a good starter—but serve it in small portions, since it can be pretty filling. If you feel like being a little more fiendish, say for a devilishly good Halloween celebration, double up on the Tabasco sauce.

Wine: California Zinfandel
Beer: Maine amber ale

2 chickens (2½ pounds each), quartered
2 onions, halved lengthwise and slivered
1 tablespoon finely minced garlic
2 tablespoons unsalted butter
2 tablespoons olive oil
2½ tablespoons Dijon mustard
2 teaspoons Worcestershire sauce
1½ teaspoons Tabasco sauce, or more to taste
1 teaspoon chili powder
½ teaspoon paprika
Generous pinch of salt
⅔ cup defatted chicken broth, preferably homemade (page 253)
Pinch of paprika, for garnish

1. Rinse the chicken pieces well and pat them dry. Snip off the wing tips and remove any excess fat. Place the chicken in a bowl and toss with the onions and garlic.

2. In a small saucepan, heat the butter and the oil. Whisk in the mustard, Worcestershire, Tabasco, chili powder, paprika, and salt. Toss the mixture with the chicken, onions, and garlic. Marinate, covered, in the refrigerator overnight.

3. Preheat the oven to 375°F, and bring the chicken to room temperature.

4. Place the chicken in a shallow roasting pan to fit, covering the pieces with the onions. Pour the broth into the pan.

5. Place the pan in the center of the oven, and immediately reduce the temperature to 350°F. Roast the chicken, basting it frequently, until it is nicely browned and the juices run clear when a sharp knife is inserted into the thickest part of the thigh, 1 hour. Skim the excess fat off the pan juices and pour into a sauce bowl. Serve the chicken hot, sprinkled with a pinch of paprika, and the sauce alongside.
Serves 6

MRS. GREEN'S SOUTHERN FRIED CHICKEN

★ ★ ★

I have enjoyed a lot of fried chicken, but after all is said and done, none can hold a candle to South Carolina–born Lula Mae Green's. Mrs. Green (Greeny to her friends) prepares her chicken two different ways, and she shared both methods with me, so that I could share them with you. In both, solid vegetable shortening is her frying medium of choice. And she covers the pan as the chicken fries, resulting in a lightly coated, golden brown, perfectly crispy chicken. Serve it as Mrs. Green does, with a pot of honey (for dipping, Southern style), alongside. And if you're looking for side dishes, I suggest Mashed Yukon Golds or Midwestern Baked Lima Beans, and Shaker Applesauce. Frosty glasses of lemonade or iced tea are my drinks of choice.

2 frying chickens (about 2½ pounds each),
   each cut into 8 pieces
2 teaspoons salt
1 teaspoon paprika
1 teaspoon freshly ground black pepper
1½ cups solid vegetable shortening
⅓ cup all-purpose flour

1. Remove any excess fat from the chicken pieces and trim off the wing tips. Rinse the pieces and pat thoroughly dry. Place them in a large bowl.

2. Combine the salt, paprika, and pepper, and rub the mixture into the chicken pieces well.

3. Heat the shortening in a deep, heavy 10-inch skillet over medium-high heat until hot (you want enough shortening to reach halfway up the chicken pieces when they're frying).

4. Meanwhile, dust the chicken pieces with the flour, shaking off any excess.

5. Fry the chicken, covered, in batches, starting with the skin side up, until golden brown and cooked through, 12 to 15 minutes per side. Drain on paper towels and serve immediately.

Serves 6

SUPER-CRISPY BUTTERMILK FRIED CHICKEN

★ ★ ★

If you're looking for an even crispier coating on your fried chicken, try this second of Lula Mae Green's recipes. Her secret to a super-crispy crust is to soak the chicken pieces in buttermilk before dredging them in flour. More flour clings to the chicken when it is soaked, and the presoaking also tenderizes the meat. Serve it up with a pitcher of fresh lemonade or iced tea garnished with mint sprigs and lemon slices.

2 frying chickens (about 2½ pounds each),
   each cut into 8 pieces
Salt and freshly ground black pepper
1 cup buttermilk
1½ cups all-purpose flour
2 teaspoons paprika
1½ cups solid vegetable shortening
Fried Chicken Gravy (recipe follows)

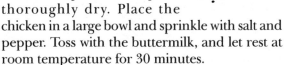

1. Remove any excess fat from the chicken pieces and trim off the wing tips. Rinse the pieces and pat thoroughly dry. Place the chicken in a large bowl and sprinkle with salt and pepper. Toss with the buttermilk, and let rest at room temperature for 30 minutes.

2. Put the flour in a large plastic bag and season it with the paprika, 1 teaspoon salt, and 1 teaspoon pepper.

3. Heat the shortening in a deep, heavy 10-inch skillet over medium-high heat until hot (you want enough shortening to reach halfway up the chicken pieces as they are frying).

4. Remove the chicken from the buttermilk and dredge it in the seasoned flour, shaking off any excess.

5 Fry the chicken, covered, in batches, starting with the skin side up, until golden brown and cooked through, 12 to 15 minutes per side. Drain on paper towels.

6. Serve hot, with Fried Chicken Gravy.

Serves 6

NOTE: Save some of the chicken-frying fat for the gravy, because even though only a small amount is used, it's full of flavor.

Fried Chicken Gravy

—★—

This white gravy for fried chicken (and mashed potatoes) is excellent. Not too thick and not too floury, it is easy to make just as soon as you finish frying the chicken. The key is to use a little of the chicken-frying fat—a tip I learned from Mrs. Green.

¼ cup chicken-frying fat
2 small onions, halved lengthwise and
  slivered
2 cloves garlic, finely minced
2 tablespoons all-purpose flour
2 cups defatted chicken broth, preferably
  homemade (page 253)
Pinch of freshly ground black pepper

   1. Heat the fat in a nonstick skillet over medium heat. Add the onions and garlic and cook, stirring, until lightly browned, 3 to 4 minutes.
   2. Add the flour and cook, stirring, until it turns golden brown, 2 minutes. Add the broth, bring to a boil, then reduce the heat and cook at a gentle simmer until thickened, 3 minutes. Add the pepper and serve hot.
   Makes about 2 cups

ICED TEA: THE CHAMPAGNE OF THE SOUTH

—❦—

When you visit the South, you'll most certainly drink "tea," meaning iced tea. It's served generously over crushed ice in everything, from Mason canning jars to fine glassware—refills encouraged. It usually comes presweetened, very presweetened, so if you like yours plain or moderately sugared, you'll need to say so.

   To get as fine a brew at home as you can get in the South, follow these simple steps. Bring a quart of fresh cold water to a boil. Pour it over 4 to 6 tea bags (use your favorite) in a heavy, heat-resistant glass or plastic 2-quart container. Let the tea bags steep 5 to 7 minutes, then remove. Add a quart of cold water and some ice, and Simple Sugar Syrup for Drinks (page 152), if you want to presweeten. Let the tea cool to room temperature before refrigerating it—this guarantees that it will remain crystal clear for at least a day. After a day, it will begin to cloud up and acquire a tannic taste. Serve with lemon slices.

   For mint iced tea (another Southern treat), add fresh mint leaves while the tea is still hot, and garnish glasses with a sprig of mint, too.

FOWL LANGUAGE

—❧—

*I*n case you're confused by the categories used in selling chicken, here's a list of the most common. They are broken down according to the bird's age and tenderness.

Squab: Not really chicken, but a young domesticated pigeon with juicy, tasty dark meat. Finding true squab will most likely require a trip to the specialty butcher. They are sold at 4 weeks old, about 1 pound or less. *Best broiled, grilled, or roasted.*

Squab Chicken: Different than a true squab, squab chicken is very small, with very tender meat. They are sold 4 to 6 weeks old, 1½ pounds or less. *Best broiled, grilled, or roasted.*

Game Hen: Descendants of Cornish chickens or of a Cornish chicken and a White Rock chicken; very flavorful. They are sold 5 to 6 weeks old, 2 pounds or less. *Split and broil or grill; roast.*

Broiler/Fryer: Young chicken with soft, smooth-textured skin; relatively lean, flexible breastbone. They are sold 13 weeks old, 3½ pounds or less. *Any cooking method, very versatile.*

Roaster: Young chicken with tender meat and smooth-textured skin; breastbone is less flexible than broilers. They range between 2½ pounds to 5 pounds. *Their higher fat content makes them good for roasting, just as their name implies.*

Hen/Stewing: Mature females; flavorful but less tender meat. Nonflexible breastbone. They are over 10 months when sold, 2½ pounds to 8 pounds. *Stew or braise.*

Capon: Surgically castrated rooster; tender meat with soft, smooth-textured skin; contains a high proportion of light to dark meat and has a relatively high fat content. They are under 8 months old when sold, 4 to 10 pounds. *Roast.*

Raising Chicken

Kosher: Kosher products are sanctioned by stringent Jewish law to adhere to specific preparation, therefore kosher chickens are generally of higher quality than other chickens. They also tend to taste saltier than conventional chicken because salting the bird is part of the koshering process.

Free-range: In contrast to mass-produced birds which are kept in small spaces, free-range chickens are permitted to roam about freely. While it is not mandatory, some free-range chickens are fed a healthier diet. Although free-range chickens cost more, many people believe they have more flavor than commercially raised chickens.

Organic: Organic chickens are fed a diet free of pesticides, antibiotics, by-products, growth promoters, and hormones; any grain that they are fed must also be organic. An organic chicken is generally thinner and has a more yellow hue, and less fat and more flavor than conventional chickens. Many organic chickens are also free-range.

GRILLED BARBECUED CHICKEN

★ ★ ★

Great barbecued chicken should be moist and tender inside, with lacquered, finger-licking skin outside. This is not easy to achieve if the chicken is cooked completely on the grill, where it can end up cooked to a crisp with skin so charred that it is impossible to enjoy. To solve this problem, I've been prebaking my chicken and then finishing it up on the grill, brushing lightly at each stage with barbecue sauce. It works! For a more intense flavor, throw some mesquite chips on the fire once you get it started.

Wine: Monterey County (CA) Petite-Sirah
Beer: American lager

2 frying chickens (2 to 2½ pounds each),
 each cut into quarters, rinsed, and
 patted dry
Salt and freshly ground black pepper, to taste
1 cup barbecue sauce, preferably Backyard
 Barbecue Sauce (page 355)

1. Preheat the oven to 400°F.
2. Place the chicken quarters in a large roasting pan. Sprinkle with salt and pepper, and lightly brush with ¼ cup of the barbecue sauce. Bake for 15 minutes, and then reduce the temperature to 350°F. Cook the chicken for 40 minutes more.

3. Meanwhile, prepare a barbecue grill with medium-hot coals.

4. Place the chicken on the grill, skin side down, 3 to 4 inches from the heat source. Cook for 15 minutes, brushing the pieces with the remaining sauce and turning them over once. Serve immediately.
Serves 8

CREAMED CHICKEN WITH ZUCCHINI AND CORN

★ ★ ★

The choice of vegetables in this creamy potted chicken gives the dish a contemporary feel. Although corn is a long-standing friend to cream sauces, zucchini is usually sauced by tomatoes. I think you'll like it equally well in this partnership, which I recommend serving over a scoop of white rice.

Wine: Napa Valley (CA) Cabernet
 Franc
Beer: Oregon pale ale

¼ *pound slab bacon, rind removed, cut into*
   ¼-inch dice

1 chicken (3½ pounds), cut into 8 pieces

Salt and freshly ground black pepper, to taste

Paprika, to taste

1 tablespoon olive oil, if needed

1 large onion, cut into ¼-inch dice

1 red bell pepper, stemmed, seeded, and
   cut into ¼-inch dice

1 yellow bell pepper, stemmed, seeded, and
   cut into ¼-inch dice

1 cup defatted chicken broth, preferably
   homemade (page 253)

2 zucchini, trimmed and cut into ¼-inch dice

2 cups fresh or frozen corn kernels,
   thawed if frozen

2 sprigs fresh thyme

1 cup heavy (or whipping) cream

Hot cooked white rice, for serving

2 tablespoons chopped fresh cilantro leaves,
   for garnish

1. Place the bacon in a large heavy pot over medium-low heat and cook until golden brown and the fat is rendered, 6 to 8 minutes. Transfer the bacon to a bowl with a slotted spoon, and set it aside.

2. Rinse the chicken pieces and pat them dry. Season with salt, pepper, and paprika. Brown the chicken in the rendered bacon fat, in batches, over medium heat until golden brown, about 5 minutes per side. If necessary, add the olive oil to the pot. Transfer the chicken to the bowl with the bacon.

3. Add the onion and both bell peppers to the pot and cook, stirring occasionally, until softened, 5 to 7 minutes. Add the broth and bring it to a boil. Reduce the heat and simmer, scraping up the browned bits on the bottom of the pan, 2 minutes.

4. Return the chicken and bacon to the pot, cover, and simmer for 10 minutes. Stir in the zucchini, corn, and thyme. Cover and simmer over medium heat for 10 minutes more.

5. Remove the chicken from the pot and set it aside. Add the cream to the vegetables and bring it to a boil. Reduce the heat slightly and simmer until the cream has thickened slightly, 3 to 5 minutes. Season with salt and pepper. Return the chicken to the pot, smother with the vegetables, and heat until cooked through, 10 minutes.

6. Serve in shallow bowls over cooked rice, sprinkled with the cilantro.

Serves 4

SAVORY CHICKEN POT PIE

★ ★ ★

I'm a great fan of chicken pot pie, and as for so many of its fans, the familiar combination of meat, carrots, and potatoes has been a tried-and-true favorite of mine since childhood. But wait till you other fans try this version—think of it as pot pie grows up. Leeks and parsnips join the chicken and carrots, as do tart-sweet dried cherries and green peppercorns. Roasting the chickens first adds a more pronounced flavor to the meat, and the defatted roasting juices makes a strong base for the pot pie's sauce. The filling can be prepared a day ahead, and the pie can be assembled shortly before baking. Served under a blanket of buttery puff pastry, the pie makes a dramatic entrée for entertaining friends and family.

Wine: Central Coast (CA) Pinot Noir
Beer: Wisconsin lager

2 small chickens (2 to 2½ pounds each),
    rinsed and patted dry
2 large lemons, halved
1 bunch fresh thyme sprigs (10 to 12 sprigs)
2 tablespoons olive oil
Salt and freshly ground black pepper,
    to taste
4 leeks (3 inches green left on), cut into
    ½-inch pieces, well rinsed
4 carrots, peeled and cut into ½-inch pieces
2 parsnips, peeled and cut into ½-inch pieces
1½ cups dried sour cherries
¼ cup chopped fresh flat-leaf parsley
¼ pound slab bacon, rind removed, cut into
    ½-inch pieces
3 cups defatted chicken broth, preferably
    homemade (page 253)
¼ cup cornstarch
1 tablespoon drained whole green peppercorns
2 teaspoons finely grated orange zest
1½ teaspoons dried thyme
1 sheet prepared puff pastry (about
    ½ pound), thawed if frozen and
    refrigerated until use
1 large egg yolk
2 teaspoons water

1. Preheat the oven to 375°F.

2. Place the chickens side by side in a shallow flameproof roasting pan. Squeeze the lemon halves over and inside each chicken. Place the 2 squeezed lemon halves and half of the thyme sprigs inside each chicken. Brush the chickens all over with the olive oil, and sprinkle inside and out with salt and pepper.

3. Roast the chickens until the juices run clear when a sharp knife is inserted into the thickest part of the thigh, 1½ hours. Set them aside to cool, reserving all the cooking juices. If you are baking the pot pies on the day you are preparing the filling, leave the oven on.

4. While the chickens are cooling, bring a pot of water to a boil. Blanch the leeks in the boiling water for 2 minutes. Remove with a slotted spoon, then drain and pat dry. Blanch the carrots and parsnips in the boiling water for 5 minutes. Drain and pat dry. Place the vegetables in a large bowl, along with the cherries and the parsley.

5. Place the bacon in a nonstick skillet over medium-low heat and cook until golden brown and the fat is rendered, about 10 minutes. Using a slotted spoon, transfer the bacon to the bowl with the vegetables.

6. When the chickens are cool enough to handle, remove and discard the skin. Shred the meat into generous pieces, about 3½ inches x 1 inch. Add the shredded chicken to the vegetables and toss together well, seasoning with salt and pepper. Set aside.

7. Skim the excess fat off the reserved chicken juices, or pour them through a gravy separator. Pour the defatted juices back into the roasting pan and place it over low heat. Add 2 cups of the chicken broth and cook, scraping up any brown bits, 10 minutes. Pour the broth through a strainer into a heavy saucepan, and bring to a boil. Reduce the heat to a simmer.

8. Mix the cornstarch with the remaining 1 cup chicken broth, and slowly add it to the simmering broth, whisking until it has dissolved and the sauce is beginning to thicken, 2 to 3 minutes. Add the green peppercorns, orange zest, and dried thyme, and simmer gently for 10 minutes.

9. Add the sauce to the chicken and vegetables, and fold all the ingredients together well. Spoon into a 2-quart round ovenproof casserole. (The pot pie can be made in advance to this point. Cover and refrigerate until ready to bake. Before baking, preheat the oven to 375°F.)

10. Roll out the pastry on a lightly floured surface so that it is 1½ to 2 inches larger than the diameter of the baking dish.

11. Beat the egg yolk with the water, and lightly brush this egg wash around the inside and outside rim of the dish. Lay the puff pastry over the dish, trim the overhang to 1 inch, and crimp the edges around the rim to form a tight seal. If you like, make a decorative pattern with any remaining scraps on the top of the pastry. Brush the entire surface lightly with the egg wash. Cut six 2-inch slits in the pastry to allow steam to escape. Place the dish on a baking sheet, and bake until the filling is bubbly and pastry is cooked through and golden brown, 50 minutes.

12. To serve, cut through the pastry with serving spoons. Spoon the chicken filling onto serving plates and top with a piece of the crust.

Serves 6 to 8

LA TASHA'S JAMBALAYA— THE REAL THING

★ ★ ★

It was pouring rain in usually sunny Charleston, South Carolina, on the October Sunday that I visited the annual Taste of Charleston. That didn't stop me. I set off for the Boone Hall plantation, where I ate my way through as many booths as possible, sampling gumbo here, red rice there, and crab cakes wherever they were offered. Filled to the brim and soaked to the bones, I sloshed my way to one last booth. There stood the crew from Robert Pinkey's restaurant, La Tasha's, serving out cups of jambalaya. As full as I was, I some-

how found room for two cups worth—that's how good the jambalaya was! I managed to meet Robert Pinkey and praise his jambalaya in person. He graciously shared the recipe with me, and here it is, the real thing. Invite your friends over and *laissez les bon temps rouler!*

Wine: Russian River Valley (CA) Zinfandel
Beer: Louisiana lager

1 cup vegetable oil
1 pound hot smoked sausage, cut into 1-inch pieces
1 pound andouille sausage, cut into 1-inch pieces
2 chickens (2 to 2½ pounds each), each cut into
    8 pieces, rinsed, and patted dry
Salt and coarsely ground black pepper, to taste
3 large onions, chopped
2 cloves garlic, minced
1 cup diced (¼ inch) celery
1 large red bell pepper, stemmed, seeded,
    and cut into ½-inch dice
1 large green bell pepper, stemmed, seeded,
    and cut into ½-inch dice
2 bay leaves
1 teaspoon dried basil
¼ teaspoon cayenne pepper
2 cups long-grain white rice
4½ cups defatted chicken broth, preferably
    homemade (page 253)
1 cup prepared tomato sauce
½ cup plus 2 tablespoons tomato paste
2 pounds medium shrimp, peeled and deveined
¾ cup chopped fresh flat-leaf parsley

1. Heat the oil in a very large heavy pot over medium heat. Add both sausages and cook, until browned, 10 minutes, turning the pieces often. Using a slotted spoon, transfer them to a bowl and set aside.

2. Sprinkle the chicken pieces with salt and pepper. Add them to the pot, in batches, and brown all over, about 10 minutes per batch. Remove and add to the bowl with the sausages.

3. Add the onions to the pot and cook over low heat until wilted, 10 minutes. Add the garlic, celery, both bell peppers, the bay leaves, basil, and cayenne and cook for another 5 minutes.

4. Add the rice to the vegetables and cook, stirring, for 5 minutes. Return the sausage and chicken to the pot. Add the broth, tomato sauce, and tomato paste and bring to a boil. Reduce the heat to a simmer and cook, covered, until the chicken is cooked through, 20 to 25 minutes.

5. Stir in the shrimp and parsley, and cook, covered, until the shrimp is cooked through, 5 minutes. Adjust the seasonings. Remove and discard the bay leaves, and serve.

Serves 8 to 10

SANDI HILLMER'S WISCONSIN CASSOULET

★ ★ ★

Besides writing cookbooks, I have enjoyed being Food Editor of *Parade* since 1986. In the fall of 1995, the editors of the magazine decided to hold a contest, asking our readers to submit the recipe for their best one-pot meal so that we could see how they really cooked at home. We received over 15,000 recipes, and after testing and tasting, Sandi Hillmer's cassoulet, sent to us from Muskego, Wisconsin, took the prize. Was it ever delicious! Sandi seems to be my soulmate—she uses as many ingredients as I do! Flavor is what I like, and Sandi's cassoulet is a winner!

Wine: Central Coast (CA) Zinfandel
Beer: Wisconsin brown lager

1 pound dried navy beans
4 celery tops (about 3 inches each) with leaves
2 bay leaves
2 sprigs fresh flat-leaf parsley
¼ pound slab bacon, rind removed, cut into
    ¼-inch dice
4 tablespoons olive oil, or more if necessary
3 skinless, boneless chicken breast halves
    (about 5 ounces each), cut into 1½-inch pieces
1 boneless pork loin (about 3 pounds), cut into
    1½-inch pieces
1 cup chopped onions
¾ cup chopped celery
¾ cup peeled and chopped carrots
3 cloves garlic, peeled and minced
3 cups defatted chicken broth, preferably
    homemade (page 253)
1 can (28 ounces) Italian plum tomatoes,
    undrained, coarsely chopped
⅓ cup pure maple syrup
¼ cup (packed) light brown sugar
1 teaspoon dried thyme
¼ teaspoon dried savory
¼ teaspoon dry mustard
¼ teaspoon cracked black pepper
½ pound kielbasa sausage, cut into 1½-inch pieces
¼ cup chopped fresh flat-leaf parsley, plus
    3 tablespoons for garnish
2 teaspoons salt, or to taste

1. Pick over the beans, discarding any stones. Soak them overnight in cold water to cover by 2 inches (or see page 336 for How to Quick-Soak Beans).

2. Drain the beans in several changes of cold water, and drain again. Place the beans in a large heavy pot, and add water to cover. Add the celery tops, bay leaves, and parsley sprigs. Simmer for 30 minutes over medium heat.

3. Meanwhile, place the bacon in a very large pot over medium-low heat and cook until golden brown and the fat is rendered, 6 to 8 minutes. Remove the bacon with a slotted spoon and set it aside. Add 2 tablespoons of the olive oil to the pot, and brown the chicken and the pork, in batches, 5 to 6 minutes per batch. Using a slotted spoon, transfer the meat to a bowl and set aside.

4. Add the remaining 2 tablespoons olive oil to the pot and cook the onions, celery, and carrots over medium-low heat until wilted, 8 to 10 minutes.

5. Return the browned meat and bacon to the pot along with the beans (discard the celery tops). Add the garlic, broth, tomatoes, syrup, brown sugar, and all of the dried herbs and spices. Simmer, stirring occasionally, for 1 hour.

6. Add the kielbasa and simmer, stirring once or twice, until all is cooked through, 30 minutes.

7. Remove the parsley sprigs and bay leaves from the cassoulet. Stir in the ¼ cup chopped parsley and season with the salt. Serve immediately, garnished with the remaining 3 tablespoons chopped parsley.

Serves 8 to 10

SAVANNAH CURRY

★ ★ ★

Miss Eliza Leslie, a nineteenth-century cookbook author, writes that this well-spiced dish, more commonly known as Country Captain, can be attributed to a British sea captain, who brought the recipe to America upon arriving here from his station in India. Georgians enjoyed its pungent flavors and were quick to adopt it as their own. Basically it is a rich chicken curry, but instead of serving it with a chutney condiment alongside, the chutney is cooked in the pot with the chicken. Serve the curry over steamy hot white rice.

Wine: Russian River Valley (CA) Gewürztraminer
Beer: Seattle India pale ale

1 chicken (2½ pounds), cut into 8 pieces
¼ pound slab bacon, rind removed,
    cut into ¼-inch dice
2 to 4 tablespoons olive oil
⅓ cup all-purpose flour
Paprika, to taste
Salt and freshly ground black pepper, to taste
1 onion, cut into ¼-inch dice
1 green bell pepper, stemmed, seeded, and
    cut into ¼-inch dice
2 teaspoons minced garlic
2 tablespoons curry powder
1 tablespoon fresh thyme leaves, or 1 teaspoon dried
2 cups canned stewed tomatoes
2 cups defatted chicken broth, preferably
    homemade (page 253)
2 tablespoons chopped mango chutney
2 tablespoons dried currants
2 tablespoons chopped fresh flat-leaf parsley
Hot cooked white rice, for serving

1. Rinse the chicken, removing any excess fat. Snip off the wing tips. Pat thoroughly dry.

2. Place the bacon in a heavy pot over medium-low heat and cook until golden brown and the fat is rendered, 6 to 8 minutes. Remove the bacon to a bowl with a slotted spoon, and set aside. Add enough olive oil to the pot to make 2 tablespoons.

3. Combine the flour, paprika, salt, and pepper in a large bowl. Dredge the chicken in the seasoned flour, shaking off any excess.

4. Brown the chicken, in batches, over medium heat, 10 minutes per batch. Remove from the pot and set aside.

5. Add another 2 tablespoons oil to the pot, along with the onion and bell pepper. Cook over low heat, stirring occasionally, until wilted, 10 minutes. Add the garlic and cook for 2 minutes more. Sprinkle with the curry powder and thyme, and cook, stirring, for 1 minute.

6. Add the tomatoes, broth, and chutney to the pot and stir to combine. Add the bacon and chicken. Bring to a boil, reduce the heat to medium, and simmer until the chicken is cooked through, 20 to 25 minutes. Add the currants and cook for another 5 minutes. Stir in the parsley, and serve immediately over the rice.

Serves 4

"YA YA" GUMBO

★ ★ ★

There are gumbos and there are gumbos, but I have never tasted one as good as Eula Mae Dore's. I was served it for lunch on Avery Island, in Louisiana's bayou country, when I was a guest of the McIlhennys, who own the Tabasco sauce company. Although this lively stew can be made with seafood, duck, and game, Ms. Dore stuck to the basics—chicken and sausage. She thickens her gumbo, not with okra, which is also traditional, but with filé powder that she prefers to make herself, gathering the leaves from nearby sassafras trees. To make her gumbo, you'll find the filé powder you need at a specialty food market or large supermarket. Just a little thickens the gumbo, and rather than adding it to the pot (filé powder that is boiled results in stringy gumbo), serve it on the table in a small dish with a tiny spoon. This way, guests can sprinkle it over their individual portions. Besides the wine, minty iced tea goes well with gumbo.

Wine: Washington State Chardonnay

1 chicken (2½ to 3 pounds), cut into 6 pieces
4 tablespoons vegetable oil
½ pound andouille sausage, cut into
    ½-inch pieces
6 cups defatted chicken broth, preferably
    homemade (page 253)
⅓ cup all-purpose flour
3 ribs celery, cut into ¼-inch dice
1 large onion, chopped
1 green bell pepper, stemmed, seeded, and
    cut into ¼-inch dice
1 tablespoon minced garlic
4 tablespoons chopped fresh flat-leaf
    parsley
2 bay leaves
½ teaspoon dried thyme
1 teaspoon Tabasco sauce
Salt and freshly ground black pepper,
    to taste
4 scallions (3 inches green left on),
    thinly sliced
2 cups hot cooked white rice, for serving
Filé powder, for serving

1. Rinse the chicken well, trimming away any excess fat, and pat the pieces dry.

2. Heat 2 tablespoons of the oil in a large heavy pot over medium heat, and cook the sausage until browned, about 7 minutes. Transfer the sausage to a bowl with a slotted spoon, and set aside. Add the chicken pieces to the pot, in two batches, if necessary, and cook until golden brown, turning, 10 minutes per batch. Pour off the fat.

3. Add the broth to the pot, cover, and simmer over medium-low heat until the chicken is tender, 20 to 25 minutes. Remove the chicken pieces and set them aside to cool. Set the pot of broth aside also. When the chicken is cool enough to handle, remove the skin and bones and cut the meat into ½-inch pieces. Set aside.

4. Meanwhile, in a cast-iron pot or skillet, combine the remaining 2 tablespoons oil with the flour and cook over medium-low heat, whisking constantly, until the mixture becomes a rich red-brown, about 30 minutes. Add the celery, onion, bell pepper, garlic, and 2 tablespoons of the parsley. Cook, stirring, for 10 minutes.

5. Add some of the reserved broth to the vegetable mixture, then pour the mixture, making sure to get it all, into the pot with the rest of the broth. Add the bay leaves, thyme, Tabasco, salt, and pepper. Bring to a boil. Reduce the heat to medium-low and simmer, uncovered, for 45 minutes. Add the chicken and sausage, and simmer for another 15 minutes.

6. Remove the pot from the heat, add the scallions, and adjust the seasonings. Let the gumbo rest for 10 minutes.

7. Ladle the gumbo into shallow bowls. Spoon ½ cup of the rice into the center of each serving, and sprinkle with the remaining chopped parsley. Serve immediately, with filé powder alongside. Allow each person to sprinkle it lightly over their gumbo. When stirred in, it will thicken the gumbo a bit.

Serves 4

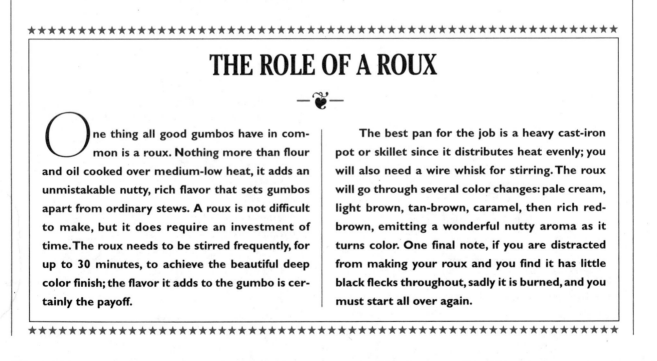

THE ROLE OF A ROUX

One thing all good gumbos have in common is a roux. Nothing more than flour and oil cooked over medium-low heat, it adds an unmistakable nutty, rich flavor that sets gumbos apart from ordinary stews. A roux is not difficult to make, but it does require an investment of time. The roux needs to be stirred frequently, for up to 30 minutes, to achieve the beautiful deep color finish; the flavor it adds to the gumbo is certainly the payoff.

The best pan for the job is a heavy cast-iron pot or skillet since it distributes heat evenly; you will also need a wire whisk for stirring. The roux will go through several color changes: pale cream, light brown, tan-brown, caramel, then rich red-brown, emitting a wonderful nutty aroma as it turns color. One final note, if you are distracted from making your roux and you find it has little black flecks throughout, sadly it is burned, and you must start all over again.

CALABACITAS

★ ★ ★

Food maven extraordinaire Betsy Schultz showed me a marvelous time during San Antonio's annual Fiesta (see page 378 for A Night in Old San Antonio). Tex-Mex cuisine has its home in south Texas, and calabacitas (the word is Spanish for zucchini) was one of the first south Texas dishes that Betsy learned to cook when she moved to the area twenty years ago. It's a recipe that is not found in cookbooks; rather it is passed along through families, and now it's popular in some local restaurants. There are many variations on the dish, but corn and squash are the constants. Pork is often added, but I've bucked the tide and substituted chicken (though I do start with slab bacon for its richness of flavor). Serve the stew with rice or warmed flour tortillas, and ice-cold beer.

Beer: Texas lager

½ pound slab bacon, rind removed,
  cut into ¼-inch dice
1 chicken (2½ pounds) cut into 8 pieces,
  rinsed and patted dry
Salt, to taste
1 cup coarsely chopped onions
1 cup coarsely chopped green bell peppers
2 cloves garlic, minced
1 teaspoon ground cumin
4 cups diced (½ inch) zucchini
2 cups fresh corn kernels
1 pound plum tomatoes, peeled and coarsely
  chopped
1 tablespoon finely chopped green jalapeño pepper
Freshly ground black pepper, to taste
¼ cup chopped fresh flat-leaf parsley
Hot cooked white rice or 8 warmed flour tortillas,
  for serving

1. Place the bacon in a large heavy pot over medium-low heat, and cook until golden brown and the fat is rendered, 6 to 8 minutes. Remove the bacon with a slotted spoon, and set it aside.

2. Raise the heat to medium and brown the chicken pieces, in batches, sprinkling them with salt and moving them so they don't stick to the bottom of the pan, 10 minutes per batch. Transfer the chicken to a bowl and set aside.

3. Add the onions and bell peppers to the pot, reduce the heat to medium-low, and cook until almost wilted, 8 minutes. Add the garlic, and cook, stirring, for 2 minutes. Add the cumin and cook for 1 minute more.

4. Return the bacon and chicken to the pot. Add the zucchini, corn, tomatoes, and jalapeño peppers. Cook, covered, until the chicken is falling off the bones, 1 hour.

5. Uncover and cook for 30 minutes longer.

6. Season the mixture with salt and pepper, sprinkle with the parsley, and serve over rice or with flour tortillas.
Serves 4

RUSTIC CHICKEN IN REPOSE

★ ★ ★

Roasted on a bed of coarsely chopped vegetables, these chicken breasts take on the sweet flavor of the fresh tarragon that is inserted between the skin and the meat. The overall flavor of the dish is enhanced by the orange and tarragon-infused sauce. Serve it directly from the oven, with a dark green salad, crusty bread, and an Oregon Pinot Noir.

Wine: Oregon Pinot Noir
Beer: California pale ale

2 cloves garlic
¼ teaspoon coarse salt
1 tablespoon finely grated orange zest
Juice of 1 large orange
1 tablespoon extra virgin olive oil
1 tablespoon finely chopped fresh tarragon leaves,
     or ½ teaspoon dried
Freshly ground black pepper, to taste
4 carrots, peeled, halved lengthwise,
     and cut into 2-inch lengths
1 pound white new potatoes, scrubbed and halved
4 large ripe plum tomatoes, halved lengthwise
     and seeded
4 small whole chicken breasts (about ¾ pound
     each), with skin and bones, rinsed and
     patted dry
8 sprigs fresh tarragon

1. Preheat the oven to 450°F.
2. Mince the garlic with the salt, and place the mixture in a small bowl. Add the orange zest, orange juice, olive oil, chopped tarragon, and pepper. Mix well and set aside.

3. Bring a pot of salted water to a boil, and blanch the carrots and potatoes for 5 minutes. Drain, and place in a bowl. Add the tomatoes to the bowl, and set aside.
4. Remove any excess fat from the chicken breasts, and place a sprig of tarragon under the skin of each side of the breasts. Replace the skin neatly. Brush the breasts well with the reserved orange mixture.
5. Add any remaining orange mixture to the vegetables and toss well. Place the vegetables in a 13 x 9 x 2-inch oven-to-table baking dish. Arrange the chicken breasts on top in a decorative row. Bake for 40 minutes, brushing the breasts once or twice with the pan juices. Test for doneness by cutting into the thickest part of a breast. The juices should run clear. Serve immediately, spooning out some vegetables and a whole breast onto each plate.
Serves 4

SAN ANTONIO FIESTA CHICKEN

★ ★ ★

The San Antonio Fiesta is held each year in April, and it celebrates Texas's independence from Mexico at the Battle of San Jacinto, April 21, 1836, forty-six days after the fall of the Alamo. This popular event is well attended and the choice of food available is mind-boggling (see page 378 for A Night in Old San Antonio). While researching the recipes for this book, I expected to find culinary surprises in unexpected places, but I was truly knocked out by what I found during my visit to San Antonio.

That visit provided a wealth of inspiration for me, and this chicken dish is one result. Serve it, as I do, with Cowboy Rice Salad alongside.

Wine: Napa Valley (CA) Chenin Blanc
Beer: California wheat beer

6 skinless, boneless chicken breast halves
 (2 to 2½ pounds total)
¼ cup extra virgin olive oil
¼ cup fresh lime juice
1 tablespoon finely minced garlic
1 teaspoon chili powder
½ teaspoon ground cumin
½ pound green beans, stem ends trimmed,
 cut into 1-inch lengths
1 cup fresh corn kernels
3 ripe tomatoes, cut into ½-inch cubes
2 red bell peppers, stemmed, seeded,
 and cut into ½-inch cubes
4 scallions (3 inches green left on),
 thinly sliced on the diagonal
6 tablespoons coarsely chopped fresh flat-leaf
 parsley or fresh cilantro leaves
Salt and freshly ground black pepper,
 to taste
¼ cup Luscious Lime Dressing (page 330)
Radicchio leaves, for serving

1. Place the chicken breasts in a bowl and toss with the oil, lime juice, garlic, chili powder, and cumin. Let rest, covered, at room temperature for 30 minutes; or refrigerate, covered, for 2 to 3 hours.

2. Meanwhile, bring a pot of water to a boil and cook the green beans for 5 minutes. Remove with a slotted spoon and set aside. Blanch the corn for 2 minutes. Drain and set aside.

3. Prepare a barbecue grill with hot coals.

4. Place the chicken breasts on the grill, 3 inches from the heat source, fanning out the small fillet on the underside. Grill the chicken until cooked through, 4 minutes per side (do not overcook). Transfer the chicken to a plate, and let it rest for 10 minutes to cool slightly. Then cut the breasts into 1-inch cubes and place them in a large bowl.

5. Add the tomatoes, bell peppers, scallions, green beans, and corn to the chicken. Toss together gently. Sprinkle with the parsley and toss lightly. Season with salt and pepper, drizzle with the dressing, and toss to combine.

6. Line a colorful serving platter with radicchio leaves. Spoon the chicken mixture on top and serve.

Serves 6 to 8

SPICED-UP GRILLED CHICKEN SALAD

★ ★ ★

Each component of this salad is a terrific dish on its own, but together they make magic. I like to use chicken straight off the grill in it. Remember when grilling the breasts to fan out the little fillet from the underside so that the breasts cook evenly.

Wine: Oregon dry Riesling
Beer: Colorado amber lager

MARINADE
¼ cup extra virgin olive oil
2 tablespoons fresh orange juice
2 cloves garlic, finely minced
2 tablespoons chopped fresh cilantro leaves
1 tablespoon finely grated orange zest
1 small dried red chile, crushed
½ teaspoon ground cumin
½ teaspoon chili powder
½ teaspoon salt, to taste

8 skinless, boneless chicken breast halves
    (about 3 pounds total)
Black Bean Salad (page 338)
1½ tablespoons fresh chopped cilantro leaves, for
    garnish
¾ cup Summer Peach Relish (page 183), for garnish

   1. Prepare the marinade: Combine all the marinade ingredients in a bowl and mix well.
   2. Flatten the chicken breasts slightly, using the flat side of a heavy knife. Add the chicken breasts to the marinade and toss to coat. Cover, and let rest for 2 to 4 hours in the refrigerator.
   3. Prepare a barbecue grill with medium-hot coals or preheat the broiler.
   4. Grill the chicken breasts, about 3 inches from the heat, until cooked through, about 3 minutes per side.
   5. Spoon the Black Bean Salad evenly in the center of four dinner plates, and top each serving with two chicken breasts. Sprinkle with the chopped cilantro and dollop with Summer Peach Relish. Serve immediately.
   Serves 4

SANTA FE BORDER GAME HENS

★ ★ ★

A soak in a marinade spiked with cumin, cinnamon, and lime juice gives a nice Southwestern flavor to these easy-to-prepare grilled butterflied game hens. To ensure evenly cooked birds, I remove the backbone with a pair of kitchen scissors, and spread out the wings as the birds cook so that they don't rest under the breast. Although I recommend buying one game hen per person, it may be too much for smaller appetites, so serve up half at a time. Accompany the hens with Vegetable-Studded Barley and Liberty Spinach Salad with Cumin Vinaigrette.

Wine: Willamette Valley (OR) Pinot Noir
Beer: Illinois amber ale

MARINADE
½ cup fresh lime juice
¼ cup extra virgin olive oil
1 tablespoon finely minced garlic
2 teaspoons ground cumin
½ teaspoon ground cinnamon
Salt and freshly ground black pepper, to taste

4 Cornish game hens (¾ to 1 pound each)
4 lime halves, for serving
1 bunch fresh cilantro, for garnish

   1. Prepare the marinade: Combine the marinade ingredients in a small bowl and set aside.
   2. Remove the giblets from the game hens (reserve them for another use, if desired). With a pair of kitchen or poultry shears, snip off the wing tips. Then, to butterfly the hens, cut each down the back to split it open. Trim away and discard the backbone. Open out the hens and place them, skin side up, on a flat surface. Press

on the breastbones, using the flat side of a heavy knife or the heel of your hand, to flatten the hens. Rinse them well under cold water and pat them dry. Place the butterflied hens in a large bowl and pour the marinade over them. Turn the hens to coat well, then set aside, loosely covered, in the refrigerator for 1 hour.

3. Prepare a barbecue grill with medium-hot coals, and oil the grill well.

4. Drain the hens, reserving the marinade. Place the hens, skin side down and wings spread out to the sides, 3 inches from the heat source. Grill them, basting with some of the reserved marinade, for 10 minutes. Then turn them over and grill on the other side, basting, until golden and cooked through, 10 minutes. Serve each person a half bird hot from the grill with a lime wedge and garnished with a cilantro sprig.

Serves 4

LACQUERED MAPLE SYRUP GAME HENS

★ ★ ★

For this butterflied game hen dish, I rest the birds in a sweet-tart mixture of maple syrup and lime juice, then baste them while they grill with

some of the reserved marinade. The sugar in the syrup gives the hens a delicious lacquered finish. Serve them with a pitcher of maple syrup on the side for drizzling over the birds.

Wine: Monterey County (CA) Pinot Noir
Beer: Louisiana lager

4 Cornish game hens (¾ to 1 pound each)
⅓ cup pure maple syrup, plus extra
*   for serving*
2 tablespoons fresh lime juice
2 tablespoons unsalted butter,
*   melted*
½ teaspoon salt
½ teaspoon freshly ground black pepper
¼ teaspoon ground allspice

1. Remove the giblets from the game hens (reserve them for another use, if desired). With a pair of kitchen or poultry shears, snip off the wing tips. Then, to butterfly the hens, cut each down the center of the back to split it open. Trim away and discard the backbone. Open out the hens and place them, skin side up, on a flat surface. Press on the breastbones, using the flat side of a heavy knife or the heel of your hand to flatten the hens. Rinse them well under cold water and pat them dry. Place the butterflied hens in a large bowl.

2. Prepare a barbecue grill with medium-hot coals or preheat the broiler. Oil the grill rack, if using.

3. Combine the ⅓ cup maple syrup, lime juice, melted butter, and all the spices in a small bowl. Pour this over the game hens and turn to coat them well. Let rest for 15 to 20 minutes.

4. If you are grilling: Place the hens, skin side down, 4 inches from the heat source and grill for 10 minutes, basting frequently with the marinade. Turn and grill on the other side, basting, until golden and cooked through, 10 minutes. Let rest for 5 minutes before serving.

If you are broiling: Arrange the hens, skin side down, on a baking sheet or in a broiler pan and broil them 4 inches from a medium-high heat source, basting frequently, for 10 minutes. Then turn and broil them on the other side, basting until cooked through, 10 minutes.

5. Arrange the hens, skin side up, on a serving platter and serve accompanied by maple syrup.

Serves 4

SWEET-AND-SOUR SQUABS

★ ★ ★

Elegant in both flavor and appearance, these diminutive autumnal game birds match up beautifully to a smooth, vegetable-laden sweet-and-sour sauce. I like to serve the birds nestled into rich egg noodles or Polenta with Mascarpone. To make them easier to eat, I cut them in half before serving and spoon the sauce over all. They're tiny, so one bird is just right for a single serving.

Wine: Oregon Pinot Noir
Beer: San Francisco Anchor Steam Beer

4 squabs (about 1 pound each)
Salt and freshly ground black pepper, to taste
3 tablespoons olive oil
1 cup diced (¼ inch) onions
¾ cup diced (¼ inch) carrots
½ cup diced (¼ inch) celery
1 tablespoon finely minced garlic
1 teaspoon dried thyme
1 teaspoon dried sage
1½ tablespoons all-purpose flour
1½ cups dry red wine
2 cups defatted chicken broth, preferably
  homemade (page 253)
¼ cup red wine vinegar
1 tablespoon red currant jelly
1 tablespoon dark brown sugar
4 tablespoons chopped fresh flat-leaf parsley

1. Rinse the squabs under cold water and pat them dry. Sprinkle them inside and out with salt and pepper.

2. Heat the olive oil in a large heavy pot or Dutch oven over medium heat, and brown the birds, two at a time, 15 minutes per batch. Transfer them to a plate.

3. Add the onions, carrots, celery, garlic, thyme, and sage to the pot and cook, stirring, over low heat until wilted, 10 minutes. Sprinkle with the flour and cook, stirring, for 1 minute.

4. Raise the heat, add the wine, broth, and vinegar, and bring to a boil. Reduce the heat to medium-low, and add the jelly and brown sugar. Return the squabs to the pot and spoon the sauce over them. Simmer gently, uncovered, basting constantly, until cooked through, 1 hour.

5. Just before serving, stir in 3 tablespoons of the chopped parsley.

6. Place the squabs on a serving platter, and spoon some of the sauce over them. Sprinkle with the remaining 1 tablespoon parsley and serve. Pass the remaining sauce.

Serves 4

SUNDAY HERB-ROASTED CAPON

★ ★ ★

Succulent and lemony, this simple roasted capon, surrounded by crisp roasted potatoes, is a delicious family weekend meal. Herbs gently slipped under the skin and into the cavity infuse the bird with a fragrant aroma and taste. Basting regularly keeps all the moisture locked in during the long roasting. Serve the carved capon, surrounded with potatoes, on a decorative platter.

Wine: Central Coast (CA) Pinot Noir
Beer: Oregon golden ale

1 capon (about 7 pounds)
Salt and freshly ground black pepper, to taste
8 cloves garlic, unpeeled
1 lemon, quartered
6 sprigs fresh thyme
6 sprigs fresh rosemary
6 sprigs fresh tarragon
4 tablespoons olive oil
½ teaspoon paprika
12 small Yukon Gold potatoes (about 3 pounds),
   scrubbed and quartered
   2 tablespoons chopped fresh rosemary leaves
   ¾ cup defatted chicken broth,
      preferably homemade (page 253)
         ¼ cup fresh lemon
            juice

1. Preheat the oven to 450°F.
2. Rinse the capon well, inside and out, under cold water. Pat it dry. With a small sharp knife, remove any excess fat from the bird, including the fat pockets around the tail.

3. Season the cavity with salt and pepper. Place the garlic cloves, lemon quarters, and 4 sprigs each of the thyme, rosemary, and tarragon in the cavity.

4. Carefully loosen the skin over the breast meat with your hands, and insert the remaining 2 sprigs each of thyme, rosemary, and tarragon between the skin and the breast meat. Carefully replace the skin. Truss the legs with kitchen string.

5. Place the capon in a roasting pan. Brush it all over with 2 tablespoons of the olive oil, and sprinkle with salt, pepper, and the paprika. Surround the capon with the potatoes, and season them with salt, pepper, and the chopped rosemary. Drizzle the potatoes with the remaining 2 tablespoons olive oil.

6. Combine the broth and the lemon juice, and pour ½ cup of the mixture into the roasting pan. Place the pan in the oven and roast for 20 minutes. Then reduce the temperature to 350°F and roast, basting every 20 minutes with the pan juices or with the broth mixture, for 2 hours. The bird is cooked when an instant-reading thermometer placed in the thickest part of the thigh registers 180°F. The juices should run clear when tested with the tip of a sharp knife in the thickest part of the thigh.

7. Transfer the bird to a carving board and let it rest for 15 minutes. Meanwhile, remove the potatoes with a slotted spoon and put them in a small baking dish. Return them to the oven to crisp while the capon is resting.

8. Pour any roasting juices through a gravy separator to remove the fat, or skim off the fat with a metal spoon. Heat the defatted juices in a small saucepan along with any juices that have gathered on the carving board.

9. Remove the string. Carve the capon and serve on a platter, surrounded by the potatoes. Pass the warmed juices in a sauceboat.
Serves 6

MY THANKSGIVING TURKEY

★ ★ ★

There are very few things that I would presume to change about America's favorite holiday meal, so if you're pleased with your Thanksgiving turkey, I'd understand why you may not feel the need to read any further. But if you're looking for a new stuffing to accompany your turkey, I have to say that the cornbread mixture I recently devised is the best I've ever made. And I've also tried roasting the turkey at a slightly lower temperature for most of its stay in the oven, and found the resulting meat to be invariably moist throughout. I hope I've tempted you to give what follows a try. It makes one delicious centerpiece.

HOW TO CARVE A TURKEY

—❧—

1. After removing your bird from the oven, always allow it to rest, loosely covered with aluminum foil, for 15 to 20 minutes, so the juices settle in.

2. Remove any strings and skewers after the bird has rested. If you've stuffed your turkey, spoon the stuffing out to a serving bowl and cover loosely with aluminum foil to keep warm.

3. Use a carving fork to hold the bird in place as you carve.

4. Remove the drumsticks first: Insert the carving fork into the meaty part of each drumstick to hold it firmly. Place the knife between the drumstick and the thigh and cut through the skin to the joint, then through the joint. Leave the drumstick whole or fans will be very disappointed.

5. Separate each thigh from the body by pressing it outward with the knife while holding the turkey in place with the fork. If the joint doesn't disengage easily, cut through it. Slice the thighs.

6. Disjoint and separate the wings in the same fashion.

7. Next, carve the breast: Make a horizontal cut across the bottom of one side of the breast with the carving knife. Slice the breast meat downward with straight, even strokes, beginning at the outside edge near where the leg was attached. When the knife reaches the incision above the wing bone, the slices will fall free. Continue slicing, working in toward the breastbone, until the breastbone is reached. Always carve across the grain. Once the first cut is made, the angle at which the knife is held should never change. Use long, sweeping strokes to ensure smooth, even slices. Once you've sliced the meat from the first half, repeat the process on the second half of the breast.

Wine: Russian River Valley (CA) Gewürztraminer
or Willamette Valley (OR) Pinot Noir

GIBLET BROTH

Giblets and neck from turkey (below)
1 cup extra giblets (about ¾ pound)
4 chicken backs (about 1¾ pounds)
2 ribs celery, with leaves
2 onions, unpeeled
2 cloves garlic, bruised
4 sprigs fresh flat-leaf parsley
4 whole cloves
3 black peppercorns
1 bay leaf
Salt, to taste

TURKEY

1 fresh turkey (18 pounds), with giblets and neck
1 orange, halved
Paprika, to taste
Salt and freshly ground black pepper, to taste
10 to 12 cups Cherry Cornbread Stuffing
*   (recipe follows)*
6 tablespoons (¾ stick) unsalted butter, at room
*   temperature*

GIBLET GRAVY

Pan juices (from turkey)
¼ cup (½ stick) unsalted butter
4 tablespoons all-purpose flour
2 tablespoons Madeira wine
1 teaspoon dried thyme
Salt and freshly ground black pepper, to taste
1 tablespoon chopped fresh flat-leaf parsley
Giblet mixture (see steps 1 and 2)
Giblet Broth, if needed

2 to 3 large bunches fresh sage, for garnish

1. Prepare the giblet broth: Wash the giblets
well. Place all the broth ingredients together in a
heavy saucepan and add water to just cover (about
6 cups). Bring to a boil. Reduce the heat and simmer, skimming any foam that rises to the surface,
until the giblets are tender, about 1 hour. Strain
the broth over a bowl, reserving the giblets, turkey
neck, and chicken backs and discarding the vegetables. You should have about 3½ cups of broth.

2. When it is cool enough to handle, shred
the meat from the turkey neck and chicken
backs, discarding any skin. Finely chop the
giblets. Mix the meats and giblets together,
cover, and refrigerate until needed.

3. Preheat the oven to 325°F.

4. Prepare the turkey: Rinse the turkey well
inside and out, and pat it dry. Remove any
excess fat.

5. Squeeze the orange halves inside the
body and neck cavities. Sprinkle the cavities with
paprika, salt, and pepper. Stuff the cavities with
the Cherry Cornbread Stuffing, using about 3
cups for the neck and 8 cups for the body. (If you
have extra stuffing, see Note, page 426.) Close
with turkey lacers, or sew closed with a large
needle and heavy thread. Tie the legs together
with kitchen string.

6. Rub the turkey all over with the butter,
and sprinkle with paprika, salt, and pepper.

7. Place the turkey, breast side up, on a rack
in a large flameproof roasting pan. Pour 2 cups
of the reserved giblet broth into the bottom of
the pan, and cover the turkey loosely with aluminum foil. Cover the remaining broth and
refrigerate it. Place the turkey in the oven and
roast for 1½ hours.

8. Remove the foil and roast the turkey,
basting with the pan juices every 30 minutes, for
2½ hours.

9. Raise the oven temperature to 350°F, and
roast for another 1 to 1¼ hours, or until an
instant-reading thermometer inserted into the
thickest part of the thigh reads 180°F. (The temperature at the thickest part of the breast should
be 160°F, and in the deepest part of the stuffing
165°F.) The juices should run clear, when the
thigh is pricked with a small sharp knife.

10. Remove the turkey, place it on a platter, and let it rest about 20 minutes, loosely covered with aluminum foil.

11. Remove the stuffing from the body and neck cavities to a bowl and cover with aluminum foil to keep warm.

12. Prepare the giblet gravy: Heat the pan

juices in the roasting pan, scraping up all of the brown bits on the bottom of the pan. Pour the juices through a gravy separator to remove the fat, or skim the fat off with a metal spoon. Pour the defatted juices into a measuring cup.

13. Melt the butter in a heavy saucepan over medium heat. Whisk in the flour and continue whisking until it browns slightly, 2 to 3 minutes. Whisking constantly, slowly pour in 2 cups of the reserved pan juices, and continue whisking until smooth. Bring the gravy to a boil, then reduce the heat to medium-low and add the Madeira, thyme, salt, pepper, parsley, and reserved giblet mixture. Simmer, stirring, until the gravy has thickened, about 10 minutes. If your prefer a thinner gravy, add more of the remaining 1½ cups giblet broth until the desired consistency is achieved. Adjust the seasonings to taste.

14. Present the turkey before carving it. Arrange the carved meat on a large decorative platter. Garnish with the fresh sage and serve accompanied by the gravy.

Serves about 16

A MENU TO GIVE THANKS FOR

—❦—

**Oyster Stew or
Creamy Fresh Morel Soup**

———

**My Thanksgiving Turkey
with Cherry Cornbread Stuffing
and Giblet Gravy**

———

**Roasted Root Vegetables
Best Brussels Sprouts Ever
Whipped Sweet Potatoes
October 31st Pumpkin Purée**

———

**Fresh Whole-Cranberry Relish
Shaker Applesauce
Sweetly Pickled Beets
Lancaster Apple Butter**

———

**Boston Brown Bread
Vermont Cheddar Cheese**

———

**Wende's Blue-Ribbon Apple Pie with
Candied Ginger
Southern Pecan Pie My Way**

Cherry Cornbread Stuffing

—★—

If you are looking for a change from the traditional turkey bread stuffing, this is the recipe to try. The dried cherries or cranberries offer a lively sweet-and-sour tang and are an interesting change from the more typical raisins. If you don't choose to eat pork but want the savory taste of sausage, well-spiced turkey sausage will do the trick.

2 recipes Country Cornbread (page 214)
    prepared 1 day ahead and left,
    loosely wrapped, at room temperature
4 tablespoons olive oil
4 tablespoons fresh thyme leaves, or
    1 tablespoon dried thyme
Salt and freshly ground black pepper, to taste
2 pounds bulk pork sausage
2 tablespoons unsalted butter
3 cups chopped onions
6 ribs celery, chopped
1 cup dried cherries or dried cranberries
1 cup pitted prunes
4 tablespoons chopped fresh sage leaves, or
    2 teaspoons dried
1/4 cup chopped fresh flat-leaf parsley
2 cups defatted chicken broth, preferably
    homemade (page 253)
Salt and freshly ground black pepper, to taste

1. Preheat the oven to 350°F.

2. Cut the cornbread into 1-inch cubes. You should have about 12 cups. Place the cubes in a large bowl with 2 tablespoons of the olive oil, 2 tablespoons of the thyme, and salt and pepper; toss well. Spread the cubes out on two baking sheets. Bake until slightly toasted, 15 minutes. Let cool at room temperature, 30 minutes. Return the cubes to the bowl.

3. Meanwhile, cook the sausage in a nonstick skillet over medium-high heat, breaking the meat up with a spatula, until cooked through and lightly browned, 15 to 20 minutes. (Pour off the fat if too much of it accumulates during cooking.) Using a slotted spoon, add the meat to the bowl with the cornbread (breaking the meat up more if necessary).

4. Heat the remaining 2 tablespoons olive oil and the butter in a heavy saucepan. Cook the onions and celery over medium-low heat, stirring, until wilted, 10 minutes. Then stir in the cherries and prunes, and cook another 5 minutes. Fold the mixture into the cornbread.

★★

A PRAYER FOR THE FIRST THANKSGIVING

—❦—

Our harvest being gotten in, our governor sent four men on fowling, that so we might after a special manner rejoice together after we had gathered the fruit of our labors. They four in one day killed as much fowl as, with a little help beside, served the company almost a week. At which time, amongst other recreations, we exercised our arms. Many of the Indians coming amongst us, and among the rest their greatest King Massasoit, with some ninety men, whom for three days we entertained and feasted, and they went out and killed five deer, which they brought to the plantation and bestowed on our governor, and upon the captain and others. And although it be not always so plentiful as it was this time with us, yet by the goodness of God, we are so far from want that we often wish you partakers of our plenty.

—EDWARD WINSLOW, THIRD GOVERNOR
OF PLYMOUTH COLONY

★★

5. Using a rubber spatula, toss the remaining 2 tablespoons thyme, the sage, and parsley with the cornbread. Slowly drizzle in the broth, ½ cup at a time, until the stuffing is moist to your liking. Adjust the seasonings to taste. Cool completely to room temperature before stuffing the turkey.

16 cups; enough for a 20- to 24-pound turkey (see Note).

NOTE: Cook the stuffing in the turkey; any extra can be cooked in an ovenproof dish, covered, at 350°F for 20 to 25 minutes.

BAYOU TURKEY BURGER

★ ★ ★

Ground turkey has such a mild flavor that it easily takes to a blast of Cajun seasoning. The avocado garnish adds a nice California-ish touch.

Since ground turkey does not brown as quickly as most other meats, you might want to cook it a bit slower to get a rich burger color. Just be sure to check the center, to see that it is cooked through.

Beer: Boston lager

1 pound ground turkey
2 scallions (3 inches green left on), thinly sliced
1 red bell pepper, stemmed, seeded, and finely chopped
1 teaspoon finely minced garlic
2 tablespoons chopped fresh cilantro leaves
¾ teaspoon dried thyme
½ teaspoon ground cumin
½ teaspoon paprika
Crushed red pepper flakes, to taste
Salt and freshly ground black pepper, to taste
4 hamburger buns, toasted
¼ cup mayonnaise, for garnish (optional)
1 small ripe avocado, sliced, for garnish (optional)

1. Prepare a barbecue grill with hot coals or preheat the broiler. Oil the grill rack, if using.

2. Place the turkey in a bowl and mix it well with the scallions, bell pepper, garlic, cilantro, thyme, cumin, paprika, and red pepper flakes. Season to taste with salt and pepper. Gently form the mixture into 4 patties.

3. Grill or broil the burgers, 3 inches from the heat source, until cooked through, 5 to 6 minutes per side.

4. Serve immediately on the toasted buns, spread with mayonnaise and topped with avocado slices, if desired.

Serves 4

TURKEY CURRY POT PIE

★ ★ ★

Although leftover turkey often takes the brunt of many a joke, those of us who plan the family meals know it as a blessing. There are so many ways to serve it, and this one is ideal for feeding a crowd on Thanksgiving weekend. The filling is curried rather than creamy and goes well with any leftover Fresh Whole-Cranberry Relish.

Wine: Dry Creek Valley (CA) Zinfandel
Beer: New York State brown ale

2 tablespoons olive oil
1 large onion, chopped
1 tablespoon minced garlic
1 tablespoon minced fresh ginger
2 tablespoons curry powder
1 tablespoon all-purpose flour
2 carrots, peeled, halved lengthwise, and
    cut into 1 inch pieces (about 1 cup)
1 cup peeled and diced (½ inch) potatoes
1 Granny Smith apple, cored and cut into
    ½-inch pieces
3 cups defatted turkey or chicken broth,
    preferably homemade (page 253 for chicken)
1 cinnamon stick (3 inches long)
½ cup golden raisins
½ cup fresh or frozen peas, thawed if frozen
1 tomato, seeded and cut into ½-inch dice
¼ cup chopped fresh flat-leaf parsley
2 cups coarsely shredded cooked turkey
Salt and freshly ground black pepper,
    to taste
1 sheet prepared puff pastry (½ pound),
    thawed if frozen
1 large egg
1 tablespoon water
Fresh Whole-Cranberry Relish (page 184)
    for serving

1. Heat the oil in a large heavy pot over low heat. Add the onion and cook, stirring occasionally, until wilted, 8 to 10 minutes. Add the garlic and ginger and cook, stirring, 2 to 3 minutes. Sprinkle with the curry powder and flour and cook, stirring constantly, to mellow the flavors, 1 to 2 minutes.

2. Add the carrots, potatoes, apple, broth, and cinnamon stick. Bring to a boil. Reduce the heat to a gentle simmer and cook, partially covered, until the vegetables are tender, 20 minutes. Then add the raisins, peas, tomato, parsley, and shredded turkey; cook 5 minutes more. Season with salt and pepper.

3. Meanwhile, preheat the oven to 350°F.

4. Place the mixture in a 2-quart round ovenproof casserole; remove and discard the cinnamon stick. On a lightly floured surface, roll the puff pastry out to form a circle about 2 inches larger than the diameter of the casserole. Beat the egg with the water, and brush this egg wash around the inside and outside rim of the casserole. Lay the pastry over the top, trim the overhang to 1 inch, and crimp the edges around the rim to form a tight seal. Cut six 2-inch slits in the center of the pastry to release the steam, and brush it with the remaining egg wash.

5. Place the casserole on a baking sheet, and bake until the crust is golden, 40 to 45 minutes. Serve piping hot, with the cranberry relish on the side.

Serves 6

ROASTED DUCK WITH A CRISPY SKIN

★ ★ ★

I know that there is more than one way to roast a duck, but I'm partial to my way—and I always get delicious results. The skin is crisp, the way I like it, and the meat perfectly moist. It is important that when preparing the duck, you remove as much of the excess fat as possible. Serve it with beautifully Caramelized Pears.

Wine: Russian River Valley (CA) Pinot Noir
Beer: Pennsylvania bock

1 duck (5 to 5½ pounds)
1 orange, halved
Salt and freshly ground black pepper, to taste
1 Granny Smith apple, quartered
1 large bunch fresh thyme
Caramelized Pears (recipe follows)

1. Preheat the oven to 400°F.

2. Rinse the duck under cold water and pat it dry. Remove all the excess fat from the cavity and around the neck area. Gently prick the skin all over with a fork; do not cut into the flesh.

3. Rub the duck all over, inside and out, with the halved orange. Sprinkle it with salt and pepper inside and out. Place the orange half in the cavity along with the apple quarters and 4 sprigs of the thyme.

4. Place the duck, breast side up, on a rack in a roasting pan, and roast it in the center of the oven for 30 minutes. Tie the legs together with kitchen string.

5. Reduce the temperature to 350°F, and roast for 1 hour and 35 minutes to 2 hours and 5 minutes more, depending on the size of your duck. Baste at regular intervals so that the skin browns nicely and gets crisp. Test for doneness by pricking with the tip of a knife in the thickest part of the thigh; if the juices run clear, the duck is done. (A meat thermometer should read 180°F when placed in the thickest part of the thigh.)

6. Remove the duck, and let rest on a platter for 15 minutes before carving. Garnish with the remaining thyme sprigs and serve with Caramelized Pears.

Serves 4

Caramelized Pears

———★———

¼ cup golden raisins
2 tablespoons fresh orange juice
3 tablespoons unsalted butter, melted
4 pears, such as Anjou, peeled, cored, and cut into
    1-inch chunks
2 tablespoons light brown sugar
1 tablespoon chopped crystallized ginger

1. Stir the raisins and orange juice together in a small bowl and let sit for 30 minutes.

2. Melt the butter in a nonstick skillet over medium heat. Add the pears and raisins, and sprinkle with the brown sugar and ginger. Cook stirring, until tender and nicely caramelized, 20 to 25 minutes.

Serves 4 to 6

MIDSEASON'S EVE DUCK

★ ★ ★

When spring is in full bloom and interest in heavy entrées wanes, a salad of substance is often the satisfying answer to our mercurial appetites. These duck breasts can be cooked a day in advance and refrigerated, then sliced before you begin the salad. Just arrange the plates when you're ready to eat.

Wine: California Rhône-style blend
Beer: American pale ale

2 whole boneless duck breasts (about ¾ pound each)
Coarse salt and freshly ground black pepper,
   to taste
2 teaspoons olive oil
¼ pound green beans, stem ends trimmed,
   halved crosswise
¼ pound wax beans, stem ends trimmed,
   halved crosswise
½ cup corn kernels, preferably fresh
4 ripe plum tomatoes, each cut into 8 pieces
6 white mushroom caps, wiped clean with
   a damp cloth and thinly sliced
¼ cup thinly slivered fresh basil leaves, plus
   more for garnish
6 tablespoons Orange Honey Vinaigrette
   (page 80)
Salt and freshly ground black pepper,
   to taste
2 heads radicchio, separated into leaves,
   rinsed and patted dry

1. Cut the whole duck breasts in half lengthwise. Trim the excess skin and fat from around the meat on each breast. If there are large fillets on the underside, separate and reserve them for another use. Score the skin of each breast 3 times on the diagonal, using a sharp knife and being careful not to pierce the meat. Season on all sides with salt and pepper.

2. Heat the oil in a nonstick skillet over medium-high heat. Place the duck breasts in the skillet, skin side down, and sauté until well browned, 3 to 4 minutes. Turn and sauté on the second side for 3 to 4 minutes more for medium-rare. Transfer the breasts to a plate, cover, and refrigerate until ready to use.

3. When you are ready to prepare the salad, thinly slice the duck breasts on the diagonal.

4. Prepare a bowl of ice water.

5. Bring a pot of water to a boil, and cook both of the beans until just crisp-tender, about 5 minutes. Remove with a slotted spoon, plunge into the ice water, drain, and pat dry. Place the beans in a large bowl. Cook the corn in the boiling water for 2 minutes, plunge into the ice water, drain, pat dry, and add to the beans with all the remaining vegetables, the ¼ cup basil, and 4 tablespoons of the vinaigrette. Fold together gently, and season with salt and pepper.

6. Arange the radicchio leaves in the center of four dinner plates. Divide the salad evenly the radicchio leaves. Arrange about 8 slices of duck, overlapping, in a row along the top of each salad. Drizzle evenly with the remaining 2 tablespoons vinaigrette, garnish with basil slivers, and serve immediately.
Serves 4

FRUITY DUCK BREASTS TWO WAYS

★ ★ ★

I like to prepare these tenderly sautéed duck breasts, arranged attractively, for a special occasion dinner. Both fruit-napped versions are well served by Fennel and Acorn Squash

Whip and wild rice accompaniments. While you can present the duck with either sauce, it is outstanding with a serving of both on the same plate.

Wine: Central Coast (CA) Pinot Noir
Beer: Oregon brown ale

*2 whole boneless duck breasts (about
    ¾ pound each)*
*Coarse salt and freshly ground black
    pepper, to taste*
2 teaspoons olive oil
*1½ cups defatted chicken broth, preferably
    homemade (page 253)*

ORANGE SAUCE
½ cup bitter orange marmalade
2 tablespoons dry white wine

CHERRY SAUCE
½ cup sweet cherry preserves
1 tablespoon dry white wine

1. Cut the whole duck breasts in half lengthwise. Trim the excess skin and fat from around the meat on each breast. If there are large fillets on the underside, separate and reserve them for another use. Score the skin of each breast 3 times on the diagonal, using a sharp knife and being careful not to pierce the meat. Sprinkle on all sides with salt and pepper.

2. Heat 1 teaspoon of the oil in each of two nonstick skillets over medium-high heat. Place 2 duck breast pieces in each skillet, skin side down, and sauté until well browned, 3 to 4 minutes. Turn and sauté on the second side, 3 to 4 minutes more for medium-rare. Transfer the breasts to a plate, cover, and let rest until serving.

3. Discard the fat in the skillets and lightly wipe them out with paper towels. Heat the skillets over medium heat. Add ¾ cup of the broth, and any accumulated juices that the duck breasts

give off, to each skillet. Bring to a boil, scraping up any brown bits on the bottom of the skillet, and boil for 1 minute. Reduce the heat to medium and stir the marmalade and white wine into one skillet. Bring back to a boil, reduce the heat, and simmer until the sauce thickens and reduces, seasoning it with salt and pepper, for 5 to 6 minutes. Repeat the same process in the other skillet with the cherry preserves and white wine.

4. Slice the duck breasts on the diagonal and fan them out on four warmed dinner plates. Spoon a little of each sauce over the top of each serving, and serve immediately.

Serves 4

JUST-NORTH-OF-THE-BORDER GRILLED QUAIL

★ ★ ★

A short stay in a marinade infuses these partially boned quail with zesty Southwestern flavor. If you are well skilled with a tiny boning knife, try removing the breast bones yourself, or better yet, leave the pesky task to the butcher. Just be sure to lay the quail out flat on the grill and not to overcook them, as they will dry out quickly. Serve them on a pool of Creamy Salsa Verde.

Wine: Amador County (CA) Barbera
Beer: Portland amber ale

8 quail (about 8 ounces each), partially boned
(see headnote)
¼ cup fresh lime juice
2 tablespoons extra virgin olive oil
2 teaspoons finely chopped garlic
1 teaspoon ground cumin
¼ teaspoon ground cinnamon
Salt and freshly ground black pepper,
to taste
2 tablespoons finely chopped fresh
cilantro leaves
1 cup Creamy Salsa Verde
(page 195), for serving
2 tablespoons coarsely chopped fresh
cilantro leaves, for garnish
Fresh yellow and orange nasturtium
blossoms, for garnish (optional)

1. Wash the quail gently under cold water. Snip off the wing tips and pat the birds dry. Place the quail in a large bowl.

2. In a small bowl, stir together the lime juice, oil, garlic, cumin, cinnamon, salt, pepper, and the finely chopped cilantro. Pour this over the quail, and toss to coat. Cover, and set aside to marinate in the refrigerator for 1 hour.

3. Prepare a barbecue grill with medium-hot coals or preheat the broiler.

4. Grill or broil the quail, 4 inches from the heat source, until golden brown and cooked through, 3 to 4 minutes per side. (Turn them with a spatula.)

5. Meanwhile, heat the salsa verde in the top of a double boiler over simmering water.

6. Divide the salsa among four dinner plates. Arrange 2 quail on top of the salsa on each plate, sprinkle with the coarsely chopped cilantro, and garnish with the nasturtiums, if desired. Serve immediately.

Serves 4

ROASTED PHEASANT WITH KENTUCKY BOURBON SAUCE

★ ★ ★

It has been said that this refined little game bird arrived in America from China via England. Benjamin Franklin's son-in-law, Englishman Richard Bache, was the first to attempt to raise pheasant in the United States, on his estate in New Jersey. I find the birds as easy to prepare as chicken and, being smaller and more delicate, far more graceful to serve. As with many game birds, there tends to be little fat, so it is necessary to drape the breast with bacon to keep it moist. Round out the meat with Down and Dirty Rice and October 31st Pumpkin Purée.

Wine: Hudson Valley (NY) Pinot Noir
Beer: Massachusetts India pale ale

1 pheasant (about 2½ pounds)
1 orange, halved
2 tablespoons olive oil
Salt and freshly ground black pepper, to taste
½ Granny Smith apple, cut into 4 pieces
2 shallots, halved
2 sprigs fresh sage, plus extra for garnish
6 slices bacon
¼ cup defatted chicken broth, preferably
homemade (page 253)
2 tablespoons bourbon
Kentucky Bourbon Sauce (recipe follows)

1. Preheat the oven to 350°F.

2. Rinse the pheasant, cleaning the cavity well. Pat it dry, and remove any excess fat. Snip off the wing tips with scissors.

3. Squeeze the orange all over the pheasant and inside the cavity. Brush the pheasant all over with the olive oil. Sprinkle it inside and out with salt and pepper. Place the apple pieces, shallots, and 2 sprigs of sage in the cavity. Tie the legs together with kitchen string.

4. Place the bird, breast side up, in a small roasting pan, and arrange the bacon slices in a single crosswise layer over the bird. Pour the chicken broth and bourbon into the pan.

5. Roast in the center of the oven, basting two or three times, for 1 hour. Remove the bacon and continue to roast until the breast is brown and the pheasant is cooked through, 15 to 20 minutes longer. When the thickest part of the thigh is tested with the tip of a knife, the juices should run clear. Let the pheasant rest for 10 minutes.

6. Carve, garnish with sage sprigs, and serve with the Kentucky Bourbon Sauce.

Serves 2

Kentucky Bourbon Sauce

★

The sweetness of honey and the silken character of the butter mellow the fine, aged flavor of Kentucky bourbon into a sauce that is richly pleasing. Swirling the butter in to finish off the sauce gives it a velvety texture.

½ cup clover honey
¼ cup bourbon
2 tablespoons unsalted butter, cut into small pieces

Combine the honey and bourbon in a small heavy saucepan, and cook over low heat, stirring

constantly, until the honey thins out, 2 minutes. Add the butter and cook, swirling the pan, until it melts and the sauce thickens, 2 minutes. Warm over low heat just before serving. Serve alongside the pheasant.

Makes about ¾ cup

PARTRIDGE AND POTATO ROAST

★ ★ ★

When steeped overnight in a pungent rosemary marinade, these partridges become infused with its strong herbaceous flavor. Accompany them in the roasting pan with potatoes, garlic, and more rosemary, and you've got an aromatically inviting midwinter meal. If you've still got a jar of Summer Peach Relish left, pass some with the partridge. It also goes well with Fresh Whole-Cranberry Relish or Sweetly Pickled Beets—or even all three!

Wine: Monterey County (CA) Pinot Noir
Beer: Oregon brown ale

4 partridges (¾ to 1 pound each)
6 tablespoons extra virgin olive oil, plus more if needed
6 cloves garlic, crushed
4 large sprigs fresh rosemary, leaves lightly bruised
Freshly ground black pepper, to taste
10 new potatoes, quartered
Salt, to taste
2 tablespoons chopped fresh rosemary leaves

1. Rinse the partridges under cold water and remove and discard the innards. Pat the partridges dry. Trim off the wing tips and necks.

2. Combine 4 tablespoons of the olive oil, the garlic, rosemary sprigs, and pepper in a large bowl. Add the partridges and toss to coat. Cover, and refrigerate for 8 hours or overnight.

3. Preheat the oven to 450°F.

4. Toss the potatoes in a bowl with the remaining 2 tablespoons olive oil.

5. Place a nonstick skillet over medium heat. Remove the partridges from the marinade, and sear them, two at a time, for 5 to 6 minutes per side. Arrange them, breast side down, in a shallow roasting pan, and surround them with the potatoes and the garlic cloves from the marinade. Sprinkle with salt and pepper, and 1 tablespoon of the chopped rosemary. Place the rosemary sprigs from the marinade on top.

6. Roast, brushing once or twice with the remaining marinade, for 10 minutes. Turn the birds breast side up, and roast for another 10 minutes. When the thickest part of the thigh is tested with a small sharp knife, the juices should run clear.

7. Arrange the partridges in the center of a large platter and surround them with the potatoes. Sprinkle the remaining 1 tablespoon chopped rosemary over the top of the partridge and potatoes, and serve.

Serves 4

BERRY-STEWED RABBIT

★ ★ ★

For fans of rabbit (I happen to be one), this slow-cooked stew—tender, sweet, sour, and so easy to make—is delectable. The cranberries blend beautifully in a rich, tart sauce with which to nap the meat. Serve this in shallow bowls over buttered egg noodles for a perfect brisk-weather meal.

Wine: Santa Barbara County (CA) Pinot Noir
Beer: American lager

1 rabbit (about 2½ pounds), cut into 8 pieces
4 carrots, peeled, halved lengthwise,
*   and cut into ½-inch pieces*
½ cup all-purpose flour
Salt and freshly ground black pepper,
*   to taste*
2 tablespoons olive oil
2 tablespoons unsalted butter
1 large onion, halved lengthwise and slivered
1 large garlic clove, minced
1½ cups defatted chicken broth, preferably
*   homemade (page 253)*
1 cup dry red wine
1 cup Fresh Whole-Cranberry Relish
*   (page 184)*
1 tablespoon red wine vinegar
2 tablespoons dark or light brown sugar
¼ teaspoon ground allspice
¼ teaspoon ground cumin
Hot cooked egg noodles, buttered, for serving
2 tablespoons chopped fresh flat-leaf parsley,
*   for garnish*

1. Rinse the rabbit pieces under cold water and pat them dry

2. Bring a small pot of water to a boil. Add the carrots and boil to soften, 5 minutes. Drain, and set aside.

3. Combine the flour, salt, and pepper in a shallow bowl. Dredge the rabbit pieces in the flour mixture, shaking off any excess.

4. Heat the oil and butter in a large heavy pot over medium-high heat. Brown the rabbit pieces, in batches, for about 4 minutes per side. Remove the rabbit from the pot.

5. Reduce the heat to medium-low. Add the onion and garlic and cook, stirring occasionally, until wilted, about 10 minutes. Return the rabbit to the pot and add the carrots, broth, wine, and cranberry relish. Stir in the vinegar, brown sugar, allspice, and cumin. Bring the mixture to a boil. Then reduce the heat to a very gentle simmer and cook, uncovered, stirring occasionally, until the rabbit is tender, 1 hour. Do not boil.

6. Serve over buttered egg noodles, garnished with the chopped parsley.

Serves 4

THYME-SCENTED RABBIT WITH ONIONS

★ ★ ★

Elegant in its simplicity, this full-bodied stew reaches the consistency of a creamy marmalade. Enhanced by the robust flavor of fresh thyme and smoky bacon, it requires nothing more than a portion of pearl barley alongside to absorb the rich juices. A frisée salad before, a fruity Pinot Noir with, and Maytag Blue after makes the perfect meal. Crusty peasant bread would be the ideal accompaniment to all courses!

Wine: Russian River Valley (CA) Pinot Noir
Beer: Washington State extra special bitter

3 tablespoons unsalted butter
1 rabbit (2½ to 3 pounds), cut into 10 to
    12 pieces
Salt and freshly ground black pepper, to taste
4 pounds onions, halved lengthwise and slivered
½ pound slab bacon, rind removed, cut into
    ¼-inch dice
1 cup dry white wine
8 large sprigs fresh thyme

1. Melt the butter in a large heavy pot over medium-high heat. Brown the rabbit pieces, on both sides, in two batches, moving the meat around so it doesn't stick to the pot, about 10 minutes per batch.

2. When the rabbit is browned, reduce the heat to low. Sprinkle with salt and pepper, and then cover the meat with the onions. Cover the pot and cook for 1 hour.

3. Meanwhile, place the bacon in a nonstick skillet over medium-low heat and cook until golden brown and the fat is rendered, 8 to 10 minutes. Transfer it to a bowl with a slotted spoon, and set aside.

4. Add the bacon, white wine, and thyme sprigs to the rabbit and cook, covered, until melting soft, 1 hour more.

5. Serve immediately, spooning the sauce over each portion.

Serves 4

fish

If you know *Huckleberry Finn,* you know how much its two heroes enjoyed fried fish. It was catfish, mostly, hauled out of the muddy Mississippi. One, Huck claims, was two hundred pounds and "big as a man." Now *that's* a fish tale!

My own tales about fish are 100 percent true—I've got snapshots and these recipes, inspired by and collected from my travels, to prove it. The photos live in albums on my bookshelf, but the recipes are here for all to try. Many of them are a bit fancier than any fish that Huck, Jim, or even Mark Twain ever ate, for we've become more sophisticated about fish since their day. For this chapter, I crusted Alaskan halibut with macadamias, topped Florida pompano with papaya salsa, seared Northwest salmon, and lightly blackened Louisiana tilapia. I flavored fish with curry sauce, oranges and limes, and a bell pepper compote. But I also made good old Boston-baked scrod and a simple grilled brook trout. I breaded Huck's favorite—most Southerners do, so I didn't think he'd disapprove. He'd more likely say, "Jim, this is nice . . . Pass me along another fish and some hot cornbread."

DEEP SOUTH CATFISH

★ ★ ★

Most catfish are now farm-raised, which turns the fish into surface feeders with a much sweeter taste than the wild channel catfish, which are bottom feeders with a slightly "swampy" taste. Some people like their fish sprinkled with unseasoned white cornmeal, others like theirs rubbed with fiery Cajun spices, but there are none who love catfish more than the townsfolk of Belzoni, Mississippi, the Catfish Capital of the World. At the annual Catfish Festival held each April, local catfish farmers dust tons of fillets with cornmeal and then fry it up to serve—along with hush puppies and coleslaw—to hungry attendees. For your own fish fry, serve the fillets with Pan-Fried Scallions, Black Bean Salad, or a bowl of Down-Home Greens.

Wine: Willamette Valley (OR) Chardonnay
Beer: American pale ale

4 catfish fillets (about ¼ pound each)
1 cup milk
1 cup yellow cornmeal
1 teaspoon salt
½ teaspoon paprika
¼ teaspoon ground cumin
¼ teaspoon cayenne pepper
Vegetable oil, for frying
4 lime halves, for serving

1. Rinse the catfish fillets and pat them dry.
2. Pour the milk into a bowl. Combine the cornmeal, salt, paprika, cumin, and cayenne in a pie plate; mix well.

3. Pour oil to a depth of ¼ inch in a heavy skillet and place it over medium heat.
4. Dip the fish fillets in the milk, shaking off any excess, and then dredge them in the cornmeal mixture, shaking off any excess.
5. Fry the catfish until deep golden brown, 5 minutes per side. Drain them on a double thickness of paper towels. Serve immediately, with the lime halves.
Serves 4

SUMMER COD POT

★ ★ ★

Lean, white, large-flaked fresh cod meat is versatile, inexpensive, and sturdy. It holds up beautifully when slowly simmered or roasted. And cod graciously accepts other flavors, so when preparing this fish I simmer it in a sweet and savory flavor combination. Orange zest and juice permeate this sauce with a sweet perfume that enhances the briny allure of olives and capers.

Wine: California Viognier
Beer: Pennsylvania German-style lager

RIVER CATS, CHANNEL CATS

—❦—

Catfish has long been a regular at the Southern dinner table, dusted with seasoned cornmeal and deep fried or blackened Cajun-style, for a crispy, peppery crust over tender flesh. Although people still go to the bayous for catfish, most of today's supply is farmed in ponds carved out of the Mississippi Delta wetlands. It's shipped north, east, and west, where it sometimes gets a different kind of treatment, winding up as catfish meunière, catfish poached in court bouillon, and the like. The farmed fish are sweeter and more delicate than the bottom-feeding "river cats," and we're discovering that we can prepare them much as we do sole, flounder, and snapper.

But I still like the classic catfish recipes best, for their soul and spice. To see them celebrated in high style, I traveled to Belzoni, Mississippi, the center of the catfish industry and home of the "World's Largest Catfish Fry," an annual feast and fair that draws forty thousand visitors to this little town. I went a day early so I could tour some farms. My hostess, Faye Janous, suggested we meet at a luncheonette. But how would she recognize me? "Don't worry," Faye laughed. "I can always spot a stranger."

The Janous farm is one of the region's biggest. Faye's husband, Billy George, walked me around a few of his ten- to twenty-acre ponds (he's got fifteen hundred acres in all) and explained the complex business of mating, hatching, feeding, and netting white "channel cats"—the tastiest of the edible American types. They go to the processing plant alive, he said, in order to maximize freshness. Fish that don't make muster there are usually just immature; these are returned to the farm for some days or weeks. I watched Billy George and his men harvest one pond with a huge, weighted net. Their catch, about a hundred gleaming cats, was a nicely whiskered bunch (the whiskers, or "barbels," act as feelers). After a luncheon at the county courthouse honoring the fair's Catfish Queen contenders, Faye rounded out my education at the Catfish Women of America's one-room catfish museum. I was an expert-in-training now, and ready for some serious eating!

I was not disappointed. By 10:30 the next morning, an army of men was already at work over massive deep fryers on the lawns before the courthouse, turning out mounds of golden hush puppies and cornmeal-battered fillets. So I lunched early—or was it breakfast? I took plenty of ketchup and coleslaw and parked myself at a picnic table swathed in red, white, and blue bunting. The Best of Elvis (who was from Tupelo, practically a local) was pumped out from the courthouse steps. More rock 'n' roll followed, and some country, too. There were games, a catfish-eating contest, farm tours, even a 10K run (not for me, thanks; I stick to eating at these affairs). The pageant came last: twelve local lovelies appeared in evening dress, thick tresses cascading down each slender back. Each girl was eager, each oh-so-hopeful, and all for the love of one homely, delicious fish.

2½ *pounds cod steaks, center bone removed*
2 *tablespoons extra virgin olive oil*
1 *large onion, coarsely chopped*
2 *tablespoons finely minced garlic*
1 *can (28 ounces) peeled Italian plum*
 tomatoes, drained and chopped,
 ½ *cup juices reserved*
Finely grated zest of 1 orange
Juice of 1 orange
¾ *cup pitted green olives, coarsely chopped*
½ *cup golden raisins*
2 *tablespoons drained tiny capers*
2 *sprigs fresh rosemary*
Salt and freshly ground pepper, to taste
½ *cup torn fresh basil leaves*
4 *cups hot cooked white rice or*
 pearl barley
4 *sprigs fresh basil, for garnish*

1. Cut the cod steaks in half lengthwise. Use tweezers to carefully remove any bones.

2. Heat the oil in a large deep skillet over medium heat. Add the onion and cook, stirring, until almost wilted, 8 to 10 minutes. Add the garlic and cook for another 2 minutes.

3. Add the tomatoes with their reserved ½ cup juices, the orange zest, orange juice, olives, raisins, capers, rosemary, salt, and pepper. Cook over medium heat, stirring, for the flavors to blend, 15 to 20 minutes.

4. Reduce the heat to medium-low so the liquid is just simmering, and add the torn basil. Add the cod, spooning the liquid over the top of the fish and making sure that the fish is covered with the sauce. Cook, shaking the pan, until the fish is cooked through (it will flake easily when tested with a fork), 10 minutes. If necessary, continue to spoon the sauce over the fish while it is cooking.

5. Serve in shallow bowls over cooked rice, with the sauce spooned over the top. Garnish with basil sprigs.

Serves 4

PAN-FRIED FLOUNDER ATOP CHOPPED GARDEN SALAD

★ ★ ★

This is how flounder was meant to be eaten—spiced up with Cajun-inspired seasonings and served over a California-style chopped salad. The contrast of textures and flavors is completely contemporary. No matter what time of year you choose to prepare the dish, all the ingredients will be available. So chop away, and let the fish fry begin!

Wine: Willamette Valley (OR) Pinot Gris
Beer: New England amber lager

½ *cup all-purpose flour*
½ *teaspoon sweet paprika*
½ *teaspoon chili powder*
½ *teaspoon ground cumin*
Salt and freshly ground black pepper,
 to taste
1 *head romaine lettuce, tough outer*
 leaves removed
1 *cup diced (¼ inch) red bell pepper*
1 *cup diced (¼ inch) carrots*
1 *cup diced (¼ inch) hothouse (seedless) cucumber*
1 *cup diced (¼ inch) ripe tomatoes*
2 *scallions (3 inches green left on), thinly sliced*
1 *ripe avocado*
1 *tablespoon fresh lime juice*
8 *tablespoons Luscious Lime Dressing*
 (page 330)
4 *flounder fillets (about ½ pound each)*
2 *tablespoons unsalted butter*
2 *tablespoons olive oil, or more as needed*
2 *tablespoons snipped fresh chives*

1. Combine the flour, paprika, chili powder, cumin, salt, and pepper in a shallow bowl. Mix well and set aside.

2. Cut the tough ribs out of the lettuce leaves, and discard the tough, darker green tops of the larger leaves. Cut the leaves into ½-inch pieces and place them in a large bowl. Add the bell peppers, carrots, cucumbers, tomatoes, and scallions.

3. Peel and pit the avocado. Cut it into ¼-inch dice and place it in a small bowl. Add the lime juice and toss well (to prevent discoloration). Add the avocado to the other vegetables and toss with 6 tablespoons of the vinaigrette. Season with salt and pepper. Divide the salad evenly among four dinner plates.

4. Cut the flounder fillets in half on the diagonal. Dredge the fillets in the reserved flour mixture, shaking off any excess.

5. Heat the butter and the olive oil in a nonstick skillet over medium-high heat. Cook the flounder, in batches, adding more oil if necessary, until dark golden brown, 3 minutes per side. Place 2 pieces of fish, overlapping, on top of each portion of salad. Drizzle the fish equally with the remaining 2 tablespoons vinaigrette, and sprinkle with the chives. Serve immediately.

Serves 4

THE HURRICANE GROUPER ON A BUN

★ ★ ★

When I was in Tampa, Florida scouting for great local eateries, the unanimous response from everyone I asked was "Don't miss the

grouper sandwich at The Hurricane in St. Petersburg." Although it was only 10:30 in the morning, I made the hour-long drive to this small, sun-bleached, wooden restaurant on Passagrille Beach. Rather than put myself through the torture of making a decision, I ordered two Hurricane specialties. I began with the fried grouper, which alone was worth the trip. Then I tried the broiled version. No disappointment here, either. With some creamy coleslaw on the side, The Hurricane delivered good eating in the fish sandwich category. Just a light coating of seasoned flour is all this flavorful fish really needs to make it a dynamite meal.

Beer: Minnesota lager

1 grouper fillet (about ¾ pound)
1 cup buttermilk
1 cup all-purpose flour
½ teaspoon paprika
Salt and freshly ground black pepper, to taste
2 tablespoons unsalted butter, or more if needed
2 tablespoons corn oil, or more if needed
4 soft multigrain or plain rolls, halved, lightly toasted if desired
½ cup Tartar Sauce (recipe follows)
Lettuce and ripe tomato slices, for serving (optional)

1. Lay the grouper on a flat surface and remove any little bones with tweezers. Going with the grain, carefully cut the grouper on the diagonal into 4 smaller fillets.

2. Place the buttermilk in a shallow dish. Combine the flour, paprika, salt, and pepper in a second shallow dish. Dip the grouper fillets into the buttermilk and then dredge them in the seasoned flour, shaking off any excess.

3. Heat the butter and the oil in a large non-stick skillet over medium heat. Add 1 to 2 fillets at a time, depending on the size of the skillet, and fry until golden brown and cooked through, about 3 minutes per side. Add a bit more butter and oil to the pan, if necessary, and repeat with the remaining fillets.

4. While the fish is cooking, spread both sides of each bun with 1 tablespoon of the Tartar Sauce.

5. Place a grouper fillet on the bottom half of each bun, top with lettuce and tomato, if desired, and cover with the top of the bun. Serve immediately.

Serves 4

Tartar Sauce

——★——

Tartar sauce originated in France, where it was made with hard-cooked egg yolks mashed into a fresh mayonnaise and then combined with onions, chives, or scallions. Here it takes on a truly American flavor with the addition of chopped sweet pickles.

When I yearn for a balanced mild tartar sauce with a silky texture and a bit of crunch, this is the one I prepare. It is perfect, whether slathered on a toasted bun holding grilled fish or

on soft-shell crabs, or used as a dip for lightly fried shrimp. If you like your tartar sauce spicy, check the Index for my recipe for Hot-Stuff Tartar Sauce.

1 cup mayonnaise
1 teaspoon Dijon mustard
1 teaspoon finely grated lemon zest
1 tablespoon fresh lemon juice
Dash of Tabasco sauce
2 tablespoons drained sweet pickle relish
2 tablespoons chopped fresh flat-leaf parsley
2 tablespoons finely minced shallots
1 tablespoon drained tiny capers
Salt and freshly ground black pepper, to taste

Combine the mayonnaise, mustard, lemon zest, lemon juice, Tabasco sauce, and relish in a bowl. Stir in the parsley, shallots, capers, salt, and pepper. Refrigerate, covered, for at least 1 hour and up to 3 days before serving, for the flavors to blend.

Makes about 1 1/4 cups

GRILLED HALIBUT TERIYAKI

★ ★ ★

Nelda and Jon Osgood, owners of the Tutka Bay Lodge, near Homer, Alaska, never have a shortage of halibut, or wonderful recipes for preparing it, and this is one of their favorites. In this recipe, halibut's firm white meat and delicate flavor fare well from a glaze of homemade teriyaki sauce that reflects a Pacific Rim influence. During grilling, the sugar in the sauce caramelizes to create a beautiful burnished finish on the fish's exterior. Because of its thickness, halibut is best grilled in a wire fish basket. If you don't have one, leave the fillet whole, but turn it very carefully during grilling.

Wine: California Gewürztraminer

TERIYAKI SAUCE
⅓ cup light soy sauce
¼ cup dry sherry
¼ cup sugar
2 tablespoons vegetable oil
4 cloves garlic, coarsely chopped
1 tablespoon coarsely chopped fresh ginger

1 halibut fillet (about 3⅓ pounds) with skin
3 scallions (3 inches green left on), thinly
*   sliced on the diagonal, for garnish*

1. Prepare the teriyaki sauce: Place all the sauce ingredients in a blender, and process until well combined.

2. Place the halibut fillet on a work surface, skin side down. Slice the halibut down to the skin at 1½-inch intervals, being careful not to cut all the way through. Place the teriyaki sauce in a shallow dish to fit the fish. Lay the prepared fillet, skin side up, in the dish, making sure that it is completely immersed in sauce. Set aside to marinate at room temperature for 30 minutes.

3. Prepare a barbecue grill with hot coals.

4. Secure the fish in a wire fish basket. Grill it, 4 inches from the heat source, skin side down, for 10 minutes, basting often with marinade. Turn the grill on the flesh side, basting, until the fish is just cooked through, 5 minutes. Remove immediately from the basket to a serving platter. Sprinkle with the scallions and serve.
Serves 6

MACADAMIA-CRUSTED HALIBUT WITH COCONUT CURRY

★ ★ ★

In Anchorage, Alaska, I had a memorable meal at the Marx Bros. Cafe, where partners Van Hale and Jack Amon have created a menu highlighting indigenous seafood. We began with fresh oysters on the half shell, followed by Van's justifiably famous Caesar salad, prepared tableside with enormous flair. The star of the meal was freshly caught halibut, encrusted with chopped macadamias and served on a bed of coconut curry sauce. Sweetly pungent fresh mango chutney added to the Pacific Rim note. A raspberry crisp (the fruit picked fresh from the garden just behind the restaurant) topped with birch syrup–butter pecan ice cream finished off the sublime summer solstice feast.

Wine: Russian River Valley (CA) Gewürztraminer
Beer: Washington State ale

MANGO CHUTNEY
¼ cup coarsely chopped fresh ginger
3 cloves garlic
3 small dried red chiles, seeds removed,
   coarsely chopped
1½ cups malt vinegar
1 cup sugar
2 ripe mangoes, peeled, pitted, and cut into
   ½-inch cubes
1 tablespoon chopped fresh cilantro leaves

COCONUT CURRY SAUCE
2 tablespoons peanut oil
3 tablespoons red curry paste (see Notes)
3 cups coconut milk (see Notes)
Salt, to taste

HALIBUT
1 cup all-purpose flour
2 large eggs
⅛ teaspoon cayenne pepper
½ pound unsalted roasted macadamia nuts,
   very finely chopped
1 pound fresh halibut, cut into ¼-pound fillets
¼ cup (½ stick) unsalted butter, melted
2 tablespoons chopped fresh cilantro leaves,
   for garnish

1. Prepare the mango chutney: Combine the ginger, garlic, chiles, and 2 tablespoons of the malt vinegar in a food processor and process until finely chopped. Transfer to a small heavy nonreactive saucepan, and add the remaining

MACADAMIAS

—❦—

Macadamias are the truffles of nuts—the creamiest and costliest of the pack, a good choice when you want to render a meal luxurious. They're named after a Dr. John Macadam, who, sadly, probably died before he could taste his namesake. Macadam's friend, botanist Baron Ferdinand von Mueller, "discovered" the nut in 1857, in the rainforest of Queensland, Australia (the aboriginals there already knew it well). It came to Hawaii in 1882; today, it's one of the state's signature crops.

One of the reasons macadamias fetch such a high price (about $17.00 a pound) is that they're so difficult to crack open. Early Hawaiian growers drove their cars over them to get the job done; today they use steel rollers. It's still a tricky job, though,

requiring three hundred pounds' worth of pressure for every square inch of nut. So dense are the hulls that an unshelled pound yields just a quarter pound of nutmeats. But what nutmeats they are.

Although macadamias are a treat in their simplest form—roasted and salted, as cocktail-hour nibblers—I can think of at least a dozen other ways to use them. Unsalted and crushed, they make a lush crust for meat and fish, such as the Macadamia-Crusted Halibut with Coconut Curry, and a buttery garnish for fruit salad, green salad, rice pilaf, and ice cream. Ground macadamias enrich cakes and pastries, and whole ones can transform humble drop cookies into an elegant dinner-party dessert. And if you've never tried them covered in chocolate, well, you have my sympathy!

malt vinegar and the sugar. Bring the mixture to a boil. Then reduce the heat and simmer, until the mixture is syrupy, about 25 minutes. Remove the pan from the heat, add the mangoes, and stir to combine. Set aside to cool. When cool, stir in the chopped cilantro.

2. Prepare the coconut curry sauce: Heat the oil in a heavy saucepan over medium-high heat. Add the curry paste and cook, stirring, to dissolve, 1 minute. Add the coconut milk and bring the mixture to a boil. Reduce the heat to a simmer and cook until the mixture has reduced by half, 25 minutes. Using a metal spoon, remove any oil from the surface of the sauce. Season the sauce with salt. Set it aside, keeping it warm.

3. Preheat the oven to 375°F. Lightly butter a baking sheet.

4. Prepare the halibut: Place the flour in a shallow bowl. In another shallow bowl, beat the eggs with the cayenne pepper. Place the chopped macadamia nuts in a third shallow bowl.

5. Dredge the halibut fillets in the flour, shaking off any excess. Dip them in the egg mixture and then dredge them in the ground nuts, being sure they are covered completely. Place the fillets on the prepared baking sheet, and drizzle each fillet with 1 tablespoon of the melted butter. Bake in the center of the oven until just done, 10 to 15 minutes (see Notes).

6. Spoon about ⅓ cup of the coconut curry sauce onto each of four warmed dinner plates. Lay a halibut fillet on top of the sauce, and then spoon about ¼ cup of the mango chutney over the fish. Sprinkle evenly with the chopped cilantro, and serve immediately.

Serves 4

NOTES: Red curry paste and coconut milk are available in Asian markets and in gourmet food shops.

Test the edge of one of the fillets for doneness by probing it gently with the tines of a fork; if the flesh flakes easily, it is done.

HALIBUT BAKED IN LEMON CURRY SAUCE

★ ★ ★

This is another recipe inspired by one I ate at Nelda and Jon Osgood's Tutka Bay Lodge just outside of Homer, Alaska. With as many as eighteen guests seated at their welcoming dining table, conversation frequently centers on lively tales of the day's catch. But when Nelda serves her sumptuous curry-baked halibut, silence descends as even the most ardent angler concentrates on the matter at hand. Personally, I don't believe that I have ever heard so many requests for a recipe!

Wine: Sonoma County (CA) Sauvignon Blanc

HOW I CAME TO CATCH A HALIBUT

—❦—

I went to Alaska intent on casting for halibut and there was no way I was going to depart without landing one. This magnificent creature migrates from its deep-sea spawning grounds to the icy waters off the Kenai peninsula each summer, followed by thousands of sportsmen lured by tales of four-hundred-pound, eight-foot specimens. The typical catch is much smaller—a sweet-fleshed twenty-eight to thirty pounds. I would have been happy with a prize of any size.

It was 7 A.M. when I boarded the thirty-foot *F/V Silver Fox I* in Homer, an arty frontier town of five thousand that's known the world over for its fishing (salmon and rockfish also collect here in record numbers). My five fellow adventurers had arrived minutes before. This was no hushed dawn gathering, for it was June, and the sun, after a brief dip below the horizon, had been up since four—raising the temperature to a balmy 30°F. Mufflers, gloves, and beefy woolen pullovers are summertime fashion essentials in these parts! Peter Karwowski, our skipper and angling instructor, began a fishing lesson that would last all day. As he plunged the *Silver Fox* through foggy Kachemak Bay and out to sea, we learned how to prepare bait, handle a fishing rod, set a hook, and reel with all our might. "The halibut's a strong fish, pretty much all muscle," Peter cautioned. "He'll break free if you don't keep the line taut."

Two hours later we were at sea, dropping our lines through the chilly drizzle. It wasn't long before the first of our party felt a nibble. "Be cool now," called Peter, "Wait until you're sure he's really got ahold of the bait." Five minutes later, a white flank flashed across the surface. Peter took over to demonstrate, slowly, painstakingly hauling the glistening fish—a fifty-pounder—upward. He threw a "gaff"—a thick hook, to contain the violent thrashing—deep into the animal's side before bringing it on the rain-soaked deck. It looked like an outsized version of its flounder cousin: flat, wide, and ghostly.

I was next to score. The initial tug on my line gave me an adrenaline rush; waiting those few beats before beginning to reel took terrific self-control. I'd hooked an even bigger beast, and needed more than a little help to bring it in. Eighty pounds . . . eighty pounds! Exhausted, I stood over its pale, four-foot bulk, blowing on my icy fingers. It wasn't long before the others began pulling, too; soon we had a mound of thirty-, forty-five-, and fifty-pound halibut in the storage bin below deck. Each fish was slashed with the mark of its owner; mine got a single notch.

When we arrived back in Homer at 4 P.M., I was all fished out and quite frozen, and more than ready for the traditional photo session (and my next fishing vacation in the Florida Keys). None of us chose to have our kills stuffed and mounted, though we could have; instead we all had a local seafood processor clean, cut, and flash-freeze them, and send them home by air. Such gorgeous steaks I returned to—three inches thick, and plenty tender and toothsome, a superb souvenir of that rousing, raw day. And they certainly helped to make the rest of the trip more memorable—I used this beautiful Alaskan fish to develop the halibut recipes I collected there.

1 cup mayonnaise

1 cup Crème Fraîche (recipe follows)

¼ cup dry sherry

2 tablespoons fresh lemon juice

2 teaspoons curry powder

1 cup thinly sliced onion

3 pounds halibut fillets, cut into 6 portions,
     patted dry

1 lemon, sliced, for garnish

1 tablespoon snipped fresh chives or chopped
     fresh flat-leaf parsley, for garnish

4 to 6 cups hot cooked white rice, for serving

1. Preheat the oven to 350°F. Lightly butter a 13 x 9 x 2-inch oven-to-table baking dish.

2. In a bowl, combine the mayonnaise, Crème Fraîche, sherry, lemon juice, and curry powder. Stir together well.

3. Scatter the sliced onions in the prepared baking dish. Arrange the halibut on top of the onions, and cover evenly with the sauce.

4. Bake until the fish flakes easily when tested with a fork, 30 minutes. Garnish with the lemon slices and snipped chives, and serve immediately with the cooked white rice.

Serves 6

Crème Fraîche

★

½ cup heavy (or whipping) cream

½ cup sour cream

Whisk the heavy cream and the sour cream together in a small bowl. Pour the mixture into a sterilized jar, cover, and let stand in a warm place for 12 hours. Then stir, and refrigerate for 24 hours.

Makes 1 cup

BAKED HALIBUT ON A BED OF PEPPERS

★ ★ ★

Tender halibut is delicious baked over bell peppers. A touch of balsamic vinegar sweetens the colorful vegetables and infuses the fish with a savory goodness. Herbes de Provence add a lusty feel to this one-dish meal. A few ripe black figs and a California goat cheese would make a terrific finish.

Wine: Napa Valley (CA) Rhône-style blend
Beer: Wisconsin dark lager

3 tablespoons extra virgin olive oil

2 red bell peppers, stemmed, seeded, and
     cut lengthwise into ½-inch strips

1 yellow bell pepper, stemmed, seeded, and
     cut lengthwise into ½-inch strips

1 onion, halved lengthwise and slivered

1 tablespoon balsamic vinegar

1 teaspoon herbes de Provence (see Note)

½ cup pitted imported black olives,
     such as Gaeta

Salt and freshly ground black pepper,
     to taste

4 tablespoons chopped fresh flat-leaf parsley

4 halibut steaks, cut 1 inch thick (about
     ½ pound each)

4 lemon halves, for garnish

1. Preheat the oven to 400°F.

2. Heat 2 tablespoons of the oil in a large nonstick skillet over medium heat. Add both of the bell peppers and the onion and cook, stirring often, until wilted, 10 minutes.

3. Stir in the vinegar, herbes de Provence, and olives, and cook 15 minutes more, stirring often. Season with salt and pepper and stir in 3 tablespoons of the parsley. Spoon the vegetables over the bottom of a baking dish large enough to hold the fish (9-inch square is perfect).

4. Brush the fish with the remaining 1 tablespoon oil, and sprinkle both sides with salt and pepper. Arrange it over the vegetables. Bake until the fish is opaque and flakes easily when tested with a fork, 20 minutes.

5. Sprinkle the fish with the remaining 1 tablespoon parsley, and serve immediately, garnished with the lemon halves.

Serves 4

NOTE: Herbes de Provence, a dried mixture of (commonly) thyme, rosemary, marjoram, oregano, summer savory, and basil, is available in specialty food stores and the spice sections of many supermarkets.

BAKED HADDOCK ON A BED OF FENNEL

★ ★ ★

This all-American fish, with its snowy white meat, can be found swimming off our Atlantic shores from April to November, as far north as Newfoundland and as far south as North Carolina. Unlike most fillets you buy, delicate, fragile haddock is always sold with the skin on. Baking haddock on a bed of fennel results in a dish of silky textures and bold flavors.

Wine: Long Island (NY) Cabernet Franc
Beer: Pennsylvania lager

3½ pounds fennel bulbs with ferns (3 to 4 bulbs)
4 tablespoons extra virgin olive oil
2 tablespoons unsalted butter
1 large onion, halved lengthwise and slivered
Salt and freshly ground black pepper,
    to taste
½ cup coarsely chopped pitted ripe California olives,
    preferably not canned
5 tablespoons chopped fresh flat-leaf parsley
4 haddock fillets (about 2 pounds)

1. Trim off the tops of the fennel bulbs. Coarsely chop enough of the fennel ferns to yield ¼ cup, and set them aside. Halve the bulbs lengthwise. Cut out the central core and slice the fennel into ¼-inch strips. Set aside.

2. Heat 3 tablespoons of the olive oil and the butter in a large heavy pot over medium heat. Add the sliced fennel and the onion, and stir well. Cover and cook, stirring occasionally, until the vegetables are very soft and jam-like, about 40 minutes.

3. Uncover the pot, raise the heat to medium-high, and cook until the mixture begins to caramelize, 7 to 10 minutes. Season with salt and pepper. Stir in the olives, 4 tablespoons of the parsley, and the reserved fennel greens.

4. Meanwhile, preheat the oven to 350°F.

5. Spread the fennel mixture evenly in a 13 x 9 x 2-inch oven-to-table baking dish.

6. Remove any bones from the haddock with a pair of tweezers. Cut each haddock fillet in half crosswise on the diagonal. Place the haddock fillets, skin side down, on top of the fennel and brush them lightly with the remaining 1 tablespoon olive oil. Sprinkle with the salt and pepper. Bake until the fish is opaque and flakes easily when tested with a fork, 30 minutes. Sprinkle with the remaining 1 tablespoon parsley and serve immediately.

Serves 4

POMPANO WITH PAPAYA CREAM AND PAPAYA SALSA

★ ★ ★

The svelte, silvery pompano is mostly at home in Florida, but it also cruises around the waters on the Gulf Coast and along our southeastern shores as far north as Virginia. In this dish, simply broiled pompano fillets, which have firm, white, somewhat oily flesh, luxuriate in a pool of delicious papaya cream. A generous dollop of spicy salsa adds an inviting spark of additional flavor. The vividly tropical pastels here look particularly attractive on the plate, echoing the vibrant Floridian style.

Wine: Monterey County (CA) Pinot Blanc
Beer: Oregon wheat beer

PAPAYA SALSA
1 cup diced (¼ inch) ripe papaya
1 cup diced (¼ inch) ripe tomato
¼ cup finely diced shallots
1 tablespoon seeded and finely minced fresh jalapeño pepper
1 tablespoon finely grated orange zest
2 tablespoons fresh orange juice
Salt and freshly ground black pepper, to taste

PAPAYA CREAM
¾ cup dry white wine
2 cups chopped ripe papaya
2 tablespoons minced shallots
½ cup heavy (or whipping) cream
2 tablespoons fresh orange juice
Salt and freshly ground black pepper, to taste

POMPANO
6 pompano fillets (about ½ pound each)
2 to 3 tablespoons olive oil
Paprika, to taste
Salt and freshly ground black pepper, to taste

1. Prepare the papaya salsa: About 1 hour before serving, combine all the salsa ingredients in a small bowl. Set aside.

2. Prepare the papaya cream: Combine the wine, papaya, and shallots in a small saucepan, and bring to a boil. Reduce the heat to medium and simmer until the liquid is reduced by about two thirds, about 5 minutes. Add the cream and simmer until the liquid has again reduced by two thirds, 5 minutes more. Remove the pan from the heat and stir in the orange juice, salt, and pepper. Set aside to cool slightly. Then purée the sauce in a blender until smooth. Set aside while you broil the fish.

3. Preheat the broiler.

4. Place the pompano fillets, skin side down, in a broiling pan. Brush lightly with some of the olive oil and season with paprika, salt, and pepper.

5. Broil the fish, skin side down, 3 inches from the heat source, for about 5 minutes. Turn the fillets over, brush with olive oil, re-season, and broil until the fish is opaque and flakes easily when tested with a fork, about 5 minutes more.

6. Spoon ¼ cup of the reserved papaya cream in the center of each dinner plate. Place a pompano fillet on top of the cream, slightly to the side, and then top with ⅓ cup of the reserved salsa. Serve immediately.

Serves 6

★★★★★★★★★★★★★★★★★★★★★★★★★

TESTING FISH FOR DONENESS
—❦—

*T*o test a fillet or steak for doneness, insert the tines of a fork gently into the thickest part of the fish. If the flesh flakes easily, it is done.

For swordfish or tuna steaks, it is best to insert a metal skewer or the tip of a small paring knife into the thickest part of the fish and pull it open slightly so that you can see the interior of the steak. If it is still translucent, allow the fish to cook a bit longer—about 1 minute—and check again. Fish continues to cook once removed from the heat, so be vigilant about checking it.

★★★★★★★★★★★★★★★★★★★★★★★★★

SEARED SALMON

★ ★ ★

In the 1980s "new wave" chefs popularized searing, a marvelous cooking method that literally and figuratively gave salmon a new lease on life, not only in professional kitchens but in home kitchens as well. Searing is a technique in which the surface of fish (or meat) is quickly browned over medium-high to very high heat in a skillet on the stove, in a very hot oven, or under a broiler. The brown sugar in this marinade caramelizes on the skin when the salmon is cooked, subtly adding to its already naturally sweet flavor.

Wine: Washington State Merlot
Beer: California porter

MARINADE
1 cup water
½ cup white wine vinegar
½ cup (packed) light brown sugar
3 tablespoons finely chopped garlic
½ teaspoon salt

4 center-cut pieces of salmon fillet, skin on
     (about ½ pound each)
1 tablespoon vegetable oil

1. Prepare the marinade: Combine all the marinade ingredients in a small nonreactive saucepan and simmer over medium heat until the sauce has reduced and thickened slightly, 30 minutes. Cool to room temperature.

2. Place the fish in a shallow baking dish and coat it with the marinade. Let it rest at room temperature for 30 minutes, turning occasionally.

3. Heat the oil in a large, heavy nonstick skillet over medium heat.

4. Remove the salmon from the marinade and place it in the hot skillet, skin side down (do this in batches, if necessary). Raise the heat to medium-high and cook for 2 to 3 minutes, shaking the pan and lifting the salmon with a spatula to loosen it from the pan.

5. Reduce the heat to medium, cover, and cook, shaking the pan occasionally, until the salmon is just cooked through, 3 to 4 minutes more. The salmon skin should be crisp and browned; the flesh should be medium-rare on the inside, more well done toward the edge. Serve immediately.

Serves 4

MANGO-MARINATED GRILLED SALMON

★ ★ ★

When cooked to perfection—the grill rack oiled just so, the timing perfect, the coals glowing—I believe that salmon can beat just about any other denizen of the sea. At home, at my grill, I watch with wonder as the fillets gradually change from deep pink to the pearly pink that signifies doneness. Lightly dressed with a sweet Maui Mango Barbecue Sauce, salmon is a superb company entrée.

Wine: Napa Valley (CA) Pinot Noir
Beer: Washington State porter

1 salmon fillet (2 pounds), cut in half crosswise
½ cup Maui Mango Barbecue Sauce (page 198)

1. Prepare a barbecue grill with medium-hot coals. Oil the grill rack well.

2. Pour half the barbecue sauce in a small bowl and set aside. Lay the salmon skin side down, on a cutting board or in a flat dish, and brush it lightly with some of the remaining barbecue sauce.

3. Place the salmon on the grill, flesh side down, 3 inches from the heat source, and cook for 8 to 10 minutes, turning after 4 minutes and brushing again with the barbecue sauce; the salmon should be lightly browned and crisp on the surface, cooked through near the edges and rarer in the center.

4. Carefully slice the salmon into 4 crosswise pieces and serve immediately, topped with a dollop of the reserved barbecue sauce.

Serves 4

BAKED SALMON ON A BED OF LEEKS

★ ★ ★

This honey and ginger marinade gives the finished salmon a lovely Asian flavor and a velvety texture. And as the leeks cook under the salmon, they develop a subtle sweetness that perfectly complements the fish.

The marinade contains citrus juice, so do not let the fish sit in it for longer than 30 minutes or it will "cook" the fish, as it does in seviche.

Wine: Willamette Valley (OR) Pinot Noir
Beer: Colorado ale

4 leeks (about 1½ pounds total)
4 salmon fillets (6 to 8 ounces each)
4 tablespoons fresh lime juice
4 tablespoons olive oil
1 tablespoon plus 1 teaspoon honey
1 tablespoon finely minced fresh ginger
Salt and freshly ground black pepper,
    to taste
2 tablespoons snipped fresh chives,
    for garnish
4 lime halves, for garnish

1. Trim the leeks, leaving 3 inches of green. Cut the leeks into a julienne (very thin strips about 4 inches x ⅛ inch). Wash them well in a strainer to remove all dirt. Bring a pot of salted water to a boil, and blanch the leeks for 2 minutes. Drain and set aside.

2. Arrange the salmon fillets in a glass or ceramic dish to fit. Combine 2 tablespoons of the lime juice, 1 tablespoon of the olive oil, the honey, ginger, salt, and pepper in a small bowl. Mix well, and pour over the salmon. Refrigerate, covered, for 30 minutes, turning once.

3. Meanwhile, preheat the oven to 450°F.

4. While the salmon is marinating, toss the blanched leeks with the remaining 2 tablespoons lime juice and up to 3 tablespoons of the remaining olive oil (you can use less oil if you wish).

FISH TIPS

—❦—

When buying fresh, whole fish, look for those with clear, bright, and shiny eyes and no "fishy" odor. The gills should be vibrant red with straight and even edges. Beware of dark, brownish-looking gills that appear bunched together like wet feathers. Fresh fish has a natural "bounce" to it. When you press it with your finger, it should come back to its original shape. Look for shiny skin and a scent reminiscent of the sea. Fillets should be moist and show no signs of drying or browning around the edges. To store your catch, wrap it tightly in plastic wrap or aluminum foil and keep it in the coldest part of the refrigerator. Fresh fish should be used within 2 days, or frozen.

When buying frozen fish, the packaging should be undamaged. There should be no signs of freezer burn, discoloration, partial thawing, or formation of ice crystals on the outside. Frozen fish stored in the coldest part of your freezer should last about 1 month. To thaw frozen fish, place it in the refrigerator and allow to slowly defrost for twenty-four hours.

As a general rule, cook fish for 10 minutes per inch of thickness, measuring at the thickest part of the fish (to test for doneness, see box, page 448). Overcooked fish will be dry and tough, so be careful. I prefer my fish just cooked to retain the greatest amount of integrity.

Season with salt and pepper. Arrange the leeks evenly on the bottom of a 13 x 9 x 2-inch oven-to-table baking dish.

5. Remove the salmon from the marinade, and place it attractively on top of the leeks, skin side down. Bake until it is cooked through (the salmon should flake easily when tested with a fork), 15 minutes. Serve immediately, sprinkled with the chives and garnished with the lime halves.

Serves 4

THE GREAT U.S.A. SALMON CAKE

★ ★ ★

Salmon from the Pacific Northwest, seasonings from Louisiana, and technique from my New York kitchen add up to this tasty American favorite. Similar to Maryland's crab cakes, these salmon cakes are light and delicate, made with poached salmon fillets that are perfumed by fresh thyme leaves. To me, homemade Tartar Sauce and a little Zesty Picnic Slaw are the natural accompaniments for these cakes, whether served alongside or on a bun. For a zesty change of pace, try Summer Peach Relish instead of Tartar Sauce.

Wine: Napa Valley (CA) Pinot Noir
Beer: Washington State India pale ale

POACHING LIQUID AND SALMON
4 cups water
1 cup dry white wine
4 sprigs celery leaves
6 sprigs fresh flat-leaf parsley
1 teaspoon coarse salt
6 black peppercorns
1 pound salmon fillets

CAKES
1¼ cups dried bread crumbs
1 tablespoon chopped fresh thyme leaves, or
  ½ teaspoon dried
1 teaspoon dried oregano
½ teaspoon dried mustard
Pinch of cayenne pepper
Salt and freshly ground black pepper, to taste
1 cup prepared mayonnaise
½ cup finely diced onion
½ cup diced (¼ inch) celery
1 tablespoon drained tiny capers, coarsely chopped
1 tablespoon chopped fresh flat-leaf parsley
1 teaspoon Worcestershire sauce
1 large egg, lightly beaten
2 tablespoons olive oil, or more if needed
Tartar Sauce (page 440), for serving

1. Prepare the poaching liquid: Combine all ingredients except the salmon in a large saucepan. Bring to a boil and then reduce the heat to a simmer.

2. Add the salmon fillets and simmer until cooked through (the salmon should flake easily with a fork), 10 minutes. Using a slotted spatula, remove the salmon from the poaching liquid and set it aside to cool. When it is cool enough to handle, remove the skin and bones and flake the salmon into a large bowl. Set aside.

3. Prepare the cakes: Combine ¼ cup of the bread crumbs with the thyme, oregano, mustard, cayenne, salt, and pepper in a small bowl. Mix well, and add to the salmon with the mayonnaise, onion, celery, capers, parsley, Worcestershire sauce, and egg. Fold the mixture together with a rubber spatula.

4. Place the remaining 1 cup bread crumbs in a shallow dish. Form the salmon mixture into 10 patties, each 2½ inches x 1 inch. Dredge the patties in the crumbs. Place them in a single layer on a plate, cover with plastic wrap, and refrigerate for at least 30 minutes and up to 1 hour.

5. Heat the olive oil in a nonstick skillet over medium heat. Sauté the cakes until golden brown, about 3 minutes per side. (Add more oil as necessary.) Drain the cakes on paper towels. Serve immediately, topped with Tartar Sauce.

Makes 10 salmon cakes; serves 5

ROASTED SCROD ON A MELTING BELL PEPPER COMPOTE

★ ★ ★

Scrod is the common marketplace name for small, young cod. A thick, mild-flavored fish, it is beautifully suited to roasting and holds up well to the assertive flavors of herbed bell pepper compote. Just a brush of oil is all the fish needs to keep it moist during cooking. This simple yet lively presentation is perfectly suited to today's more casual entertaining styles. If you've prepared the compote ahead of time, all you have to do is quickly arrange the vegetables and the fish, and bake just before it's time to eat.

Wine: Hudson Valley (NY) Pinot Noir
Beer: Boston lager

6 tablespoons extra virgin olive oil
2 yellow bell peppers, stemmed, seeded, and cut into ¼-inch slivers
2 red bell peppers, stemmed, seeded, and cut into ¼-inch slivers
1 large onion, halved lengthwise and slivered
2 teaspoons chopped fresh rosemary leaves, or ¾ teaspoon crushed dried
Salt and freshly ground black pepper, to taste
1 tablespoon finely minced garlic
6 tablespoons chopped fresh flat-leaf parsley
2 pounds scrod fillets (1 or 2 fillets)

1. Heat 4 tablespoons of the oil in a large heavy pot over low heat. Add both the bell peppers, the onion, rosemary, salt, and pepper and cook for 20 minutes, stirring occasionally. Stir in the garlic and cook until the vegetables are very soft, 10 minutes. Add 4 tablespoons of the chopped parsley. Spread the vegetables evenly in a 13 x 9 x 2-inch oven-to-table baking dish.

2. Meanwhile, preheat the oven to 350°F.

3. Cut the scrod into 4 portions crosswise. Lay the scrod, skin side down, on top of the vegetables. Brush the fish with the remaining 2 tablespoons olive oil and sprinkle with salt and pepper. Bake until the fish is cooked through (it will flake easily with a fork), 30 minutes. Sprinkle with the remaining 2 tablespoons chopped parsley, and serve immediately.

Serves 4

BOSTON BAKED SCROD

★ ★ ★

For a healthful, easy-to-prepare dinner with plenty of flavor, I suggest you try scrod fillets topped with a julienne of fresh vegetables. Baking in a foil packet, with a drizzle of olive oil and some fresh lemon juice squeezed over all before sealing the bundle, creates a perfectly cooked piece of fish. Any fresh green herb that you have on hand will add to the great flavor. You can put these packets together an hour or two ahead of baking, which makes them a natural for entertaining. (If you do prepare them in advance, refrigerate them, but be sure to bring them to room temperature before baking.) Each person opens the sealed packet on his or her plate to reveal their invitingly fragrant dinner serving.

Wine: Long Island (NY) Chardonnay
Beer: Pennsylvania pilsener

6 scrod fillets (½ pound each)
Salt and freshly ground black pepper, to taste
4 ripe plum tomatoes, seeded and slivered lengthwise
1 red bell pepper, stemmed, seeded, and slivered lengthwise
1 small onion, halved and slivered lengthwise
1 tablespoon drained tiny capers
2 tablespoons chopped fresh flat-leaf parsley
2 tablespoons fresh lemon juice
3 tablespoons extra virgin olive oil

1. Preheat the oven to 400°F. Set out six 14 x 12-inch pieces of aluminum foil, shiny side up.

2. Lay a scrod fillet in the center of the bottom half of each piece of foil. Sprinkle the fillets with salt and pepper. Arrange all the vegetables on top of each piece of fish, and sprinkle them evenly with the capers and parsley. Drizzle each fillet with 1 teaspoon of the lemon juice and 2 teaspoons of the olive oil.

3. Fold the top half of the foil over the fish, and seal the packets tightly on all sides.

4. Place the packets on a baking sheet, leaving 2 inches between them, spaced evenly for proper heat circulation. Bake for 15 minutes. Remove the baking sheet from the oven and let the packets rest for 5 minutes.

5. Serve immediately, placing one unopened packet on each plate. Open them carefully, because a puff of herb-infused steam will billow out.

Serves 6

CITRUS AND HERB-INFUSED SEA BASS

★ ★ ★

Whole roasted fish make a beautiful presentation and succulent eating, especially when they are infused with aromatic herbs. I always bring the finished dish to the table so that diners—whether family, guests, or both—can ooh and aah before I retreat back to the kitchen to do the boning away from prying eyes. Very few of us feel comfortable enough to bone a fish at the table—if you do, more to your credit. Once the fish are cooked and boned, you'll have four delicious fillets to serve. A light drizzle of extra virgin olive oil and fresh lemon juice, and a good grinding of black pepper, and you'll be enjoying sea bass my favorite way.

PLANKING SHAD

—❦—

*f*or Mid-Atlantic residents, the term "shad planking" conjures up memories of mouth-watering morsels of sweet white fish, served up at an afternoon seafood extravaganza that combines the pleasures of a picnic with plenty of local politics. For the past forty-eight years since 1939, when the local branch of the Ruritan Club held their first festival with about a dozen attendees, a huge, smoky fire surrounded by colorful tents has lured generations of "plankers" to the annual Shad Planking Festival in Wakefield, Virginia. Wakefield's hundred-member Ruritan Club is one of the oldest and largest in this organization, which was founded in Holland, Virginia, in the 1920s. The purpose of the clubs then (and now) was to foster goodwill between rural farm families and town dwellers by bringing everyone together over a good meal. Since the first cookout, Ruritans have raised thousands of dollars for scholarships and become a mainstay in civic affairs.

The pre-festival action begins on Tuesday afternoon when one ton of shad is trucked into a scenic glen of loblolly pines and unloaded onto more than ninety yards of plastic-covered tables. An enthusiastic committee of all-male volunteers immediately sets about cleaning and scaling the fish, gently lifting out the roe, a delicacy they will enjoy later in the evening as their reward for a job well done. After dinner, everyone beds down early in anticipation of the crack-of-dawn action on festival day. At 5:00 A.M. Wednesday, the "fire" committee sets a match to a hundred feet of wood and

pine branches arranged beneath a rustic shelter. Spirals of smoke encircle the boughs, then drift slowly into the cool morning air. An hour later the "planking" committee begins tacking the cleaned, split shad onto cured oak planks. By 9:00 A.M. the coals are red-hot, and the planks are lined up like a drill team on either side. The shad, which will cook for about six hours, will be brushed no fewer than five times with Carter Nettle's top-secret basting sauce. In the clubhouse kitchen, a hearty breakfast of bacon, fried apples, biscuits, and coffee awaits volunteers. Hunger staunched, the volunteers continue about their tasks until the gates are thrown open and eager attendees begin streaming across the clearing. Immediately, long food lines form as local Republican and Democrat representatives

assemble to meet and mingle with their constituents. In election years the political action gets more intense, and the governor of the state is likely to be the guest of honor. Civic affairs aside, the festival is a red-letter day on the local calender. And as anyone who's ever attended Wakefield's Shad Planking Festival will tell you—the proof is right there in the eating.

Wine: Virginia Chardonnay
Beer: New York State amber lager

*2 whole sea bass (about 1½ pounds each), heads
and tails left on, scaled and gutted*
*2 to 3 tablespoons extra virgin olive oil,
plus more for serving*
*Salt and freshly ground black pepper,
to taste*
2 orange slices, halved
2 lemon slices, halved
*4 sprigs fresh rosemary, plus more
for garnish*
*4 sprigs fresh tarragon, plus more
for garnish*
¼ cup fresh orange juice
¼ cup dry white wine
4 lemon halves, for garnish

1. Preheat the oven to 350°F. Oil a shallow baking dish large enough to hold both fish.

2. Brush the cavity of the fish lightly with some of the olive oil, and season with salt and pepper. Lay half of the the orange and lemon slices in each cavity. Place 1 to 2 sprigs of rosemary and tarragon in the cavity of each fish, depending on size. Tie the fish closed, loosely, at two intervals with kitchen string.

3. Place the fish in the prepared baking dish, and brush them all over with olive oil. Sprinkle with salt and pepper. Combine the orange juice and wine in a small saucepan, and cook over medium heat for 2 to 3 minutes. Set this aside for basting.

4. Bake the fish until it flakes easily when tested with a fork, 40 minutes, basting with the juice mixture once or twice.

5. Remove the strings and present the whole fish on a platter garnished with herb sprigs. Bone the fish, removing the fillets to dinner plates. Serve with a pitcher of extra virgin olive oil, the lemon halves, and a peppermill.

Serves 4

SHAD ROE ON A BED OF GREENS

★ ★ ★

I consider it nothing short of a miracle that I got to sample the cornmeal-battered shad roe that's fried up and served at the workmen's dinner held on the eve of the annual Shad Planking Festival in Wakefield, Virginia. Traditionally the occasion is an all-male affair of eating and drinking, a sociable reward for all the hard work these men have put in preparing the more than 2,000 pounds of shad for the next day's festivities. Plenty of rainbow trout, tubs of tangy coleslaw from the Virginia Diner, piping hot hush puppies and cornbread, and kegs of cold beer round out this lively evening, which is hosted by the local Ruritan Club. When I returned home after the festival, I bought my own shad roe and realized, in retrospect, that although fried roe had tasted wonderful in the midst of all the celebration and camaraderie, slow, careful cooking is the method most likely to bring out the best in this springtime delicacy.

Wine: Virginia Viognier
Beer: Louisiana ale

2 pairs shad roe
8 slices bacon
Salt and freshly ground black pepper, to taste
½ pound mesclun (mixed baby salad greens)
¼ cup Orange Honey Vinaigrette (page 80)
1 tablespoon snipped fresh chives
4 long fresh chives, for garnish

1. Gently rinse the roe in a bowl of ice water, and pat dry with paper towels. Trim the membrane that joins the two sides of the shad roe, separating each pair into two lobes.

2. Cook the bacon in a nonstick skillet over medium heat until crisp, 6 to 8 minutes. Transfer the bacon to paper towels to drain. Reduce the heat under the skillet to low.

3. Place the shad roe in the skillet. Cover and cook, gently turning them often, until the roe is golden on the outside and cooked through (the interior should be gray). Season with salt and pepper.

4. Lightly dress the salad greens with the vinaigrette. Place 1 lobe of roe in the center of each plate, and surround them with the dressed greens. Sprinkle with the snipped chives. Lay one slice of the bacon over each lobe, and garnish with a single chive. Crumble the remaining bacon over the greens, and serve immediately.

Serves 4

PAN-FRIED SOLE ON A BUN

★ ★ ★

Here's a fish sandwich that rises above the rest—a touch sophisticated and very satisfying. A light dusting of seasoned flour is all that's necessary to get a crispy crust on pan-fried sole. Meld the juicy sweetness of this fine fish with a little fresh Tartar Sauce, a layer of lettuce, and a toasted bun, and you'll dig into a tasty American favorite.

Wine: Long Island (NY) Sauvignon Blanc
Beer: Midwestern lager

2 fillets of sole (about 6 ounces each)
½ cup all-purpose flour
½ teaspoon paprika
Salt and freshly ground black pepper, to taste
2 tablespoons peanut or other vegetable oil
¼ cup Tartar Sauce (page 440)
4 soft multigrain rolls, halved and toasted
1 head Bibb lettuce, leaves separated, rinsed, and dried

1. Cut the fish fillets in half crosswise.

2. Place the flour, paprika, salt, and pepper in a paper or plastic bag. Place the fish in the bag and shake gently to dredge it, shaking off the excess flour.

3. Heat the oil over medium-high heat in a nonstick skillet. Cook the fish, carefully turning the pieces once, until browned and cooked through, 3 to 4 minutes per side.

4. Spread 2 teaspoons of the Tartar Sauce on each bun, and place a lettuce leaf on the bottom half of each. Top with a piece of fish, cover with the remaining bun half, and serve. Pass additional Tartar Sauce, if desired.

Serves 4

LIME-BROILED LEMON SOLE

★ ★ ★

For generations, when Americans thought of fish they immediately envisioned sole, especially served in classic fashion with a traditional buttery amandine sauce. You rarely see it served this way any more. These days there are newer, more healthful, zippier ways to enjoy it, such as with this sweet, delicate citrus sauce. Fresh lemon, orange, or grapefruit juice and zest make delightful substitutes for lime, giving the same results.

Wine: Napa Valley (CA) Sauvignon Blanc
Beer: Your favorite American lager

4 lemon sole fillets (about 6 ounces each)
¼ cup olive oil
Salt and freshly ground black pepper, to taste
¼ cup fresh lime juice
1 clove garlic, pressed
1½ tablespoons drained tiny capers
½ teaspoon finely grated lime zest
1 tablespoon chopped fresh basil leaves

1. Preheat the broiler. Line a baking sheet with aluminum foil.

2. Brush the fillets lightly with 1 tablespoon of the olive oil, and sprinkle them with salt and pepper. Arrange the fish in a single layer on the prepared baking sheet. Broil, 4 inches from the heat source, until the fish is cooked through (it should be opaque and should flake easily when tested with a fork), 8 minutes.

3. Meanwhile, combine the remaining 3 tablespoons olive oil, the lime juice, garlic, capers, and lime zest in a small saucepan. Cook over low heat, swirling the pan constantly, for 2 to 3 minutes. Season to taste with salt and pepper. Cover the sauce to keep it warm. Just before serving, swirl in the chopped basil.

4. Serve the fish on a platter or on individual plates, with the sauce spooned over it.

Serves 4

SOUTH BEACH RED SNAPPER

★ ★ ★

Red snapper, with its distinctive red-pink coloration, is an American favorite. Although simple preparations can often be the best, this sweet fish is one that inspires creativity. Here I broil the fish, then serve it atop a bowl of fragrant jasmine-scented rice, surrounded by a tropical fruit salsa. It's an exciting and unusual dish that mirrors the food served in Miami's stylish, colorful South Beach.

Wine: California Gamay
Beer: Vermont lager

SALSA
2 cups diced (¼ inch) ripe pineapple
2 cups diced (¼ inch) peeled hothouse (seedless)
  cucumber
2 cups diced (¼ inch) ripe plum tomatoes
1 cup diced (¼ inch) red onion
¼ cup pineapple juice
2 tablespoons minced garlic
2 tablespoons minced fresh ginger
1 teaspoon cornstarch
Salt, to taste

FISH
6 fillets red snapper (about 6 ounces each)
2 tablespoons olive oil
2 tablespoons fresh lime juice
Salt and freshly ground black pepper, to taste

½ cup chopped fresh basil leaves
Hot cooked white rice, preferably jasmine-scented
  (see Note) for serving

1. Preheat the broiler. Line a broiling pan with aluminum foil.

2. Prepare the salsa: In a heavy nonreactive saucepan, combine the pineapple, cucumber, tomatoes, onions, and pineapple juice. Simmer over medium-high heat, stirring occasionally, for 5 minutes. Reduce the heat to medium, add the garlic and ginger; cook, stirring, until the onions and tomatoes have softened, 5 minutes.

3. Pour ¼ cup of the liquid from the saucepan into a small bowl. Add the cornstarch and mix together until smooth. Stir the mixture back into the simmering fruit and cook, stirring, until slightly thickened, about 2 minutes. Season generously with salt, and set aside.

4. Prepare the fish: Place the fish, flesh side up, in the prepared pan. Brush the fillets with the olive oil and drizzle with the lime juice. Sprinkle with salt and pepper. Broil the fish, 3 inches from the heat source, until the flesh is cooked through and flakes easily when tested with a fork, 7 minutes.

5. While the fish is cooking, heat the salsa over medium heat, and stir in the basil.

6. Serve the fish over rice in shallow pasta bowls, and spoon the sauce over the fish.

Serves 6

NOTE: Jasmine rice is a flavorful aromatic variety, grown primarily in Thailand. But Jasmati, a jasmine-type rice, is now grown in the United States by RiceTec, the folks who produce Texmati rice. The American jasmine rice has a soft texture, nutty flavor, and sweet aroma.

BROILED SWORDFISH WITH LEMON-CAPER SAUCE

★ ★ ★

Swordfish is so meaty and flavorful it hardly needs more than a grinding of pepper and a generous squeeze of lemon juice to finish it off. Well, you may not need to top your fish with this zesty lemon and garlic sauce, but you'll be glad you did. (For a variation of this dish using lime, see page 456.)

Although the finished dish will always be tasty, a little care is required to keep swordfish from drying out during cooking. I give it a light brush of oil to help retain moisture. The fish continues to cook for a minute or two after it's removed from the broiler, so bear this in mind when testing it. To test for doneness, insert a metal skewer or a small paring knife into the thickest part of the swordfish steak. Then pull it slightly sideways so that you can peek at the inside. If it looks uncooked (still translucent), cook it a bit longer, and test again for doneness.

Wine: Sonoma County (CA) Sauvignon Blanc
Beer: Pennsylvania extra-bitter ale

4 pieces of swordfish (6 to 8 ounces each),
    cut 1 inch thick
¼ cup olive oil
Salt and freshly ground black pepper,
    to taste
¼ cup fresh lemon juice
1 clove garlic, pressed
1½ tablespoons drained tiny capers
½ teaspoon finely grated lemon zest
1 tablespoon chopped fresh flat-leaf parsley

1. Preheat the broiler.

2. Brush the fish lightly on both sides with 1 tablespoon of the oil, and sprinkle with salt and pepper. Place the fish on a small wire rack set inside a broiling pan. Broil, 4 inches from the heat source, for 4 minutes. Carefully turn the fish over and broil for another 4 minutes.

3. Meanwhile, combine the remaining oil with the lemon juice, garlic, capers, and lemon zest in a small saucepan. Place over low heat and cook, swirling the pan, to heat through, 2 to 3 minutes. Stir in the parsley.

4. Place the swordfish on dinner plates, spoon the sauce over it, and serve immediately.

Serves 4

NOT-QUITE-BLACKENED TILAPIA

★ ★ ★

The first time I tasted tilapia was at The Inn at Le Rosier in New Iberia, Louisiana, where chef Hallman Woods III prepared it in a simply delicious manner. The second time was a Cajun-inspired moment in my own kitchen, when I liberally spiced and semi-blackened up some. Originally, the tilapia available in markets was fished wild and had a salty, muddy taste. Nowadays the white-fleshed fish is farmer raised

and sweet. Blackened tilapia is particularly tasty when served with Garlicky Red Jacket Mashed Potatoes and Maque Choux.

Wine: Monterey County (CA) Pinot Blanc
Beer: California pale ale

SPICE MIXTURE
1 teaspoon salt
1 teaspoon sweet paprika
½ teaspoon ground cumin
¼ teaspoon Old Bay Seasoning
¼ teaspoon garlic powder
¼ teaspoon dried thyme
¼ teaspoon dried oregano
¼ teaspoon dry mustard
⅛ teaspoon freshly ground black pepper
⅛ teaspoon cayenne pepper

¼ cup (½ stick) unsalted butter, melted
4 tilapia fillets (about 6 ounces each)
4 lime halves, for garnish

1. Prepare the spice mixture: Combine all the ingredients for the spice mixture in a small bowl.

2. Place the melted butter in a bowl.

3. Heat a heavy nonstick skillet over high heat for 5 minutes (see Note).

4. Meanwhile, dip the fish fillets in the butter. Sprinkle them all over with the spice mixture.

5. Reduce the heat very slightly and sear the coated fish, 2 fillets at a time until very dark brown and crispy, 2 minutes per side. Repeat with the remaining 2 fish fillets.

6. Serve immediately, garnished with lime halves.

Serves 4

NOTE: Working with a skillet that's been heated over high heat for this length of time means you've got to take some precautions. Make sure

BEST WAYS TO COOK AND BONE A TROUT, A LA SOUTH DAKOTA

—❧—

After a glorious trout-fishing expedition at Trout Haven, a fishing camp and cafe outside of Deadwood, South Dakota, the chef dusted my freshly caught 13-inch beauty with cornmeal, then cooked the whole thing—from head to tail—and served it up with terrific creamy coleslaw, crispy fries, and plenty of homemade tartar sauce. Every last morsel was nothing short of splendid.

The folks at Trout Haven shared the following rules for cooking and boning trout with me. You'll want to follow them, because these guys really know their fish.

• Always cook trout with the head on; this will keep the skeleton intact and easy to remove later after cooking.

• Don't bother to scale trout. The scales are so small they fry up when cooked.

• Do not overcook. Trout should be moist and fork-tender, and overcooking will dry and toughen them. Trout are done when they no longer have a semitransparent look, but are solid white.

Trout Haven Cooking Methods

Frying in butter, bacon grease, or vegetable oil: In a heavy pan, heat enough fat or oil to coat the surface of the pan with about an ⅛-inch layer. Coat the cleaned fish in a light breading of half flour and half cornmeal. Fry at a moderate temperature until browned on each side (approximately 8 minutes per side) for a 12-inch trout. Turn only once, and never overload the pan. The skin is delicious when cooked this way.

Baking: Place the cleaned trout on an aluminum foil–lined baking sheet. Bake in a preheated 350°F oven for 20 minutes for a 10- to 11-inch trout. Do not turn.

Broiling: Trout can be broiled 10 to 15 minutes, 4 inches from the heat. Baste with oil or butter, but do not turn.

Microwave: Microwave trout in a shallow glass dish covered with vented plastic wrap. Microwave on High for 2½ to 3½ minutes, then let stand, covered, for 2 minutes. These directions are to microwave one trout.

Boning Cooked Trout

Place the cooked trout on its side. Remove the back fin, the fin at the bottom of the opening, and the fins on either side of the opening. Slide a fork down the back just enough to open the skin. Raise the head with your fingers, and pull the meat from the skeleton on the underside with a fork, lifting the head upward as you do. When all the meat on that side is off the bone, turn the trout over and repeat the procedure. Discard the head and the skeleton. Any remaining bones can be discarded as the fish is eaten.

the nonstick surface on your skillet will be able to withstand such intense heat; or else use a well-seasoned cast-iron skillet. Use your stove fan to draw away any smoke generated once the fish is added, and stand back to avoid splatters. Protect your hands, when lifting the skillet, with insulated potholders.

PAN-FRIED TROUT

★ ★ ★

Well-seasoned flour adds a nice flavor coating to pan-fried trout, but I find size is also an important factor—the smaller the trout, the better the taste. And don't stint on the fresh lemon. I prefer serving a lemon half per person rather than just a wedge. With wedges, people always seem to run out of juice before they've finished eating. Great accompaniments include East Norwalk Cole Slaw, Piccalilli Corn Salad, and Bread-and-Butter Pickles.

Wine: Washington State Chenin Blanc
Beer: Vermont lager

½ cup all-purpose flour
½ teaspoon paprika
½ teaspoon salt
¼ teaspoon freshly ground black pepper
1 tablespoon unsalted butter
1 tablespoon vegetable oil
4 brook trout (about ¾ pound each),
    cleaned (innards removed) but with
    heads and tails left on
4 lemon halves, for serving

1. Combine the flour, paprika, salt, and pepper in a bag that is large enough to hold one fish at a time.

2. Heat the butter and the oil in a large nonstick skillet over medium-low heat.

3. When the butter is melted, place the trout, one at a time, in the bag with the flour mixture, shaking off the excess. Raise the heat under the skillet to medium-high. When the butter and oil are bubbling, add the trout and cook until a light crust has formed and the fish flakes easily when tested with a fork at the thickest point, about 5 minutes per side.

4. Serve immediately, with lemon halves; bone the fish before eating as described in the box on the facing page .
Serves 4

GRILLED TROUT

★ ★ ★

To my way of thinking, grilling a whole trout is the single most delicious way of preparing it, especially when the fish is cooked outdoors the day it's caught. Trout done this way is very easy to prepare, needing just a light brushing of oil and a sprinkle of seasoning before cooking. Grill as many fish as there are hungry mouths to feed, making sure each fish comes with its own lemon half.

Wine: Napa Valley (CA) Viognier
Beer: California pale ale

4 whole brook trout (about ¾ pound each),
cleaned (innards removed) but with heads
and tails left on
3 tablespoons olive oil
Salt and freshly ground black pepper, to taste
4 lemon halves, for serving

1. Prepare a barbecue grill with medium-hot coals

2. Brush the fish well with the olive oil, and sprinkle with salt and pepper.

3. Place the fish on the grill and cook until they are browned and the flesh flakes easily when tested with a fork at the thickest point, about 5 minutes per side. Serve immediately, with a lemon half for each serving; bone the fish before eating as described in the box on page 460.

Serves 4

POACHED TROUT

★ ★ ★

The secret to great-tasting poached trout is the very essence of simplicity—all you need is a shiny, clear-eyed fish and a simple, yet full-of-flavor liquid in which to delicately simmer it. An agreeable, reasonably priced white wine, combined with a few of the vegetables customarily used in basic soup stock, and flavored with a bit of parsley and some bay leaves, does the job nicely. If you wish to add them, a few sprigs of fresh thyme or rosemary will gently urge the flavor along ever further. While using a fish poacher is the ideal method, the large pot called for in this recipe will work almost as well—just be careful when removing the fish.

I love trout prepared this way. It tastes so fresh and clean, and the flesh is indescribably succulent. The greatest trout treat, however, is a very tiny one that most people don't know about, though it's my favorite part of the fish—the little, sweet cheek located just below the eye.

Wine: Washington State Sauvignon Blanc
Beer: Oregon lager

POACHING LIQUID
8 cups water
1½ cups dry white wine
2 ribs celery with leaves, coarsely chopped
1 large carrot, coarsely chopped
6 sprigs fresh flat-leaf parsley
2 bay leaves
6 black peppercorns
1½ teaspoons salt

2 whole brook trout (about ¾ pound each),
cleaned (innards removed) but with heads
and tails left on
2 lemon halves, for serving

1. Prepare the poaching liquid: Place all the poaching liquid ingredients in a nonreactive pot large enough to hold the fish, and bring to a boil over high heat. Reduce the heat, cover partially, and simmer for 20 minutes. Strain the liquid and discard the vegetables. Return the poaching liquid to the pot.

2. Add the trout and simmer gently, partially covered, until the fish flakes easily when tested with a fork at the thickest point, 10 to 12 minutes. Do not let the liquid boil.

3. Using a long spatula, carefully remove the fish from the liquid and serve immediately, with the lemon halves. If desired, the trout may be boned before serving, as described in the box on page 460.

Serves 2

SEARED TUNA STEAKS

★ ★ ★

I think this is *the* way to cook tuna, although grilling is a close second. When selecting fish, look for yellowfin tuna that is at least 1 inch thick. The result you are striving for is a moist steak with a firm exterior and a pale pink interior, and the skillet you use is important. I have a heavy one that allows for uniform heat throughout the pan, and I get a good sear over medium-high heat. But you may need to go higher. Cast iron will sear the steak well. Just be sure to pay close attention to the fish as you're cooking it. After the fish is removed from the skillet, it will continue to cook as it rests, so remove it from the pan while it's still a little rarer than you'd like. Serve the tuna with a generous spoonful of Fresh Pineapple Relish.

Wine: Dry Creek Valley (CA) Zinfandel
Beer: California porter

Coarsely ground black pepper
2 tuna steaks (6 to 8 ounces each),
    cut 1 inch thick
1 tablespoon olive oil

1. Generously pepper the tuna steaks on both sides, patting the pepper down lightly.
2. Heat the olive oil in a nonstick skillet over medium-high heat. Add the tuna steaks and sear the first side until lightly browned, 5 minutes. Turn them over and cook for 3 minutes on the other side, or until cooked to your liking (see testing box, page 448). Let rest for a minute or two before serving.

Serves 2

SEARED FRESH TUNA AND NOODLES

★ ★ ★

What's old often becomes new. Once welcome at nearly every American table, tuna noodle casserole fell into gastronomic oblivion at the end of the 1960s. The mere mention of this starchy amalgam, topped with a layer of crushed cornflakes or potato chips, made eaters turn up their noses in disdain. But this true American classic was once a family favorite, and there's no reason why it shouldn't become one again. In this updated recipe, chunks of fresh, marinated tuna are served on top of noodles dressed with a flavorful peanut sauce, then garnished with chopped peanuts and fresh cilantro. Exciting and contemporary, these flavors will easily please diners in the twenty-first century.

Wine: Santa Barbara County (CA) Pinot Noir
Beer: Oregon ale

DRESSING

2 tablespoons soy sauce

2 tablespoons rice wine vinegar

2 tablespoons water

2 teaspoons sugar

¼ teaspoon salt

1 teaspoon finely minced fresh ginger

1 teaspoon finely minced garlic

2 tablespoons smooth peanut butter

¼ cup peanut oil

MARINADE

1 tablespoon peanut oil

1 tablespooon dark sesame oil

1 tablespoon light soy sauce

1 tablespoon finely minced fresh ginger

2 tuna steaks (½ pound each),
*   cut 1 inch thick*

½ pound fettuccine or other noodles

¼ cup coarsely chopped peanuts

¼ cup diced (¼ inch) hothouse (seedless) cucumber

3 tablespoons chopped fresh cilantro leaves

4 lime halves, for garnish

1. Prepare the dressing: Whisk together the soy sauce, rice wine vinegar, water, sugar, salt, ginger, garlic, and peanut butter in a large bowl until smooth. Slowly whisk in the oil and continue whisking until slightly thickened. Set aside.

2. Prepare the marinade: Combine the marinade ingredients in a shallow baking dish. Add the tuna steaks and coat well with the marinade. Let rest at room temperature for 15 minutes, turning once or twice.

3. Meanwhile, bring a large pot of salted water to a boil.

4. Remove the tuna from the marinade. Heat a nonstick skillet over medium-high heat. Add the tuna steaks and sear until lightly browned on the outside and pale pink inside, 5 minutes on the first side and 3 minutes on the second side. Let rest at room temperature for 3 to 4 minutes. Then cut the steaks into 1-inch chunks and set aside.

5. Cook the fettuccine in the boiling water until just tender, 10 to 12 minutes. Drain. Rinse under water, and drain again. Toss the noodles with the reserved dressing.

6. Divide the noodles among four dinner plates, and sprinkle evenly with the peanuts. Sprinkle the cucumbers over each portion, and top with the tuna chunks. Sprinkle with the chopped cilantro, garnish each plate with a lime half, and serve.

Serves 4

WHITE GULL INN TRADITIONAL FISH BOIL

★ ★ ★

No visit to Door County, Wisconsin—the peninsula that extends off the eastern coast of the state into Green Bay and Lake Michigan—would be complete without savoring that famous local feast called a "fish boil." The delicious meal originated with Scandinavian settlers and lumberjacks, who found it a nourishing way to enjoy local ingredients. Now a well-established local tradition, "the boil," as it is called, is served at restaurants all over the peninsula. I had mine at the White Gull Inn at Fish Creek, where it is cooked outside over a wood fire using a 22-gallon pot and two baskets, one to hold the fish steaks and the other to hold the potatoes. This recipe is for creating a fish boil at home on the kitchen stove. You will need a pot that holds at least 5 gallons, preferably with a removable bas-

A DOOR COUNTY FISH BOIL

*I*f you go to Door County, Wisconsin, and don't attend a fish boil, well, you haven't been to Door County. It's the region's signature ritual that, like Thanksgiving, celebrates heritage and environment with a feast. Unlike Thanksgiving, it takes place all the time—nightly, in summer—in restaurants and inns everywhere. Finding one is easy. Just follow the signs; or look around at suppertime for a billow of smoke and steam, the output of a huge kettle over a blazing wood fire.

Door County is all peninsula, a narrow, seventy-five-mile-long finger that juts north into Lake Michigan. Early Scandinavian settlers made their living off the lake, which is rich in trout and whitefish. Men out on the water in steamships would eat a few of their catch as "domers," stuffed with onion, wrapped in newspaper, and steamed in the domes of their engine boilers. These meals became fish boils once the ships grew large enough to accommodate the galleys with pot-bellied stoves. Eventually the boil moved ashore and became fodder for all kinds of celebrations. The first public one was held in 1961; visitors have been flocking here for more ever since.

The county, popularly known as "the Cape Cod of the Midwest," has a bounty of state parks and pretty fishing villages throughout. I stayed in Fish Creek, a long-time tourist favorite for its performing arts, shops, lodgings, and, of course, fish boils. I found mine at the White Gull Inn, where master boiler Russ Ostrand has been staging the event (and playing the accordion during interludes) for thirty years. An eager crowd of twenty-five watched and listened as he narrated over the roar of flames. He began with a "pinch" of salt—a whole pound for every two gallons of water, not, in fact, to make the boil salty but to encourage the fish oil to float. Potatoes followed, then whitefish chunks in the final minutes. Finally, *whoosh:* A little kerosene thrown into the fire got the liquid to "overboil," carrying all that fishy-tasting oil with it.

Dinner, fished out in a basket with a long pole, was served minutes later. We dressed the boiled masterpiece in tartar sauce, butter, and lemon and had it with coleslaw and blueberry, banana, lemon, and Swedish limpa breads. We ate to the bursting point, washing all down with Golden Rail, a Wisconsin microbrew. Tradition dictates cherry pie for dessert, made from tart Door County fruit. Saving room took planning—and great self-control!

For more information on visiting Door County and attending a fish boil, contact the Door County Chamber of Commerce at (800) 527-3529.

ket for draining (a canning pot with a rack or a pot with a pasta insert will also work). If your pot does not have a removable basket, you can make cheesecloth bags to hold the potatoes and fish, or you can drain the boil in a colander. Don't forget the coleslaw and cherry pie that make this feast authentic.

Wine: Virginia Chardonnay
Beer: Wisconsin dark lager

12 small red new potatoes
8 quarts (2 gallons) water
2 cups salt (see Note)
12 whitefish or lake trout steaks, 2 inches thick
  (3 to 4 ounces each, 2½ to 3 pounds total)
2 tablespoons coarsely chopped fresh flat-leaf parsley
Tartar Sauce (page 440) for serving
½ cup (1 stick) unsalted butter, melted, for serving
4 lemon halves, for serving

1. Wash the potatoes well and cut a thin slice off each end (this allows for better flavor penetration). Set them aside.

2. Pour the water into a 5-gallon pot and bring it to a rolling boil. Keep it boiling as much as possible during the cooking procedure.

3. Add 1 cup of the salt and the potatoes to the pot. Cook until the potatoes are nearly done (test with a fork), 20 minutes. Add the remaining 1 cup salt and the whitefish. Cook until the fish is still firm but beginning to pull away from the bone when lifted with a fork, 8 to 10 minutes. While the fish is cooking, skim the oil off the surface of the water with a spoon.

4. Lift the cooked potatoes and fish from the water and drain well.

5. Arrange the fish and potatoes on a large platter and sprinkle with the parsley. Serve immediately with the Tartar Sauce, melted butter for dipping or spooning over, and the lemons alongside.

Serves 4 generously

NOTE: The amount of salt is based on the amount of water. If you're increasing the amount of water, add 1 cup of salt for each additional gallon of water.

Shellfish

Imagine the delight of the earliest settlers in the New World when they discovered its shellfish—vast beds of oysters, clams, and mussels, more varieties of sweet crab than they'd ever seen before, oceans teeming with shrimp and huge, meaty lobsters. All these jewels of the sea soon became staples.

Much of America's favorite seafood cookery—clambakes and lobster boils—goes back to those early days. The gifted Creole cooks of New Orleans weighed in early, too, and to this day their cuisine relies heavily on local shellfish. When Italian immigrants arrived they introduced shellfish marinara and shrimp scampi. So, here is a collection of my favorite influences: some modern creations—a refreshing spring pasta with shrimp and peas, summery Grilled Soft-Shell Crabs with Roasted Tomato Sauce, and the Southwestern-minded Seared Sea Scallops in Chipotle Cream. And some recipes that are inspired by seaside classics—Connecticut-style broiled stuffed lobster, Cajun soft-shell crab on a bun, South Carolina shrimp burgers. Try them in your kitchen, whether inland or seaside—they'll taste plenty authentic.

PACIFIC NORTHWEST LIGHT MUSSELS

★ ★ ★

Today some of the best mussels in the country are being cultivated in the Pacific Northwest, bedded among the rocks in Washington's Puget Sound. There, within the past ten years, researchers have discovered a different breed of mussel, *Mytilus galloprovincialis,* growing abundantly off the coast of California and in Puget Sound. Naturally grown in Spain and Italy, no one is exactly sure how they came to America, but one theory is that they attached themselves to the hulls of Spanish galleons traveling to the New World. However they got here, they are a boon to all of us mussel lovers, and you should use them if you can get them. They are sand-free, plump, and simply delicious, especially in a flavorful broth, like the one in this recipe. Make sure you have some crusty bread for dipping into the flavorful broth.

Wine: Oregon Müller-Thurgau
Beer: Washington State India pale ale

4 pounds mussels
¼ cup (½ stick) unsalted butter
1 leek, white part only, well washed,
*   patted dry, and thinly sliced*
1 cup diced (¼ inch) fennel bulb
¼ cup finely chopped shallots
2 cups diced (¼ inch) seeded tomatoes
½ cup chopped fresh flat-leaf parsley
1 tablespoon finely minced garlic
Salt and freshly ground black pepper,
*   to taste*
1 cup dry white wine

1. Clean the mussels as described in the box, this page.

2. Melt the butter in a large, heavy nonreactive pot over medium heat. Add the leeks, fennel, and shallots and cook, stirring, until wilted, 8 minutes.

3. Add the tomatoes, parsley, and garlic and cook for 2 minutes. Season with salt and pepper.

4. Add the mussels and the wine and raise the heat to high. Cover and cook, shaking the pan occasionally, until all the mussels have opened, 6 to 8 minutes. Discard any that do not open. Serve immediately, in shallow bowls with the vegetables and broth.

Serves 4

TO CLEAN MUSSELS

—❧—

When you're buying mussels, be sure to ask for the freshest available. Scrub the shells well with a stiff brush, and rinse in several changes of cold water. Just before cooking them, pull off the "beards" (the tough, fibrous material the mussels uses to suspend themselves from the rocks or pilings); if you remove them ahead of time, the mussels will die and be unsuitable for eating.

TINY COCKLES AND FRESH TOMATOES OVER LINGUINE

★ ★ ★

Diminutive cockles—those tiny sweet-tasting clams—are easy to cook, and when served still in their shells, they are attractive to look at and fun to eat. Whether you spoon them over pasta or heap them high in a bowlful of broth, a good-size wedge of crusty peasant bread is a must for dunking. Garnish the cockles with plenty of fresh basil.

Wine: Sonoma County (CA) Sauvignon Blanc

4 pounds cockles or littleneck clams
3 tablespoons extra virgin olive oil
3 tablespoons minced garlic
½ cup dry white wine
½ cup clam juice
4 cups diced (¼ inch) seeded plum tomatoes
4 scallions (3 inches green left on),
  thinly sliced
⅓ cup slivered fresh basil leaves
Salt and freshly ground black pepper, to taste
¾ pound linguine, cooked

1. Rinse the cockles in cold water and drain them well in a colander.

2. Heat the oil in a large, heavy nonreactive pot over low heat. Add the garlic and cook, stirring, until wilted, 2 to 3 minutes.

3. Add the wine and clam juice, cover, and raise the heat to medium. Simmer until the flavors are blended, 3 to 5 minutes.

4. Add the cockles, cover, and simmer to steam, shaking the pan, until the cockles open, 3 to 5 minutes. Discard any that do not open. Transfer the cockles to a large serving bowl, along with the juices. Toss with the tomatoes and scallions. Sprinkle with the basil and salt and pepper.

5. Divide the linguine among four shallow pasta bowls, and top with the cockles and broth. Serve immediately.
Serves 4

SUPER BOWL CLAMBAKE

★ ★ ★

I've been known to get a hankering for a clambake on completely nontraditional occasions—say, Super Bowl Sunday—but even in summer, it's not always possible to throw a clambake on the beach. So, I've devised an indoor method in order to have this extravaganza any time of the year.

First I dig out the large turkey roasting pan that goes to the back of the shelf after the holiday season. Then I shop for large bunches of thyme and rosemary in place of seaweed, since fresh herbs are usually available all year round. Good fresh corn is the one difficult ingredient to find out of season, but it is available. As long as the ears have nice tight husks, and a tested kernel spurts a bit of milky liquid when poked, it's okay

★★★

A TRADITIONAL CLAMBAKE

—❦—

When it came to my first clambake, I was perhaps too ambitious. But with the misty shore at Malibu, California for a backdrop, who wouldn't be? I wanted the *real* thing—in a pit in the sand, over white-hot rocks, and with wild seaweed for seasoning. This was the tradition, after all, established by New England's Native Americans long before the *Mayflower* turned up. The digging was no problem; a few friends volunteered for that. But two key ingredients proved hard to come by in southern California—large, round beach stones (sedimentary rock preferred) and plump Maine lobsters. I got the lobsters, eventually, but our rocks were all wrong. They wouldn't heat up in time, and so, with twenty-five guests on the way, the lobsters, seaweed, chicken, corn, and shellfish wound up in the biggest pot I could find. Inauthentic, perhaps, but everyone still had a great time.

That was 1972. When I attempted my second clambake, twenty-one years later, I was older and wiser. This time I was on Nantucket, expecting another party of twenty-five. Islanders usually hire a team of experts for occasions like this, and so did I. I was nervous nonetheless, because the weather on the June day I chose was cold and drizzly. There was nothing to do but throw on a slicker and watch as the local pros dug a four-foot pit on Miacomet Beach, lined it with rocks (the right kind!), and shoveled in blazing coals.

Four hours later, there was still no break in the clouds. Grim, I ordered a canopy for the table.

A pickup truck delivered wooden pallets, which were burned over the coals one at a time, to build up the heat in the rocks. Once the rocks were ready, the workers removed the embers and laid down wet rockweed. This native seaweed has tiny sacs full of saltwater, which burst and release briny vapor when heated. Next came the lobsters, in wire baskets, followed by mussels, steamer clams, sweet onions, new potatoes, corn, and a heavy tarp over all (the chicken, which is typically prepared at a clambake, was barbecued separately, on a nearby grill). I looked up from the pit and saw a patch of blue sky, then another. The late afternoon would be beautiful; the weather was turning fine in time for my clambake.

When the tarp was lifted, an hour later, a magnificent puff of steam masked the finished treasure for mere seconds: scarlet lobsters, open clams and mussels, bright red potatoes, moist green corn husks—all very promising indeed. We downed our feast with ice-cold beer, by the light of a glorious June sunset.

Now *that* was a real clambake. It was special; it was an "occasion." But a clambake needn't be outdoors, or even a summer thing. However, it should be an occasion, and what better one than the Super Bowl? Next year, try my indoor clambake (page 469) in place of (or along with) chili, or whatever is traditional with you. Blue skies may be out of the question, but there's no beating a clambake to add a bit of summer to a midwinter party.

★★★

for this dish. If the ears look old and unappetizing, pass them by and use frozen corn on the cob instead. They won't have their husks, but that doesn't matter. For this indoor version, I like to include lobsters and exclude chicken, but if you prefer, you can include pieces of grilled or broiled chicken alongside. Serve the bake in large bowls with some broth for cleaning the clams, melted butter for dipping, and lots of lemons. Finally, may the big game be as good as the food—and may you win the office pool.

TO CLEAN CLAMS

— ❧ —

*T*o clean hard-shell clams, first scrub them with a stiff brush under cold running water, discarding any clams with broken shells. Place the clams in a large bowl and cover with cold water. Sprinkle with 1 tablespoon each cornmeal and salt and let stand 1 hour. Drain the clams, rinse, and drain again.

To clean soft-shell (steamer) clams, wash in several changes of cold water and drain, discarding any with broken shells.

Wine: Sonoma County (CA) Chardonnay
Beer: San Francisco Anchor Steam Beer

4 live lobsters (about 1¼ pounds each)
16 small red new potatoes
8 small onions
3 large bunches fresh thyme, rinsed
2 large bunches fresh rosemary, rinsed
5 pounds cherrystone clams, cleaned
  (see box, this page)
8 ears corn, cleaned (see Note)
2 pounds steamer clams, cleaned (see box, this page)
2 pounds mussels, cleaned (see page 468)
4 cups Fish Broth (page 254) or bottled clam juice
4 cups water
4 to 6 lemons, halved, for serving
Unsalted butter, melted, for serving (optional)

1. Precook the lobsters: Bring a large kettle of salted water to a boil. Add the lobsters, head first, and boil them for 2 minutes. Remove them from the water, place them on a flat surface, and press down on the tails to flatten them.

2. Place the potatoes and onions in a large deep (turkey) roasting pan, about 16 x 12 x 5 inches, with a cover. Scatter one third of the herbs over the vegetables. Arrange the cherrystone clams evenly over the vegetables, and then cover with the corn. Spread the steamers and mussels over and around the corn. Scatter the remaining herbs evenly over the top.

3. Add the broth and water to the roasting pan, cover, and bring to a boil. Reduce the heat to medium-high and steam, covered, for 10 minutes.

4. Lay the precooked lobsters evenly and flat over the top and cover with the reserved corn husks, if you have any. Cover, and cook over medium heat for 15 minutes.

5. Cut the lobsters in half and return them to the pan. Place the roasting pan on the table, and dig in (discard any unopened clams or mussels)! Serve in large deep bowls with lemons, melted butter, if using, and some of the remaining broth in the roaster for dipping the clams to clean them.

Serves 8

NOTE: Remove 1 or 2 of the outermost husks from the corn and set them aside. Carefully peel back the remaining husks without removing them. Remove and discard the silks. Press the husks back into place.

FREDDIE GAUTREAU'S BEER STEAMERS

★ ★ ★

Cabbage Island in Maine is located about 30 minutes by ferry from Boothbay Harbor, and it was there that I attended a mid-July lobster bake, which is similar to a clambake. My friends and I had made reservations for the bake right by the harbor, and the price of the ticket included the appetite-invigorating and breathtakingly scenic ferry trip. Once on the island and while attending to the business at hand—devouring freshly caught and cooked lobster—I managed to get into conversation with another diner at my table, Barbara Miller. Somehow the subject turned to clams, and Barbara told me about her father's way of steaming them. Once home, I worked up the recipe, and have enjoyed steamers à la Freddie Gautreau ever since. Here they are.

Beer: Your favorite American lager

4 pounds steamer clams, cleaned (see To Clean Clams, page 471)
1 large onion, halved lengthwise and slivered
½ teaspoon cracked black peppercorns
3 bottles pale lager beer
½ cup (1 stick) unsalted butter, melted, for serving (optional)

1. Place the clams in a large pot and add the onions, peppercorns, and beer. Bring to a boil over high heat, then reduce the heat slightly, cover, and cook, shaking the pot once or twice, until the clams open, 5 to 7 minutes.

2. Serve up immediately in shallow bowls, discarding any clams that haven't opened. Pour the cooking broth through a fine strainer into small bowls and place one at each setting, along with a little ramekin of melted butter, if desired. To eat the clams, first dip them into the broth to remove any sand that still might be clinging to them and then dip them into the butter. Afterwards, if you wish, you can drink the flavorful clam broth—just avoid drinking the last few drops, where any sand from the clams will have settled.

Serves 4

LOUISIANA FRIED OYSTERS

★ ★ ★

Fried oysters, crisp from a coating of crushed saltines, are a favorite of mine. I serve them up hot and fresh, sometimes with just plenty of fresh lemon and Tabasco, sometimes as Po' Boys with Rémoulade Sauce on soft rolls, sometimes both ways. You can easily adjust the quantities in this recipe, depending on the number of people you'll be feeding. Just be sure to use fresh vegetable oil for frying, so that the flavor of the oysters is not sullied.

Wine: Monterey County (CA) Pinot Blanc
Beer: California pale ale

12 oysters, shucked, in their liquor
1 large egg
2 tablespoons milk
Dash of Tabasco sauce
½ cup all-purpose flour
Paprika, to taste
Salt and freshly ground black pepper,
    to taste
1 cup finely crushed saltine crackers
    (about 12 crackers)
Vegetable oil, for frying

FOR SERVING
Lemon halves
Soft white or French rolls (optional)
Rémoulade Sauce (page 89; optional)
Sliced ripe yellow tomatoes (optional)
Mesclun (mixed baby salad greens;
    optional)

1. Drain the oysters and set them aside.
2. In a small bowl, beat the egg with the milk and Tabasco sauce. Set aside.

3. Place the flour in another bowl and season with the paprika, salt, and pepper. Place the crushed saltines in another bowl.

4. Pour oil to the depth of 1½ inches in a medium-size pot, and heat to 350°F.

5. Dredge the oysters, one at a time, in the seasoned flour, shaking off any excess. Dip them into the egg mixture and then dredge them in the cracker crumbs. Let them rest on waxed paper until you are ready to begin frying. Do not crowd them on the paper.

6. Fry the oysters, 2 or 3 at a time, until they are just golden brown, 2 minutes. Using a slotted spoon, transfer them to paper towels, to drain. Serve immediately, as is, with the lemons for squeezing, or, if desired, on rolls garnished with Rémoulade Sauce, ripe yellow tomatoes, and mesclun.

Serves 3 to 4

SHELLFISH AND SHELLS MARINARA

★ ★ ★

Littleneck clams and shrimp easily cook up into a simply prepared, robust Italian-inspired meal. For maximum flavor, I've infused the oil for the sauce with garlic and added the seafood just before dishing the sauce over the pasta shells. Please, no cheese with seafood sauces—or so tradition dictates!

Wine: Napa Valley (CA) Zinfandel
Beer: New York State amber lager

3 tablespoons extra virgin olive oil

2 large cloves garlic, bruised

2 cans (28 ounces each) Italian plum tomatoes, drained and coarsely chopped

¼ cup dry red wine

¼ cup coarsely chopped fresh flat-leaf parsley

¼ cup torn fresh basil leaves

1 teaspoon dried oregano

Salt and freshly ground black pepper, to taste

Pinch of sugar

¾ pound medium shell pasta

20 littleneck clams, cleaned (see To Clean Clams, page 471)

½ pound large shrimp, peeled and deveined

1. Heat the oil in a large, heavy, nonreactive pot over medium-low heat. Add the garlic and cook until it colors slightly (do not let it burn), 3 to 4 minutes. Remove the pot from the heat and gently stir in the tomatoes.

2. Return the pot to medium-low heat. Add the wine, parsley, basil, oregano, salt, pepper, and sugar. Cook slowly, uncovered, stirring occasionally, for 30 minutes.

3. Shortly before serving, bring a large pot of salted water to a boil. Add the pasta and cook, until just tender, 10 to 12 minutes.

4. While the pasta is cooking, add the clams to the sauce, cover, and cook, shaking the pot once or twice, until they just begin to open, 8 minutes. Add the shrimp and cook until they turn pink, 5 minutes more. Remove and discard the garlic.

5. Divide the pasta among four shallow bowls. Spoon the hot sauce over the top, distributing the clams and shrimp evenly (discard any clams that have not opened). Serve immediately.

Serves 4

RIAD'S LINGUINE WITH FRESH SEAFOOD

★ ★ ★

Riad Aamar, former chef-owner of Doc's Restaurant in New Preston, Connecticut, is known for, among other things, his terrific pastas. His combination of fresh seafood in this simple preparation is one of my favorites, and I prepare it at home, using my Fresh Herbed Tomato Sauce as its base. Crusty warmed peasant bread, briny olives, and a bitter green salad are the best accompaniments.

Wine: California Rhône-style blend

3 tablespoons extra virgin olive oil

2 cloves garlic, sliced

12 jumbo shrimp, peeled and deveined

12 sea scallops

12 mussels, cleaned and debearded (see To Clean Mussels, page 468)

12 littleneck clams, cleaned (see To Clean Clams, page 471)

½ cup dry white wine

1 teaspoon crushed red pepper flakes

3 cups Fresh Herbed Tomato Sauce (page 307)

2 tablespoons chopped fresh flat-leaf parsley

Salt and freshly ground black pepper, to taste

¾ pound linguine

1. Heat the olive oil in a large, heavy nonreactive pot over medium-low heat. Add the garlic and cook, stirring occasionally, until lightly browned, about 5 minutes.

2. Add the shrimp and cook for 1 minute, stirring. Add the scallops and cook for 2 minutes more.

3. Add the mussels, clams, wine, red pepper flakes, tomato sauce, and 1 tablespoon of the parsley. Raise the heat to medium-high and bring the sauce to a boil. Reduce the heat, cover the pot, and cook until all the shellfish have opened (discard any that haven't), 5 minutes. Season with salt and pepper.

4. Meanwhile, bring a large pot of salted water to a boil. Cook the linguine until just tender, 10 to 11 minutes. Drain.

5. Divide the linguine among four shallow pasta bowls, and ladle the sauce on top, distributing the seafood evenly. Sprinkle the remaining 1 tablespoon chopped parsley over the seafood, and serve immediately.

Serves 4

SEARED SCALLOPS IN CHIPOTLE CREAM

★ ★ ★

The mingling of chipotle cream with delicate scallops results in an exciting East-meets-Southwest flavor. Chipotles in adobo, available in cans or jars in many specialty food stores, are smoked dried jalapeños that have been slowly stewed in a spicy liquid. I purée the chipotles before adding them to the rich, mildly piquant sauce.

Wine: Napa Valley (CA) Pinot Noir
Beer: New York State India pale ale

2 tablespoons olive oil
3 cloves garlic, bruised
1½ pounds sea scallops
Freshly ground black pepper, to taste
1 cup defatted chicken broth, preferably
*   homemade (page 253)*
1 tablespoon puréed chipotles in adobo
*   (see headnote)*
½ cup heavy (or whipping) cream
Salt, to taste
½ cup thinly slivered fresh
*   basil leaves*

1. Heat the oil in a nonstick skillet over low heat. Add the garlic and cook, stirring occasionally, until just golden, about 5 minutes. Remove and discard the garlic. Remove and reserve 1 tablespoon of the oil.

2. Raise the heat to medium-high and sear the scallops in small batches until just cooked through, 3 minutes on each side, adding the reserved oil if necessary. Season them with black pepper, transfer to a plate, and keep warm in a very low oven (250°F).

3. Add the chicken broth to the skillet and bring it to a boil. Boil for 2 minutes, stirring up any brown bits on the bottom of the pan. Reduce the heat to medium, add the chipotle sauce, and cook for 2 minutes, stirring occasionally. Add the cream and simmer until it has reduced slightly and thickened, 2 to 3 minutes. The sauce should coat the back of a spoon, and a finger should leave a trail when drawn through it. Season with salt.

4. Spoon a generous tablespoon of the sauce in the center of each dinner plate. Arrange 6 scallops on the sauce, scatter the slivered basil over the scallops, and serve immediately.

Serves 6

LOW COUNTRY SHRIMP AND SAUSAGE GRAVY

★ ★ ★

After I returned home from a glorious week in Charleston, South Carolina I was still hankering for another plateful of shrimp gravy over creamy grits. Some experimenting in the kitchen resulted in this savory and satisfying dish, perfect for a weekend brunch or as a light supper. I use rock shrimp, if I can get them, but regular large shrimp, cut crosswise into thirds, can be easily substituted. (For a bit more on rock shrimp, see page 167 for Hot Time Party Shrimp.)

Wine: Monterey County (CA) Riesling
Beer: Louisiana lager

½ *pound shrimp, preferably rock shrimp,*
   peeled and deveined (see step 1)
1 tablespoon olive oil
2 Cajun sausages, such as andouille
   (¼ pound each), cut into ½-inch-thick slices
½ *pound baked ham, cut into ¼-inch-thick*
   slices and coarsely shredded
1 tablespoon unsalted butter
1 clove garlic, minced
Pinch of Old Bay Seasoning
3 ripe tomatoes, seeded and cut into ½-inch dice
3 scallions (3 inches green left on), thinly sliced
   on the diagonal
1 tablespoon water
1 tablespoon chopped fresh flat-leaf parsley
Creamy Grits (page 45), for serving

1. Rock shrimp have a hard shell and are best bought already peeled. If you can't buy yours out of the shell, peel them carefully by cutting along the outer curve of the tail with kitchen scissors. Pull the shell away to release the meat. Devein the shrimp, then rinse them and pat dry with paper towels. If using regular shrimp, buy large ones, and cut them into thirds once they're peeled and deveined.

2. Heat the oil in a large nonstick skillet over medium-high heat. Add the sausages and brown lightly, turning for about 5 minutes. Add the ham and cook for 3 minutes more.

3. Add the butter and the shrimp, and cook, shaking the pan, until the shrimp are cooked through, 3 to 5 minutes.

4. Add the garlic and Old Bay Seasoning, and cook stirring, for 1 minute more.

5. Add the tomatoes, scallions, and water and cook, shaking the pan, to wilt the vegetables, 1 to 3 minutes. Sprinkle with parsley and serve over Creamy Grits.
Serves 4

BLUSHING SPRING SHRIMP AND PEAS

★ ★ ★

When spring finally arrives and lighter flavors are called for, seasonal fresh peas should be cooked up as often as possible. I think there's no more delightful way to enjoy them than tossed with shrimp, ripe tomatoes, and prosciutto. If you're lucky enough to find fresh pea tendrils (sold separately from the peas themselves) in your farmers' market, snap them up and add them to the sauce just before you serve it over a bed of orzo.

Wine: Anderson Valley (CA) Gewürztraminer
Beer: New York State extra-special bitter

ORZO

*5 cups defatted chicken broth, preferably homemade
    (page 253)*
2 cups orzo pasta
¼ cup slivered fresh basil leaves
1 tablespoon finely grated lemon zest
1 tablespoon extra virgin olive oil
1 tablespoon fresh lemon juice

SHRIMP

6 ripe plum tomatoes, peeled
¼ cup olive oil
1 tablespoon minced garlic
1 teaspoon tomato paste
*¼ pound prosciutto, sliced ⅛ inch thick,
    slivered*
*½ cup fresh or frozen (thawed) peas,
    blanched for 3 to 5 minutes
    if fresh*
*1 pound medium shrimp, peeled and
    deveined*
*Salt and freshly ground black pepper,
    to taste*
½ cup torn fresh basil leaves

1. Prepare the orzo: Bring the broth to a boil in a medium saucepan. Add the orzo, reduce the heat, and simmer, uncovered, until just tender, 7 to 9 minutes. Drain, and return the orzo to the pan. Add the remaining ingredients and stir well to combine. Cover to keep warm.

2. Prepare the shrimp: Cut the tomatoes in half lengthwise, and remove and discard the seeds and core. Set aside.

3. Heat the oil in a large nonstick skillet over medium-low heat. Add the garlic and cook, shaking the pan, until wilted, 5 minutes. Stir in the tomatoes, tomato paste, prosciutto, and peas. Cook, shaking the pan, until the tomatoes are softened, 5 minutes.

4. Raise the heat to medium-high and add the shrimp. Season with salt and pepper. Stir in the basil and cook, shaking the pan and turning the shrimp, until the shrimp are cooked through, 3 to 4 minutes.

5. Serve the shrimp over the orzo in shallow bowls.
    Serves 4

GRILLED SCAMPI
ON A STICK

★ ★ ★

Grilled shrimp make for some of my favorite cookout food. I like to bathe them first in a good garlicky marinade that has red pepper flakes added for spice. Take care when grilling not to overcook the shrimp, as they will toughen. Leave the little tail shell on to act as a handle.

Wine: Idaho dry Riesling
Beer: Oregon red ale

2 pounds large shrimp
2 tablespoons extra virgin olive oil
2 tablespoons dry white wine
1½ tablespoons finely minced garlic
¼ teaspoon paprika
Pinch of crushed red pepper flakes
*Salt and freshly ground black pepper,
    to taste*
*2 tablespoons coarsely chopped fresh
    flat-leaf parsley*
6 lemon halves, for serving

1. Peel and devein the shrimp, leaving the tail shells on.

2. In a large bowl, combine the oil, wine, garlic, paprika, red pepper flakes, salt, pepper, and 1 tablespoon of the parsley. Add the shrimp and toss well. Refrigerate, covered, for 1 hour.

3. Meanwhile, prepare a barbecue grill with hot coals.

4. Thread 4 to 6 shrimp, crosswise, on each of 4 to 6 metal skewers. Grill the shrimp, 3 inches from the heat source, brushing them with any remaining marinade, until cooked through, 3 to 4 minutes per side. (Do not overcook them.)

5. Arrange the skewers on a large platter, sprinkle with the remaining 1 tablespoon parsley. Serve with the lemon halves for squeezing.

Serves 4 to 6

FROGMORE STEW FOR A CROWD

★ ★ ★

Ben Moise, a game warden in South Carolina, first introduced me to Frogmore Stew, a tasty example of low country cuisine that is named after a former town center of St. Helena Island. It is not a stew in the usual soup-like sense, instead it is a melange of smoked sausage, shrimp, and corn on the cob, cooked in seasoned water and, for full effect, best served on newspaper-covered picnic tables in the height of corn season. There's cocktail sauce for shrimp dipping (you could use my Tartar Sauce or Rémoulade Sauce) and butter for the corn. Guests help themselves, and the only utensils required are fingers. If you serve an accompani-

OLD BAY SEASONING

—❦—

In 1939, when Gustav Brunn arrived in the United States from his native Germany, he had few possessions, one of which was a small spice grinder. In Germany, Gustav made his living grinding spices for pickling, so when he arrived in Baltimore, he set up business as the Baltimore Spice Company, and sold spices to sausage and pickle makers. Then cooks at local restaurants asked him to grind the spices they used in their popular Maryland dish, steamed crabs. Wisely, he noted what they wanted and eventually developed his own eleven-spice combination—celery seeds, mustard seeds, pepper, bay leaves,

paprika, allspice, ginger, mace, cloves, cardamom, and cinnamon—and called it India Girl Shrimp and Crab Seasoning, since many of the spices in the mixture came from India. Later the name changed to Old Bay Seasoning, after the steamship, *Old Bay*, which ran from Baltimore to Norfolk, Virginia.

The same recipe, developed over fifty years ago, is still used today in Old Bay Seasoning, now owned by McCormick & Company. From coastal towns to landlocked cities, steamed blue crabs to fish boils, people who like to spice up their seafood reach for the familiar blue and yellow cans of Old Bay.

ment like Zesty Picnic Slaw as well, then forks are probably a good idea. This recipe serves eight, but you can easily adjust it by figuring per person: ½ pound shrimp, ¼ pound sausage, and 1½ ears corn. Ben has been known to add crawdads (crawfish), or cleaned blue crabs when the corn goes in, for color and taste variety. A large pot with a perforated basket liner makes cooking and draining a snap. This is Ben's favorite recipe because, he says, it is hard not to have a good time when you're eating with your fingers, and I agree.

Beer: Your favorite American lager

4 tablespoons Old Bay Seasoning
2 pounds smoked sausage, cut into 2-inch pieces
12 ears freshly shucked corn, broken into 3- to
    4-inch pieces
4 pounds medium shrimp

Fill a large stockpot, ideally fitted with a perforated basket insert, two-thirds full of water. Add 3 tablespoons of the Old Bay Seasoning to the water and bring to a vigorous boil. Insert the perforated basket, if using, and add the sausage. Return the water to a boil and cook the sausage, uncovered, for 5 minutes. Add the corn and cook 2 minutes. Add the shrimp and cook 3 minutes (do not let the water return to a boil before timing the corn and shrimp; otherwise they will overcook). Drain by lifting out the basket, if using, or carefully pour the contents into a large colander. Dust the stew with the remaining tablespoon of Old Bay Seasoning. Serve by dumping out the contents on a newspaper-lined picnic table and let your guests go wild.
Serves 8

BEAUFORT SHRIMP BURGERS

★ ★ ★

I discovered these delicious shrimp burgers on a visit to Beaufort, South Carolina, where there is no shortage of shrimp or ideas on how to use them. It's best not to complicate matters here—Tartar Sauce and fresh lettuce is all that you need to enhance the delicate seasonings.

Wine: New York State dry Riesling
Beer: Wisconsin bock

1 pound medium shrimp, peeled and deveined
⅓ cup minced onion
¼ cup mayonnaise
1 large egg, lightly beaten
2 teaspoons chopped fresh tarragon leaves, or
    ¾ teaspoon dried
¼ teaspoon paprika
Salt and freshly ground black pepper,
    to taste
1 tablespoon vegetable oil, plus more
    if needed
1 tablespoon unsalted butter, plus more
    if needed
½ cup Tartar Sauce (page 440)
6 best-quality hamburger rolls,
    lightly toasted
1 head Bibb lettuce, leaves separated, rinsed,
    and patted dry

1. Place the shrimp in a food processor and pulse until they are just ground up. Do not overprocess. Transfer the shrimp to a bowl.

2. Add the onion, mayonnaise, egg, tarragon, paprika, salt, and pepper to the shrimp, and combine well.

3. Form the mixture into 6 patties, each 3 inches in diameter.

4. Heat the oil and butter in a nonstick skillet over medium heat. Fry the shrimp patties, in batches, until golden brown, 4 minutes per side. Reduce the heat, and add more oil and butter, if necessary.

5. Spread Tartar Sauce over both sides of each hamburger roll. Place a shrimp burger on the bottom of each roll, top with a lettuce leaf, and cover with the other half of the roll. Serve immediately.

Serves 6

SHRIMP AND LOBSTER ETOUFFEE

★ ★ ★

Etouffée literally means "smothered," and it refers to a method used for many richly sauced Cajun classics. This one is traditionally made with crawfish tails, their perfumed liquor, and their prized fat. While I have enjoyed many delicate pale-pink-hued étouffées, there are none that I have savored more than Paul Prudhomme's, colored a rich, deep red-brown by the roux on which it is based.

I try to eat at Paul Prudhomme's renowned restaurant, K-Paul's Louisiana Kitchen, whenever I am in New Orleans. Of course, when you eat there, you're eating the genuine article, the real Louisiana crawfish, or "mudbug." These local shellfish are in season only from December to June, when they're not burrowing under the soil of the wetlands. However, as with many shellfish, crawfish are now being farmed, and are more easy to find. If crawfish are unavailable, shrimp and lobster make perfectly delicious substitutes.

For my étouffée, I decided to follow the example set by Paul Prudhomme and begin with a rich roux. I wasn't fearless enough to get my oil heated up to 500°F, as Paul suggests, so I cooked the flour for a longer time than he requires, in order to achieve that red-brown color (see page 414 for The Role of the Roux for more on the subject). The result was a delicious dish without the danger. Serve over bowls of hot, fluffy rice.

Wine: Mendocino (CA) Gewürztraminer
Beer: Louisiana lager

6 tablespoons vegetable oil
½ cup plus 2 tablespoons all-purpose flour
1 cup finely chopped onion
½ cup finely chopped celery
½ cup finely chopped green bell pepper
¼ cup thinly sliced scallions
1½ tablespoons finely minced garlic
1½ cups Fish Broth (page 254) or bottled
    clam juice, heated
4 ripe plum tomatoes, peeled and cut into
    ¼-inch dice
2 teaspoons Worcestershire sauce
½ teaspoon Tabasco sauce
1 teaspoon dried thyme
¾ teaspoon dried oregano
½ teaspoon salt
¼ teaspoon freshly ground black pepper
2 pounds medium shrimp, peeled and
    deveined
½ pound cooked lobster meat, cut into
    1-inch pieces, or lump crabmeat,
    picked over to remove any cartilage
2 tablespoons chopped fresh flat-leaf parsley
6 to 8 cups hot cooked white rice,
    for serving

1. Make the roux: Heat the oil in a cast-iron Dutch oven over medium heat. When the oil is very hot, slowly whisk in the flour. Continue to whisk constantly until the roux turns a rich red-brown color, about 30 minutes.

2. Add the onions, celery, bell peppers, scallions, and garlic, and cook, stirring, until the vegetables have softened, 5 minutes.

3. Stirring constantly, pour in the hot fish broth in a slow thin stream. Continue stirring until smooth. Then raise the heat and bring the mixture to a boil, still stirring constantly. Reduce the heat to a simmer and cook until thickened, 5 to 10 minutes.

4. Add the tomatoes, Worcestershire, Tabasco, thyme, oregano, salt, and pepper. Cover partially, and simmer to blend the flavors, 30 minutes.

5. Just before serving, stir in the shrimp and lobster and cook through, 2 to 3 minutes. Stir in the chopped parsley, and serve immediately over hot, fluffy rice.

Serves 6 to 8

BROILED STUFFED LOBSTER

★ ★ ★

When I was growing up in East Norwalk, Connecticut, going to The Pier restaurant, which was situated along the Saugatuck River, was a great treat, usually reserved for Mother's Day or Father's Day. I always ordered a broiled stuffed lobster, and my fond memories of that dish led to this re-creation. Although the proportions are for two, it is an easy recipe to double.

Wine: Willamette Valley (OR) Pinot Noir
Beer: San Francisco Anchor Steam Beer

CAJUN VS. CREOLE: THE SHORT COURSE

— ❦ —

What's the difference betwen Cajun and Creole cuisine? Louisianans know; many could even discourse on this question. But I'll spare you the long answer. The short one is this: Both styles have French roots, and both use the so-called "holy trinity" of chopped bell peppers, onions, and celery as their flavor base. Woodsy, potent filé powder (ground sassafras leaves) is key to both, too; it's prominent in the thickening for gumbos and stews.

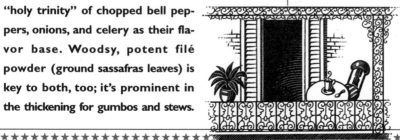

But Creole cooking is New Orleans city cooking, more sophisticated and worldly than its Cajun country cousin (the Creoles' ancestors were African and Spanish, too). Creole cooking uses lots of butter and cream in exquisite sauces. The Cajuns, who are of French Acadian descent, have a spicier, more robust cuisine. They use a darker, stronger roux, and plenty of game in hearty dishes that are less fussy, but no less delicious.

HOW TO BOIL AND EAT LOBSTERS

—ಲ—

Before you boil lobsters, you have to buy lobsters. This I suggest you do on the day you are serving them. At the market, look for ones that are energetic, at least in lobster terms. Those are the ones that move around, even when the tank in which they are held seems crammed. When removed from the tank, they should wiggle their antennas and move their claws. I like to buy lobsters in the 1¼- to 1½-pound range. I find that there's plenty of meat in ones that size, and I figure on 1 lobster per diner. Once home, place the lobsters on an ice pack in a pan on the bottom shelf of your refrigerator until cooking time.

When ready to cook the lobsters, bring a large kettle of salted water to a rolling boil. Hold the lobsters by the tail and plunge them, head first, into the boiling water to instantly kill them. Once the water returns to a boil, cook the lobsters until they are bright red and cooked through. A 1¼-pound lobster will take 6 to 8 minutes. Remove the lobsters from the water and let them rest for 4 to 5 minutes to settle. Serve hot with clarified butter and lemon halves, or chilled or at room temperature with lemons or your favorite mayonnaise dressing.

Eating a Lobster

To eat a lobster, you need nothing more than a nutcracker, a lobster pick, and plenty of napkins.

1. To begin, using a gentle twist, break off the tail where it is connected to the fore part of the body. Using your thumb and index finger, push and pull the meat out of the tail in one piece. If you find a dark vein running down the center, remove and discard it.

2. Break off the large claws and arms at the top of the joint. Crack the claws with a nutcracker in one or two places, depending on the size and age of the lobster. A small, young lobster will have a very soft shell. Pull out all the moist claw meat with a pick.

3. There isn't much meat per se in the lobster body (remove what there is with your pick), but if you are an aficionado, you know to avoid the sand sac near the lobster's head, and to enjoy the red coral (roe), found only in female lobsters, and the green tomalley (the liver). If you're a beginning lobster lover, don't be afraid to try them.

4. Last but not least, pull off the small legs from the inner section of the body and suck out the scant, yet sweet, moist meat. This activity can take some time when you really get into it. But if you've chosen the perfect lobster-loving friends and the day is warm and summery, why worry about time?

2 lobsters (1½ to 2 pounds each)
½ cup dried bread crumbs
1 large ripe plum tomato, seeded and cut into
  ¼-inch dice
2 tablespoons chopped fresh flat-leaf parsley
1 teaspoon finely grated lemon zest
½ to 1 teaspoon finely minced garlic
Salt and freshly ground black pepper, to taste
½ cup (1 stick) unsalted butter, melted
2 lemon halves, for serving

1. Have your fishmonger kill and split the lobster, or prepare the lobsters at home, as follows: Grasp each one by the tail on a flat surface and jab the tip of a large sharp knife between the eyes. This will kill the lobsters instantly. (Alternately, insert a sharp knife between the head and body to sever the spinal cord.)

2. Place the lobsters on a flat surface, belly up, and split them from head to tail, separating the thin membrane that covers the tail meat. Do not cut through the back outer shell. Remove and discard the intestine that runs down the length of the tail, and the sac from the head. Hold open the cavity and remove the tomalley (greenish liver) and coral (reddish roe), if any, and place them in a bowl. Bend the tail back until you hear it crack so that it lies flat.

3. Add the bread crumbs, tomatoes, parsley, lemon zest, garlic, salt, and pepper to the tomalley and coral, and stir well. Bind together with 2 tablespoons of the melted butter. Set the stuffing aside.

4. Preheat the broiler.

5. Arrange the lobsters belly side up on a baking sheet, and place the sheet 5 to 6 inches from the heat source. Broil, basting often with melted butter, until cooked through, 12 to 15 minutes (depending on size). The meat should be opaque and the shells red.

6. Add the stuffing to the body cavities, drizzle with 1 teaspoon of the melted butter, and broil until the stuffing is golden, 2 minutes. (If the stuffing begins to burn, cover it with aluminum foil.)

7. Serve immediately, with the lemon halves and with any remaining melted butter (heated, if desired).

Serves 2

CHESAPEAKE LOBSTER CRAB CAKES

★ ★ ★

There are hundreds of versions of the classic Maryland crab cake. Chefs across the country have taken the liberty of making the basic recipe their own by adding favorite herbs and spices. As far as I'm concerned, the Worcestershire, Tabasco, and onion are givens, along with, of course, the luscious white meat from the famous blue crab. Here I've made the crab cake *my* own by adding lobster, orange zest, and some complementary spices. These cakes are loosely packed, light, and delicate, and require some careful handling.

Wine: Santa Barbara County (CA) Marsanne
Beer: Maryland pale ale

12 slices best-quality white bread, crusts removed
4 tablespoons olive oil, plus more if needed
1 tablespoon Old Bay Seasoning
½ pound lump crabmeat, picked over to
    remove any cartilage
½ pound shredded cooked lobster meat
1 tablespoon drained tiny capers
½ cup finely diced onion
½ cup diced (¼ inch) celery
½ cup diced (¼ inch) red bell pepper
1 cup mayonnaise
1 tablespoon chopped fresh flat-leaf parsley
2 teaspoons finely grated orange zest
1 teaspoon Worcestershire sauce
½ teaspoon dry mustard
⅛ teaspoon ground mace
Dash of Tabasco sauce, or to taste
1 large egg, lightly beaten
1 tablespoon unsalted butter, plus more if needed
Joe's Mustard Sauce (recipe follows) or
    Tartar Sauce (page 440)

1. Preheat the oven to 350°F.

2. Cut the bread into cubes, and toss them in a bowl with 2 tablespoons of the oil and the Old Bay Seasoning until coated. Spread the bread cubes in a single layer on a baking sheet, and bake until toasted, 10 to 12 minutes. Let rest at room temperature for 30 minutes, and then crush into medium-fine crumbs. Set aside.

3. In a large bowl, combine the crab, lobster, capers, onion, celery, bell pepper, mayonnaise, parsley, orange zest, Worcestershire, mustard, mace, Tabasco, and egg with ¼ cup of the bread crumbs. Toss the mixture lightly but thoroughly.

4. Place the remaining bread crumbs in a shallow dish. Form the crab mixture into twelve 2-inch-diameter patties. Carefully dredge the patties in the crumbs. Place in a single layer on a platter, cover with plastic wrap, and refrigerate for at least 30 minutes to 1 hour to chill well.

5. Heat 1 tablespoon butter and the remaining 2 tablespoons oil in a nonstick skillet over medium heat. Cook the cakes, in batches, until golden brown, about 3 minutes per side, adding more butter and oil as necessary. Drain the cakes well on paper towels, and serve immediately, topped with a spoonful of Joe's Mustard Sauce or Tartar Sauce.

Serves 4 to 6

Joe's Mustard Sauce

—★—

Joe's Stone Crab Restaurant in Miami is one of my all-time favorite eateries. In season (October through May), the fresh stone crab claws they serve there are sublime. Accompanying the white-meat claws is Joe's famous mustard dipping sauce, which I've found is great with other seafood dishes, such as the preceding Chesapeake Lobster Crab Cakes, The Great U.S.A. Salmon Cake, and Savannah Cocktail Crab Bites. If you make a stop at at Joe's, be sure to have the sliced tomatoes and onions to start, and Key lime pie for dessert.

3½ teaspoons Coleman's dry English mustard
1 cup mayonnaise
2 tablespoons light cream
2 teaspoons Worcestershire sauce
1 teaspoon A.1. steak sauce
⅛ teaspoon salt

Place the mustard and mayonaise in a small bowl and whisk together to blend. Add the remaining ingredients, and continue to whisk until the mixture is creamy. Refrigerate, covered, until ready to use. Serve at room temperature.

Makes about 1⅓ cups

DO AS BLUE CRAB LOVERS DO—MEET AND EAT!

—❧—

Blue crabs are found in abundance along the eastern shore of Maryland, preferring waters that move from ocean saltiness to fresh. Thus the Chesapeake Bay provides ideal conditions. Life begins when female, or "sponge," crabs deposit their eggs between May and October. The baby crabs, which at birth are about $\frac{1}{25}$ inch long, look like a swimming question mark with seven pairs of legs and a long tail. This "zoea" molts, or sheds its shell, several times, by which time it begins to resemble an adult and is then called "megalops."

In the process of reaching full maturity as a hard-shell blue crab, the crab must shed its shell a number of times, and it's during one of these "molts"—ideally when the crab is 4 to 6 months old and 3½ to 4 inches across—that it becomes the completely edible (shell and all) soft-shell crab, velvety yet slightly chewy in texture when grilled or sautéed. These are best harvested from mid-May to mid-June. At 12 to 14 months they reach full majestic maturity as hard-shell crabs.

How to Clean Soft-Shell Crabs

Place the crab, on its stomach, on a flat surface. Using a pair of kitchen shears, cut off the face, just behind the eyes. Lift up the edges of the shell on either side and remove the spongy gills and innards, then turn the crab over and cut off the tail flap, or "apron." Rinse the crab and pat dry with paper towels. They are now ready to sauté or grill (see page 486)—the best ways to enjoy them.

How to Eat Hard-Shell Crabs

Whole hard-shell blue crabs are usually sprinkled liberally with a seafood seasoning and steamed in a large cauldron over boiling water that may be mixed with beer or vinegar. Covered, they take about 25 minutes to cook, taking on a bright red color when ready. It's traditional to serve the crabs in a big pile directly on a table that is well covered with newspaper or brown paper. Coleslaw and bread or muffins should accompany the crabs.

Although some effort is required to open the crab, the prize of sweet succulent meat is well worth it. You'll need a wooden mallet or a meat pounder to get to the claw meat.

1. With your thumb or a small knifepoint, pry off the apron flap on the underside of the crab and discard it.

2. Next, again with your thumb or a small knifepoint, lift off the top shell and discard it. Break off the large toothed claws on both sides and save them for eating.

3. Scrape off and discard the feathery gills on both sides.

4. Hold the crab at each side and break it apart at the center. Discard the little side legs and begin the feast: Pick out the body meat with a small knifepoint, a seafood fork, or your fingers. Use a mallet to gently crack the large claws and pick out the meat from them.

CAJUN SOFT-SHELL CRABS ON BUNS

★ ★ ★

These spicy sandwiches taste best when served with a heap of creamy coleslaw and a salad of sliced ripe tomatoes and oranges drizzled with a little oil and a splash of fresh lime juice. When preparing the crabs, use the seasonings judiciously, keeping an eye on the cayenne! The seasoned flour for dredging the crabs echoes the flavor of the spicy mayonnaise slathered on the buns.

Wine: Napa Valley (CA) Sauvignon Blanc
Beer: Texas white beer

4 soft-shell crabs, cleaned (see box, page 485)
1 cup milk
¾ cup all-purpose flour
½ teaspoon paprika
¼ teaspoon garlic powder
⅛ teaspoon cayenne pepper, or more to taste
¼ cup (½ stick) unsalted butter
4 toasted round whole-wheat or seven-grain sandwich buns or rolls
4 tablespoons Cajun Mayonnaise (recipe follows) or more to taste
2 scallions (3 inches green left on), thinly sliced

1. Soak the prepared crabs in the milk for 30 minutes. Meanwhile, combine the flour, paprika, garlic powder, and cayenne in a bag and shake well.

2. Remove the crabs from the milk and shake them, one at a time, in the bag of seasoned flour. After removing from the bag, shake off any excess flour.

3. Melt the butter in a large skillet over medium-high heat. Sauté the crabs, 2 at a time, until crispy and browned, 4 to 5 minutes per side. Transfer them to paper towels to drain.

4. Spread each toasted bun with 1 tablespoon of the mayonnaise (or more if desired). Sprinkle the scallions on the bottom half and top with the crab. Cover with the top half of the roll and serve immediately.

Serves 4

Cajun Mayonnaise

★

If you have any of this mayonnaise left over after using it for the soft-shell crab recipe, mix it with a little plain mayo and canned salmon for a tasty salad and serve with sliced ripe tomatoes.

¼ cup mayonnaise
¼ cup plain nonfat yogurt
¼ teaspoon dried oregano
⅛ teaspoon garlic salt
⅛ teaspoon ground cumin
Pinch of cayenne pepper, or more to taste
Pinch of freshly ground black pepper

Combine all the ingredients in a small bowl, stirring well. Cover and refrigerate for at least 24 hours for the flavors to blend before serving.

Makes about ½ cup

GRILLED SOFT-SHELL CRABS WITH ROASTED TOMATO SAUCE

★ ★ ★

Jonathan Waxman, one of America's great chefs, and in my opinion the best of all on the grill, was generous enough to share his delicious recipe for grilled soft-shell crabs with me. If serving as an entrée, accompany the crabs with Fabulous Fennel Bread Salad or Eggplant-Zucchini Compote. If you choose to serve the crabs as an appetizer, one on the center of a large plate, topped with its spoonful of sauce, makes a wonderful presentation.

Wine: Santa Barbara County (CA) Nebbiolo
Beer: California pale ale

4 soft-shell crabs (about ¼ pound each)

CRAB MARINADE
½ cup olive oil
2 tablespoons dry white wine
1 tablespoon minced shallots
1 tablespoon chopped fresh rosemary leaves
1 tablespoon diced (¼ inch) red bell pepper
¼ teaspoon minced garlic
¼ teaspoon crushed red pepper flakes
Salt, to taste

ROASTED TOMATO SAUCE
2 tablespoons red wine vinegar
2 tablespoons extra virgin olive oil
¼ teaspoon finely minced garlic
3 ripe tomatoes, cored
Salt and freshly ground black pepper,
    to taste

1. Clean the crabs following the directions on page 485.

2. Prepare the crab marinade: Combine all the marinade ingredients in a medium-size bowl and mix well. Add the crabs and cover them well with the marinade. Refrigerate, covered, for 3 to 5 hours. Remove from the refrigerator 15 to 20 minutes before grilling. Brush off any excess marinade.

3. Prepare a barbecue with medium-hot coals.

4. Prepare the roasted tomato sauce: Combine the vinegar, olive oil, and garlic in a bowl and set aside. Grill the tomatoes, turning them until they are soft and slightly charred, 10 to 12 minutes. Add them to the bowl and mash with a fork, mixing all the ingredients together. Season with salt and pepper. Set aside.

5. Grill the crabs shell side down, 3 inches from the heat source, for 3 minutes without turning. Then turn them over carefully with a spatula and grill for 2 to 3 minutes more. The crabs will be hot to the touch when they are cooked through. Place 2 crabs in the center of each dinner plate, top each with a generous tablespoon of the tomato sauce, and serve immediately.

Serves 2 as an entrée; 4 as an appetizer

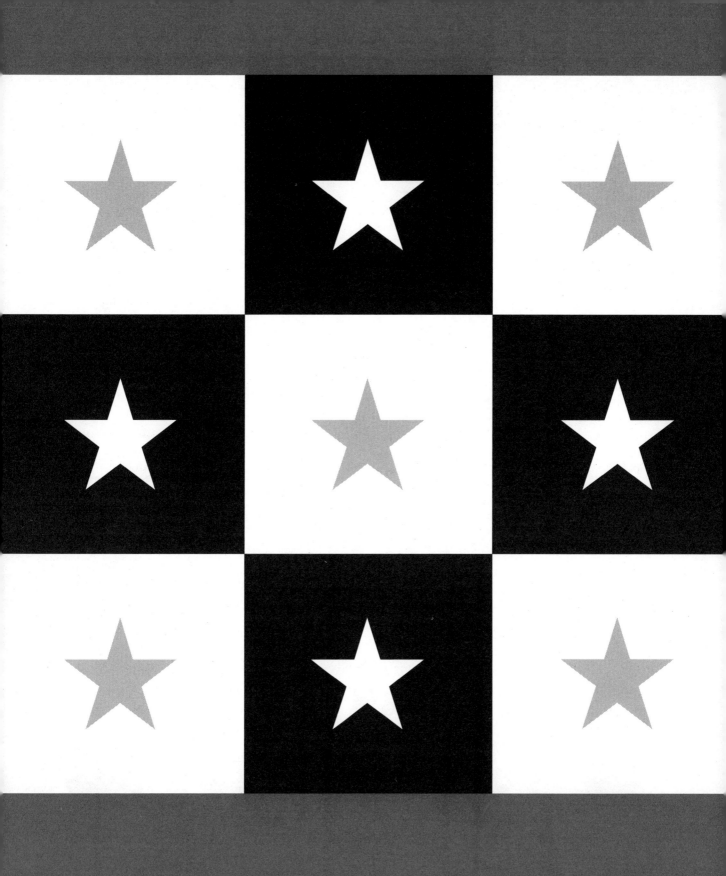

PART SIX

FOR

DESSERT

Fruit Desserts, Puddings & Pies

I like my pies, crisps, crumbles, and buckles heaping with fruit, oozing just a little out of their crusts or streusel toppings and stuffed to near bursting with the most splendid apples, cherries, pears, peaches, plums, or berries the season has to offer. I like them American—homey, generous, and earnest.

Pie in particular—fruit or other—is a cultural icon. It turns up in dozens of American folk songs, and it's been stolen off windowsills in dozens of cartoons. My explanation? We're simply crazy about it! Think about the surfeit at most family Thanksgivings—two, three, four kinds! And those people who say they'll have just a "little" of each are usually back for more.

Every dessert here, including rich, creamy puddings, will be familiar to you, for this is a collection of tried-and-true favorites.

HARVEST BAKED PEARS

★ ★ ★

Fruit as dessert is not only a summer thought. Autumn gives us a wealth of apples and pears to turn into compotes, pies, and crisps, as well as to eat out of hand. During the fall, I often poach pears in wine to serve as a light final course, but recently I've taken to baking them, much as I do apples, with excellent results. Add a slice of Maytag Blue cheese and it becomes a surprising savory accent to roast pork or turkey.

4 ripe Anjou pears
2 tablespoons fresh lemon juice
1/3 cup coarsely chopped walnuts
1/4 cup golden raisins
2 teaspoons (packed) light brown sugar
1 teaspoon finely grated lemon zest
1/8 teaspoon ground cinnamon
4 tablespoons pure maple syrup
1 tablespoon unsalted butter, cut into
*   quarters*
2/3 cup apple juice or sweet cider

1. Preheat the oven to 350°F.
2. Core the pears from the top with a swivel-blade vegetable peeler, leaving the last inch or so at the bottom intact. Cut a thin slice from the bottom of each pear so they stand upright. Peel 1 inch of the skin from around the top of the pear and drizzle the exposed flesh with the lemon juice to prevent discoloration. Place the pears standing upright in a baking dish to fit.
3. Combine the walnuts, raisins, brown sugar, lemon zest, cinnamon, and 2 tablespoons of the maple syrup in a small bowl. Stir to mix well, then stuff the pear cavities with the mixture

and dot each portion with a pat of the butter. Pour the apple juice and remaining maple syrup into the bottom of the dish.
4. Bake the pears until they are tender to your liking, about 1 hour, basting frequently with the juices. Serve warm, drizzled with any remaining juices.
Serves 4

BIG BEAUTIFUL BERRY SALAD

★ ★ ★

Fresh berries make a welcome end to a meal during the long days of summer. They look beautiful, have a fresh, sweet taste, and say dessert without weighing heavily. The accent of mint leaves provides the salad with a pleasant pepperiness. Do not wash the berries, but barely sprinkle them clean with the sprayer hose in your kitchen sink so they retain their integrity. For the best results, toss together not more than 1 hour before serving.

3 pints fresh, ripe strawberries
1 pint fresh blueberries
1 pint fresh blackberries
1 pint fresh raspberries
2 tablespoons unsweetened apple juice concentrate,
*   thawed if frozen*
2 tablespoons fresh orange juice
2 tablespoons finely grated orange zest
1/4 cup chopped fresh mint leaves
8 fresh mint sprigs, for garnish
Sweetened Whipped Cream (page 515),
*   for serving*

1. Rinse all the berries very gently and pat dry carefully with paper towels. Hull the strawberries and cut into quarters. Place in a large bowl with the blueberries, blackberries, and raspberries.

2. Mix the apple juice concentrate, orange juice and zest, and the chopped mint leaves together in a small bowl. Add to the berries and gently toss. Let rest at room temperature for 1 hour before serving.

3. To serve, spoon the berries into a large decorative serving bowl and garnish with the mint sprigs gathered into a small bouquet. Serve with Sweetened Whipped Cream.

Serves 12

PEACH RHUBARB COMPOTE

★ ★ ★

I serve this gently stewed summer compote in wine goblets. Sweet peaches complement the tart rhubarb, and dolloped with whipped cream and garnished with dainty blackberries and mint sprigs on top, it makes a splendid dessert.

6 ripe peaches, peeled, halved, and pitted
10 large stalks rhubarb, trimmed and cut
　　into 1-inch lengths (about 4 cups)
1 cup sugar
½ cup fresh orange juice
1 tablespoon finely grated orange zest
2 teaspoons ground ginger
½ teaspoon ground mace
½ teaspoon salt
Sweetened Whipped Cream (page 515),
　　for garnish
Fresh blackberries, for garnish
Mint sprigs, for garnish

1. Cut the peaches into large coarse pieces, to make about 4 cups. Place the peaches and rhubarb in a large heavy saucepan and stir in the sugar, orange juice and zest, ginger, mace, and salt.

2. Bring to a boil over medium heat. Reduce the heat to a simmer, and cook, uncovered, until the rhubarb is tender, 10 to 12 minutes, stirring once or twice and skimming off any foam that rises to the surface.

3. Remove from the heat and let the compote cool to room temperature or to the desired temperature. If not serving immediately, cover and refrigerate for up to 3 days. It may be served cold. Spoon out into goblets and garnish each with Sweetened Whipped Cream, blackberries, and a mint sprig.

Makes about 10 cups; 12 to 14 servings

BLUSHING PEACH CRUNCH

★ ★ ★

When summer is in high heat and a seasonal fruit seems to arrive in the market daily, I remain on the lookout for gorgeous white peaches. During the July that I was developing recipes for this book, the wait seemed interminable. When these favorites of mine finally showed up, I made the fastest dessert I could think of— saving a few peaches to eat as is. I served the marvelous result while it was still warm—and I suggest you do the same. It's absolutely peachy— especially with a scoop of Homey Vanilla Ice Cream or a drizzle of heavy cream.

6 to 8 ripe peaches, peeled, halved, and pitted
½ cup (1 stick) unsalted butter
1 cup sugar
¾ cup all-purpose flour
¼ cup old-fashioned rolled oats
½ teaspoon ground cinnamon
½ teaspoon ground nutmeg

1. Preheat the oven to 400°F.
2. Coarsely slice the peaches, to make about 6 cups, and place them in a 9-inch square baking pan.
3. Melt the butter in a small saucepan over low heat. Remove from the heat and stir in the remaining ingredients to mix well.
4. Scatter the mixture evenly over the fruit. Bake in the center of the oven until the top is golden brown and bubbly, about 40 minutes. Allow the dessert to cool slightly before serving.
Serves 6

COMFY FRUIT DESSERTS

— ❦ —

Cobbler, crisp, crunch, and crumble sound so similar (and so much like sound effects!) that it's easy to get them confused. In fact, these all-American desserts are more alike than they are different. Each is just fruit baked under a topping. A **cobbler** is topped with biscuit dough or batter that, once baked, will have a bumpy, "cobbled" surface. **Crisps** are similar to cobblers, except they have a buttery topping (flour, sugar, butter, spice) sprinkled over or in place of the biscuit dough. A **crunch** is the same thing as a crisp, but with nuts or oats added for a thicker streusel. Crumble a pastry mix- ture over the fruit base and you've got ... a **crumble**. For something cakier, try any one of these toppings on a **buckle**—fresh fruit mixed with cake batter.

I base the amount of sugar used to sweeten the fruit on how naturally sweet a fruit is. Whether it needs a thickener or not (cornstarch or tapioca) also depends on the fruit, since the finished product won't need to hold together much. The challenge (if I can call it that—these are so easy!) is figuring out what nuts, seasonings, and fruit combinations to use, and how to serve—with whipped cream, ice cream, heavy cream, or nothing at all.

ORANGE RHUBARB CRUMBLE

★ ★ ★

Every year at the end of April, the rhubarb comes up at the end of my asparagus garden. These two spring favorites seem to be content sharing a bed. The first stalks of rhubarb appear pale red and delicate in size as the asparagus wanes and turns to ferns. As summer waxes, the rhubarb turns a dark ruby, thickens, and really flourishes. When I'm ready to pick it, I hold my hand toward the bottom of the stem, wiggle gently and pull the stalk out of the earth (no harm to the plant), and then proceed with it to the kitchen. For this dessert, the addition of orange zest contributes a delicate sweetness to the tart fruit, while a basic crumble topping enhanced with pecans adds an interesting dimension.

3 pounds fresh rhubarb, preferably thin
*   stalks*
1¾ cups all-purpose flour
¾ cup old-fashioned rolled oats
½ cup (packed) light brown sugar
1 teaspoon ground cinnamon
½ cup (1 stick) unsalted butter, cold,
*   cut into small pieces*
½ cup coarsely chopped pecans
1 large egg, lightly beaten
1 cup granulated sugar
2 tablespoons chopped crystallized ginger
Finely grated zest of 1 orange
⅓ cup fresh orange juice
2 tablespoons cornstarch

1. Preheat the oven to 350°F.
2. Remove and discard all leaves from the rhubarb stalks, then trim 1½ inches from both ends. Cut into 1-inch pieces, to make about 8 cups, and set aside.
3. Combine the flour, oats, brown sugar, and cinnamon in a bowl and cut in the butter with a pastry cutter or two knives, or use your fingertips, until the mixture is crumbly. Add the pecans and the egg and toss until mixed. Set aside.
4. Combine the rhubarb, granulated sugar, crystallized ginger, and orange zest in a 3-quart baking dish.
5. Stir the orange juice into the cornstarch in a small bowl to blend well, then add to the rhubarb. Toss thoroughly to coat.
6. Spread the oat topping evenly over the rhubarb. Bake in the center of the oven until golden and bubbly, 45 to 50 minutes. Allow the crumble to cool slightly before serving.

Serves 6

DOUBLE BERRY COBBLER

★ ★ ★

A dip of the spoon through a buttermilk crust blanket reveals the sumptuous fruits beneath. Delicately coated with sugar to enhance their natural juices, blackberries and blueberries seem to have an affinity for each other, but other combinations, including raspberries and strawberries, are delightful too. When huckleberries are in season, don't pass them by!

BERRY FILLING

1 pint fresh blackberries, gently rinsed
1 pint fresh blueberries, gently rinsed
¾ cup sugar
1½ teaspoons cornstarch
1 teaspoon fresh lemon juice

DOUGH

1½ cups all-purpose flour
¼ cup plus 1 teaspoon sugar
1½ teaspoons baking powder
1 teaspoon baking soda
1 teaspoon salt
⅛ teaspoon ground cinnamon
2½ tablespoons unsalted butter, cold
1 teaspoon finely grated lemon zest
¾ cup buttermilk

Homey Vanilla Ice Cream (page 555) or heavy
(or whipping) cream, for serving

1. Preheat the oven to 400°F. Lightly grease and sugar a 9-inch pie plate.

2. Prepare the berry filling: Dry the berries and toss the filling ingredients together gently in a small bowl and then spoon them into the pie plate in an even layer. Set aside in a cool place.

3. Prepare the dough: Combine the flour, ¼ cup sugar, baking powder, baking soda, and salt in a medium-size bowl. In another bowl, mix together the 1 teaspoon of sugar and the cinnamon and set aside.

4. With a pastry cutter or two knives, cut the butter into the flour mixture until it resembles coarse meal. Mix in the lemon zest.

5. Make a well in the center of the flour mixture and slowly pour in the buttermilk. Using a fork, stir just until the dry ingredients are moistened and a dough forms. Turn the dough out onto a lightly floured surface and pat or roll it into a rough 9-inch circle. Lift it carefully and place it over the berries.

6. Using your fingers, rough the dough to get a "cobbled" effect by pinching it between your thumb and forefinger, then lifting it slightly. Do this all over the top of the dough. If you tear it, patch the hole by pinching the dough together. Don't be afraid to rough it up! Prick the pastry all over with the tines of a fork, then sprinkle with the reserved cinnamon-sugar. Bake until the crust is golden brown, 35 to 40 minutes. Transfer to a rack to cool for 10 to 15 minutes before serving with vanilla ice cream or heavy cream.

Serves 6

DOUBLE DIP OF CHOCOLATE PUDDING

★ ★ ★

My mother always made chocolate pudding from the familiar supermarket box, and probably yours did, too, but once you try this home-made version—richer, denser, much more flavorful—you might find it difficult to go back to the shelf. When making this pudding, don't worry if it seems a little lumpy. Just keep on whisking and it will smooth out. To top it all off,

reach for a dollop of whipped heavy cream or a drizzle of plain cream. Sophisticated or not, chocolate pudding will always please anyone of any age from anywhere in the country.

½ cup sugar
3 tablespooons unsweetened cocoa powder
2½ tablespoons cornstarch
Pinch of salt
1 large egg plus 2 yolks
2 cups milk
4 ounces best-quality semisweet chocolate, chopped
2 tablespoons unsalted butter
1 teaspoon instant espresso coffee powder
1 teaspoon pure vanilla extract
Heavy (or whipping) cream, whipped if desired,
    for serving

1. Combine the sugar, cocoa powder, cornstarch, and salt in a medium-size bowl.

2. Whisk the egg and egg yolks together in a small bowl. Add to the sugar mixture and whisk well to make a smooth paste. Set aside.

3. Scald the milk in a medium-size heavy saucepan over medium heat. Remove from the heat immediately. Whisking constantly, add ½ cup of the hot milk to the egg mixture and continue whisking until smooth. Slowly pour this mixture back into the hot milk in the saucepan and continue whisking until smooth.

4. Place the saucepan over medium heat and cook, whisking constantly, until thickened and the mixture boils slowly (large bubbles will form), 5 to 7 minutes. Remove from the heat and add the chopped semisweet chocolate, butter, instant coffee, and vanilla. Continue whisking until smooth.

5. Scrape the pudding into four individual serving dishes or into one bowl and allow to cool to room temperature. Cover with plastic wrap and refrigerate until well chilled. Serve with cream, whipped or plain.

Serves 4

CAROLINA RICE PUDDING

★ ★ ★

There is no comfort food that can beat a rice pudding, fragrantly warm and drizzled with some fresh, thick cream and pure New England maple syrup. For me, the best way to make rice pudding is on top of the stove, rather than in the oven. I use long-grain rice, which is less starchy than short- or medium-grain, and am pleased by the result. The taste seems cleaner and less heavy and altogether delicious.

2½ cups water
Peel of 1 orange in strips, white pith removed
1 cinnamon stick (3 inches long)
Pinch of salt
1 cup long-grain rice
½ cup golden raisins
⅓ cup dark rum
2 cups milk
2 cups heavy (or whipping) cream, plus
    extra for serving
1 cup sugar
2 tablespoons unsalted butter
Pure maple syrup, warmed, for serving

1. Place the water, orange peel, cinnamon stick, and a pinch of salt in a heavy saucepan and bring to a boil over medium-high heat. Add the rice and stir well. Reduce the heat to low, cover the pan, and simmer until the rice is very tender and all of the liquid has been absorbed, about 20 minutes.

2. While the rice is cooking, soak the raisins in the rum.

3. Add the milk, cream, sugar, butter, and the raisins and rum to the rice and cook over medium-low heat, stirring frequently, until the mixture thickens, 35 to 40 minutes. Reduce the heat if the mixture boils too rapidly. Remove from the heat and remove and discard the peel and cinnamon stick.

4. Serve the rice pudding warm with pitchers of heavy cream and warmed maple syrup.

Serves 8 to 10

LOW COUNTRY BREAD PUDDING

★ ★ ★

I headed down to South Carolina looking for red rice and Frogmore Stew, which I found amidst marvelous architecture, beguiling house tours, and local oysters. But I also found unexpected treasures, such as Miss Daisy Mae Brown's cafe, tucked in the BP gas station on Edisto Island. I'd read about the cafe in a magazine feature on the low country, and as soon as I had the opportunity, I set out to find it.

I timed it so that I left Charleston in the late morning, making the forty-mile trip in time for lunch. From the outside, the BP looked like a small rural gas station, but once inside, it was crystal clear that food was the order of business—there were steam tables laden with it, plus seating at comfortable Formica-topped tables and cafeteria-style service, making lunch a bustling affair. I just couldn't get enough of Miss Daisy's red rice, ribs, collards, squash, or cornbread, but fortunately I managed to leave room for her bread pudding, all moist, dark, and studded with raisins—the best I ever tasted. Half in a stupor from all I had eaten, I sought out Miss Daisy, hoping to get her pudding recipe for this book. No go—Miss Daisy said she was waiting for a contract from a large company for the

recipe. I said that I was sure I tasted cloves. She said they were canned peaches. I hope Miss Daisy gets her contract. Until then, she has inspired me enough to come up with a bread pudding of my own. No peaches, and no cloves either!

1 loaf (about 1¼ pounds) brioche or
*   challah bread, or other egg bread*
2½ cups milk
2¼ cups half-and-half
½ cup golden raisins
½ cup dark raisins
3 tablespoons Grand Marnier or
*   other orange liqueur*
3 tablespoons orange marmalade
1 tablespoon unsalted butter, for greasing
*   baking dish*
3 large eggs
1 cup sugar
2 tablespoons pure vanilla extract
Homey Vanilla Ice Cream (page 555) or
*   heavy (or whipping) cream, for serving*

1. Slice the bread 1 inch thick. Place on a baking sheet in one layer and dry out overnight by letting it stand, uncovered, at room temperature.

2. Tear the dried-out bread into 1½-inch pieces and place in a large bowl. (You should have about 12 cups.) Add the milk and the half-and-half and toss well with the bread, making sure all of the pieces are moistened. Let stand for 1 hour, tossing occasionally.

3. Meanwhile, combine both of the raisins, the Grand Marnier, and orange marmalade in a small bowl and let stand for 1 hour.

4. Preheat the oven to 325°F. Using the butter, grease a 13 x 9 x 2-inch baking dish.

5. Whisk together the eggs, sugar, and vanilla in a medium-size bowl and add to the bread along with the raisin mixture. Toss gently but thoroughly to mix. Spoon the mixture into the prepared baking dish and bake until nicely golden and set, 45 minutes to 1 hour. Serve warm with ice cream or a pitcher of cream to drizzle over the top.

Serves 8

DIXIE BANANA PUDDING

★ ★ ★

The first time I ever tasted a sinfully rich banana pudding was in Savannah, Georgia. This velvety-textured milk-based custard, redolent with the essence of banana, is nothing short of celestial, with its fluffy meringue resting on top. While some recipes call for instant pudding instead of "scratch" custard, don't be tempted to use it. The extra time spent on the real thing is essential, so don't cut corners here!

1¾ cups sugar
¼ cup all-purpose flour
2 tablespoons cornstarch
Salt
5 cups milk
8 large eggs, separated
2 tablespoons unsalted butter
1½ tablespoons pure vanilla extract
1 box (12 ounces) vanilla wafers
8 ripe bananas, peeled and cut crosswise
*   into ¼-inch slices*

1. Sift 1½ cups of the sugar, the flour, cornstarch, and a pinch of salt into a large heavy saucepan and set aside.

2. Scald the milk in a medium-size heavy saucepan over medium heat. Remove immediately from the heat. Whisking constantly, slowly pour the hot milk into the sugar mixture in the saucepan. Continue whisking until smooth.

3. Place the mixture over medium heat and cook, whisking constantly, until it starts to thicken (a finger drawn across the back of a spoon coated with the mixture should leave a trail), 10 minutes. Remove from the heat. Whisking constantly, add the egg yolks, one at a time, and continue whisking until thoroughly blended.

4. Return the saucepan to low heat and cook, whisking constantly, until the mixture is very thick, 2 to 3 minutes more. Remove from the heat and stir in the butter and vanilla. Set aside for 5 minutes to cool slightly.

5. Preheat the oven to 400°F.

6. Line the bottom of a 13 x 9 x 2-inch baking dish with half of the vanilla wafers, overlapping as necessary, and cover with half of the banana slices. Cover evenly with half of the custard. Make another layer of wafers, followed by banana slices, then spread the remaining custard evenly over the top.

7. Place the egg whites in a bowl with a pinch of salt and beat with an electric mixer until foamy. Add the remaining ¼ cup of sugar, 1 tablespoon at a time, and continue to beat until the whites hold stiff peaks.

8. Spoon the meringue all over the surface of the pudding, making sure to spread it all the way to the outer edges, so it touches the sides of the baking dish. Use the back of the spoon or a rubber spatula to make some decorative swirls.

9. Bake the pudding in the center of the oven for 5 to 8 minutes, watching carefully, until the meringue is nicely colored—a golden brown with some white valleys. Serve at room temperature, or chill and serve cold.

Serves 10 to 12

GRANNY REESMAN'S SUMMER BERRY PIE

★ ★ ★

While I was growing up, my Granny Reesman baked these glorious pies every summer when the berries were just right. Barely more than a pinch of cinnamon was ever necessary to bring out the juicy flavor of perfectly ripe seasonal favorites. I remember her pies so well and take great delight in sharing her recipe with you.

*Buttery Pie Crust for a 9-inch double-crust pie
    (page 522)*
2 cups fresh ripe strawberries
2 cups fresh blueberries, picked over
2 cups fresh raspberries, picked over
1 cup plus 1 tablespoon sugar
¼ cup cornstarch
¼ teaspoon ground cinnamon
2 teaspoons finely grated lemon zest
1 teaspoon pure vanilla extract
*1 large egg white, lightly beaten with
    1 tablespoon water*

1. Preheat the oven to 400°F.
2. Prepare the pie dough as directed through step 4, rolling out the bottom crust to fit a 9-inch pie plate. Roll out the top crust and fold it into quarters. Beginning ³/₄ inch from the center point, use a knife to cut 3 slits on both of the straight sides, leaving ½ inch between each. This will allow steam to escape as the pie bakes. Place the top crust on a plate. Cover both crusts with plastic wrap and refrigerate until ready to use.
3. Lightly rinse each type of berry separately, using the spray-hose attachment at your kitchen sink. Drain and pat dry with paper towels. Hull and quarter the strawberries, then combine in a large bowl with the blueberries and raspberries. Toss gently with the 1 cup sugar, the cornstarch, cinnamon, lemon zest, and vanilla.
4. Remove the prepared pie shell from the refrigerator and brush bottom and sides with the egg white mixture to prevent sogginess. Spoon the berry mixture into the shell.
5. Remove the top crust from the refrigerator and unfold it over the filling. Trim the overhang to 1 inch. Moisten the edges of the crusts with water where they meet, then press them together lightly and turn under. Crimp the edge

decoratively. Brush the top crust lightly all over with water and sprinkle evenly with the 1 tablespoon sugar.

6. Bake the pie in the lower third of the oven until the filling is bubbly and the crust is golden brown, 1 to 1¼ hours. Let cool on a rack before serving warm or at room temperature.

Serves 6 to 8

SWEET CHERRY PIE

★ ★ ★

There is something about human nature that makes us crave anything short-lived and elusive. The elusiveness is what makes capturing the prize so revered. In this vein, there is the too-short cherry season heralded by delicate white and pink blossoms in the springtime.

Since most people expect to find sour cherries in a pie, the taste of one baked with sweet Bings may come as an unexpectedly pleasant surprise, and, with a scoop of Homey Vanilla Ice Cream, could begin a whole new taste sensation. Some cherry hints: Wash just before using and don't store them wet. The best flavor comes at

room temperature when eaten right from a bowl on your table.

Sweet Pie Crust for a 9-inch double-crust pie (page 523)
4 cups pitted sweet cherries
2 tablespoons fresh orange juice
2 tablespoons fresh lemon juice
2 tablespoons cornstarch
1 to 1½ cups sugar (depending on the sweetness of the fruit)
¼ teaspoon ground cinnamon
Pinch of salt
1 tablespoon finely grated orange zest
¼ teaspoon pure almond extract
1 large egg white, lightly beaten with 1 tablespoon water
1½ tablespoons unsalted butter, cold, cut into small pieces

1. Preheat the oven to 450°F.

2. Prepare the pie dough as directed through step 4, rolling out the bottom crust to fit a 9-inch pie plate. Roll out the top crust and fold it into quarters. Place the top crust on a plate. Cover both crusts with plastic wrap and refrigerate until ready to use.

3. Place the cherries in a large bowl. Stir the orange and lemon juices into the cornstarch in a small bowl, then stir in the sugar, cinnamon, and salt. Add the sugar mixture to the cherries and toss gently to combine. Let stand at room temperature for 15 minutes.

4. Add the orange zest and almond extract to the cherries and toss well.

5. Remove the prepared pie shell from the refrigerator. Brush the bottom and sides with the egg white mixture to prevent sogginess. Spoon in the cherry filling. Dot the filling with the butter.

6. Remove the top crust from the refrigerator and unfold it over the filling. Trim the overhang to 1 inch. Moisten the edges of the crusts

★★★

THE CHERRY ORCHARD

—❦—

*I*t was an offer I couldn't refuse: a harvest dinner in one of loveliest cherry orchards in Michigan, under a full moon and surrounded by trees heavy with fruit. It would be quite a trip, requiring two planes to reach Traverse City, on the Lower Northwest Peninsula, then an hour's drive north along Lake Michigan. But this was well worth the trouble. I was the guest of Charles and Julia Eisendrath, who were not only gracious hosts but great chefs. Friends who attend this annual feast looked forward to it all year. Michigan's cherries, once ripe, don't last long. They're in season for a glorious three weeks, usually between mid-July and early August.

The Eisendrath place was inland, on Lake Charlevoix. Half of the nation's tart cherries come from around here, as does a significant quantity of sweet ones. The temperate microclimate created by the lake is friendly to this fussy fruit: never too hot or cold, with just the right amount of sun and rain. Orchards carpet the hills; and the translucent sour cherries seem to glow against the big lake in the background. I arrived to find tables draped in blue-and-white-checked cloths and set for seventy-five guests. At sunset candles came out, and Charles fired up his grill, a stainless-steel creation of his own design, with seasoned cherry wood cuttings.

Cherries are terrific with game birds, which is exactly what Charles had for us: mallards, black ducks, teals, and redheads that he had bagged in the fall. He basted them in drippings mingled with cher-

ries and cherry juice, garlic, Cognac, and kirsch. Once done, the carved breasts were presented on a huge board, framed with fruit-laden branches. There was a rich cherry sauce for the ducks and salads of grains and summer vegetables on the side. And, of course, there were plenty of cherries for dessert, served over celebratory sundaes and in sour cherry pies.

I spent the next day touring the region and sampling the summer crop, which would be gone in another week or two: yellow Queen Annes, as flavorful as crimson Bings; the intense, yet mellow sweet black cherries; and the red, gem-bright sour Montmorencies. (These last are rarely sold in stores; most wind up in pie filling or jam. If they're not sugared immediately after they're picked, they quickly turn brown.) Farm stands boasted a half dozen different kinds, along with homemade cherry salsas, barbecue sauces, jams, juices, and jellies. And such pies—sugar-crusted, lattice-topped, their juices oozing!

I came home inspired, ready to create sour cherry recipes with several fresh quarts I'd brought from the Eisendrath orchards. I also returned with renewed passion for the fruit—the best of it, that is, which is firm and shiny outside and silky, not mushy, inside. A good cherry shouldn't have a sticky skin (that means it's overripe), and should not be so hard as to be crunchy (that means it's underripe). How else can I determine quality? I can't, at least not without tasting. So buyers beware; try a sample if you can. And eat what you purchase within a day or two—but need I say that? How could you not?

★★★

where they meet with water, then press together lightly and turn under. Crimp the edge decoratively. Decorate the top crust, if you wish, by cutting several cherry shapes, with leaf and stem, from any remaining dough scraps. Moisten the undersides lightly with water and press them gently to the top crust. Cut several 1-inch slits in the top crust to allow steam to escape during baking.

7. Bake the pie in the center of the oven for 10 minutes. Then reduce the oven temperature to 350°F and bake until the filling is bubbly and the crust is golden brown, 45 to 55 minutes more. Let cool on a rack before serving warm or at room temperature.

Serves 6 to 8

KING ORCHARDS' SOUR CHERRY PIE

★ ★ ★

Everybody that I spoke to in Michigan during the all-too-brief sour cherry season—mid-July to early August—froze the delectable fruit immediately so they could use it in pies all year round. The fresh cherries are so, so good, and since my first taste directly from the tree, I've been hooked.

This recipe comes from King Orchards, located in Central Lake, Michigan, close to Charles Eisendrath's Overlook Farm (where I spent a memorable evening celebrating the sour cherry harvest). No spices necessary here—a drop of almond extract just pops the flavor!

Sweet Pie Crust for a 9-inch double-crust pie
   (page 523)
3 cups pitted sour cherries
1 cup sugar
⅓ cup all-purpose flour
¼ teaspoon pure almond extract
1 large egg white, lightly beaten with
   1 tablespoon water

1. Preheat the oven to 400°F.

2. Prepare the pie dough as directed through step 4, rolling out the bottom crust to fit a 9-inch pie plate. Roll out the top crust and fold it into quarters. Place the top crust on a plate. Cover both crusts with plastic wrap and refrigerate until ready to use.

3. Combine the cherries, sugar, flour, and almond extract in a large saucepan. Stir well and bring the mixture to a boil over medium heat. Boil for 1 minute, stirring, until the mixture thickens. Remove from the heat and cool the filling to room temperature.

4. Remove the prepared pie shell from the refrigerator. Brush with some of the egg white mixture to prevent sogginess, then spoon the cooled cherry filling into the shell.

5. Remove the top crust from the refrigerator and unfold it over the filling. Trim the overhang to 1 inch. Moisten the edges of the crusts where they meet with water, then press together lightly and turn under. Crimp the edge decoratively. Cut several 1-inch slits in

the top crust to allow steam to escape during baking.

6. Bake the pie in the center of the oven until the filling is bubbly and the crust is golden brown, 35 minutes. Let cool on a rack before serving warm or at room temperature.

Serves 6 to 8

PEACHY KEEN PIE

★ ★ ★

There is no time like peach time—that season of luscious, juicy, and summery fruits—and no dessert like a fresh peach pie. To preserve the delicate peach flavor and color, I use tapioca as a thickener, since it is less "starchy" than cornstarch or flour. And for the easiest peach peeling, I boil a pot of water, blanch the peaches in it for no more than 30 seconds, then lift them out and slip off the skins. I love this pie served warm, topped with homemade peach ice cream.

Buttery Pie Crust for a 9-inch double-crust pie
  (page 522)
4 pounds ripe peaches
1 tablespoon fresh lemon juice
⅔ cup plus 1 tablespoon sugar
¼ cup instant tapioca
½ teaspoon ground nutmeg
1 large egg white, lightly beaten with
  1 tablespoon water
2 tablespoons unsalted butter, cut into
  small pieces

1. Preheat the oven to 375°F.
2. Prepare the pie dough as directed through step 4, rolling out the bottom crust to fit a 9-inch pie plate. Roll out the top crust and fold it into quarters. Beginning ¾ inch from the center point, use a knife to cut 3 slits on both of the straight sides, leaving ½ inch between each. This will allow steam to escape as the pie bakes. Place the top crust on a plate. Cover both crusts with plastic wrap and refrigerate until ready to use.

3. Peel and halve the peaches, discarding the pits. Cut into thick slices and place in a large bowl. Toss gently with the lemon juice.

4. Combine the ⅔ cup sugar, the tapioca, and the nutmeg in a small bowl. Add to the peaches and toss well.

5. Remove the prepared pie shell from the refrigerator. Brush the bottom and sides with some of the egg white mixture to prevent sogginess. Spoon in the peach filling. Dot the filling with the butter.

6. Remove the top crust from the refrigerator and unfold it over the filling. Trim the overhang to 1 inch. Moisten the edges of the crusts where they meet with water, then press together lightly and turn under. Crimp the edge decoratively. Brush the top crust lightly all over with the remaining egg white mixture and sprinkle evenly with the 1 tablespoon sugar.

7. Bake the pie in the center of the oven until the filling is bubbly and the crust is golden brown, 1 hour. Let cool on a rack before serving warm or at room temperature.

Serves 6 to 8

WENDE'S BLUE-RIBBON APPLE PIE WITH CANDIED GINGER

★ ★ ★

There are apple pies and then there are *apple pies*. If I were giving out blue ribbons, my good friend Wende would certainly be taking one home, because her pie really takes the cake! The apple filling is perfect, moist but not soupy, and the crust is delicious. I'd say it's an all-around winner. The ginger combined with the bite of Granny Smith apples creates just the right not-too-sweet taste, and the Calvados—a very fine apple brandy from Normandy, France—adds a deep flavor note.

Buttery Pie Crust for a 9-inch double-crust pie
(page 522)
5 to 6 large Granny Smith apples
(to make 5 cups sliced)
1½ tablespoons fresh lemon juice
½ cup (packed) light brown sugar
4 ounces crystallized ginger
2 tablespoons cornstarch
1½ teaspoons ground cinnamon
2 tablespoons Calvados (apple brandy)
1 large egg white, lightly beaten with
1 tablespoon water
2 tablespoons unsalted butter, cut into
small pieces
2 tablespoons milk
1 teaspoon granulated sugar

1. Preheat the oven to 375°F.
2. Prepare the pie dough as directed through step 4, rolling out the bottom crust to fit a 9-inch pie plate. Roll out the top crust and fold it into quarters. Beginning ¾ inch from the center point, use a knife to cut 3 slits on both of the straight sides, leaving ½ inch between each. This will allow steam to escape as the pie bakes. Place the top crust on a plate. Cover both crusts with plastic wrap and refrigerate until ready to use.
3. Peel, core, and thickly slice the apples. Place them in a large bowl, and toss gently with the lemon juice.
4. Combine the brown sugar, crytallized ginger, cornstarch, and 1 teaspoon of the cinnamon in a food processor. Pulse the machine on and off until well mixed and the ginger has been finely chopped. Add this mixture to the apples, along with the Calvados, and toss gently to combine.
5. Remove the prepared pie shell from the refrigerator. Brush the bottom and sides with the egg white mixture to prevent sogginess. Spoon in the apple filling. Dot the filling with the butter.
6. Remove the top crust from the refrigerator and unfold it over the filling. Trim the overhang to 1 inch. Moisten the edges of the crusts where they meet with water, then press together lightly and turn under. Crimp the edge decoratively. Brush the top crust lightly with milk. Mix the remaining ½ teaspoon of cinnamon with the granulated sugar and sprinkle the mixture over the pie.
7. Bake the pie in the center of the oven until the apples are tender, the juices are bubbly, and the crust is golden brown, 1 hour. Let cool on a rack before serving warm or at room temperature.

Serves 6 to 8

A BIT ABOUT APPLES

—🍎—

What's a cook to do about the myriad varieties of apples that are suddenly (or so it seems) vying for attention? The array at some orchards and farmers' markets can be daunting, and the picturesque names of the new exotics only add to the confusion. An apple called Honey Crisp is hard to resist, but what does one do with it? Who could pass up a Winter Banana, whatever it turns out to be? What's to know about Jonathans, Jonamacs, and Jonagolds—are they more alike than different, or what? And are those Mutsus, Sensyus, Tsugarus, and Fujis American, Japanese, or both?

Apples have clearly come a long way since the days when the itinerant orchardist John Chapman (a.k.a. Johnny Appleseed, 1774 to 1845) planted hundreds of thousands of trees in Ohio, Illinois, Indiana, and Iowa. They now grow from coast to coast, in more than three hundred varieties (and a few thousand distinct genetic lines). Each is unique: To know them, just start tasting! We've borrowed many new ones from abroad (hence the Japanese names), and developed dozens of modern hybrids on our own. This healthy biodiversity has virtually guaranteed us bounty and a splendid selection for generations to come.

At New York City's Union Square Greenmarket, where I often buy my apples, vendors distribute sample slices to the curious and dispense advice about which types are good for pies, applesauce, baked apples, and just eating out of hand. With up to thirty-five different kinds for sale on many days, customers need help. But don't worry if you're not getting satisfactory answers. You'll wind up with an apple suited to your needs if you follow these guidelines:

Pies, pancakes, muffins, and cakes: Look for assertive-tasting fruit that's not too watery. The apples should have some tartness—a little to a lot, depending on your taste. Examples include Granny Smith, Pippin, Rhode Island Greening, Ida Red, Jonathan, and Jonamac.

Applesauce: Apples that are suitable for pies are usually good for sauce, too, as are a few strongly flavorful types that are too watery or not firm enough for pies. McIntoshes, in season, make excellent sauce.

Baked: Firm fruit makes the best baked apples. This includes Cortland, Northern Spy, and Rome Beauty, whose ability to hold its shape makes it very popular for baking.

Out-of-hand: Most apples that are good for pies, applesauce, and baked apples are delicious raw, too, with the exception of very tart or mealy types. Very delicate-flavored types should only be eaten out-of-hand or in salads. Try Empire, Fuji, Honey Crisp, Red Delicious, Royal Gala, and Winter Banana.

Apple butter: The kind of apples you need when you want to make apple butter are those that are dry, even mealy. They'll likely produce a thicker, richer apple butter than those you'd choose for sauce or pie, although I've found that McIntoshes work well.

OLD-FASHIONED APPLE PIE

★ ★ ★

American as . . . Everyone has their favorite recipe for apple pie. Mine is similar to the pie my aunt used to make when I was young. The cinnamon permeated every warm bite of apple. Today I serve this topped with a thin slice of Vermont Cheddar cheese, and as the pie still represents the best of American cooking—simple and delicious—it remains a classic staple in my home.

Classic Pie Crust for a 9-inch double-crust pie
   (page 521)
5 to 6 large apples, such as Granny Smith,
   Pippin, or Rhode Island Greening
   (to make 5 cups sliced)
1 tablespoon fresh lemon juice
¾ cup sugar
1½ tablespoons cornstarch
1 teaspoon ground cinnamon
Pinch of ground nutmeg
1 large egg white, lightly beaten with
   1 tablespoon water
1 to 2 tablespoons unsalted butter,
   cut into small pieces

1. Preheat the oven to 450°F.

2. Prepare the pie dough as directed through step 4, rolling out the bottom crust to fit a 9-inch pie plate. Roll out the top crust and fold it into quarters. Beginning ¾ inch from the center point, use a knife to cut 3 slits on both of the straight sides, leaving ½ inch between each. This will allow steam to escape as the pie bakes. Place the top crust on a plate. Cover both crusts with plastic wrap and refrigerate until ready to use.

3. Peel, core, and thickly slice the apples. Place them in a large bowl and toss gently with the lemon juice, then with the sugar, cornstarch, cinnamon, and nutmeg.

4. Remove the prepared pie shell from the refrigerator. Brush the bottom and sides with some of the egg white mixture to prevent sogginess. Spoon in the apple filling. Dot the filling with the butter.

5. Remove the top crust from the refrigerator and unfold it over the filling. Trim the overhang to 1 inch. Moisten the edges of the crusts where they meet with water, then press together lightly and turn under. Crimp the edge decoratively. Decorate the top crust, if you wish, by cutting out an apple shape, with a stem and leaf, from any remaining dough scraps. Moisten the undersides lightly with water, and press them gently to the top crust. Brush the top crust lightly all over with the remaining egg white mixture.

6. Place the pie on the center rack of the oven and immediately reduce the heat to 350°F. Bake until the apples are tender, the juices are bubbly, and the crust is golden brown, 1 hour. Let the pie cool on a rack before serving just slightly warm or at room temperature.

Serves 6 to 8

APPLE-RASPBERRY PIE

★ ★ ★

The sweet flavor of berries gives a summery feel to this apple pie. While fresh raspberries are my first choice, IQF (individually quick frozen) raspberries, blueberries, or blackberries, will do quite nicely in this case. Just be sure not to use berries packed in syrup and thaw before adding them to the apples.

Classic Pie Crust for a 9-inch double-crust pie (page 521)
5 to 6 large Ida Red or Granny Smith apples (to make 5 cups sliced)
1½ tablespoons fresh lemon juice
½ cup plus 3 tablespoons sugar
2 tablespoons all-purpose flour
1 teaspoon pure vanilla extract
1 cup fresh raspberries, gently rinsed
1 large egg white, lightly beaten with 1 tablespoon water

1. Preheat the oven to 450°F.

2. Prepare the pie dough as directed through step 4, rolling out the bottom crust to fit a 9-inch pie. Roll out the top crust and fold it into quarters. Beginning ¾ inch from the center point, use a knife to cut 3 slits on both of the straight sides, leaving ½ inch between each. This will allow steam to escape as the pie bakes. Place the top crust on a plate. Cover both crusts with plastic wrap and refrigerate until ready to use.

3. Peel, core, and slice the apples. Place in a large bowl and toss gently with the lemon juice, then with the ½ cup sugar, the flour, and vanilla. Dry the raspberries and toss gently but thoroughly with the apples.

4. Remove the prepared pie shell from the refrigerator. Uncover and brush the bottom of the chilled crust with the egg white mixture to prevent sogginess. Spoon in the fruit filling.

5. Remove the top crust from the refrigerator and unfold it over the filling. Trim the overhang to 1 inch. Moisten the edges of the crusts where they meet with water, then press together lightly and turn under. Crimp the edge decoratively.

6. Brush the top crust lightly all over with water and sprinkle evenly with the 3 tablespoons sugar.

7. Bake the pie in the lower third of the oven for 20 minutes, then reduce the heat to 350°F and bake for 1 hour more. If the crust browns too quickly, cover it with aluminum foil, removing the foil in the last 20 minutes of baking so it doesn't create too much steam and a soggy crust. Let cool on a rack before serving warm or at room temperature.

Serves 6 to 8

PEAR-CRANBERRY CRUMBLE TART

★ ★ ★

Every fall, when fresh cranberries start arriving in the markets, I start plotting out the different ways to use this indigenous American fruit before it disappears soon after Christmas. One special combination is as an accent to sweet pears. A blanket of crumble mixture makes this festive tart ideal for the holidays. For a real splurge, top a warm wedge with a scoop of Homey Vanilla Ice Cream or New Orleans Praline Ice Cream.

CRUST

½ cup (1 stick) unsalted butter,
*   cut into pieces*
¼ cup granulated sugar
½ teaspoon pure vanilla extract
1 cup all-purpose flour
Pinch of salt

FILLING

4 ripe pears (about 2 pounds)
2 tablespoons fresh lemon juice
1¼ cups fresh cranberries
½ cup granulated sugar
2 tablespoons all-purpose flour
2 tablespoons finely chopped crystallized
*   ginger*

CRUMBLE

⅓ cup granulated sugar
⅓ cup all-purpose flour
3 tablespoons cold unsalted butter,
*   cut into pieces*

2 teaspoons confectioners' sugar (optional)

1. Prepare the crust: Place the butter in a food processor and process a few seconds until creamy. Add the granulated sugar and vanilla and process until the mixture is light and fluffy, about 20 seconds, stopping to scrape the sides of the bowl once or twice.

2. Combine the flour and salt in a small bowl and add it to the food processor. Process until the dough comes together around the sides of the bowl, then scrape the sides of the bowl, and process for a few extra seconds.

3. With lightly floured hands, press the dough evenly over the bottom and up the sides of a loose-bottom 10½-inch tart pan, pressing particularly around the bottom edge to make sure the dough is not too thick.

4. Trim off any excess dough at the top of the tart pan with a knife, then lightly press the dough around the inside of the rim with your thumb so it extends about ⅛ inch above the pan. Prick the dough all over with a fork, then chill the prepared pan, covered with plastic wrap, in the freezer for at least 30 minutes or overnight.

5. Preheat the oven to 375°F.

6. Bake the tart shell until golden brown, about 25 minutes. Cool on a wire rack.

7. Prepare the filling: Halve, core, and peel the pears. Cut crosswise into ¼-inch slices. Place in a bowl and toss with the lemon juice. Add the cranberries, granulated sugar, flour, and ginger. Spoon the pear mixture into the tart shell.

8. Prepare the crumble: Combine the granulated sugar, flour, and butter in the food processor bowl and process until the mixture resembles coarse meal. Sprinkle the crumble over the entire surface of the tart.

9. Return the tart to the oven and bake until the top is golden brown and the pears are tender, about 1 hour. If the crust is getting too brown while baking, cover the edges with aluminum foil. Cool the tart on a rack to room temperature or until still warm, then remove the sides of the pan and place the tart on a serving plate. Sprinkle the top with confectioners' sugar, if desired, to serve.

Serves 8 to 10

PLUM TART WITH GINGER CRUST

★ ★ ★

When red plums become available in June, turn some of them into this easy tart. No rolling is necessary for the crust—simply press it evenly into a tart pan. The bite of ginger in the crust enhances both the ripe sweetness of the plums and the pleasant, underlying tartness.

CRUST

½ cup (1 stick) unsalted butter, cut into
    small pieces
¼ cup sugar
¼ teaspoon pure vanilla extract
1 cup all-purpose flour
¼ cup finely ground gingersnap cookies
    (about 1 ounce)
½ teaspoon ground ginger
⅛ teaspoon salt

FILLING

1½ pounds red plums, pitted and
    quartered
3 tablespoons sugar
¼ teaspoon ground ginger
¼ teaspoon ground cinnamon
¼ cup red currant jelly or apricot jam,
    melted

1. Prepare the crust: Place the butter in a food processor and process a few seconds until creamy. Add the sugar and vanilla and process until the mixture is light and fluffy, about 20 seconds, stopping to scrape the sides of the bowl once or twice.

2. Combine the flour, ground gingersnaps, ginger, and salt in a small bowl and add them to the food processor. Process until the dough comes together around the sides of the bowl, then scrape the sides of the bowl and process for a few extra seconds.

3. With lightly floured hands, press the dough evenly over the bottom and up the sides of a loose-bottom 9-inch tart pan, pressing particularly around the bottom edge of the pan with your fingers, making sure that the dough is not too thick.

4. Trim off any excess dough at the top of the tart pan with a knife, then lightly press the dough around the inside of the rim with your thumb so it extends about ⅛ inch above the pan. Prick the dough all over with a fork, then chill the prepared pan, covered with plastic wrap, in the freezer for at least 30 minutes or overnight.

5. Preheat the oven to 375°F.

6. Prepare the filling: Place the quartered plums in a bowl with the sugar, ginger, and cinnamon. Toss well and set aside.

7. Bake the chilled or frozen tart shell until golden brown, 25 minutes. Cool completely, in the pan, on a wire rack. Reduce the oven temperature to 350°F.

8. Brush half the jelly all over the inside of the cooled tart shell. Arrange the plums decoratively in the tart shell, skin side up, starting at the outside rim and working toward the center. The plums should overlap slightly. Brush them all over with the remaining jelly.

9. Place the tart on a baking sheet. Cover the rim of the tart shell with aluminum foil to prevent the crust from overbrowning, then bake the tart until the plums are tender, about 30 minutes. Let cool on a rack to room temperature or until slightly warm, then remove the sides of the pan, place the tart on a serving plate, and serve.

Serves 8

SOUTHERN PECAN PIE MY WAY

★ ★ ★

I like my pecan pie heavy on the pecans, and you can bet this one is. For my pie, I only use nice big pecan halves, not weensy pieces, so that each slice is rich with a deep nutty flavor. Bourbon, instead of vanilla extract, partners well with pecans, resulting in an even more seductive filling. And remember, the fresher your pecans, the better your pie will be. I never say no to a dollop of whipped cream and so suggest it as a finishing touch. But the pie is delicious as is.

PECANS

—❦—

What's more American than apple pie? Pecan pie, no question about it. Europeans were making apple pastries long before they colonized the New World, but pecans are native to North America. Explorers got their first taste in the Mississippi Valley, from Native American traders who called the nuts *pakan, pagan,* and the like. George Washington and Thomas Jefferson cultivated them on their estates, and they grew in popularity throughout the nineteenth century (with some help from a Louisiana slave named Antoine, the first person to successfully graft a pecan tree). Today there are pecan orchards throughout the South.

This buttery, toasty nut stars in dozens of other sweets—ice cream, cookies, cakes, and candies (including irresistible New Orleans–style pralines). It's widely used in stuffing at holiday time; and many cooks (including me) toss it into pilafs and salads year-round. Folks in Cajun country like them spiced, and my version of Cajun Spiced Pecans appears on page 157.

Some pecan fans buy theirs right after the fall harvest, just-picked and still in their shells. Freshness does matter, since the oily pecan can easily turn rancid. When buying them unshelled, look for heavy, smooth specimens that don't rattle when shaken. Store shelled pecans in airtight containers, up to 9 months in your refrigerator and up to 2 years in your freezer.

Classic Pie Crust for a 9-inch single-crust pie
    (page 521)
3 large eggs, beaten
1 cup dark corn syrup
½ cup (packed) dark brown sugar
¼ cup (½ stick) unsalted butter, melted
2 tablespoons bourbon
Pinch of salt
1½ cups pecan halves
Sweetened Whipped Cream (page 515),
    for serving

1. Preheat the oven to 425°F.

2. Prepare the pie dough as directed through step 3, rolling out the crust to fit a 9-inch pie plate. Cover with plastic wrap and refrigerate until ready to use.

3. Combine the eggs, corn syrup, brown sugar, melted butter, bourbon, and salt in a bowl and mix well.

4. Remove the prepared pie shell from the refrigerator and arrange 1 cup of the pecan halves evenly over the bottom. Pour the filling carefully over the pecans, then arrange the remaining ½ cup pecans decoratively on top of the filling.

5. Place the pie on a baking sheet and bake in the center of the oven for 15 minutes. Reduce the oven temperature to 350°F and bake until the filling is set, for 40 minutes more. If necessary, cover the rim of the pie crust with aluminum foil to prevent burning. Let cool on a rack before serving warm or at room temperature with Sweetened Whipped Cream.

Serves 6 to 8

QUICK CRUSTS

— ❦ —

*f*ast and tasty, crusts from cookie crumbs take the tension out of pie-making and give real meaning to the phrase "easy as pie." These foolproof shells, simple mixtures of crumbs and butter, are pressed into a pie plate with your fingers, so there's no rolling to worry about, and they bake up flavorful in little time, ready to take a custard or ice cream filling.

Favorite cookies to crumble include vanilla wafers, chocolate wafers, graham crackers, and gingersnaps. All are tasty as is, but occasionally I'll add a little cinnamon or nutmeg to a vanilla wafer crust, or sugar to the graham crackers, as I do in the Key Lime Pie recipe (page 517), because I think it better sets off the filling.

CHOCOLATE-PECAN BANANA CREAM PIE

★ ★ ★

American pie-bakers seize the moment when it comes to using favorite fruits at their seasonal peak to enclose in a pastry crust. However, the best pies are not necessarily made only from summer or autumn fruits; cream pies can be appreciated all year round. During the 1800s housewives had a penchant for these creamy indulgences, and this one remains a favorite. While it is delicious all dressed up as it is here, it is also good without the extra toppings.

CRUST
1¼ cups chocolate wafer cookie crumbs
    (almost 5 ounces)
¼ cup (½ stick) unsalted butter, melted

FILLING
3 large egg yolks
¾ cup sugar
3 tablespoons cornstarch
¼ teaspoon salt
1½ cups milk
1 tablespoon unsalted butter
1 teaspoon pure vanilla extract
½ cup heavy (or whipping) cream, plus
    additional for garnish (optional)
3 ripe bananas
½ cup finely chopped pecans,
    for garnish

1. Preheat the oven to 375°F.

2. Prepare the crust: Combine the cookie crumbs and the melted butter in a small bowl and mix well. Press the mixture evenly over the bottom and sides of a 9-inch pie plate. Bake the crust in the center of the oven for 7 minutes, then cool completely on a rack.

3. Prepare the filling: Beat the egg yolks in a heavy medium-size saucepan. Mix in the sugar, cornstarch, and salt, then stir in the milk.

4. Add the butter to the mixture and set the pan over medium heat. Cook, stirring constantly, until the butter is melted and the mixture is bubbling and thick, 5 to 7 minutes.

5. Remove the pan from the heat and stir in the vanilla. Transfer the custard to a glass bowl and cover, laying plastic wrap directly on the surface to prevent a skin from forming. Chill in the refrigerator for 2 hours.

6. Whip the heavy cream to stiff peaks and, using a rubber spatula, fold it gently but thoroughly into the chilled custard. Peel and evenly slice 2 bananas and arrange in one layer over the bottom of the prepared crust. Spoon the custard over the bananas. Cover with plastic wrap and refrigerate at least 6 hours or overnight.

7. Before serving, remove the plastic wrap. Peel and evenly slice the remaining banana and arrange the slices decoratively around the edge of the pie. Sprinkle the center with the chopped pecans and garnish with additional whipped cream, if desired.

Serves 6 to 8

HARVEST SWEET POTATO PIE

★ ★ ★

This is an easy dessert to put together on Thanksgiving weekend. Either my Sweet or Classic Pie Crust recipe makes a good base for the mashed sweet potato filling.

Sweet or Classic Pie Crust for a 9-inch single-crust
    pie (page 523 or 521)
1¼ cups cooked, mashed sweet potatoes
½ cup (packed) light brown sugar
½ teaspoon salt
¼ teaspoon ground cinnamon
Pinch of ground nutmeg
2 large eggs, lightly beaten
½ cup plain nonfat yogurt
¼ cup milk
1 tablespoon unsalted butter, melted
12 pecan halves, for garnish (optional)
Sweetened Whipped Cream (facing page),
    for serving

1. Prepare the pie dough as directed through step 3. Cover with plastic wrap and refrigerate until ready to use.

2. Preheat the oven to 400°F.

3. Combine the mashed sweet potatoes, brown sugar, salt, cinnamon, and nutmeg in a large bowl and stir to blend well. Stir in the eggs, yogurt, milk, and butter.

4. Remove the prepared pie shell from the refrigerator and unwrap it. Spoon the sweet potato mixture into the shell. Arrange the pecan halves in a decorative circle around the edge of the pie, if desired. Bake in the center of the oven until the filling is set (the tip of a knife inserted in the center comes out clean) and the crust is golden brown, 45 minutes. Let cool on a rack before serving warm or at room temperature, accompanied by Sweetened Whipped Cream.
Serves 8

SPICED CARROT PIE

★ ★ ★

During those months when sweet potatoes are not up to par, or when pumpkins are only a memory, carrot pie, laced with aromatic spices in a cinnamon crust, makes an absolutely delicious dessert. It would be equally welcome after roast turkey or Shaker Cranberry Brisket for a holiday feast. I actually prefer this filling because it is less dense than either the sweet potatoes or canned pumpkin purée used for traditional pies. While puréeing the carrots by machine is perfectly acceptable, I prefer to pass them through a coarse strainer to obtain just the right texture.

CRUST
1¼ cups all-purpose flour
½ teaspoon ground cinnamon
Pinch of salt
½ cup (1 stick) unsalted butter, cold, cut into
    small pieces
6 tablespoons ice water

FILLING
1¼ pounds carrots, peeled and cut into ¼-inch
    slices
½ cup sugar
½ teaspoon ground ginger
¼ teaspoon ground cinnamon
¼ teaspoon ground cloves
¼ teaspoon ground nutmeg
Pinch of salt
2 large eggs, lightly beaten
1 cup heavy (or whipping) cream
Sweetened Whipped Cream (optional; recipe follows),
    for serving

1. Prepare the crust: Place the flour, cinnamon, and salt in a food processor and pulse on and off to mix. Add the butter and pulse the machine on and off just until the mixture resembles coarse meal.

2. With the machine running, trickle in the ice water through the feed tube and process just until the dough gathers together. Remove the dough from the machine, and flatten it with the palm of your hand to form a thick disk. Wrap it in plastic wrap and chill in the refrigerator for at least 1 hour.

3. Remove the dough from the refrigerator and roll it out on a lightly floured work surface or between two sheets of waxed paper to form an 11-inch circle, to fit a 9-inch pie plate. The rolled-out dough should be about ⅛ inch thick. Work quickly, as the dough can become sticky. Remove 1 sheet of waxed paper. Use a spatula to help lift the dough and fold it loosely in half, then into quarters. Gently transfer it to the pie plate, centering the corner of the dough in the center of the plate. Open up the dough and press it lightly into the plate to fit. Trim the dough, leaving a 1-inch overhang. Prick the dough all over with the tines of a fork, cover with plastic wrap, and refrigerate until ready to use.

4. Preheat the oven to 450°F.

5. Prepare the filling: Place the carrots in a saucepan, cover with cold water, and bring to a boil. Reduce the heat and simmer, uncovered, until the carrots are very tender, about 15 minutes. Drain.

6. Pass the carrots through a coarse strainer, pressing them with the back of a wooden spoon. Measure out 1 cup of the puréed carrots and place it in a bowl (reserve any remaining carrots for another use).

7. Add the remaining ingredients except the Sweetened Whipped Cream to the carrots and mix well.

8. Remove the prepared pie shell from the refrigerator and spoon in the filling. Bake the pie in the center of the oven for 20 minutes, then reduce the heat to 350°F and bake until the

filling is set (the tip of a knife inserted in the center comes out clean) and the crust is golden brown, 30 minutes. Let cool on a rack for at least 30 minutes before serving with a dollop of Sweetened Whipped Cream.

Serves 6 to 8

Sweetened Whipped Cream

───★───

1 cup heavy (or whipping) cream
2 tablespoons sugar
½ teaspoon pure vanilla extract

Beat the cream in a large bowl with an electric mixer at medium speed until it becomes frothy. Add the sugar and vanilla and continue beating until the cream holds soft peaks. Do not overbeat. Refrigerate the cream, covered with plastic wrap, for no more than 1 hour if not using immediately.

Makes 2 cups

LEMON CHESS PIE

★ ★ ★

There are a number of stories about how chess pie, a simple pie long associated with the South, got its name. Some people believe it's a derivation of cheese pie, although it contains no cheese (its filling is, however, curd-like). The best chess pie I have ever tasted, a lemon chess, was at Virgil's Barbecue on West 44th Street in New York City. This recipe is inspired by one given to me by Virgil's chef, Daniel Russo. While the filling does bear some resemblance to that of lemon meringue pie, the lemon meringue is creamier, while the lemon chess is firmer, grainier. It would be most delicious served on a sultry summer afternoon along with a glass of sparkling iced tea or lemonade garnished with a sprig of mint.

*Simple Pie Crust for a 9-inch single-crust pie
    (page 519)*
1½ cups sugar
*6 tablespoons (¾ stick) unsalted butter,
    at room temperature*
3 tablespoons cornstarch
2 tablespoons finely grated lemon zest
4 large eggs
⅓ cup fresh lemon juice
*Sweetened Whipped Cream (page 515), for
    serving*
Fresh mint sprigs, for garnish

1. Preheat the oven to 350°F.

2. Prepare the pie dough as directed through step 3, rolling the crust out to fit a 9-inch pie plate. Prick the crust all over with the tines of a fork, then line with aluminum foil and fill with dried beans or pie weights. Bake in the center of the oven until very lightly golden, 8 minutes. Remove the foil and dried beans or pie weights and cool the shell on a rack. Leave the oven on.

3. Using an electric mixer on medium speed, beat the sugar and the butter in a large bowl until light and fluffy. Beat in the cornstarch and the lemon zest. Add the eggs, one at a time,

beating well after each addition. Beat in the lemon juice, then spoon the mixture into the prebaked pie shell.

4. Bake the pie in the center of the oven for 40 to 45 minutes, until the filling is set and the top is golden. Let cool on a rack to room temperature. Serve dolloped with Sweetened Whipped Cream and garnished with a small mint sprig.
Serves 8

LEMON MERINGUE PIE

★ ★ ★

A great American classic, lemon meringue pie, with its billowy cloud of golden-edged meringue atop a light-as-air lemon filling, is a perfect ending to almost any meal. The best meringues have edges defined with color and some nice areas of white too. To ensure meringue perfection, spread the mixture out all the way to the very edge of the pie crust, keeping a nice mounded center. Check on the pie while it bakes so that it doesn't get too brown. Cool your pie away from extreme heat, humidity, and draft—these conditions are not meringue friendly! Garnish with a fresh or candied violet for a final touch of pizzazz.

Classic Pie Crust for a 9-inch single-crust pie
   (page 521)

LEMON FILLING
1¼ cups sugar
⅓ cup cornstarch
¼ teaspoon salt
1½ cups tepid water
4 large egg yolks
¼ cup fresh lemon juice
2 tablespoons finely grated lemon zest
2 tablespoons unsalted butter

MERINGUE
5 large egg whites
¼ teaspoon cream of tartar
¼ teaspoon salt
½ cup sugar

1. Preheat the oven to 350°F.

2. Prepare the pie dough as directed through step 3 to fit a 9-inch plate. Prick the crust all over with the tines of a fork, then line with aluminum foil and fill with dried beans or pie weights. Bake the crust in the center of the oven, until very lightly golden, 8 minutes. Remove the foil and beans or pie weights and bake until light golden, 5 minutes more. Cool the shell on a rack. Raise the oven temperature to 400°F.

3. Prepare the filling: Combine the sugar, cornstarch, and salt in a heavy 2-quart saucepan. Slowly add the water, stirring until smooth. Place over medium heat and bring to a gentle boil, stirring constantly. Boil to thicken, 1 minute, and remove from the heat.

4. Place the egg yolks in a small bowl and whisk to mix. Whisking constantly, slowly pour about ¼ cup of the hot sugar mixture into the yolks and continue whisking until smooth. Slowly pour the egg mixture back into the saucepan, whisking constantly until smooth. Stir in the lemon juice, the lemon zest, and butter and return the pan to the heat. Bring to a boil,

stirring constantly, and boil to thicken for 1 minute, then remove from the heat. Pour the filling into the prepared crust.

5. Prepare the meringue: Place the egg whites, cream of tartar, and salt in a large bowl and beat with an electric mixer at low speed until soft peaks begin to form. Increase the speed to medium and add the sugar, a tablespoon at a time, beating just until stiff peaks form. Do not overbeat.

6. Spoon the meringue all over the surface of the filling, mounding it in the center and making sure to spread it all the way to the outer edge, so it touches the crust. Use the back of the spoon or rubber spatula to make some decorative swirls.

7. Bake the pie in the center of the oven until the meringue is lightly browned on the edges, or 5 to 7 minutes. Do not allow the meringue to overcolor. Cool the pie on a rack in a cool, draft-free area to room temperature and then refrigerate for at least 3 hours before serving.

Serves 8

KEY LIME PIE

★ ★ ★

A visit to the Florida Keys is synonymous with eating Key lime pie. It's so smooth and refreshing, and while everyone seems to have their own delicious version, sweetened condensed milk is a universal ingredient. Key limes are grown in southern Florida and have a very thin, greenish-yellow peel; the juice is tangier and more intense than a regular lime. If you cannot find fresh Key limes, the juice is available, sold in bottles, in specialty food stores and fine supermarkets. Regular lime juice just doesn't give the same pucker, and is not a good substitute. Be sure to chill the pie thoroughly before serving so that the filling sets up nicely.

CRUST

1¼ cups graham cracker crumbs
    (about eleven 5 x 2½ -inch crackers)
¼ cup granulated sugar
⅓ cup unsalted butter, melted

FILLING

4 large egg yolks
1 can (14 ounces) sweetened condensed milk
½ cup Key lime juice

TOPPING

1 cup heavy (or whipping) cream
¼ cup confectioners' sugar
Thin lime slices, for garnish

1. Preheat the oven to 350°F.

2. Prepare the crust: Combine the graham cracker crumbs, sugar, and melted butter in a small bowl and mix well. Press the mixture evenly over the bottom and sides of a 9-inch pie plate. Bake in the center of the oven for 8 minutes, then cool completely on a rack.

3. Prepare the filling: Beat the egg yolks in a medium-size bowl with an electric mixer at medium speed until light. Add the sweetened condensed milk and the Key lime juice and beat until well blended. Pour the filling into the prepared crust and bake the pie in the center of the oven until the filling is set but still creamy, about 15 minutes. Cool the pie completely on a rack and then chill thoroughly in the refrigerator for at least 4 hours.

4. Prepare the topping: Before serving, whip the cream with the confectioners' sugar until it holds firm peaks. Use a rubber spatula to swirl it over the surface of the pie, or use a pastry bag to pipe it decoratively. Decorate the cream with the lime slices and return the pie to the refrigerator until serving time.

Serves 6 to 8

DEBBIE'S BALL PARK ICE CREAM PIE

★ ★ ★

Debbie Glassman Shenkel, a longtime friend and terrific cook, described her delicious-sounding mile-high ice cream pie to me, and once I made it, I watched in amazement as it magically disappeared, a slice at a time, directly from the freezer. This is definitely one for a party because it is *huge*. I do recommend making it with homemade ice cream and sauces. They are easy to prepare, and this is just a great dessert.

40 vanilla wafers
3 tablespoons unsalted butter, melted
2 quarts Homey Vanilla Ice Cream (page 555),
    softened
½ cup Old-Fashioned Butterscotch Sauce (page 564)
½ cup chopped peanuts
2 Snickers bars (2 ounces each), chopped
Silky Hot Chocolate Sauce (page 562), warmed,
    for serving

1. Place the wafers in a large plastic bag with a zip top and crush them with a rolling pin, or place them in a food processor and process until pulverized. Place the crumbs in a 10-inch spring-form pan, add the butter, and mix well so that all the crumbs are moistened. Press the crumbs evenly over the bottom of the pan, pushing them up about 1 inch on the sides. Cover with plastic wrap and freeze until the crust is firm.

2. Spread half of the ice cream over the crust. Freeze until firm.

3. Spread the butterscotch sauce over the ice cream and sprinkle with the peanuts. Freeze until firm.

4. Spread the remaining ice cream over the peanuts and freeze until firm.

5. Top with the chopped Snickers bars, pressing them in slightly. Freeze until ready to serve.

6. If frozen solid, let the pie soften in the refrigerator at least 1 hour before serving. Run a warm knife around the inside of the pan and remove the sides of the pan. Cut the pie into wedges and serve with warmed chocolate sauce.

Serves 10 to 12

SIMPLE PIE CRUST

★ ★ ★

This pie dough, with the texture almost of a cookie dough, can be fragile, so handle it with care. If it should break while you're transferring it from the rolling surface to the pie plate, just gently press and patch it together. It's lovely for fruit pies, and works well with creamy fillings, too.

1¼ cups all-purpose flour
½ cup sugar
½ teaspoon salt
½ cup (1 stick) unsweetened butter, cold,
    cut into small pieces
6 tablespoons heavy cream
1 teaspoon pure vanilla extract

1. Combine the flour, sugar, and salt in a food processor, and pulse on and off to mix. Add the butter and pulse the machine on and off until the mixture resembles coarse meal.

2. Add the cream and vanilla, and process the dough just until it gathers together. Remove the dough from the machine and divide it in half. Flatten each half with the palm of your hand to form a thick disk. Wrap the disks in plastic wrap and chill in the refrigerator for at least 1 hour.

3. Remove one disk of dough from the refrigerator. Unwrap it and roll it out on a lightly floured surface or between two sheets of waxed paper to form a circle about ⅛ inch thick and 2 inches larger than the pie plate. Work quickly, as the dough can become sticky. Use a spatula to help lift the dough, and fold it loosely in half, then into quarters. Gently transfer it to the pie plate, centering the corner of the dough in the center of the plate. Open up the dough and press it lightly into the plate to fit. If the dough should tear, just press it gently together. Trim the dough, leaving a 1-inch overhang. If making a single-crust pie, turn the edges under and flute it decoratively.

4. Repeat the rolling process for a top crust or for another bottom crust. The circle for a top crust should be 9 inches for an 8-inch pie and 10 inches for a 9-inch pie.

5. Follow the individual pie recipes for filling and baking.

Makes enough for an 8- or 9-inch double-crust pie

TIPS FOR MAKING A BETTER PIE

1. When making pie crust, do not overmix the dough after the liquid has been added to the other ingredients; overmixing will result in a tough crust.

2. Once the dough is gathered into a ball, flatten it into a disk shape and dust it very lightly with flour, then wrap in plastic wrap, and chill for at least 1 hour. For a double crust, divide the dough in half, form each half into a disk, and wrap and refrigerate each disk separately; keep the second half of the dough refrigerated while you work on the first.

3. To roll out the crust, place the chilled disk of dough on a lightly floured work surface. Flatten the dough with the palm of your hand or, if the dough is hard, hit it lightly with the rolling pin several times to flatten. Roll the dough from the center outward, lifting and turning it frequently to prevent sticking. Dust the work surface and rolling pin lightly with flour as necessary. Roll the dough out to a thickness of about ⅛ inch and a diameter 2 inches greater than the diameter of the pie plate for the bottom crust, 1 inch greater for the top crust.

4. To transfer the rolled-out dough to the pie plate, dust the surface of the dough very lightly with flour, then fold the dough loosely in half and then into quarters. Lift the dough gently, place it in the pie plate, with the center tip of the fold in the center of the plate, and unfold it carefully.

5. To fit the dough in the pie plate, gently ease it over the bottom and up the sides of the plate, making sure it fits comfortably, with no air pockets left between the dough and the surface of the plate. If the dough should tear, patch it by pressing the torn edges together with your fingertips or by adding a small scrap of rolled-out dough and pressing it in place, first moistening it with a little water if necessary.

6. For a single-crust pie, trim the dough overhang to 1 inch. Turn the overhanging edge underneath and press it gently but firmly against the rim of the pie plate; crimp the edge decoratively by pressing it between the thumb of one hand and the thumb and first finger of the other hand, continuing all the way around. The length of time you need to bake an unfilled crust will depend on the oven temperature. Each of the pie recipes in this chapter includes the proper time for the temperature called for. The following are some general guidelines for prebaking. **For a partially baked crust:** Preheat the oven to 350°F. Prick the bottom and sides of the crust all over with the tines of a fork. Line the crust with aluminum foil, parchment paper, or waxed paper and fill with dried beans or pie weights. Bake the crust in the center of the preheated oven for 8 minutes until very lightly golden, then carefully remove the foil and weights, prick the crust again, and bake 5 minutes longer until light golden. **For a fully baked crust:** After removing the foil and weights and repricking the crust, bake it for another

✶✶✶✶✶✶✶✶✶✶✶✶✶✶✶✶✶✶✶✶✶✶✶✶✶✶✶✶✶✶✶✶✶✶✶

10 to 12 minutes, until it is golden brown.

7. Fill the pastry-lined pie plate, baked or unbaked, with the prepared filling. If using fruit to fill an unbaked pie shell, first brush the bottom and sides of the crust with a mixture of lightly beaten egg white and water; this will prevent the crust from becoming soggy.

8. The following easy method of cutting steam vents in a top crust works for all my crusts except the Sweet Pie Crust, which is too delicate to handle this way. For that dough, wait until the top crust is on the pie before cutting vents. For the other double-crust pies, roll out the second disk of dough as for the first in step 3 above and fold it into quarters. Beginning ¾ inch from the center point, use a knife to cut 3 slits on both of the straight sides, leaving ½ inch between each. This will allow steam to escape as the pie bakes. Place the crust on top of the filling with the center tip of the fold in the center of the filling. Unfold the dough carefully and trim the edges so there is a 1-inch overhang. Moisten the top and bottom crusts where they meet with a little water, then turn the top crust edge under the bottom. Crimp the edge decoratively as described for the single crust in step 6 above.

9. To give the top crust an attractive finish, brush it lightly with water, egg white, or milk and, if desired, sprinkle with a little granulated sugar.

10. Bake the pie in the center or lower third of a preheated oven, placing fruit pies on a baking sheet to catch spills from a bubbling filling.

11. To keep pie crust edges from overbrowning, check after the first 20 or 25 minutes and then cover the edges with strips of aluminum foil if necessary.

12. Cool the pie on a wire rack to the desired temperature for serving.

✶✶✶✶✶✶✶✶✶✶✶✶✶✶✶✶✶✶✶✶✶✶✶✶✶✶✶✶✶✶✶✶✶✶✶✶

CLASSIC PIE CRUST

One of the most important recipes to have in your culinary repertoire is a versatile pie crust, one suitable for everything from cream pies like lemon meringue to fruit pies like Old-Fashioned Apple Pie. This is made with vegetable shortening, for a crust that is light, flaky, tender yet crisp. Butter, on the other hand, makes a flavorful, rich, firm but crumbly dough. If you love butter you can use a combination of the two here—say, ½ cup shortening and ¼ cup butter—for a flavorful, sturdy yet flaky crust.

Once you've mastered this easy crust, you'll never find yourself at a loss. Make up an extra batch and keep it well wrapped in the freezer for last-minute emergencies.

2 cups all-purpose flour
1 teaspoon salt
¾ cup solid vegetable shortening,
    cut into small pieces
4 to 5 tablespoons ice water

1. Combine the flour and salt in a food processor, and pulse on and off to mix. Add the shortening and pulse the machine on and off until the mixture resembles coarse meal.

2. With the machine running, trickle in 4 tablespoons of ice water through the feed tube, just until the dough gathers together. (If the dough seems dry, add up to 1 tablespoon more

water, ½ teaspoon at a time.) Remove the dough from the machine and divide it in half. Flatten each half with the palm of your hand to form a thick disk. Wrap the disks in plastic wrap and chill in the refrigerator for at least 1 hour.

3. Remove one disk of dough from the refrigerator. Unwrap it and roll it out on a lightly floured work surface or between two sheets of waxed paper to form a circle about ⅛ inch thick and 2 inches larger than the pie plate. Work quickly, as the dough can become sticky. Use a spatula to help lift the dough and fold it loosely in half, then into quarters. Gently transfer it to the pie plate, centering the corner of the dough in the center of the plate. Open up the dough and press it lightly into the plate to fit. If the dough should tear, just press it gently together. Trim the dough, leaving a 1-inch overhang. If making a single-crust pie, turn the edge under and flute it decoratively.

4. Repeat the rolling process for a top crust, or for another bottom crust. The circle for a top crust should be 9 inches for an 8-inch pie and 10 inches for a 9-inch pie.

5. Follow the individual pie recipes for filling and baking.

Makes enough for an 8- or 9-inch double-crust pie

NO MORE WEEPY PIE SHELLS

—❧—

To keep the bottom crust of fruit pies from weeping and becoming soggy, lightly beat 1 large egg white with 1 tablespoon of water and brush it over the bottom of the uncooked shell before adding the filling.

BUTTERY PIE CRUST

★ ★ ★

This buttery dough creates a rich, tasty crust that really sets off fruit pies. I combine the ingredients by hand to prevent overworking the dough.

3 cups all-purpose flour
⅛ teaspoon salt
¾ cup plus 2 tablespoons (1¾ sticks) unsalted butter, cold, cut into small pieces
1 large egg
6 tablespoons ice water

1. Combine the flour and salt in a large bowl. Add the butter and mix together with your fingertips or a pastry cutter until the mixture resembles coarse meal.

2. Mix the egg with the water in a small bowl. Toss the mixture gently with the butter mixture just until the dough comes together; do not overwork it. Divide the dough in half. Flatten each half with the palm of your hand to form a thick disk. Wrap them in plastic wrap and chill in the refrigerator for at least 1 hour.

3. Remove one disk of dough from the refrigerator. Unwrap it and roll it out on a lightly floured work surface or between two sheets of waxed paper to form a circle about ⅛ inch thick and 2 inches larger than the pie plate. Work quickly, as the dough can become sticky. Use a spatula to help lift the dough, and fold it loosely in half, then into quarters. Gently transfer it to the pie plate, centering the corner of the dough in the center of the plate. Open up the dough and press it lightly into the plate to fit. If the dough should tear, just press it gently together. Trim the dough, leaving a 1-inch overhang. If making a single-crust pie, turn the edge under and flute it decoratively.

4. Repeat the rolling process for a top crust or for another bottom crust. The circle of a top crust should be 9 inches for an 8-inch pie and 10 inches for a 9-inch pie.

5. Follow the individual pie recipes for filling and baking.

Makes enough for an 8- or 9-inch double-crust pie

SWEET PIE CRUST

★ ★ ★

This crust, made with both butter (for rich flavor and sturdiness) and shortening (for flakiness), and sweetened with a bit of sugar, is another basic to keep on file for all your dessert pies or tarts. A hint of cinnamon or allspice, no more than ¼ teaspoon, can be added along with the dry ingredients to complement different fillings. Roll the crust in a cool spot in your kitchen, as a warm area or surface will make the dough sticky and difficult to manage.

*2 cups all-purpose
    flour*
2 tablespoons sugar
1 teaspoon salt
*½ cup (1 stick) unsalted butter, cold,
    cut into small pieces*
⅓ cup solid vegetable shortening, cold
5 to 6 tablespoons ice water

1. Combine the flour, sugar, and salt in a food processor, and pulse on and off to mix. Add the butter and shortening and pulse the machine on and off until the mixture resembles coarse meal.

2. With the machine running, trickle about 5 tablespoons of ice water through the feed tube just until the dough gathers together. (If the dough seems dry, add up to 1 tablespoon more water, ½ teaspoon at a time.) Remove the dough from the machine and divide it in half. Flatten each half with the palm of your hand to form a thick disk. Wrap the disks in plastic wrap and chill in the refrigerator for at least 1 hour.

3. Remove one disk of dough from the refrigerator. Unwrap it and roll it out on a lightly floured work surface or between two sheets of waxed paper to form a circle about ⅛ inch thick and 2 inches larger than the pie plate. Work quickly, as the dough can become sticky. Use a spatula to help lift the dough, and fold it loosely in half, then into quarters. Gently transfer it to the pie plate, centering the corner of the dough in the center of the plate. Open up the dough and press it lightly into the plate to fit. If the dough should tear, just press it gently together.

Trim the dough, leaving a 1-inch overhang. If making a single-crust pie, turn the edge under and flute it decoratively.

4. Repeat the rolling process for a top crust or for another bottom crust. The circle for a top crust should be 9 inches for an 8-inch pie and 10 inches for a 9-inch pie.

5. Follow the individual pie recipes for filling and baking.

Makes enough for an 8- or 9-inch double-crust pie

Cakes & Cookies

When I was small, one of the high points of each year was our elementary school carnival. The students played a version of Musical Chairs, vying for the opportunity to select from the homemade goodies loaded on a long table. There were high angel-food cakes with pastel glazes and sturdy chocolate layer cakes, thickly spread with frosting. All the kids loved them, but I think I loved them *more*.

We grownups relish cake just as much as children do, though we eat it with less abandon. The most American of recipes tend to be our favorites: devil's food, coconut, Lady Baltimore, New York–style cheesecake (the world's richest), Boston cream pie, and brownies – of course, brownies.

You'll find many native cookies in this section, too. Chocolate chips were born in the U.S.A., by happy accident. I've got oatmeal cookies, nicely jazzed with dried cherries, Southern pecan sandwich cookies, and campfire s'mores (from scratch!). For a real taste of the past, try the gingerbread cookies from Williamsburg, Virginia—a recipe that's been with us since Patrick Henry's day.

LADY BALTIMORE CAKE

★ ★ ★

This glamorous cake, said to have been a specialty of the Lady Baltimore Tea Room in Charleston, South Carolina, in the late 1800s, remains a popular dessert today, with very good reason. Immortalized in Owen Wister's 1906 book *Lady Baltimore*, moist white cake layers, filled with pecans, figs, and raisins, are encased in a billowy frosting made from egg whites and a sugar syrup. It bakes up into an altogether lovely confection, but a word to the wise: For making the frosting, you will need a candy thermometer, and remember—organization is critical here!

CAKE
3 cups cake flour
1 tablespoon baking powder
½ teaspoon salt
1 cup (2 sticks) unsalted butter, at room temperature
2 cups sugar
1 teaspoon pure vanilla extract
1 cup milk
8 large egg whites, at room temperature
Pinch of salt

FROSTING
4 large egg whites, at room
*   temperature*
Pinch of salt
1½ cups sugar
½ cup water
¼ teaspoon cream of tartar
2 teaspoons pure vanilla extract

FILLING
1 cup coarsely chopped pecans
½ cup chopped dried figs
½ cup dark raisins

1. Preheat the oven to 350°F. Grease three 9-inch round cake pans. Line the bottom with waxed or parchment paper and grease the paper. Dust the bottom and sides of the pans with flour, tapping out any excess.

2. Prepare the cake: Sift together the flour, baking powder, and salt. Set aside.

3. Beat the butter and the sugar in a large bowl with an electric mixer at medium speed until creamy. Add the vanilla. Add the flour mixture alternately with the milk and beat until well combined.

4. In a separate bowl, using clean beaters, beat the egg whites with the pinch of salt at medium-high speed until they hold soft peaks. Stir one third of the whites into the cake batter until well blended. Fold the remaining whites into the batter with a rubber spatula until just combined; do not overmix. Scrape the batter evenly into the prepared pans and bake in the center of the oven until a wooden pick inserted in the center of the layers comes out clean, 25 to 30 minutes. Cool the layers in the pans on a rack for 20 minutes, then turn them out into the rack, carefully peel off the paper, and cool completely.

5. Prepare the frosting: Place the egg whites in a large bowl with the pinch of salt, then beat with the electric mixer at medium-high speed until the whites hold soft peaks. Set aside.

6. Combine the sugar, water, and cream of tartar in a heavy saucepan. Bring to a boil over medium-high heat and cook until a candy thermometer registers 245°F (just past soft ball and on its way to firm ball). Remove from the heat immediately and, with the mixer at

medium speed, slowly drizzle the syrup into the beaten egg whites until it has been completely mixed in. (Do not drizzle the syrup directly into the beaters, as they will spin the sugar onto the sides of the bowl, where it will harden.) Increase the speed to medium-high and continue beating until the frosting has completely cooled, 7 minutes. Mix in the vanilla.

7. Prepare the filling: Place one third of the frosting in another bowl and combine with the pecans, figs, and raisins.

8. Assemble the cake: Place one cake layer on a serving platter. Spread it with half of the filling and top with another layer. Spread this layer with the remaining filling and top with the remaining layer. Cover the sides and top of the cake with the remaining frosting.

Serves 12

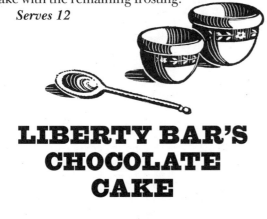

LIBERTY BAR'S CHOCOLATE CAKE

★ ★ ★

When Dwight Hobart, owner of the Liberty Bar in San Antonio, opened the restaurant in 1985, he wanted a great chocolate cake on his menu, so his mother, Minerva, pointed him in the direction of her friend, Virginia Green of Pampa, Texas. Sure enough, Virginia's cake turned out to be just what Dwight was looking for, and onto the menu it went—aptly named Virginia Green's Chocolate Cake. It's simply the best chocolate cake—dense and rich—I've ever tasted.

The cake batter is very easy to put together in the food processor as long as all of the ingredients are measured in advance. The frosting, however, requires careful attention, as it must boil for precisely 9 minutes. Use a large saucepan and watch the heat so that the frosting base does not boil over. Allow plenty of time for the frosting to cool and thicken before you assemble the cake. Then, go to town!

CHOCOLATE FROSTING
2 cups sugar
2 cups evaporated milk
11 ounces unsweetened chocolate,
*   cut into small pieces*
1 cup (2 sticks) unsalted butter, cold,
*   cut into 1-inch cubes*
1 teaspoon pure vanilla extract

CAKE BATTER
2¼ cups cake flour
1½ teaspoons baking powder
1 teaspoon baking soda
¼ teaspoon salt
1⅓ cups unsweetened cocoa powder
1 cup boiling water
3 large eggs, at room temperature
1 cup granulated sugar
1 cup (packed) light brown sugar
¾ cup (1½ sticks) unsalted butter,
*   at room temperature, cut up in*
*   small pieces*
1¼ cups buttermilk, at room temperature

1. Prepare the chocolate frosting: Combine the sugar and evaporated milk in a large saucepan (3 quarts is best) and bring to a boil over medium heat. When the mixture reaches a boil, continue to boil for *exactly* 9 minutes *without stirring*, watching carefully that the pot does not boil over. Remove the pan from the heat and add the chocolate, butter, and vanilla. Stir with a wooden spoon until the mixture is smooth. Cool to room temperature, cover, and refrigerate for 2 to 3 hours or overnight.

2. Preheat the oven to 350°F. Grease two 9-inch round cake pans. Line the bottoms with waxed or parchment paper, and grease the paper. Dust the bottom and sides of the pans with flour, tapping out any excess.

3. Prepare the cake: Sift the flour, baking powder, baking soda, and salt together. Set aside.

4. Sift the cocoa powder and place it in a 2-cup glass measure. Gradually stir in the boiling water, continuing to stir until thoroughly blended and smooth. Set aside.

5. Place the eggs and both the sugars in a food processor and process for 1 minute. Stop the machine and scrape down the sides of the bowl. Process for 30 seconds more, then add the butter and process for 1 minute. Stop the machine, scrape down the sides of the bowl, and process 30 seconds more.

6. Add the buttermilk and pulse the machine on and off four times. Stop the machine, scrape down the sides of the bowl, and pulse the machine on and off four more times. Add the cocoa mixture and pulse the machine on and off four times. Scrape down the sides of the bowl. Add the flour mixture and pulse the machine on and off four times. Scrape down the sides of the bowl and pulse the machine a final four times. Scrape the batter into the prepared pans and bake in the center of the oven until a wooden pick inserted in the center of the layers comes out clean, 35 minutes. Cool the layers in the pans on a rack for 10 minutes, then turn them out onto the rack, and cool completely.

Carefully peel off the paper.

7. Remove the frosting from the refrigerator at least 30 minutes before spreading it on the cake and stir it well.

8. Assemble the cake: Place one layer on a serving plate (even the top off with a serrated knife, if necessary) and spread with some of the frosting. Top with the remaining layer and use the remaining frosting to cover the sides and top of the cake.

Serves 10 to 12

THE QUEEN OF COCONUT CAKES

★ ★ ★

This coconut cake, Ark Restaurants's version of a Paul Prudhomme classic, is such a delicious dessert, and with its three yummy layers of golden cake and lots of coconut filling and cream cheese frosting, it makes a stunning presentation. There are four components to the cake: the filling, cake layers, frosting, and syrup, which can be made over the course of two days if you don't have time to do it all at once. The filling needs time to thicken up in the refrigerator, so make it as far ahead as possible.

FILLING

1¼ cups heavy (or whipping) cream
¾ cup granulated sugar
2 tablespoons coconut cream (Coco Lopez)
1 tablespoon cornstarch
1 tablespoon milk
½ cup (1 stick) unsalted butter, at room
    temperature
1 cup shredded coconut

CAKE

3 cups all-purpose flour
1 tablespoon baking powder
¼ teaspoon salt
1½ cups granulated sugar
4 large eggs
¾ cup (1½ sticks) unsalted butter, at room
    temperature, cut up in small pieces
1 cup milk
1 tablespoon pure vanilla extract

FROSTING

6 ounces cream cheese, at room temperature
½ cup (1 stick) unsalted butter, at room temperature
¼ teaspoon salt
1 pound confectioners' sugar
3 tablespoons milk
1 tablespoon vanilla extract

SYRUP

1 cup granulated sugar
1 cup water
¼ teaspoon pure vanilla extract

½ cup shredded coconut, for garnish

1. Prepare the filling: Place the cream, granulated sugar, and coconut cream in a heavy saucepan over medium heat and bring it to a simmer. Stir the cornstarch and the milk together in a small bowl until there are no lumps. Whisk the cornstarch mixture into the simmering cream until smooth and cook, stirring, until slightly thickened, 3 minutes. Add the butter and the coconut and continue cooking, stirring, 3 minutes more. Remove from the heat and cool to room temperature, then refrigerate until thickened, about 2 hours. Keep refrigerated until ready to assemble the cake.

2. Preheat the oven to 350°F. Grease three 9-inch round cake pans. Line the bottoms with waxed or parchment paper, and grease the paper. Dust the bottom and sides of the pans with flour, tapping out any excess.

3. Prepare the cake: Sift the flour, baking powder, and salt together and set aside.

4. Beat the granulated sugar and the eggs in a large bowl with an electric mixer at medium speed for 1 minute. Gradually add the butter, milk, and vanilla and continue beating for 2 minutes more. Reduce the speed to low, add the flour mixture, and beat for 1 minute.

5. Scrape the batter evenly into the prepared pans and bake in the center of the oven until a wooden pick inserted in the center of the layers comes out clean, 20 minutes. Cool the layers in the pans on a rack for 20 minutes, then turn them out onto the rack, carefully peel off the paper, and cool completely.

6. Prepare the frosting: Place the cream cheese and the butter in a bowl and beat with the mixer at medium speed until creamy. Add the salt, confectioners' sugar, milk, and vanilla and mix until smooth and soft. Set aside.

7. Prepare the syrup: Combine the granulated sugar, water, and vanilla in a heavy saucepan and bring to a boil. Boil for 3 minutes, stirring occasionally. Remove from the heat and use a pastry brush to brush the top of each cake

layer with the syrup, just enough for a light imbibing—you don't have to use all the syrup.

8. Assemble the cake: Place one cake layer on a serving platter. Spread it with half of the filling and top with another layer. Spread this layer with the remaining filling and top with the remaining layer. Cover the sides and top of the cake with the frosting, then sprinkle the top with the shredded coconut.

Serves 12

★★

THE FINAL FINISH

—❦—

*f*or some people, cakes are just the vehicle for frostings—never can they be too rich. Frostings are thick and suitable for between layers, as well as on the sides and top of the cakes. Icings (including the special chocolate icing called *ganache*) and glazes are thinner coatings, with icings a bit thicker than glazes. Icings will set on the cake quickly and harden as the sugar dries. Glazes will also set but will not harden because they have less sugar. When icing or glazing a cake, protect the platter from drips by cutting four 12 x 3-inch strips of waxed paper or foil and inserting one long side of each strip under the edges of the cake on all sides, so the plate is covered. Once done, remove the strips by pulling each toward you from one long end, turning the platter to position each strip for removal. Once the topping on a cake is set, place it under a domed cake cover until ready to serve.

To Frost a Layer Cake

*P*lace the cooled bottom layer upside down on the cake plate so the flattest surface is on top. If you are working with split layers, the cut side should be up. Brush off any crumbs on or around the cake.

Spread the bottom layer evenly with frosting or filling (about ¾ cup of either for an 8-inch cake). You should never spread the frosting as if you're buttering toast (hard, downward strokes) because you will inevitably incorporate crumbs into your frosting. Instead, use a thin metal frosting spatula to gently push the frosting where you want it to go. Once the bottom layer is frosted, position the top layer, right side up (for whole and split cakes), and press it down lightly.

The sides of the cake should be frosted first, the top of the cake last. To finish most cakes, use the spatula to spread the frosting onto the sides with smooth back-and-forth strokes. Finish with smooth gliding strokes across the top of the cake. Let the frosting set for 30 minutes after finishing.

To Ice or Glaze a Cake

*T*o apply an icing or a glaze to a cake, spoon or pour a generous amount of icing or glaze over the center of the cake, then allow it to drip down the top and sides of the cake. Use the back of a spoon or thin spatula to spread it over thin areas. Stop spreading once the icing or glaze begins to set so that the smooth finish will not be lost.

★★

STEPHAN PYLES'S HEAVEN AND HELL CAKE

★ ★

Stephan Pyles, chef-owner of the famous Star Canyon in Dallas, Texas, serves this spectacular cake at his restaurant. If you always save room for dessert, then I wholeheartedly recommend this one! It is some work of art, and the best word for it is "statuesque"—four layers of cake, two each of devil's food and angel food, sandwiched together with peanut butter mousse and thickly iced with a creamy milk chocolate ganache. You'll want to allow plenty of time to make the cake, but believe me, it is worth every minute. If you have a heavy-duty mixer, now is the time to pull it out, as it will make the job go more quickly. However, an electric hand mixer will also work.

You must be sure that the ganache is chilled until it is thick enough to frost the sides of the cake. It is also necessary to let the cake chill for about 2 hours before slicing so that the layers hold together well. Use a warm, wet knife for the honors. The very first slice may have to be larger than the others so you can get into the rest of the cake to slice neatly.

ANGEL FOOD CAKE
⅔ cup cake flour
1 cup confectioners' sugar
1 cup egg whites (7 or 8 large eggs),
    at room temperature
Pinch of salt
1 teaspoon cream of tartar
⅔ cup granulated sugar
1 teaspoon pure vanilla extract
½ teaspoon pure almond extract

DEVIL'S FOOD CAKE
½ cup unsweetened cocoa powder
1 cup strongly brewed coffee
½ cup vegetable shortening
1½ cups granulated sugar
1 teaspoon pure vanilla extract
2 large eggs
1½ cups cake flour
1 teaspoon baking soda
¾ teaspoon salt
¼ teaspoon baking powder

PEANUT BUTTER MOUSSE
12 ounces cream cheese, at room temperature
1¾ cups confectioners' sugar
2 cups creamy peanut butter, at room temperature
2 tablespoons heavy (or whipping) cream

CHOCOLATE GANACHE
2 cups heavy (or whipping) cream
2 pounds milk chocolate, coarsely chopped

1. Preheat the oven to 375°F. Line the bottom of a 10-inch round cake pan with waxed or parchment paper. Do not grease the pan or the paper.

2. Prepare the angel food cake: Sift together the flour and the confectioners' sugar. Set aside.

3. Place the egg whites in a bowl and beat with an electric mixer at low speed while adding the salt and the cream of tartar. Continue beating until soft peaks form, 1 minute. Increase the speed to medium, and add the granulated sugar to the egg whites, tablespoon by tablespoon, until all is incorporated, then continue to beat 1½ minutes more. When the egg whites have stiff peaks, mix in the vanilla and almond extracts.

4. Sprinkle half of the flour mixture over the egg whites and fold it in with a large rubber spatula. Sprinkle the egg whites with the remaining flour mixture and fold it in. Do not overmix or the egg whites will deflate. Gently spoon the mixture into the prepared pan, mounding slightly in the center, and bake in the center of the oven until golden brown, 40 to 50 minutes. Do not overbake or the cake will sink in the center. Cool the cake in the pan on a rack for 30 minutes, then turn it out onto the rack, carefully peel off the paper, and cool completely.

5. Prepare the devil's food cake: Reduce the oven temperature to 350°F. Butter a 10-inch round cake pan. Line the bottom with waxed or parchment paper, and butter the paper. Dust the bottom and sides of the pan lightly with flour. Sift the cocoa powder into a bowl. Drizzle with the coffee and whisk the mixture until smooth. Set aside.

WHIP IT GOOD

Since many of my cake recipes call for beaten egg whites, here are some tips for getting them whipped to perfection.

• The purpose of beating egg whites is to incorporate as much air as possible. If you have good arm strength, the best method involves a copper bowl and a large balloon whisk. Most home cooks use a mixer with the whisk attachment, which is fine.

• Remember egg whites will expand up to six times their natural volume. Choose your bowl accordingly.

• Be sure the bowl and whisk you are using are dry and clean; any amount of moisture will prevent the egg whites from whipping up properly.

• When separating an egg white from the yolk, break the egg in half, cup your hand over a bowl and place the egg in your cupped hand. Let the white slip through your fingers and you will be left with a perfect whole yolk. Passing the egg yolk from shell half to shell half is a riskier method, since there is more of a chance of the yolk breaking and contaminating the whites.

• Let egg whites come to room temperature for maximum volume when whipped.

• A pinch of salt helps break up the gelatinous texture of the egg whites; a pinch of cream of tartar helps to stabilize them.

• Beating whites to soft peaks means the whites will flop gently over when the beater is removed. Stiff peaks will hold their shape when the whisk is lifted.

6. Combine the shortening, granulated sugar, vanilla, and eggs in a large bowl and beat with the electric mixer for 2 minutes at medium speed. Sift together the flour, baking soda, salt, and baking powder and add to the shortening mixture alternately with the cocoa mixture. Beat until all is incorporated, then pour the batter into the prepared pan, and bake in the center of the oven until a wooden pick inserted in the center of the cake comes out just clean, 30 minutes. Cool the cake in the pan on a rack for 30 minutes, then turn it out onto the rack, carefully peel off the waxed paper, and cool completely.

7. Prepare the peanut butter mousse: Beat the cream cheese in a large bowl with the electric mixer at medium speed until it is light and creamy. Gradually beat in the confectioners' sugar and then the peanut butter. Add the cream and continue beating until thoroughly incorporated and fluffy. Set aside.

8. Prepare the chocolate ganache: Bring the cream to a boil over medium-high heat in a heavy saucepan. Remove from the heat, add the chocolate, and stir until smooth. Whisk the mixture to combine thoroughly and then set aside to cool to room temperature.

9. Assemble the cake: Carefully slice the completely cooled cakes in half horizontally with a long serrated knife so you have four layers in all. Place one of the devil's food layers, cut side up, on a cake plate and spread with one third of the peanut butter mousse. Top with an angel food layer, again cut side up, and spread with half the remaining peanut butter mousse. Add another cake layer and the remaining mousse, then top with the final cake layer.

10. Whisk the chocolate ganache and pour it over the top and sides of the cake. Use an icing spatula to spread the ganache to cover completely. Chill the cake in the refrigerator for at least 2 hours before serving. Serve chilled.

Serves 12 to 14

"SCHOOL'S OUT" STRAWBERRY SHORTCAKE

★ ★ ★

If you consider yourself a strawberry shortcake aficionado, don't think you've eaten the best, until you've tasted this version. I was visiting Seattle when seafood consultant Jon Rowley invited me to his daughter Megan's fifth grade graduation from Perkins Elementary School. After the ceremony, I joined the kids while they picked strawberries. Then it was off to a great party, one given every year for the children at school's end, where Jon taught us all the secret of his great shortcake. It begins with great biscuits, and his are baked and donated to the party by Sally McArthur, executive chef at Anthony's, a seafood restaurant on Pier 66 in Puget Sound. Jon Rowley likes his berries with three textures for an ideal filling. First, some of the berries are coarsely sliced, then combined with more berries, these gently crushed. Just before serving, freshly sliced berries are mixed in. After eating several helpings, I understand why he is not the only one who thinks he has perfected the best strawberry shortcake.

3 pints ripe strawberries, lightly rinsed,
*   patted dry, and hulled*
¼ cup plus 1 tablespoon sugar
2 cups heavy (or whipping) cream
6 Sally McArthur's Shortcake Biscuits
*   (recipe follows)*

1. Slice 1 pint of the strawberries (irregularity is preferred) and reserve in a medium-size bowl.

2. Place the berries from the second pint between the palms of your hands, and lightly crush them by gently rubbing your palms together. The object is to break the berries and release the juice but not to smash them. The result should be torn chunks.

3. Combine the crushed berries in the bowl with the sliced berries and stir in the ¼ cup sugar. Let stand for 1 hour.

4. Just before serving time, slice the remaining pint of berries into the berry mixture, reserving 6 small whole perfect berries for garnish. Whip the cream with the 1 tablespoon of sugar until it holds soft peaks.

5. To serve, split the shortcakes by cutting off the top third of each biscuit. Place the bottoms on six dessert plates and top each with approximately ⅓ cup of the prepared berries and juice and a spoonful of whipped cream. Cover with the top of the shortcake. Spoon over more berries and more cream, then garnish with a reserved whole strawberry and drizzle with strawberry juice. Serve immediately.

Serves 6

Sally McArthur's Shortcake Biscuits

★

Sally McArthur, executive chef of Anthony's Restaurant in Seattle, uses self-rising flour in her rustic dropped biscuits to avoid the aluminum undertaste baking powder can sometimes give. For the lightest biscuits, do not overwork the dough.

2 cups self-rising flour
2½ tablespoons sugar
⅛ teaspoon salt
½ cup (1 stick) unsalted butter, cold, cut into small pieces
¾ cup milk
2 tablespoons light cream

1. Preheat the oven to 400°F. Grease a baking sheet.

2. Combine the flour, sugar, and salt in a bowl. Add the butter and rub it into the flour mixture with your fingertips until it resembles coarse meal. Stir in the milk until a very soft dough is formed. Do not overwork.

3. Drop the dough in six equal portions onto the prepared baking sheet. Lightly pat each portion into a round and lightly brush the tops of the rounds with the cream.

4. Bake the biscuits in the center of the oven for 15 to 20 minutes, or until golden brown. Cool on a wire rack.

Makes 6

JUNIOR'S FAMOUS CHEESECAKE

★ ★ ★

Junior's, the Brooklyn landmark restaurant that has been synonymous with overstuffed deli sandwiches, cheeseburgers, blintzes, and skyscraper desserts since 1949, is most famous for "the best cheesecake in Brooklyn . . . New York . . . USA . . . the world!" Although Junior's cheesecake at one time faced stiff competition from Lindy's, Reuben's, and the Brass Rail, all popular New York establishments with creamy cheesecakes, Junior's secret weapon was

German baker Egil Peterson, who raised Junior's cheesecake to an art form. (Mr. Peterson retired in the late 1960s.)

The Rosen family, owners of Junior's, were kind enough to share their famous recipe with me. While Junior's original version uses a sponge-cake base as the crust, I've simplified the recipe by beginning with a graham cracker crust, which is a snap to put together right in the pan. As the top of the cheesecake will get very brown during baking, I suggest covering it with aluminum foil during the last 15 minutes of baking to prevent burning.

This is the best cheesecake you'll ever taste! If you ever need a great food gift, Junior's ships its cakes anywhere in the continental U.S.A. Just call (800) 958-6467.

CRUST
1½ cups graham cracker crumbs
6 tablespoons (¾ stick) unsalted butter, melted

FILLING
1 cup less 2 tablespoons sugar
3 tablespoons cornstarch
1 pound 14 ounces cream cheese, at room
*   temperature*
1 extra-large egg
½ cup heavy (or whipping) cream
¾ teaspoon pure vanilla extract

1. Preheat the oven to 350°F.
2. Prepare the crust: Combine the graham cracker crumbs and melted butter in a 9½-inch springform pan and mix well. Press the mixture evenly over the bottom and 1 inch up the sides of the pan. Bake the crust, in the center of the oven, for 10 minutes, then cool completely on a rack. Increase the oven temperature to 450°F.
3. Prepare the filling: Combine the sugar and the cornstarch in a large bowl. Add the cream cheese and beat with an electric mixer at medium speed until smooth and creamy.

4. Add the egg and beat well. Add the cream gradually, beating until the mixture is smooth. Beat in the vanilla.
5. Scrape the filling into the prepared crust. Bake in the center of the oven until the top is browned and the filling is set around the edges, 40 minutes. (It may be necessary to cover the cheesecake with aluminum foil for the last 15 minutes of baking if it is overbrowning.) The center will still be slightly loose. Cool to room temperature, in the pan, on a rack. Then place the cheesecake in the refrigerator for at least 3 hours or overnight before removing the sides of the pan and serving.
Serves 12

CHERRY-STUDDED POUND CAKE

★ ★ ★

Lush and buttery with the added delight of moist summer cherries, this cake is delectable with a cup of tea, especially one with a natural orange scent. A scoop of "Hot" Red Cherry Sorbet in a pretty glass goblet alongside may gild the lily, but it's a gilding nobody will mind.

1 cup (2 sticks) unsalted butter, at room
*   temperature*
1 cup sugar
4 large eggs, separated
1 teaspoon pure vanilla extract
½ cup sour cream
1½ cups all-purpose flour
1 teaspoon baking powder
Pinch of salt
1¾ cups pitted fresh
*   Bing cherries*

1. Preheat the oven to 350°F. Lightly grease a 9 x 5 x 2¾-inch loaf pan. Line the bottom with a piece of waxed or parchment paper and grease the paper. Dust the bottom and sides of the pan with flour, tapping out any excess.

2. Beat the butter and the sugar in a large bowl with an electric mixer at medium speed until light and fluffy. Add the egg yolks and the vanilla and beat until smooth. Add the sour cream and beat until blended in.

3. Sift the flour, baking powder, and salt together and add all but 2 tablespoons of the mixture to the batter in three batches, stirring with a wooden spoon until just combined. Toss the remaining 2 tablespoons flour mixture with the cherries in a bowl and set aside.

4. Using clean beaters, beat the egg whites in a separate bowl with the mixer at medium speed until they hold soft peaks. Stir one third of the egg whites into the batter until combined, then fold in the remaining egg whites with a rubber spatula until just combined. Do not overmix the batter.

5. Fold the cherries into the batter, then scrape the batter into the prepared pan. Bake the cake for 35 minutes, then reduce the oven temperature to 325°F and bake until golden brown and a wooden pick inserted in the center comes out just clean, 45 minutes more. Cool the cake in the pan on a wire rack for 15 minutes, then turn it out onto the rack, peel off the paper, and cool completely.

Makes 1 loaf; serves 8 to 10

CHOCOLATE SILK CAKE

★ ★ ★

When I decided to make this cake, I wanted it as rich as possible, with buttery depth in every bite. There's no doubt that I've met my goal.

While the cake is not difficult to make, there are a few important tips to follow. For the smoothest texture, be sure that the chocolate is cool before adding it to the egg mixture. Once the dry ingredients are added, do not overwork them or the cake will be tough. Stir until they just disappear into the batter.

For an extra sinfully delicious treat, serve the cake warm with heavy cream or your favorite ice cream.

8 ounces bittersweet chocolate, broken into
*   small pieces*
1 cup (2 sticks) unsalted butter, at room
*   temperature*
1 cup sugar
4 large eggs
1 teaspoon pure vanilla extract
½ cup sour cream
1½ cups all-purpose flour
1 teaspoon baking powder
Pinch of salt

1. Preheat the oven to 350°F. Lightly grease a 9 x 5 x 2¾-inch loaf pan. Line the bottom with a piece of waxed or parchment paper and grease the paper. Dust the bottom and sides of the pan with flour, tapping out any excess.

2. Melt the chocolate in a small saucepan over very low heat, stirring until smooth. Set aside to cool.

3. Beat the butter and the sugar in a large bowl with an electric mixer at medium speed until light and fluffy. Add the eggs, one at a time,

beating well after each addition. Add the vanilla and the sour cream and beat well. Stir in the cooled chocolate.

4. Sift the flour, baking powder, and salt over the batter and stir it in until just combined.

5. Scrape the batter into the prepared pan. Bake in the center of the oven until a wooden pick inserted in the center comes out just clean, 1 hour to 1 hour 10 minutes. Cool the cake in the pan on a wire rack for 15 minutes, then turn it out onto the rack, carefully peel off the paper, and cool completely.

Makes 1 loaf; serves 8 to 10

BOSTON CREAM PIE (OR CAKE?)

★ ★ ★

During the mid 1800s, Boston's Parker House Hotel was a culinary hotbed of creativity, giving us everything from those meltingly soft Parker House rolls to Boston cream pie. Whether this luscious confection is a cake or a pie is inconsequential, although I see it as a cake. Once I bite into the double layers of moist yellow cake, rich custard filling, and heavenly chocolate glaze, all controversy comes to an immediate halt. Who cares about the name when it is so, so sublime!

CAKE
1 cup cake flour
1 teaspoon baking powder
½ teaspoon salt
½ cup (1 stick) unsalted butter, at room temperature
1 cup granulated sugar
1½ teaspoons pure vanilla extract
1 tablespoon finely grated
*   orange zest*
2 large eggs
½ cup milk

CUSTARD FILLING
3 large egg yolks
6 tablespoons granulated sugar
3 tablespoons all-purpose flour
1½ cups milk
1½ tablespoons unsalted butter
1½ tablespoons fresh orange juice
½ teaspoon pure vanilla extract

CHOCOLATE GLAZE
4 ounces semisweet chocolate, cut into small pieces
2 tablespoons confectioners' sugar
¼ cup heavy (or whipping) cream

1. Preheat the oven to 350°F. Lightly grease an 8-inch springform pan. Line the bottom with waxed or parchment paper, then grease the paper and flour the bottom and sides of the pan, tapping out any excess.

2. Prepare the cake: Sift the flour, baking powder, and salt together and set aside.

3. Beat the butter and the granulated sugar in a large bowl with an electric mixer at medium speed until light and fluffy. Add the vanilla and orange zest and beat well. Add the eggs, one at a time, beating well after each addition.

4. Add the flour mixture, alternately with the milk, at low speed, beating well after each addition. Scrape the batter into the prepared pan and bake in the center of the oven until the cake is golden and a wooden pick inserted in the center comes out just clean, 40 minutes. Cool the cake in the pan on a rack for 30 minutes, then turn it out onto the rack, carefully peel off the paper, and cool completely.

5. Prepare the custard filling: Whisk the egg yolks in a small bowl. Add the granulated sugar and the flour and whisk well to make a smooth paste.

6. Scald the milk in a medium-size heavy saucepan. Remove from the heat. Slowly whisk ½ cup of the scalded milk into the egg mixture until smooth. Whisking constantly, slowly pour this mixture back into the scalded milk and continue whisking until smooth. Return the pan to medium heat and bring the mixture to a boil, stirring constantly with a wooden spoon. Once the mixture comes to a boil, boil for 1 minute, stirring until thickened and a finger drawn across the back of the spoon holds a trail. Remove from the heat and stir in the butter, orange juice, and vanilla until smooth. Pour the custard into a bowl. Lay a piece of plastic wrap directly on the custard's surface (to prevent a skin from forming), and cool to room temperature.

7. Assemble the cake: Using a long serrated knife, split the completely cooled cake in half horizontally so you have two layers. Place the bottom layer, cut side up, on a serving plate.

8. Stir the custard until smooth, then spoon it evenly over the cake layer on the plate. Cover with the remaining cake layer, cut side down.

9. Prepare the glaze: Melt the chocolate in a small saucepan over very low heat, stirring until smooth. Remove from the heat and stir in the confectioners' sugar and cream until smooth. Slowly pour the chocolate mixture over the top of the cake, allowing it to drip and run down the sides. Use a spatula to smooth the top of the cake, if necessary, but not the sides; the icing should run down these. Set the cake aside for at least 1 hour before serving.

Serves 8 to 10

BLUEBERRY CORNMEAL CAKE

★ ★ ★

This lovely, uncomplicated cake is splendid in summer, when blueberries are in season. It is delicious at teatime with a tall glass of iced tea, or as dessert to end a light summer dinner. Don't be hasty to taste; let the cake sit for 1 hour to settle in. Vanilla or cinnamon-flavored ice cream tops it off to perfection.

1 cup plus 2 tablespoons self-rising flour
¾ cup fine cornmeal
⅛ teaspoon salt
¾ cup (1½ sticks) unsalted butter,
  at room temperature
⅔ cup plus 3 tablespoons
  granulated sugar
1 large egg
1 pint blueberries, picked over,
  lightly rinsed, and patted dry
1 tablespoon confectioners' sugar, for dusting

1. Preheat the oven to 375°F.

2. Sift the flour, cornmeal, and salt together in a medium-size bowl, and set aside.

3. Beat the butter and the ⅔ cup granulated sugar in a large bowl with an electric mixer at medium speed. Add the egg and beat well. Add the flour mixture at low speed and mix until just blended.

4. Press three fourths of the dough evenly over the bottom and about 1 inch up the sides of an 8½-inch springform pan.

5. Toss the blueberries in a bowl with the 3 tablespoons granulated sugar and pour them over the dough in the pan. Top the blueberries with the remaining dough, pinching it off in small amounts and arranging it evenly over the surface.

HAWAIIAN VINTAGE CHOCOLATE

—❦—

Although cocoa came from the New World, for centuries it was the Old World that used it best. But now, at last, European masters have a serious American rival. Jim and Marie Walsh of Kona, Hawaii, are making the world's first "vintage" chocolate, from the only cacao beans grown commercially in the United States. *Newsweek* said "the richness is amazing!" and I agree. The chocolate is silky textured and, like wine, changes in character from year to year. Dry weather results in fruity, floral flavor, while ample rain brings out a heartier chocolate essence. The beans, which are blended, come from two sites on the Big Island, one quite sunny and the other damp and jungly. They're grown without pesticides and pollinated naturally, by tiny native midges. Once harvested (by hand), the beans are fermented in wooden boxes, dried in the sun, and shipped to San Francisco for processing—painstaking roasting, grinding, blending, smoothing, and aging. All this fuss is costly, of course, making Hawaiian Vintage Chocolate more expensive than any European type. I think it's worth paying extra for, and so do many of the nation's leading pastry chefs. If you're passionate about chocolate, you owe yourself a try. To order call (800) HAWNCHO.

---

6. Bake the cake in the lower two thirds of the oven until nicely browned, 40 to 50 minutes, covering the top with aluminum foil if it browns too quickly. Cool in the pan on a rack for at least 1 hour before slicing. Just before serving, dust the cake with the confectioners' sugar and remove the side of the pan.

Serves 8

GRANNY RUTH'S BROWNIES

★ ★ ★

When my friend Enid married her husband, Alexander Fisher, she learned of his passion for rich chocolate desserts, particularly brownies. She alerted her mother, Ruth, a great and inventive baker, who began a quest for the perfect brownie. Ruth and Alexander would analyze, diagnose, appraise, and investigate all desserts that remotely resembled a brownie. She tried many different recipes culled from magazines and cookbooks, while Alexander procured samples from bakeries all over town. Some were too dry, too cakey, had too many nuts, weren't chocolatey enough. Finally, after many experiments, the following recipe was perfected and named in honor of Enid's mom.

6 ounces unsweetened chocolate
1 cup (2 sticks) unsalted butter
6 large eggs
2½ cups sugar
2 teaspoons pure vanilla extract
1¾ cups all-purpose flour, sifted
½ teaspoon salt
2 cups chopped walnuts (optional)

1. Preheat the oven to 325°F. Lightly grease a 15 x 10-inch jelly-roll pan. Dust the pan with flour, shaking out the excess.

2. Melt the chocolate and the butter in a small heavy saucepan over very low heat, or in the top of a double boiler over simmering water. Stir until smooth and set aside to cool slightly.

3. Beat the eggs and the sugar in a bowl with an electric mixer on medium speed until thick and fluffy. Add the vanilla and mix well.

4. Stir the chocolate into the egg mixture. Add the flour and salt and mix until just combined; do not overmix. Stir in the chopped walnuts, if desired. Spoon the batter into the prepared pan and spread it out evenly.

5. Bake in the center of the oven until the center is just set, 25 to 30 minutes. Allow to cool completely before cutting into desired portions.

Makes thirty-five 2-inch brownies

MARBLED CREAM CHEESE BROWNIES

★ ★ ★

I find it hard to pass up a good cream cheese brownie. When made right, the creamy cheese mixture is a marvelous foil for the chewy denseness of the chocolate mixture. Not only delicious, but beautiful to look at, they are surprisingly easy to make. Swirling a knife through the batter before baking creates the marbled surface and a very professional look.

CREAM CHEESE MIXTURE
3 ounces cream cheese, at room temperature
2 tablespoons unsalted butter, at room temperature
¼ cup sugar
1 large egg, lightly beaten
1 tablespoon all-purpose flour
½ teaspoon pure vanilla extract

BROWNIE MIXTURE
2 ounces unsweetened chocolate
½ cup (1 stick) unsalted butter
2 large eggs
1 teaspoon pure vanilla extract
¾ cup sugar
½ teaspoon salt
½ cup all-purpose flour, sifted

1. Preheat the oven to 350°F. Grease an 8-inch square baking pan.

2. Prepare the cream cheese mixture: Beat the cream cheese and butter in a medium-size bowl with an electric mixer at medium speed until fluffy. Add the sugar and beat until smooth.

3. Beat in the egg, flour, and vanilla to blend well and set aside.

4. Prepare the brownie mixture: Melt the chocolate and butter in a large heavy saucepan over very low heat, or in the top of a double boiler over simmering water. Stir until smooth and set aside to cool slightly.

5. Add the eggs, one at a time, mixing well after each addition. Add the vanilla, sugar, and salt and mix well.

6. Add the flour and stir just to combine; do not overmix. Set aside ½ cup of the brownie mixture and scrape the rest of the batter into the prepared pan.

7. Pour the reserved cream cheese mixture evenly over the brownie mixture, using a rubber spatula to gently spread it all over. Spoon the reserved chocolate mixture evenly over the top. Swirl the tip of a knife through the batter to create a marbled effect.

8. Bake the brownies on the middle rack of the oven until the center is just set, 35 to 40 minutes. They should be slightly moist in the center. Cool the brownies completely before cutting.

Makes sixteen 2-inch brownies

MORE THAN S'MORES

★ ★ ★

In my formative years, I was a Brownie and advanced all the way up to Senior Girl Scout. Of the many pleasures of those years, our troop's camping trips and evenings around the campfire stand out. They never ended without roasting marshmallows and making s'mores, that ubiquitous treat created from two graham crackers sandwiched together with a toasted marshmallow and piece of chocolate bar, then devoured around the campfire. (I'll spare you my camp songs!) I never dreamed then that one day I'd make s'mores from scratch.

I first tasted Melissa Kelly's extraordinary confection at Larry Forgione's Beekman Arms Tavern in Rhinebeck, New York. She has since moved on to the Old Chatham Sheepherding Company & Inn in Old Chatham, New York, but was generous enough to share her recipe with me. Somewhat untraditional (these include ice cream and chocolate sauce), they are, of course, more work than layering s'mores from store-bought ingredients, but with planning it's not so daunting a job. Roll up your sleeves and make all the components ahead of time—the ice cream and sauce up to 1 week, the marshmallows a few days before, and the graham crackers the day before. All I can say is that they are the most delicious s'mores in the world—and in my book, that's really something.

Homemade Graham Crackers
   (recipe follows)
Marshmallows (page 543)
Homey Vanilla Ice Cream (page 555)
Silky Hot Chocolate Sauce (page 562),
   warmed

1. Preheat the broiler. Line a baking sheet with parchment paper or aluminum foil. Place a second baking sheet in the freezer to chill.

2. Place 6 graham crackers on the lined baking sheet and top each one with a 2½-inch marshmallow. Place 6 of the 1½-inch marshmallows directly on the lining.

3. Place the baking sheet under the broiler and broil until the marshmallows start to brown, 3 to 6 minutes. Remove the baking sheet from the broiler. Remove the chilled baking sheet from the freezer and quickly slide the parchment paper from the hot sheet to the chilled one. (The chilled baking sheet will make it easier to remove the marshmallows that are not sitting on crackers.)

4. Using a spatula, transfer the crackers with the marshmallows to 6 dessert plates. On top of each marshmallow, place a small scoop of vanilla ice cream and cover with a second graham cracker. Spoon some of the warmed chocolate sauce onto each plate, and place a 1½-inch marshmallow in the center of the sauce (use a spatula to remove the marshmallow from the parchment paper). Serve immediately. You're family or friends will definitely want s'more!

Serves 6

Homemade Graham Crackers

★

¾ cup all-purpose flour
½ cup plus 1 tablespoon whole-wheat flour
¼ cup rye flour
3 tablespoons sugar
½ teaspoon baking powder
¼ teaspoon baking soda
½ teaspoon ground cinnamon
¼ teaspoon salt
2 tablespoons unsalted butter, cold,
  cut into ½-inch cubes
2 tablespoons solid vegetable shortening,
  cold
2 tablespoons cold water
2 tablespoons honey
1 tablespoon molasses
1 teaspoon pure vanilla extract

1. Combine all of the flours, the sugar, baking powder, baking soda, cinnamon, and salt in a food processor. Pulse three or four times, just to blend. Evenly distribute the butter and shortening in a circle around the chopping blade and pulse again to combine. Add the water, honey, molasses, and vanilla and process for 5 to 10 seconds, until the dough starts to pull away from the sides of the workbowl. Scrape the dough out onto a smooth surface, gather into a ball, and flatten into a 5-inch disk.

2. Place the disk of dough between two sheets of waxed paper. Using a rolling pin, roll the dough into an 11-inch square about ⅛ inch thick. Slide a baking sheet underneath the bottom sheet of waxed paper and refrigerate the dough until firm, 30 to 40 minutes.

3. Peel off the top sheet of waxed paper and invert the dough onto another baking sheet. Peel off the second piece of waxed paper. Using a sharp knife or a pizza cutter, trim the edges of the square. Prick the dough all over with a fork, then cut it into approximately 2½-inch squares. Refrigerate the baking sheet with the cut squares until the squares are firm, 20 to 30 minutes.

4. Preheat the oven to 350°F.

5. Using a wide spatula, spread the chilled dough squares out on the baking sheet, leaving 1½ inches between crackers. Bake in the center of the oven until the crackers are lightly browned, 12 to 15 minutes.

6. Cool the crackers, on the baking sheet, on a wire rack for 5 minutes. Using a metal spatula, transfer the crackers from the sheet to the rack to cool completely. Store the crackers in an airtight container for up to 5 days at room temperature.

Makes 16 crackers

Marshmallows

—★—

Vegetable oil, for preparing the pan
½ cup cornstarch
½ cup confectioners' sugar
1 cup granulated sugar
1 cup light corn syrup
¾ cup cold water
Pinch of salt
2 envelopes unflavored gelatin
1½ teaspoons pure vanilla extract
1 large egg white, at room temperature

1. Line a 9-inch square baking pan with aluminum foil, leaving a 2-inch overhang on two opposite sides. Fold the overhangs down along the outside of the pan. Generously oil the bottom and sides of the foil-lined pan. Combine the cornstarch and confectioners' sugar in a small bowl. Sift half of the mixture over the bottom and sides of the pan. Do not tap out the excess. Reserve the remaining cornstarch mixture.

2. Combine the granulated sugar, corn syrup, ¼ cup of the water, and salt in a heavy medium-size saucepan. Stir with a wooden spoon over medium-low heat until the sugar dissolves completely. Dip a clean pastry brush in warm water and use to wash down the sides of the pan, to remove any clinging sugar crystals. Raise the heat to medium-high and bring the syrup to a boil. If using a candy thermometer that is mounted on a metal frame, insert it into the boiling syrup, resting it on the bottom of the pan. If using a thermometer that attaches to the side of the pan, do not let the tip touch the bottom. Cook the syrup until the thermometer registers 240°F (soft ball stage), 8 to 12 minutes.

3. While the syrup is cooking, place the remaining ½ cup of water into a small cup and sprinkle with the gelatin. Let the gelatin soften for at least 5 minutes.

4. When the syrup is at the proper temperature, remove it from the heat and let cool for 1 minute, then stir in the softened gelatin mixture and the vanilla.

5. In the large bowl of a heavy-duty electric mixer, using the wire whip attachment, beat the egg white at low speed until frothy. Gradually increase the speed to medium-high and beat until stiff peaks start to form. While continuing to beat, slowly pour the hot syrup into the egg white. Beat until the mixture is tepid and forms soft, shiny peaks, 10 to 15 minutes.

6. Scrape the marshmallow into the prepared pan and spread it evenly. Sift the remaining cornstarch mixture evenly over the top. Cover with plastic wrap and refrigerate for at least 12 hours.

7. Invert the chilled marshmallow onto a cutting board and peel off the foil. Using a sharp knife, cut the marshmallow into six 2½-inch squares and at least six 1½-inch squares. Dust the marshmallows all over with the cornstarch mixture that has fallen onto the board during the cutting process. Store in an airtight container in the refrigerator for up to 5 days.

Makes six 2½-inch marshmallows, and at least six 1½-inch marshmallows

PINWHEEL COOKIES

★ ★ ★

The first time I tasted these buttery cookies, my sister, Elaine, was making up batches to send to her fiancé, who was in the Air Force and stationed at Langley Field in Virginia. I was, as usual, annoying her by stealing as many cookies as possible while she was carefully packing them in decorative tins between sheets of waxed paper. I do remember being fascinated by the loving care with which she prepared them. And here they are with love, from Elaine and me, for you to try.

3 cups all-purpose flour
2 teaspoons baking powder
½ teaspoon salt
1 cup (2 sticks) unsalted butter, at room
    temperature
1 cup sugar
2 large eggs
2 teaspoons pure vanilla extract
1½ ounces bittersweet chocolate,
    melted and cooled

1. Sift together the flour, baking powder, and salt, and set aside.

2. Cream the butter and the sugar in a large bowl with an electric mixer at medium speed until light and fluffy. Add the eggs and the vanilla and beat well. Gradually add the flour mixture, and beat on low speed to mix well.

3. Remove half of the dough from the bowl. Divide it in half, form each half into a disk, wrap them separately in plastic wrap, and place them in the refrigerator.

4. Add the chocolate to the remaining dough and mix to blend. Divide the chocolate dough in half, form each half into a disk, wrap them separately in plastic wrap, and place them in the refrigerator. Chill the dough for 2 hours.

5. Remove one portion of dough from the refrigerator. Remove the plastic wrap and place the dough between two sheets of waxed paper. Roll the dough out to a rectangle approximately 12 x 8 inches and ⅛ to ¼ inch thick. Return the dough to the refrigerator and roll out the remaining dough portions in the same way.

6. Remove the top sheet of waxed paper from one white dough rectangle and one chocolate rectangle. Carefully stack the chocolate dough on top of the white dough by inverting it onto the white dough and peeling away the waxed paper. Trim the edges so that the two layers are similar in size. Roll the dough up lengthwise, jelly-roll fashion, making sure the roll is tight. Use the remaining sheet of waxed paper to help you along. Discard the waxed paper. Place the dough on a baking sheet, cover with plastic wrap, and chill until firm, about 1 hour. Repeat with the remaining dough portions.

7. Preheat the oven to 375°F. Lightly grease two baking sheets.

8. Remove the dough rolls from the refrigerator and slice into ¼-inch-thick rounds. Place on the prepared baking sheets, 1 inch apart. Bake, one sheet at a time, in the center of the oven until just lightly colored, 10 to 12 minutes. Do not allow to overbrown, which will result in a less distinctive design. Using a metal spatula, transfer to a rack to cool. Store in an airtight container for up to 1 week.

Makes about 5 dozen cookies

TOLL HOUSE COOKIES

★ ★ ★

No book about food in America would be complete without at least one recipe for chocolate chip cookies—and the tale of how they came to be. The story begins in 1930, when Ruth Wakefield and her husband bought the Toll House Inn in Whiteman, Massachusetts. While making a batch of brown sugar dough for her butter "drop-do" cookies, a traditional colonial recipe, she cut a chocolate bar into chunks to mix in, hoping it would melt and give her chocolate dough. The bits of chocolate softened ever so slightly, never melting throughout, and history was made! The chocolate chip cookie was born. Pleased with their success when she served them, Mrs. Wakefield named them after her inn. Subsequently, the Nestlé Company bought the Toll House name and developed the little chocolate chips we all know and love so well. While this recipe is based on one provided courtesy of the Nestlé Company, I have adapted it somewhat by adding raisins and coconut for a chewier cookie. Store these cookies in an airtight container for up to a week.

2¼ *cups all-purpose flour*
1 *teaspoon baking soda*
1 *teaspoon salt*
1 *cup (2 sticks) unsalted butter, softened*
¾ *cup granulated sugar*
¾ *cup (packed) light brown sugar*
1 *teaspoon pure vanilla extract*
2 *large eggs*
2 *cups (12-ounce package) semisweet*
  chocolate chips
½ *cup chopped walnuts or pecans*
½ *cup golden raisins*
½ *cup shredded coconut*

1. Preheat the oven to 375°F.

2. In a small bowl, combine the flour, baking soda, and salt. Set aside.

3. In a large mixing bowl, cream the butter, granulated sugar, brown sugar, and vanilla with an electric mixer or a wooden spoon. Add the eggs, one at a time, beating well after each addition.

4. Gradually beat in the flour mixture. Stir in the chocolate chips, walnuts, raisins, and coconut.

5. Drop the dough by rounded tablespoonfuls onto ungreased baking sheets. Bake until golden brown, 9 to 11 minutes. Let the cookies stand on the baking sheets for 2 minutes before removing with a spatula to wire racks to cool completely.

Makes about 5 dozen cookies

STEFFI'S BEST CHOCOLATE CHIP COOKIES

★ ★ ★

Steffi Berne, author of the *Cookie Jar Cookbook*, keeps her jars filled with some of the best cookies in the world. As she is my neighbor, she is always bringing me a treat and I am always asking her for the recipe. These oatmeal–chocolate chip cookies, whipped up in a processor, make for one of my favorite variations.

1¼ cups quick-cooking oats

1 cup all-purpose flour

½ teaspoon baking powder

½ teaspoon baking soda

Pinch of salt

½ cup granulated sugar

½ cup (packed) light or dark brown
    sugar

2 ounces semisweet or bittersweet chocolate,
    cold

½ cup (1 stick) unsalted butter, cold

1 large egg

½ teaspoon pure vanilla extract

¾ cup walnuts

1 cup (6-ounce package) semisweet
    chocolate chips

1. Position two oven racks to divide the oven into thirds and preheat the oven to 375°F. Line baking sheets with parchment paper or aluminum foil, shiny side up.

2. Process the oatmeal in a food processor until it is fine, almost a powder. Remove to a medium-size bowl and stir in the flour, baking powder, baking soda, and salt. Set aside.

3. Place both the sugars and the cold chocolate in the food processor and pulse the machine on and off until the chocolate is grated. Cut the butter into 8 pieces and add it to the processor. Process until blended. With the machine off, scrape the bowl with a rubber spatula. Add the egg and the vanilla extract and process to mix well.

4. Add the flour mixture and pulse the machine on and off five or six times. Add the walnuts and pulse the machine on and off just until the flour disappears into the dough. Remove the dough to a large bowl. Add the chocolate chips and mix well.

5. Roll level tablespoonfuls of the dough into uniform balls and place them 2 inches apart on the lined baking sheets. Flatten the balls into ½-inch-thick rounds with the heel of your hand. Bake, two sheets at a time, until the center of the cookies are barely firm to the touch, 12 to 15 minutes. Reverse the sheets front to back and top to bottom after 7 minutes to ensure even baking. Allow the cookies to rest on the sheets for 3 to 4 minutes before transferring them with a metal spatula to a rack to cool. Store in an airtight container for up to 1 week.

Makes about 3 dozen cookies

COOKIE JAR PEANUT BUTTER COOKIES

★ ★ ★

When I was a child, I loved making peanut butter cookies. I'm not sure where my fail-safe recipe came from, but I do know it produced great cookies. My grown-up version may not be exactly the same, but it creates cookies that are a little crispy on the outside and chewy on the inside. With a cold glass of milk, they bring back wonderful memories for me. When you bake them, they should be golden brown on the bottom, which takes anywhere from 10 to 12 minutes. Keep an eye on these cookies! Even slightly too dark cookies lose their fresh taste.

2½ cups all-purpose flour
1 teaspoon baking powder
½ teaspoon baking soda
½ teaspoon salt
½ cup (1 stick) unsalted butter, at room temperature
½ cup solid vegetable shortening, at room temperature
1 cup (packed) dark brown sugar
1 cup granulated sugar
2 large eggs
1 cup creamy peanut butter, at room temperature

1. Preheat the oven to 350°F.

2. Sift together the flour, baking powder, baking soda, and salt and set aside.

3. Cream the butter, shortening, and both sugars in a large bowl with an electric mixer at medium speed until light and fluffy. Add the eggs, one at a time, beating well after each addition. Beat in the peanut butter.

4. Add the reserved flour mixture by the cupful, beating at low speed to mix well.

5. Shape the dough into 1-inch balls and place on ungreased baking sheets 1½ to 2 inches apart. Press each cookie twice in each direction with the back of a fork to make a crosshatch design and to flatten the cookie to about ¼ inch thick.

6. Bake in the center of the oven until golden, 10 to 12 minutes. Using a metal spatula, transfer to a rack to cool. Store in an airtight container for up to 1 week.

Makes about 5 dozen cookies

★★★

PEANUTS

—❦—

Peanuts are an American original—South American, that is. First domesticated in ancient Peru and Brazil, they didn't find their way north until the eighteenth century. By the mid nineteenth century, low-lying peanut plants were flourishing throughout the Southern states, but it wasn't until the turn of the twentieth century and Dr. George Washington Carver's active research and promotion of the peanut as a nutritious food with hundreds of uses that its popularity took off. Today Americans consume over 600 million pounds of peanuts and 700 million pounds of peanut butter annually—in fact the average American child will eat 1,500 peanut butter sandwiches by the time he or she graduates from high school. But peanut butter consumption doesn't stop with grade school—once out, we continue to eat about 3 pounds of peanut butter per person each year.

Here are the four basic varieties of peanuts grown in America:

Runner peanuts: Used primarily for peanut butter and candies because of their uniform size.

Virginia peanuts: The largest, making them the first choice for roasting and snacking.

Spanish peanuts: Smaller, with a reddish brown skin, principally used for candy and for peanut oil.

Valencia peanuts: Typically have three or more nuts per pod, and are usually roasted and sold in the shell, or boiled.

★★★

OATMEAL CHERRY COOKIES

★ ★ ★

Oatmeal cookie aficionados fall into two camps, either chewy or crisp. I myself fall into the chewy camp. My favorite variation these days contains dried cherries or cranberries for a bit of tartness and extra moistness.

1¾ cups all-purpose flour
1 teaspoon baking soda
½ teaspoon ground cinnamon
Pinch of salt
1 cup (2 sticks) unsalted butter, at room
    temperature
1⅓ cups (packed) light brown sugar
⅓ cup granulated sugar
2 large eggs
¼ cup milk
1 teaspoon pure vanilla extract
2½ cups old-fashioned rolled oats
1 cup dried cherries or cranberries

1. Preheat the oven to 350°F.
2. Sift together the flour, baking soda, cinnamon, and salt, and set aside.
3. Cream the butter and both the sugars in a large bowl with an electric mixer at medium speed until light and fluffy. Add the eggs, milk, and vanilla, and beat well. Gradually add the reserved flour mixture, beating well after each addition.
4. Stir in the oats and dried cherries, mixing well.

5. Drop the dough by teaspoonfuls onto ungreased baking sheets 1½ to 2 inches apart, and bake until golden brown, about 10 minutes. Using a metal spatula, transfer the cookies to a rack to cool. Store in an airtight container for up to 1 week.
Makes about 5 dozen cookies

WILLIAMSBURG SUGAR COOKIES

★ ★ ★

As you most likely know, a visit to Williamsburg, Virginia, is like a step back in time to the colonial period in American history. When I was there one bright October day, these old-fashioned sugar cookies, sold by colonial-clad vendors at small stands around town, were one of my two preferred snacks (along with the Colonial Gingerbread Cakes), accompanied by a cup of cold cider and a crisp red apple. If you bake them up in colder weather, hot chocolate or hot cider would be perfect.

2 cups all-purpose flour
2 teaspoons cream of tartar
1 teaspoon baking soda
¼ teaspoon salt
¼ cup (½ stick) unsalted butter,
    at room temperature
¼ cup solid vegetable shortening,
    at room temperature
1¼ cups sugar
1 large egg
3 tablespoons milk
1 teaspoon pure vanilla extract
1½ teaspoons finely grated orange zest

1. Preheat the oven to 350°F.

2. Sift together the flour, cream of tartar, baking soda, and salt, and set aside.

3. Cream the butter, shortening, and 1 cup of the sugar in a large bowl with an electric mixer at medium speed until light and fluffy. Add the egg, milk, vanilla, and orange zest, and beat well. Gradually add the reserved flour mixture, and beat on low speed to mix well.

4. With your hands, form the dough into small balls about 1½ inches across. Roll the balls in the remaining ¼ cup sugar and place 1½ inches apart on ungreased baking sheets. Flatten the balls with the bottom of a glass—they should be about 3 inches across and ¼ inch thick.

5. Bake the cookies in the center of the oven until very lightly golden brown, 8 to 10 minutes. Cool for 10 minutes on the baking sheet, then use a metal spatula to transfer the cookies to a rack to cool completely. Store in an airtight container for up to 1 week.

Makes about 2 dozen cookies

COLONIAL GINGERBREAD CAKES

★ ★ ★

The Raleigh Tavern Bake Shop in Colonial Williamsburg sells lots of traditional baked goods from linen-lined baskets set in front of an enormous hearth. Alongside are big kegs of cider and chilled bottles of root beer, encouraging instant consumption. These gingerbread cakes, moist, chewy, and subtly flavored, are one of two cookies that I enjoyed with my cider. They are just as good with ice cream or a wedge of Cheddar cheese and an apple.

1 cup sugar
2 teaspoons ground ginger
1 teaspoon ground nutmeg
1 teaspoon ground cinnamon
1½ teaspoons baking soda
½ teaspoon salt
1 cup (2 sticks) unsalted butter, melted
1 cup unsulfured molasses
½ cup evaporated milk
¾ teaspoon pure vanilla extract (optional)
¾ teaspoon lemon extract (optional)
4 to 4½ cups all-purpose flour, sifted

1. Preheat the oven to 375°F. Lightly grease two baking sheets.

2. Combine the sugar, ginger, nutmeg, cinnamon, baking soda, and salt in a bowl. Add the melted butter, molasses, and evaporated milk, along with the vanilla and lemon extracts, if desired, and mix well with a wooden spoon.

3. Add 4 cups of flour, 1 cup at a time, mixing well with the wooden spoon. The dough should be stiff enough to handle without sticking to your fingers. Knead the dough on a lightly floured surface until smooth, adding up to ½ cup of flour as necessary so that it is not sticky.

4. Divide the dough in half. Wrap one half in plastic wrap and refrigerate until ready to use. Roll the other half out ¼ inch thick on a lightly floured surface. Dust the surface of the dough lightly with flour (this gives the cookies a nice rustic finish when they come out of the oven) and use a 2½-inch round cookie cutter to cut out cookies. Transfer the cookies to the prepared baking sheets with a metal spatula, leaving 1 inch between them. Repeat with the remaining dough. Re-roll the dough scraps and cut out as many additional cookies as possible.

5. Bake the cookies in the center of the oven until they spring back when lightly touched, 10 to 12 minutes. Use the metal spatula to transfer the cookies to a wire rack to cool. Store in an airtight container for up to 1 week.

Makes about 3½ dozen cookies

GEORGIA PECAN SANDWICH COOKIES

★ ★ ★

I was inspired to make these rich-tasting sandwich cookies by the fresh pecans I brought home from Georgia. They are one of my favorites to serve with tea or a tall glass of lemonade for an afternoon snack. The cookies are easy to mix up and roll out—just make sure the dough is well chilled before cutting out the shapes. Nicely packed in decorative tins, they also make a lovely gift for the holidays.

3 cups all-purpose flour
1 teaspoon ground cinnamon
½ teaspoon ground cloves
½ teaspoon salt
1 cup (2 sticks) unsalted butter, softened
½ cup granulated sugar
¼ cup (packed) light brown sugar
2 tablespoons pure maple syrup
1 large egg
2 cups finely chopped pecans (about 8 ounces)
2 large egg whites, lightly beaten
¼ cup raspberry jam
¼ cup apricot jam
¼ cup confectioners' sugar, for dusting

1. Sift together the flour, cinnamon, cloves, and salt, and set aside.

2. Beat the butter, both sugars, and the maple syrup in a large bowl with an electric mixer at medium speed until light and creamy. Add the egg and beat well. Add gradually the flour mixture, and beat on low speed to mix well. Stir in the pecans.

3. Gather the dough into a ball and cover with plastic wrap. Refrigerate for at least 2 hours.

4. Preheat the oven to 375°F. Lightly grease several baking sheets.

5. Roll the dough out about ⅛ inch thick on a lightly floured surface. Using a 3-inch star-shaped (or other) cookie cutter, cut out the cookies. Re-roll the scraps and cut out as many additional cookies as possible. You should have an even number. Use an apple corer or thimble to cut a small circle from the center of half of the stars. (These will be the sandwich tops.) Using a metal spatula, carefully arrange the cookies on the prepared baking sheets, spacing about 1 inch apart. Brush the cutout stars lightly with the beaten egg whites.

6. Bake the cookies until lightly browned, 8 to 10 minutes. Transfer to racks with the metal spatula to cool.

7. Spread about ½ teaspoon of jam on the flat side of each whole star and top with a cutout star, shiny side up, to make a sandwich. Press the cookies gently together. Dust with confectioners' sugar to serve. Store in an airtight container for up to 1 week.

Makes about 3 dozen sandwich cookies

The Big Scoop

Norman Rockwell painted soda fountains, and Thornton Wilder wrote one into *Our Town*. Why? Because they were the most sociable, friendly fixtures of American life for well over a century. The confections they sold were fantasy food—sugary, frosty, fizzy—in dreamy hues of pink, green, tawny brown, and creamy white.

Once upon a time, every town had such a place (often at a drugstore), complete with cool marble or Formica counters and spinning stools. On Nantucket Island, Massachusetts, I found two old-fashioned fountains happily coexisting on the same cobblestone street. No need to compete—summer business is good! A steady stream of customers kept both humming, their screen doors creaking and banging, their blenders noisily churning.

In this chapter, I pay soda fountains homage with a collection of recipes for classic cold confections, including peanut butter ice cream, a cherry milkshake, and some of America's sweetest, wettest lemonades.

SWEET CHERRY ICE CREAM

★ ★ ★

When cherries arrive in the market in May, my cravings crescendo for the intense flavor of my favorite fruit. I long for cheery, fresh cherry ice cream and pies. Garnet-red, sweet Bing cherries are perfect for this recipe. Big and juicy, they are almost black when fully ripened in June and July.

3 cups heavy (or whipping) cream
1 cup milk
½ cup sugar
1 tablespoon pure vanilla extract
4 large egg yolks
2 cups pitted, coarsely mashed sweet
  cherries

1. Combine the cream, milk, sugar, and vanilla in a heavy saucepan. Cook, stirring frequently, over medium heat until the milk is hot but not boiling and the sugar is dissolved, about 10 minutes. Remove from the heat.

2. Place the egg yolks in a small bowl and whisk to mix. Whisking constantly, slowly pour in 1 cup of the hot milk mixture and continue whisking until smooth.

3. Slowly pour the egg mixture back into the hot mixture in the saucepan, whisking constantly until well combined. Place the saucepan over medium heat and stir the mixture constantly until it is thick enough to coat the back of a spoon, 6 to 8 minutes. The mixture should never boil.

4. Strain the mixture into a bowl and cool to room temperature.

5. Freeze in an ice cream maker according to the manufacturer's instructions. During the last 5 minutes of freezing, add the mashed cherries.

Makes about 1½ quarts

SUMMERTIME PEACH ICE CREAM

★ ★ ★

Nothing is better in the summertime, when fruit is at its juicy ripest perfection, than home-made ice cream—especially old-fashioned peach. Cooking the custard with the peach peels and pits infuses it with an extra-rich flavor. Slice some fresh, ripe peaches into a bowl and top with a scoop of this ice cream. Serve it with Granny Ruth's Brownies. Yummy!

2 pounds fresh, ripe peaches
1 tablespoon fresh lemon juice
¾ cup sugar
3 cups heavy (or whipping) cream
1 cup milk
1 tablespoon pure vanilla extract
4 large egg yolks

1. Peel, pit and slice the peaches, reserving the peels and pits. Place the peach slices in a bowl with the lemon juice and ¼ cup of the sugar. Toss well and set aside.

2. Combine the cream, milk, remaining ½ cup sugar, vanilla, and reserved peach peels and pits in a heavy saucepan. Cook, stirring frequently, over medium heat until the milk is hot but not boiling and the sugar is dissolved. Remove from the heat.

3. Place the egg yolks in a small bowl and whisk to mix. Whisking constantly, slowly pour in 1 cup of the hot milk mixture and continue whisking until well combined.

4. Slowly pour the egg mixture back into the hot mixture in the saucepan, whisking constantly until smooth. Place the saucepan over medium heat and stir the mixture constantly until it is thick enough to coat the back of a spoon, 6 to 8 minutes. The mixture should never boil.

5. Cool to room temperature and then strain into a bowl.

6. Purée the peaches in a food processor until smooth. Stir into the cream mixture and freeze in an ice cream maker according to the manufacturer's instructions.

Makes about 2 quarts

STRAWBERRY FAIR ICE CREAM

★ ★ ★

One of the more pleasant things to do in the early summer is to go to a "pick-your-own" strawberry farm. I load a basket with plump, juicy berries for the particularly special treat of fresh strawberry ice cream. To begin, I purée most of the berries and stir them into the custard, but always save some of the whole mashed berries to mix in at the end of freezing for added texture. Sometimes I use the ice cream in a soda by blending 2 tablespoons each Strawberry Syrup and milk in the bottom of a tall glass. Then I add 2 scoops of strawberry ice cream and top with seltzer. A little swizzle and I have a better-than-soda-fountain soda for the perfect end to a hot summer afternoon.

3 pints fresh, ripe strawberries, lightly rinsed
½ cup plus 2 tablespoons sugar
3 cups heavy (or whipping) cream
1 cup milk
1 tablespoon pure vanilla extract
4 large egg yolks

1. Pat the strawberries dry, then hull and quarter them. Toss 2 pints of the berries with the 2 tablespoons sugar and set aside. Coarsely mash the remaining pint of berries and set aside.

2. Combine the ½ cup sugar, cream, milk, and vanilla in a heavy saucepan. Cook, over medium heat, until the milk is hot but not boiling and the sugar is dissolved, about 10 minutes. Remove from the heat.

3. Place the egg yolks in a small bowl and whisk to mix. Whisking constantly, slowly pour in 1 cup of the hot milk mixture and continue whisking until smooth.

4. Slowly pour the egg mixture back into the hot mixture in the saucepan, whisking constantly until well combined. Place the saucepan over medium heat and stir the mixture constantly until it is thick enough to coat the back of a spoon, 6 to 8 minutes. The mixture should never boil.

5. Strain the mixture into a bowl and cool to room temperature. Purée the reserved 2 pints berries in a food processor until smooth. Stir into the cream mixture and freeze in an ice cream maker according to the manufacturer's instructions.

6. During the last 5 minutes of freezing, add the remaining pint of mashed berries.

Makes about 2 quarts

BITTERSWEET CHOCOLATE ICE CREAM

★ ★ ★

When craving chocolate ice cream, I always go for broke and make it with as much premium chocolate as possible. This is definitely the time to splurge at a specialty food shop. For the richest flavor, do not use milk chocolate, as it will result in a pale-hued, weak-flavored ice cream.

3 cups heavy (or whipping) cream
1 cup milk
½ cup sugar
4 large egg yolks
12 ounces best-quality bittersweet chocolate,
   broken into small pieces

1. Combine the cream, milk, and sugar in a heavy saucepan. Cook, stirring frequently, over medium heat until the milk is hot but not boiling and the sugar is dissolved, about 10 minutes. Remove from the heat.

2. Place the egg yolks in a small bowl and whisk to mix. Whisking constantly, slowly pour in 1 cup of the hot milk mixture and continue whisking until smooth.

3. Slowly pour the egg mixture back into the hot mixture in the saucepan, whisking constantly until well combined. Place the saucepan over medium heat and stir the mixture constantly until it is thick enough to coat the back of a spoon, 6 to 8 minutes. The mixture should never boil.

4. Place the chocolate in a large heavy saucepan and stir over very low heat until just melted and smooth. Remove from the heat.

5. Strain the custard mixture into the melted chocolate, whisking constantly until completely blended. Cool to room temperature.

THE ESKIMO PIE

— ❦ —

Not really a pie but rather America's first chocolate-covered ice-cream bar on a stick, Eskimo Pie was invented in 1921 by Iowa school teacher and candy-store owner Christian Nelson. Intrigued by a little boy's indecision between a chocolate candy bar and an ice-cream sandwich, Nelson asked the child which it would be. The boy replied, "I want 'em both, but I only got a nickel!" With the seed of a clever idea planted, and after a lot of experimenting, Nelson figured out how to combine chocolate and ice cream in what later would be known as the Eskimo Pie. The first bar was named the "I-Scream-Bar," but in a later collaboration with an Omaha ice cream company superintendent and chocolate genius, Russell Stover (yes, there really was a Russell Stover), it was decided that the name Eskimo Pie had more appeal. Wrapped up in a shiny foil wrapper, this frozen treat has sold untold millions, and made decision-making in the sweet shop a little less difficult for all of us.

6. Freeze in an ice cream maker according to the manufacturer's instructions.

Makes about 5 cups

HOMEY VANILLA ICE CREAM

★ ★ ★

When all is said and done, I still sometimes think that there is no better homemade ice cream than vanilla. You can dress it up or dress it down, and for me, it remains a most seductive flavor.

3 cups heavy (or whipping) cream
1 cup milk
½ cup sugar
2 vanilla beans, split in half lengthwise
1 tablespoon pure vanilla extract
4 large egg yolks

1. Combine the cream, milk, sugar, and vanilla beans in a heavy saucepan over medium heat. Cook, stirring frequently, until the milk is hot but not boiling and the sugar is dissolved, about 10 minutes. Remove from the heat and stir in the vanilla extract.

2. Place the egg yolks in a small bowl and whisk to mix. Whisking constantly, slowly pour in 1 cup of the hot milk mixture and continue whisking until smooth.

3. Slowly pour the egg mixture back into the hot mixture in the saucepan, whisking constantly until well combined. Place the saucepan over medium heat and stir the mixture constantly until it is thick enough to coat the back of a spoon, 6 to 8 minutes. The mixture should never boil.

4. Strain the mixture into a bowl and cool to room temperature.

5. Freeze in an ice cream maker according to the manufacturer's instructions.

Makes about 1 quart

LAURIE'S WINTER LEMON ICE CREAM

★ ★ ★

Whether in the form of tarts, cookies, sherbets, or sorbets, I find lemon desserts always the most refreshing. My associate, Laurie, agrees with me on this point and created a creamy lemon ice cream with just the right amount of velvet tartness. Topped with blueberries, raspberries, or Fresh Strawberry Sauce, it is the consummate summer treat. But it is also perfection after a heavy winter meal, scooped beside a slice of chocolate cake with a bit of Silky Hot Chocolate Sauce drizzled over the top.

3 lemons
1 cup Simple Sugar Syrup for Sorbets (page 561)
3 cups heavy (or whipping) cream
1 cup milk
½ cup sugar
4 large egg yolks

1. Remove the zest from 2 of the lemons in long strips, using a lemon zester. Place the strips in a small saucepan with the sugar syrup and bring to a boil. Cook for 5 minutes, then remove from the heat. Remove the zest from the syrup with a slotted spoon and set aside. Cool the syrup to room temperature.

2. Remove the zest from the remaining lemon and finely chop it. Set aside. Squeeze the lemons to obtain ½ cup of juice and set aside.

3. Combine the cream, milk, and sugar in a heavy saucepan. Cook, stirring frequently, over medium heat until the milk is hot but not boiling and the sugar is dissolved, about 10 minutes. Remove from the heat.

4. Place the egg yolks in a small bowl and whisk to mix. Whisking constantly, slowly pour 1 cup of the hot milk mixture into the eggs and continue whisking until smooth.

5. Slowly pour the egg mixture back into the hot mixture in the saucepan, whisking constantly until well combined. Place the saucepan over medium heat and stir the mixture constantly until it is thick enough to coat the back of a spoon, 6 to 8 minutes. The mixture should never boil.

6. Strain the mixture into a bowl and cool to room temperature.

7. Stir in the cooled sugar syrup, ½ cup lemon juice, and finely chopped lemon zest. Freeze the mixture in an ice cream maker according to the manufacturer's instructions. Just before the mixture has finished freezing, with the motor off, add the reserved lemon strips and stir to combine.

Makes about 1½ quarts

CREAMY PEANUT BUTTER ICE CREAM

★ ★ ★

Smooth, creamy, and intense with peanut butter flavor, this ice cream, with hot fudge sauce dripping over the top, is quite spectacular. The only thing better would be the addition of a heaping spoonful of Fresh Strawberry Sauce to top it all off. No chunky peanut butter here, please!

3 cups heavy (or whipping) cream
1 cup milk
1½ cups creamy peanut butter
½ cup sugar
1 teaspoon pure vanilla extract
4 large egg yolks

1. Combine the cream, milk, peanut butter, sugar, and vanilla in a heavy saucepan. Cook, stirring frequently, over medium heat until the mixture is hot but not boiling, the sugar is dissolved, and the mixture is smooth, about 10 minutes. Remove from the heat.

2. Place the egg yolks in a small bowl and whisk to mix. Whisking constantly, slowly pour in 1 cup of the hot milk mixture and continue whisking until smooth.

3. Slowly pour the egg mixture back into the hot mixture in the saucepan, whisking constantly until well combined. Place the saucepan over medium heat and stir the mixture constantly until it is thick enough to coat the back of a spoon, 6 to 8 minutes. The mixture should never boil.

4. Strain the mixture into a bowl and cool to room temperature.

5. Freeze in an ice cream maker according to the manufacturer's instructions.

Makes about 5 cups

NEW ORLEANS PRALINE ICE CREAM

★ ★ ★

Pralines, one of New Orleans's confectionery stars, are made from a mixture of cream, pecans, and brown sugar. Most familiar as a candy, this combination is also sumptuous when transformed into ice cream. A rich, gooey spoonful is irresistible served with beignets, a rich, aromatic dessert coffee, or anything gingerbread!

3 cups heavy (or whipping) cream
1 cup milk
1 cup (packed) light brown sugar
4 large egg yolks
1½ cups coarsely chopped pecans

1. Combine the cream, milk, and sugar in a heavy saucepan. Cook, stirring frequently, over medium heat until the milk is hot but not boiling and the sugar is dissolved, about 10 minutes. Remove from the heat.

2. Place the egg yolks in a small bowl and whisk to mix. Whisking constantly, slowly pour in 1 cup of the hot milk mixture and continue whisking until smooth.

3. Slowly pour the egg mixture back into the hot mixture in the saucepan, whisking constantly until well combined. Place the saucepan over medium heat and stir the mixture constantly until it is thick enough to coat the back of a spoon, 6 to 8 minutes. The mixture should never boil.

4. Strain the mixture into a bowl and cool to room temperature.

5. Freeze in an ice cream maker according to the manufacturer's instructions. Just before the mixture has finished freezing, with the motor off, add the chopped pecans and stir to combine.

Makes about 5 cups

RED-AND-WHITE PEPPERMINT ICE CREAM

★ ★ ★

When I was a child, good behavior was occasionally rewarded with a trip to the local soda fountain. And invariably I'd order my favorite ice cream flavor, which at the time was peppermint. This recipe honors that memory, resulting in a concoction of the palest, most delectable pink flecked with bits of crushed red-and-white peppermint candy. For really good behavior, allow yourself a peppermint ice cream sundae—Scoops of Peppermint Ice Cream topped with Silky Hot Chocolate Sauce, crushed peppermints, and a cap of whipped cream.

1¼ cups coarsely crushed red-and-white
*   peppermint candies*
3 cups heavy (or whipping) cream
1 cup milk
½ cup sugar
4 large egg yolks

1. Place ¾ cup of the crushed peppermint candies in a food processor and process until powdery. Set aside.

2. Combine the cream, milk, and sugar in a heavy saucepan. Cook, stirring frequently, over medium heat until the milk is hot but not boiling and the sugar is dissolved, about 10 minutes. Remove from the heat.

3. Place the egg yolks in a small bowl and whisk to mix. Whisking constantly, slowly pour in 1 cup of the hot milk mixture and continue whisking until smooth.

4. Slowly pour the egg mixture back into the hot mixture in the saucepan, whisking constantly until well combined. Place the saucepan over medium heat and stir the mixture constantly until it is thick enough to coat the back of a spoon, 6 to 8 minutes. The mixture should never boil.

5. Strain the mixture into a bowl. Add the powdered peppermint and stir until completely dissolved. Cool to room temperature.

6. Freeze in an ice cream maker according to the manufacturer's instructions. Just before the mixture has finished freezing, turn the motor off, add the remaining ½ cup crushed candies, and stir to combine.

Makes about 5 cups

JUNE STRAWBERRY SORBET

★ ★ ★

This gorgeous seasonal sorbet, splendidly garnished with the tiniest of fresh berries and fresh mint leaves, is so good and so light, you may have trouble sharing. But do—the compliments are worth it.

2 pints fresh, ripe strawberries, lightly rinsed, dried, hulled, and halved
1 cup Simple Sugar Syrup for Sorbets (page 561)
2 tablespoons fresh lemon juice

1. Purée the strawberries in a food processor with ¼ cup of the sugar syrup.

2. Transfer the purée to an ice cream maker along with the remaining syrup and the lemon juice and freeze according to the manufacturer's instructions.

Makes about 4 cups

STRAWBERRY-RHUBARB SORBET

★ ★ ★

Along with other harbingers of spring, rhubarb and strawberries say summer's on the way. Here I combine these natural partners in a sorbet with the consistency of a sherbet for a slightly tart, yet surprisingly sweet dessert—so welcome at the point when winter fruits have lost their charm.

4 cups sliced fresh rhubarb
1¼ cups sugar
½ cup water
1 pint fresh, ripe strawberries, lightly rinsed, dried, hulled, and halved
¾ cup fresh orange juice

1. Combine the rhubarb in a saucepan with the sugar and water. Bring to a boil, then reduce the heat slightly and simmer until the rhubarb is very tender, about 20 minutes.

2. Purée the rhubarb in a food processor and remove to a large bowl.

3. Add the strawberries and orange juice to the food processor and purée, then stir into the rhubarb. Cool to room temperature.

4. Freeze in an ice cream maker according to the manufacturer's instructions.

Makes about 5 cups

BLOOD ORANGE SORBET

★ ★ ★

Blood oranges are plentiful during the colder months, and their delicate red juice results in a jewel-like sorbet. This recipe could not be easier to make, and what a surprising, refreshing finale to a winter stew. The sugar syrup can be made anytime and kept on hand for occasions like this.

2 cups fresh blood orange juice (about 8 oranges)
2 cups Simple Sugar Syrup for Sorbets (page 561)

Place the juice and sugar syrup in an ice cream maker and freeze according to the manufacturer's instructions.

Makes about 4 cups

"HOT" RED CHERRY SORBET

★ ★ ★

When succulent Bing cherries are in season, it takes a lot of control not to put them in everything I make. Other than my Sweet Cherry Pie, there is no other dessert that comes near "Hot" Red Cherry Sorbet for concentrated flavor. A small sprig of fresh mint, or a perfect red rosebud, is all that you need for a bright garnish.

4 cups pitted Bing cherries
2 cups Simple Sugar Syrup for Sorbets (page 561)
¼ cup fresh lemon juice
½ teaspoon pure almond extract

1. Combine the cherries and ½ cup of the sugar syrup in a food processor and purée until very smooth.

2. Scrape the mixture into a large bowl and stir in the remaining sugar syrup, the lemon juice, and the almond extract.

3. Freeze in an ice cream maker according to the manufacturer's instructions.

Makes about 1½ quarts

A SODA FOUNTAIN SAMPLER

— ❧ —

While soda fountains have not disappeared entirely from America's landscape, they are generally reserved for summertime beach resorts. Lucky for us, the dreamy concoctions they made so popular live on.

Ice cream soda/float: History tells us that, in 1874, Robert Green of Philadelphia was selling a concoction of syrup, cream, and soda water at the Franklin Institute's fifty-year celebration when he ran out of cream, substituted vanilla ice cream, and met with instant success. Ice cream sodas today are made by mixing syrup in a little milk, adding seltzer, then a scoop of ice cream. Floats are carbonated soft drinks made fancy by the addition of a scoop of ice cream.

Flip: A rich drink made with syrup, a whole egg or egg yolk, spice, and soda water. The drink should always be "flipped," which means shaken rapidly over crushed ice so it is foamy and very cold.

Fizzes: Refreshing, light beverages consisting of syrup, soda, and powdered sugar stirred in to make it fizz.

Egg cream: If you grew up in New York City, you know what an egg cream is. While this chocolatey concoction contains no egg and no cream (just milk), the nomenclature is thought to have come from the flavor being as rich as a drink made from eggs. Plus the ingredients, if mixed properly, make a foamy egg-white-like head that tops off the drink. Even though the ingredients are simple: chocolate syrup, milk, and seltzer, the flavor and texture are completely dependent on the correct proportions. Ideally, your seltzer should come from a real old-fashioned seltzer bottle; the pressure from the jet of water will combine the ingredients together perfectly, resulting in ½-inch head of foam, the trademark of a good egg cream. If you want the true egg cream experience, see if you can find Fox's U-Bet Chocolate Syrup at your supermarket. It has been around as long as the egg cream, and is the syrup of choice. U-Bet gives the egg cream the perfect chocolate taste. New Yorkers swear by it, and it is available nationwide.

Milkshake: Traditionally, the milkshake was the most unadulterated of the soda-fountain milk-based drinks. Originally, it was just milk combined with a flavored syrup, and sometimes ice cream, blended until it was frothy and creamy. In more recent times, ice cream became the dominant ingredient. Richer milk shakes also included eggs, cream, or buttermilk, and were called nogs. Milkshakes, like malteds (below), are typically prepared in a special blender and the container used to make the drink often holds enough for seconds.

Malted: Malteds are prepared with milk, flavored syrup, ice cream, and a scoop of malt powder (dehydrated whole milk, wheat extracts, and malted barley). If an egg is added, it becomes a malted nog.

Frappé/frappe: Once simply a mixture of fruit juices, frozen to a slushy consistency and served as a drink, this is now another name for "milkshake."

Sundaes: Soda-fountain drinks were considered so seductive in the nineteenth century that the sale of sodas on Sunday was prohibited. Around the 1880s, in order to get around this "blue law," soda fountains came up with the sundae, a mixture of ice cream, syrup, and whipped cream, but no soda, to serve on the Lord's Day. Today, popular sundaes include the hot fudge (scoops of vanilla ice cream blanketed by a warm, thick chocolate sauce that is topped by whipped cream and a maraschino cherry) and the hot butterscotch, the same thing, only with butterscotch sauce replacing the hot fudge. There are those who go for a sprinkling of chopped nuts added to the sundae mix, as well. Of course, vanilla ice cream isn't a must—it just goes nicely with all the sauces. Any favorite ice cream flavor can be used in a sundae.

Parfait: Meaning "perfect" in French, the parfait is a refined sundae made with softer, creamier ice cream, served in a tall fluted glass. Its appearance is more delicate and was, at one time, very popular with the ladies. Traditionally, a glass of soda water is served alongside.

Banana split: Some consider the banana split to be the *ne plus ultra* as far as sundaes go. Served in a special elongated dish, it includes a whole split banana, three different ice creams and syrups, plus luscious garnishes. Do try my recipe, which starts on this page.

SIMPLE SUGAR SYRUP FOR SORBETS

★ ★ ★

This syrup is very easy to make and it is convenient to have on hand when making sorbets. Tightly covered, it lasts for an indefinite amount of time in the refrigerator.

4 cups sugar
4 cups water

Place the sugar and water in a saucepan; bring to a boil. Reduce the heat and simmer gently until the sugar has dissolved, about 5 minutes. Cool to room temperature. The syrup can be used immediately or stored indefinitely, in a covered container in the refrigerator.

Makes about 5 cups

BIG-TIME BANANA SPLIT

★ ★ ★

Few folks will deny that a good old-fashioned banana split wins the Triple Crown in the gooey dessert category. Three ice creams, three sauces, lots of fresh whipped cream, and three cherries to top it all off—what could be more celebratory? While it's a favorite soda-fountain treat, this delectable dessert is easy enough to make at home with store-bought ice cream and sauce if you're not ambitious enough to make your own. It's the combination of carefully planned flavors side by side that makes the finished creation so good when the melt-down begins. But even if you don't make your own ice cream and sauces, please do whip your own cream!

1 ripe banana, peeled and split lengthwise
1 scoop Bittersweet Chocolate Ice Cream
   (page 554)
1 scoop Sweet Cherry Ice Cream (page 552)
1 scoop New Orleans Praline Ice Cream
   (page 557)
1 tablespoon Silky Hot Chocolate Sauce
   (this page), warmed
1 tablespoon Cherry Sauce (facing page)
1 tablespoon Old-Fashioned Butterscotch Sauce
   (page 564), warmed
1 to 2 tablespoons chopped dry-roasted peanuts
½ cup Sweetened Whipped Cream (page 515)
3 maraschino cherries with stems

   1. To assemble the banana split, lay each banana half, cut side in, along each side of a banana split dish or similar long, oval dessert dish. Arrange the ice cream scoops between the bananas down the center of the dish.
   2. Spoon the chocolate sauce over the chocolate ice cream, the cherry sauce over the cherry ice cream, and the butterscotch sauce over the praline ice cream. Sprinkle with peanuts and top each scoop with a dollop of whipped cream and a cherry. Serve immediately.
   Serves 1 or 2

DRIVE-IN CHERRY MILKSHAKE

★ ★ ★

Save this cherry milkshake for those decadent days of cherry season. If you don't have fresh cherry sauce on hand, a fine-quality dark cherry preserve will do just fine. Don't be frightened by the amount of ice cream—it's a genuine soda-fountain proportion! Of course, you may have to use all your strength to empty your glass, if you're drinking this as is traditional—through a straw. If you prefer, another fruit sauce or preserve may be substituted for the cherry.

½ cup milk
2 tablespoons Cherry Sauce (facing page) or
   cherry preserves
3 scoops (about 3 ounces each) Homey
   Vanilla Ice Cream (page 555)

   1. Place the milk and the cherry sauce in a blender and blend to mix.
   2. Add the ice cream and blend until smooth. Serve immediately in a 14-ounce glass.
   Serves 1

SILKY HOT CHOCOLATE SAUCE

★ ★ ★

Chocolate sauce is perfect for topping soda-fountain favorites, but it can do double duty when drizzled over thick slices of pound cake or fresh fruit salads. Vanilla extract adds to the flavor, but you can customize the sauce for the adult crowd by replacing the vanilla with a preferred liqueur: Chambord, Grand Marnier, Amaretto, or Kahlúa are but a few suggestions.

12 ounces best-quality bittersweet
   chocolate
1 cup heavy cream
2 teaspoons pure vanilla extract

1. Finely chop the chocolate and set it aside.

2. Place the cream in a heavy saucepan and bring it almost to a boil over medium heat. Remove it from the heat just before it boils. Add the reserved chopped chocolate and the vanilla and whisk until smooth. Refrigerate in a covered container for up to 2 weeks. Reheat in the top of a double boiler over simmering water.

Makes about 2 cups

CHERRY SAUCE

★ ★ ★

When you're longing for a fresh cherry shake or a black cherry ice cream sundae, this lush sauce will answer the call. Bring out the pitters during the June high season and make plenty. Because sugar acts as a natural preservative, the sauce should keep for up to 3 to 4 weeks, refrigerated. The drained syrup also freezes well.

1½ pounds Bing cherries, stems and pits
   removed
1½ pounds sugar (about 3⅔ cups)
¾ cup water
¼ teaspoon pure almond extract
1 tablespoon fresh lemon juice

1. In a medium-size heavy saucepan, alternate layers of cherries and sugar. Set the saucepan aside and allow the cherries to macerate for at least 1 hour.

2. Add the water and almond extract to the pan and bring the mixture to a boil over high heat, stirring occasionally. Reduce the heat slightly and simmer until the mixture starts to thicken, about 15 minutes, skimming off any scum that rises to the surface. Stir in the lemon juice and remove the pan from the heat. Cool to room temperature and refrigerate until chilled before serving.

Makes about 4 cups

FRESH STRAWBERRY SAUCE

★ ★ ★

Wait until your local strawberries are in season and then make up batches of this sauce. The microwave embraces fruit. If you have one, the sauce will be quick to make, and turn out beautiful to look at, and delicious tasting. Fresh lemon juice keeps it from being cloyingly sweet. Because of the amount of sugar used, the sauce will keep, refrigerated, for up to 1 month. Serve over strawberry ice cream or give it your best go on a banana split.

3 cups fresh, ripe strawberries, lightly rinsed, dried, hulled, and quartered
2 cups sugar
2 teaspoons finely grated lemon zest
1 tablespoon fresh lemon juice

1. Combine all the ingredients in a 4-quart microwave-safe dish.
2. Cook, uncovered, on high power (see Note) for 10 minutes. Remove from the microwave, stir, and return to the microwave to cook 5 minutes longer.
3. Cool completely before pouring into containers, covering, and storing in the refrigerator.
Makes about 3 cups

NOTE: This recipe was tested in a full-power carousel microwave oven of 650 to 700 watts, using microwave-safe equipment.

LANAI SWEET PINEAPPLE-GINGER SAUCE

★ ★ ★

During a visit to Hawaii, I spent time on the island of Lanai, where I had the opportunity to tour a pineapple plantation. Once home, I was inspired by my trip to create a lot of new recipes that incorporate fresh pineapple, and this is one of them. It makes a fresh-tasting ice cream topper and has become a member of my banana split sauce trinity. It would be equally delicious spooned over a slice of Chocolate Silk Cake dolloped with whipped cream. A word of caution: Even when cooked, fresh pineapple does not store well, so use the sauce within 24 hours.

1 fresh, ripe pineapple, peeled and cored
1 cup sugar
2 tablespoons finely chopped crystallized ginger

1. Cut the pineapple into ¼-inch dice, reserving the juices. Place in a large heavy saucepan along with any reserved juices, the sugar, and ginger.
2. Bring to a boil, reduce the heat to medium, and cook at a gentle boil for 15 minutes, stirring occasionally, or until the sauce thickens slightly. Let cool to room temperature, then refrigerate, covered, for up to 24 hours.
Makes about 3 cups

OLD-FASHIONED BUTTERSCOTCH SAUCE

★ ★ ★

Although indispensable in making banana splits, I am sure that once you make and taste this sauce, you'll find many other desserts to pour it over. It is *the* topping for New Orleans Praline Ice Cream and would be splendid drizzled over warm Old-Fashioned Apple Pie,

Harvest Baked Pears, or Granny Ruth's Brownies topped with Homey Vanilla Ice Cream. Delicately dipped fresh fruit would be less extravagant but equally as good!

1⅓ cups (packed) light brown sugar
¾ cup light corn syrup
4 tablespoons (½ stick) unsalted butter
2 tablespoons water
Pinch of salt
6 tablespoons heavy (or whipping) cream

Combine the brown sugar, corn syrup, butter, water, and salt in a heavy saucepan over medium heat. Bring to a boil, stirring, and boil for 2 minutes. Remove the pan from the heat and set it aside to cool. Once cool, stir in the cream. Refrigerate in a covered container up to 2 weeks.

Makes about 2 cups

VANILLA BEAN SYRUP

★ ★ ★

If you plan on making any vanilla-flavored ice cream treats, you won't want to be without this important soda-fountain syrup. It is very easy to make and keeps well, so make a batch in May and use it all summer long for your kitchen soda-fountain specialties. It will make a professional soda jerk out of anyone!

1 cup sugar
1 cup water
1 vanilla bean, split

Combine the sugar, water, and vanilla bean in a saucepan. Bring to a boil, stirring to dissolve the sugar. Once the mixture boils, reduce the heat slightly and simmer for 5 minutes, swirling the pan occasionally. Cool the mixture completely and refrigerate in a covered container for up to 4 months. Remove the vanilla bean before using.

Makes about 1¼ cups

FRESH STRAWBERRY SYRUP

★ ★ ★

This syrup is a soda fountain essential. A banana split or strawberry soda or sundae just can't be made without it, and for me, those two ice cream favorites are particular necessities. When you're straining the crushed berries through the cheesecloth, be careful not to get too much pulp into the liquid or the syrup will be cloudy.

4 cups fresh, ripe strawberries,
*   lightly rinsed*
1¾ cups water
2 teaspoons finely grated
*   lemon zest*
1¼ cups sugar

1. Crush the berries in a large heavy saucepan. Add 1 cup of the water and the lemon zest and bring to a boil over medium-high heat. Reduce the heat to medium and simmer for 5 minutes, skimming any foam off the top. Set the mixture aside to cool.

2. Meanwhile, combine the sugar and remaining ¾ cup water in a small heavy saucepan. Bring to a boil, stirring to dissolve the sugar, and cook until the syrup reaches 260°F on a candy thermometer. Remove from the heat and set aside.

3. Strain the cooled strawberry mixture through a strainer lined with a double thickness of cheesecloth into a bowl. Squeeze well until all the juice is extracted and the pulp and seeds are left behind. Discard the pulp.

4. Return the clear, strained strawberry liquid to the cleaned-out large saucepan and add the sugar syrup. Bring to a boil over medium heat and cook for 8 minutes. Transfer to a pint jar, cover, and refrigerate for up to 2 weeks.

Makes about 2 cups

DEEP BLUEBERRY SYRUP

★ ★ ★

Fresh blueberry syrup is indeed a very rare commodity and a fine treat. I came up with my recipe when a compote I was developing just didn't work. Rather than throw it all away, I strained the potful of blueberries and ended up with a rich, flavorful syrup. It was such a success that I have since perfected the recipe.

Because the amount of sugar added to the blueberries acts as a natural preservative, the syrup will keep, covered and refrigerated, for up to 2 months. It makes a super-special topping for waffles, pancakes, and French toast, as well as for ice cream sundaes.

1½ pounds blueberries, lightly rinsed
3 cups sugar
1 vanilla bean, split lengthwise
¾ cup water
1 tablespoon fresh lemon juice

1. Combine the blueberries and sugar in a large heavy saucepan. Toss gently with a rubber spatula to mix, then stick the vanilla bean into the center. Let stand for 1 hour.

2. Add the water and lemon juice to the blueberry mixture and bring to a boil over high heat, stirring occasionally. Reduce the heat slightly and simmer, skimming off any foam that rises to the surface, until the mixture starts to thicken, about 15 minutes.

3. Remove from the heat and strain through a fine sieve. Cool to room temperature and refrigerate, tightly covered, until ready to use.

Makes about 2 cups

THREE LEMONADES AND A CHERRY COLA

★ ★ ★

Nothing quenches your thirst like an icy tall glass of sweet-tart lemonade. Satisfying on its own or as an accompaniment to a favorite sandwich, here are three variations to suit the hottest of summer days. County Fair Lemonade tames the puckery taste of fresh lemon juice with sugar syrup, making it delicious and refreshing. Old-Fashioned Lemonade is easy to make and has a turn-of-the-century feel to it (and I don't mean the one coming up!). Bernice "Toots" Zipperman's version adds an unusual twist—a little orange juice. It's a good choice when you are looking for something a bit different, but still rejuvenating.

If you're not in the mood for lemonade, yet want a cooling soda fountain treat, nothing could be easier to put together than Cameron's Cherry Cola. Maraschino cherries and their juice combine with a favorite U.S. soft drink for a hard-to-beat taste.

Bernice "Toots" Zipperman's Old-Fashioned Lemonade

★

When I was a guest on Sue Zelickson's radio show in Minneapolis, I mentioned that I had noticed fresh lemonade stands replacing soda stands at the fairs I had attended around the country. After a brief discourse on the subject, Sue gave me her mother's excellent recipe, where the taste is softened and enhanced by an orange. She guarantees that this will evoke memories of the "penny lemonade stand" and old-fashioned screened porches.

2 large lemons
1 medium orange
½ cup sugar
4 cups water
12 to 16 fresh mint leaves
Ice, for serving

Squeeze the lemons and the orange into a pitcher (preferably clear glass). Add the sugar, water, and mint leaves and stir until the sugar is dissolved. Serve over ice cubes.

Makes about 1 quart without ice

County Fair Lemonade

★

During the summers of 1994 and 1995, I went to more local fairs than I ever dreamed of, and between ox pulling, sheep shearing, and crafts, there were numerous lemonade booths draped in familiar red, white, and blue bunting. Here is one of more than a few versions of fresh American lemonade made with sugar syrup. You can adjust the sweetness to your taste, as my proportions are a tad tart. Once you have the syrup made, it will keep indefinitely in the refrigerator. Fresh lemon juice is a must!

2 cups sugar
6 cups water
2 cups fresh lemon juice (about 12 lemons),
    strained
1 to 2 lemons, very thinly sliced,
    for garnish
Ice, for serving

1. Place the 2 cups sugar and 2 cups of the water in a heavy saucepan. Bring the mixture to a boil, stirring to dissolve the sugar, and continue to boil for 2 minutes. Remove from the heat and cool to room temperature. (This makes 2½ cups of syrup, which can be kept indefinitely in the refrigerator in a covered container.)

2. Pour the strained lemon juice into a large pitcher (preferably clear glass). Add the remaining 4 cups water and 1 cup of the sugar syrup, or more to taste. Add the sliced lemons and fill the pitcher with ice before serving. Serve in tall glasses.

Makes about 2 quarts without ice

Old-Fashioned Lemonade

—★—

Sweep off the porch, pinch off the dead geranium blossoms, pull up the rockers, fill your pitchers, and please invite me. This is the lemonade that Grandma used to make when you finished picking gooseberries and blackberries for her pies. One glass is incentive enough to keep bowls of lemons on your kitchen table all summer long, always ready for the juicer.

2 cups fresh lemon juice (about 12 lemons),
strained
4 cups water
½ cup sugar
1 to 2 lemons, very thinly sliced, for serving
Ice, for serving
Sprigs of lemon mint, for garnish

Pour the strained lemon juice into a large pitcher (preferably clear glass). Add the water and the sugar and stir until the sugar is dissolved. Add the sliced lemons and fill the pitcher with ice before serving. Serve the lemonade in tall glasses garnished with a sprig of mint.

Makes about 1½ quarts
without ice

Cameron's Cherry Cola

—★—

The cherry cola as concocted by my friend Cameron Wright is made from cola combined with a small ladleful of minced maraschino cherries in their syrup. The beverage is served over crushed ice, with a straw, which constantly becomes clogged with bits of cherry flesh (which can then be catapulted out of the straw—especially charming for the under-twelve set). The vanilla cola, a variation on the theme, substitutes Vanilla Syrup to taste for the cherries, and your straw remains clog-free.

1 jar (3½ ounces) maraschino cherries
Crushed ice, for serving
1¼ cups (10 ounces) cola

1. Drain the cherries, reserving the syrup and discarding the stems, if any. Mince the cherries and return to the syrup.
2. Fill two 12-ounce glasses three fourths full with crushed ice.
3. Ladle 2 heaping tablespoons of the cherry-syrup mixture over the ice and fill the glasses to the rim with cola. Stir, and sip through a straw!

Serves 2

CONVERSION TABLE

—❧—

U.S. Dry & Liquid Measures

★ ★ ★

The following equivalents are based on U.S. fluid measure, since in the U.S. measurements for dry ingredients, as well as for liquid, are by volume, not by weight.

1 pinch = less than ⅛ teaspoon (dry)
1 dash = 3 drops to scant ⅛ teaspoon (liquid)
3 teaspoons = 1 tablespoon (dry and liquid)
2 tablespoons = 1 ounce (liquid)
4 tablespoons = ¼ cup = 1 ounce (liquid)
5⅓ tablespoons = ⅓ cup (dry and liquid)
8 tablespoons = ½ cup = 4 ounces (liquid)
16 tablespoons = 1 cup = 8 ounces (liquid)
2 cups = 16 ounces (liquid) = 1 pint (liquid)
4 cups = 32 ounces (liquid) = 1 quart (liquid)
16 cups = 128 ounces (liquid) = 1 gallon (liquid)

Temperatures

★ ★ ★

°Fahrenheit (F) to °Celsius (C)

– 10°F	=	– 23.3°C (freezer storage)
0°F	=	– 17.7°C
32°F	=	0°C (water freezes)
50°F	=	10°C
68°F	=	20°C (room temperature)
100°F	=	37.7°C
150°F	=	65.5°C
205°F	=	96.1°C (water simmers)
212°F	=	100°C (water boils)
300°F	=	148.8°C
325°F	=	162.8°C
350°F	=	177°C (baking)
375°F	=	190.5°C
400°F	=	204.4°C (hot oven)
425°F	=	218.3°C
450°F	=	232°C (very hot oven)
475°F	=	246.1°C
500°F	=	260°C (broiling)

Approximate Equivalents

★ ★ ★

1 quart (liquid) = about 1 liter
1 stick butter = 8 tablespoons = 4 ounces = ½ cup
1 cup all-purpose presifted flour = 5 ounces
1 cup stone-ground yellow cornmeal = 4½ ounces
1 cup granulated sugar = 7 ounces
1 cup (packed) brown sugar = 6 ounces
1 cup confectioners' sugar = 4½ ounces
1 large egg = 2 ounces = about ¼ cup
1 egg yolk = about 1 tablespoon
1 egg white = about 2 tablespoons

Conversion Factors

★ ★ ★

If you need to convert measurements into their equivalents in another system, here's how to do it.

ounces to grams: multiply ounce figure by 28.35 to get number of grams

grams to ounces: multiply gram figure by .0353 to get number of ounces

pounds to grams: multiply pound figure by 453.59 to get number of grams

pounds to kilograms: multiply pound figure by 0.45 to get number of kilograms

ounces to milliliters: multiply ounce figure by 29.57 to get number of milliliters

cups to liters: multiply cup figure by 0.24 to get number of liters

Fahrenheit to Celsius: subtract 32 from the Fahrenheit figure, multiply by 5, then divide by 9 to get Celsius figure

Celsius to Fahrenheit: multiply Celsius figure by 9, divide by 5, then add 32 to get Fahrenheit figure

inches to centimeters: multiply inch figure by 2.54 to get number of centimeters

centimeters to inches: multiply centimeter figure by 0.39 to get number of inches

FAIRS & FESTIVALS

★ ★ ★

American Royal International Invitational Barbecue Contest

Held first weekend in October.
For information:
1701 American Royal Court
Kansas City, Missouri 64102
(816) 221-9800; fax (816) 221-8189

This is the largest barbecue cooking competition in the world, with continuous live music (bluegrass, jazz, and rock 'n' roll) and family entertainment (clogging contest, fiddling contest, games, crafts, petting zoo, and more). There is a large food court that serves barbecued specialties (you cannot taste the contestants's barbecue dishes due to health regulations). The contest begins on Friday night, when the contestants fire up their smokers and cook all night. Visitors are welcome to come see all of the ingenious home-built smokers and learn barbecuing techniques from the contestants as well as enjoy the music and activities.

Castroville Artichoke Festival

Held end of September for 2 days.
For information:
California Artichoke Advisory Board
P.O. Box 747
10719 Merritt Street
Castroville, California 95012
(408) 633-4411

This festival celebrates artichokes with specialties as well as a parade, artichoke demonstration, artichoke eating contest, games, arts and crafts, the crowning of the Artichoke Festival Queen, 10K run and walk, and more.

World Catfish Festival

Held the first Saturday in April
  (unless it falls on Easter weekend).
For information:
Belzoni-Humphreys County Industrial Development Foundation, Inc.
528 North Hayden Street
Belzoni, Mississippi
(601) 247-4238

The catfish is honored with a day-long event—a catfish, hush puppy, and coleslaw lunch, live music, the crowning of the Catfish Queen, activities for children, and a catfish eating contest. There is also a 10K run, tours of local catfish ponds, craft booths, and more. A museum honoring the catfish is located across the street from the courthouse.

Fiesta San Antonio

Held during the second half of April.
For information:
Fiesta San Antonio Commission
122 Heiman Street
San Antonio, Texas 78205
(210) 227-5191

Ten days of parades, festivals, street parties, band concerts, sporting events, art shows, elegant balls, all celebrating Texas's independence from Mexico at the Battle of Jacinto, which took place on April 21, 1836, forty-six days after the fall of the Alamo. A favorite event, called "Night in Old San Antonio," is actually a four-night extravaganza—lots of food and entertainment in different theme areas and in the Marketplace (El Mercado). Don't forget to visit the Alamo!

Georgia Peach Festival

Held for one week in early June.
For information:
Georgia Peach Festival
P.O. Box 2001
Fort Valley, Georgia 31030
(912) 825-4002

Peach County, Georgia, celebrates the annual harvest with a peach dessert recipe contest, the world's largest peach cobbler, arts and crafts, sporting events, musical entertainment, 5K road race, historic displays, and peaches, peaches, peaches. Visit local peach packing plants, too. Don't forget to try the fresh peach ice cream and cobbler that's available everywhere!

Gilroy Garlic Festival

Held at the end of July for 3 days.
For information:
Gilroy Garlic Festival
P.O. Box 2311
Gilroy, California 95021
(408) 842-1625

The heart of the garlic festival is in an area called Gourmet Alley, where you can sample such garlic treats as pepper steak, calamari, scampi, garlic bread, and even garlic ice cream! Other events include live music, children's activities and entertainment, and the crowning of the Garlic Queen.

Great Wisconsin Cheese Festival

Held the first weekend in June.
For information:
Great Wisconsin Cheese Festival
1940 Buchanan Street
Little Chute, Wisconsin 54140
(414) 788-7390

Thousands of people celebrate their love of cheese in the nation's dairyland. There is the Big Cheese Parade on Saturday morning and a Big Cheese Breakfast on Sunday. Other events include a cheese-curd eating contest, cheese carving demonstrations, cheese tastings, and a cheesecake contest, along with gladiator pedestal jousting, magic shows, children's games, crafts/novelty booths, and rides. Lots of live music throughout.

The Gumbo Festival

Held in mid-October.
For information:
The Gumbo Festival
P.O. Box 9096
Bridge City, Louisiana 70094
(504) 436-4712

Bridge City's world-famous gumbo is cooked daily at the festival grounds—over 2,000 gallons of both seafood and chicken/sausage. Other native Louisiana dishes such as jambalaya, red beans and rice with sausage are available, along with homemade cakes, funnel cakes, and more. There is a gumbo cooking contest, live entertainment—Cajun, country, zydeco, jazz, blues, and rock music—and Miss Creole Gumbo and King Creole Gumbo are on hand to greet visitors. Also a 5K run and games.

Lima Bean Festival

Held the first Saturday in October in
West Cape May, New Jersey.
For information:
Alys Dolmetch
(609) 884-4086

A day-long affair celebrating the harvesting of the Fordhook lima bean with live music, food booths serving every type of lima bean preparation, antique and crafts booths, and the crowning of the Lima Bean Queen.

Marysville Strawberry Festival

Held for one week in mid-June in
Marysville, Washington
For information:
(360) 659-7664

This is the biggest strawberry festival held in Washington State, the heart of the strawberry country. Started by local berry growers in the 1930s, it now draws over 100,000 visitors. Week-long festivities include the Grand Parade, arts and crafts booths, an auto show, go-cart races, talent shows, golf and softball tournaments, lots of food to sample, and, of course, the Official Strawberry Shortcake. Go berry picking at one of the local strawberry farms.

National Mushroom (Morel) Hunting Championship

Held every May in Boyne City, Michigan.
For information:
Boyne City Chamber of Commerce
(616) 582-6222

Besides the hunt, other events include pancake breakfasts, arts and crafts, activities for children, live music, area restaurants preparing morel mushroom specialties, and amusement rides.

Taste of Charleston

Held in October at Boon Hall Plantation.
For information:
Charleston Restaurant Association
(803) 577-4030

Booths featuring the Creole, Cajun, and low-country cooking of Charleston's better restaurants, plus wine tastings and ice-carving competition.

Wakefield Ruritan Club Shad Planking

Held on the third Wednesday in April,
3 miles west of Wakefield, Virginia,
on Brittles Mill Road.
For information:
(800) 642-6887; tickets available in March

Besides a marvelous lunch of plank-cooked shad served with a secret sauce, hush puppies, coleslaw, and iced tea, activities include speeches by distinguished Virginia politicians. Nearby is the First Peanut Butter Museum in the U.S.A. and the Virginia Diner, which serves up every peanut specialty imaginable.

Yarmouth Clam Festival

Held the third weekend in July in
Yarmouth, Maine.
For information:
Yarmouth Chamber of Commerce
(207) 846-3984

Three days of great food and free entertainment. Highlights include a parade, concerts, crafts, sports competitions, carnival rides, fireworks, and special kids' entertainment. Great festival foods: besides clams—steamed, fried, or in chowder—other foods include lobster and scallop rolls, homemade pies, fried doughboys, lime rickeys, peach shortcake, cotton candy, and watermelon.

ON THE ROAD

★ ★ ★

Here are the addresses and phone numbers for many of the restaurants and other places I visited while preparing this book.

Al's Breakfast
413 14th Avenue, S.E.
Minneapolis, Minnesota 55414
(612) 331-9991

American Classic Tea
Charleston Tea Plantation
P.O. Box 12810
Charleston, South Carolina
29412
(803) 559-0383

American Spoon Foods, Inc.
P.O. Box 566
1668 Clarion Avenue
Petoskey, Michigan 49770
(800) 222-5886; (616) 347-9030;
fax: (616) 347-2512

Anchor Bar
1047 Main Street
Buffalo, New York 14209
(716) 886-8920

Antoine's Restaurant
713 St. Louis Street
New Orleans, Louisiana 70130
(504) 581-4422

Arcadia
21 East 62nd Street
New York, New York 10021
(212) 223-2900

Avalon
844 Front Street
Lahaina, Hawaii 96761
(808) 667-5559

Bayona
430 Dauphine Street
New Orleans, Louisiana 70112
(504) 525-4455

Beekman Arms
4 Mill Street, Routes 9 and 308
Rhinebeck, New York 12572
(914) 876-7077

Ben & Jerry's Ice Cream
Route 100
P.O. Box 240
Waterbury, Vermont 05676
(802) 244-5641

Elizabeth Berry
Heirloom Beans
Box 706
Abiquiu, New Mexico 87510
(505) 685-4888

Big Six Farm
P.O. Box 981
Fort Valley, Georgia 31030
(912) 825-7504

Biringer Strawberry Farm
Highway 529 between
Marysville and Everett
4625 40th Place N.E.
Marysville, Washington 98271
(206) 259-0255

The Blue Willow Inn
Restaurant
294 North Cherokee Road
Georgia Highway 11
Social Circle, Georgia 30279
(404) 464-2131

BP Gas Station of Edisto
Miss Daisy Mae Brown's
101 Palmetto Boulevard
Edisto Island, South Carolina
29438
(808) 869-3434

Broken Arrow Ranch
104 Highway 27
West Ingram, Texas 78025
(210) 367-5875
For mail order:
(800) 962-4263

The Brown Hotel
335 West Broadway
Louisville, Kentucky 40202
(502) 583-1234

Arthur Bryant's
1727 Brooklyn Avenue
Kansas City, Missouri 64127
(816) 231-1123

Butternut Mountain Maple Syrup Farm
Main Street
P.O. Box 381
Johnson, Vermont 05656
(802) 635-7483

Cabbage Island Clambakes
The Moore Family
Boothbay Harbor, Maine 04538
(207) 633-7200
June 24th through Labor Day

Cabot Creamery
P.O. Box 128
Cabot, Vermont 05647
(802) 563-2231

Cafe du Monde
800 Decatur Street
New Orleans,
Louisiana 70130
(504) 525-4544

Cafe Pasqual's
121 Don Gasper Avenue
Santa Fe, New Mexico 87501
(505) 983-9340

Campanile
624 South La Brea Avenue
Los Angeles, California 90036
(213) 938-1447

Capriole, Inc.
P.O. Box 117
Greenville, Indiana 47124
(812) 923-9408

Carolina Gold Rice
Route 3, Box 258
Grahamville, South Carolina 29943
Write for the latest rice prices

Central Grocery
923 Decatur Street
New Orleans, Louisiana 70130
(504) 523-1620

Cheyenne Crossing Cafe
Junction of Highways 14A and 85
Lead, South Dakota 57754
(605) 584-3510

Chinois on Main
2709 Main Street
Santa Monica, California 90405
(310) 392-9025

Coach Farm, Inc.
105 Mill Hill Road
Pine Plains, New York 12567
(518) 398-5325

Colonial Williamsburg
P.O. Box 1776
Williamsburg, Virginia 23187-1776
(800) HISTORY or
(804) 220-7645

Commander's Palace
1403 Washington Avenue
New Orleans, Louisiana 70130
(504) 899-8231

Congdon's Pharmacy
47 Main Street
Nantucket, Massachusetts 02554
(508) 228-0020

The Convention Grill
3912 Sunnyside Avenue
Edina, Minnesota 55424
(612) 920-6881

Corky's Bar-B-Q
5259 Poplar Avenue
Memphis, Tennessee 38119
(901) 685-9744

Dahlia Lounge
1904 Fourth Avenue
Seattle, Washington 98101
(206) 682-4142

Doc's
62 Flirtation Avenue at Route 45
New Preston, Connecticut 06777
(860) 868-9415

The Dog Team Tavern
Dog Team Road P.O. Box 421
Middlebury, Vermont 05753
(802) 388-7651

Henry Dykeman's Farm Market
Route 22
Pawling, New York 12564
(914) 855-5166
Opens May 1st for the summer

Ed's Tastee Freeze
Highway 90 West
(88 College Avenue)
De Funiak Springs,
Florida 32433
(904) 892-9843

Elizabeth's on 37th
105 East 37th Street
Savannah, Georgia 31401
(912) 236-5547

Empress Chili
5675 Rapid Run Road (other locations all over town)
Cincinnati, Ohio 45233
(513) 922-6669
Open 11 A.M. to 10 P.M. every day, Friday nights until 11 P.M.

Ferry Plaza Farmers' Market
On the Embarcadero, in front
of the Ferry Building at the
foot of Market Street
San Francisco, California
(415) 981-3004
Open 8 A.M. to 1:30 P.M.
Saturdays year-round

**First Peanut Museum in
the U.S.A.**
Route 460 West (near
intersection with Route 40)
Waverly, Virginia 23890
(804) 834-2969;
(804) 834-2151
Open 2 P.M. to 5 P.M.
Thursday through Monday,
voluntary donation

Flaherty's Mapleworks
HCR, Box 120
Boy River, Minnesota 56632
(218) 889-2258

Fog City Diner
1300 Battery Street
San Francisco, California
94111
(415) 982-2000

The French Laundry
6640 Washington Street
Yountville, California 94599
(707) 944-2380

Frontera Grill
445 N. Clark Street
Chicago, Illinois 60610
(312) 661-1434

Gold's Delicatessen
421 Post Road East
Westport, Connecticut 06880
(203) 227-0101

Goode Company BBQ
5109 Kirby, two blocks south of
Highway 59
Houston, Texas 77098
(713) 522-2530 and
8911 Katy Freeway
Houston, Texas 77024
(713) 464-1901

Gosman's Dock
500 West Lake Drive
Montauk, New York 11954
(516) 668-5330

Gordon's
500 N. Clark Street
Chicago, Illinois 60610
(312) 467-9780

Hancock Shaker Village
P.O. Box 898
Junction of Routes 20 and 41
Pittsfield, Massachusetts 01202
(413) 443-0188

The Herbfarm
32804 Issaquah-Fall City Road
Fall City, Washington 98024
(206) 784-2222

The Heritage Diner
80 River Street
Hackensack, New Jersey 07601
(201) 342-6757

Hotel Bel-Air
701 Stone Canyon Road
Los Angeles, California 90077
(310) 472-1211

**The Hume Beefalo
Farm**
R.D. 1-Andover
Chester, Vermont 05143
(802) 875-3352

**The Hurricane
Seafood Restaurant**
807 Gulf Way
St. Petersburg Beach,
Florida 33741
(813) 360-9558

Inn of the Anasazi
113 Washington Avenue
Santa Fe, New Mexico 87501
(505) 988-3236

Janous Fish Farms, Inc.
Route 1, Box 255
Belzoni, Mississippi 39038
(601) 247-2221

Jesperson's Restaurant
312 Howard Street
Petoskey, Michigan 49770
(616) 347-3601

Joe's Stone Crab
227 Biscayne Street
Miami Beach, Florida 33139
(305) 673-0365

Joyner of Smithfield
315 Main Street
Smithfield, Virginia 23430
(804) 357-2161

Junior's
386 Flatbush Avenue
Brooklyn, New York 11201
(800) 958-6467

**K.C. Masterpiece
Restaurant**
10985 Metcalf
Overland Park, Kansas 66210
(913) 345-1199

Katz's Delicatessen
205 Houston Street
New York, New York 10002
(212) 254-2246

Kea Lani Restaurant
Kea Lani Hotel
4100 Wailea Alanui
Wailea
Maui, Hawaii
96753
(808) 875-4100

Keys Diner
767 Raymond
St. Paul, Minnesota 55114
(612) 646-5756
(The original—there are ten
altogether)

King's Orchards
4620 North M 88
Central Lake, Michigan 49622
(616) 544-6479

**Konriko Rice Mill &
General Store**
307 Ann Street
New Iberia, Louisiana 70560
(800) 551-3245; (318) 367-6163
Open 9 A.M. to 5 P.M.
Monday through Saturday;
small fee for tour

K-Paul's Louisiana Kitchen
416 Chartres Street
New Orleans, Louisiana 70130
(504) 524-7394

Lancaster Central Market
Penn Square
Lancaster, Pennsylvania 17607
(717) 291-4723

Lane Packing Co.
Highway 96 E and Lane Road
Fort Valley, Georgia 31030
(912) 825-2891

La Tasha's
43A Cannon Street
Charleston, South Carolina
29403
(803) 723-3222

Laura Chenel's Chèvre, Inc.
4310 Fremont Drive
Sonoma, California 95476
(707) 996-4477

**Leech Lake Indian
Reservation**
Route 3, Box 100
Cass Lake, Minnesota 56633
(218) 335-8200

Liberty Bar
328 East Josephine
San Antonio, Texas 78215
(210) 227-1187

Lively Run Goat Dairy
8978 County Road 142
Interlaken, New York 14847
(607) 532-4647

Manganaro's Hero Boy
492 Ninth Avenue
New York, New York 10018
(212) 947-7325

The Marx Bros. Cafe
627 West Third Avenue
Anchorage, Alaska 99501
(907) 278-2133

Maytag Dairy Farms
P.O. Box 806
Newton, Iowa 50208-9986
(515) 792-1133
For mail order: (800) 247-2458

McIlhenny Company (Tabasco)
Avery Island, Louisiana 70513
(318) 365-8173

Mrs. Wilkes's Boarding House
107 West Jones Street
Savannah, Georgia 31401
(912) 232-5997

Mulate's
325 Mills Avenue
Breaux Bridge, Louisiana 70517
(318) 332-4648

Mustard's Grill
7399 St. Helena Highway
Napa Valley, California 94558
(707) 944-2424

Nantucket Pharmacy
45 Main Street
Nantucket,
Massachusetts
02554
(508) 228-0180

Nathan's Famous
1310 Surf Avenue at
Stillwell Avenue
Brooklyn, New York 11224
(718) 946-2202

Ocean Spray Cranberries, Inc.
One Ocean Spray Drive
Lakeville-Middleboro,
Massachusetts 02349
(508) 946-7488

**Old Chatham Sheepherding
Company & Inn**
P.O. Box 190
99 Shaker Museum Road
Old Chatham, New York 12136
(518) 794-9774

The Old Inn on the Green
Route 57
New Marlborough,
Massachusetts 01230
(413) 229-3131

Pete's Kitchen
1962 East Colfax
Denver, Colorado 80206
(303) 321-3139

The Pig Stand
1508 Broadway
San Antonio, Texas 78215
(210) 222-2794

Pike Place Market
Pike Street to Virginia Street
and First Avenue to
Western Avenue
Seattle, Washington 98101
(206) 682-7453

The Rainbow Room
30 Rockefeller Plaza (between
49th and 50th Streets),
65th floor
New York, New York
10112
(212) 632-5000

Randol's
2320 Kaliste Saloom Road
Lafayette, Louisiana 70508
(318) 981-7080
Open 7 days, live music
5 P.M. to 10 P.M. weekdays,
until 11 P.M. weekends

Reading Terminal Market
12th and Arch Streets
Philadelphia, Pennsylvania
19107
(215) 922-2317
Open 8 A.M. to 6 P.M.,
Monday through Saturday

Red's Eats
Water Street
Wiscasset, Maine 04578
(207) 882-6128

Reuben's
244 Madison Avenue
New York,
New York
10036
(212) 867-7800

Rosario's Cafe y Cantina
1014 South Alamo
San Antonio, Texas 78210
(210) 223-1806

Le Rosier
314 East Main Street
New Iberia, Louisiana 70560
(318) 367-5306

Royal Hawaiian Hotel
2259 Kalakaua Avenue
Honolulu, Hawaii 96815
(808) 923-7311

Shelburne Farms
102 Harbor Road
Shelburne, Vermont
05482
(802) 985-8686

Short Stop Diner
315 Franklin Street
(exit 148 on the
Garden State Parkway)
Bloomfield, New Jersey 07003
(201) 429-1591

Silver Fox Halibut Charters
P.O. Box 402
Homer, Alaska 99603
(907) 235-8792

Simon's Specialty Cheese
Highways 41 and N
Little Chute, Wisconsin
54140-0223

(414) 788-6311
Open 8 A.M. to 6 P.M. Monday
to Friday, Saturday 8 A.M. to
5 P.M.

Skyline Chili
1007 Vine Street (at Court
Street; other locations all
over town)
Cincinnati, Ohio 45202
(513) 721-4715
Open 10 A.M. to 6 P.M.,
Monday through Friday

**Slightly North of Broad
Restaurant**
102 East Bay Street
Charleston, South Carolina
29401
(803) 723-3424

Sole Mio Restaurant
917 West Armitage
Chicago, Illinois 60614
(773) 477-5858

**The Solie House Bed and
Breakfast**
914 East Hancock Street
Appleton, Wisconsin 54911
(414) 733-0863

Sonny Bryan's Smokehouse
2202 Inwood Road
Dallas, Texas 75235
(214) 357-7120

Sonoma Cheese Factory
2 Spain Street
Sonoma, California 95476
(707) 996-1931
Open 8:30 A.M. to 5:30 P.M.,
Monday through Friday, until
6 P.M. Saturday and Sunday

Spago
1114 Horn Avenue
West Hollywood, California
90069
(310) 652-4025

**The Spent Grain Baking
Company, Inc.**
P.O. Box 127
Edmonds, Washington 98020
(206) 776-6010

The Stage Deli
834 Seventh Avenue
New York, New York 10019
(2120 245-7850

Star Canyon
3102 Oaklawn Avenue
Dallas, Texas 75219
(214) 520-7827

Stars
150 Redwood Alley
San Francisco, California 94102
(415) 861-7827

Stroud's Restaurant & Bar
1015 East 85th Street
Kansas City, Missouri 64131
(816) 333-2132

Tapawingo
9502 Lake Street
Ellsworth, Minnesota 49729
(616) 588-7971

Tecolote Cafe
1203 Cerrillos Road
Santa Fe, New Mexico 87501
(505) 988-1362

The Tick Tock Diner
281 Allwood Road
Route 3
Clifton, New Jersey 07011
(201) 777-0511

Tip Top Diner
2814 Fredericksburg Street
San Antonio, Texas 78231
(210) 735-2222

Tony Luke's
39 East Oregon Avenue
Philadelphia, Pennsylvania 19148
(215) 551-5725

Tra Vigne
1050 Charter Oak Street
St. Helena, California 94574
(707) 963-4444

Trout Haven Ranch
9 miles north of Hot Springs,
just off Highways 385 and 79
Deadwood, South Dakota 57732
(605) 342-6009
Open 8 A.M. to 8 P.M., June 1
through Labor Day

Tutka Bay Lodge
Nelda and Jon Osgood
P.O. Box 960
Homer, Alaska 99603
(907) 235-3905

Union Square Greenmarket
17th & Broadway
New York, New York 10003
(212) 477-3220
Open Monday, Wednesday,
Friday, and Saturday, year-round

Vella Cheese Company
315 Second Street East
Sonoma, California 95476-0191
(707) 938-3232

Virgil's
152 West 44th Street
New York, New York 10036
(212) 921-9494

Virginia Diner
U.S. Route 460
Wakefield, Virginia 23888
(804) 899-3106
Open 7 days a week, breakfast,
lunch, and dinner

Walker Art Center
725 Vineland Place
(at Lyndale Avenue)
Minneapolis, Minnesota
55403
(612) 375-7600

The Whistle Stop Cafe
Route 1, Box 54
McCrackin Street
Juliette, Georgia
31046
(912) 994-3670

The White Gull Inn
P.O. Box 160
Main Street
Fish Creek, Wisconsin 54212
(414) 868-3517
Fish boils on Wednesday,
Friday, Saturday, and Sunday
in summer and Saturdays only
in winter

Woodenknife Cafe
Box 104
Interior, South Dakota 57750
(605) 433-5463

Zuni Cafe and Grill
1658 Market Street
San Francisco, California 94102
(415) 552-2522

BIBLIOGRAPHY

★ ★ ★

Adler, Jerry. "Caviar." *Martha Stewart Living,* vol. 25, Dec. 1994/Jan. 1995, pp. 106–111.

Alters Jamison, Cheryl, and Bill Jamison. "A Flavorful History." *The Official 1994 Santa Fe Guide.*

The American Heritage Cookbook and Illustrated History of American Eating and Drinking. By the Editors of *American Heritage: The Magazine of History.* New York: Simon & Schuster, 1964.

Angers, Trent (ed.). *Louisiana Festivals Cookbook: Book One.* Lafayette, LA: Acadian House, 1992.

Bear, John, and Marian Bear. *How to Repair Food.* Berkeley, CA: Ten Speed Press, 1987.

Beard, James A. *American Cookery.* Boston, MA: Little, Brown and Company, 1972.

Belsinger, Susan, and Carolyn Dille. *The Chile Pepper Book.* Loveland, CO: Interweave Press, 1994.

Bianchini, Francesco, Francesco Corbetta, and Marilena Pistoia. *The Complete Book of Fruits and Vegetables.* New York: Crown Publishers, 1976.

Bissell, Frances. *The Book of Food.* New York: Henry Holt and Company, 1994.

Bittman, Mark. *Fish: The Complete Guide to Buying and Cooking.* New York: Macmillan Publishing Company, 1994.

Black, Maggie, and Susan Dixon. *Mrs. Beeton's Cookery and Household Management.* Great Britain: Ward Lock Limited, 1980.

Bradley, Susan. *Pacific Northwest Palate.* New York: Addison-Wesley Publishing Company, 1989.

Carson, Jane. *Colonial Virginia Cookery.* Williamsburg, VA: The Colonial Williamsburg Foundation, 1968.

Chalmers, Irena, and Milton Glaser. *Great American Food Almanac.* New York: Harper & Row, 1986.

Chandonnet, Ann. *The Alaska Heritage Seafood Cookbook.* Anchorage: Alaska Northwest Books, 1995.

Chiarello, Michael. *Flavored Oils: 50 Recipes for Cooking with Infused Oils.* San Francisco: Chronicle Books, 1995.

Claiborne, Craig. *The New York Times Food Encyclopedia.* New York: Wing Books, 1985.

Collins, Douglas. *America's Favorite Food—The Story of Campbell Soup Company.* New York: Harry N. Abrams, 1994.

Czarnecki, Jack. *A Cook's Book of Mushrooms.* New York: Artisan, 1995.

Damrosch, Barbara. *The Garden Primer.* New York: Workman Publishing Company, 1988.

Davidson, Alan. *Seafood: A Connoisseur's Guide and Cookbook.* New York: Simon & Schuster, 1989.

Delmar, Charles. *The Essential Cook: Everything You Really Need to Know About Foods and Cooking.* Chapel Hill, NC: Hill House Publishing Company, 1989.

DeWitt, Dave. "Where There's Fire . . ." *Food Arts,* vol. 6, June 1993, pp. 56–61.

DeWitt, Dave, and Nancy Gerlach. *The Whole Chile Pepper Book.* Boston: Little, Brown and Company, 1990.

DeWitt, Dave, and Mary Jane Wilan. *The Food Lover's Handbook to the Southwest.* Rocklin, CA: Prima Publishing, 1992.

Dubit, Wendy. "Apples." *Martha Stewart Living,* vol 10, Oct./Nov. 1992, pp. 74–81.

Ellis, Merle. *The Great American Meat Book.* New York: Alfred A. Knopf, 1996.

Fuss, Edward, and Susan Hazen-Hammond. *Chile Pepper Fever: Mine's Hotter Than Yours.* Stillwater, MN: Voyageur Press, 1993.

Fussell, Betty. *The Story of Corn.* New York: Alfred A. Knopf, 1992.

Garfinkel, Perry. "Striking Oil." *Saveur,* no. 4, Jan./Feb. 1995, pp. 75–80.

Geffen, Alice M., and Carole Berglie. *Food Festival: The Guidebook to America's Best Regional Food Celebrations.* 2nd ed. Woodstock, VT: The Countryman Press, 1994.

Greene, Bert. "An Apple Scrapbook." *Cook's,* vol. 9, Sept. 1988, pp. 32–35.

Guste, Roy F., Jr. *The Tomato Cookbook*. Gretna, LA: Pelican Publishing Company, 1995.

Herbst, Sharon Tyler. *The New Food Lover's Companion*. 2nd ed. Hauppauge, NY: Barron's Educational Series, 1995.

Hirasuna, Delphine, et al. *Vegetables*. San Francisco: Chronicle Books, 1985.

Idone, Christopher. *Lemons: A Country Garden Cookbook*. San Francisco: Collins Publishers, 1993.

Iggers, Jeremy. "Rice." *Martha Stewart Living*, vol. 22, Sept. 1994, pp. 78–87.

James, Michael. *Slow Food: Flavors and Memories of America's Hometowns*. New York: Warner Books, 1992.

Johnston, Ruth Mossock. *The Buffalo Cookbook*. Blaine, WA: Hancock House Publishers, 1995.

Kavasch, Barrie. *Native Harvests*. New York: Vintage Books, 1979.

Kavasch, E. Barrie. *Earth Maker's Lodge*. Peterborough, NH: Cobblestone Publishing, 1994.

———. *Enduring Harvests*. Old Saybrook, CT: The Globe Pequot Press, 1995.

Keegan, Marcia. *Southwest Indian Cookbook*. Santa Fe, NM: Clear Light Publishers, 1987.

Kimball, Christopher. *The Cook's Bible*. New York: Little, Brown and Company, 1996.

Kimball, Marie. *Thomas Jefferson's Cookbook*. Charlottesville: The University Press of Virginia, 1976.

King, Shirley. *Fish: The Basics*. New York: Simon & Schuster, 1990.

Kummer, Corby. "Tomatoes." *Martha Stewart Living*, vol. 8, June/July 1992, pp. 76–83.

———. "Potatoes." *Martha Stewart Living*, vol. 9, Aug./Sept. 1992, pp. 43–53.

———. *The Joy of Coffee*. Shelburne, VT: Chapters Publishing Limited, 1995.

Land, Leslie. "Real Tomatoes." *Food & Wine*, vol. 14, Aug. 1991, pp. 48–55, 87.

Lang, Jennifer Harvey. *Larousse Gastronomique*. New York: Crown Publishers, 1984.

Leonard, Jonathan N. *American Cooking: New England*. New York: Time-Life Books, 1971.

Loomis, Susan H. *The Great American Seafood Cookbook*. New York: Workman Publishing Company, 1988.

———. *Farmhouse Cookbook*. New York: Workman Publishing Company, 1991.

Luckett, Pete. *Fresh Fruits & Vegetables*. Tucson, AZ: Fisher Books, 1990.

Manning, Jo. *Seasonal Florida*. Ponte Vedra Beach, FL: Yardbird Productions, 1994.

Mariani, John F. *The Dictionary of American Food and Drink*. Rev. ed. New York: William Morrow and Company, 1994.

Marshall, Lydie. *A Passion for Potatoes*. New York: Harper Perennial, 1992.

———. "Potatoes, Please." *Food & Wine*, vol. 17, Feb. 1994, pp. 60–65, 92, 96.

Martin, Alexander C. *Trees: A Guide to Familiar American Trees*. New York: Golden Press, 1956.

McGee, Harold. *On Food and Cooking*. New York: Collier Books, 1984.

McLaughlin, Michael. *The Mushroom Book*. San Francisco: Chronical Books, 1994.

Miller, Mark. *The Great Chile Book*. Berkeley, CA: Ten Speed Press, 1991.

Morris, Dan, and Inez Morris. *The Complete Fish Cookbook*. New York: Macmillan Publishing Company, 1972, 1986.

Pierson, Stephanie. "Seeing Red." *Saveur*, no. 4, Jan./Feb. 1995, p. 36.

———. "The Queen of Lima Beans." *Saveur*, no. 6, May/June 1995, pp. 69–76.

Rain, Patricia. *The Artichoke Cookbook*. Berkeley, CA: Celestial Arts, 1985.

Rolnick, Harry. *The Complete Book of Coffee*. Hong Kong: Rolf Stacker Associates Advertising Limited, 1982.

Root, Waverley. *Food*. New York: Konecky & Konecky, 1980.

Rosengarten, Frederic, Jr. *The Book of Edible Nuts*. New York: Walker Publishing Company, 1984.

Schapira, David, Karl Schapira, and Joel Schapira. *The Book of Coffee & Tea*. New York: St. Martin's Press, 1982.

Schneider, Elizabeth. *Uncommon Fruits and Vegetables: A Commonsense Guide*. New York: Harper & Row, 1986.

———. "One Potato, Two Potato, Three Potato, More. . . " *Food Arts,* vol. 7, Sept. 1994, pp. 34–40.

Schrambling, Regina. "Harvesting the American Feast." *Saveur,* no. 3, Nov./Dec. 1994, pp. 42–52.

Schremp, Gerry. *Celebration of American Food: Four Centuries in the Melting Pot*. Golden, CO: Fulcrum Publishing, 1996.

Seyfer, Eudora. "Beloved Blue Willow." *House Beautiful Magazine,* Nov. 1995.

Stall, Gaspar J. "Buddy." *Proud, Peculiar New Orleans: The Inside Story*. Baton Rouge, LA: Claitor's Publishing Division, 1970.

Taylor, John Martin. *Hoppin' John's Lowcountry Cooking*. New York: Bantam Books, 1992.

Toussaint-Samat, Maguelonne. *A History of Food* (trans. by Anthea Bell). Cambridge, MA: Blackwell Publishers, 1992.

Trager, James. *The Food Chronology*. New York: Henry Holt and Company, 1995.

Travers, Carolyn Freeman (ed.). *The Thanksgiving Primer*. Plymouth, MA: Plimouth Plantation Inc., 1987.

Wolf, Bruce. "Citrus." *Martha Stewart Living,* vol. 11, Dec. 1992/Jan. 1993, pp. 83–87.

Worth, Helen. *Down-on-the-Farm Cookbook*. New York: Greenberg Publisher, Inc. 1943.

Yorkshire, Heidi. "Washington State Apples." *Bon Appetit,* vol. 38, Nov. 1993, pp. 44–46.

INDEX

★ ★ ★